The
ENGLISH
REGIONAL
CHAIR

Frontispiece. Thomas Rosoman and his family on the Thames at Hampton, by Johann Zoffany, c.1780. In the 18th century painted Windsor chairs were often used in the grounds of fashionable households. (Private Collection)

The
ENGLISH
REGIONAL
CHAIR

Bernard D. Cotton

ANTIQUE COLLECTORS' CLUB

Published for the Antique Collectors' Club
by the Antique Collectors' Club Ltd.

British Library CIP Data
Cotton, Bernard *1939-*
    English regional chairs
    1. English domestic chairs, history
    I. Title
    749.320942

Printed in England by
the Antique Collectors' Club Ltd.
Woodbridge, Suffolk

THE ANTIQUE COLLECTORS' CLUB

The Antique Collectors' Club was formed in 1966 and now has a five figure member-ship spread throughout the world. It publishes the only independently run monthly antiques magazine *Antique Collecting* which caters for those collectors who are interested in widening their knowledge of antiques, both by greater awareness of quality and by discussion of the factors which influence the price that is likely to be asked. The Antique Collectors' Club pioneered the provision of information on prices for collectors and the magazine still leads in the provision of detailed articles on a variety of subjects.

It was in response to the enormous demand for information on "what to pay" that the price guide series was introduced in 1968 with the first edition of *The Price Guide to Antique Furniture* (completely revised, 1978 and 1989), a book which broke new ground by illustrating the more common types of antique furniture, the sort that collectors could buy in shops and at auctions rather than the rare museum pieces which had previously been used (and still to a large extent are used) to make up the limited amount of illustrations in books published by commercial publishers. Many other price guides have followed, all copiously illustrated, and greatly appreciated by collectors for the valuable information they contain, quite apart from prices. The Antique Collectors' Club also publishes other books on antiques, including horology and art reference works, and a full book list is available.

Club membership, which is open to all collectors, costs £17.50 per annum. Members receive free of charge *Antique Collecting,* the Club's magazine (published ten times a year), which contains well-illustrated articles dealing with the practical aspects of collecting not normally dealt with by magazines. Prices, features of value, investment potential, fakes and forgeries are all given prominence in the magazine.

Among other facilities available to members are private buying and selling facilities, the longest list of "For Sales" of any antiques magazine, an annual ceramics conference and the opportunity to meet other collectors at their local antique collectors' clubs. There are over eighty in Britain and more than a dozen overseas. Members may also buy the Club's publications at special pre-publication prices.

As its motto implies, the Club is an amateur organisation designed to help collectors get the most out of their hobby: it is informal and friendly and gives enormous enjoyment to all concerned.

For Collectors — By Collectors — About Collecting

The Antique Collectors' Club, 5 Church Street, Woodbridge, Suffolk

CONTENTS

COLOUR PLATES

8

PREFACE

The need for a major study of regional chair traditions has long been felt by everyone seriously interested in English furniture. A useful start has already been made on analysing the stylistic character of seventeenth century provincial oak furniture in terms of local decorative preferences but there is little reliable published information on later vernacular chairs. Dr. Bill Cotton was one of the first scholars to insist that the regional origin of turned chairs — Windsors, spindle and ladder backs — could also be charted and this impressive volume contains the results of his investigations.

The vital factor that led on to a major advance in chair studies was a dawning awareness that more vernacular chairs than anyone previously realised bear a maker's name, initials or a trade label. This is not to say they are exactly numerous, but we now know that many chair turners working before 1870 identified their products, although not always on a regular basis.

The next step was, with the assistance of his wife Gerry, to compile a master index of chair makers and turners from contemporary sources such as Trade Directories and Census Returns so that bridges could be built between names found on chair seats or frames and individual craftsmen. A few Windsor chair makers helpfully incorporated a town or village in their name stamp, but this often laborious method was generally the only sure way to provenance the majority of chairs. Groups illustrating local design types and workshop practices gradually emerged. Micro-research could then be started on inventories, newspapers and parish registers, recording oral history and attempts made to contact families who had inherited chairs, all of which served to illuminate regional chair making traditions. This personal approach, used to good effect by students of folklore, had seldom previously been employed by furniture historians. Another novel feature is the intelligent use of diagrams, charts and graphs to illustrate points.

In the course of research many obviously once important chair making centres were identified from documentary evidence where the custom of marking chairs was never practised. This offered a different sort of challenge which required mounting an intensive search to discover seat furniture that had descended in local families and expressed a consistent personality which it could reasonably be assumed represented the output of workshops in the district. Old photographs also provided many valuable clues to provincial idioms.

No previous book on English regional furniture has united such a powerful combination of fieldwork, archival research and sociology; it is a towering achievement and puts this branch of English furniture studies alongside the most progressive work being done by American scholars who, by and large, know so much more about their furniture than we do about ours. Dr. Cotton has not by any means, as he would be the first to admit, said the last word on his chosen subject, some of his theories deserve to be challenged, but it is a real threshold book, for the landscape of English furniture will never look quite the same again. Dr. Cotton has established a firm foundation on which members of the Regional Furniture Society (of which he is chairman) and others can build with confidence, we need no longer despair that rush seated, spindle or ladder back and simple turned chairs are irretrievably anonymous.

Furthermore, common furniture has at last been brought out of its antiquarian backwater into the mainstream of art history. The author has been most fortunate in finding a publisher whose enthusiasm and commitment are equal to his own. Their inspired partnership must be saluted for producing this huge, splendidly illustrated book, which is surely destined to become a modern classic.

Christopher Gilbert
Temple Newsam House
Leeds, England

ACKNOWLEDGEMENTS

There can be few opportunities in life more fulfilling than creating new knowledge from an apparently random mass of information, for that is exactly what furniture historians have confronted when studying British vernacular furniture traditions. The task of recording and analysing England's regional chair designs has offered an exciting and sometimes frustrating search to bring order and recognition to one such tradition, albeit a very diverse and widely interpreted one.

This text is not intended to represent every chair style made, or necessarily every regional group, rather it is a record of those traditions which have emerged through the decoding of an immense amount of documentary and visual information about chairs, chair makers, and the social life of different regions. Handling many chair examples was part of this experience, and through this, a sense of stylistic compatibility and difference was developed in a very direct and sensory way. That more chair variants remain to be recorded is certainly true, and through this route other regional traditions may yet be identified. Some dynasties of chair makers worked over a long period and no identified work has yet been suggested for either them or their locality. These traditions are the absent pieces of the jigsaw puzzle which, set against the background of the information gained so far, may eventually be fitted into place.

To undertake the work of identifying regional furniture traditions, a number of difficulties have had to be overcome. For example, the umbrella terms so often applied to vernacular furniture such as 'country', 'folk', or 'rustic' have obscured both the rural and urban origins of regional furniture, and have created romanticised notions of 'cottage' life. These stereotypes fail to recognise that in the eighteenth and nineteenth centuries, Britain was not a homogenous nation, but rather a series of distinct regions, some persistently rural, others becoming increasingly industrialised, all of which developed their own special form of cultural life, both material and social. Probably the best single identifier of specific regions was the use of dialect, for within eighteenth and nineteenth century Britain, speech was both the divider and unifier of different social classes and regional cultures. The metaphor of regional language differences is useful, too, when extended to an examination of objects, for within these terms, each region displays evidence, not of random forms of architecture, furniture, or other manufactured items, but in the same way that language is organised within a system of implicit rules: grammar, syntax, and punctuation, so too are many of the material expressions of regional life.

To adopt this structuralist view of the study of objects has many advantages for the researcher, since it guides the principles of exploration in particular ways. For example, adopting the linguistic code as a way of exploring traditions of furniture making, is to embark with the belief that, like language, furniture design will be systematic in its principles of construction, and that since it is the product of a particular culture, it will hold meaning and nuance within the terms of that society. Of course a theoretical model of this kind is ultimately of little assistance unless it provides an agenda which will guide research towards new insights. In relation to this study of vernacular chair design, so diverse were the styles made in England alone that a long and demanding process of recording designs from traditions which were often completely unrecognised or half known, was accompanied by the identification of key design signatures. These recurring stylistic motifs may be said to form the dialect of a particular tradition, and were recognised as the key variables through which other chairs could be grouped by association. In turn, these chairs often introduced new stylistic elements into the regional design code. In this sense, the premise of structuralism has actively aided the decoding of many traditions. For example in the North West tradition, the identification of nine principal underarm turning motifs and nine spindle turnings for backs, led to yet ever more complex and interesting conclusions about combinatory laws: what motifs can be mixed with which others, and which could not. Such observance of the rules of stylistic code has resulted in increasingly close comparisons between the grammar of language and the grammar of design. In these and other terms, the field of vernacular furniture studies is now making headway, especially with the formation of the Regional Furniture Society, and the steady flow of scholarly work which this organisation publishes.

If this study goes some way to support this initiative in exhibiting that an interpretive framework can successfully be brought to the study of vernacular furniture on a regional basis, then I shall be delighted, since beyond the information it provides about English chair design, the exciting promise will have been made that other branches of vernacular furniture may similarly yield to systematic recording and analysis. Such a venture will require persistence, since much so-called country furniture has been displaced from its place of origin. Much has gone abroad, and as with the interpretation of chair design, this new programme of work will lean heavily on the relatively rare examples of maker identified pieces. Like chairs, there are probably many more pieces of regional furniture which are so identified than we have imagined, and the recording of these will lead us ever closer to mapping the vernacular furniture traditions of this country.

Of course, all research programmes of this kind rely enormously on the goodwill and encouragement of others to point out new material and to sustain enthusiasm. The number of people from many walks of life who have helped me in producing this work is considerable, and includes museum curators, librarians, archivists, auction houses, antiques dealers, furniture restorers, and owners of chairs. To all go my grateful thanks for their contributions.

A number of people either inspired me to undertake this work, or have been so consistent in their help and support, that they must be mentioned by name. My thanks and affection go firstly to the late Fred Lambert, a gifted and pioneering teacher, who first introduced me to chair making and coppice crafts some thirty years ago at Worcester College of Education. It is a great sadness to me that he died in 1989, before this book was published.

Christopher Gilbert has been a constant inspiration and friend who has provided the encouragement to continue the work, especially when other alternatives looked more attractive. Many others have contributed in numerous ways to the book: in providing documentary information, or consistently loaning chairs for photographic documentation. In this connection, my thanks go particularly to Pauline Agius, Christopher Baylis, John Boram, William Brear, Michael and Sheila Golding, Nancy Goyne-Evans, Bob Morley, Danny Robinson, Ivan Sparkes, and Timothy Wilson. Particular thanks are due to Paul Griffiths of Oxford University Computer Centre who ran the statistical data on the Mendlesham chair project as an act of generosity from one researcher to another. Keith Barnes of the Oxford Photographic Workshop developed and printed countless photographs for the project, and by his professionalism has made a major contribution to this work. James Forsyth found many stamped chair examples in his work as a furniture restorer, and without his vigilance and good sense, many critical revelations would have remained undiscovered. The index of chair makers was so laboriously extracted from Trade Directories and other sources as a team effort, and Sue Burch and Ruth Jones should have particular thanks for help with this project. Checking data and compiling interpretive information sheets were the province of Elizabeth Randall, and grateful thanks are due to her. My heartfelt thanks go to Jill Champion, who edited this book in a caring and sympathetic way, Steven Farrow, who worked so hard on the design and layout, and Lynn Taylor for the mammoth typesetting task. Finally, it is to my wife Gerry that my unqualified thanks must go. She has worked unstintingly and uncomplainingly as my co-worker, typist, driver, field work organiser, photographic assistant, and in all the other aspects of the work needed to be done. Her contribution has been of the highest order and may she feel equal satisfaction, with me, in the publication of this work.

INTRODUCTION

This book records a series of remarkable chair making traditions which developed in England during the late eighteenth and nineteenth centuries and, in some cases, continued into the twentieth century. The apparently spontaneous development of regional chair styles which differed markedly from area to area, represented a radical and important event in the social and material culture of this country. Before the eighteenth century, furniture which could make claims to skilled construction, was commonly produced by turners and joiners for use in prosperous households. In contrast, the labouring and artisan classes typically owned little other than very basic, roughly made furniture which reflected their often transient and impoverished life styles.

The chairs which began to appear in the eighteenth century for use in poorer households were quite different from those produced by joiners in earlier times from seasoned timber, usually oak, and constructed with conventional mortice and tenon joints as a system of right-angled parts, in the manner of other pieces of 'case' furniture. Such seating, although durable and typically carved and embellished with symbols and other stylistic devices, often reflecting regional origins, was essentially unsympathetic to the needs of bodily comfort. Indeed, it often relied upon the padded clothing styles worn by the user to provide a layer of 'upholstery' to an otherwise unyielding chair.

In contrast the largest group of chairs made for common use during the eighteenth and nineteenth centuries were rush seated (although some chairs of this type were made in the West Midlands with thin wooden seats). Made by wood turners or specialist makers, they were simply constructed with either a series of horizontal cross splats or, alternatively, with a number of vertical spindles composing the back design.

This form of seating was an advance on the rough stools which had been made for centuries as primitive seating for the poor, and in offering support for the back, combined with a rush or woven willow seat, provided a degree of comfort previously unavailable to the working population.

A second distinct group of chairs made during this period were described as 'Windsor' chairs, and were distinguished from other turned chairs in having a shaped wooden seat into which the legs and back support spindles and splats were morticed. The development of this chair style was to have a far reaching influence on the production of common seating and was to be differently interpreted in many regions.

The first Windsor chairs were probably largely, if not entirely, made as armchair varieties only, until about the second half of the eighteenth century, whereas the documentary evidence of domestic life in the seventeenth and eighteenth centuries suggests that both arm and side chairs of the rush seated varieties were made during this period. This perhaps indicates that the first Windsor chairs, although progenitors of what was to become a widely available chair for vernacular use, were originally intended for middle class homes and perhaps prosperous inns and other gathering places, or were painted for use as garden furniture in manorial households.

Whether the first rush and willow seated ladder and spindle back chairs and 'Windsor' chair varieties displayed regional design characteristics is not clear, or indeed, whether all regions produced prototype common chairs. However, it seems probable that turned chairs were universally made during this period, since probate inventories record the existence of rush seated chairs in many parts of England, and genealogical research

of chair making dynasties from different regions indicates the existence of both rush seat chair turners and 'Windsor' chair makers from the early eighteenth century.

The evidence of chairs from the first half of the eighteenth century suggests that in many parts of England, a spontaneous and progressive need for common chairs grew steadily, and by the middle of the century vernacular chair making traditions had appeared in many, if not all geographic regions. These local traditions usually developed in particular towns or groups of towns and villages, where traditions often continued for a number of generations, typically involving particular families who supplied a local need. Later, certain successful local centres tended to attract other families into the trade, enabling the craft to develop into a regional industry.

Indeed, so strongly developed were certain of these centres by the beginning of the nineteenth century, that in some cases there was a tendency for particular traditions to supply the surrounding population with chairs to the extent that they suppressed the need for other chair making traditions to arise in the immediate surrounding counties. This was particularly true, for example, in the Southern and Home Counties, where the Buckinghamshire Windsor chair making trade, centred in High Wycombe, supplied chairs to a wide region, and largely dominated the production of common chairs in the whole of the south of England. For this reason, perhaps, not every county in England has provided firm evidence of a local chair making tradition, and the regional surveys included in this book therefore represent only strongly identified and generally persistent traditions.

INTRODUCTION

CONSTRUCTION

Chair makers who produced ladder and spindle back chairs during the late seventeenth and early eighteenth centuries, universally rejected the long favoured oak for the strong and more flexible ash (although other woods were occasionally used, including alder, birch, beech, cherry, elm, sycamore, walnut and yew). The makers of turned chairs employed the technique of creating segments for turning by splitting or 'cleaving' round sections of mature or coppice timbers down the length of the grain. These segments were then turned in freshly felled or 'green' condition, rather than as sawn, dry or 'seasoned' timbers.

Such technology was doubly attractive to chair turners, since in addition to allowing relatively low powered 'pole' lathes to operate effectively, the use of wet timber incorporated an effective principle of construction hitherto not widely used in furniture making. This method of making chairs exploited the tendency of wet wood to dry to an oval shape, since the water conducting cells of which hardwood is composed, are made of differentially thickened cells, depending on the time of year in which they are created, with larger cells being produced in the peak growing times of spring and summer, and with bands of smaller cells being formed in the autumn and winter. On drying, different layers of cells distort to different degrees, which results in a differential distortion of the bands of cells, causing an ovalling effect.

The characteristic of ovalling was used as a key element in 'green' chair construction. When round mortices are drilled into the green back and front legs to hold the previously dried, dowel shaped mortices of the stretchers, the wet uprights tend to oval in shape on drying out, gripping the end of the dry, oval tenon and holding it tight. Figure 1 shows the tightly fitting union of a chair stretcher when morticed into the leg.

The processes of cleaving and shaping freshly felled timber or coppice, although newly adopted in furniture making, essentially represented techniques which had been practised for centuries in other coppice crafts, particularly in the production of cleft ash and chestnut fence hurdles used to house animals, or to provide wattle frameworks on to

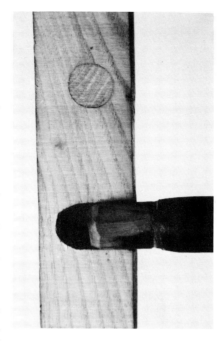

Figure 1. A section through the leg of a 19th century spindle back chair from the North West region, showing the tenon which became ovalled on drying, being firmly held by the ovalling of the back leg as it dried out. The lower dowel mortice and tenon shows the considerable depth to which the tenons were bored, and the rounded ending which was produced by round headed bits.

which plaster was applied. Other crafts such as 'riven' spale basket-making, cleft fencing of various regional styles, peg and thatch roof spar making, spoon, bowl and tool-handle making, were all ancient crafts which required the essential use of cleaving and shaping of green wood to produce the basic item. Steaming and bending cleft segments, a skill adopted to bend 'ladders' or 'splats' for the backs of chairs, was also practised by at least one other trade, that of the barrel-maker, in which the individual oak staves were steamed prior to being bent to shape. 'Common' chair making, therefore, represented a more complex development of pre-existing coppice crafts, and was, in these terms, quite different as a manufacturing concept from the joiner's method of chair making.

The paramount requirement of chairs in common use was essentially similar in whatever region they were made: that of being able to withstand hard, daily use. The necessary strength was successfully achieved by a marked variety of designs, although the central principle of construction

remained the same, the creation of a strong framework from the production of a number of small parts which needed only simple technology to produce them. The assembly of these parts into a complex structure provided acceptable forms of seating within a given regional code of furniture design.

However, although the process of green wood construction techniques worked well enough in the short term, and was well adapted to the simple tools and devices available to the rural turners and coppice workers, it was not ideal for direct translation into making chairs which were to last for a long time. The defects of this method of construction in chairs became obvious after a period of use, since although cottage homes of the seventeenth and early eighteenth centuries were typically poorly heated, and had high humidity arising from the use of earth and stone floors, nevertheless as drying of the wood continued, the once tight joints tended to become loose. Once this process had begun, continued use caused movement in the joints which led inevitably to the chairs falling apart. Even the common practice of securing the top ladder or cross splat with a square peg was not sufficient to prevent disintegration of many of the common chairs made during this period.

The realisation of the long-term problems of green wood construction gradually altered the approach which many regional chair makers adopted towards their craft, and as the eighteenth century progressed, examples of turned chairs, particularly from the North West region, indicate that extensive use was made of sawn, dry, timber. This practice was made possible by the increased mechanisation which workshops adopted, using water power to drive machinery of various kinds, including belt driven circular saws. See Chapter 7, pp.321-5 for details of the highly mechanised workshop of one Lancashire chair turner.

The inside surface of the chair leg from a Lancashire spindle back chair shown in Figure 2 illustrates the circular saw marks made when producing parts for turning, which the turner has left in situ, and which are quite commonly found on chairs from this region. The use of sawn, dry timbers required a powerful lathe on which to turn this relatively hard material, and water driven, and later

Figure 2. The inside facet of a front leg from a Lancashire spindle back chair, c.1800, showing circular saw teeth marks which indicate that, in common with the usual practice in this region's chair making, this chair leg was turned from sawn seasoned timber, rather than from cleft 'green' wood.

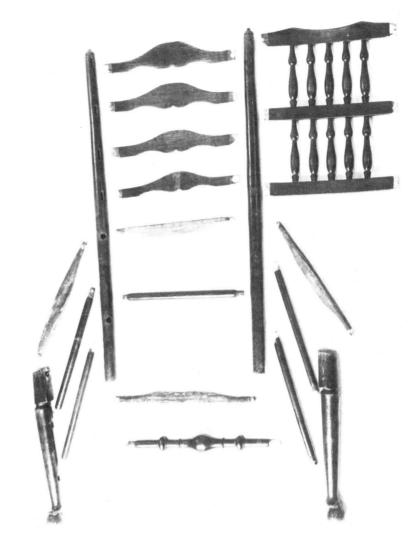

Figure 3. Skeletal plan of the parts of a typical rush seated chair from the North West region, made from ash and alder, c.1820, showing both ladder and spindle forms of back design which were interchangeable in this particular design.

steam driven machinery was developed, although foot treadled lathes using a reciprocating flywheel were also commonly used.

However, although it is probable that industrialised techniques were common in workshops in or near to large conurbations, chair makers in more rural regions maintained the older techniques of turning green wood on relatively low powered treadle or 'pole' lathes. It seems likely that the inefficient qualities of green construction were avoided by drying the parts before assembly, and by using glue to form a strong joint. Chairs were made in this way particularly in Lincolnshire and the West Midlands, and examples remain in tight condition after over one hundred years of use.

LADDER AND SPINDLE BACK CHAIRS

Within individual regional chair making traditions, varying degrees of craft specialisation were required to produce chair parts, and of the many regional preferences, the rush and thin wooden seated ladder and spindle back varieties probably represented the least complex form of structure. An example of the components of a typical rush seated side chair of ladder back design from the North West region is shown in Figure 3, in which a common alternative back structure composed of spindles and cross rails is also illustrated. In this chair type, the majority of parts are turned, with the exception of the seat rush rails which were shaped with a draw knife, and the ladders which were typically made from sections of cleft wood, which after steaming to make them more supple, were bent in a 'former' to create the curved shape. In this common type of turned chair, the major turnery skill occurred in producing the front legs, where an offset pad foot necessitated the use of two centres in the turning process. A straight front leg avoided this complication, being turned with one centring process, and chairs thus made were probably less costly. An example of this second form of front leg is shown in Figure 4 as one of the components of an essentially similar chair to that shown in Figure 3, but in this case the chair is made with a thin wooden seat, typical of those made in the West Midland Counties.

A further alternative front leg assembly was produced which was composed of a straight front seat rush bar with squared raised corners, into which the turned front legs were morticed. The different forms of front legs described above were preferred in chairs of particular back designs, and were all commonly produced throughout the North West Midlands, and North West region, as

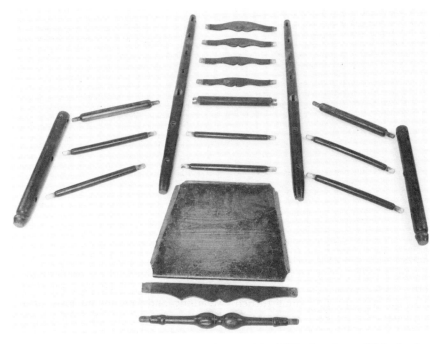

Figure 4. Skeletal plan of a ladder back chair from the West Midlands region, c.1820, showing the thin wooden seat form which was used as an alternative to rush and willow seating in this region. The front legs are turned on one centre only, and represent a less complex form of turning than those with pad feet, shown in Figure 3, which were turned on two centres.

well as in the Lincolnshire tradition.

Within the repertoire of ladder back chairs from each region, the ladders or cross splats are typically graduated in size, and dome shaped on top with three common shapes below: those which are straight along the bottom of the ladder, those shaped with a downward tip and those with an upward indentation. In addition to these, various other ladder shapes were made, including a further major style made in Lancashire which has a so-called wavy line shape (see Chapter 7, pp.414-19). Other less common ladder forms include those with plain parallel splats, those which are Cupid's bow shaped, or those which are decoratively fretted below. The number of ladders or splats varies with the style and may include those with either six, five, four, or three in the side chairs, with four and five being the most common numbers, and the armchair counterpart to a particular side chair being typically made with one more splat than the side chair.

Ladder back chairs typically have continuous round back uprights, as in the case of the chairs shown in Figures 3 and 4, which often taper upwards and terminate in a decorative finial, and which may be square in section below seat level or, in examples from the North West region, shaped to an octagon.

A variation of the standard ladder back form occurs in a major sub-group of sturdy chairs made in Lancashire and Cheshire which provide a style which rather than having a ladder which joins the top of the back uprights, utilises various designs of top rails which are square in section and which join the legs across the top. Examples of these chairs are shown in Chapter 7, pp.377-90.

Related to this group in design terms is a further chair group made in the West Midlands which are lighter in construction than those made in the industrial North West but which also have top stay rails. These are commonly associated with ladder back and spindle back chairs made with both wooden and rush seats. See Chapter 6 for examples of these designs. A further group of chairs known to have been made particularly in the Cheshire town of Macclesfield have an alternative turned form of curved top stay rail which is round in section, terminating in barrel shaped ends joined to the back uprights. Examples of this chair design are shown in Chapter 7, pp.366-75.

The alternative group of rush seated chairs to the ladder back styles have backs composed of one, two or three rows of spindles. Sometimes such chairs have a ladder back counterpart made of otherwise similar parts. In this way some chair makers made a repertoire of different designs, incorporating parts from one style into the structure of another. Figure 3 illustrates the framework of the chair which could be modified to provide either a ladder back or a spindle back version. However, other individual styles of spindle back from the Lancashire and Cheshire tradition particularly, have quite specific forms, and have little relationship to an equivalent ladder back form. These styles include a major sub-group which has a square section cross stay rail which joins sawn back uprights, and terminates in ear shaped projections. See Chapter 7, Figures NW113-30.

The turnery styles of the spindles used in these chairs are not idiosyncratic, rather they fall within regional conventions in which, for example, nine different styles have been identified for the double and treble row spindle back chairs made in Lancashire and Cheshire, and fifteen for those included in the single row spindle back chairs from the North West Lakeland region (see Chapter 7, pp.327-55). Hearsay has suggested that the different spindle turnings and chair styles from the North West were representative of chair traditions from particular towns and were peculiar to them. The evidence of known chair makers' work, however, suggests that rather than a design being specific to one town or village, a number of distinct spindle back chairs existed within a larger region offering a wider choice, from which it seems probable that individual chair makers produced a repertoire of styles. The individual spindle types may, therefore, be the product of a particular maker rather than a particular place. This notion is supported by the evidence that chair makers working at considerable distances from each other were making similar spindle turnings. See for example, those included in chair styles made in the towns of Macclesfield in Cheshire, and Todmorden on the Lancashire/Yorkshire border (Chapter 7, Figures NW93 and NW138).

It also seems that makers working in the same area produced different spindle turnings from each other.

See, for example, a spindle back chair design made in Salford, Manchester, compared with a further design made by a maker recorded working at Hanging Ditch, Manchester. Both chairs have typical but different regional spindle turnings from each other, and are both made by makers who worked in the outer Manchester area. See Chapter 7, Figures NW84 and NW106.

In addition to these distinctions, it may also be the case that makers produced different spindle profiles for different chair styles. See, for example, a low nursing chair and a standard spindle back side chair, both stamped by J. Shackleton of Todmorden, Yorkshire (Chapter 7, Figures NW93 and NW100), where both chairs have different spindle turnings from each other.

However, further evidence of the work of known makers is needed before a definite sense of the boundaries of local and more extended regional design codes can be firmly defined, and this remains as a research project for those interested in the regional furniture from the North West region.

Above all other design devices, however, the front stretcher turnings exhibit the greatest degree of regional identification, with particular forms being associated with both ladder and spindle back styles, and others which are quite specific to a particular chair type. The conventional nature of the front stretcher turnings has been highly significant in the search for regional attribution, since firmly provenanced styles exhibiting a particular front stretcher turning have suggested a regional relationship with one or more previously unattributed styles which, in turn, have lead to the identification of further chairs by design association. The formation of a regional code of turnery 'signatures' is complex, and relies on establishing a profile of recurring devices. The number of different turnery expressions varies from region to region and includes, for example, twenty-four attributed to ladder back chairs from the Lancashire/Cheshire region, compared with perhaps three or four from the West Midlands tradition. Examples of regional front stretcher turnings from the North West region are shown in Figure NW289 in Chapter 7. Rush seated armchairs also exhibit a limited range of regionally specific turning devices in

the underarm support turnings, and examples of these are shown in Chapter 7, Figure NW71. Interestingly, the underarm turning devices are commonly composed of half of the front stretcher turning, creating points of common unity in the design. In other examples, the underarm turnings are equally conventional, but are quite unlike the stretcher motifs.

Although the use of spindles and ladders in the back design was the most common form, other back designs occurred in chairs made in the Lancashire and Cheshire tradition during the nineteenth century. Some basic grades of rush seated kitchen chairs had backs with vertical square sectioned parts, or were made with plain curved cross splats or narrow cross splats supporting small turned spindles. This group of chairs is illustrated in Chapter 7, pp.420-29.

The production of great quantities of rush seated chairs in the North West region during the nineteenth century must have resulted in an army of rush workers who generally produced the finest quality work. This craft is an arduous one to perform, with each seat taking about three hours of tightly twisting the rush to create thin strands which fit tightly and symmetrically over the seat frame. Because of the physical strength needed to do this craft over a long period of time, it was predominantly executed by men, probably as home-based workers. The source of their material was both the local rivers and meres, where the freshwater rush, *scirpus lacustris,* was gathered in the first three weeks of July from the water's edge, and dried for later use; and also much saltwater rush, *scirpus maritimus,* was imported from the Low Countries, and brought into ports such as Liverpool, and sold to rush importers who, in turn, sold it in bundles to rush 'bottomers'.

The craft of rush seating is highly skilled in order to produce fine work, although the conditions of work were particularly onerous, since the dry rush has to be made wet in order to twist it without breaking. Given the difficulties of the trade and the generally high level of skill achieved, it is surprising that the craft has received so little recognition, and is often associated only with the itinerant seat menders who wandered through the countryside repairing chair seats at the door.

WINDSOR CHAIRS

The second major group of regional chairs, 'Windsor' chairs, differed significantly from the rush seated chairs in both constructional and ergonomic terms. Its development also signified a radical departure from earlier, right-angled joined or turned chairs, since evidently for the first time, chair makers observed that the human body was rounded in shape, and they provided a curved back, and usually a sympathetically contoured wooden seat to accommodate this. Such genuinely innovative moves in chair making involved the application of the techniques of cleaving and turning which were used in ladder and spindle back chair production, and also incorporated techniques of steaming and bending to form arm bows, and later in the eighteenth century, to create bent top hoops, and bent stretchers to connect the legs. Making a Windsor chair involved a further process too, that of the use of the pit saw to convert trees into planks, prior to being sawn into seats which were finally adzed to shape. Adzing was a craft known to other trades, particularly the shipwright who had used it since archaic times.

The differences in construction techniques between the rush seated turned ladder and spindle back chairs and the wooden seated Windsor chairs was such that Windsor chair makers did not make rush seated chairs, or vice versa. This resulted in the majority of regions being generally host to one or other of these major chair styles. For example, Windsor chairs with distinct regional characterstics were made in such geographically diverse regions as the West of England counties of Cornwall, Devon and Somerset; the central region based in Buckinghamshire and the Thames Valley area; the North East Midlands region centred in certain Lincolnshire and Nottinghamshire towns. In Yorkshire a Windsor tradition arose generally later in the nineteenth century, particularly in the industrial cities of South Yorkshire; and to a less developed extent, in the far North East county of Durham. With the exception of Lincolnshire, where an important rush seated ladder back chair making tradition was continued by several generations of chair turners, these areas were almost entirely dominated by the Windsor chair as the common seating form.

INTRODUCTION

Conversely, other geographically linked regions produced rush seated chairs in great numbers and with great variation of turnery and other design differences, to the virtual exclusion of Windsor chairs. This particularly occurred in the North West region which fostered vigorous traditions in Cheshire, Lancashire and the Lakeland region of Westmorland and Cumberland.

The realisation of the shortcomings of 'green' wood technology which had been experienced in the first ladder and spindle back turned chairs was largely avoided in the production of Windsor chairs, since although parts were initially often produced from green wood, they were typically thoroughly air dried before assembly, and animal glues made from hide and bones were used to produce bonded joints for stretchers and back spindles. The use of tapered leg tenons which were morticed through the seat and secured with a wooden wedge, represented a further application of a known technique from other crafts, particularly for securing the tool handles into tool heads. This mode of fixing legs into the chair seat was especially efficient since the seat was constantly forced down on to the taper of the upper leg, reinforcing the joint union. This form of construction was successfully used in Windsor chair manufacture throughout the eighteenth century and into the first third of the nineteenth century, in the Thames Valley/Chilterns tradition particularly, when blind socket mortice and tenons and the use of glue, gradually replaced this earlier mode of fixing.

The distinction between 'green' wood constructed chairs, and those which used dry wood, glue bonded joints, and through morticed leg fixing was dramatic, since where 'green' wood constructed chairs tended progressively to loosen with the user's movements, and eventually to disintegrate, well-made examples of Windsor furniture using dry wood remained tight and firm. Such chairs were made with the taut qualities of a strung musical instrument, in which the juxtaposition of opposing forces created a finely tuned piece of furniture. Such was the skill of many of the eighteenth century Windsor chair makers, that their techniques were emulated and continued well into the nineteenth century, when mass production techniques gradually

replaced much of the handmade content of the chairs, and massiveness was used to create the strength which hitherto a refined craftsman's sense of the practical use of opposing structures had supplied.

WEST COUNTRY WINDSORS

The styles of Windsor chairs vary from area to area, showing wide regional interpretation. Those made in the West Country, for example, fall into three major categories, and include a rare group of elegant continuous arm Windsors attributed to the village of Yealmpton near to Plymouth in Devon. This chair style is unique in the English tradition, although a similar style was also made in New York, Rhode Island, and in parts of Connecticut. See Chapter 5, pp.275-8 for a fuller discussion of this chair style. In this version of the Windsor, the arm and raised cresting bow of the back are made from one bent, flowing segment which is often supported by turned spindles having simulated bamboo turnings. In common with virtually all West Country Windsors, these chairs were typically painted in blue, green or a muddy red paint, and more rarely in yellow ochre.

In the heartland of Devon, and in Cornwall, other primitive forms of Windsors of both arm and side chair varieties were made. These styles are typified by the elliptical hand-shaped, rather than turned, back spindles which are typically morticed through the hoop and pegged through from the front to secure them. In the majority of examples, the hoop is flattened rather than domed in section, as is typically the case in other English Windsors. In some examples two or more decoratively turned underarm supports were employed, whilst in others a crudely shaped curved support was used. Side chair equivalents to these primitive West Country Windsor armchairs were sometimes made with a wedge to the rear of the seat from which two spindles supported the hoop.

The leg turnings used in chairs from this group often have an 'egg and reel' turning near the bottom of the leg, and in others a plain undecorated leg was used. In all cases, an 'H' form stretcher is used to connect the legs, and the alternative 'crinoline' stretcher, widely used elsewhere in the English tradition, was not fashionable in this region.

Some chair seats were made in the usual seating wood of elm, but many were made from sycamore, with a number of distinct 'waisted' seat shapes, many of which have counterparts in American Windsors.

Many of the chair styles commonly used in South Devon and Cornwall cottage homes were illustrated in the genre paintings of West Country regional life created by the late nineteenth century Newlyn School of painters, and illustrations of chairs painted by members of this school, as well as photographs of different modes of primitive Windsor chair construction are shown in Chapter 5, Figures SW17 and SW65 and p.262, Figures SW5-7.

A third type of Windsor chair was made in Cornwall, Devon and Somerset which is characterised in having an arm bow which is constructed of sawn parts rather than a bent hoop. In this form of construction, two sawn outer arm parts are joined by a raised curved back section which fits between the arms. The top hoop is morticed into the arm, and the back design is entirely constructed of spindles. The seats in this Windsor style are typically made of elm, and the leg design includes the 'egg and reel' motif in the late eighteenth and early nineteenth century examples. Examples made later in the nineteenth century have either a single ring and concave turning or a raised triple ring turning on the legs. This style of chair has swept, round arm supports in the earlier examples and, as is the case in other regional traditions, has turned arm supports in chairs made from about 1840 onwards.

Although the Yealmpton group of chair makers described themselves as such from about 1811 until their decline in about 1860, and other chair makers were also recorded scattered throughout the West Country, the majority of chairs from this region were probably made by carpenters, cabinet makers or joiners as part of a general repertoire of furniture. This is illustrated by the makers of the 'three-part armchairs' provenanced to Cullompton, Devon, and Axbridge, Somerset, which are shown in Chapter 5, Figures SW23 and 25, who advertised themselves as cabinet makers and joiners. Conversely, the Windsor chairs which were made in the Thames Valley, London and Buckinghamshire region during most of the eighteenth

Plate 1. High hoop back Windsor armchair. Yew with elm seat. Attributed to Jack Goodchild, chairmaker, of Naphill, Bucks., 1885-1950.

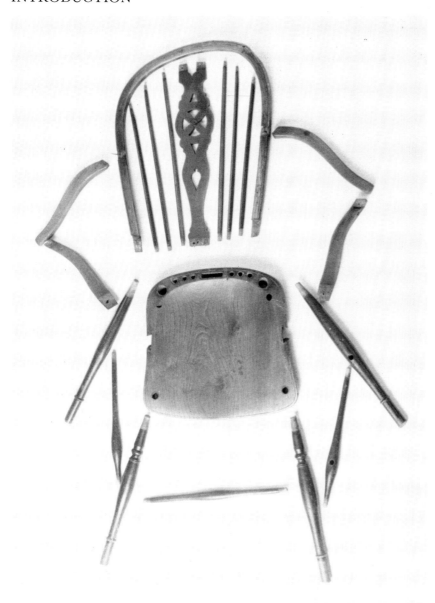

Figure 5. Skeletal plan of a low back armchair from High Wycombe, Bucks. Made from beech, ash, fruitwood and elm, c.1810. This chair design was essentially a development of a side chair and incorporated a larger seat and arms which were screwed to the hoop and supported on curved supports. This style of chair was made in large numbers as a counterpart to side chairs, and they were probably intended as dining rather than fireside chairs.

splat. Other 'best' chairs were made in yew wood with elm seats, and in these examples, the legs were usually connected by a 'crinoline' shaped stretcher.

This extremely durable form of seating was to be used throughout the Midlands and the south of England, to the exclusion of virtually all other forms of common chairs. As the nineteenth century dawned, the Windsor chair makers of this region rapidly extended their repertoire to include an increasing number of hoop-backed side chairs and armchairs. These were sometimes made with spindles alone composing their back design, but more commonly had a central fretted splat with motifs which included the ubiquitous wheel, as well as a star, urn, Prince of Wales' feathers, roundel, crown, tulip, petalate, and Gothic motifs. Examples of this style of chair and the different forms of splat motifs are shown in Chapter 2, pp.53-72.

A further armchair style began to be made towards the end of the eighteenth century which was probably intended to be part of a set with side chairs. This style has one bow only, in the manner of a side chair, and the arms are morticed and screwed to the hoop, and typically supported by curved sawn underarm supports. An illustration of the components of this chair is shown in Figure 5. The development of this form of armchair is significant in that it reflected a social change in family life, where families increasingly ate together at a dining table, and thus created a need for seating for all the family members. Hitherto, the tall backed armchairs, with the double bows, were essentially made as fireside chairs, and were probably brought to the table at meal times.

A further Windsor style arose in this region towards the end of the eighteenth century in which the typical hoop was abandoned in favour of sawn, shaped back uprights which were connected by curved plain top stay rails, and varying forms of central turned and shaped cross rails. This style of Windsor is commonly described as a 'scroll' back Windsor, a title which reflects the scrolled shaping of the uprights.

As the nineteenth century progressed, changes occurred in the styles of turnery used in making these chairs; legs which morticed through the seat and legs turned with a high single ring and concave turning

century, were produced by turners who described themselves clearly as 'Windsor chair makers'.

THAMES VALLEY/CHILTERN WINDSORS

During the first half of the eighteenth century, the Thames Valley and Chilterns trade essentially produced high quality Windsors of comb back, hoop back, and Gothic shaped back designs, with cabriole legs. Examples of these designs are illustrated in Chapter 2, pp.45-48.

During the second half of the eighteenth century, other styles began

to appear including the archetypal 'wheel' back Windsor chairs which were made with single ring and concave turned legs, elegantly made double bow structure and a central fretted splat. This new form of Windsor was the precursor of chairs which were to epitomise English Windsors made for everyday use, and which became the primary product of a craft which grew into a major industry in the Buckinghamshire town of High Wycombe. This form of Windsor chair was typically made with turned beech legs, connecting stretchers, and back spindles, and an elm seat, ash hoop, and fruitwood gradually gave way to those with heavier single ring, as well as those with raised three ring turnings and blind socket jointing. After about 1850, the leg turnings included the heavier turned triple ring motif. At the same time there was a rise in the weight of material used in the chairs, and a decline in the fine handwork manifest in the earlier styles. The general increase in massiveness coincided, too, with the introduction of new chair forms including low and high 'smokers' bow' chairs, as well as the lath back varieties. An anthology of styles made in this region, and illustrations of splat and leg turning devices is given in Chapter 2.

NORTH EAST WINDSORS

The Windsor chairs made in Lincolnshire, in the North East Midlands, reflect design influences from Buckinghamshire chairs made in the late eighteenth and early nineteenth centuries. These include the use of a single ring and concave leg turnings, as well as the use of egg and reel turnings found in some early eighteenth century Thames Valley chairs. The typical double hoop construction was adopted, too, with curved round 'crook' underarm supports being common. However, the Lincolnshire styles, although showing an awareness of Windsor designs from the south of England, display much less uniformity than those from Buckinghamshire. This is often reflected in imprecise bending techniques in the arm, arm supports, top bow and crinoline stretchers. The single ring and concave turning in this tradition is also typically of a more elongated nature than the Buckinghamshire varieties and, in common with many North Country Windsors, the major splat fretting device was that of the stylised fleur-de-lis, although some chairs were made with modifications of the urn motif, and turned roundels common in the Buckinghamshire tradition.

Around 1830, the Lincolnshire trade developed rapidly in many towns, including Grantham, Sleaford, Boston and Caistor. At this time, the earlier, finely made Windsors began to give way to heavier styles which were to typify the later regional characteristics of North Country Windsors. These features include a generally weightier structure than those made in the southern region, with a bent arm bow, and a top hoop, made in both high and low form,

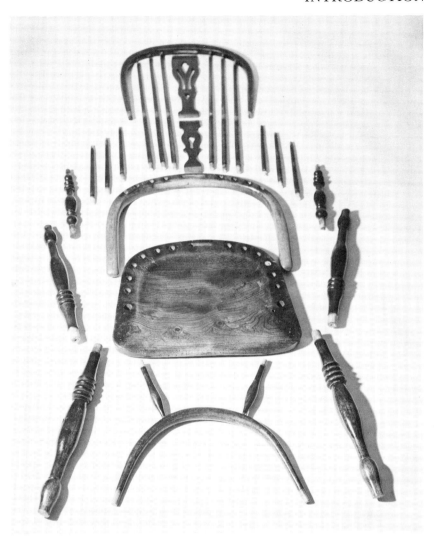

Figure 6. Skeletal plan of a high Windsor chair made in Worksop, Nottinghamshire. Ash with elm seat, c.1850. This style of chair was the most common design of Windsor armchair in the North East Midlands, and it was made in a low back form too. The double bow form exhibited in this chair, represents the essential mode of construction for Windsors from other regions, including the high double bow Windsor chairs from High Wycombe and the high primitive Windsors from the West Country.

with upper and lower splats in which the stylised fleur-de-lis was most commonly used.

In this tradition, the single ring and concave leg turning was less commonly made than the more usual two and three ring turnings, and examples made in ash with elm seats were made with both 'H' and 'crinoline' leg stretchers, whereas examples of 'best' chairs made in yew typically have a crinoline stretcher form.

In addition to the simple fleur-de-lis splat, some chairs had more elaborate splat fretting, and these were commonly made in yew with an elm seat, and occur in association with decoratively turned legs. Within the Lincolnshire tradition, Windsors

of the plainest model were made in both high and low back styles without the central splat, using turned spindles alone. This style of chair usually had a very shallow seat, front to back, and unlike the Buckinghamshire tradition in the south, side chairs formed a relatively small part of the chair maker's repertoire.

The Windsor chair making trade which arose in the county of Nottinghamshire in Retford, Worksop, Newark, Wellow and Rockley, similarly produced a range of typically North Country Windsors of the low and high backed varieties, and in these too, the fleur-de-lis splat was used most commonly (see Figure 6). However, unlike many Lincolnshire made chairs, the two ring leg turning

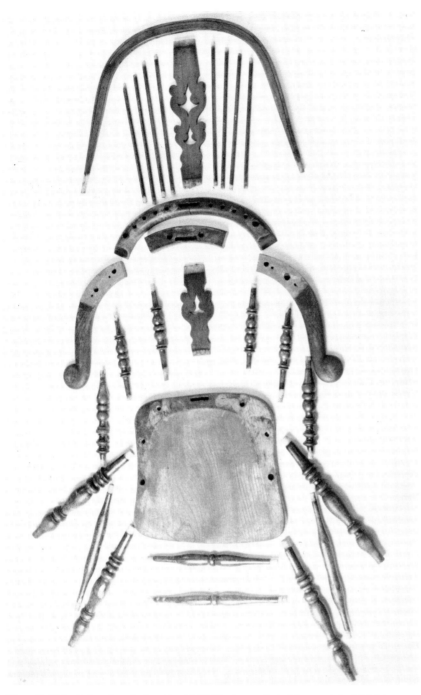

Figure 7. Skeletal plan view of a 'smoking high' Windsor, typical of those made in High Wycombe, Nottinghamshire, Yorkshire and Durham, showing the relatively large number of parts needed to make this type of chair, and the correspondingly high number of separate skills required to produce the turned, fretted, sawn and adze shaped sections for this, the most structurally complex of all the English regional chair styles.

Country, the two curved outer arm rests are either joined in the middle, or sometimes linked with a separate short member, and were joined by a raised applied back section, into which the top hoop was morticed (see Figure 7). These styles, too, were made as standard chairs in ash and elm, as well as in the prestigious yew wood.

'Scroll back' Windsors of a heavier type than those made in the south of England were also made in Worksop, and known as 'Grecian' and 'Roman' chairs. Some of these chairs are illustrated on a trade card produced by a firm of Windsor Chair Makers in Worksop shown in Chapter 3, Figures NE269 and 270.

In Yorkshire, the Windsor chair making trade was less developed than in the North East Midlands, and no doubt, the makers to the south supplied many chairs to markets in Yorkshire during the first half of the nineteenth century. However, throughout the nineteenth century, a few Windsor chair makers worked in towns and cities scattered throughout Yorkshire producing regional styles of Windsor chairs. See Chapter 3, pp.191-209 for illustrations of chairs attributed to this county. As the nineteenth century progressed, the number of Windsor chair makers in the region gradually increased, and while the trade was declining elsewhere in the North East Midlands, the makers in the industrial centres of South Yorkshire were increasing, reaching a peak during the last twenty years of the nineteenth century.

The chairs made by these tradesmen were generally inelegant and utilitarian in design. Double bow Windsors of high and low form were made, with a broad form of fleur-de-lis fretted splat being commonly used. The smoking High Windsor and smokers' bow chairs were also made in large numbers, and were widely used in working men's clubs, homes, inns and offices throughout the North East region. Other forms of high back Windsors were also made which exhibit wide variation in splat designs, and an anthology of designs from this region is shown in Chapter 3, pp.200-4.

The far north eastern counties of Durham and Northumberland had even fewer Windsor chair makers than Yorkshire, and produced similar chairs, including the high smoking and smokers' bow chair. Examples of chairs from this region

was not favoured by this region's chair turners, who preferred a three ring turning. The finest quality Windsors from the Nottinghamshire tradition were commonly made from yew, with highly decorative fretting in the splats. Chairs of this high quality were described as 'best' chairs, and the makers from the Nottinghamshire region sent their

products to retail outlets in many parts of northern England.

In addition to the repertoire of double bow Windsors, the Worksop makers also made 'smokers' bow' or 'office' chairs as well as the 'high smoking' styles of Windsors. These robust chairs were made with three sawn parts composing the arm, but unlike the form made in the West

are shown in Chapter 3, Figures NE424-34.

EAST ANGLIAN CHAIRS

Although the majority of vernacular chair making traditions in England may be divided into those which made either predominantly Windsor or ladder and spindle back chairs, one further cultural region, that of East Anglia, developed a chair making tradition which largely ignored the turner's art and placed chair making firmly within the province of the cabinet maker's trade, to the degree that in this area alone, chair makers are typically listed in trade directories as 'Cabinet and Chair Makers'. Vernacular chairs made in this area usually took their inspiration from the classical eighteenth century designers' styles, particularly those of Chippendale, Hepplewhite and Sheraton. Within this tradition, the possibilities for interpretation of the basic design forms were formalised in the *Norwich Chair-makers' Book of Prices*, 1801, for use by journeymen cabinet and chair makers and their employers. Within these terms, customers could choose their own design from different individual parts which were combined with a range of basic frame designs. These included chairs with both flat and hollow wooden seats, as well as those with drop in rush or upholstered seats. The basic forms of back design particularly were open to individual interpretation, using different arrangements of cross splats, stay rails, reeding, inlay, and the incorporation of turned wooden balls or 'buttons'.

The woods which the East Anglian chair makers used commonly included oak in the eighteenth century examples, with elm the most common wood in the first half of the nineteenth century. Mahogany was increasingly being brought into the repertoire of woods as the nineteenth century progressed. See Figure 8 showing the components of a common elm East Anglian chair.

Provincial styles of dining and corner chairs which adopt versions of fretted splats and shaped stay rails reminiscent of the work of classical designers, and which are commonly called either 'Country Chippendale', 'Hepplewhite' or 'Sheraton', were probably made in many parts of England, and are among the most difficult of the English vernacular chairs to attribute to a particular region. Such styles have been identified

Figure 8. Skeletal plan of a typical chair from the East Anglian cabinet and chair making tradition. Made in elm, c.1820. Chairs from this region were predominantly made from sawn and shaped parts, and commonly made with a 'hollow' seat. The only turned parts used in this chair are the balls or 'buttons' used as back decoration, and the overall style is reminiscent of chair designs produced by Thomas Sheraton.

to the East Anglian tradition, however, and the general reliance on classical design in this tradition resulted in these chair styles being a natural part of the East Anglian chair repertoire. See Chapter 4, pp.216-27 for illustrations of this style of chair.

There is, therefore, an essential distinction between the East Anglian chair tradition, and that of the other English regions, a tradition with a general dependence on the cabinet making techniques of sawing and shaping parts, as well as the use of conventional mortice and tenon joints rather than the round dowel jointing form of the turned chair. The use of the styles of the classical metropolitan designers of the eighteenth century, albeit greatly modified, rather than the spontaneous generation of a 'pure' vernacular tradition is another characteristic of in this region's chairs. A full discussion of this tradition is given in Chapter 4, pp.212-16.

MANUFACTURING TECHNIQUES

If the styles of chairs varied from area to area, so too did the workshop practices necessary to make the different types of chairs. Chair turners who made ladder and spindle back chairs used fewer specialised processes than those who made Windsor chairs. Within the manufacture of ladder and spindle back chairs, turning was the only essential craft with steaming and bending of ladders, and in some cases, stay and cross rails being ancillary skills. Seating was a separate task, often undertaken by outworkers who specialised in rush or willow seating, and those chairs which incorporated thin elm seats, were hand sawn by the makers. The manufacture of these chairs consequently required relatively little specialised division of labour, and it was possible for individual chair turners to make complete chair frames.

Conversely, the making of Windsor chairs involved a number of specialist skills which often resulted in larger workshops employing men to work in one branch of the trade only. The workshops of High Wycombe are typical of this specialisation. Men were employed to work in one skill area alone, for example in wood turning, seat making, steaming and bending parts, staining and polishing, as well as the bench crafts of making fretted and turned splats and other sawn parts, or assembling ('framing') a chair. (See footnote, Chapter 2, p.35 which gives a detailed list of the many chair making trades in High Wycombe.) However, smaller workshops, such as those in the North East Midlands, often employed fewer men, and this involved individual craftsmen undertaking a number or all of the different trades.*

Although a greater variety of tasks was required to produce Windsor rather than ladder and spindle back chairs, many of the stages involved in the sequence of wood preparation for 'green' wood turnery and the turnery itself were similar. These included sawing the freshly felled timber to the approximate length of the part to be turned, and then cleaving or splitting the round section into triangular shaped segments using a mallet and wedge. These sections were then initially shaped with a flat sided axe to remove some surplus wood, and further shaping with a draw knife was then undertaken, holding the section of wood in a primitive foot operated vice known as a 'draw' or 'shave horse'. John Shadford's drawing of his workshop tools, shown in Figure 18, p.27, illustrates that this Lincolnshire chair maker used a mallet and wedge (items 22 and 23) to cleave round sections of wood. However, no shaving horse is shown as part of his workshop devices, and it may be that this maker held the segment to be turned in a vice whilst shaping it with the draw knife. The photographs of chair turners shown in Figures 9 to 14 (overleaf) illustrate the various stages in producing chair legs from 'green' timber, from sawing the beech trunk to finally air drying the turned legs and stretchers. The illustrations used in this sequence depict different chair turners, all of whom worked close to their timber sources in the Chiltern Hills near to High Wycombe during the first half of this century. The turners from the region had worked in an unbroken line from the eighteenth century, and the processes shown in these twentieth century photographs depict practices which are probably identical to those used by 'green' wood turners since the craft began.

The principal tool of the chair turner was the lathe, and the design of these varied according to the maker and the context in which he

worked. For example, those turners who worked with 'green' wood, and especially those who worked in rural areas close to the source of their raw materials, often operated simple lathes which relied on the motive power of a flexible pole. This form of lathe was relatively low powered, and relied upon the soft qualities of freshly felled timber in order to be efficient. Working at such lathes, the turner tied a leather cord to the tip of the bent pole, and having wound the cord once around the segment, fixed it to the apex of a triangular shaped foot treadle. The part to be turned was held between the two pivots of a fixed or 'tail' stock and the movable head stock, which in turn were held in a strong wooden bed made of two substantial sections of wood supported on heavy legs.

With this type of lathe, the turner could shape the parts only on the downward thrust of the treadle, and relied on the upward movement of the tip of the pole to return the treadle to the position where it could again be depressed. Such lathes were used over many centuries, and were used for chair turning both as fixed devices in workshops, as well as portable structures which could be moved around to different woodland sites, and housed in temporary shelters. Examples of this form of lathe are shown overleaf. The first, illustrated in Figure 15, is a pole lathe, dating from the seventeenth century which has probably been used by many generations of turners. The example in Figure 16 shows a pole lathe being operated in the Chiltern woodlands in Buckinghamshire to turn chair legs from the indigenous beech wood which provided much of the raw material for this important regional Windsor chair making tradition. The practice of turning with pole lathes continued in this region until the 1920s when the last peripatetic turner retired (see Chapter 1, p.26). This picture shows the clean and smoothly turned shavings which typify the soft green turnery of the pole lathe.

As well as the pole lathe favoured by rural chair turners, the use of treadle lathes became increasingly popular during the eighteenth century. These lathes had the advantage over pole lathes in that working on the principle of either a wooden or metal reciprocating flywheel, the revolving action was constant, and thus turning could take place continuously. These

lathes also had gearing systems which could be applied to assist in turning different densities of wood.

This form of lathe was used from archaic times using wooden reciprocating flywheels, and they were adopted by chair makers in many parts of the country. An example of this form of lathe with a metal wheel, abandoned in a turner's workshop in the Chiltern Hills, is shown in Figure 17. Unusually, this lathe has the addition of a grindstone permanently fixed on the same shaft as the head stock, so that the sharpening of the turnery tools was made easier. Another example of this form of lathe shown in use in a village workshop in the Chiltern Hills some time during the 1950s is shown in Figure 13 being used by Samuel Rockall, who was one of the last turners working outside the town of High Wycombe, making legs and stretchers. This form of lathe is also known to have been used in Lincolnshire workshops and an example is illustrated in the drawing of tools shown in Figure 18.

In addition to treadle and pole lathes, other workshops harnessed water power to drive belt-driven machinery from an overhead system of wheels attached to a revolving shaft. Such a workshop was operated by Mark Chippindale, a chair and bobbin turner of Aighton Bailey and Chaigley in Lancashire in 1815, whose inventory of machinery, given in detail in Chapter 7, p.322, shows that in addition to lathes and a bench drill, he had a circular saw. Such lathes required heavy frameworks to withstand the movement and pressures of the belt drive, although the metal tail and head stocks were similar to those used in other forms of wood turning lathes.

---

* Paradoxically, in individual chair making workshops, turning was not always undertaken, and in at least one of the major Windsor chair making centres in the North East Midlands, at Worksop in Nottinghamshire, the production of turned parts was the province of a specialist turnery firm, leaving the other chair making trades to be accomplished in the individual workshops. The great standardisation of the underarm turnings, legs, connecting stretchers and back spindles typically found in Windsors from this region is accounted for by their common origin. However, the specialist turnery workshop in Worksop probably used a steam engine to power the lathes in order that the large numbers of parts needed in this town's prolific industry could be turned, and later in the 19th century, as the number of chair making firms declined, some, if not all these remaining workshops purchased engines and did produce their own turned parts. See Chapter 3, p.164 for further details. In the Buckinghamshire tradition, too, specialist turners worked in the Chiltern Hills, either working in small workshops behind their houses or occasionally in makeshift huts in the woodlands. These turners produced legs and stretchers in great quantities from freshly felled timber which were then air dried before being collected by the chair making firms in High Wycombe.

Figure 9. A photograph of chair turners sawing a freshly felled beech tree into sections to the length of the parts to be turned. This arduous work was undertaken with a double handed, cross cut saw, and the sections were either split into 'billets' of wood for turning in situ, or carried on a cart back to the home-based village workshops.

(Courtesy Museum of English Rural Life, University of Reading.)

Figure 10. George Dean, one of the last of the Chiltern chair turners who worked in the woods until the early 1950s, splitting a round section of beech in two, using a mallet or 'beetle', and an axe as a wedge. The number of felled trees in the background awaiting conversion indicates the prodigious amounts of wood used in this craft.

(Courtesy Museum of English Rural Life, University of Reading.)

Figure 11. Samuel Rockall who worked as a chair turner on the edge of Summer Common, Buckinghamshire, for nearly sixty-two years, felled his timber for all of that time in the nearby Turville Woods. This maker learned his trade from his uncle, also Samuel, who died in 1913 at the age of eighty-nine, and who had also been a chair maker all his life. Between them, these two turners worked for 116 years, and provided a continuity of the craft from the early part of the 19th century until the 1960s. Here, Samuel Rockall is shown shaping a cleft billet of wood with a flat sided axe to remove the bark and the sharp edges, prior to further shaping with a draw knife. The workshop is characteristic of many used by chair turners, full of shavings and the clutter of the trade, with drying billets of wood yet to be shaped. This maker felled his trees a year before use and left them lying in the woodland until needed. He then took his own shire horse to haul the trunks back to his workshop on a timber carriage which had iron wheels to withstand the weight of the timber.

(Photograph by C.F.F. Snow. Museum of English Rural Life, University of Reading)

Figure 12. Samuel Rockall is shown here roughly shaping a leg segment using a draw knife and a primitive foot-operated 'draw' or 'shave horse' to hold the wood. Shaped sections lie to the left of the 'horse', and show that quite precise shaping was made prior to them being turned. The large metal treadle lathe stands to the left, embedded in a deep layer of shavings.

(Courtesy Museum of English Rural Life, University of Reading)

Figure 13. A crisp three ring leg being deftly turned by Samuel Rockall, showing the typical skill of the Windsor chair maker. The foot of the turned leg is left deliberately long in order that it can be cut off to adjust to the warping of the seat. For this reason, the feet of Windsor chair legs are often of different lengths from each other, depending on the seat shape.

(Photograph by C.F.F. Snow. Museum of English Rural Life, University of Reading)

Figure 14. Chair legs stacked to air dry after turning in the beech woods of Buckinghamshire. After drying, these were put into sacks and collected by chair manufacturers who came by cart from High Wycombe. Chair turners who worked in the Chiltern village of Radnage chose a more unusual way of drying legs, by pushing them into the hedges around the village. *(Courtesy Museum of English Rural Life, University of Reading.)*

Figure 15. A pole lathe of venerable age, probably 17th century. This simple form of lathe was commonly used from archaic times to produce domestic turnery ware. This example bears the scars of continuous use, probably by several generations of turners. *(Courtesy Science Museum, London.)*

Figure 16. A pole lathe set up in a temporary shelter in the beech woods of the Chiltern Hills, Buckinghamshire, c.1940. The pole lathe was inexpensive to make, and offered a skilled turner the opportunity to produce chair parts in situ *close to his source of raw material. The head and tail stocks and wooden framework are similar to those found in other forms of lathe, but the power was provided by a bent sapling. A leather cord was tied to the top of the pole, and then wound once around the segment to be turned, and was finally attached to the apex of the foot treadle. Turning could only take place on the downward action of the treadle, which was returned to its upward position by the power of the pole. An experienced turner could produce parts quickly, but the continuous rotation of treadle and belt driven lathes was more efficient and generally, though not always, preferred in permanent workshops. (See Figure 17)*

(Courtesy High Wycombe Chair Museum.)

Although the types of lathes differed according to the regional context and the organisation of a particular workshop, the hand tools used were probably similar, and essentially contained part of the inventory of tools which cabinet makers used, but without the range of moulding planes and ploughs which were commonly used by cabinet makers. Although detailed records of the hand tools and devices used in chair making workshops are scarce, amongst those that exist is an inventory of some thirty-seven different items which were drawn by John Shadford, a Windsor chair maker from Caistor in Lincolnshire, in his workshop notebook (see Figure 18) during the nineteenth century. These included, in addition to hand tools, a treadle lathe, a steaming tank, a large bending bench, a small bending bench, a metal worker's vice, and a vat of red lead in which to stain chairs.

Further evidence is provided by a collection of tools owned by James Thomlinson, a 'turner chair maker' of Lancaster who, in his will dated

Figure 17. A treadle lathe photographed in the disused workshop of Samuel Saunders in the Chiltern Hills of Buckinghamshire, c.1940. This form of lathe was typical of those used by chair turners in many parts of England, and shows the large reciprocating flywheel which was rotated by a foot treadle, allowing continuous turning which made it more efficient than the simple pole lathe.

(Courtesy Museum of English Rural Life, University of Reading.)

Figure 18 (Below). A drawing from the workshop notebook of John Shadford, Windsor chair maker of Caistor, Lincolnshire (fl.1851-88), showing the tools and devices used in his workshop, as well as some chair parts, and one of the chairs he made. This naive drawing represents a unique visual record of the hand tools and other equipment probably used by chair makers all over England. John Shadford's work is discussed in Chapter 3, pp.144-6.

(Courtesy Lincoln Record Office)

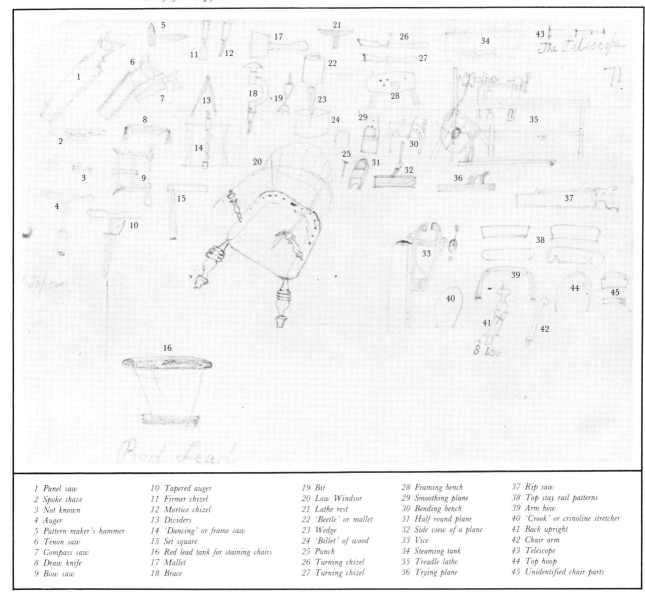

1 Panel saw	10 Tapered auger	19 Bit	28 Framing bench	37 Rip saw
2 Spoke shave	11 Firmer chizel	20 Low Windsor	29 Smoothing plane	38 Top stay rail patterns
3 Not known	12 Mortice chizel	21 Lathe rest	30 Bending bench	39 Arm bow
4 Auger	13 Dividers	22 'Beetle' or mallet	31 Half round plane	40 'Crook' or crinoline stretcher
5 Pattern maker's hammer	14 'Dancing' or frame saw	23 Wedge	32 Side view of a plane	41 Back upright
6 Tenon saw	15 Set square	24 'Billet' of wood	33 Vice	42 Chair arm
7 Compass saw	16 Red lead tank for staining chairs	25 Punch	34 Steaming tank	43 Telescope
8 Draw knife	17 Mallet	26 Turning chizel	35 Treadle lathe	44 Top hoop
9 Bow saw	18 Brace	27 Turning chizel	36 Trying plane	45 Unidentified chair parts

Figure 19. Jack Goodchild of Naphill, Buckinghamshire, c.1950, bending a steamed yew branch to form a Windsor arm or top bow. The steaming tank stands to the left. The 'bed' of the bending bench, to which alternative sizes of formers could be bolted, is made of cast iron. The physical effort needed to bend the hoops around the former can be appreciated from this photograph. (Courtesy High Wycombe Chair Museum)

Figure 20. Jack Goodchild holding the bent branches of yew which were roughly shaped before being steamed and bent to form bows. The string tied across the bow is to prevent the bent wood from straightening out while it is drying. Such bows, when shaped, show the decorative variegation of dark heart wood and yellow sap wood common to yew, which helped to make this the most favoured of chair making woods.
(Courtesy Museum of English Rural Life, University of Reading)

1847, gives a comprehensive list of tools, including 'six chair bows and an adze', and more than fifty different tools, although, inexplicably, a lathe is not mentioned (see Chapter 7, pp.324-5). However, the list does include a 'large glue kettle' and an 'oilstone', both of which might also be expected to have been part of the Shadford workshop contents, though not included in his drawing; and it may be that both lists do not mention every item in the particular workshop. One major difference, however, is apparent between the contents of these two North of England workshops and those which developed in

Figure 21. A pit saw in use in the early part of this century. One man stands on the trunk, gripping the saw and pulling it to the upward position, while another in the pit below pulls the saw down on the cutting stroke. This method was used to make the planks from which Windsor chair seats were made.

(Courtesy High Wycombe Chair Museum)

Figure 22. Jack Goodchild using a razor sharp adze to create the saddle shaped seats for which Windsors are noted. The seat maker or 'bottomer' held the seat in position on the floor with his feet, and needed great skill not only to produce the required shaping, but also to avoid injuring himself.

(Courtesy Museum of English Rural Life, University of Reading)

Figure 23. An illustration of one of the bench trades involved in making Windsor chairs. Jack Goodchild is shown making a complex Gothic fretted splat and using a file to clean and sharpen the fretting profile. A wide range of different splat designs was made, particularly in the High Wycombe tradition, and different examples of these are hung on the wall of this workshop. See Chapter 2 for more details of splat designs from this region. (Courtesy High Wycombe Chair Museum)

the Buckinghamshire tradition, since a brace and separate bits are recorded in both the Thomlinson and Shadford tool lists, whereas a set of fixed stocks or braces and spoon bits were typically used in Buckinghamshire to produce the different sized mortice holes, in order to avoid having to constantly change bits. Fixed stocks of this kind were used by the Oxford Windsor chair maker,

Walter Puddifer, and two of his stocks are illustrated in Chapter 2, Figure TV217.

In addition to turning, the practice of steaming short, flat sections of wood prior to bending them over a former, to create the typical curved ladder shape, was amongst the skills used by some chair turners making ladder back chairs. However, it was the Windsor chair makers who needed

to perfect the art of steaming the relatively long sections of cleft wood, shaped branches or coppice poles, which were needed to make arm and top bows, and then at the moment of required suppleness, to bend the section around a former and hold it to shape with wood or iron pegs. Such a process required great understanding of the material being used, as well as considerable physical

Figure 24. Jack Goodchild boring leg mortices into a seat using a fixed 'stock' or bit and brace. He is shown making the angle of entry, using his experience rather than a template. The seat was held on to a heavy low bench in order to gain sufficient downward pressure to make the mortice.

(Courtesy Museum of English Rural Life, University of Reading)

strength. Any failure of timing resulted in a bent section whose fibres broke away at some point, causing a 'feathering' effect which rendered the bow useless. Figure 19 shows a Buckinghamshire Windsor chair maker bending a roughly shaped yew branch around a former, using pegs to hold it in shape. The tank used for steaming the part stands to the left of the scene, and another size of former is shown to the right. Figure 20 shows the same maker holding two bent yew branches tied to hold them in shape whilst they dried.

A further major craft was involved in producing Windsor chairs, that of making elm seats. This process began with the sawing of the elm trunks in a pit saw. In this arduous work, the trunk was placed over a pit and one man stood on top to guide and pull a double handled saw upwards through the timber. His mate worked in the pit below pulling the saw down to cut the wood, and in so doing, became showered with sawdust. The photograph shown in Figure 21 taken early this century, shows such a pit saw being used to convert an elm trunk. The resulting planks were then sawn into outline seat shapes, and adzed to the correct profile whilst in green condition, and then stacked to dry. This drying process was necessary since elm is prone to extreme distortion as it dries, and the fitting of legs could only be accurately undertaken after the wood had completed its 'movement'. The making of elm seats was the province of the chair 'bottomer' or seat maker who used the ancient skill of adzing to shape the sawn seat 'blank' to create

Figure 25. A further bench craft, that of 'framing' or assembling the chair was an important skill in creating the right balance and style of the chair. Here Jack Goodchild is shown hammering the leg assembly of a side chair in place. Later, the feet will be cut to length.

(Courtesy Museum of English Rural Life, University of Reading)

the sympathetically dished shaping which made the seat comfortable to sit on. This was a highly skilled craft, requiring the precise use of a razor sharp cutting edge to pare away thin shavings. To achieve this, the maker held the seat in place on the floor with his feet and cut the wood away, taking great care to avoid injuring himself. Such was the skill of these men that, particularly in the eighteenth century, chair seats were also shaped on the bottom, to create lightness and elegance, and seats from this period often bear the delicate adze marks on the underside. The bottomer shown working in Figure 22 shows the back bending action required to use the adze.

The skilled bench trade of fretted splat making, morticing, and assembling were learned last in a sequence of skills taught to apprentices who followed a full course of instruction. Each of these processes required different forms of adeptness in producing accurate shaping for the frets, drilling the many correct angles of mortice into the seat, and in assembling and levelling the chairs to produce the competence of style for which Windsor chairs were noted. Illustrations of these various aspects of chair making are shown in Figures 23-25.

The final stage of staining and polishing completed chairs at this maker's workshop is also shown in Figure 26 which shows a chair after dipping into a tank of stain, probably a mixture of alum and urine or tartar, which produced a yellow/brown colour, prior to being varnished when dry. However, other techniques of staining had been used in the first half of the nineteenth century in the Thames Valley area, and Loudon, writing in 1833, recorded that these chairs 'are sometimes painted, but more frequently stained with diluted sulphuric acid and logwood; or by repeatedly washing them over with alum water, which has some tartar in it. They should afterwards be washed over several times with an extract of Brasil wood... Quicklime slacked in urine and laid on the wood while hot is said to be the general practice with the Windsor chair manufacturers in the neighbourhood of London.'

However, the process of staining finished chairs, or not, varied considerably from region to region. For example, some ladder and spindle back chair makers working in the

Figure 26. The final process in making a Windsor chair was to stain and polish it. Here a chair is being removed from a vat of stain which may have been a mixture of alum and either urine or tartar, or a commercial water stain mixture. In either case, staining would have been followed by a coat of Shellac varnish and, perhaps, a final coat of beeswax for the 'best' chairs.

(Courtesy Museum of English Rural Life, University of Reading)

nineteenth century in Lincolnshire, Herefordshire and Worcestershire regions did not stain their chairs at all, with the result that surviving chairs have now often become an attractive pale golden yellow through the process of ageing alone.

Other chair makers, particularly those working in the North West region and Scotland, commonly used alder in making their chairs. This wood oxidises to a pink colour on being cut, and the natural colour of the wood was augmented by the use of a mahogany stain to simulate this wood. Other chair makers, for example those who mass-produced Windsors in the Yorkshire tradition in the late nineteenth century, advertised their wares as stained with 'Mahogany, Walnut or brown stain', and in these cases stains were used to enhance the appearance of chairs made with inferior mixed woods such as birch and willow. The Lincolnshire workshop of John Shadford contained a vat of red lead used to stain the chairs (see Figure 18, p.27). Varnish was applied over this finish,

and the total effect was presumably intended to simulate mahogany. In the West Country, chairs were frequently painted and on occasion the nodes of simulated bamboo turnings were picked out in a different colour (see Chapter 5, Figure SW57.

✳✳✳✳✳✳✳✳✳✳✳✳✳✳✳✳

In studying the regional variations of the seating furniture made for everyday use, often in the humblest of homes, one can only be filled with respect for the skill and artistry of the makers. Chairs which may at first sight appear the same, are seen to be the product of a particular region or even a particular individual. As the different regional styles are discussed in the following chapters, the author hopes the reader will share his delight in the great diversity of design of these objects which, although simply made to fulfil a basic human need, reflect the richness of English vernacular life and the originality of English craftsmen.

Chapter 2
THE THAMES VALLEY
AND THE CHILTERNS

The chair making tradition which arose in the South of England was centred on the area where the Chiltern Hills run through Buckinghamshire and into the South East of Oxfordshire. The Chilterns were densely forested, particularly with beech trees, isolating their inhabitants from the developing life of London and the Thames Valley during the eighteenth century. The compact villages, typical of other parts of England, were rare, and the Chiltern communities tended to live in scattered houses and hamlets built in the valleys.

The Windsor chair making craft which developed in Buckinghamshire, and particularly in the town of High Wycombe, came ultimately to satisfy much of the need for common seating furniture for the whole of the South of England, as well as the Midlands and East Anglia.

The origins of Windsor chair making in this region can certainly be traced back to the beginning of the eighteenth century, and probably the earliest reference to Windsor chairs being made in Wycombe is provided in an account book of the Overseers of the Poor of West Wycombe, which states that David Pisis (Pusey) was paid 6/6d. in 1732 for a 'Wins [Windsor] chair ordered by the Vestry'.[1] However, although Windsor chairs are known to have been made in other parts of Buckinghamshire, as well as in Middlesex and London during the eighteenth century (see Figures TV18 and 148), evidence of the growth of this trade in the major centre of High Wycombe during this period is scarce, and it awaits the military census of the High [Chepping] Wycombe area in 1798, recording men between the ages of fifteen and sixty and their occupations, for

evidence of the trade to be revealed, when fifty-eight chair makers, master men and workmen were recorded in the Wycombe area.[2]

The location of what was to become the centre for the chair making industry, the High Wycombe area, was not a random choice, but probably reflected three major conditions which were important in its development. Firstly, raw material was readily available. Beech for legs, stretchers and back spindles, ash for hoops, elm for the seats and fruitwood for splats; all these woods abounded in the Chiltern Hills. As early as 1725 Daniel Defoe wrote of the '... vast quantity of beechwood which grows in the woods of Buckinghamshire more plentifully than in any other part of England... [provided] beech quarters for diverse uses, particularly chair makers and turnery wares... The quantity of this brought down from hence is almost incredible, yet so is the county overgrown with the beech in these parts that it is bought very reasonably, nor is there likely to be any scarcity of it for time to come'.[3]

If the materials needed by the trade were present, so equally was a market for its products; the large population of London and its environs provided an insatiable and growing market for the chairs, particularly as the eighteenth century

came to a close and the population here, as in all parts of England, was expanding (see table below).

The vital link bringing together the chairs and their buyers was provided by the third crucial element, that of transport. The busy London-Oxford road, which was a main route for the Midlands and the South West, passed through High Wycombe, and provided the means for transporting the chairs by horse-drawn cart to these areas, as well as to London.

By the end of the eighteenth century, the chair making trade in Wycombe had become strongly developed, and was essentially organised by owners of small firms. Four chair making businesses are recorded in 1790,[4] and by 1830, the number of firms in the High Wycombe area had grown to twenty.[5] These businesses tended to be owned by members of a few chair making families including the Cannons, Harrises, Howlands, Sewells, Skulls, Treachers, and Widgintons, who raised substantial businesses which were to continue throughout the nineteenth century and in some cases continue today.

At the same time that the trade expanded in High Wycombe, chair making businesses were established in other Buckinghamshire towns, and by 1830 there were firms in Amersham, Chesham and Wendover.[6] This growth continued, and by 1847

Table I Population Growth [1921 Census Report]			
Date	Berks.	Bucks.	London
1801	110,752	107,900	958,791
1831	146,702	146,977	1,654,632

Plate 2. Comb back Windsor chair with four cabriole legs. Yew with elm seat. Thames Valley, c.1740-70.

Figure TV1. The interior of a cottage at Great Barrington, near Burford, Oxfordshire, taken in 1953, is evocative of many of the cottage homes in the Cotswolds largely occupied by farm workers. The cottage retains its 19th century iron fireplace and 'over-mantel' (the curtain below the mantelshelf used to restrict smoke eddying into the room). To the right of the mantelshelf hang useful household objects — fire tongs, a balance to weigh vegetables and meat, and a padded cloth kettle holder. The turned leg dining table has a decorated fabric cover which was placed over the table between meals. The 'pegged' rug in front of the hearth is a typical product of 19th and early 20th century working class culture; hessian sacks, used for agricultural purposes, were pegged through with strips of cloth, usually from old clothes, to form a rug pile.

The two armchairs situated either side of the fire are representative of the region's 19th century Windsor chairs. That on the left is a double bow Windsor with a roundel turned central splat characteristic of the Buckinghamshire region (see Figure TV75). The 'crook' underarm supports probably date this chair to the first half of the 19th century.

The chair in which the elderly lady sits, is a typical scroll back Windsor style, with the 'raised' three ring leg turning motif and a regionally specific arm support. This style of chair was made widely in the Oxfordshire and Buckinghamshire chair making centres (see Figures TV163 and TV214). The use of a high and low back armchair perhaps reinforces the view that chairs purchased during the 19th and early 20th centuries had cultural connotations with a 'father' (or larger chair) and a 'mother' (or smaller) chair placed either side of the fire. (Photograph Edwin Smith)

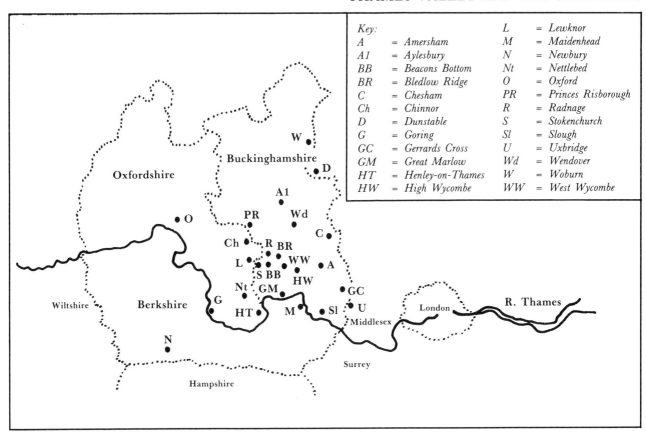

Key:
A = Amersham
A1 = Aylesbury
BB = Beacons Bottom
BR = Bledlow Ridge
C = Chesham
Ch = Chinnor
D = Dunstable
G = Goring
GC = Gerrards Cross
GM = Great Marlow
HT = Henley-on-Thames
HW = High Wycombe
L = Lewknor
M = Maidenhead
N = Newbury
Nt = Nettlebed
O = Oxford
PR = Princes Risborough
R = Radnage
S = Stokenchurch
Sl = Slough
U = Uxbridge
Wd = Wendover
W = Woburn
WW = West Wycombe

Figure TV2. Chair making centres in the Thames Valley region, 1800-1850.

the chair making industry had spread to further centres in Buckinghamshire (see Figure TV2). The skill of the Buckinghamshire Windsor chair makers spread further afield as craftsmen left the area to set up as independent chair makers in Oxfordshire.

Within the major centre of High Wycombe, the owners of firms worked in a ruthlessly competitive milieu, in which the quality and cheapness of their chairs were primary factors which caused them to flourish or fail. In order to function competitively, the manufacturers sought to keep operating costs as low as possible, and they typically provided double storey workshops of single brick, or more usually wood-clad structures, in which their skilled craftsmen rented space at the rate of 2/- per week, in the nineteenth century, and a few pence more for oil and lights and for the use of the grindstone.[7] Apart from the polishing and drying areas, these workshops were unheated and glass for the windows was considered a luxury. The illustration in Figure TV3 shows

a two storey chair making factory, typical of those erected throughout High Wycombe. These particular buildings were owned by C. Gibbons of Oxford Road, High Wycombe. The photograph, taken in the early twentieth century, also shows a cart being loaded with layers of chairs prior to being transported to customers.

Although the premises in which the chair makers worked were clearly of a very basic nature, the payment of the craft-workers by piece-work rates had advantages and disadvantages for employer and worker alike. Under this system the employer held little responsibility other than to provide a roof over his workers' heads, and to pay them at the end of the week for the work that they achieved. For the chair maker, the system rewarded him poorly, in terms of his working conditions, and in the payment he received. However, under the system, he was essentially self-employed, and could choose to work, or not. These men were usually skilled in one or more of the crafts of turning, seat making, making sawn parts, including fretted splats,

assembling, finishing and staining chairs. Some tradesmen could undertake all of these tasks: others were specialised tradesmen and a review of chair making trades given in the 1851 census for High Wycombe lists twenty-three different chair trades and occupations.*

The chair makers usually received their week's wages at the end of Saturday's work, often resulting in a weekend of drinking, with high absenteeism from work on Monday. If there was any money left by Monday, then they often congregated at the well-known public houses in Wycombe, where they drank, played games and had 'an impromptu fry-up'.[8] Given the generally poor

---

* The 1851 Census for High Wycombe illustrates the very specialised nature of the chair making industry there, and lists the following as separate occupations:

Journeyman Chair Maker; Chair Worker; Chair Labourer; Chair Borer; Chair Manufacturer; Chair Framer; Chair Matter; Chair Maker, back Feet; Chair Maker, seats; Chair Maker, seat Borer; Chair Caner; Chair Back Maker; Chair Turner; Master Chair Turner; Chair Traveller; Chair Bow Maker; Chair Carver; Chair Maker, sweep Backs; Chair Maker, cane Seats; Chair Maker, grainer; Chair Maker, benchman; Chair Painter; Chair Top Maker.

35

Plate 3. Low Windsor armchair. Yew with elm seat. Stamped 'ROBERT PRIOR MAKER UXBRIDGE' (fl.1816-45).

Plate 4. Low Windsor armchair. Yew with elm seat. Stamped 'J. PRIOR UXBRIDGE'. This stamp refers to John Prior, chair maker (fl. 1768-1816).

Plate 5. High hoop back Windsor chair. Yew with elm seat. (Feet missing.) Stamped 'ROBERT PRIOR MAKER UXBRIDGE' (fl. 1816-45).

Plate 6. Windsor side chair. Ash and beech with elm seat. Stamped 'ROBERT PRIOR MAKER UXBRIDGE' (fl. 1816-45).

Plate 7. Low Windsor armchair. Ash and fruitwood with elm seat. Stamped 'PRIOR'. Attributed to Samuel Prior of Cricklewood (fl. 1816-39).

37

Figure TV3. Chair makers loading chairs in the factory of C. Gibbons, 'chair manufacturers of Oxford Road, High Wycombe', c.1900. The double storey, wooden framed and clad buildings to the left and rear are characteristic of the workshops built in the 19th century to house the chair makers. The chairs being loaded are stratified, with the lower layer composed of the plain, heavy stick back type which were supplied in thousands to meet contracts given by the War Department.

Rush seated chairs made in large numbers for institutional use, are packed in two layers above, and finally large smokers' bow or office chairs are being loaded on top. The difficulty in moving large consignments of chairs such as this on the unmade roads of the time must have been an enormous labour, requiring regular changes of horses.

(Courtesy High Wycombe Chair Museum)

working conditions of the mid-nineteenth century, the lives of the High Wycombe chair makers apparently did not seem exceptional to them, and one chair framer, who had worked under the piece-work system commented:

'I was a framer. I worked in another man's factory it's true, but I was really working for myself, because every chair I framed, provided that I made a good sound job of it, I was paid for... All right then, I couldn't make chairs without a roof over my head, so it was only fair I should pay for my bench room; likewise if I wanted to frame on after dark I needed a light to do it by, and it only seems reasonable that a master would jib at paying you for chairs that you had made by the light he had paid for. ... No, if you like piece-work, and I did, for I was a good workman and could make a bit extra any time I wanted to and could leave off too

and have a day's holiday when I chose, well, if you liked piece-work you accepted the conditions and the customs that went with it.'[9]

A major concern of the chair masters was to find markets for their chairs, and towards the mid-nineteenth century many firms provided catalogues of their wares. From these, they received mail orders from furniture warehouses, retailers and institutions. Some firms also employed travellers to take waggon loads of chairs to sell to anyone who would buy them in the surrounding counties, and one can see from photographs of high laden horse-drawn waggons taking chairs to their destination how difficult transport by road must have been (see Figure TV3). One such 'chair traveller', and later factory owner, was Benjamin North, of West Wycombe, a former paper maker who became unemployed with the advent of mechanisation in

that industry. He became a traveller for Mr Randel, a chair turner of Thame, and in his memoirs (1882) recorded: 'So I took my first journey with a load of chairs, starting from Thame in the night, going through Wheatley, on to Headington, where I took my horse out and gave it the usual bait and also refreshed myself.' He travelled through Witney and Burford to the 'beautiful town of Cheltenham', and so on to Tewkesbury where 'I sold my chairs and returned home, thus finishing my first journey with satisfaction to my master.'[10]

Mechanisation came to chair making towards the middle of the nineteenth century, and steam engines began to be introduced into the Wycombe factories to power machinery. The hand crafts which relied entirely on muscle power began to be supplemented by belt-driven band and circular saws, wood turning lathes, tenoning and boring machines, seat adzers, planing machines, sanders and polishers. These machines which gradually revolutionised production, were installed with little regard for the safety of their operators. Machines were frequently unguarded, with exposed moving belts which came down from overhead wheels, and in which workers could catch their clothes or their hands. Mayes reports that, 'For the first half century of the machine age, an operator with all his fingers was a rarity'.[11] However, the greater use of machines in the chair making industry did not cause redundancy amongst chair makers, and it is reported that by 1877, there were almost a hundred chair making factories in High Wycombe, producing 4,700 chairs per day.[12]

Although High Wycombe was the centre for creating many of the chair parts and assembling the completed chairs, most of the ordinary turnery work of producing the legs and stretchers required by the manufacturers, was undertaken by turners who lived in villages and hamlets of the Chiltern Hills, close to the source of wood, and who sold their work to the factory owners. This turnery trade arose particularly a few miles to the north west of High Wycombe in the forested hills in the area of Stokenchurch, Chinnor, Bledlow Ridge, Princes Risborough, Great Hampden, Radnage, and Beacon's Bottom. In the late nineteenth century, the turners bought their wood at annual sales of standing timber which was sold by auction at the Stokenchurch Hotel. Here, estate owners would offer a 'fall' of twelve to twenty beech trees which, when sold, would be felled by the vendor, usually during the winter when the sap was low. The turners would then be responsible for sawing the trunks into lengths suitable for leg and stretcher turning, and lopping and burning up the unwanted branches.[13] Some of these turners preferred to make a rough shelter at the woodland site from wood, bracken and the woodshavings they produced. Here, the turner used a froe or fromard to split the wood and a side axe to roughly shape the section. Then a draw knife, used in conjunction with a simple wooden draw horse, was used to further shape the segments, and the green wood was finally turned on a pole lathe. The resulting unseasoned, turned legs and stretchers were stacked in neat piles or poked into a 'hedgehog' of legs to dry.

Figure TV4. The workshop of a High Wycombe chair manufactory, c.1880. The use of belt driven machinery, powered by steam engines, improved productivity, and assisted the expansion of the chair making trade during the second half of the 19th century. This was often achieved at the cost of safety, with unguarded machines and the belts which drove them presenting a constant hazard to the chair makers.   (Courtesy High Wycombe Chair Museum)

Figure TV5 illustrates such a turner's camp in the Chilterns in the early twentieth century, and shows chair legs drying to the right of the hut and cleft sections in the foreground await shaping. A boy sits on a draw horse outside the hut, and the man to the left of the scene is roughly shaping cleft segments with a side axe. The pole which provided power for the lathe is shown entering the front of the hut. See Chapter 1, pp.24 and 26 for further discussion of the use of the pole lathe in the chair making trade.

The lives of woodland turners (also known as bodgers*) must have been lonely, although an insight into one chair turner's thoughts and life, when looking back over the years, is sensitively given by Mr George Dean, brother of Owen Dean of Great Hampden, who was one of the last turners to work in the Chiltern Woodland. George Dean expressed himself thus:

'It was a strangely enjoyable life, carefree and a bit lonesome if your mate was away. In the spring it was lovely as the trees took on their fresh green leaf, and in the winter, the sighing of the wind and the sight of the birds gathering in the branches when the smoke ascended at meal times. Occasionally the robins would build by the lathe side in the thatch, and hatch the eggs and rear the young. Now and then a wren would make a cosy nest and flit about. Once a flock of pigeons descended on the trees round our shops just after dark. The noise of their flapping wings was alarming as they settled in the tree tops, too exhausted to heed us very much as we worked by candlelight in our primitive way.'[14]

However, the majority of the turners preferred to work in a shed near to their homes, similar to that

---

* The term 'bodger' appears to be a popular twentieth century name applied to turners who worked in the woodland using pole lathes. However, this term, which is usually applied to someone who 'bodges' or 'botches' his work, producing a poor result, seems a singularly inappropriate term to apply to these excellent craftsmen, and was a description probably not known to the original turners. This is reinforced since no reference to 'bodgers' is made in the Census returns for the High Wycombe area in either 1841 or 1851, although a few references are made in these returns to workers recorded in 'hut in woods'.[15] This probably refers to turners working in the woodland setting. The introduction of the word 'bodger' is probably a journalistic term introduced by writers in the early twentieth century when describing this craft, a word which has been erroneously repeated in subsequent texts.

39

*Plate 8. Child's high table chair. Beech with elm seat. Stamped 'R.B.'
Buckinghamshire, c.1840.*

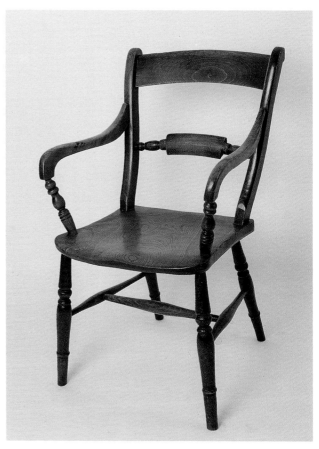

*Plate 9. Scroll back Windsor armchair. Beech with elm seat. Stamped
'S. HAZELL OXFORD' (fl.1846-92).*

*Plate 10. Ladder back side chair. Oak with rush seat. Stamped
'GLENNISTER MAKER WYCOMBE G.R.V.', c.1920.*

*Plate 11. Bergère Windsor chair. Fruitwood with elm seat. Stamped
'J.S.', Wycombe, c.1870.*

Figure TV5. A turner's camp in the Chiltern beech woods, late 19th century. The hut in the centre houses the pole lathe on which the legs and stretchers were turned. The man to the left roughly shapes cleft segments of beech with a side axe, prior to their being further shaped with a draw knife by the boy on the 'draw horse'. There is a stack of turned legs in the foreground and a 'hedgehog' of plain back legs on the far right.

(Courtesy High Wycombe Chair Museum)

Figure TV6. A shed based turner's workshop in the Chiltern Hills, 1902. This form of small workshop was found in many Buckinghamshire towns and villages, and presented an alternative to the large manufacturers which developed in High Wycombe. Beech trunks have been brought to the workshop for sawing and splitting into sections, to provide turnery parts. Stacks of legs are shown to the left and centre and these would probably have been turned on a metal treadle lathe with a fly-wheel mechanism, rather than on a pole lathe. *(Photograph C.F. Snow)*

shown in Figure TV6, rather than work in the woodland, and to use a metal foot-treadled lathe, with a reciprocating flywheel, rather than a pole lathe of the kind shown in Figure TV5. Elderly relatives of craftsmen who remember the chair turning trade in the village of Radnage recall that it was the children's job to push freshly turned legs into the hedges around the cottage gardens to dry, and then to count them into sacks ready for the chair manufacturers from High Wycombe, who collected them by horse and cart.[16]

Traditionally the Wycombe factory owners exploited their strength as buyers of the chair turners' work, and before the First World War paid 5/- (25p) for a gross of legs and stretchers, each gross being made up of 144 legs and 108 stretcher parts. The turner would have to produce 2½ gross per week in order to earn a living wage of 12/6d. (62p),[17] and to achieve this he had to work relentlessly from seven in the morning till seven in the evening, five and a half days a week.

Both turning in situ in the woodland, using a pole lathe, and the use of workshop based treadle lathes, continued well into the twentieth century. The last known member of the singular group of craftsmen who worked in the woodland was Mr

Figure TV7. A Chiltern turner, Mr Samuel Rockall, working at a metal treadle lathe, which has a reciprocating flywheel mechanism. Mr Rockall was born in 1878 and continued in his trade until 1961, living all his life in Summer Cottage, Turville, some seven miles west of High Wycombe. The shed form of workshop (usually sited close to their homes) was preferred by the majority of the Chiltern turners.

(Courtesy Museum of English Rural Life, University of Reading)

Owen Dean, who continued turning in Great Hampden Wood, until the 1920s.[18]

A few turners who worked in sheds, continued after this time, and prior to the Second World War, some tried to modernise their production methods by bringing in electrically driven machinery. One such workshop, now in disrepair (1984), lies at Beacon's Bottom, Radnage. It was owned by the Avery family who had a long history throughout the nineteenth century as chair turners. An extract from their accounts book from the early part of the twentieth century, reproduced in Figure TV8, shows

something of the economic difficulties which the turners experienced in dealing with the chair manufacturers. Entries for turned chair parts supplied to one of his customers, J. Cox and Son Ltd., begins with a delivery in January 1916, and subsequent deliveries in February, March and May. Payment for these consignments was not made until June. Today the Buckinghamshire chair industry still flourishes in Stokenchurch and High and West Wycombe, but the turnery is usually undertaken by the same businesses who market the completed chairs.

Early Windsors

If the growth of the chair making industry itself was one of change and development during the eighteenth and nineteenth centuries, then the development of the Windsor chair form followed a similar progression. 'Windsor' is a generic term used to describe a chair composed of a wooden seat into which legs are morticed below, and where a number of either turned or sawn and shaped uprights are morticed above, to create the back. This simple term, whilst perhaps doing less than justice to the great variety of designs which were to derive from the earliest chairs of this type, serves to divide this basic style from the other major English regional chair traditions which include, for example, the turned rush seated chairs from the North West Region (see Chapter 7); and those which are turned and have thin elm seats from the West Midlands tradition (see Chapter 6); as well as the wide range of chairs made with wooden seats from the East Anglian tradition (see Chapter 4).

The origins of the term 'Windsor chair' are not clear although the tracing of 'innocent' references to Windsors, in letters and other writings, make it plain that the Windsor chair was known by the early eighteenth century. Nancy Goyne Evans, in her excellent paper (1979) concerned with the emergence of the Windsor seating form, claims that the earliest known reference to Windsor furniture is used by Stephen Switzer in his publication, *Ichnographica Rustica* in 1718, which is an expanded treatise on rural gardening, devoting space to a description of a garden at Dyrham, near Bath. In this he describes a 'large seat called a Windsor seat which is contrived to turn round any way'.[19] This probably referred to a type of seat which was similar to one described by Daniel Defoe, writing of a house in Windsor in 1725, in which he describes a further seating device which pivoted in order that the sitter could orientate the seat.[20]

A further early reference to a Windsor chair, given by Lord Percival writing to his brother-in-law Daniel Dering, commenting on a visit to the grounds of Hall Barn, Buckinghamshire, said 'My wife was carry'd in a "Windsor" chair like those at Versailles, by which means she lost nothing worth the seeing.'[21] Whether this device was intended to push or carry Lady Percival is not clear. Certainly Windsors with wheels were made in the eighteenth century, and such a chair appears on the trade cards of Lock[n] Foulger of Walham Green in 1777.[22]

These early references suggest that Windsor furniture was originally designed for the garden. However, eighteenth century Windsor chairs of a more conventional variety were made for use in both the home and the garden. These styles were probably identical to each other, but those made for the garden were painted green to protect the chairs from the weather. Such chairs, for example, were advertised by John Brown, 'At

the 3 Chairs and Walnut Tree at St. Paul's Churchyard' (1727), and this maker's merchandise included 'all sorts of Windsor Garden chairs of all sizes painted green or in the wood'.[23] (See Figure TV16).

Although many documentary references confirm that Windsors were known from at least the second quarter of the eighteenth century, the earliest provenanced Windsor chairs date from the third quarter of the eighteenth century. However, it is probable that Windsor chairs originated in the late seventeenth or early eighteenth century, prior to the earliest documentary references, and the

unprovenanced early English comb back Windsor, from the collection of the late Edwin Skull, shown in Figure TV11, is probably an example of a Windsor prototype. The positioning of the barley twist decoration in the front and middle cross stretchers and central back spindles is typical of those found in Carolean cane seated chairs from the second half of the seventeenth century (see Figure TV10). This and the stylised crown motif in the comb rail suggest that the Skull chair was made in the late seventeenth or early eighteenth century, adopting contemporary features in a newly emerging seating form.

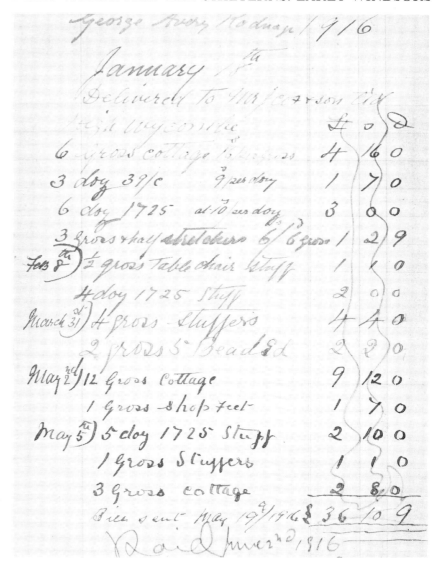

Figure TV8. An extract from the early 20th century account book of George Avery, of Beacon's Bottom, Radnage. This family of chair turners worked throughout much of the 19th century and were in existence until the outbreak of the Second World War. The details of the supply of chair parts to the firm of J. Cox & Son, Ltd., of High Wycombe, shows the difficulty which turners often had in being paid for their work; turned parts supplied in January, February, March and May of 1916 were finally paid for in June of that year. The entries also show that parts were referred to by numbers, which presumably related to style specifications.

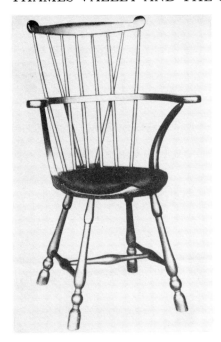  

Figure TV9. The 'Oliver Goldsmith' comb back Windsor chair, with painted surface. This chair was bequeathed by Oliver Goldsmith in 1774. (Courtesy Victoria and Albert Museum)

Figure TV10. A 'barley twist' turned walnut armchair with cane seat and back, c.1670-90. The juxtaposition of the three cross stretchers connecting the legs shows a typical form of construction found in cane seated Carolean chairs. This feature is found in the Windsor chairs shown in Figures TV11, 12 and 13. The 'Skull' chair shown in Figure TV11 also embodies barley twist connecting stretchers.

Figure TV11. Comb back Windsor chair, late 17th/early 18th century. From the collection of the late Edwin Skull, chair manufacturer of High Wycombe, Buckinghamshire. This chair has residual original surface paint and barley twist turnings which reflect stylistic awareness of similar turnings typically used in Carolean cane seated chairs (see Figure TV10) and other furniture from the second half of the 17th century. The crown motif carved in the stay rail is also reminiscent of the design of many elaborately carved cross rails found in examples of caned Carolean chairs.

Until recently this notable chair, although unprovenanced, was considered the earliest known English Windsor. However, a further group of four low backed Windsor chairs painted green, and having marked stylistic similarities to the Skull chair, have been recorded, and may be equally early in date. They have exaggerated saddle-seat shaping, scribed edge decoration to the arms and arm bow supports, the incorporation of plain H-stretchers, as well as decoratively turned stretchers connecting the front legs, and plain stretchers connecting the rear legs. Although these chairs do not have the high back support of the Skull chair, the arm bow in Figure TV12 is raised and fretted towards the rear of the chair, in a manner reminiscent of the comb rail fretting of the Skull chair. The chair shown in Figure TV13 has a separate decorative vestigial comb, slightly raised on spindles above the arm bow. The evidence of these further examples of chairs of the Skull type, suggests that rather than

the Skull chair being an isolated early example of a Windsor chair, a tradition of naïve Windsors may have existed during the late seventeenth/early eighteenth century in which these examples are stylistically related.

Although many existing Windsors can be stylistically attributed to the period 1720-1770, few are provenanced to maker or owner. One which does have a reliable pedigree, is the comb back Windsor, now in the Victoria and Albert Museum, which belonged to the poet Oliver Goldsmith who died in 1774 (see Figure TV9). Interestingly, this chair has a sawn and scroll shaped arm bow, which is unlike the bent arm bow construction typically found in the mid-eighteenth century comb and hoop back Windsors from the Thames Valley tradition. Chairs of this kind, painted green, appear in a number of eighteenth century family portraits painted out of doors. The painting by Zoffany of the Rosoman family on the Thames at Hampton, c.1780, illustrates two similar chairs

clearly being used as outside furniture (see Frontispiece).

The two earliest Windsors ascribed to known makers from this region were made around the middle of the eighteenth century. Both of these chairs were produced at Slough, Buckinghamshire, some two miles from the town of Windsor.

The first chair shown in Figure TV14 has a paper label declaring the maker to be John Pitt of Slough, who was buried in January 1759.[24] The second, shown in Figure TV15, has the remnants of a trade card under the seat declaring 'Richard Hewett Chair-Maker at Slough in the... Windsor. Makes and s[ells] ... Forest and all s...' A Richard Hewett, who was probably the maker of this chair, was buried on 7 September 1777 in the parish of Upton-cum-Chalvey, of which Slough was then part.[25] These two chairs are similar in design, except that the Pitt chair has four cabriole legs, whereas the Hewett chair has cabriole legs at the front only, and

Figure TV12. Low Windsor armchair. Ash with elm seat. One of a group of four attributed to the late 17th/early 18th century, with original green paint. This naïve style of chair has qualities similar to the chair shown in Figure TV11, including the broad, saddle seat, the leg stretcher formation, the top front leg turning motif, the scribed arm bow, and the pierced back decoration. The similarity between the designs of this chair and that of Figure TV11 illustrates that a group of Windsors were made with a common design theme. See Figure TV13 for a further example.

Figure TV13. Low Windsor armchair. Ash with elm seat. One of a group of four attributed to the late 17th/early 18th century, with original green paint. This chair has similar characteristics to the chairs in Figures TV11 and 12. In addition, it has an unusual, slightly raised decorative comb section in the centre of the arm bow.

Figure TV14. Comb back, cabriole legged, Windsor chair with applied label under the seat indicating the maker to be John Pitt of Slough, Buckinghamshire, who was buried in 1759. This is the earliest provenanced English Windsor chair to whom a maker can be attributed, and illustrates that by the mid-18th century, the cabriole leg had become fashionable.

(Courtesy Dr. J. Stabler)

turned rear legs. The back designs of both chairs are composed of rectangular sectioned uprights supporting shaped comb rails with three elliptical shaped spindles each side of a plain unfretted vasiform splat. The arm bows are connected to the seat by elliptical spindles and thin flattened arm supports in both examples, with four spindles in the Pitt chair and five in the Hewett chair. The incorporation of broad, deeply shaped saddle seats, flattened underarm supports and comb rails in these two chairs particularly articulate with the design and the general demeanour of the seats and underarm supports found in the three naïve Windsors illustrated in Figures TV11, 12 and 13 and with the comb rail found in the Skull chair (Figure TV11). The correspondence of these features suggests that a design transition occurred between late seventeenth/ early eighteenth and mid-eighteenth century Windsor chairs, in which these primary components were maintained, and other features became

modified or replaced; for example, the adoption of cabriole legs rather than turned legs and of a splat rather than a turned decorative central spindle.

The Hewett and Pitt chairs give positive evidence of comb back chairs from the mid-eighteenth century. However, comb back chairs were certainly made in the first half of the eighteenth century, and were characterised in having four turned legs, and an example of this style is shown in Figure TV16. This chair has residual original green paint and was probably made for use as a garden chair (see p.43) and, given the early references to painted Windsors,[26] may serve to support the view that this form of turned leg chair preceded those with cabriole legs. Symonds, writing on the Windsor chair in 1935, endorses this view and claimed that 'one of the features of an early comb backed chair is when the legs are turned... This turned leg preceded the cabriole legs.'[27]

Other distinguished Windsor chairs,

Figure TV15. Comb back, cabriole legged, Windsor chair with paper label applied underneath the seat, stating 'Richard Hewett. Chairmaker at Slough in the.... Windsor. Makes and s[ells] ... Forest and all s...'. This maker died in 1777. *(Courtesy Dr. J. Stabler)*

Figure TV16. Comb back Windsor chair. Ash with elm seat, with traces of original green paint. Attributed to Thames Valley, c.1720-40. Comb back Windsors with turned legs probably developed before those with cabriole legs. The paint may well reflect its use as an item of garden furniture, which was an early 18th century function for Windsor seating. See p.43 for further discussion.

Figure TV17. Comb back cabriole legged Windsor chair. Mahogany. Attributed to London, c.1750. This sophisticated example of a Windsor chair shows many refinements, including finely carved foliar motifs to the front legs, and the use of French scroll feet, as well as the elegant use of scrolling to the front seat edges and to the arm terminals. This form of Windsor was made for the homes of wealthy patrons, and would probably have been used as a library chair.   (Courtesy J. Steel)

Figure TV18. Cabriole legged, hoop back Windsor chair. Yew with elm seat, c.1800. A trade card under the seat reads: 'W. Webb. Newington, Surrey'. (W. Webb, fl.1792-1808.) This elegant style of chair probably originated in the 1740s and continued to be made throughout the 18th and into the early 19th centuries.

which were probably of the comb back variety, were made in the first half of the eighteenth century, and were far removed from those intended either as garden furniture or for common use. Symonds, in *The Windsor Chair* (1935), noted that these were made from mahogany, and the example shown in Figure TV17 may be similar to that supplied by Henry Williams (fl.1728-1758) a joiner of London who supplied 'a very neat mahogany Windsor chair for £4' for the Prince of Wales' Library at St. James's Palace, and '2 Mahogany Windsor chairs, richly carved' at £8 for the Blue Room there.

Eighteenth Century Double Bow or Hoop Back Windsors

A further major form of Windsor chair to develop towards the middle of the eighteenth century was that of double bow or hoop back Windsors. This chair design had cabriole legs to the front and turned legs to the rear, and a back design which was characterised by a top hoop rather than a comb rail, with either a central fretted splat with turned spindles each side, see Figure TV18, or with turned spindles alone, see Figure TV19. The date of introduction of these hoop back chairs is not clear. Symonds, writing in 1935, suggests that they appear to come into vogue about 1740.[28] Sparkes, writing in 1975, agrees with this dating, suggesting that the hoop backs developed from the comb back Windsor, and argues that, 'From the principle of the curved arm bow which was introduced to strengthen the comb back chair, it was a short step to replace the comb piece with a similarly bent bow, and so produce what we now call the bow-back.'[29] A further distinction is observed too, in that the eighteenth century hoop back style of chair has a crinoline stretcher connecting the legs, rather than the H-form stretcher found in the comb back varieties. Chairs in this group conform to a particularly elegant style, and those with central splats have piercings reminiscent of Chippendale chair splats.

Figure TV19. Cabriole legged, hoop back Windsor armchair. Yew with elm seat. Attributed to Thames Valley, c.1775-1800. This Windsor form, made without a central splat, appears to have been less commonly made than those with splats.   (Collection B. Morley)

Figure TV20. Gothic Windsor armchair. Yew with elm seat. Attributed to Thames Valley., c.1740-80. The incorporation of Gothic splats within a conventional double bow Windsor form is unusual, and creates a design which is less obviously Gothic in form than those made with an arched bow. See Figure TV22.

(Courtesy Ivan Sparkes)

Figure TV21. Triple Gothic arch Windsor settee. Yew with elm seat. Attributed to London/Thames Valley, c.1730-60. This visually complex and exciting example of Windsor seating furniture probably epitomises the best work in the London/Thames Valley chair making tradition during the mid-18th century.

(Private Collection, Middleburgh, Virginia)

Figure TV22. Gothic Windsor chair. Yew with elm seat. Attributed to London/Thames Valley, c.1740-60. Unusually, the arch of the top bow is surmounted by a decorative scrolled crest which probably also assisted in strengthening the bow joint. *(Courtesy Bonsor Pennington, Horsham)*

Gothic Windsors

It is, however, a further group of chairs characterised by their Gothic fretted splats which probably shows the peak of Windsor design. This elaborated form of seating was made in the first half and into the second half of the eighteenth century, both in armchair and settee form, and it is probably the style referred to in a description given in the accounts of George Bowes, 1733-4, in which he records:

'1734. 13 May. Paid John Willis rect. in Paul's Church yard for 1 Windsor Settee with 4 seats, Two Ditto with 3 seats each, and 8 Single chairs at 6 ye Seat £5. 8. 0. Pd. Waterage and drink money to the Ship's Crew of Thos and Francis on board of whom they were sent to Gibside. 2/6. £5. 10. 6.'[30]

The style of this furniture, with elaborate Gothic central splats, narrower upper and lower fretted splats each side, and short fretted splats supporting the arm bows, owes much to the Gothic revival which took place in the second quarter of the eighteenth century, when design motifs which incorporated Gothic arches, were fashioned into furnishings and architecture of many kinds. This revival was epitomised in the house at Strawberry Hill, purchased by Horace Walpole (1717-1797), which was converted into a cottage with arched Gothic tracery windows, and has become synonymous with this seating style. The Gothic Windsor is unusual in that it is usually characterised in having a top bow made in two parts which join as in a Gothic arch (see Figures TV21 and 22). Alternatively, but less commonly, this back design was also made in the typical double hoop form (see Figure TV20). These Gothic splat chairs were apparently considered to be 'best' Windsor seating furniture, since no examples have been recorded made in other than prized yew, with elm seats.

47

Figure TV23. Cabriole legged Windsor comb back side chair. Fruitwood with elm seat. Attributed to Thames Valley, 1775-1800. This chair incorporates the fretted splat style and leg design typically found in cabriole legged double bow chairs, combined with a back framework characteristic of the comb back style.

(Courtesy Ivan Sparkes)

Figure TV24. Cabriole legged Windsor comb back armchair. Fruitwood with elm seat. Attributed to Thames Valley, c.1775-1800. This chair illustrates an amalgamation of styles, including a comb back design with the cabriole legs typical of double hoop back chairs.

Figure TV25. Tall comb back Windsor armchair. Fruitwood with elm seat. Attributed to Thames Valley, c.1775-1800. This chair shows a merging of 18th and 19th century elements, including a comb back framework with a wheel fretted splat, and turned legs typical of the 19th century Windsor chair tradition.

Transitional Windsors

Mid-eighteenth century Windsors with cabriole legs, with both Gothic and Chippendale splats, gradually gave way to those with a new form of turned legs which were to become the predominant style for the late eighteenth/nineteenth century Windsors. The transition between these styles appears to have been a gradual one, and during the mid to late eighteenth century chairs incorporated new splat designs which were commonly used in later nineteenth century traditions. Stylistic hybrids were also made which reflected the synthesis of mid and late eighteenth century Windsor designs. For example, the chair shown in Figure TV23 illustrates a rare side chair form which incorporates a decorative comb rail design, with fretted splat and cabriole front legs typical of those found in double hoop

chairs (see Figure TV18). The armchair illustrated in Figure TV24 combines a comb back design in the back, with the leg design of a double hoop back. The chair in Figure TV25 also dates from the last quarter of the eighteenth century, combining a comb back design with the new style of turned legs made from the late eighteenth century to the mid-nineteenth century, and with the addition of the wheel motif fretted splat which was to typify the High Wycombe hoop back Windsor tradition. The side chair illustrated in Figure TV27 is a rare form which incorporates the back design typical of the comb backs from the late eighteenth century with a star shaped fretted motif splat more commonly found in hoop back chairs of the nineteenth century (see Figure TV89).

Figure TV26. Comb back Windsor armchair. Fruitwood with elm seat. Attributed to Thames Valley, c.1840-60. This chair has typical features of double hoop chairs with turned legs, but incorporates a comb rail, which is a design feature associated with 18th century chairs.

Figure TV27. Comb back Windsor side chair. Fruitwood with elm seat. Attributed to Thames Valley, c.1780-1800. This chair illustrates the merging of 18th and 19th century Windsor design, and includes a comb back framework with a star fretted splat, and turned legs typical of 19th century Windsors.

Figure TV28. A cottage interior in Berkshire, showing a typical armchair from this region. This style of high back Windsor chair with the wheel fretted splat, provided comfortable seating in many cottage homes throughout Buckinghamshire, Oxfordshire, Berkshire, and the counties surrounding them during the 19th century, and has provided a persistent image of the English Windsor chair.

Figure TV29. High hoop back Windsor armchair. Yew with elm seat, with scribed edge line. Attributed to Buckinghamshire, c.1779-83. This chair is the earliest provenanced example of this Buckinghamshire regional chair style and was part of an original group of six. A hand-written inscription under the seat reads, 'Mr. Longridge. Gateshead, Durham. By the Vulcan. Capt, R. Hawkes, or by the first ship in that Trade',[31] The transportation date of these chairs by this ship has been identified by Dr John Stabler as being at some point between 1779 and 1783.

Single ring and concave turned legs; lower ring and straight feet; legs connected by a crinoline stretcher. Hoop with scribed edge line supporting four tapered and splayed long spindles each side of an accentuated wheel motif fretted splat, with small central applied roundel. Arm hoop supported by four elliptical spindles and bent arm supports.

(Courtesy Dr John Stabler)

The Emergence of the Nineteenth Century Tradition

Eighteenth century Windsor chairs from the Thames Valley gradually gave way to two further major styles of chairs which incorporated turned legs; those made with a back framework of a bent hoop or hoops, and those made with sawn back uprights and cross stay rails.

The first group includes chairs which retained the upper bent hoop and bent arm bow, and a back design composed either of long turned spindles alone (see Figure TV130) or with the option of a central, fretted splat (see Figure TV29) or were more rarely made with triple back splats (see Figure TV115). These features were essential characteristics of the double bow cabriole legged chairs of the eighteenth century, but in the new design of Windsors, the cabriole leg was abandoned in favour of turned legs, and a range of splat designs not found in the cabriole legged chairs, was also introduced. A further style of armchair was also produced, probably towards the end of the eighteenth century, which had no direct counterpart in previous eighteenth century Windsor design, that is, a low arm chair which incorporated one back hoop only, and sawn, shaped arms connected to the hoop, supported by curved and flattened underarm supports (see Figures TV73 and 74). The back design of this style of chair was also made with one of a range of fretted central splats, or, less commonly, triple splats, or with turned spindles alone.

In addition to armchairs of double and single hoop construction, side chairs of single hoop form were made, with an arrangement of plain turned spindles alone, or with the incorporation of different fretted splats. These designs of side chairs were made as compatible counterparts to the late eighteenth century hoop back armchairs. Their inclusion as a principal part of the chair maker's repertoire may have been a late eighteenth and early nineteenth century innovation, since although some comb back side chairs with cabriole legs have been recorded (see Figure TV23 for an example which dates from the last quarter of the eighteenth century), no hoop back side chairs with spindles and splats have been recorded which can be firmly provenanced to the eighteenth century. This lack of information concerning eighteenth century hoop back side chairs is not necessarily evidence that such chairs were not made, but chairs which have been recorded with positive attribution to the eighteenth century are all of the

49

armed variety. However, the apparent lack of side chairs attributable to the eighteenth century, strikingly contrasts with the wide manufacture of side chairs during the whole of the nineteenth century in the Wycombe tradition. The manufacture of side chairs probably reflects a change in dining habits of working people, and the increased possibilities for family meals which the greater prosperity of the nineteenth century brought. These changes produced a subsequent need for a comfortable seating form for all the family which encouraged the production of side chairs on a large scale.

The precise point of introduction of the double hoop Windsors with the turned leg forms associated with the late eighteenth and nineteenth century Windsor tradition, is unclear. However, two double bow Windsors of a type commonly made in the Buckinghamshire tradition which have central wheel motif fretted splats, have been positively dated to the last quarter of the eighteenth century (see Figure TV29). These chairs are part of an original group of six, and a handwritten inscription under the seat reads, 'Mr. Longridge. Gateshead, Durham. By the Vulcan. Capt. R. Hawkes, or by the first ship in that Trade'. In his excellent analysis of these chairs,[32] Dr. John Stabler traces the history of the *Vulcan* under Hawkes' captaincy and concludes that although the precise date of the manufacture of these chairs cannot be decided, since the ship is recorded visiting home ports under Hawkes between 1779 and 1783, they must have been made before 1783.

The date of these chairs is of considerable significance, since important evidence follows from it. These chairs represent, for example, the first provenanced Windsors which incorporate the union of stylistic devices which were to be commonly employed in the nineteenth century Windsor chairs from this region, particularly those of the fretted wheel motif splat, and single ring and concave turned legs with a lower ring and straight feet.

It is these features which designate this chair as different from the cabriole legged double bow Windsors, for other design features are common to both of them. For example, they both incorporate the thin, generous sized seat which flares out at the front corner edges to display the through-morticed and wedged tenons of the

Figure TV30. A pair of high hoop back Windsor armchairs. Yew wood with elm seats. Attributed to Buckinghamshire, c.1770-1820. These chairs epitomise the finest qualities which this region's chairs provide, with broad elegant seats and spacious curved backs which fit the human body in a way which chairs had not, before this style developed. The chair materials too, display the acute awareness of the characteristics of native woods, with the use of yew, a strong pliable wood, with glorious coloration which develops particularly as the wood becomes exposed to use, joined with the contoured graining and strength of elm seats.

legs. The arm hoop, which is through-morticed with four long spindles either side of the central splat and supported by four elliptical underarm support spindles, and the crook shaped front support are all closely similar features in both chair designs.

However, if the mode of transition from one form to the other is clearly centred in alteration of leg style, from cabriole to turned legs, then the change was probably a gradual one. This is evidenced in the cabriole legged double bow chair made by William Webb who worked at Newington, Surrey, between 1792 and 1808,[33] which is shown in Figure TV18. This chair was evidently made later than the Longridge double bow wheel back chairs (see Figure TV29), which were made before 1783, and confirms the continuity of the cabriole legged chair style at the same time that the turned leg variety was coming into fashion.

Examples of different types of leg turnings used in the Thames Valley area are shown in Figure TV31. The particular form of turning of the Longridge chair is a single ring with concave turning below (type B). This turning device is located near to the

top of the legs below where the tenon is morticed and wedged through the seat. This precise mode, the positioning of the leg turning, and the through seat morticing practice, probably suggest design features which were common to the late eighteenth and early nineteenth century hoop back Windsors. However, this style was, in turn, gradually discontinued during the first half of the nineteenth century, and although the single ring and lower concave turning persisted, it became heavier in profile, and the turning motif occurred lower down the leg. The advent of this second form of turning also coincided with the abandonment of the through-mortice and tenon mode of fixing the leg into the seat (see Figure TV32) in favour of blind socket morticing, where the leg tenon was turned to a dome shape to fit exactly a domed ended mortice. See Figure TV33 for an illustration of this form of construction.

A plain elliptical leg with a turned ring and straight foot below was made as an optional rear leg form for chairs with the single ring turning, and occurs in chairs with both the higher and lower ring turned legs.

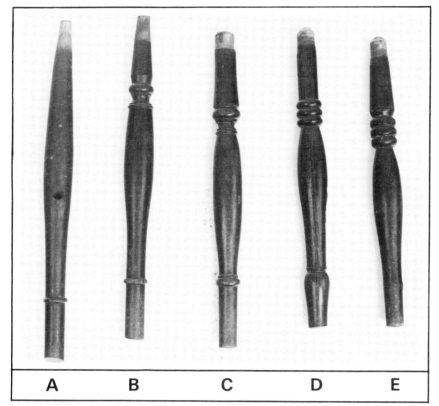

A   B   C   D   E

Figure TV31. A sequence of leg turnings used in the Thames Valley Windsor chair making tradition. Turnings altered in style from the second half of the 18th century until the late 19th century, and the legs illustrated offer an approximate sequence of designs:

A: A plain elliptical turned leg with single ring and straight foot below, c.1770-1850. This type was used as a more economical form than those with more elaborate turnings, as a rear leg. This example has a tapered and wedged tenon which passed through the seat in a similar way to leg B. This essential form of plain leg continued to be used throughout the 19th century, and into the 20th century.

B: This form represents a style made c.1770-1840 and has a narrow ring and concave motif turned high on the leg with a tapered and wedged tenon above, and a ring and straight foot below.

C: A heavier form of single ring and concave motif turning with a blind socket tenon above and ring and straight foot below. This design essentially developed from leg style B, and was used extensively in the Wycombe tradition, c.1835-70.

D: A three ring turning motif with a blind socket tenon above, and a vase shaped foot below. The ring turning is raised above the level of the leg above, and is a type of turning peculiar to this region's chairs. This style was made contemporaneously, as an alternative to leg style C, c.1835-70.

E: A leg with a heavy three ring turnery motif, where the rings are set at the same level as the leg turning above and below. This style is typically found in many kinds of hoop and scroll back Windsors made in the last thirty years of the 19th century, and represents a less elegant form of leg turning than those which had preceded it, c.1870-1900.

Figure TV33. A blind socket seat mortice with an appropriately turned domed leg tenon. The use of this form of leg jointing into the seat was commonly adopted by the Thames Valley chair makers from around 1840. This mode superseded the method of jointing typically used in 18th century Windsors where the legs were morticed through the seat.

Figure TV32. A front leg from a double hoop Windsor, morticed and wedged through the front of the seat. The tenon stands slightly proud of the seat surface, showing how use has forced the seat down on to the tapered leg turning, causing some wear which has allowed the leg to protrude. This form of leg morticing was extremely effective since the joint was constantly tightened in use.

This was a less elaborate leg to produce, and was, no doubt, an economy measure used in the production of some chairs. However, this rear leg form was evidently used less frequently than the ring and concave turned rear leg (see Figure TV31, types B and C).

Contemporary with the heavy single ring and lower concave leg turning, a further leg type was produced in the first half of the nineteenth century, which had a three ring turning to the upper leg, and vase shaped feet. This leg was also fitted to the seat by the use of a blind socket. The ring turnings used in this form represent a unique style made only in the High Wycombe tradition, and are characterised by being turned so that they are raised above the surrounding leg, rather than level with the upper and lower leg, as is typically found in other regional three ring turned legs produced at this time. Plain elliptical back legs terminating in vase shaped feet were also made to accompany the use of the raised three ring turned legs, but were used less often than rear legs with ring turnings (see Figure TV31, type D).

Much evidence in the form of name and initial stamped chairs, with the larger, lower ring and concave turned leg, as well as those with raised three ring turnings exists to confirm that these styles were turned during the first half of the nineteenth century. For example, the wheel back side chair shown in Figure TV65, made by William Sewell, who was working in West Wycombe in 1830, illustrates a chair with lower ring and concave turned, blind socketed legs, as does the chair made by C. Cannon & Co, who worked in High Wycombe

between 1827 and 1844, illustrated in Figure TV67. The use of the raised three ring leg also appears to have been introduced by about the 1840s, since this form of leg occurs in chairs which are stylistically similar to those with the lower ring and concave turned legs, and initial stamped examples of chairs with the raised three ring legs indicate makers who began work before 1850. For example, the stick back side chair shown in Figure TV135 stamped 'J. Mead' (fl.1841-51).

After 1850, a fourth type of leg, heavier than its predecessors, was introduced which has three ring turnings which are not raised above the outline of the upper and lower legs (see Figure TV91). This design lacks the elegance of the other leg forms used in the High Wycombe tradition, and was incorporated in chairs which became increasingly heavy in structure as the nineteenth century progressed. By the turn of the twentieth century, this style of leg had become the most common in this tradition, and photographs taken of chair turners producing legs in the Chiltern woodlands during the 1920s and 1930s show this type of leg alone being produced (see Chapter 1, Figure 13).

Although transitional changes occurred in the forms of leg turnings and their mode of morticing, it is emphasised that no absolute date of change of style from the refined single ring and concave turning to the heavier form of this design, and to the raised three ring leg can be absolutely ascribed, since it is likely that change came about gradually, and that three forms of leg turning

were being made simultaneously in the second quarter of the nineteenth century. The persistence of the refined single ring turning into the first half of the nineteenth century was perfectly possible, since makers who would have trained to produce chairs in this way, during the late eighteenth century, may well have continued to do so as a habit of trade practice throughout their working lives. This is evidenced, for example, in the work of Robert and John Prior of Uxbridge, who were trained by their father, a Windsor chair maker during the second half of the eighteenth century, and whose business Robert inherited. Chairs stamped by Robert Prior are illustrated in Figures TV151-159, all of which exhibit the high ring and lower concave turned legs, as well as through seat mortices and tenons, a mode of production which Robert and John probably used throughout their lives as workshop owners between 1816 and 1845.

Turned Stretchers

Interestingly, armchairs made with the high ring and through-morticed legs commonly either have a crinoline stretcher if they are made in yew with elm seats or, when they are made with the typical combination of other woods used in this region — ash, elm, beech and fruitwood — the legs are joined by H-form stretchers in which the cross stretcher is more usually of a decorative turnery style (see Figure TV36, type A). This stretcher design was common to some eighteenth century Windsors

Figure TV34. High hoop back Windsor armchair. Beech with ash top hoop, and arm bow, fruitwood splat and underarm supports, and elm seat with scribed edge line. Stamped 'R.F.' on rear of seat. Attributed to Buckinghamshire, c.1830-70.

Raised three ring turned legs with lower rings and vase shaped feet. Legs connected by H-form elliptical turned stretchers. Hoop with scribed edge line supporting three parallel long spindles either side of central splat with wheel fretted motif and applied turned central roundel. Arm hoop supported by four elliptical spindles and crook shaped arm supports.

Figure TV35. The stamp 'R.F.' impressed on the back seat edge of the chair illustrated in Figure TV34. For makers with these initials see Appendix.

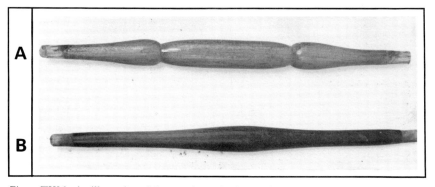

Figure TV36. An illustration of the two alternative forms of cross stretcher found in the Thames Valley Windsor chair tradition. Stretcher A: This style has antecedents in late 18th century Windsors from the region (see Figures TV23 and 25), and is a mode of turning which is also found in some Windsor chairs from the Lincolnshire tradition (see Chapter 3, Figure NE20). Stretcher B: Elliptical turning commonly used in Thames Valley Windsors was an alternative to the more elaborately turned version.

Figure TV37. High hoop back Windsor arm-chair. Beech with ash hoop and elm seat with scribed edge line. Stamped 'J.P.' on rear of seat. Attributed to Buckinghamshire, c.1840-60.

Single ring and concave turned legs. Lower ring and straight turned feet. Legs connected by H-form elliptical turned stretchers. Hoop with scribed edge line supporting three tapered long spindles either side of central splat with wheel fretted motif, with central roundel turned in situ. Arm bow supported by four elliptical turned short spindles and a regionally common style of turned underarm support. See for example the scroll back kitchen armchair illustrated in Figure TV175, and the high wheel back chair shown in Figure TV41.

Figure TV39. A view of the rear of two hoop back side chairs showing, to the left, the use of a rear seat wedge with two splayed support spindles attached to the hoop. The right hand chair shows the alternative mode which has no wedge and support spindles. Both of these methods of construction are structurally sound and the use of a rear wedge appears to be an embellishment rather than a superior form of construction. Inexplicably no side chairs of this style, but without the rear wedge, have been recorded with makers' stamps.

Figure TV38. The stamp 'J.P.' impressed on the back seat edge of the chair illustrated in Figure TV37. For makers with these initials see Appendix.

from this region (see Figures TV23 and 25), but no more so than the plain elliptical form of stretcher shown in Figure TV36, type B. Therefore, the significance of the combination of the high ring and through-morticed legs with this stretcher is not clear. However, no examples of Windsors with the larger lower ring and concave turning, or three ring turned legs have been recorded incorporating the regional stretcher form, type A.

Splat Designs

The incorporation of the wheel motif fretted splat in the 'Longridge' chair is highly significant, since this is the earliest provenanced example of this splat being used in a double bow Windsor armchair, although this device was incorporated in unprovenanced comb back chairs attributed to the late eighteenth century (see Figures TV25 and 30). This splat style became popular from the late eighteenth century, and was used throughout the nineteenth century and continues to be used in the twentieth century in the Wycombe tradition.

However, a number of splats with different motifs also arose, either simultaneously or shortly after the introduction of the wheel splat, including, for example, those with urn, roundel, star, crown, tulip, Prince of Wales' feathers, and Chippendale style motifs, as well as those which displayed Gothic tracery design. A comprehensive, but not necessarily exhaustive anthology of these styles is illustrated in Figures TV46-128. The proliferation of these alternative splat designs was a dominant feature of early nineteenth century Windsor forms, since many of the variant splat chairs illustrated here occur in combination with the high ring and through-morticed legs, features which suggest a time of production from the second half of the eighteenth century until the 1840s. Although variant splat forms appear in combination with the later lower ring and concave turned legs, as well as those with raised three ring turned legs, they are less commonly found, suggesting that a greater standardisation of chair splat designs occurred during the second quarter of the nineteenth century, with the wheel motif becoming pre-eminent at this time.

Chairs with Splayed Rear Support Spindles

Many of the single hoop back arm-chair and side chair varieties were made with a rear seat wedge supporting two long spindles, which were splayed outwards to mortice into, and support the hoop. Although commonly used, many chairs do not have this extra feature, and are straight along the back seat edge (compare the chairs in Figure TV39). Both seat forms are found in combination with the whole range of fretted splat styles, in side chairs and single hoop back arm-chairs. However, the double hoop back armchairs appear not to have been made with the supporting spindles in the late eighteenth and early nineteenth centuries, although some late nineteenth century examples were made with these supporting spindles (see Figure TV139).

Underarm Supports

During the second quarter of the nineteenth century a major stylistic alteration occurred in the form of underarm supports used in double hoop Windsors. The Longridge chairs, shown in Figure TV29, illustrate the use of curved crook shaped supports similar to those adopted in the cabriole legged double hoop Windsors of the eighteenth century. These supports were tenoned into the seat and fixed to the arm bow by either metal pins, as in the case of the Longridge chair, or were screwed to the arm from below (see Figure TV40). This form of underarm support continued in use into the second quarter of the nineteenth century, when it appears to have declined in favour of turned supports, the styles of which are typically, but not invariably, one of two popular forms. Examples are illustrated in Figures TV41 and 43. No exact point for the introduction of turned supports can be ascribed, but it is likely that they began to appear by about 1840. This is evidenced by the illustrations of both wheel and stick back Windsors shown in Edwin Skull's catalogue, c.1849, illustrated in Figures TV60 and 129, which show chairs with turned underarm supports only. No chairs are shown in this, or any of the later chair manufacturers' catalogues from the High Wycombe area with crook

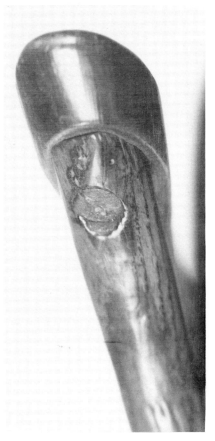

Figure TV40. A detailed illustration showing the use of a steel screw to fix a crook shaped underarm support to the arm. The head of the screw was usually covered over with a 'stopping' mixture or putty and stained over. In some examples a small nail was used as an alternative form of fixing.

shaped underarm supports, and it appears that by 1850, the turned underarm form had become dominant. Further evidence that the crook underarm support was entirely a feature of the early double bow Windsors is provided in that no armchairs with the high ring and concave turned legs have been recorded with turned underarm supports; all have crook shaped arm supports. The crook arm support is, however, found in chairs with the later, occasionally raised three ring legs (see Figure TV34) and the lower ring and concave leg (see Figure TV47).

The second form of armchair made in this tradition, during the first half of the nineteenth century, has a single hoop and sawn, shaped arms, with flattened underarm supports, in a similar style to those used in the 'Oliver Goldsmith' chair in Figure TV9. A minority of armchairs with

single hoop backs were made, too, with turned arm supports, an example of which is shown in Figure TV71. The single hoop armchair style probably entered the range of this region's repertoire of designs a little later than the double hoop armchair with turned legs, although the precise point at which it was first used is not clear. However, some chairs, for example those with

Figure TV41. High hoop back Windsor arm-chair. Beech with ash top hoop and arm bow, fruitwood splat, and plain elm seat. Stamped 'R.H.' on rear of seat. Attributed to Buckinghamshire, c.1850-80. The form of underarm turning adopted in this chair is one of the most common styles found in this region, and other examples are shown in Figures TV37 and 175.

Raised three ring turned legs with lower ring and straight turned feet. Legs connected by H-form elliptical turned stretchers. Plain hoop supporting four parallel long spindles either side of central splat with wheel fretted motif and central roundel turned in situ. Arm bow supported by four short spindles and turned underarm supports.

Figure TV42. The stamp 'R.H.' impressed on the back seat edge of the chair illustrated in Figure TV41. For makers with these initials see Appendix.

Chippendale style splats shown in Figures TV95 and 96, and a chair with a simple floral motif in Figure TV101, show the features of high ring and concave turned and through-seat morticed legs attributed to the earlier period of production. Further evidence that they may have

been made in the second half of the eighteenth century is indicated by the chair of this style shown in Figure

TV148 which was made in the workshop of John Prior of Uxbridge who is known to have worked between 1768 and 1816.

The shaped arms and flattened underarm supports are also held in place by metal screws, in a similar way to the upper fixing commonly used on crook shaped arm supports. See Figure TV45 for an illustration of this feature.

The variety of splats found in double hoop Windsor armchairs is also found in single hoop armchairs, examples of which are illustrated in Figures TV73, 84 and 87. It has been suggested that the development of this armchair, in combination with the comparable side chairs, coincided with changing social habits within a growing population,[34] and that whereas the double bow Windsor was essentially used as a fireside chair, the low single hoop back armchair was for use at the head of the dining table. This is probably true, and is supported by nineteenth century photographs of cottage interiors from this region which commonly include examples of double hoop Windsors, stood by the fireside, but seldom the single hoop variety (see Figure TV28).

Figure TV45. Detail showing the use of a steel screw to fix the arm of a low single hoop Windsor to the hoop. The screw head was typically covered over with a 'stopping mixture' of putty and stained. A further example of the use of a screw in forming a joint in Windsor construction is shown in Figure TV40.

Figure TV43. High hoop back Windsor arm-chair. Beech with ash hoop and seat with scribed edge line. Stamped 'J.V.' on rear of seat. Attributed to Buckinghamshire, c.1840-70. The underarm turning adopts one of the most common forms found in this region, and is illustrated, for example, in the catalogue of B. North of High Wycombe, c.1860, an extract of which is shown in Figure TV145, as well as in other chairs made in this region. See Figure TV131 for example.

Single ring and concave turned legs with lower ring and straight turned feet. Legs connected by H-form elliptical turned stretchers. Hoop with scribed edge line supporting three parallel long spindles either side of central splat with wheel fretted motif and central turned roundel. Arm bow supported by four tapered short spindles and turned arm supports.

Figure TV44. The stamp 'J.V.' impressed on the back of the seat wedge of the chair illustrated in Figure TV43. The number '27' probably refers to the chair's place in a batch of similar chairs. A James Veary is recorded as working in West Wycombe between 1841 and 1861.

Figure TV46. A group of four side chairs made to identical specifications, but bearing the initial stamps of three different makers. From left to right they are impressed on the rear of the seats, 'A.R.', 'T.B.', 'J.P.' and 'T.B.'. The close similarity in the construction of these chairs, and the different makers' marks suggest that these makers were working in the same workshop using the same patterns and templates, and that the use of their initial stamps was simply a method of identifying their own work.

Figure TV47. High hoop back Windsor arm-chair. Ash with fruitwood splat, beech legs and stretchers, elm seat with scribed edge line. Stamped 'T.B.' on rear edge of seat. Attributed to Buckinghamshire, c.1800-40. This style of hoop back Windsor, with the wheel splat motif, is the most common design of its type in the tradition and the use of the crook shaped underarm supports dates its production prior to c.1840.

Single ring and concave turned legs with lower ring and straight turned feet. Legs connected by H-form elliptical turned stretchers. Hoop with scribed edge line supporting three tapered long spindles either side of central splat with wheel fretted motif without the central turned roundel. Arm bow supported by four elliptical short spindles and crook shaped underarm supports.

Figure TV49. Hoop back Windsor side chair. Beech with ash hoop, fruitwood splat and elm seat with scribed edge line. Stamped 'T.B.' on rear edge of seat. Attributed to Buckinghamshire, c.1800-40. This delightful form of splat motif is extremely rare, and an alternative form of tulip motif is shown in Figure TV99.

Single ring and concave turned legs with lower ring and straight turned feet. Legs connected by H-form elliptical turned stretchers. Hoop with scribed edge line supporting three tapered long spindles either side of central splat with tulip fretted motif. Seat with rear wedge supporting two spindles connected to top of hoop.

Figure TV51. Hoop back Windsor 'Gothic' side chair. Beech with ash back and elm seat with scribed edge line. Stamped 'T.B.' on rear of seat. Attributed to Buckinghamshire, c.1800-40. This elegant style of chair was made by many of the Wycombe makers during the 19th century. See the B. North Catalogue No.3, c.1860, Figure TV145, and the Skull Catalogue, c.1849, in Figure TV53.

Single ring and concave turned legs with lower ring and straight turned feet. Legs connected by H-form elliptical turned stretchers. Hoop with scribed edge line enclosing a simple 'Gothic' tracery design.

Figure TV48. The stamp 'T.B.' impressed on the back seat edge of the chair illustrated in Figure TV47. For makers with these initials see Appendix.

Figure TV50. The stamp 'T.B.' impressed on the back of the seat wedge of the chair illustrated in Figure TV49. For makers with these initials see Appendix.

Figure TV52. The stamp 'T.B.' impressed on the back seat edge of the chair in Figure TV51. For makers with these initials see Appendix.

Makers' Marks

A common, but not universal, feature of the Thames Valley chair tradition was the tendency for makers, probably the framers, to initial stamp their chairs. This practice probably arose not as a form of public advertising, but simply to enable individual makers who were working in the same workshop to identify their work from that of others. This would have been particularly necessary where makers were using a common set of templates and formers, their chairs being consequently closely similar to each other. This is illustrated in Figure TV46 which shows four similar chairs which have stamps by three different makers, T.B., J.P., and A.R. The chairs so closely resemble each other as to suggest that

Figure TV53. An illustration from the catalogue, c.1849, of Edwin Skull, chair manufacturer of High Wycombe, showing to the left, a scroll back Windsor chair with arcaded cross and stay rail, supporting turned spindles. The chair to the right is a hoop back Windsor with a Gothic tracery design of bent bows. The presentation of these two styles, side by side, clearly shows that the seat and legs were made from similar components in both designs and that the makers evidently saw these two distinct types of Windsors, scroll and hoop back, to be compatible alternative styles.

(Courtesy High Wycombe Chair Museum)

Figure TV54. Hoop back Windsor side chair. Beech with ash hoop, fruitwood splat, and elm seat with scribed edge line. Stamped 'T.B.' on rear edge of seat. Attributed to Buckinghamshire, c.1800-40. This style of chair is similar to the chair shown in Figure TV56 which has single ring turned legs and straight feet, indicating that this maker incorporated different turned parts.

Raised three ring turned front legs and plain turned rear legs with vase shaped feet. Legs connected by H-form elliptical turned stretchers. Hoop with scribed edge line supporting three elliptical long spindles either side of central splat with wheel fretted motif and applied central roundel. Seat with rear wedge supporting two spindles connected to top of hoop.

Figure TV55. The stamp 'T B' impressed on the back of the seat wedge of chair illustrated in Figure TV54. For makers with these initials see Appendix.

they were made at the same time in one workshop using the same manufacturing devices, and subsequently stamped to identify each individual maker's work.

Other chairs show full name and place stamps of workshop owners (see Figures TV66 and 152), and in these cases, it may be assumed that the intention was to advertise the maker's products.

In addition to offering information about makers or possible makers, the documenting of initials and name stamped chairs has also served to show that makers were typically involved in making a range of chairs rather than one type. Examples of one maker who stamped his work 'T.B.' on the rear of the seats of the chairs he made, are shown in Figures TV46-57, as an illustration of the recorded repertoire of the work of one maker. A number of other makers' work whose stamps relate a small group of chairs together are also interspersed in the anthology of illustrations shown. These include

Figure TV56. Hoop back Windsor side chair. Beech with ash hoop, fruitwood splat and elm seat with scribed edge line. Stamped 'T B' on rear of seat. Attributed to Buckinghamshire c.1800-40.

Single ring and concave turned legs with lower ring and straight turned feet. Legs connected by H-form elliptical turned stretchers. Hoop with scribed edge line supporting three elliptical long spindles either side of central splat with wheel fretted motif and central roundel turned in situ. Seat with wedge supporting two spindles connected to top of hoop.

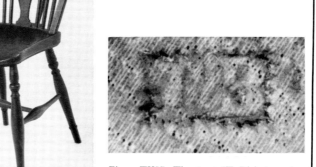

Figure TV57. The stamp 'T B' impressed on the back of the seat wedge of chair illustrated in Figure TV56. For makers with these initials see Appendix.

makers with the initial stamps, 'J.P.' and 'S.M.', for example. Many of the chairs included in the wheel splat section below are also stamped, as well as some chairs with variant splats.

Not all stamps or brands found on Windsor chairs refer to their makers, however, and since large numbers of the common wheel back varieties of side chairs, particularly, were sold for use in institutions and public meeting places throughout London and the Home Counties, it is not unusual to find inventory marks of ownership on chairs. An example of this is shown in Figure TV69 which illustrates a Windsor side chair dating from the first half of the nineteenth century, which carries the stamp of St. Paul's School on the edge of the seat. This chair probably formed part of a consignment purchased for this famous boys' public school, and evidently supported many generations of boys through the rigours of daily use until the 1980s when they were abandoned in favour of contemporary seating.

Figure TV58. Hoop back Windsor side chair. Beech with ash hoop, fruitwood splat, and elm seat with scribed edge line. Stamped 'W. LOW' on rear of seat wedge. Attributed to Buckinghamshire, c.1770-1820. This chair embodies the features of a broad thin elm seat splayed to the front edge, and the legs morticed and wedged through the seat which suggest a chair design from the late 18th or early 19th centuries.

Single ring and concave turned legs which are morticed and wedged through the seat surface. Lower ring and straight turned feet. Legs connected by H-form elliptical turned stretchers. Hoop with scribed edge line supporting three tapered long spindles either side of central splat with scribed and fretted wheel motif with applied central roundel. Seat with rear wedge supporting two spindles connected to top of hoop.

Figure TV59. The stamp of 'W. Low' impressed on the rear seat wedge of the chair illustrated in Figure TV58. No maker of this name has yet been traced.

Figure TV60. An illustration from the catalogue, c.1849, of Edwin Skull, chair manufacturer of High Wycombe. The three drawings clearly show a progression of styles with wheel motif fretted splats, including, from left to right, a side chair, a single hoop armchair, and a double hooped armchair. The armchairs have turned arm supports which became fashionable towards the mid-19th century. (Courtesy High Wycombe Chair Museum)

Figure TV61. Hoop back Windsor side chair. Ash hoop, legs and stretchers, beech splat and plain elm seat. Stamped 'W. SMART' on rear of seat.

Raised three ring turned legs with lower ring and vase shaped feet. Legs connected by H-form elliptical turned stretchers. Hoop with scribed edge line supporting three elliptical long spindles either side of central splat with wheel fretted motif and applied turned roundel. Seat with rear wedge supporting two spindles connected to top of hoop.

Figure TV63. Hoop back Windsor side chair. Beech with ash hoop, fruitwood splat and elm seat with scribed edge line. Stamped 'J. MEAD' on rear of seat. Attributed to Buckinghamshire, c.1830-50. See Figure TV135 for another chair made by this maker.

Single ring and concave turned legs with lower ring and straight turned feet. Legs connected by H-form elliptical turned stretchers. Hoop with scribed edge line supporting three elliptical long spindles either side of central splat with wheel fretted motif and turned central roundel. Seat with rear wedge supporting two spindles connected to top of hoop.

Figure TV65. Hoop back Windsor side chair. Beech with ash hoop, fruitwood splat and plain elm seat. Stamped 'SEWELL. MAKER. W. WYCOMB. BUCKS.' on rear of seat (fl.1830-45).

Single ring and concave turned legs with lower ring and straight turned feet. Legs connected by H-form elliptical turned stretchers. Hoop with scribed edge line supporting three parallel long spindles either side of central splat with raised fretted wheel motif with central roundel turned in situ. Seat with rear wedge supporting two spindles connected to top of hoop.

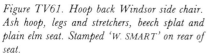

Figure TV62. The stamp 'W. Smart' (fl.1823-35), impressed on the back of the seat wedge of chair illustrated in Figure TV61. This maker worked in Lewes, Sussex.

Figure TV64. The stamp of J. Mead impressed on the back of the seat wedge of chair illustrated in Figure TV63. For makers with this name see Appendix.

Figure TV66. The stamp of William Sewell of West Wycombe, Bucks. (fl.1830-1845), impressed on the back seat edge of the chair illustrated in Figure TV65.

Figure TV67. Hoop back Windsor side chair. Beech with ash hoop, fruitwood splat and elm seat with scribed edge line. Branded 'C. CANNON & CO.' underneath seat. High Wycombe, c.1830-45.

Decoratively turned legs with lower ring and straight turned feet. Legs connected by H-form elliptical turned stretchers. Hoop with scribed edge line supporting three elliptical long spindles either side of central splat with wheel fretted motif without turned roundel. Seat with rear wedge supporting two spindles connected to top of hoop.

Figure TV68. The brand of Charles Cannon, chair manufacturer of High Wycombe (fl.1827-44), branded underneath the seat of the chair illustrated in Figure TV67.

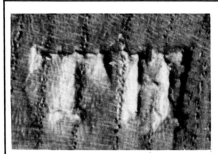

Figure TV72. The stamp of 'T.H.' impressed on the backs of the seats of the chairs shown in Figure TV71. For makers with these initials see Appendix.

Figure TV71. Pair of low hoop back Windsor armchairs. Beech with ash hoops, fruitwood splats and elm seats with scribed edge lines. Stamped 'T.H.' on rear of seats. Attributed to Buckinghamshire, c.1820-60. This form of chair was probably made as a dining chair, and the natural counterpart to the side chairs of this design; whereas the tall backed variety of the wheel back style was essentially intended as a fireside chair.

Single ring and concave turned legs with lower ring and straight turned feet. Legs connected by H-form elliptical turned stretchers. Hoops with scribed edge lines supporting three tapered long spindles either side of central splats with wheel fretted motifs and central roundels turned in situ. Shaped arms, morticed and screwed to the hoop and supported by decoratively turned underarm supports.

Figure TV69. Hoop back Windsor side chair. Beech with ash hoop, fruitwood splat and elm seat with scribed edge line. Stamped 'ST. PAUL'S SCHOOL' on edge of seat. Attributed to High Wycombe, c.1820-50.

Single ring and concave turned legs with lower ring and straight turned stretchers. Plain hoop supporting three elliptical long spindles either side of central splat with wheel fretted motif and applied roundel. Seat with rear wedge supporting two spindles connected to top of hoop.

Figure TV70. The chair owner's stamp, St. Paul's School, impressed on the edge of the seat of the chair illustrated in Figure TV69. It is not unusual to find the owner's identification stamped or branded on to Windsor chairs, particularly where the owner was an institution or other place of public gathering. The identifying stamp is interesting since it illustrates that this chair, bought as one of a number of chairs, survived the rigours of school life for over one hundred years.

Figure TV73. Low hoop back Windsor arm and side chair from the Buckinghamshire tradition, c.1835-70, with the roundel motif splat. These chairs epitomise the robust structure and simple, well designed appearance which enabled this type of chair to become a major regional style throughout many of the southern shires of England. They are made in the combination of woods commonly used in these chairs; ash bows, beech spindles, legs and stretchers, elm seats and fruitwood splats. The arms and arm supports are also in fruitwood.

Figure TV74. Low hoop back Windsor armchair. Fruitwood with ash hoop and elm underarm supports and seat with scribed edge line. Attributed to Buckinghamshire, c.1820-40. The wheel form of spindles radiating from a central roundel is indicative of the early chair making tradition in which certain chair makers were also wheelwrights. This particular expression of the wheel motif is an unusually interesting and rare form, and suggests that the central roundel turning, commonly found as a feature of many styles of chairs from this region, may have been analogous to the hub of a wooden wheel.

Single ring and concave turned legs. Lower ring and straight turned feet. Legs connected by H-form elliptical turned stretchers. Hoop with scribed edge line supporting wheel back form. Shaped arms, morticed and screwed to the hoop and supported by shaped and flattened underarm supports screwed and morticed into edge of seat.

Figure TV75. High hoop back Windsor armchair. Fruitwood with ash hoops and underarm supports and elm seat with scribed edge line. Attributed to Buckinghamshire, c.1830-70. The form of raised three ring turning used in the legs of this chair is peculiar to this region's turners and this motif is shown in Figure TV31.

Raised three ring turned legs with lower ring and vase shaped feet. Legs connected by H-form elliptical turned stretchers. Hoop with scribed edge line supporting four parallel long spindles either side of central splat with turned roundel motif. Arm bow supported by four short spindles and crook shaped arm supports.

Figure TV76. Hoop back child's Windsor armchair. Beech with ash hoop, fruitwood splat and elm seat with scribed edge line. Attributed to Buckinghamshire, c.1830-50. Children's chairs were made in great variety and abundance in this tradition. However, hard use has led to the destruction of many. A number of designs of scroll back low and high children's chairs are illustrated in the Skull Catalogue of 1849, see Figure TV164.

Heavy single ring and concave turned front legs, plain turned rear legs with lower ring and straight turned feet. Legs connected by H-form elliptical turned stretchers. Hoop with scribed edge line supporting three heavy tapered long spindles either side of central splat with turned roundel motif. Shaped arms morticed and screwed to the hoop and supported by turned underarm supports.

Figure TV77. High hoop back Windsor armchair. Yew with elm seat with scribed edge line, and legs morticed and wedged through the seat. Attributed to Buckinghamshire, c.1790-1820. The relatively unusual splat motif occurs here in a chair with a thin, elegantly shaped seat, the legs morticed and wedged through the seat. The hoop and underarm supports are secured with a dowel through the side edge of the seat. These latter features are commonly found in combination with chairs which also have unusual splat designs. Interestingly, this style of splat was also used by early 19th century chair makers from Lincolnshire. See the chair made by John Taylor of Grantham, Lincolnshire illustrated in Chapter 3, Figure NE33.

Single ring and concave turned legs with lower ring and straight turned feet. Legs connected by H-form elliptical turned stretchers, with regional turnery device in centre stretcher. Hoop with scribed edge line supporting three tapered long spindles either side of central splat with urn fretted motif. Arm hoop supported by four elliptical turned spindles and crook shaped arm supports.

Figure TV78. Low hoop back Windsor armchair. Ash hoop, legs and stretchers, fruitwood splat, spindles, arms, and underarm supports, elm seat with scribed edge line. Attributed to Buckinghamshire, c.1820-50.

Single ring and concave turned legs with lower ring and straight turned feet. Legs connected by H-form elliptical turned stretchers. Hoop with scribed edge line supporting three parallel long spindles either side of central splat with urn fretted motif. Shaped arms, morticed and screwed to the hoop and supported by shaped and flattened (replaced) underarm supports morticed into the edge of the seat.

Figure TV79. Hoop back Windsor side chair. Beech with ash hoop, fruitwood splat, and elm seat with scribed edge line. Attributed to Buckinghamshire, c.1820-40.

Single ring and concave turned legs with lower ring and straight turned feet. Legs connected by H-form elliptical turned stretchers. Hoop with scribed edge line supporting three tapered long spindles either side of central splat with urn fretted motif. Seat with rear wedge supporting two spindles connected to top of hoop.

Figure TV80. High hoop back Windsor armchair. Beech with ash hoop and elm seat with scribed edge line and legs morticed and wedged through the seat. Attributed to Buckinghamshire, c.1790-1820.

Single ring and concave turning on front legs. Plain turned rear legs. Lower ring and straight turned feet. Legs connected by H-form elliptical turned stretchers with regional turnery motif in cross stretcher. Hoop with scribed edge line supporting three tapered long spindles either side of central splat with Prince of Wales' feathers fretted motif with three small applied turned roundels. Arm hoop supported by three elliptical spindles and crook shaped arm supports.

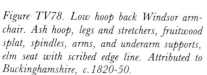

Figure TV81. High hoop back Windsor armchair. Beech with ash hoop and elm seat with scribed edge line. Stamped 'W. LOW' on rear edge of seat. Attributed to Buckinghamshire, c.1790-1820. A side chair with a wheel motif splat made by this maker is shown in Figure TV58.

Single ring and concave turned legs with lower ring and straight turned feet. Legs connected by H-form elliptical turned stretchers. Hoop with scribed edge line supporting three tapered long spindles either side of central splat with Prince of Wales' feathers fretted motif. Arm hoop supported by four parallel spindles and crook shaped arm supports.

Figure TV82. The stamp of W. Low impressed on the rear seat edge of the chair shown in Figure TV81. This maker is currently untraced.

Figure TV83. Hoop back Windsor side chair. Beech with ash hoop, fruitwood splat, and elm seat with scribed edge line. Attributed to Buckinghamshire, c.1790-1830. The turning incorporated in the legs of this chair displays a deep concave below the single ring which is closely similar in style to that found in many early 19th century leg turnings from the Lincolnshire tradition. See Figures NE12-16, Chapter 3.

Single ring and concave turned legs with lower ring and straight turned feet. Legs connected by H-form elliptical turned stretchers. Hoop with scribed edge line supporting three tapered long spindles either side of central splat with Prince of Wales' feathers fretted motif with three small applied turned roundels. Seat with rear wedge supporting two spindles connected to top of hoop.

Figure TV84. Low hoop back Windsor armchair. Beech with ash hoop, fruitwood arms and splat, and elm seat with scribed edge line. Attributed to Buckinghamshire, c.1830-40.

Single ring and concave turned legs with lower ring and straight turned feet. Legs connected by H-form elliptical turned stretchers. Hoop with scribed edge line supporting three parallel long spindles either side of central splat with Prince of Wales' feathers fretted motif with three small inset turned roundels. Shaped arms morticed and screwed to the hoop, and supported by shaped and flattened underarm supports morticed and screwed into edge of seat.

Figure TV85. Low hoop back Windsor armchair. Beech with ash hoop, fruitwood splat, and elm seat with scribed edge line. Stamped 'A R' on back edge of seat. Attributed to Buckinghamshire, c.1800-40.

Single ring and concave turned legs with lower ring and straight turned feet. Legs connected by H-form elliptical turned stretchers. Hoop with scribed edge line supporting three parallel long spindles either side of central splat with Prince of Wales' feathers fretted motif. Shaped arms morticed and screwed to the hoop, and supported by shaped and flattened underarm supports morticed and screwed into edge of seat.

Figure TV86. The stamp 'A R' impressed on the back of the seat wedge of chair illustrated in Figure TV85. The only recorded maker from the Buckinghamshire region with these initials is Arthur Redding (fl.1823-30), of Amersham.

Figure TV87. Low hoop back Windsor armchair. Beech with ash hoop and elm seat with scribed edge line and legs morticed through the seat. Attributed to Buckinghamshire, c.1820-40.

Single ring and concave turning on front legs. Plain turned rear legs. Lower ring and straight turned feet. Legs connected by H-form elliptical turned stretchers. Plain hoop with scribed edge line supporting three parallel long spindles either side of central splat with star fretted motif and central turned roundel. Seat with rear wedge supporting two spindles connected to top of hoop. Shaped arms, morticed and screwed to the hoop and supported by shaped and flattened underarm supports morticed into edge of seat. (An iron brace has been added to the left arm.)

Figure TV88. High hoop back Windsor armchair. Beech with ash hoop, fruitwood splat, and thin elm seat. Attributed to Buckinghamshire, c.1800-30. This chair has an unusual star splat motif, and in common with many chairs from this region which incorporate unusual splats, the seat is thin, and elegantly swept outwards to the front, and the legs mortice through the seat. See p.17 for a discussion on the implications of this point.

Single ring and concave turning on front legs. Plain turned rear legs. Lower ring and straight turned feet. Legs connected by H-form elliptical turned stretchers. Hoop with scribed edge line supporting three tapered long spindles either side of central splat with star fretted motif with turned central roundel. Arm bow supported by four tapered short spindles and heavy crook shaped arm supports.

Figure TV89. Hoop back Windsor side chair. Beech with ash hoop, fruitwood splat and elm seat with scribed edge line. Attributed to Buckinghamshire, c.1800-30.

Single ring and concave turned legs with lower ring and straight turned feet. Legs connected by H-form elliptical turned stretchers. Hoop with scribed edge line supporting three tapered long spindles either side of central splat with star fretted motif and central applied turned roundel. Seat with rear wedge supporting two spindles connected to top of hoop.

Figure TV90. Hoop back Windsor side chair. Beech with ash hoop, fruitwood splat and plain elm seat. Attributed to Buckinghamshire, c.1880-1900. The splat motif is uncommon, and shows some similarities to the designs incorporated in the high back armchairs shown in Figures TV91 and 92.

Three ring turned legs with lower ring and straight turned feet. Legs connected by H-form elliptical turned stretchers. Plain hoop without scribed edge line supporting three elliptical long spindles either side of central splat with fretted motif. Seat with rear wedge supporting two spindles connected with top of hoop.

Figure TV91. High hoop back Windsor armchair. Yew with plain elm seat. Attributed to Buckinghamshire, c.1780-1830. This elegant design of chair has many of the features found in 'best' quality chair designs from the region, including the broad, thin seat and legs which mortice through the seat. It also incorporates four spindles either side of the splat which is a typical feature of chairs made in yew.

Single ring and concave turned legs with lower ring and straight turned feet. Legs connected by H-form elliptical turned stretchers with cross stretcher turned with regional motif. Hoop with scribed edge line supporting four elliptical long spindles either side of central splat with raised fretted cruciform motif. Arm hoop supported by four elliptical spindles and crook shaped arm supports.

Figure TV92. High hoop back Windsor armchair. Yew with thin elm seat with scribed edge line. Attributed to Buckinghamshire, c.1840-80. The use of two parts to the back splat is relatively uncommon in this region, and more commonly occurs in chairs from the North East Windsor chair tradition.

Raised three ring turned legs with lower ring and vase shaped feet. Legs connected by H-form elliptical turned stretchers. Hoop with scribed edge line supporting four elliptical long spindles either side of central splat constructed in two parts, with cruciform fretted motif. Arm hoop supported by four elliptical underarm spindles and turned arm supports.

Figure TV93. Hoop back Windsor side chair. Beech with ash hoop, fruitwood splat, and plain elm seat. Attributed to Buckinghamshire, c.1830-50. The use of vase shaped feet as part of a single ring turned leg is unusual in this tradition. The use of 'Gothic' style fretting is a design feature utilised in various ways in this region's chairs. See Figures TV51 and 110.

Single ring and concave turned front legs, plain turned rear legs, and vase shaped feet. Legs connected by H-form elliptical turned stretchers. Plain hoop supporting three elliptical long spindles either side of central fretted splat with Gothic tracery motif. Seat with rear wedge supporting two spindles connected to top of hoop.

Figure TV94. High hoop back Windsor armchair. Ash with beech splat and plain elm seat. Attributed to Buckinghamshire, c.1835-50. The legs show the pronounced graining of parts turned from thin branches rather than from cleft segments.

Single ring and concave turning on front legs. Plain turned rear legs. Lower ring and straight turned feet. Legs connected by H-form elliptical turned stretchers. Plain hoop supporting three elliptical long spindles either side of central fretted splat with Gothic tracery motif, constructed in two parts. Arm hoop supported by three elliptical short spindles and crook shaped arm supports.

Figure TV95. Low hoop back Windsor armchair. Ash with fruitwood splat and elm seat with scribed edge line. Attributed to Buckinghamshire, c.1820-40. The design of this chair is unusual both in its pierced splat form and in having both spindle and crook arm supports.

Single ring and concave turned legs with scribe lines (back legs replaced). Lower ring and straight turned feet. Legs morticed and wedged through the seat and connected by crinoline stretcher. Hoop with scribed edge line supporting three tapered long spindles either side of central Gothic tracery fretted splat. Shaped arms with notch underneath hand grip, morticed and screwed to the hoop and supported by an elliptical turned spindle and crook shaped arm supports.

Figure TV96. Low hoop back Windsor armchair. Beech spindles, legs and stretchers, ash hoop, fruitwood splat, oak arms and underarm supports, plain elm seat. Attributed to Buckinghamshire, c.1800-40.

Single ring and concave turned legs with lower ring and straight turned feet. Legs connected by H-form elliptical turned stretchers. Hoop with scribed edge line supporting three tapered long spindles either side of central fretted Gothic tracery splat. Seat with rear wedge supporting two spindles connected to top of hoop. Shaped arms morticed and screwed to the hoop and supported by shaped and flattened underarm supports morticed and screwed into edge of seat.

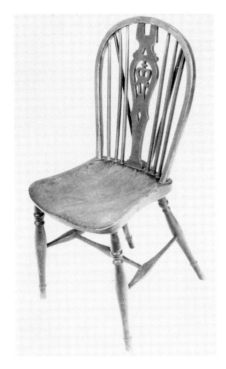

Figure TV97. Hoop back Windsor side chair. Beech with ash hoop, fruitwood splat, and elm seat with scribed edge line. Stamped 'J.P.' on rear of seat. Attributed to Buckinghamshire, c.1840. A further chair made by this maker is illustrated in Figure TV37.

Single ring and concave turned legs. Lower ring and turned feet. Legs connected by H-form elliptical turned stretchers. Hoop with scribed edge line supporting three tapered long spindles either side of central splat with unusual crown motif. Seat with rear wedge supporting two spindles connected to top of hoop. Of the range of splat motifs recorded in this tradition, this is perhaps the least common design.

Figure TV99. Hoop back Windsor side chair. Beech with ash hoop, fruitwood splat, and elm seat with scribed edge line. Attributed to Buckinghamshire, c.1820-50. The tulip motif in the splat is extremely unusual and an alternative form of this design is shown in Figure TV49.

Single ring and concave turned legs with lower ring and straight turned feet. Legs connected by H-form elliptical turned stretchers. Hoop with scribed edge line supporting three tapered long spindles either side of central splat with tulip fretted motif. Seat with rear wedge supporting two spindles connected to top of hoop.

Figure TV100. High hoop back Windsor armchair. Beech with ash hoop, fruitwood splat, and elm seat with scribed edge line and legs morticed and wedged through the seat. Attributed to Buckinghamshire, c.1820-1840.

Single ring and concave turned legs. Lower ring and tapered feet. Legs connected by H-form stretchers. Hoop with scribed edge line supporting four long spindles either side of central splat with a six petal shaped motif with a central small applied turned yew roundel, and a further one inset below. This splat motif is exceptionally rare. Arm hoop supported by four spindles and crook shaped arm supports.

Figure TV98. The stamp 'J.P.' impressed on the back of the seat wedge of the chair illustrated in Figure TV97. For makers with these initials see Appendix.

Figure TV101. Low hoop back Windsor armchair. Beech with ash hoop, fruitwood splat, and elm seat with scribed edge line. Attributed to Buckinghamshire, c.1800-30.

Single ring and concave turning on front legs which mortice through top of seat. Plain turned rear legs. Lower ring and straight turned feet. Legs connected by H-form elliptical turned stretchers. Hoop with scribed edge line supporting three splayed and tapered long spindles either side of central splat with unusual simple flower fretted motif and central turned roundel. Shaped arms, morticed and screwed to the hoop and supported by shaped and flattened underarm supports morticed and screwed into edge of seat.

Figure TV102. Detail of the fretted splat motif of the chair shown in Figure TV101, showing a typical form of applied central roundel which appears as a feature of many splat designs in the Buckinghamshire Windsor tradition. This motif may represent the hub of a wooden wheel and perhaps reflects the craft of wheelwrighting which some 18th century chair makers also followed. Roundels of this applied kind were typically turned in either fruitwood or yew: other central roundels were turned in situ as part of the splat.

Figure TV103. Hoop back Windsor side chair. Beech with ash hoop, fruitwood splat, and elm seat with scribed edge line and legs morticed through the seat. Attributed to Buckinghamshire, c.1790-1820.

Single ring and concave turning on front legs. Plain turned rear legs. Lower ring and straight turned feet. Legs connected by H-form elliptical turned stretchers. Hoop with scribed edge line supporting three tapered long spindles either side of central splat with unusual lyre motif and small central turned roundel.

Figure TV104. Low hoop back Windsor armchair. Yew with elm seat with scribed edge line. Attributed to Buckinghamshire, c.1830-60. This style of chair was made extensively in the High Wycombe tradition, and was featured in a number of chair manufacturers' catalogues. See, for example, the B. North Catalogue, c.1860, illustrated in Figure TV145, and an illustration from Edwin Skull's catalogue, c.1849, Figure TV53.

Single ring and concave turned legs with lower ring and straight turned feet. Legs connected by crinoline stretcher (left hand stretcher support replaced). Hoop with scribed edge line supporting a Gothic tracery back design. Shaped arms, morticed and screwed to the hoop and supported by shaped and flattened underarm supports morticed and screwed into edge of seat.

Figure TV105. Hoop back Windsor side chair. Yew with elm seat with scribed edge line. Attributed to Buckinghamshire, c.1830-60. This chair is the natural counterpart of the armchair shown in Figure TV104.

Single ring and concave turned legs with lower ring and straight turned feet. Legs connected by crinoline stretcher. Hoop with scribed edge line supporting Gothic tracery back design.

Figure TV106. Child's high Windsor table chair. Yew with elm seat with scribed edge line. Attributed to Buckinghamshire, c.1800-60.

Single ring and concave turning on front legs with removable foot rest. Plain turned rear legs. Lower ring and straight turned feet. Legs connected by H-form elliptical turned stretchers. Hoop with scribed edge line supporting Gothic tracery design. Turned arms of a type used in many children's chairs (see Figure TV164) supported by turned arm supports, and with holes bored to take a restraining bar.

(Courtesy Huntington Antiques)

Figure TV107. Hoop back Windsor side chair. Yew with beech legs and stretchers and plain elm seat. Stamped 'R.F.' on rear of seat. Attributed to Buckinghamshire, c.1820-50. This chair has a thin, broad seat typical of the early 19th century tradition. A further chair, a high back Windsor with a wheel fretted motif, which also has this maker's stamp is shown in Figure TV34.

Single ring and concave turned legs with lower ring and straight turned feet (worn). Legs connected by H-form elliptical turned stretchers. Hoop with scribed edge line with Gothic tracery back design.

Figure TV108. The stamp 'R.F.' impressed on the back of the seat edge of the chair illustrated in Figure TV107. For makers with these initials see Appendix.

Figure TV110. Windsor armchair. Beech with ash back and elm seat with scribed edge line. Stamped 'T N' on rear of seat. Attributed to Buckinghamshire, c.1840-60. The shortened arms probably reflect a need to draw the chair closely to a table. This chair is one of a group of chairs made for a Birmingham Almshouse.

Single ring and concave turned front legs. Plain turned rear legs. Lower ring and straight turned feet. Legs connected by H-form elliptical stretchers. Curved stay rail passing over sawn and reeded back uprights. Back design consisting of three interlocking Gothic tracery forms. Sawn scroll shaped arms which are unusually short, morticed into the back uprights. Back uprights fixed by dowel through the side of the seat. Shaped and flattened underarm supports morticed into edge of seat.
(Courtesy Christie's)

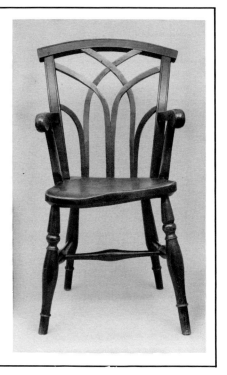

Figure TV111. The stamp 'T N' impressed on the back of the seat edge of the chair shown in Figure TV110. For makers with these initials see Appendix.

Figure TV109. Low hoop back Windsor armchair. Ash hoop and back, fruitwood arms and arm supports, beech legs and stretchers, and elm seat with scribed edge line and legs morticed through and wedged. Attributed to Buckinghamshire, c.1800-40. This chair is the natural counterpart to the chair illustrated in Figure TV107.

Single ring and concave turned legs with lower ring and straight turned feet. Legs connected by H-form elliptical turned stretchers with regional turnery device in cross stretcher. Hoop with scribed edge line enclosing Gothic tracery back design. Shaped arms morticed and screwed to the hoop and supported by shaped and flattened underarm supports morticed and screwed into edge of seat.

Figure TV112. High hoop back Windsor armchair. Beech with ash top hoop and arm bow, fruitwood splat and elm seat with scribed edge line. Attributed to Buckinghamshire, c.1800-40. This chair has stylistic similarities to cabriole legged chairs from the earlier 18th century tradition. The fretting of the splat and the general design has been maintained in this 19th century chair, but the cabriole leg has been abandoned in favour of the more economical turned leg.

Single ring and concave turned legs with lower ring and straight turned feet. Legs connected by H-form elliptical turned stretchers. Hoop with scribed edge line supporting four tapered long spindles either side of central fretted splat showing Chippendale influence, and constructed in two parts. Arm hoop supported by four turned spindles and crook arm supports.

Figure TV113. Hoop back Windsor side chair. Beech with ash hoop, fruitwood splat, and elm seat with scribed edge line. Attributed to Buckinghamshire, c.1835-50. This chair is the side counterpart to the armchair shown in Figure 112. The inclusion of two turned spindles either side of the splat is unusual, and made necessary by the atypical width of the splat.

Heavy single ring and concave turned legs with lower ring and straight turned feet. Legs connected by H-form elliptical turned stretchers. Hoop with scribed edge line supporting two elliptical long spindles either side of a central fretted splat showing Chippendale influence. Seat with rear wedge supporting two spindles connected to top of hoop.

Figure TV114. Tall hoop back Windsor arm-chair. Beech with ash hoop, arm bow, and underarm supports, fruitwood splat and elm seat with scribed edge line. Attributed to Buckinghamshire, c.1800-40. The splat in this chair is constructed in two parts, which is relatively uncommon in this tradition, where typically splats are made in one section exposed to the front of the arm bow. This unusually tall chair was probably made as a special order for a large person, and would have required a special set of formers to produce the curved bows.

Single ring and concave turned legs with lower ring and straight turned feet. Legs connected by H-form elliptical turned stretchers. Hoop with scribed edge line supporting four tapered long spindles either side of central splat with wheel fretted motif and central roundel. Arm hoop supported by four elliptical spindles and crook shaped arm supports.

(Collection B. Morley)

Figure TV115. High back Windsor arm and side chair. Attributed to Buckinghamshire, c.1780-1820. The armchair is made from a mixture of woods: ash for the arm and top hoops, and underarm supports, fruitwood for legs, stretchers, spindles and splats, and elm for the seat. The side chair is made from ash, with fruitwood back legs and stretchers (front legs replaced) and an elm seat. The hoop is secured to the seat by a dowel through the side edge of the seat. These chairs have four tapered long spindles alternating with three fretted splats with pierced urn motifs. The use of alternate spindles and splats is a feature of some visually striking designs from this region, and other examples of this style are shown in Figure TV116, as well as the chairs illustrated in Figures TV151-153 which were made by Robert Prior of Uxbridge, Middlesex.

Figure TV116. Hoop back Windsor side chair. Beech with ash hoop, fruitwood splats, and elm seat with scribed edge line. Attributed to Buckinghamshire, c.1790-1830. This chair has construction and design features in common with the chairs in Figure TV115 including the elegant, thin shaped seat which is waisted and flared to the front; the single ring turnings are set high on the legs which mortice through the seat. These features are typical of the best quality early 19th century chairs from this region. The unusual practice of securing the hoop in place with a wooden dowel through the side of the seat is common to the group, shown in Figures TV115-117 and suggests that they may have been the product of the same maker or workshop.

Single ring and concave turning on front legs. Plain turned rear legs. Lower ring and straight turned feet. Legs morticed and wedged through seat, and connected by H-form elliptical turned stretchers. Hoop with scribed edge line supporting two long spindles alternated with three shaped splats incorporating an outline urn motif. Seat with rear wedge supporting two spindles connected to top of hoop.

Figure TV117. Hoop back Windsor side chair. Beech with ash hoop and fruitwood splats, elm seat with scribed edge line. Attributed to Buckinghamshire, c.1830-50.

Single ring and concave turning on legs. Lower ring and straight turned feet. Legs connected by H-form elliptical turned stretchers. Plain hoop with scribed edge line supporting four tapered long spindles and two shaped splats with applied central roundels.

Figure TV118. High hoop back Windsor armchair. Ash hoop, arm bow and underarm spindles, fruitwood splat, spindles, legs and stretchers, plain elm seat. Attributed to Buckinghamshire, c.1800-40. This chair has an unusual fretted splat design and is the natural counterpart to the side chair shown in Figure TV119. This style of splat is also found in some Windsor chairs made in the North Eastern tradition. See Figure NE33, Chapter 3.

Single ring and concave turned front legs. Plain turned rear legs. Lower ring and straight turned feet. Legs connected by H-form elliptical turned stretchers. Hoop with scribed edge line supporting four long tapered spindles either side of central fretted splat. Arm hoop supported by four turned spindles and crook shaped arm supports.

Figure TV119. Hoop back Windsor side chair. Beech with ash hoop, fruitwood splat and spindles, and elm seat with scribed edge line and legs morticed and wedged through the seat. Attributed to Buckinghamshire, c.1780-1830.

Single ring and concave turning on front legs. Plain turned rear legs. Legs connected by H-form elliptical turned stretchers. Hoop with scribed edge line supporting three tapered spindles either side of central splat with fretted motif. Seat with rear wedge supporting two spindles connected to the top of the hoop. Hoop fixed by dowel through side edge of seat.

Figure TV120. Hoop back Windsor side chair. Beech with ash hoop, fruitwood splat and spindles, and elm seat with scribed edge line and legs morticed and wedged through the seat. Attributed to Buckinghamshire, c.1780-1830. This chair has an unusual splat design which is combined with the features of a broad, thin seat, flared outwards to the front, with the legs morticed and wedged through the seat. See pp.17 and 18 for a discussion of the implications of this combination of design features.

Single ring and concave turning on front legs. Plain turned rear legs. Lower ring and straight turned feet. Legs connected by H-form elliptical turned stretchers. Hoop with scribed edge line supporting three tapered long spindles either side of central fretted splat.

Figure TV121. Hoop back Windsor side chair with residual later paint. Beech with ash hoop, fruitwood splat, and elm seat with scribed edge line and legs morticed and wedged through the seat. Attributed to Buckinghamshire, c.1780-1830.

Single ring and concave turning on front legs. Plain turned rear legs. Lower ring and straight turned feet. Legs connected by H-form elliptical turned stretchers. Hoop with scribed line supporting three tapered long spindles (one spindle missing), either side of central unusual fretted splat. Seat with rear wedge supporting two spindles connected to top hoop.

Figure TV123. A raised brass emblem or insignia fixed by a brass screw to the centre of the splat of the chair shown in Figure TV122. This plaque probably represents a civic insignia rather than military, and suggests that this chair was probably part of a group used in a place administered by local government.

Figure TV122. Hoop back Windsor side chair. Yew with elm seat with scribed edge line and legs morticed through seat. Attributed to Buckinghamshire, c.1780-1820.

Single ring and concave turning high on the legs with lower ring and straight turned feet. Legs connected by crinoline stretcher. Hoop with scribed edge line supporting three tapered long spindles either side of central fretted splat with central wheel and applied metal emblem (see Figure TV123 for detail illustration). Seat with rear wedge supporting two spindles connected to top of hoop. Hoop fixed by dowels through sides of seat. (Collection B. Morley)

Figure TV124. Hoop back Windsor side chair. Yew with ash crinoline supports and back legs, and plain elm seat with legs morticed and wedged through the seat. Attributed to Buckinghamshire, c.1790-1820.

Single ring and concave turning high on legs with lower ring and straight turned feet. Legs connected by crinoline stretcher. Hoop with scribed edge line supporting three tapered long spindles either side of central fretted splat with undecorated raised disc which was probably intended to accommodate a metal badge or emblem. Seat with rear wedge supporting two spindles connected to top of hoop. Hoop fixed by dowels through sides of seat.

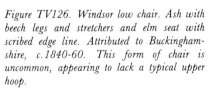

Figure TV126. Windsor low chair. Ash with beech legs and stretchers and elm seat with scribed edge line. Attributed to Buckinghamshire, c.1840-60. This form of chair is uncommon, appearing to lack a typical upper hoop.

Single ring and concave turned legs with lower ring and straight turned feet. Legs connected by H-form elliptical turned stretchers. Arm bow supported by eleven tapered spindles and elliptical turned underarm supports.

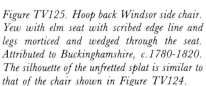

Figure TV125. Hoop back Windsor side chair. Yew with elm seat with scribed edge line and legs morticed and wedged through the seat. Attributed to Buckinghamshire, c.1780-1820. The silhouette of the unfretted splat is similar to that of the chair shown in Figure TV124.

Single ring and concave turning high on the legs with lower ring and straight turned feet, which are worn. Legs connected by crinoline stretcher. Hoop with scribed edge line supporting three tapered long spindles either side of central splat without frets or decoration, damaged at top. Seat with rear wedge supporting two spindles connected to top of hoop. Hoop fixed by dowels through sides of seat. (Collection B. Morley)

Figure TV127. Windsor low chair. Ash hoop splat and spindles, beech legs and stretchers, plain elm seat. Attributed to Buckinghamshire, c.1840-60.

Single ring and concave turned legs with lower ring and straight turned feet. Legs connected by H-form elliptical turned stretchers. Arm bow with slightly raised central section supported by seven elliptical turned spindles either side of central fretted splat with turned roundel motif, and turned arm supports of regional style.

Figure TV128. Windsor low chair. Yew with plain elm seat. Attributed to Buckinghamshire, c.1800-30. This elegant and unusual chair shows a further example of the fretted and roundel turned splat which was particularly used, in this form, by Robert Prior, Windsor chair maker, of Uxbridge, Middlesex. See Figures TV160 and 161.

Single ring and concave turned legs with lower ring and straight turned feet. Legs connected by crinoline stretchers. Arm bow with raised central section supported by six faux bamboo turned spindles either side of central fretted splat with raised roundel motif, and faux bamboo turned arm supports (left hand support replaced).

(Collection B. Morley)

Figure TV130. High stick back Windsor side chair and armchair. Yew with elm seats, with scribed edge lines. Attributed to Buckinghamshire, c.1800-40. These stick back Windsors are made in yew, a wood which was reserved for the best chairs in each design category. The interesting markings in the hoops, legs, and spindles in these chairs show the graining of yew to its best advantage.

Figure TV129. An illustration from the catalogue of Edwin Skull of High Wycombe, chair manufacturer, c.1849. These superb (hand coloured) drawings show the typical progression of Wycombe stick back Windsors, including a side chair, a low single bow armchair and a double bow armchair, with turned underarm supports, and heavy single ring and concave turned legs, design features which became fashionable towards the mid-19th century.

(Courtesy High Wycombe Chair Museum)

Figure TV131. Low hoop back stick Windsor. Beech with ash hoop and elm seat, with scribed edge line. Stamped 'S.M.' on rear of seat. Attributed to Buckinghamshire, c.1845-80. This style of underarm turning was commonly used by High Wycombe makers of the mid-19th century, and is extensively illustrated in the B. North catalogue No.5, c.1860. See chair number 19 in Figure TV145 for an identical illustration of this chair.

Single ring and concave turned legs with lower ring and straight turned feet. Legs connected by H-form elliptical turned stretchers. Hoop with scribed edge line supporting seven tapered long spindles. Seat with rear wedge supporting two spindles connected to top of hoop. Shaped arms, morticed and screwed to the hoop and supported by turned underarm supports.

Figure TV133. Windsor side chair. Ash hoop, beech with plain elm seat. Stamped 'J.O.' on rear of seat. Attributed to Buckinghamshire, c.1840-60. This style of chair was made by many makers in High Wycombe throughout the 19th century and an illustration of a similar chair, advertised by the chair making firm of E. Skull in their c.1849 catalogue shown in Figure TV129.

Raised three ring turned legs. Lower ring and vase shaped feet. Legs connected by H-form elliptical turned stretchers, with replaced cross stretcher. Plain hoop supporting seven elliptical long spindles. Seat with rear wedge supporting two spindles connected to top of hoop.

Figure TV135. Windsor side chair. Ash hoop with scribed line, plain elm seat with scribed edge line, remainder beech. Stamped 'J. MEAD' on rear edge of seat. Attributed to High Wycombe, c.1841-51. For another chair design by this maker see TV63.

Single ring and concave turning on front legs. Plain turned rear legs. Lower ring and straight turned feet missing. Legs connected by H-form elliptical turned stretchers. Plain hoop with scribed edge line supporting seven tapered long spindles. Seat with rear wedge supporting two spindles connected to top of hoop. The hoop is reinforced at seat level with later metal brackets.

Figure TV136. The stamp of 'J. Mead' impressed on the back of the seat wedge of the chair illustrated in Figure TV135. For makers with this name see Appendix.

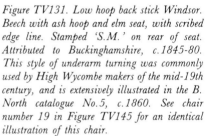

Figure TV132. The stamp 'S.M.' impressed on rear seat edge of the chair in Figure TV131. For makers with these initials see Appendix.

Figure TV134. The stamp 'J.O.' impressed on the back of the seat wedge of the chair illustrated in Figure TV133. For makers with these initials see Appendix.

Figure TV137. Stick back Windsor armchair. Ash with elm seat. Attributed to Buckinghamshire, c.1800-40. The incorporation of an additional top hoop, which extends the chair's height, illustrates that some experimentation of design was practised in this tradition.

Single ring and concave turning on front legs. Plain turned rear legs, lower ring and straight turned feet. Legs connected by H-form elliptical turned stretchers. Plain lower hoop supporting seven tapered long spindles surmounted by upper hoop supported by four tapered spindles. Shaped arms morticed and screwed to the hoop and supported by shaped and flattened underarm supports screwed and morticed into edge of seat. Notches on under surface of arms.

Figure TV138. Unusually high, high back Windsor. Yew with alder seat. Attributed to Buckinghamshire, c.1830-60.

Single ring and concave turned legs with lower ring and straight turned feet. Legs connected by H-form elliptical turned stretchers. Hoop with scribed edge line supporting eleven tapered long spindles. Seat with rear wedge supporting two spindles connected to top of hoop. Arm hoop supported by five short elliptical spindles and crook shaped arm supports. The arm bow has two attached 'platforms' to broaden the arm shape.
(Collection B. Morley)

Figure TV139. High stick back Windsor. Ash with elm seat. Stamped 'J.W. WEBB' and 'J.F.S.' on rear edge of seat. Attributed to High Wycombe, c.1890-1910. This late example has a conspicuously heavy demeanour typical of Windsor chairs made in the late 19th century.

Heavy three ring turned legs. Lower ring and straight turned feet. Legs connected by H-form elliptical turned stretchers. Plain hoop supporting nine parallel long spindles. Seat with rear wedge supporting two spindles connected to top of hoop. Arm hoop supported by four turned underarm spindles and turned underarm supports.

Figure TV141. High stick back Windsor. Ash with elm seat. Stamped 'GLENISTER MAKER WYCOMBE 1892' on rear seat edge. This chair is closely similar to the one made by the firm of Gibbons shown in Figure TV143 and, in common with this chair and the chair in Figure TV139, exhibits the manner in which late 19th century Windsor chairs in this tradition became heavier and clumsier in appearance than those made earlier in the 19th century.

Decoratively turned legs with large lower ring and straight turned feet. Legs connected by H-form decoratively turned stretchers. Hoop supporting nine parallel long spindles. Arm hoop supported by turned underarm supports and five short elliptical spindles.

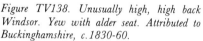

Figure TV140. The stamp of J.W. Webb impressed on the rear seat edge of the chair shown in Figure TV139. This manufacturer was part of a large family dynasty of chair makers who worked in High Wycombe, West Wycombe, Stokenchurch, Henley and Chesham during the 19th century. See Appendix for details. The initials J.F.S. stamped next to the manufacturer's name refer to the framer of the chair.

Figure TV142. The stamp of Thomas Glenister, chair manufacturer of Hughenden Road, High Wycombe (fl.1883-99), impressed on the back seat edge of chair illustrated in Figure TV141. This firm of chair makers, under the ownership of different members of the Glenister family, has been recorded working from 1825 to 1988.

Figure TV144. The stamp of C. Gibbons, chair manufacturer of Oxford Road, High Wycombe (1883-89), impressed on the back seat edge of chair illustrated in Figure TV144. The firm of Glenister and Gibbons is recorded between 1869 and 1877. After this time, these makers continued as separate chair manufacturers at different addresses. The initial stamp 'W.H.' also impressed on the rear seat edge refers to the (untraced) framer who assembled the chair.

Figure TV143. High stick back Windsor. Ash with elm seat with scribed edge line. Stamped 'GIBBONS WYCOMBE 1897' and 'W.H.' on rear of seat.

Decoratively turned legs with large lower ring and straight turned feet. Legs connected by H-form decoratively turned stretchers. Hoop with scribed edge line supporting nine parallel long spindles. Arm hoop supported by turned underarm supports and five short elliptical spindles. This chair model is identical to the Glenister chair shown in Figure TV141.

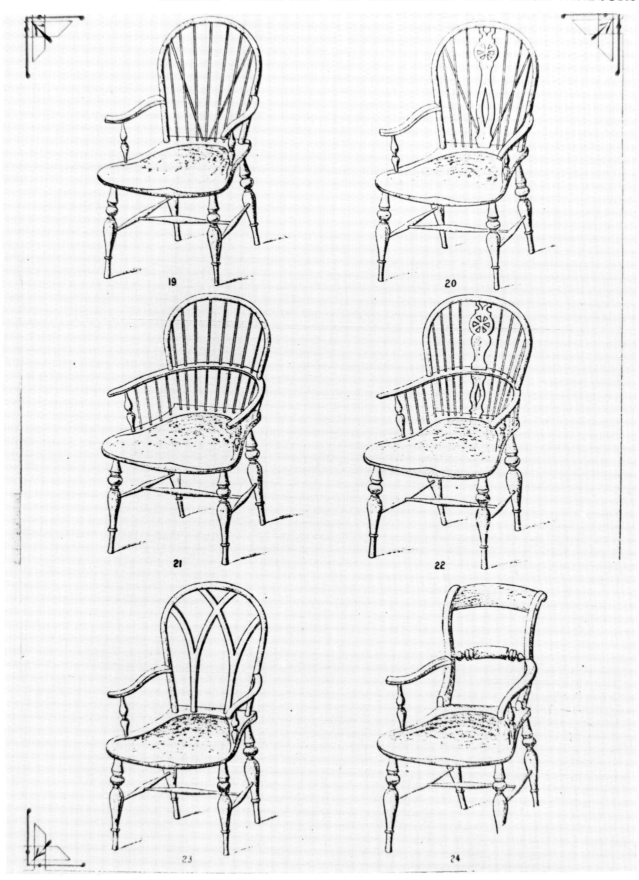

Figure TV145. A plate from the c.1860 catalogue of B. North, chair manufacturer of West Wycombe, Buckinghamshire. This firm is recorded working between 1863 and 1899, and produced a wide range of both hoop and scroll back Windsors. The chairs shown in this extract illustrate plain single and double hoop stick back Windsor armchairs in items 19 and 21; single and double hoop back Windsor armchairs with fretted wheel motif splats in items 20 and 22; and a single hoop back armchair with Gothic tracery form back design in item 23. Chair No.24 shows an example of a scroll back Windsor chair made with sawn back uprights rather than a hoop. In each case these chairs are shown with the turned underarm supports typical of Windsor chairs made after c.1840. The leg turnings are shown to be entirely of the lower single ring and concave variety which are generally associated with Windsor chairs made in the late first half, and into the third quarter of the 19th century. (Courtesy High Wycombe Chair Museum)

The Prior Family

Of the many Windsor chair makers to work in towns and villages outside the major chair making centre of High Wycombe, few could claim a more distinguished place in the history of English Windsor chair making than the Prior family of Uxbridge, Middlesex. Members of this family were Windsor chair makers for at least three generations, from the second half of the eighteenth century until the third quarter of the nineteenth century. The first recorded member was John Prior who worked in Hillingdon, Uxbridge, during the last half of the eighteenth century and into the nineteenth century, until his death in 1816.[35] He and his wife Martha had six children, two of whom, John and Robert, were to follow in their father's craft to become 'chair and hurdle makers'[36] in Hillingdon, and a further son, Samuel, followed in this trade at Cricklewood. The title of their occupation seems to accurately describe the orientation of these craftsmen, for in addition to producing the finest and most striking designs of Windsor chairs, they did not despise the materials with which they worked in any sense, and offered for sale sundry by-products of their chair making woods which they evidently harvested in both coppice and mature woodland. These subsidiary products included rustic garden seats made from coppice thinnings, and an invoice raised by John Prior in 1768 describes such a seat as a 'Rurall Chair' (see Figure TV146). A further bill raised by the firm of John and Robert Prior in 1822 itemises other coppice products including poles for making rose harbors (arbours), stakes for supporting espalier fruit trees, and sticks for staking garden peas (see Figure TV147). The hurdles which they made would probably have included both cleft hazel hurdles used as garden and livestock wind-breaks and fencing, and ash hurdles used in penning sheep.*

Of the chairs made by the Priors, the earliest style appears as the logo on the invoice issued by John Prior in 1768 which illustrates a classical style of Windsor chair made with a pierced splat, cabriole front legs joined by a crinoline stretcher, and with a splayed seat form, typical of best Windsor styles made from the mid- to late eighteenth century in the Thames Valley region (see Figure

Figure TV146. An invoice raised by John Prior of Uxbridge, Middlesex on 9 July, 1768, for 'One Rurall Chair'. This probably refers to a rustic seat which formed part of the repertoire of sundry items supplied by this maker in addition to high quality Windsor chairs.

Figure TV147. An invoice raised by John and Robert Prior in 1820 for the sale of (Rose) 'harbor poles' of two sizes, espalier supports and pea sticks. Although the Prior logo portrays them as Windsor chair makers and turners who made chairs for 'Wholesale, Retail & for Exportation', they clearly did not despise selling the coppice materials, for garden use, which they harvested as a by-product to their main craft of chair making. (Courtesy Hillingdon Borough Libraries)

TV146). This illustration probably displays the most prestigious style of chair made by John Prior, and although no chair of this type bearing his stamp has been recorded, a further style made and stamped by this maker is shown in Figure TV148. This chair is a conventional style of low wheel back Windsor, typical of those made in great numbers in High Wycombe during the late eighteenth century, and throughout the first half of the nineteenth century. The example made by Prior is made in yew with an elm seat, and has the refined high single ring and concave turned leg made during the last quarter of the eighteenth century, and may indicate

that this design was a later addition to John Prior's repertoire of chair styles.

Some years before his death, John Prior had apparently taken Robert, the eldest son, and also Samuel, and John the youngest son into the business and taught them his trade

---

* The making of hurdles as well as Windsor chairs is an interesting combination of crafts. Cleaving wood to produce hurdles and, in the case of 'gate' hurdles, the rough shaping of tenons using a side axe and draw knife, and the cutting of the mortices into the side parts with a 'twyvil', or double ended morticing knife, are ancient uses of materials and tools within a 'green' wood technology. The extension of the 'archaic' use of green wood as well as the relatively sophisticated adaptions and new techniques used to create Windsor chairs, suggests a historic continuum of coppice usage which directly links the Windsor chair to its antecedents.

Figure TV149. The stamp of John Prior of Uxbridge, Middlesex (fl.1768-1816), impressed on both seat side edges of the chair shown in Figure TV148.

Figure TV148. Low splat back Windsor. Yew with elm seat. Stamped 'J. PRIOR UXBRIDGE' on both sides of seat (fl.1768-1816). This conventional pattern of chair was made extensively in the Buckinghamshire tradition, and indicates that in addition to making their very individual patterns, the Priors also made regionally standard designs.

Single ring and concave turned legs with lower ring and straight turned feet. Legs morticed and wedged through the seat and connected by a crinoline stretcher. Hoop with scribed edge line supporting three parallel long spindles either side of a central splat with accentuated wheel fretted motif and applied central roundel. Shaped arms, morticed and screwed to the hoop and supported by shaped and flattened underarm supports screwed and morticed into edge of seat.

(see Figure TV150 in which the workshop on the left is described as Prior and Son). He ultimately passed on the business to his eldest son, Robert, at some time around his death in 1816 and it was he who carried on the business for the next twenty years, either employing his younger brother John in the business, or working with him as junior partner. Samuel did not join his two brothers, and by the time Robert had taken over the family workshop, he had moved to establish his own business as a chair and hurdle maker at Cricklewood, a few miles from Uxbridge.[37]

By the time of John senior's death, the business was apparently a flourishing concern, and the premises which Robert inherited were situated at the Hillingdon end of Uxbridge High Street*, and were of considerable size. These buildings were drawn in about 1810, as part of a panorama of the main street (see

Figure TV150) and show a range of linked premises which apparently have large showroom windows, as well as yard gates in the centre. The workshops were probably situated above the showrooms as well as in other buildings shown to the rear, and what was probably a loading area for the chairs can also be seen in the centre of the premises.

Evidence that this was a business of some size, employing others, is suggested in the hand written caption above the buildings which reads, 'Prior and Son, Windsor Chair Manufactury'. This description was also written on a signboard above the large right hand lower windows, and suggests that advertising was a significant part of the business, perhaps appealing to potential customers who would have passed along this important route, now the A40, to and from London from Oxford and Buckinghamshire as well as the West Midlands.

Robert and John junior continued to work at Uxbridge over a relatively long period of time, from about 1816 until 1845 when they are last recorded in a trade directory.[38] Samuel continued in his trade beyond this time, and is last recorded working at Cricklewood in 1851.[39] A further chair maker, Charles Prior, who was probably Samuel's son, had

---

* These premises have now been demolished, and the Civic Centre now stands approximately on this site.[40]

Figure TV150. A panorama of Uxbridge High Street, drawn by W.J. Burgiss, c.1810, shows an extensive workshop premises to the left which is described above as 'Prior & Son, Windsor Chair Manufactury'. This caption refers to John Prior, chair and hurdle maker, and his son, Robert, who inherited the business following his father's death in 1816, when he was joined by his brother, also John. The advertising signboard above the right hand window, and the large showroom window to the left suggest that sales to travellers passing along the main (now the A40) route to London from the West Midlands, as well as Oxfordshire and Buckinghamshire, formed part of their trade. The large gate in the centre of the buildings, and the first floor rooms above the showroom suggest that there were extensive workshops. John Prior senior lived at the house to the left of the Green Dragon Inn, shown to the right of the drawing.

(Courtesy Hillingdon Borough Libraries)

become a chair maker/turner at Brentford in Middlesex,[41] being last recorded as a chair maker in High Street, Brentford, in 1862.[42] Robert, too, had a son named Robert who was also trained as a turner and chair maker. Robert junior probably worked with his father and appears to have continued in his trade after his father had retired, since he is recorded as a turner living at Windsor Street, Uxbridge in 1851.[43] No further record exists of Priors working in the town after that point, and it appears that Robert junior was the last of the Prior chair makers in Uxbridge.*

Of the six known chair making members of the Prior family, it is the low wheel back chair shown in Figure TV148, and the cabriole legged Windsor shown as the logo on the bill-head (see Figure TV146) which firmly indicate at least part of the range of chairs made by John Prior, the originator of the firm. In contrast, the repertoire of recorded chairs bearing the stamp of his son, Robert Prior, is more comprehensive, and examples of these are shown in Figures TV151-159. These chairs show a considerable range of designs, from the simplest form made in fruitwood and elm shown in Figure TV158, to the most elaborate in Figures TV151 and 153, and indicates that under Robert Prior's ownership, the firm made chairs to appeal to different markets. The firm also probably extended its range of sales outlets, since the bill-head issued by Robert Prior (see Figure TV147) in 1820 differs from the invoice raised by his father, in advertising sales for 'wholesale, retail, and exportation' purposes. It would be of the greatest interest to know if the Priors did export chairs, since firm records of an export trade in English Windsors are scarce.

Although the Priors' business at Uxbridge was not remarkable in its size and location, since there were many large chair manufactures located close to High Wycombe, the quality of the chairs made in Robert Prior's workshops distinguish this maker as an important designer and craftsman, producing styles which were probably unique to his workshop. The chairs which he made are characterised by bold details which emphasise pleasing aspects of the basic form in a way which was uncommon elsewhere in this regional tradition. For example, the use of

Figure TV151. Low hoop back Windsor arm-chair. Ash hoop, fruitwood elsewhere, with elm seat with scribed edge line. Stamped 'ROBERT PRIOR MAKER UXBRIDGE' on side of seat (fl.1816-45). The use of the H-form stretcher is typically reserved for those chairs made principally with ash, beech, and fruitwood parts, whereas those made in yew with elm seats usually have a crinoline stretcher, as in Figure TV153.

Single ring and concave turned legs with lower ring and straight turned feet. Legs connected by H-form elliptical turned stretchers with regional turnery motif on cross stretcher. Hoop with scribed edge line supporting three narrow fretted splats with central roundel alternating with two tapered long spindles. Shaped arms, morticed and screwed to the hoop and supported by short fretted splats with central roundel as well as shaped and flattened underarm supports screwed and morticed into edge of seat.

Figure TV152. The stamp of Robert Prior of Uxbridge, Middlesex (fl.1816-45), impressed on the side seat edge of the chair in Figure TV151.

triple splats was an elegant, if relatively costly way of producing a chair back design, and was adopted within a regional tradition which typically produced chairs which had only one central back splat. One of the triple splat forms of back design made by the Priors is shown in Figure TV151 which illustrates fretted splats with central roundel turnings, and in order to present a harmonious design curve, are made in two lengths, so that the roundels

Figure TV153. Low hoop back Windsor arm-chair. Yew with elm seat with scribed edge line. Stamped 'ROBERT PRIOR MAKER UXBRIDGE' on side of seat (fl.1816-45).

Single ring and concave turned legs with lower ring and straight turned feet. Legs connected by crinoline stretcher. Hoop with scribed edge line supporting three narrow splats with Prince of Wales' feathers motif, alternating with two tapered long spindles. Shaped arms, morticed and screwed to the hoop and supported by short fretted splats with Prince of Wales' feathers motif, as well as shaped and flattened underarm supports morticed and screwed into edge of seat. Back hoop fixed with turned dowel through side of seat. This chair probably represents the finest design qualities produced by this region's chair makers, where a number of fretted splats were incorporated to achieve perfect stylistic balance within a regional tradition of chairs which were typically economical in their use of fretted parts. (Courtesy Huntington Antiques)

Figure TV154. The stamp of Robert Prior, chair maker, of High Street, Uxbridge, Middlesex (fl.1816-45), impressed on the side seat edge of the chair in Figure TV153. This maker, in common with his brothers Samuel and John, was probably apprenticed to their father, John senior. Robert appears to have inherited the business after his father's death in 1816, and he continued to produce a range of chairs of outstanding quality and innovation until approximately 1845, probably employing his brother, John, as well as other chair makers.

---

* A Robert Thomas Prior, a Cabinet Maker and Turner of Coggeshall Road, Bocking, in Essex is recorded working between 1855 and 1874, and it is possible that this refers to Robert Prior junior, formerly of Uxbridge, who had perhaps moved after his father's death.[44]

Figure TV155. High hoop back Windsor armchair. Yew, elm seat with scribed edge line. Stamped 'ROBERT PRIOR MAKER UXBRIDGE' on side of seat (fl.1816-45). This magnificent example of a high hoop back Windsor is made in yew, as were many 'best' Windsors, and was probably made as a special order for a large person. Making the chair would have required large formers, around which the large top hoop and arm bow, which were bent, to be specially made.

Single ring and concave turned legs with lower ring, and straight turned feet (missing). Legs connected by crinoline stretcher. Hoop with scribed edge line, morticed into arm bow, supporting five parallel long spindles either side of central splat with Prince of Wales' feathers fretted motif, with three small inset roundels. Arm bow supported by five underarm support spindles and crook shaped arm supports.

Figure TV156. Low hoop back Windsor. Beech with ash hoop, fruitwood arms, underarm supports and splat, and elm seat. Stamped 'ROBERT PRIOR MAKER UXBRIDGE' on side of seat (fl.1816-45). This conventional pattern of chair was made extensively in the Buckinghamshire tradition, and indicates that in addition to their very individual patterns, the Priors were making standard designs.

Single ring and concave turned legs with lower ring and straight turned feet. Legs morticed and wedged through the seat and connected by H-form elliptical turned stretchers; cross stretcher with regional turnery motif. Hoop with scribed edge line supporting three parallel long spindles either side of central splat with accentuated wheel fretted motif and applied central roundel. Shaped arms, morticed and screwed to the hoop and supported by shaped and flattened underarm supports screwed and morticed into edge of seat.

(Courtesy M. and D. Robinson, Key Antiques)

Figure TV158. Windsor armchair. Fruitwood with elm seat. Stamped 'ROBERT PRIOR MAKER UXBRIDGE' (fl.1816-45). The simple design of this Windsor chair is in sharp contrast with the elegant hoop back styles made by the Priors, and illustrates that a range of chairs was made at different price levels, including the most economical styles.

Single ring and concave turned legs which mortice through the seat, terminating in lower ring and straight turned feet. Legs connected by turned H-form stretchers. Sawn back uprights with connecting curved stay rail. Two narrow plain cross rails below with scribed edge lines. Shaped arms morticed and screwed to the back uprights, supported by shaped and flattened arm supports morticed and screwed into the sides of the seat.

are presented in a curve in line with the shape of the hoop. This form of design was also used in the chairs made by Robert Prior which have triple splats with Prince of Wales' feathers (see Figure TV153).

A penchant for adopting the Prince of Wales' feathers splat design by Prior is also shown in the very large chair illustrated in Figure TV155 which prominently shows this motif, but in this case, in a more conventional single splat form. It may be that this splat design was employed since it had popular royalist connotations at the beginning of the nineteenth century, when the Prince of Wales, later to become George IV, was titular monarch as the Prince Regent, from 1811 to 1820.

Although numerous examples of individualistic designs by Robert Prior have been recorded, it is clear

Figure TV157. The stamp of Robert Prior of Uxbridge, Middlesex (fl.1816-45), impressed on the side edge of the seat of the chair shown in Figure TV156.

that this firm also made regionally standard chair designs as well, and an example of a single hoop back Windsor armchair with a wheel motif splat, stamped by Robert Prior, typical of those made in nearby High Wycombe, is shown in Figure TV156. This chair is made in ash, beech and elm, with a fruitwood splat, and in common with chairs made in these woods throughout the

Figure TV159. The stamp of Robert Prior of Uxbridge, Middlesex (fl.1816-45), impressed on the rear seat edge of the chair shown in Figure TV158.

region, has H-form leg stretchers. In all other respects, however, the chair closely resembles the example in yew and elm made by John Prior senior, shown in Figure TV148.

A further chair stamped by Robert Prior, illustrated in Figure TV158, shows a style similar in essence, but different in detailed design to the scroll back Windsors which formed part of the simplest form of Windsor

Figure TV160. Low hoop back Windsor armchair. Yew with elm seat with scribed edge line. Attributed to Prior family, Middlesex, c.1790-1845.

Single ring and concave turned legs with lower ring and straight turned feet. Legs morticed through seat and connected by H-form elliptical turned stretchers. Hoop with scribed edge line supporting three narrow fretted splats with central roundels alternating with two slightly elliptical long spindles. Shaped arms, morticed and screwed to the hoop and supported by fretted underarm supports similar in design to the back splats, and flattened underarm support screwed and morticed into edge of seat. This chair has the extra design detail which typifies the work of Robert Prior, for example, in terms of the inclusion of extra underarm decorative splats which mirror the design of the back splats. Although this chair is unstamped, it is identical to the chair shown in Figure TV151, with the exception of the leg stretcher form.   (Collection P. Bune)

Figure TV161. Hoop back Windsor side chair. Beech with ash hoop and elm seat with scribed edge line. Attributed to Prior family, Middlesex, c.1800-45. This style of chair is the natural counterpart to the armchair stamped by Robert Prior shown in Figure TV151. This chair is not stamped, but its finesse in design detail, shown for example, in the use of two different splat lengths to create a crescent of roundel positions, suggests that this may be Prior's work.

Single ring and concave turned legs with lower ring and straight turned feet. Legs connected by H-form elliptical turned stretchers. Hoop with scribed edge line supporting three narrow fretted splats with central roundels, alternating with two slightly elliptical long spindles.

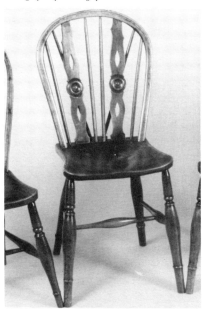

Figure TV162. Hoop back Windsor side chair. Fruitwood with elm seat with scribed edge line, and ash hoop. Attributed to Buckinghamshire, c.1800-40. This chair has some similarities with the chair shown in Figure TV161 but lacks the stylistic finesse typical of Prior's chairs, and was probably made by a maker elsewhere, but is included here to record an alternative mode of the roundel back design.

Single ring and concave turning on front legs. Plain turned rear legs. Lower ring and straight turned feet. Legs connected by H-form stretchers. Hoop with scribed edge line supporting four slightly elliptical long spindles and two narrow fretted splats with central roundels. Seat with rear wedge supporting two spindles connected to top of hoop.

designs made extensively in High Wycombe, and elsewhere, throughout the nineteenth century. This style of chair relied on two sawn uprights connected by two shaped splats to form the back, rather than utilising a bent hoop. The example made by Robert Prior has a simple back made of sawn back uprights, joined by a plain curved stay rail with two narrow rails below, but in other respects, exhibits the fine balance of legs and seat common to this maker's work.

However, the total range of designs made by the Priors has probably not yet been fully recorded, and other styles by Robert or other members of the family may yet be identified, and in this way further extend the typology of styles attributable to this important dynasty of chair makers who were at the same time producing standard regional styles, as well as significantly different designs, to form an important contribution to this regional tradition of chair making.

Square Back Windsors

The second major regional chair style to develop in the Buckinghamshire and Oxfordshire areas was that of chairs whose seats and range of leg turning styles were similar to those used in the hoop back varieties, with the exception that seats with rear wedges were not used. Their back designs, however, were not made from bent hoops but rather from two sawn back uprights, of which two basic forms were made, both of which were connected by a curved top stay rail.

The first of these two types incorporates sawn and shaped uprights which 'scroll' over at the top towards the rear, and are connected by a curved stay rail set below the top of the uprights. The uprights are also connected at a mid-point by various cross splat designs, which may be either plain, carved, turned and centrally flattened, or completely turned.

The second group of chairs has sawn shaped uprights which commonly terminate in turned finials, but in this design the curved stay rail passes over the back uprights. Chairs of this style typically have back designs composed of vertical parallel or elliptical turned spindles or of narrow flattened and curved splats (laths).

Interestingly, the Wycombe chair makers of the nineteenth century appear not to have hierarchically distinguished between the hoop and square back Windsors, and made both styles as part of their repertoire, and presented them on an equal design basis. This is illustrated by the nineteenth century trade catalogues produced by various makers from High and West Wycombe, who illustrated sawn back and hoop back Windsors side by side (see Figure TV186).

The scroll back*, and other related square back styles of chairs have popularly been considered to have originated in the late nineteenth century. However, the chairs shown in Figures TV165-171 illustrate extremely elegant forms of square back Windsors, which have lower ring and concave leg turnings, typical of those made prior to 1850,

---

* In common with other chair terms, the original makers' terms are unavailable to us, and others have been invented by writers, particularly in this century. The term 'scroll' back has been so created and adopted by numerous writers as a descriptive title. See for example, F. Gordon Roe, Mayes and Sparkes.

Figure TV163. A plate from the catalogue, c.1849, of Edwin Skull, chair manufacturer of High Wycombe (fl.1844-77), showing a range of closely related scroll and other square back Windsors, with spindles as well as plain and turned cross splats composing the back designs.

(Courtesy High Wycombe Chair Museum)

and the chair in Figure TV166 has high ring and concave turned legs, through morticing the seat, which are features of late eighteenth and early nineteenth century hoop back Windsors. These examples of square back chairs embody too, roundel turnery devices, common to many Wycombe and Uxbridge chairs made in the first half of the nineteenth century, either as part of a solid splat decoration, as in Figures TV167, 170 and 171, or as a silhouette form in Figures TV169 and 172.

The evidence of this group of chairs suggests that the use of sawn back uprights was adopted in the early nineteenth century, although these particular styles are uncommon. As the century progressed, further designs of scroll back Windsors developed, amongst which five cross splat designs have been recorded, including a plain curved cross splat (see Figure TV178), a curved, turned and centrally flattened cross splat (see Figure TV181), and more rarely, a curved, turned rope motif cross splat (see Figure TV177), a turned hexagonal shaped middle section, turned at each end, and carved cross splats (see Figures TV183 and 185 for examples).

Of these styles, the variety made with the turned and flattened central cross splat appears to have been the most commonly made, and were certainly made in the first half of the nineteenth century. Chairs of this design were shown in Edwin Skull's catalogue, c.1849, which illustrates a row of naïvely drawn and hand coloured images of these styles (see Figure TV163). A further illustration taken from the Skull catalogue shows

Figure TV164. A (hand coloured) plate from the catalogue, c.1849, of Edwin Skull, chair manufacturer of High Wycombe (fl.1844-77). This illustration shows an anthology of children's low rocking chairs, both arm and side varieties, and a 'high table chair' on the right. This latter style of chair was made to seat a child at the dining table, and a removable restraining bar was used to prevent the child falling out.

(Courtesy High Wycombe Chair Museum)

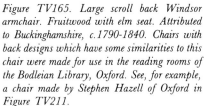

Figure TV165. Large scroll back Windsor armchair. Fruitwood with elm seat. Attributed to Buckinghamshire, c.1790-1840. Chairs with back designs which have some similarities to this chair were made for use in the reading rooms of the Bodleian Library, Oxford. See, for example, a chair made by Stephen Hazell of Oxford in Figure TV211.

Single ring and concave turned legs which mortice through the seat, terminating in lower ring and straight turned feet. Legs connected by crinoline stretcher. Decorative scribed turning at mid-point on legs and on crinoline stretcher supports. Sawn and shaped back uprights with shaped stay rail set below top level of back uprights. Narrow plain cross splats with crossed thin rails below, with a turned reeded circle at their inter-section and a small turned roundel at the centre. Shaped arms morticed and screwed to the hoop, supported by shaped and flattened arm supports morticed and screwed into the sides of the seat.

Figure TV166. Square back Windsor armchair. Fruitwood with elm seat. Attributed to Bucking-hamshire, c.1790-1840. This unusual and highly elaborate chair style illustrates many of the design features of this region's chairs, brought together to create a single ebullient style.

Single ring and concave turned legs which mortice through the seat, terminating in lower ring and straight turned feet. Legs connected by crinoline stretcher. Sawn back uprights with curved stay rail connecting back uprights. Cross splat below with turned central roundel supporting three small fretted splats with reeded cross motifs. Crossed reeded rails below with a turned circle at their intersection, and a small roundel at the centre. Shaped arms morticed and screwed to the uprights, supported by shaped and flattened arm supports, morticed and screwed into the sides of the seat. Two small underarm fretted splats with reeded cross motifs.

(Courtesy Christie's)

Figure TV167. Scroll back Windsor armchair. Fruitwood with elm seat with scribed edge line. Stamped 'W. MARKHAM' twice on rear seat edge. Attributed to Buckinghamshire, c.1790-1830. The cross splat design in this chair is reminiscent of those adopted by Robert Prior of Uxbridge in his chairs shown in Figure TV151.

Single ring and concave turned legs with lower ring and straight turned feet. Legs connected by crinoline stretcher. Sawn and shaped back uprights with scribed edge lines. Shaped stay rail set below top level of back uprights. Two decoratively shaped cross splats below with turned central roundels. Shaped arms, morticed and screwed to the back uprights, supported by curved and flattened arm supports morticed and screwed into the sides of the seat.

Figure TV168. The stamp of W. Markham impressed twice on the rear seat edge of the chair shown in Figure TV167. This maker is untraced. However, Thomas Markham is recorded as a chair maker in High Wycombe in 1841,[46] and Henry and Joseph Markham are recorded working there in 1861,[47] and it may be that W. Markham was a relative of these makers.

examples of these styles as children's chairs, both with and without arms or rockers (see Figure TV164).

Further evidence of the date of production of this design are the chairs attributed to William Wardell (fl.1839-54), and Stephen Hazell senior (fl.1846-65), both of whom worked as Windsor chair makers in the city of Oxford. Examples of chairs attributed to these makers are shown in Figures TV208-216. It is equally true that this style of scroll back Windsor was made continuously in the City of Oxford tradition until 1930, by Walter Puddifer, the last Windsor chair maker in Oxford, who worked until this time[45] making identical scroll back styles to those made by Hazell (see Figure TV218).

The group of square back chairs which have either long parallel or elliptical turned plain spindles fixed between the stay rail and the seat were also probably designed during the same period as the scroll back

varieties, and again, Edwin Skull's catalogue of 1849 illustrates an armchair of this style, which is shown in an extract from the catalogue in Figure TV206. A similar chair to this is shown in Figure TV198.

Other chairs were made by the High Wycombe makers which incor-porated short, elaborately turned spindles to produce decorative back designs. Of these, the most widely made style had a curved and arcaded stay rail connected by three turned spindles to a lower cross rail which is similarly arcaded. This style was widely made by the Wycombe chair manufacturers, and is illustrated in the catalogue produced by Benjamin North, c.1860, in item no.4, Figure TV186, as well as in W. Ellis's catalogue, chair manufacturer of West Wycombe, c.1870, item no.35, shown in Figure TV205. This type of chair is an unusually decorative style in a range of scroll back Windsors, which are essentially plain in design.

This style was often made in fruit-wood with an elm seat, a combination of woods reserved for prestigious styles of chairs. An example of this design is shown in Figure TV203.

A further style which incorporates decorative spindles is shown in Figure TV207. This chair has the elegant swept 'Grecian' arms, and a broad curved stay rail connecting four turned spindles to a lower cross rail. A side chair of this design was advertised by Edwin Skull in his catalogue, c.1849, and is shown in Figure TV206.

Figure TV169. Scroll back Windsor armchair. Fruitwood, with elm seat with scribed edge line. Attributed to High Wycombe, c.1820-40.

Single ring and concave turned legs with lower ring and straight turned feet. Legs connected by H-form elliptical turned stretchers. Sawn and shaped back uprights with curved stay rail set below top level of back uprights. Two plain curved narrow cross rails supporting turned central roundel with a floral fretted motif each side. Curved shaped arms, morticed and screwed to the back uprights, supported by shaped and flattened underarm supports morticed and screwed into the seat edge.

Figure TV170. Windsor armchair. Yew, with elm seat with scribed edge line. Attributed to Buckinghamshire, c.1790-1830. This chair has some design similarities with the chair made by W. Markham shown in Figure TV167 and is the natural counterpart to the side chair shown in Figure TV171.

Double ring and concave turned legs with lower double ring and straight turned feet and decorative turnings at mid-point. Legs connected by crinoline stretcher. Straight sawn uprights with edge scribed lines. Curved plain tablet shaped stay rail, with edge scribed line, passing over back uprights. Two decoratively shaped cross splats below with central turned roundel motifs. Curved shaped arms morticed and screwed to the back uprights, supported by shaped and flattened underarm supports morticed and screwed into the seat edge.

Figure TV171. Square back Windsor side chair. Yew, with elm seat with scribed edge line. Attributed to Buckinghamshire, c.1780-1830. The splat designs have similarities with those used in certain chair styles attributed to Robert Prior of Uxbridge (see Figure TV151), which adopt a pierced version of this splat set in a vertical position.

Double ring and concave turned legs with decorative turning at mid-point, and lower double ring and straight turned feet. Legs connected by a crinoline stretcher. Straight sawn back uprights with scribed edge lines. Tablet shaped stay rail with scribed edge line, passing over back uprights. Two decoratively shaped cross splats below with central roundel motifs.

Figure TV172. Scroll back arm and side chairs. Fruitwood, elm seat with scribed edge line. Stamped 'R.F.' on rear seat edge. Attributed to High Wycombe, c.1840-70. A side chair of this design was advertised by Benjamin North, Chair Manufacturer of West Wycombe in his catalogue, c.1860, an illustration of which is shown in Figure TV186, item number 7.

Raised three ring turned legs with vase shaped feet. Legs connected by H-form elliptical turned stretchers. Sawn and shaped back uprights with decorative scribed lines. Curved stay rail with lower decorative scribed lines set below the top level of back uprights. Two scribed curved cross rails supporting two decorative roundels. The armchair has curved shaped arms morticed and screwed into the back uprights, supported by shaped and flattened underarm supports morticed and screwed to side edges of seat.

Figure TV173. The stamp 'R.F.' impressed on the back seat edge of the chairs illustrated in Figure TV172. For makers with these initials see Appendix.

Figure TV174. Scroll back Windsor side chair. Yew with plain elm seat. Attributed to High Wycombe, c.1790-1830. The use of the turned roundel shown in this chair as a decorative feature of the stay rail is a further example of the use of this turnery device in this region's chairs. Other examples are shown in Figures TV167-171.

Single ring and concave turning on front legs. Plain turned rear legs. Lower ring and straight turned feet. Legs connected by H-form elliptical turned stretchers. Sawn and shaped back uprights connected by curved stay rail, with two decoratively turned roundels, set below top level of back uprights. Two decoratively turned cross splats below.

Figure TV175. Scroll back armchair. Beech with elm seat with scribed edge line. Stamped 'S.M.' on rear of seat. Attributed to Buckinghamshire, c.1845-80. The underarm turning was commonly used in many high wheel back chairs from the mid to late 19th century High Wycombe tradition. See for example Figure TV143. Other examples of chairs made by 'S.M.' have been recorded and one is shown in Figure TV131.

Single ring and concave turned legs with lower ring and straight turned feet. Legs connected by H-form elliptical stretchers. Sawn, shaped and turned back uprights supporting curved rectangular tablet shaped stay rail which passes over back uprights. Central horizontal turned and flattened cross splat. Curved shaped arms morticed and screwed into back uprights and supported by turned underarm supports.

Figure TV177. Scroll back Windsor side chair. Beech, elm seat with scribed edge line. Attributed to High Wycombe, c.1840-80. This alternative design was produced from a standard scroll back frame, by the addition of a different cross splat.

Three ring turned legs with lower ring and straight turned feet. Legs connected by H-form elliptical turned stretchers. Sawn and shaped back uprights with curved stay rail set below top level of back uprights. Decoratively turned and curved cross splat in the form of a central rope twist motif with turned finials at each end.

Figure TV176. The stamp 'S.M.' impressed on the back seat edge of chair illustrated in Figure TV175. For makers with these initials see Appendix.

Figure TV178. Scroll back Windsor side chair. Beech with plain elm seat. Stamped 'W. BRISTOW' on rear edge of seat. Attributed to High Wycombe, c.1830-80. The use of the undecorated lower cross splat creates this as the plainest of the scroll back chair styles, made by many of the Wycombe chair manufacturers. See Figures TV186 and 205 which show illustrations of this style of chair advertised by B. North, c.1860, and Walter Ellis, c.1870.

Heavy three ring turned legs with lower ring and straight turned feet. Legs connected by H-form elliptical turned stretchers. Sawn and shaped back uprights with a curved stay rail set below top level of back uprights, and plain, curved cross splat set below.

Figure TV179. The stamp of William Bristow impressed on the rear seat edge of the chair illustrated in Figure TV178. This maker is recorded as living at Downley, High Wycombe, in 1841.[48]

Figure TV180. Child's scroll back Windsor armchair. Beech with plain elm seat. Attributed to High Wycombe, c.1840-80. Many styles of children's chairs were made in the Wycombe tradition, and a range of these designs is illustrated in Figure TV164 taken from the catalogue of Edwin Skull, c.1849.

Single ring and concave turning on front legs. Plain turned rear legs. Lower ring and straight turned feet fitted to rockers. Legs connected by H-form elliptical turned stretchers. Sawn and shaped back uprights with narrow stay rail set below top level of back uprights. Plain curved cross splat below. Curved shaped arms morticed and screwed into back uprights, supported by simple turned underarm supports.

(Courtesy I. Sparkes)

Figure TV181. Scroll back Windsor side chair. Beech with plain elm seat. Stamped 'J. ALDRIDGE' on rear of seat, c.1840-80.

Heavy three ring turning to legs. Lower ring and straight feet. Legs connected by H-form elliptical turned stretchers. Sawn and shaped back uprights with stay rail set below top level of back uprights. Decoratively turned and flattened cross splat.

Figure TV182. The stamp of James Aldridge of High Wycombe (fl.1840-60), impressed on the rear seat edge of the chair in Figure TV181.

Figure TV183. Scroll back Windsor side chair. Beech with plain elm seat. Attributed to High Wycombe, c.1840-80. A carved cross splat was used in a range of Wycombe chairs, examples of which were advertised by Walter E. Ellis, chair manufacturer of High Wycombe, in his catalogue, c.1875 (see Figure TV184).

Three ring turning on the front legs, plain turned back legs; lower ring and straight turned feet. Legs connected by H-form elliptical turned stretchers. Sawn and shaped back uprights with broad stay rail set below top level of back uprights. Decoratively carved shaped cross splat.

51

Figure TV184. Scroll back Windsor side chair advertised by Walter E. Ellis, chair manufacturer of High Wycombe, c.1875. This chair shows a similar cross splat style to that exhibited in the chair in Figure TV183.

(Courtesy High Wycombe Chair Museum)

Figure TV185. Scroll back Windsor side chair. Beech with plain elm seat. Attributed to Buckinghamshire, c.1840-80. The use of a carved cross splat creates a further style of chair, within a basic scroll back frame. Many chair styles in this group were created by the simple expedient of incorporating a variety of turned, plain and carved cross splats.

Heavy three ring turned legs with lower ring and straight turned feet. Legs connected by H-form elliptical turned stretchers. Sawn and shaped back uprights with broad curved stay rail set below top level of back uprights. Decoratively shaped and carved cross splat.

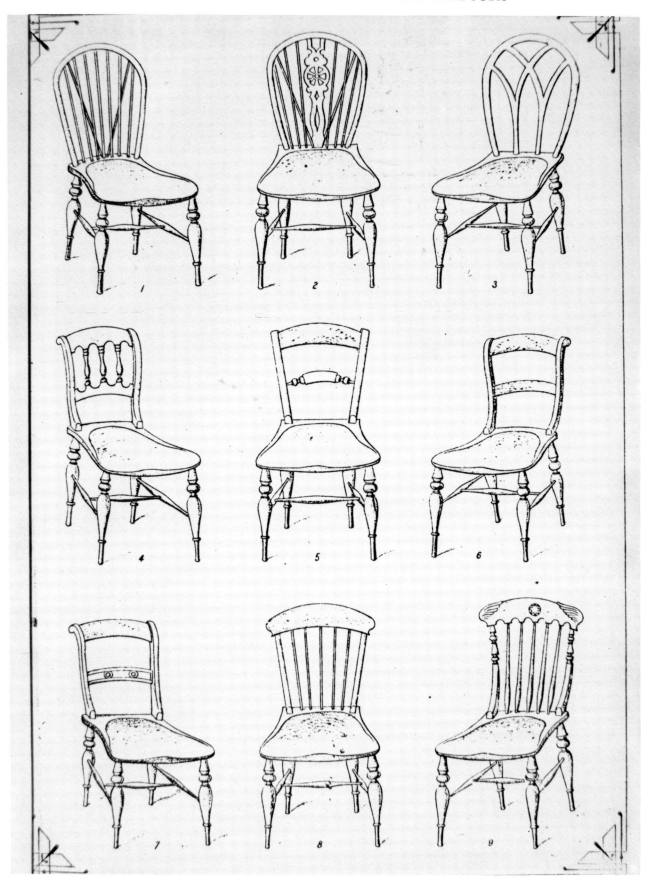

Figure TV186. A plate from the c.1860 catalogue of Benjamin North, chair manufacturer of West Wycombe, Buckinghamshire. This firm is recorded working between 1864 and 1899, producing a wide range of hoop and square back Windsors. Interestingly, the inclusion of these styles on the same page of the catalogue, suggests that these designs were seen as equivalent categories of chairs able to be ranked together. In this illustration, for example, scroll back and other square back chairs were offered in items 4 to 9, and three styles of hoop back chairs offered in items 1 to 3. These three latter styles were offered as the major hoop back side chair styles, and, significantly, by this time, the less common forms of fretted splat designs shown in Figures TV73-125 appear not to be offered by this or any other firm in the region producing a catalogue.

(Courtesy High Wycombe Chair Museum)

Figure TV187. *Scroll back Windsor armchair. Beech with plain elm seat. Attributed to High Wycombe, c.1830-60. This basic design was made widely in the mid to late 19th century Wycombe tradition, and an example of a similar style is shown in item 24 of the B. North catalogue, c.1860, in Figure TV145. This style of chair was used widely in cottage homes throughout the south of England, and chairs of the type are shown being used in an Essex house in Figure TV215 where they provided comfortable seating in an otherwise austere setting.*

Single ring and concave turned legs with lower ring and straight turned feet. Legs connected by H-form elliptical turned stretchers. Sawn and shaped back uprights with broad curved stay rail set below top level of back uprights. Decoratively turned and flattened shaped cross splat. Swept 'Grecian' style arms unusually supported by two turned underarm supports each side. (Courtesy I. Sparkes)

Figure TV192. *A plate from the hand-drawn and coloured catalogue of Edwin Skull, chair manufacturer of High Wycombe (fl.1844-77). This firm was highly productive, employing 30 men in 1851[49] and 60 in 1861.[50] The range of chairs which they made was comprehensive, and included hoop, scroll and other sawn back chairs, as well as smoking high and bow chairs, 'fancy' chairs and those with cane and rush seats. The catalogue produced by the firm in 1849 provides the earliest known anthology of illustrations of chair styles from High Wycombe, and is an important record in describing and dating this region's chairs. The two styles shown in this plate, for example, are respectively, a lath back armchair of the kind shown in Figure TV193 and a smoker's bow chair of the type illustrated in Figure TV226. Both of these styles are commonly believed to be designs originating in the late 19th century. Skull's catalogue evidences that they were being made at least by c.1849, and probably for some time before this, since this firm was established by 1844.* (Courtesy High Wycombe Chair Museum)

Figure TV188. *Lath back Windsor side chair. Beech with plain elm seat. Stamped 'G.B 31' on rear edge of seat. Attributed to Buckinghamshire, c.1860-1900. This was one of the most common of the Wycombe made chairs, and was made by many of the manufacturers. An example of this design can be seen in the extract from the catalogue, c.1870, of Walter Ellis, chair manufacturer of High Wycombe, shown in Figure TV205, item 36.*

Three ring turned legs with lower ring and straight turned feet. Legs connected by H-form elliptical turned stretchers. Sawn, shaped and turned back uprights with curved shaped stay rail passing over back uprights. Four curved vertical splats or laths supported between the stay rail and the seat.

Figure TV189. *The stamp of 'G.B 31.' impressed on the rear seat edge of the chair shown in Figure TV188. The initials G.B represent those of the framer and the figure 31 refers to a batch number.*

Figure TV190. *Lath back side chair. Fruitwood with elm seat. Stamped 'T.A.' on rear of seat. Attributed to High Wycombe, c.1840-80. This unusually elaborate form of kitchen Windsor chair, combined with its manufacture in fruitwood, create this as a superior model of its type. A similar chair was advertised by B. North & Co. in their catalogue, c.1860, shown in Figure TV186.*

Heavy decoratively turned legs and H-form stretchers with two cross stretchers. Sawn and shaped back uprights, broad shaped stay rail with central carved floral motif. Five curved flattened laths connecting the stay rail and seat.

(Collection B. Pearce)

Figure TV191. *The stamp 'T.A.' impressed on the rear seat edge of the chair in Figure TV190. For makers with these initials see Appendix.*

Figure TV193. Lath back Windsor armchair. Beech with plain elm seat. Attributed to High Wycombe, c.1840-80. This essential design of chair was widely made by makers in the High Wycombe tradition, and is a similar to the armchair shown in Figure TV194 but with the absence of the fretted splat. An illustration of a similar chair to this was advertised in Edwin Skull's catalogue, c.1849, shown in Figure TV192.

Heavy decoratively turned legs with lower ring and vase shaped feet. Legs connected by H-form elliptical turned stretchers with two cross stretchers with central egg shaped motif. Shaped, sawn and turned back uprights with broad curved shaped stay rail passing over back uprights. Curved shaped arms supported by two turned underarm supports.

(Courtesy I. Sparkes)

Figure TV194. Lath and splat back Windsor armchair. Fruitwood with plain elm seat. Attributed to High Wycombe, c.1820-70. This very large example of a Wycombe chair embodies the highest levels of constructional quality in producing what was probably a commemorative chair. Examples of chairs of this essential style were advertised by many of the Wycombe chair manufacturers, and examples are shown in Figure TV223 taken from Glenister and Gibbons' catalogue (fl.1865-79). The chair shown as item 124, closely resembles the chair in Figure TV194 and cost £1.00 at the time the catalogue was published.[51]

Large ball and concave turned legs with lower accentuated ring and vase shaped feet. Legs connected by H-form decoratively turned side and double cross stretchers. Sawn and shaped back uprights with curved shaped stay rail passing over back uprights. Central elaborately fretted splat with initials 'M.H.' carved at the top, with two curved plain splats or laths each side. Curved shaped arms supported by three decoratively turned underarm supports.

(Collection B. Morley)

Figure TV195. Lath back Windsor side chair. Beech with plain elm seat. Stamped 'Js COX HIGH WYCOMBE BUCKS.' on rear of seat (fl.1864-1907).

Elliptical legs with upper and lower narrow ring turnings. Legs connected by H-form elliptical turned stretchers with extra stretcher connecting rear legs. Sawn, slightly shaped back uprights with narrow stay rail set below top level of back uprights. Four plain laths connecting stay rail to seat.

Figure TV196. The stamp of James Cox and Sons impressed on the rear seat edge of the chair illustrated in Figure TV195. This chair manufacturer is recorded between 1864 and 1907 working in Oxford Road, High Wycombe.

Figure TV197. Stick back Windsor armchair. Beech with plain elm seat. Attributed to High Wycombe, c.1840-80. This form of chair was made by many of the chair manufacturers in the High Wycombe tradition, and an armchair of this style is shown in Skull's catalogue of c.1849, shown in Figure TV206.

Single ring and concave turned legs with lower ring and straight turned feet. Legs connected by H-form elliptical turned stretchers. Sawn and shaped back uprights with curved shaped stay rail passing over back uprights. Six long elliptical spindles supported between the stay rail and the seat. Curved shaped arms, morticed and screwed to the back uprights, supported by curved, flattened arm supports, morticed and screwed into the side edges of the seat.

Figure TV198. Stick back Windsor armchair. Beech with plain elm seat. Attributed to High Wycombe, c.1840-80. The underarm supports are reminiscent of those adopted by certain Lincolnshire chair makers. See for example, the chair by J. Marsh of Sleaford in Figure NE40, Chapter 3.

Narrow triple ring and concave turned legs with lower ring and straight turned feet. Legs connected by H-form elliptical turned stretchers. Shaped, sawn and turned back uprights with broad curved shaped stay rail passing over back uprights. Curved shaped arms morticed and screwed into back uprights, supported by turned underarm supports.

Figure TV199. Stick back Windsor side chair. Beech with plain elm seat. Stamped 'Hy GOODEARL & SONS' on rear edge of seat. Attributed to High Wycombe (fl.1877-99). This style of chair was widely made in the Wycombe tradition, and a similar design is illustrated in the catalogue produced by B. North, c.1860, shown in Figure TV186.

Elliptical turned legs with upper and lower narrow ring turnings. Legs connected by H-form elliptical turned stretchers with extra stretcher connecting rear legs. Legs morticed through seat. Sawn, shaped and turned back uprights with broad curved stay rail passing over back uprights. Five elliptical spindles between the stay rail and the seat.

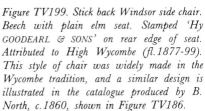

Figure TV200. The stamp of Henry Goodearl and Sons, impressed on the back of the seat edge of chair illustrated in Figure TV199. This firm of chair manufacturers is recorded working between 1877 and 1899 in West End Road and Mendy Street, High Wycombe.

Figure TV201. Stick back Windsor side chair. Beech with plain elm seat. Stamped 'GIBBONS' on rear edge of seat. Attributed to High Wycombe (fl.1883-99).

Heavy three ring turned legs with lower ring and straight turned feet. Legs connected by H-form elliptical turned stretchers. Decoratively turned back uprights with curved shaped stay rail passing over back uprights. Four elliptical spindles connecting the seat and stay rail.

Figure TV202. The stamp of Gibbons impressed on the rear of the seat edge of the chair illustrated in Figure TV201. Charles Gibbons is recorded as a chair manufacturer in Oxford Road, High Wycombe, between 1883 and 1899.

Figure TV203. Scroll back Windsor side chair. Beech with fruitwood spindles and elm seat. Stamped 'J.N.' on rear edge of seat, c.1830-80. This style of chair was made by many of the High Wycombe chair manufacturers, and a similar example is illustrated in the catalogue of Walter Ellis of High Wycombe, c.1890, shown in Figure TV205, except that the chair illustrated by Ellis has single ring leg turnings, whereas the chair here has three ring leg turnings.

Three ring turned legs with lower ring and straight turned feet. Legs connected by H-form elliptical turned stretchers. Sawn and shaped back uprights with curved, arcaded stay rail set below top level of back uprights connected by three turned spindles to a lower arcaded cross rail.

Figure TV204. The initial stamp of 'J.N.' impressed on the rear seat edge of the chair shown in Figure TV203. For makers with these initials see Appendix.

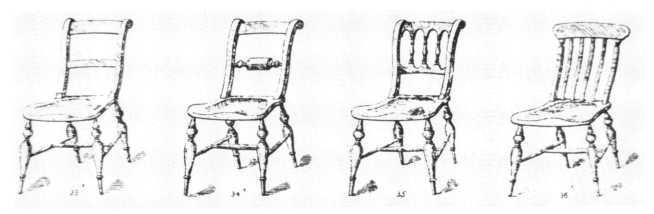

Figure TV205. A plate from the catalogue, c.1890, of Walter Ellis, chair manufacturer, who worked at Desboro Road and West End Road, High Wycombe, between 1887 and 1899. This maker advertised a range of scroll back Windsors for sale which were similar in design to those produced earlier in the 19th century by other makers who also offered catalogues of chairs. See for example Figures TV53 and 163 which show common forms of scroll back Windsors from Edwin Skull's catalogue, c.1849. This continuity of design by the Buckinghamshire and Oxfordshire chair makers was a common feature of this region's trade, and successful designs were typically made, with minor alterations, over some sixty or more years of the 19th century, and some designs, including the lath back design shown in item 36, continue to be made today. (Courtesy High Wycombe Chair Museum)

Figure TV206. A hand drawn and coloured plate from the catalogue, c.1849, of Edwin Skull, chair manufacturer of High Wycombe (fl.1844-77), showing square back armchairs of spindle and plain cross splat design, as well as a side chair with turned spindles connecting the stay rail and cross splat. An example of an armchair of this latter variety is shown in Figure TV207.

(Courtesy High Wycombe Chair Museum)

Figure TV207. Square back Windsor arm-chair. Beech with plain elm seat. Attributed to High Wycombe, c.1840-80.

Three ring turned legs with lower ring and straight turned feet. Legs connected by H-form elliptical turned stretchers. Shaped, sawn and turned back uprights with curved shaped stay rail passing over back uprights. Two plain curved narrow cross splats with the top one supporting four decoratively turned spindles between itself and the stay rail. Swept Grecian style arms supported by turned underarm supports. A side chair of this type was advertised by Edwin Skull, in his catalogue, c.1849, and is reproduced in Figure TV206.

(Collection Mr and Mrs Cordeaux)

Figure TV208. An arm and side chair of the scroll back Windsor chair variety made by Stephen Hazell of Oxford (fl.1846-92), illustrating the sturdy, well proportioned qualities which this region's turners produced in chairs which were intended for everyday domestic use. Their existence, some one hundred years after their manufacture, says much for the exacting workmanship with which these makers practised their craft.

Oxford Chair Makers

Scroll back Windsors were also made in centres outside High Wycombe, and a number of chair turners who were typically trained in Buckinghamshire, moved away to work in towns outside the county where a local need for chairs might be met. Such local traditions have typically been little researched, presumably since they fall outside the main epicentre of the region's chair trade in High Wycombe. However, these ancillary traditions are worthy of investigation since, in addition to their local historical significance, they can offer clearly defined terms of reference for micro-studies of the chair making trade. Such detailed studies are more difficult to make in the High Wycombe trade, since the large population of makers working there during the nineteenth century creates difficulties in identifying individual maker's work, the products of which were often dispersed to fulfil orders distanced from their place of production. One local chair making tradition which was mainly concerned with the production of scroll back Windsors was founded in Oxfordshire, where a persistent chair making tradition has been identified within the city of Oxford itself from 1779. The manufacture of scroll back Windsor chairs was probably begun by William Wardell, who was born around 1801 in the chair making town of West Wycombe,[52] close to High Wycombe, where he was probably taught his trade of chair turner. Little is known of his early life except that his wife came from the Oxfordshire chair making town of Stokenchurch, but by 1839 he had become Oxford's only recorded maker of 'Windsor, garden and cane chairs', working and residing at 101 Summertown.[53]

During this period, two further chair makers were to emerge; Thomas Slater and Stephen Hazell, both of whom were born in Summertown, Slater in 1824[54] and Hazell in 1819.[55] It seems fair to assume that both of these craftsmen learned their craft from William Wardell and that they both, in due course, branched out as craftsmen working in their own right. Slater's career seems to have been short lived, however, and his only advertisement as a chair maker was made in 1851 when he was twenty-seven years of age.[56] No other record can be traced of his having worked further in the industry.

Figure TV209. Scroll back Windsor side chair. Beech with plain elm seat. Stamped 'Wm W' on rear of seat. Attributed to William Wardell of Oxford, c.1840. This maker advertised himself as a 'Windsor, garden, and cane chair maker' at 101 Summertown, Oxford, in 1839. He probably trained Stephen Hazell senior and Thomas Slater in the craft, both of whom were to become independent Windsor chair makers in Oxford. The turnery device used either end of the cross splat is identical to that used by Hazell in his chair shown in Figure TV214.

Single ring and concave turned legs with lower ring and straight turned feet. Legs connected by H-form elliptical turned stretchers. Sawn and shaped back uprights with stay rail set below top level of back uprights. Decoratively turned and centrally flattened cross splat.

Figure TV210. The stamp of 'Wm W' impressed on the rear edge of the seat of the chair shown in Figure TV209. This is probably the stamp of William Wardell who worked as a Windsor chair maker at 101 Summertown, Oxford (fl.1839-54). This maker was born in the chair making centre of West Wycombe, and by 1861 had returned to High Wycombe with his chair maker sons, George and William, towards the end of his working life.

Stephen Hazell was to become one of Oxford's most significant Windsor chair makers. Unlike Slater, he chose to stamp his name on his chairs, thus leaving behind him a firmly identifi-

Figure TV211. Windsor armchair. Yew with elm seat with scribed edge line. Stamped 'S. HAZELL OXFORD' on rear of seat (fl.1846-92). This chair was probably part of a group made for the Reading Rooms of the Bodleian Library, Oxford. After Stephen Hazell junior had finished working in 1892, it is known that Glenister's Chair Manufactury in High Wycombe were commissioned to make further chairs of this design for the library, c.1900.

Single ring and concave turned legs with lower ring and straight turned feet. Legs connected by H-form elliptical turned stretchers. Sawn back uprights with curved tablet shaped stay rail passing over back uprights, and back design composed of two crossed plain narrow rails with central turned circle. Curved shaped arms supported by flattened curved arm supports morticed into the edges of the seat.

(Courtesy Pauline Agius)

able record of the types of chairs which he made. Stephen Hazell first advertised as a chair maker in 1846 when he, like Slater, was twenty-seven years of age.[57] At this time he described himself as a 'Turner and Windsor chair-maker', working in South Parade, Summertown, where he worked until 1854 when he and his family moved to the centre of Oxford, to a workshop in Friar Street and later at 36 Speedwell Street. During this time his wife had given birth to a son, Stephen Charles Hazell, who duly followed his father into the chair making trade. He worked with his father until 1875, when Stephen Hazell senior was last advertised as a chair maker working from 10 Albert Street, Oxford.[58]

The complete range of chairs made by the Hazells has probably not yet been fully identified. However, in addition to two forms of scroll back Windsor armchair, a more elaborate chair style, illustrated in Figure TV211, is known to have been made by the Hazells for use in the Reading Rooms of the Bodleian Library, Oxford.[59]

The order to produce this chair, and presumably others like it, must have represented a prestigious commission for Stephen Hazell but it may be that he produced relatively few chairs of this design.*

Hazell's most readily identifiable chair design is of the scroll back Windsor chair type. This style was made extensively in the Wycombe centres and most probably elsewhere in Oxfordshire. Nowhere was it made with greater finesse, however, than in the city of Oxford. The chairs were typically made with beech legs, arms and cross rails and with seats made of elm.

The armchairs were made in two styles: one with projecting arms (see Figure TV214) and the second with an elegant swept arm reminiscent of earlier Regency chair styles (see Figure TV212).

Throughout the English chair making tradition, individual chair makers gave their work a 'signature' with small differences of turnery. Both of the Hazells produced the same pattern in the barrel-shaped turning situated on either side of the centre back cross rail and this provides a feature which identifies their work.

Their single ball or acorn turning on the legs is also typical of most refined Windsor chairs — in contrast to the somewhat clumsier leg which has a three ring turning and is common to many of the late nineteenth century High Wycombe made chairs. In addition to the stamp 'S. HAZELL OXFORD' and a general dynamic precision of construction and lightness of design, the 'Oxford' chair is also characterised by the sharply finished corners at the back of the seat. These contrast with the rounded rear corners of many of the seats produced at High Wycombe for this style of chair.

Stephen Hazell (the elder) continued making chairs until the mid-1870s but by 1877 Stephen Charles Hazell was working on his own account. He continued as a chair maker until 1892 when he retired at the relatively early age of forty-five. Local newspapers record that he was a member of the Oxford Liberal Club and his obituary in 1898 hints at a personal life full of troubles. The *Oxford Journal*

Figure TV212. Scroll back Windsor armchair. Beech with plain elm seat. Stamped 'S. HAZELL OXFORD' on rear of seat (fl. 1846-92).

Single ring and concave turned legs. Lower ring and straight turned feet. Legs connected by H-form elliptical turned stretchers. Shaped and sawn back uprights with broad, curved stay rail set below top level of back uprights. Decoratively turned and flattened cross splat. Swept Grecian style arms supported by turned underarm supports.

Figure TV213. The stamp of Stephen Hazell of Oxford, impressed on the rear seat of the chair shown in Figure TV212. Stephen Hazell senior worked as a chair maker at South Parade, Summertown, Oxford, from 1846 until 1854. He then moved to Friar Street, and later to Speedwell Street, and is last recorded as a chair maker working at 10, Albert Street, Oxford, in 1875. Stephen Hazell junior then continued as a Windsor chair maker in his own right until 1892 when he retired from his craft at the early age of 45 years. Both father and son appear to have used the same identification stamp.

Figure TV214. Scroll back Windsor armchair. Beech with elm seat with scribed edge line. Stamped 'S. HAZELL OXFORD' on rear of seat (fl.1846-92). This chair shows a further style made by Stephen Hazell, and illustrates the broad elegance of the seats which he made, with typical precise chamfering to the underside edges and rear corners of the seat.

Single ring and concave turned legs with lower ring and straight turned feet. Legs connected by H-form elliptical turned stretchers. Sawn and shaped back uprights with stay rail and lower scribed line set below top level of back uprights. Turned and flattened cross splat. Curved shaped arms supported by turned underarm supports.

and *County News* of Saturday, 27 August, 1898, reveals that:
'The flag of the Liberal Club ran at half mast on Wednesday for the late Mr Stephen Charles Hazell, of Kingston Road, who died on Sunday morning last, and was interred at Osney Cemetery. The deceased was formerly an active member of the Old West Ward Liberal Association, and was for some time secretary. He

retired from business some years ago, though only 53 at the time of his death. He, and his father before him, carried on business in Speedwell Street as chair makers, and were the only makers, in the City, of Windsor chairs. Mr Hazell was not lacking in capacity, but his domestic affairs had been for some years of a most unhappy character and thus doubtless militated against his public usefulness.'

The void left in the Oxford chair making tradition by Stephen Charles Hazell's early death was not left unfilled for long. In the year of Hazell's death, the last of the Oxford Windsor chair makers, Walter Puddifer, moved into the city.[60] Puddifer came from an established chair making background and had probably been trained

---

* Later in the nineteenth century when more of these chairs were required by the Bodleian Library, the long-established Windsor chair making firm of Glenisters from High Wycombe was commissioned to provide replacement chairs in the same style.[61]

Figure TV215. The interior of a labourer's cottage in Essex during the late 19th century, showing scroll back Windsors in a setting where they provided a rare source of comfort for these working people.

Figure TV216. Scroll back Windsor armchair. Beech with elm seat with scribed edge line. Stamped 'S. HAZELL OXFORD' on rear of seat (fl.1846-92). The underarm supports are of a design commonly found in both hoop and scroll back Windsors from the Buckinghamshire/ Oxfordshire tradition. See Figures TV41 and 175 for other examples. This chair is heavier in construction than the other Hazell armchairs illustrated here, and may indicate a late 19th century example.

Single ring and concave turned legs with lower ring and straight turned feet. Legs connected by H-form elliptical turned stretchers. Sawn and shaped back uprights with stay rail set below top level of back uprights. Decoratively turned and flattened cross splat. Curved shaped arms supported by turned underarm supports.

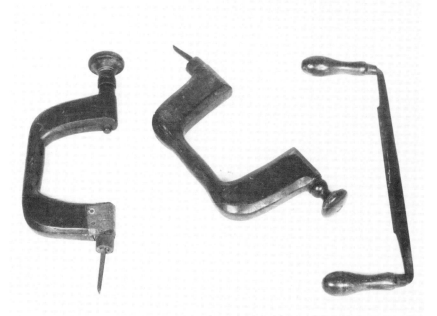

Figure TV217. The remaining tools of Walter Puddifer, the last Windsor chair maker to work in the city of Oxford (fl.1892-1930). The draw knife on the right of the picture, and the two fixed bits and braces were typical of this region's chair makers' tools. The 'fixed stocks' or braces would have been part of a set of perhaps ten, and each held a different sized spoon bit so that spending time changing sizes of bit was avoided. These tools are stamped with Walter Puddifer's father's initials, 'J.P.', Joseph Puddifer, who had probably trained Walter Puddifer in his workshop at the chair making centre of Stokenchurch on the Oxfordshire/Buckinghamshire border.

by his father, Joseph Puddifer, who was a beer retailer and chair maker in Stokenchurch.[62]

Such was the continuity of the Windsor chair making craft in Oxford that Walter Puddifer continued to make virtually identical chairs to those made by the Hazells. He, too, stamped his chairs on the rear edge of the seat. Figure TV219 shows an example of his mark and one of his chairs is shown in Figure TV218. The final workshop of this last Oxford Windsor chair maker still exists in Circus Street, close to Magdalen Bridge, and is now used as a garage. His son, Mr Philip Puddifer, still lives close by and recalls that in 1930 the historical link of the Oxford Windsor chair makers with High Wycombe remained active. He remembers that his father used to load those chairs which were

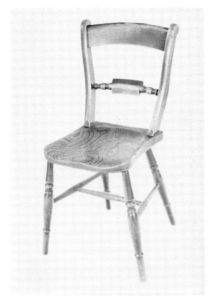

Figure TV218. Scroll back Windsor side chair. Beech with plain elm seat. Stamped 'W. PUDDIFER OXFORD' on rear of seat (fl.1892-1930). The style of chair made by Puddifer was virtually identical to those made by the Hazells, and his chairs, therefore, continued an unbroken line of design from the first half of the 19th century until the second quarter of the 20th century.

Single ring and concave turned legs with lower ring and straight turned feet. Legs connected by H-form elliptical turned stretchers. Sawn and shaped back uprights with plain stay rail set below top level of back uprights. Decoratively turned and flattened cross splat.

(Collection Mr and Mrs G. Pulzer)

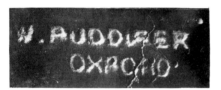

Figure TV219. The stamp of Walter Puddifer of Circus Street, Oxford. This maker came from Stokenchurch in 1899, the year that Stephen Hazell junior, Oxford's only Windsor chair maker, died, and continued making scroll back Windsors until about 1930. He sold his chairs locally, and took others to the wholesale market in High Wycombe on his horse and cart. His small workshop still stands, within a close distance of Magdalen Bridge, and is used today as a garage. Some of his tools still exist, and are shown in Figure TV217.

Figure TV220. Scroll back Windsor side chair. Beech with plain elm seat. Stamped 'SEWELL C NORTON' on rear of seat, c.1830-80. This chair has the unusual stylistic feature of splayed feet. In other respects it follows the common regional pattern for this chair style.

Single ring and concave turned front legs. Lower ring and splayed feet. Legs connected by H-form elliptical turned stretchers. Sawn and shaped back uprights with stay rail set below top level of back uprights. Decoratively turned and flattened cross splat.

Figure TV221. The stamp of Sewell of Chipping Norton, Oxfordshire, c.1830-80, impressed on the rear edge of the seat of the chair in Figure TV220. This maker has not been traced in local records. However, S. Sewell, chair maker of West Wycombe, is recorded, and a chair made by him is illustrated in Figure TV65.

Figure TV222. Best high smoker's Windsor chair. Beech with elm top hoop, arms, raised arm section and seat, fruitwood splat. Attributed to High Wycombe, c.1850-80. This form of chair was also made extensively in the Nottinghamshire and Yorkshire region, examples of which can be seen in Figures NE338-346, Chapter 3. However, the Wycombe made versions are often characterised in having particularly vase shaped legs and narrower turnings to those adopted in the North. A number of the Wycombe manufacturers made this style of chair, an example of which is shown in the catalogue of Glenister and Gibbons (fl.1865-79), illustrated in Figure TV223, item 122, which is a virtually identical design to that of the Windsor shown above. The cost of this style of chair was 8/- (40p) at the time that the catalogue was produced.[63]

Heavy, elaborately turned legs with feet missing, H-form stretchers with two cross stretchers. Central ball motif in cross stretchers. Sawn and shaped arms made in two sections joined by raised connecting section. Four elliptical spindles either side of central decoratively fretted splat with a fir tree motif. Two turned spindles either side of decoratively fretted splat with fir tree motif below the arms, and turned underarm supports.

named Sewell are recorded working in West Wycombe, Buckinghamshire, and the movement of a member of this family out of the county is, therefore, suggested as a further example of the spread of the trade into Oxfordshire.

Office or Smokers' Bow Chairs

The repertoire of chairs made in the Wycombe tradition also includes the smoker's bow or office chair, whose arms and raised back rest are entirely

not sold locally, on to a horse and cart and took them to the wholesalers in High Wycombe.

A further example of a tradition which appears to have developed for a short period in the Oxfordshire market town in Chipping Norton is shown in Figure TV220. This chair is stamped 'Sewell C. Norton'. No maker of this name has yet been traced to the town, but chair makers

sawn and shaped, and the smoking high, or broad arm Windsors which embody essentially the same structural features but are extended with an upper top hoop with a splat and turned plain spindles. Both of these latter styles of chairs were made extensively in the North Eastern chair making tradition, particularly in Worksop, Nottinghamshire, and in many cities in Yorkshire. The equivalent styles made in High Wycombe are largely regionally characterised by leg turnery devices

Figure TV223. A plate from the catalogue of Glenister and Gibbons, chair manufacturers of Oxford Road, High Wycombe (fl.1865-79). This firm made a range of both best quality and utilitarian Windsors, and the examples shown here include the most elaborate and substantial of the lath and splat back varieties, in items 123 and 124. These chairs were often made in fruitwood with elm seats, and had elaborately fretted splats. An example of this style of chair is shown in Figure TV194 which has commemorative initials carved at the top of the splat, and indicates that these were probably 'best' rather than everyday chair designs. The smoking high or broad arm Windsor chair in item 122 was a style of chair also made extensively in the North East Windsor chair making tradition. *(Courtesy High Wycombe Chair Museum)*

Figure TV225. Office or smoker's bow Windsor chair. Beech with elm seat. Stamped 'A C' on rear seat edge. Attributed to High Wycombe, c.1845-85. The ring and inverted cup turning on the legs, as well as the double cross stretchers with central ball motif, are closely similar to those shown in the illustration taken from Glenister and Gibbons' catalogue, 1865-79,[65] Figure TV224 and suggest that these turnery devices were a regional style.

Heavy elaborately turned legs with vase shaped feet. H-stretchers with double cross stretchers. Sawn and shaped arms made in two sections surmounted by raised curved back support. Six turned spindles connecting arms and back rest to the seat, with two turned underarm supports.

Figure TV226. The stamp of 'A.C.' impressed on the rear seat edge of the chair in Figure TV225. For makers with these initials see Appendix.

Figure TV224. A drawing of a smoker's bow chair taken from the catalogue of Glenister and Gibbons (fl.1865-79). Their price list for this period shows the chair cost 10/- (50p). A similar chair to this is shown in Figure TV225.[64]   (Courtesy High Wycombe Chair Museum)

Figure TV228. A detail of the leg turning device commonly found as a characteristic part of the design of smoker's bow and best high smoking chairs from the High Wycombe tradition, c.1840-1900.

Figure TV227. An inn fireside in Essex photographed in the late 19th century. Smokers' bow chairs sit either side of the fire, and to the right of the room, next to the bureau, is a scroll back armchair. These robust and comfortable Windsors, made in the High Wycombe tradition, were made for exactly this kind of setting, and were common forms of seating throughout the south of England, found in homes, inns, schools, and offices.

Figure TV229. Office or smoker's bow Windsor chair. Ash legs and stretchers, elm splats, stay rail, seat and underarm supports. Attributed to High Wycombe, c.1860-90.

Elaborately turned legs with straight feet. Decoratively turned side and cross stretchers connecting legs. Three elaborately fretted splats connecting the arms to the seat. Two shaped and flattened underarm supports.

Figure TV230. Office or smoker's bow chair. Elm, stamped 'GLENISTER MAKER WYCOMBE', c.1890.

Thin ring and large 'egg' shaped motif turned legs with lower turned cup and straight feet. H-stretchers with elaborately turned side and double cross stretchers. Two sawn and turned underarm supports. Sawn and shaped arms in bow section, surmounted by raised curved back support. Three turned arm support spindles with thin ring and double egg shaped turning motifs either side of central splat with large turned roundel, connecting the back rest to the seat. The turned roundel splat shows a further use of this decorative device which was used in different ways in a range of Wycombe chairs.
(Collection B. Morley)

Figure TV232. Bergère style, office or smoker's bow chair. Fruitwood with elm seat. Stamped 'J.S.' on rear edge of seat. Attributed to High Wycombe, c.1850-80. A similar chair to this was advertised by Glenister and Gibbons of High Wycombe in their mid-19th century catalogue, and was priced at 14/- (70p) per chair, compared with 10/- (50p) for the more orthodox style of smoker's bow shown in Figure TV224.

Elaborately turned legs with inverted cup turnings and vase shaped feet. H-form stretcher with two cross stretchers incorporating central ball motif. Six turned spindles and two turned underarm supports, graduated in height, connecting the curved swept arms to the seat. The arms and back are made from three separate sections; the middle section curved to fit the shape of the back, and the arms scrolled.

Figure TV233. An illustration of a bergère style, office or smoker's bow chair illustrated in the catalogue of Glenister and Gibbons of High Wycombe (fl.1865-79). A similar chair to this is illustrated in Figure TV232 which incorporates the regional turnery devices of double cross stretchers with central ball motifs and leg turnings which include ring and inverted cup turnings.
(Courtesy High Wycombe Chair Museum)

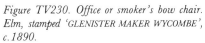

Figure TV231. The stamp of Glenister impressed on the rear seat edge of the chair in Figure TV230. This chair was made in the manufactory of T. Glenister, Hughenden Road, High Wycombe (1883-the present).

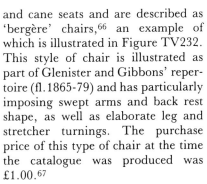

alone, particularly the inclusion of the inverted cup turnings as part of the leg turnery style (see Figure TV228 for detail). A further form of smoker's bow which incorporates a roundel motif, turned back splat and sawn arm supports is shown in Figure TV230 and is stamped 'Glenister Maker Wycombe'. Other forms of smokers' bows have elaborately fretted splats between the arm and the seat (see Figure TV229).

Further chair styles which have some similarity to the smokers' bow chairs were made with both solid elm

and cane seats and are described as 'bergère' chairs,[66] an example of which is illustrated in Figure TV232. This style of chair is illustrated as part of Glenister and Gibbons' repertoire (fl.1865-79) and has particularly imposing swept arms and back rest shape, as well as elaborate leg and stretcher turnings. The purchase price of this type of chair at the time the catalogue was produced was £1.00.[67]

Stools

A minor but important part of the Windsor chair making trade was the production of stools. These simple items of seating furniture were important in various settings both at work and at leisure. The different uses for which stools were made dictated that different heights of stools were manufactured, and these include low stools for children to sit on, those of normal height which were used instead of chairs, and others which were made in a high

form to seat those engaged, for example, in clerical work, or for teachers, who typically sat at a high desk.

Certain of the Thames Valley and Chiltern makers advertised stools as part of their repertoire of children's chairs, and an example is shown in Figure TV234 taken from the catalogue of Glenister and Gibbons.

Other stools are illustrated in Figures TV235, 237, 241, 243 and 244, and these show the same use of materials as in chair making, including elm tops, and legs and connecting stretchers of ash or beech. The turnings, too, are typical of those used in the Windsor chairs of the region, including single ring and concave turned, as well as three ring turned legs, joined by elliptical turned stretchers. Primitive stools were also made, with hand-shaped legs which mortice through the seat in the manner of the simplest stick furniture. The examples shown in TV239 and TV244 illustrate both three and four legged stools, both of which are stamped by their makers.

97

Figure TV234. An illustration of a stool taken from the catalogue of Glenister and Gibbons, chair manufacturers of High Wycombe (fl.1865-79). Stools of different heights were made for a variety of uses, including low stools for use by school children, tall stools for use by clerks or teachers who typically sat at high desks, and stools of normal chair seat height.

(Courtesy High Wycombe Chair Museum)

Figure TV235. Stool with oval elm top with edge scribe line. Stencilled 'TRIBE MAKER 25 OLD STREET' under seat (fl.1817-39). This simple form of seating has many of the characteristics of the Windsor chairs from this region, including the combination of beech for the legs and elm seats. The leg turnings and connecting stretchers, too, are similar in design to those used in many Windsors from this region.

Beech legs with single ring and concave turning below and lower ring and straight turned feet. Legs connected by H-form elliptical stretchers made of beech.

Figure TV236. The stencil of Tribe. Maker. 25, Old Street on the underneath of the stool shown in Figure TV235. Thomas Tribe (fl.1817-39), is recorded as a furniture and Windsor chair maker at 25 Old Street, St. Lukes, London.

Figure TV239. Primitive stool with rectangular elm top with pronounced chamfer to lower edge. Four ash legs, hexagonal in section. Stamped 'T. HEWITT' numerous times on lower chamfered edge of seat. Attributed to Buckinghamshire, c.1820-40. T. Hewitt is untraced, but chair makers with this surname are recorded in the Buckinghamshire region, including John Hewitt who is listed as a chair maker in High Wycombe in 1841, and Richard Hewett who is recorded as a chair maker living in Slough in the mid-18th century (see Figure TV15).

(Collection Mr and Mrs Hardwick)

Figure TV237. High stool. Round elm top with scribe line and central curved fretted hand grip. Stamped 'H.E. MILES H. WYCOMBE' on edge of seat (fl.1860-1900). This form of tall stool was made for sitting at a clerk's or teacher's desk, or for sitting at the bar of an inn. The example appears to have been used by a short person who put his feet on the top rear stretcher, causing it to wear away.

Four ash legs with three ring turnings and single ring and straight turned feet. Legs joined by box form ash stretchers, composed of double elliptical stretchers connecting each pair of legs.

Figure TV238. The stamp of Henry E. Miles of High Wycombe, Buckinghamshire (fl.1860-1900). This maker worked at Boudery's Lane in 1899[68] and no doubt made stools as part of a repertoire of other Windsor seating furniture.

Figure TV240. The stamp of T. Hewitt impressed on the chamfered edge of the stool shown in Figure TV239.

Figure TV241. Stool with rectangular top with central hand fret. Stamped 'B. NORTH WEST WYCOMBE' on edge of seat (fl.1864-99). This simple form of seating has many of the design characteristics typical of the utility Windsor chairs made in this region at the end of the 19th and into the 20th centuries.

Four elliptical beech legs with two single narrow ring turnings. Legs connected by H-form elliptical stretchers made of beech. Beech top with fretted hand grip.

(Collection Mr and Mrs Hardwick)

Figure TV242. The stamp of Benjamin North, chair manufacturer of West Wycombe, Buckinghamshire (fl.1864-99), impressed on the seat edge of the stool shown in Figure TV241.

Figure TV243. High stool. Elm top, alder legs. Attributed to Buckinghamshire, c.1850-80. This form of high stool, designed to seat a person at a high desk, or at the bar of an inn, appears to have been used by people who alternately placed their feet on the rear (front) and side stretchers causing wear on these surfaces.

Plain square elm top, hollowed to be used as a seat either to the front or rear. Four alder legs with three ring turnings and vase shaped feet; legs connected by single elliptical box form stretchers with the side stretchers set lower than the front and rear stretchers.

Figure TV244. Primitive stool. Three hand-drawn legs morticed through an elm octagonal shaped top. Stamped 'R. STILES' twice on underneath of top. (Collection B. Morley)

Figure TV245. The stamp of Robert Stiles, chair turner of Radnage, near Stokenchurch, Oxon. (fl.1851), on underside of the stool in Figure TV244.

* * * * * *

Epilogue

The designs of chairs included in this chapter, although extensive, are, however, part of a much larger repertoire of chairs made by the Wycombe makers, many of which were variously upholstered, cane seated, made with imported woods, painted and japanned, and may be generally described as fashionable chairs. Designs so classified fall outside the terms of reference of this book, since they are essentially the products of current taste, and lack the qualities which would designate them as vernacular or regional in design.

The chairs which have been included in this section embody the necessary qualifications of being Windsor chairs of regional style and manufacture, and were substantially the product of hand manufacture using indigenous, largely locally grown timbers. Their use, too, was widespread and very largely satisfied the demand for 'common' chairs in the whole of the South Midlands and the South East of England. It is not surprising, therefore, that in combination with the hoop back Windsor styles, scroll back and other related square back Windsors have come to be synonymous with the term Windsor, and represent one of the major regional traditions of English vernacular chairs.

Figure NE1. The Old Vicarage, Horbling, Lincolnshire, in the second half of the 19th century, showing an elderly lady sitting in a stick back Windsor chair of local design. Her companion, who reads to her, sits in a child's Windsor chair, probably of the same design. (Courtesy Wellholme Gallery, Grimsby)

Chapter 3

THE NORTH EAST REGION

This chapter initially illustrates the distinctive regional chair making traditions which developed in the North East Midlands counties of Lincolnshire (pp.102-159) and Nottinghamshire (pp.160-190). These areas were the home of dynamic Windsor chair making traditions, with rush seated chairs being made by a separate group of makers in Lincolnshire and possibly in Leicestershire and Rutland. This chapter subsequently considers the styles of chairs made to the north of these counties, where a less extensive but identifiable tradition of Windsor chair making developed, particularly in the industrial cities of Sheffield, Leeds, Hull and Bradford in the West Riding of Yorkshire (pp.191-209) as well as in a few towns in other parts of the county. The text continues its review northwards to examine the small number of chair makers who worked in the far north eastern counties of

Northumberland and Durham; the Windsor chairs made in these areas show close similarities in design to those produced in Yorkshire and the North East Midlands counties.

To the south of Nottinghamshire and Lincolnshire, in the counties of Rutland, Leicestershire and Northamptonshire, several families of chair turners worked at the trade, including John March of Geddington, Northamptonshire*, William Rowe of Hallaton, Leicestershire, as well as many extended families of chair turners who worked over a number of generations including the Peggs of Loughborough, the Baines of Uppingham and Leicester, and the Cants of Uppingham. Of these makers, only work by John March and William Rowe has been recorded to illustrate examples of chairs made in these counties (see Figures NE57, 59 and 114). It may be that other makers in this region made turned

rush seated chairs, since a group of such chairs has been recorded bearing regional turnery features found in rush seated chairs from Lincolnshire, but which seem sufficiently different to place them outside the recognised Lincolnshire patterns (see Figures NE213-215 which form a group which may have been made by the Leicestershire, Rutland or East Anglian chair turners).

---

* That the Windsor chairs made in Leicestershire, Rutland and Northamptonshire may have been part of the North Eastern tradition is circumstantially reinforced by the work of one Windsor chair maker, John March, who worked in the village of Geddington, Northamptonshire.[1] Of the two name stamped chairs recorded for this maker, one has close similarities with the Lincolnshire side chairs shown in Figures NE53 and 55 made in Grantham, Lincolnshire, and the second (see Figure TV172, Chapter 2) has characteristics of certain chair styles made in Buckinghamshire to the south. This bridging of styles between two prominent Windsor chair making areas, the Chiltern Hills in the South of England, and the North East Midlands, perhaps indicates the outer boundaries of design influence for these two major traditions.

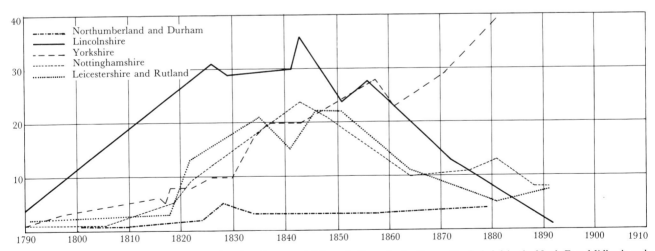

Figure NE2. This graph shows the numbers of chair makers recorded in trade directories for the counties included in the North East Midlands and North East chair making tradition.[2]

The distribution of chair makers within this large region, or rather series of adjoining regions, indicates that Lincolnshire formed the most populous centre for the chair making trade, with many more chair makers working in this county during the first sixty years of the 19th century, than any other county in the region.

The number of chair makers working in the counties surrounding Lincolnshire, including the combined counties of Leicestershire and the small county of Rutland to the South, Nottinghamshire to the West, and Yorkshire to the North, all sustained approximately the same number of chair makers from the beginning of the 19th century until about 1850, when the numbers of chair makers in all the counties of the region began to decline, with the exception of Yorkshire, where the numbers of chair makers increased towards the end of the 19th century. The chair making trade in Northumberland and Durham was relatively undeveloped during the 19th century, even though the combined population levels for these counties was larger than that for all the separate counties of this region, except Yorkshire.

NORTH EAST MIDLANDS: LINCOLNSHIRE

The North East and North East Midlands chair tradition, however, was predominantly that of the Windsor chair, and throughout this broad area, chair makers produced a multitude of Windsor chair designs which were made within the framework of local traditions whose members have, in some cases, left strongly identified legacies of their craft in the form of name and place stamped chairs. To a more limited degree, rush seated ladder back chairs were also made in this region, particularly by one established family dynasty of chair turners who are believed to have produced consistent patterns of chairs in Spilsby, Louth and Alford in North Lincolnshire, and Boston and Spalding in the South.*

The graph shown in Figure NE2 indicates the development in numbers of chair makers during the nineteenth century in the counties of this region.

The distribution of the chair makers within this extensive region is particularly interesting in that the pronounced development of the trade in Lincolnshire and the surrounding counties appears to have largely satisfied the needs of the people in their own areas, and probably to a great extent those living in the counties of the North East of England as well, since few chair makers are recorded for the far northern regions[3] despite the larger populations (see table below).

However, towards the end of the nineteenth century, a decline in the Windsor chair making trade occurred throughout the North East Midlands counties. Paradoxically, this event corresponded with a pronounced rise in the number of chair makers working in Yorkshire from about 1880 to the end of the century. Some of these chair manufacturers, who were typically based in the large industrial cities, were no doubt making 'fancy' or fashionable mahogany chairs, whereas others were responsible for producing large numbers of late nineteenth century Windsors which show signs of much standardisation of parts, and mechanised production techniques. Many examples of these latter chairs have been recorded with Yorkshire makers' marks and trade labels attached to them, advertising cabinet makers and household furniture suppliers (see Figures NE386-390).

* It may be assumed that this region's chair turners worked in a similar way to other regional English chair making traditions, where rush seated chairs and Windsors were either typical of individual regions or were made in separate workshops in the same area. This dichotomy may have arisen simply because of the differences in construction techniques, in the seating mode, and in the equipment and devices needed to make the two types of chairs.

POPULATION FIGURES FOR THE REGION[4]

	1801	1831	1861	1891
LEICESTERSHIRE AND RUTLAND	146,382	216,365	259,273	394,095
LINCOLNSHIRE	208,625	317,288	412,246	472,907
NORTHUMBERLAND AND DURHAM	317,462	476,215	851,691	1,522,896
NOTTINGHAMSHIRE	140,350	225,394	293,867	445,792
YORKSHIRE	859,133	1,371,966	2,033,610	3,218,440

LINCOLNSHIRE

Within the interrelated cultural regions of the North East, the earliest examples of Windsor chairs to be recorded were made in Lincolnshire. This county was predominantly agriculturally based during the nineteenth century, and has a varied terrain, with fen land and marsh bordering the seaboard, rising to a central area of heathland which, in turn, gives way to the fertile clay land of the western boundary. The architecture of the region reflects the soils and stone underlying it; attractive red-brick buildings under clay pantile roofs are the most common form of housing and other buildings during the eighteenth and early nineteenth century, but attractive stone houses were built as well,

particularly in the south of the county.

Within Lincolnshire, the chair making tradition was, inexplicably, the most widespread and populous of any of the counties of the region, with groups of makers working throughout the nineteenth century in many different towns (see Figures NE3-5).

Given the concentration of chair makers in these Lincolnshire towns it is, perhaps, not surprising that many different designs of Windsors were made as a response to the intense competition which must have prevailed. This is particularly illustrated in the products of the early Lincolnshire chair makers where wide and idiosyncratic variations in leg, splat and underarm design were made.

This variance is more experimental and innovative than that found in any other related northern region, where fewer, more conventional designs remained unchanged over a long period.

Within the diversity of Lincolnshire designs, it is evident that certain chair styles were highly regarded and copied by different makers, often working in the same town, with the result that virtually identical chairs have been recorded, stamped with different makers' marks (see Figures NE12-16). Competition between makers may account for the numerous name and place stamped Windsors recorded for certain towns in this county. This was particularly true for chairs made

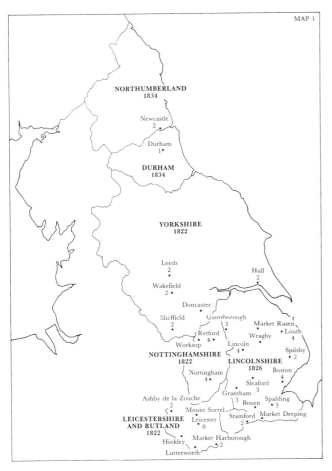

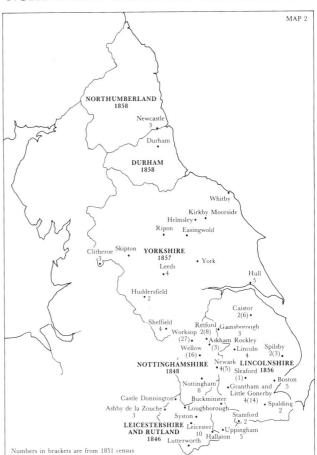

in the chair making centres of Grantham, Sleaford, and Boston. However, the tradition of makers from these towns identifying their products is in contrast to equally developed Windsor chair making traditions from other towns whose makers evidently did not stamp their chairs.*

Of the many design features which provenanced chairs from Lincolnshire exhibit, certain of the more distinctive elements have been isolated from the complete chair to form the basis of a survey of the stylistic characteristics of the work of a number of known Lincolnshire makers' work, and is shown in Figures NE6-8 on the following pages.

---

* In isolating design elements from name and place stamped chairs it should be noted that these chairs carry the workshop owner's stamp, not that of the many turners, framers, and benchmen typically involved in making Windsor chairs. Consequently, name stamped chairs are a reflection of larger numbers of chair makers' work. This point is graphically evidenced in the bar graph shown in Figure NE9 which illustrates the large number of chair makers recorded in Grantham, Sleaford and Boston, and the relatively small number of 'named' chairs to be recorded. However, the Sleaford makers do appear to be an exception to this rule, since James Marsh and John Brand, who name stamped their Windsor chairs, appear not to have employed labour but made complete chairs.

Figure NE3. Distribution of chair makers in the North East region, from trade directory sources, 1822-34.

Figure NE4. Distribution of chair makers in the North East region, from trade directory sources, 1846-58. Numbers in brackets indicate chair makers listed in the 1851 Census.

Figure NE5. Distribution of chair makers in the North East region, from trade directory sources, 1879-94.

Note: *Town names only indicate one maker recorded.*

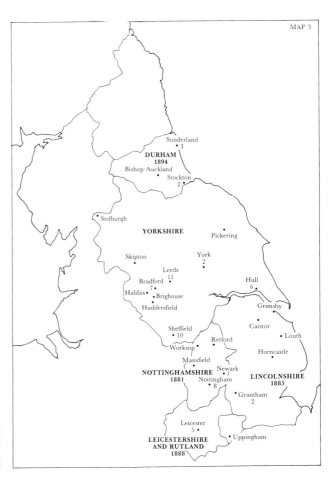

Figure NE6 demonstrates the strong tendency which existed for Windsor chair makers to express a code of practice in the production of emblematic forms of underarm turnings. Researchers including Crispin[5] and Cotton (1983)[6] have produced evidence to illustrate this view in tracing variations in Windsor arm turnings throughout many of the distinct Windsor chair making areas of England. However, evidence provided by the schematic key shown right extends this idea and indicates that underarm turning devices not only differed between centres, but in the case of the Lincolnshire makers particularly, changed over time within the same region, as makers died and others continued in the tradition. By contrast in other areas including, for example, the Nottinghamshire Windsor chair making centres, changes in underarm turning designs remained relatively unaltered even when makers changed.

In many, but not all cases, splat designs also show pronounced local differences within the Lincolnshire

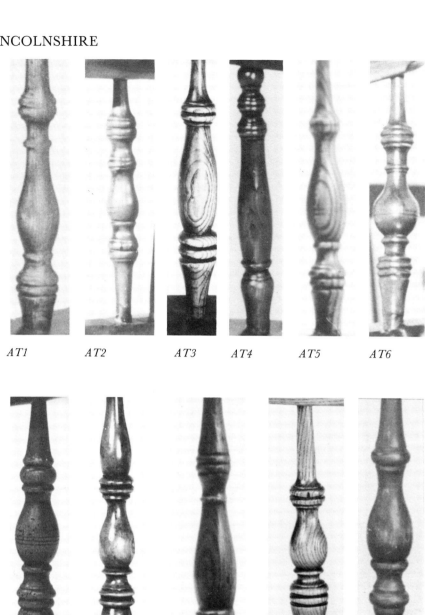

AT1   AT2   AT3   AT4   AT5   AT6

Figure NE6. Representative underarm turning designs adopted by Lincolnshire Windsor chair makers during the 19th century.

Key: AT1. N. Allen, Boston, fl.1790-1829, low back stick Windsor. AT2. T. Simpson, Boston, fl.1819-56, low back stick Windsor. AT3. T. Simpson, Boston, fl.1822-56, low back Windsor. AT4. J. Amos, Grantham, fl.1814-42, low back Windsor. AT5. Marsh, Sleaford, Thomas, fl.1822-26, James, fl.1842-61, low back stick Windsor. AT6. Marsh, Sleaford, fl.1822-61, high splat Windsor. AT7. Marsh, Sleaford, fl.1822-61, high hoop back Windsor. AT8. J. Taylor, Grantham, John, fl.1800-43, Joseph, fl.1841-89, low back Windsor. AT9. J. Taylor, Grantham, fl.1826-89, low stick back Windsor. AT10. J. Taylor, Grantham, fl.1826-89, low splat back Windsor. AT11. T. Camm, Grantham, fl.1828-51, low stick back Windsor. AT12. T. Camm, Grantham, fl.1828-51, comb back stick Windsor. AT13. G. Wilson, Grantham, fl.1841-92, low stick back Windsor. AT14. G. Wilson, Grantham, fl.1841-92, low comb back splat Windsor. AT15. G. Wilson, Grantham, fl.1841-92, low splat back Windsor. AT16. G. Wilson, Grantham, fl.1841-92, low splat back Windsor. AT17. Shirley, Grantham and Caistor, William, fl.1808-43, William jun., fl.1841-89, Frederick, 1851-71, Alfred, 1871-81, high splat back Windsor.

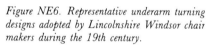

AT7   AT8   AT9   AT10   AT11

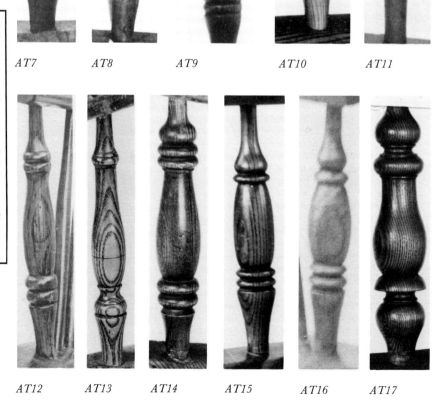

AT12   AT13   AT14   AT15   AT16   AT17

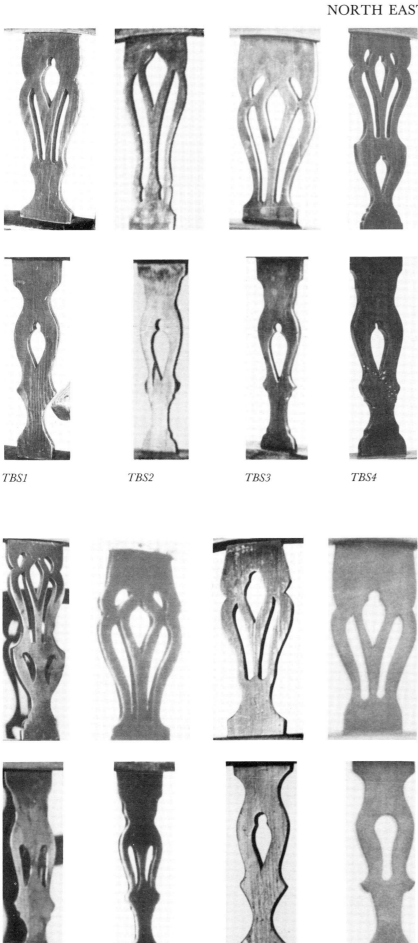

TBS1   TBS2   TBS3   TBS4

TBS5   TBS6   TBS7   TBS8

tradition, particularly during the first half of the nineteenth century, with motifs being produced which were specific to a group of makers at one time, and where different generations of craftsmen created altered splat designs (Figure NE7). This was, again, particularly true for Lincolnshire Windsor chairs, and less true for the established designs produced in Nottinghamshire and Yorkshire.

If arm turnings and many splat designs may be firmly ascribed to particular makers, or to a regional tradition, leg designs are less obviously so (see Figure NE8). Within this group of turned parts, certain motifs seem universal and conventionally correct for the known makers in this region, and these extend essentially to other regions too, at least in their broad outline. However, detailed examination of leg turnings from provenanced chairs indicates that more or less subtle differences do exist which illustrate a typology sufficient for some turnery signatures to be attributable to particular makers in the Lincolnshire region.

Although the illustration of chair elements is offered as a reflection of this region's Windsor chair making characteristics, it seems probable that the early nineteenth century tradition was more stylistically localised and identifiable than that of the later nineteenth century. As time progressed, the dispersal of chairs made their designs readily available over a wide area, and makers may have

Figure NE7 (left and overleaf). Representative splat designs adopted by Lincolnshire Windsor chair makers during the 19th century, with both upper and lower splats made in pairs.

Key: TBS1. T. Simpson, Boston, fl.1819-56. TBS2. J. Amos, Grantham, fl.1814-42. TBS3. J. Amos, Grantham, fl.1814-42. TBS4. Marsh, Sleaford, Thomas, fl.1822-26, James, fl.1842-61. TBS5. Marsh, Sleaford, Thomas, fl.1822-26, James, fl.1842-62. TBS6. J. Hubbard, Grantham, fl.1841. TBS7. G. Wilson, Grantham, fl.1841-92. TBS8. G. Wilson, Grantham, fl.1841-92. (Overleaf). TBS9. G. Wilson, Grantham, fl.1841-92. TBS10. T. Simpson, Boston, fl.1819-56. TBS11. G. Wilson, Grantham, fl.1841-92. TBS12. Shirley, Grantham and Caistor, William, fl.1808-43, William jun., fl.1841-89, Frederick, fl.1851-71, Alfred, fl.1871-81. TBS13. J. Amos, Grantham, fl.1814-42. TBS14. J. Taylor, Grantham, John, fl.1800-43, Joseph 1841-89.

    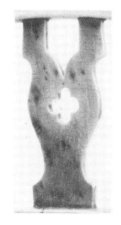 

  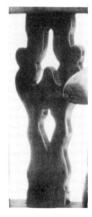   

| TBS9 | TBS10 | TBS11 | TBS12 | TBS13 | TBS14 |

adopted turnery and other stylistic devices from other regions, causing regional shifts in design characteristics. This aspect of stylistic alteration is evidenced in the large anthology of anonymous Windsors which have been recorded and shown in Figures NE71-74, 83-92 and 96-99, which although showing characteristics of the region, are seldom precisely similar enough to be firmly ascribed to the work of a known maker's workshop. Rather, they represent a visual code of chair designs which is indicative of this region, but whose precise origins remain to be ascribed. Their inclusion serves the important function of illustrating the wide variety of nineteenth century North East Windsor chairs which were made within a highly conventional tradition but one that allowed the possibility for some experimentation within it.

Figure NE8 (opposite). Representative leg turning designs adopted by Lincolnshire Windsor chair makers during the 19th century.

Key: L1. J. Amos, Grantham, fl.1814-42, low splat back yew Windsor. L2. J. Amos, Grantham, fl.1814-42, mid splat back yew Windsor. L3. Marsh, Sleaford, fl.1822-61, mid splat back yew Windsor. L4. G. Wilson, Grantham, fl.1841-92, high splat back yew Windsor. L5. N. Allen, Boston, fl.1790-1829, low stick back Windsor. L6. Shirley, Grantham and Caistor, fl.1808-89, side stick back Windsor. L7. T. Camm, Grantham, fl.1830-51, low stick back Windsor. L8. T. Camm, Grantham, fl.1830-51, comb back arm Windsor. L9. T. Camm, Grantham, fl.1830-51, side splat back Windsor. L10. T. Simpson, Boston, fl.1819-56, low stick back Windsor. L11. T. Simpson, Boston, fl.1819-56, low splat back Windsor. L12. J. Brand, Sleaford, fl.1826-51, low stick back Windsor. L13. Marsh, Sleaford, fl.1822-61, low stick back Windsor. L14. Marsh, Sleaford, fl.1822-61, comb back side Windsor. L15. Marsh, Sleaford, fl.1822-61, side splat back Windsor. L16. Marsh, Sleaford, fl.1822-61, side stick back Windsor. L17. J. Amos, Grantham, fl.1814-42, low yew splat Windsor. L18. J. Taylor, Grantham, fl.1826-89, low stick back Windsor. L19. J. Taylor, Grantham, fl.1826-89, low splat back Windsor. L20. J. Taylor, Grantham, fl.1800-89, comb back side Windsor. L21. J. Taylor, Grantham, fl.1800-89, low stick back Windsor. L22. J. Taylor, Grantham, fl.1800-89, mid splat back Windsor. L23. J. Taylor, Grantham, fl.1800-89, side splat back Windsor. L24. J. Hubbard, Grantham, fl.1841, low splat back Windsor. L25. J. Hubbard, Grantham, fl.1841, low stick back Windsor. L26. J. Hubbard, Grantham, fl.1841, side splat back Windsor. L27. G. Wilson, Grantham, fl.1841-92, low stick back Windsor. L28. T. Simpson, Boston, fl.1819-56, low splat back Windsor. L29. G. Wilson, Grantham, fl.1841-92, comb back arm Windsor. L30. G. Wilson, Grantham, fl.1841-92, low splat back Windsor. L31. G. Wilson, Grantham, fl.1841-92, low splat back Windsor. L32. G. Wilson, Grantham, fl.1841-92, low splat back Windsor. L33. Marsh, Sleaford, fl.1822-61, side splat back Windsor.

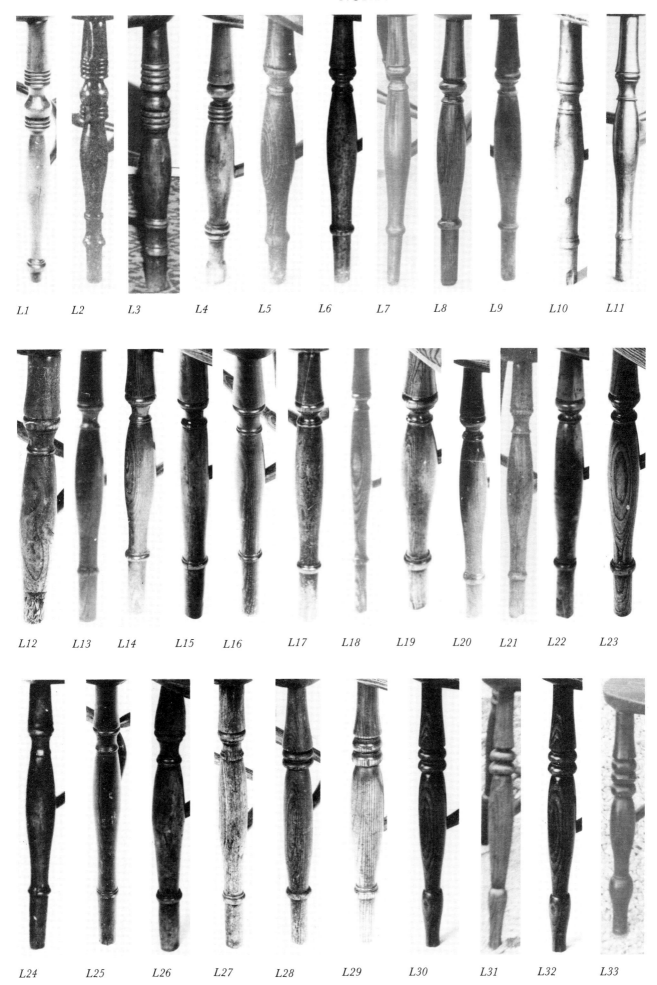

L1   L2   L3   L4   L5   L6   L7   L8   L9   L10   L11

L12   L13   L14   L15   L16   L17   L18   L19   L20   L21   L22   L23

L24   L25   L26   L27   L28   L29   L30   L31   L32   L33

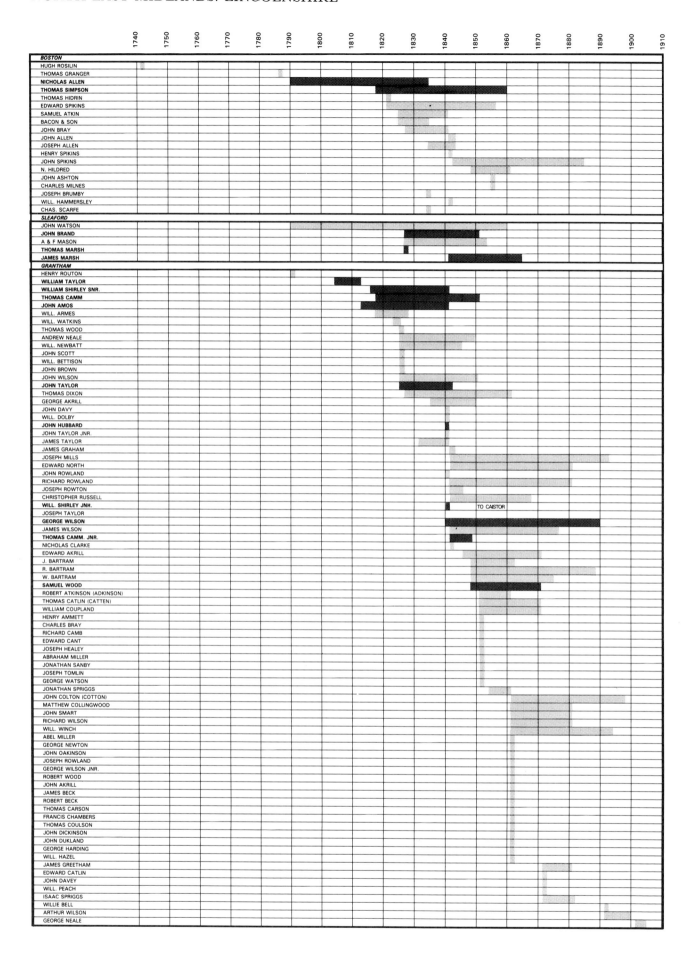

Figure NE9. Bar graph indicating the known working periods of the chair makers in the three Lincolnshire centres of Boston, Sleaford and Grantham, 1740-1900. Those makers whose names and working times are more heavily shaded are those for whom provenanced work has been identified.

Figure NE10. This photograph of Manthorpe Road, Grantham, c.1900, shows a row of houses to the left of the picture in which many chair and cabinet makers lived throughout the 19th century.[7] At the time that this picture was taken, the chair workshop opposite to these houses at the side of 50 Manthorpe Road, was still operating, and the last of the chair makers were still living in these houses. (Courtesy Michael Pointer)

Lincolnshire Windsors 1790-1840

Of the many distinct styles of Lincolnshire Windsors, the greatest variety was made between c.1790 and c.1840. The major centres of this tradition were the towns of Grantham and Sleaford which jointly produced the greatest number of chair makers of any of the thirteen towns and villages where other chair makers worked in the county.

Certain chair makers in Grantham and Sleaford, Boston and Caistor, identified their products with name and place stamps, and recorded chairs from these local traditions have allowed the illustration of the designs of chairs made in these regions, as well as at least a partial indication of the range of different styles of chairs made by individual chair makers.

Within the busy market town of Grantham, in sight of the high spire of its imposing church, a vigorous tradition of cabinet and Windsor chair making flourished, and many

men of the town were employed in these crafts throughout the nineteenth century (see Figure NE9 for details of the individual chair makers who worked here). The majority of these craftsmen lived and worked at Westgate just outside the town boundary, in the areas of Little Gonerby and Spittlegate where a group of them lived as neighbours in a row of terraced houses on Manthorpe Road, and walked just a few yards each morning to a workshop which stood opposite to their houses (see Figure NE10).

This particular workshop, which can be seen in relation to the chair makers' cottages in the plan view in Figure NE11, was owned by different chair makers in succession. These owners were evidently responsible for maintaining employment and the organisation of the workshop, and it is their names which were typically stamped on the finished chairs. However, the distinction between the owner and the other employed chair makers did not apparently reflect any great social differences between

them, for chair turners and workshop owners lived in the same type of terraced houses, and no doubt shared the vicissitudes of life together.*

Other chair makers who name stamped their work also lived in the area of Little Gonerby, and it may be assumed that they, too, employed other chair makers. The combined output of chairs from this large community of craftsmen must have been considerable, and the high quality and variety of the designs which they made must place Grantham Windsors at a pinnacle in the development of the English regional chair.

Name stamped chairs were also produced in Sleaford, a small town some fourteen miles from Grantham. Here the chair making trade was relatively small, and the two chair makers for whom name stamped

---

* The Grantham chair makers tended to live in close proximity to each other, and lived in the area of Little Gonerby, including Manthorpe Road, as well as New Street, Wharf Road, Vine Street, Castlegate, and Well Lane. See Appendix for addresses.

Plate 12. Low splat back Windsor armchair. Yew with elm seat. Stamped 'AMOS GRANTHAM'. This stamp refers to John Amos, chair maker (fl.1814-42).

Plate 13. Low comb back Windsor armchair. Ash and beech with elm seat. Stamped 'G. WILSON GRANTHAM'. This stamp refers to George Wilson, chair maker (fl. 1841-91).

Plate 14. Low stick back Windsor armchair. Ash with elm seat. Stamped 'MARSH SLEAFORD'. This stamp refers to James Marsh, chair maker (fl. 1842-61).

Plate 15. High splat back Windsor armchair. Yew with elm seat. Stamped 'G. WILSON GRANTHAM'. This stamp refers to George Wilson, chair maker (fl. 1841-91).

Plate 16. High splat back Windsor armchair. Fruitwood with elm seat. Stamped 'HUBBARD GRANTHAM'. This stamp refers to John Hubbard, wheelwright and chair maker (fl. 1841).

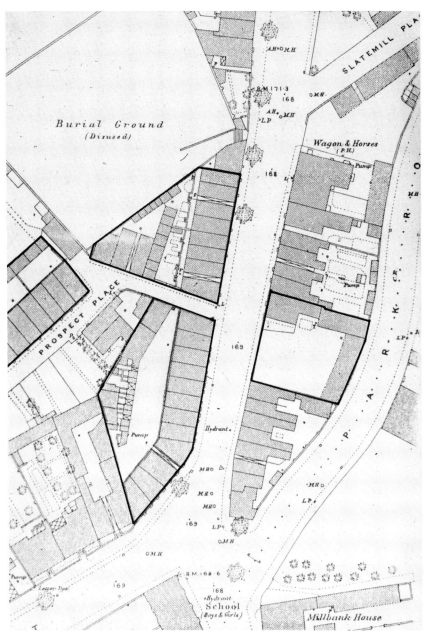

Figure NE11. Plan view of the Manthorpe Road area of Grantham, Lincolnshire 8 1866, showing the rows of terraced cottages in which a succession of chair makers lived during the 19th century. These cottages were without gardens, and had small washing/toilet and fuel storage areas behind the houses. The chair making workshop in which many of the craftsmen worked was opposite to the houses, to the rear and side of 50 Manthorpe Road. A petrol filling station was built on the workshop site in the 1970s, although the houses opposite remain substantially unchanged.

in the sale of James Marsh's cottage and turner's workshop which, with two stone and tiled houses with large gardens, was sold in 1865 for £580.[16] Clearly Marsh worked in his own workshop behind his house, and it may be that he and the other Sleaford chair makers rejected the division of skills typical of many workshops, and made complete chairs. It is not recorded whether Marsh and the other Sleaford makers supplied their chairs to markets outside their region, but since the developed chair making centre of Grantham would probably have operated a trade wholesale market, in addition to making chairs for local people, the Sleaford makers would probably have taken their chairs to be sold in Grantham.

Stool making, common in industrial areas, appears not to have been an important part of the Lincolnshire chair maker's craft, although examples were made, perhaps to order. The stool shown in Figure NE137, a rare example, made by Marsh (probably Thomas) of Sleaford, shows many of the features of this maker's Windsor chairs, with the single ring and concave turned motif incorporated into the legs, and connected by H-form stretchers. Both the legs and stretchers of this stool are made in yew which usually indicated that it was a prized item of seating furniture.

A further Lincolnshire centre of Windsor chair making from which name stamped chairs have been recorded is Boston. Of the fourteen chair makers who worked in the town during the nineteenth century, seven were working before 1830, and of these early makers, two name stamped their work, Nicholas Allen (fl.1790-1829),[17] and Thomas Simpson (fl.1819-56)[18] (see Figures NE21, 63, 125 and 129). Only six of the total number of chair makers were working after 1850.[19] It may be that rush seated chairs were also made in the Boston tradition, since the Ashton family, rush seat chair turners of Spilsby, Louth and Alford, and the Spikins family, chair turners of Boston,[20] intermarried.*

chairs have been recorded were part of a group of six within the town. The Sleaford tradition began at least as early as 1790, when John Watson (fl.1790-1861), is recorded as a chair maker.[9] Three other makers, Thomas Marsh,[10] John Brand,[11] and a woman, Ann Mason,[12] who probably inherited her business from her late husband, were first recorded in the 1820s, and a further maker, her son Frederick, was first recorded in 1841.[13] The last maker to begin work in Sleaford was James

Marsh,[14] who seems to have taken over from his father, Thomas Marsh, in 1842 and worked on until the tradition died out in Sleaford in the 1860s, when he and John Watson are last recorded.[15]

The Sleaford makers made a similarly wide range of styles to those made in Grantham, but the craft here was essentially a local trade in which three or four small turnery workshops arose, perhaps employing one other maker besides the owner. One of these workshops is described

---

* The Ashton dynasty of chair turners worked in the towns of Spilsby and Louth, and in the village of Alford in North Lincolnshire during the 18th and 19th centuries (see Appendix for genealogical details). In 1805, Ann Ashton married Edmund Spikins, a chair maker in Boston: their son, John Ashton Spikins, also became a chair maker.[21] Both the Ashtons and the Spikins families involved a number of their families in the chair making craft, and it may be that the linking of these families encouraged the cross-fertilisation of chair designs.

Figure NE12. Stick back Windsor armchair, medium back height. Ash with elm seat, stamped on rear of seat 'J. TAYLOR GRANTHAM' (fl.1800-43).

Single ring and concave turned front legs, plain turned back legs. Crook or crinoline stretcher connecting the legs. Crook arm supports. Four elliptical underarm spindles, nine long back spindles. *(Courtesy Tom Crispin)*

Figure NE14. Stick back Windsor armchair, medium back height. Ash with elm seat, stamped on rear of seat, 'HUBBARD GRANTHAM' (fl.1841).

Single ring and concave turned legs. Crinoline stretcher connecting the legs. Crook arm supports. Four elliptical underarm spindles, nine long back spindles.

Figure NE16. Stick back Windsor armchair, medium back height. Ash with elm seat, stamped on rear of seat, 'BRAND' (fl.1826-51).

Single ring and concave turned front legs, plain turned back legs. H-form stretchers connecting the legs. Crook arm supports. Four elliptical underarm spindles, nine long back spindles.

Figure NE13. The stamp of John Taylor, who lived at various times at Swinegate, Church Hill, and Manthorpe Road, Grantham[22] (fl.1800-43). Taken from upper rear seat surface of the chair shown in Figure NE12. Other Taylor stamps found on later chairs show the surname only (see Figures NE31 and 33).
(Courtesy Tom Crispin)

Figure NE15. The stamp of John Hubbard of Northgate, Grantham, Lincolnshire, whose only record is that as a wheelwright in 1841, when he was aged 40 years;[23] taken from the rear upper seat surface of the chair in Figure NE14.

Figure NE17. The stamp of John Brand (fl.1826-51), taken from the rear of the upper seat of the chair shown in Figure NE16. John Brand lived variously at Southgate and Spittlegate, Sleaford, Lincolnshire. Other chairs stamped by this maker include the title Sleaford below the surname (see Figure NE36).

Some Lincolnshire Windsor chair designs may have been influenced by chairs made in the High Wycombe tradition to the South, and many apparent similarities exist. However, specific aspects of design, although superficially similar between these traditions, on close examination reveal regional differences in construction. For example, amongst the earliest name and place stamped Windsor chairs from Lincolnshire which are similar to each other in their essential design, are three hoop back armchairs of medium back height which have nine turned sticks or spindles composing the back design (see Figures NE12, 14 and 16). Although these are apparently similar to Buckinghamshire made chairs of related design, differences are clear between them, including the method of morticing the top hoop into the arm. High Wycombe hoops typically have a distinct parallel tenon cut at the end of the hoop, narrower than the hoop diameter, which in turn is parallel throughout its length. Lincolnshire hoops are tapered towards the point at which they enter the arm, and this tenon fits into a tapered mortice.

The early arm supports are crook shaped and round in section, in both traditions. In the Lincolnshire made Windsors, however, the three short underarm spindles to the rear of this support are typically elliptical in shape, unlike the High Wycombe

113

Plate 17. 'Roman' kitchen chair. Yew with elm seat. Paper label below seat printed 'I. ALLSOP & SON, WINDSOR CHAIR MANUFAC-TURERS, WORKSOP, NOTTS.' (fl.1871-87).

Plate 18. Comb back side chair. Fruitwood with elm seat. Stamped 'F. WALKER ROCKLEY'. This stamp refers to Frederick Walker, chair maker (fl.1823-71).

Plate 19. High splat back Windsor armchair. Yew with elm seat. Stamped 'F. WALKER ROCKLEY'. This stamp refers to Frederick Walker, chair maker (fl.1823-71).

Plate 20. Low splat back Windsor armchair. Yew with elm seat. Stamped 'WHITWORTH GAMSTON'. This stamp refers to John Whitworth, wheelwright and chair maker (fl.1841-51).

Plate 21. Splat back side chair. Ash with rush seat. Lincolnshire, c.1780.

Figure NE18. Low back Windsor armchair. Yew with elm seat, stamped 'AMOS GRANTHAM' (fl.1814-42) on side of seat. Ornately turned front legs as in Figure NE20, except that in this chair, the rear legs are similarly turned to the front legs, and connected with a crinoline stretcher. See also Plate 12.

Upper and lower splats pierced with unusual cruciform or floral motifs. Four elliptical underarm spindles, and crook shaped underarm supports.

(Collection Mrs Diana Harding-Hill)

Figure NE20. Windsor armchair, medium back height. Yew with elm seat, stamped 'AMOS GRANTHAM' (fl.1814-42) on upper rear of seat. The ornately turned front legs are similar to the Brand of Sleaford chair shown in Figure NE35.

Plain turned rear legs, connected by H-form stretchers. Central cross stretcher turned in a regional pattern. Three long spindles either side of central fretted splat. Stylised fleur-de-lis fretting in the upper splat, and petal shaped fret in lower splat. Four elliptical underarm spindles, and crook shaped underarm supports.

(Courtesy Leeds Art Galleries)

Figure NE19. The stamp of John Amos who worked at Little Gonerby, Grantham (fl.1814-42). The stamp is from the chair seat of Figure NE18 and is, unusually for this maker, struck on the side edge of the seat and not in the more usual position on the rear upper surface of the seat.

examples which employ parallel turned spindles. This regional turnery difference is a significant one since Lincolnshire Windsors from later periods often exhibit the feature of elliptical underarm spindles, and in so doing, illustrate a primary and continuous regional design signature.

Leg turnings are similar in both traditions in general outline, and follow similar chronological changes in design. In both traditions, the single ring and lower concave

turning motif was produced during the first quarter of the nineteenth century. Often this turning appeared only on the front legs, with plain, elliptical turned legs being used on the rear, although this is not an invariable rule, since ring turnings are sometimes found on back legs too.

Although superficially similar in both traditions, the concave shape below the single ring turnings in some Lincolnshire chair legs is more elongated than that found in the High Wycombe legs of this style, where the single ring is typically a flattened ball shape, and the lower concave turning more strongly indented than that adopted in the Lincolnshire counterpart. Other single ring turned legs are, however, identical between the traditions, and examples of both variants may be seen in Figures NE12 and 33.

In both regional traditions around 1840, the single ring turning began to give way to triple ring turned legs in

the Buckinghamshire tradition, and in the North East Midlands tradition, double ring turnings became common, with triple ring turning following this, particularly for use in high back Windsors. Less commonly a large ball turned motif in both high and low back Windsors is found in the Lincolnshire tradition alone.

Of the three Lincolnshire chairs from the group of plain stick back Windsors made in ash and elm (see Figures NE12, 14 and 16), two have crinoline stretchers: the third has an H-form stretcher design with a cross stretcher motif typical of chairs in this region. This also contrasts with the Buckinghamshire tradition, where the use of a crinoline stretcher is usually limited to 'best' chairs made in yew.

Given these distinctions between the Windsor stick back styles, the pronounced similarities between the finely balanced Lincolnshire styles and the Buckinghamshire made counterparts, suggest clear design influences between these regions, although the exact direction of this transmission is unclear, but would appear to have been facilitated by the movement of the chairs rather than their makers, since searches of census returns in both areas show no evidence of chair makers born in one area moving to the other.

In addition to the stick back Windsors with crook shaped underarm supports made in the early nineteenth century, were those with similar arm supports but which had fretted back splats and usually more ornately turned legs. Although chairs from this group are rare, a small range of examples has been recorded with the stamps of early nineteenth century makers from workshops in both Grantham and Boston.

Amongst the earliest recorded examples of this chair style is one made by William Taylor of Westgate, Grantham, shown in Figure NE28. This finely balanced chair exhibits many of the conventional features of Windsor chairs from the Lincolnshire tradition made during the first half of the nineteenth century, including the single ring and long concave turning motif combined with plain, elliptically turned rear legs, the short underarm and long back spindles which are also elliptical in profile, and the crook shaped underarm supports typical of those used in both the Lincolnshire and Thames Valley traditions. The urn shaped splat was

Figure NE21. Windsor armchair, medium back height. Yew with elm seat, stamped on the side edge of the seat, 'T. SIMPSON BOSTON' (fl.1819-56). The ornately fretted top splat appears properly proportioned for its position. The lower splat design is, however, ambiguous in relation to the upper splat, and either may therefore be replacements.

Single ring and concave turning motif on front legs, plain turned rear legs, connected by crinoline stretcher. Three long spindles either side of central fretted splat. Three very slightly elliptical underarm spindles, with crook shaped underarm supports. (Courtesy Victoria and Albert Museum)

Figure NE22. High back Windsor armchair. Yew with elm seat. Attributed to Lincolnshire, c.1780-1830.

Turned front legs with lower ring and pear shaped turning connected by crinoline stretcher. Plain turned rear legs, connected by plain stretcher. Three long spindles either side of central fretted splat. Stylised fleur-de-lis fretting in the upper splat and double pierced lower splat. Four elliptical underarm spindles, and crook shaped terminal underarm supports. (Courtesy Garth Denham Associates)

Figure NE23. High stick back Windsor armchair. Yew with elm seat. Attributed to Lincolnshire.

Turned front legs with lower ring and pear shaped turning. Rear legs plain turned; legs connected by H-form stretcher (replaced). Nine long back spindles and four elliptical underarm spindles. Crook shaped underarm supports. (Courtesy B. Morley)

reproduced in various forms in chairs made by members of the Taylor family, as well as by other chair makers in the Grantham and Sleaford traditions throughout the nineteenth century. (See Figures NE26 and 33).

William Taylor advertised his chairs in the *Lincoln, Rutland and Stamford Mercury* on 25 June, 1813. 'William Taylor, the Original Windsor Chairmaker. no.11 Westgate, Grantham, returns thanks for the liberal encouragement he has for several years experienced at Stow Green Fair etc. he will have an assortment of Yew and other Windsor chairs at the above fair on the 2nd. and 3rd. of July. Observe none are his works but those marked "Taylors. Grantham" on the seat.'

Further examples of chairs from the early nineteenth century tradition are those from the workshop of John Amos (fl.1814-42), who lived and worked at Little Gonerby, Grantham, which exhibit considerable diversity

in terms of their design detail, including certain features which are not entirely typical of the region (see Figures NE18 and 20). Amongst these are ornately turned legs, with narrow ring motifs above and below a ball turning. The feature of narrow ring turnings articulates with a similar turnery device sometimes found in East Anglian chair, stool, and table leg turnings, and perhaps reflects an exchange of design ideas between these adjoining counties. (See Figures EA56 and 98, Chapter 4 for examples.)

A further Windsor, from the workshop of T. Simpson of Boston, fl.1819-56, is illustrated in Figure NE21. This chair shows the regionally typical features of single ring and elongated concave turned legs on the front of the chair, and plain turned legs to the rear. The maker's stamp is just visible on the right hand of the seat.

Examples of chairs made in John Hubbard's workshop in Northgate,

Grantham (fl.1841), are restrained, and more regionally obvious in their design than the others in the group, and exhibit the simple stylised fleur-de-lis splat, and the single ring and concave indented motif to the leg turnings (see Figure NE24).

Other examples adopting these conventions, made by Marsh of Sleaford, John Amos of Grantham and Taylor of Grantham, are shown in Figures NE26-28. Within this group of both plain stick and splat back chairs which have crook underarm supports, a further rare subgroup with a distinctive leg turning style has been recorded, and is shown in Figures NE22-23. The bell shaped turnery motif incorporated in the front legs of these chairs is similar to turnings found in some rush seat ladder back chairs attributed to the North East Midlands (see Figure NE213) and is also a common turnery device in East Anglian chairs.

Figure NE24. Two low back Windsor armchairs. Yew with elm seats, both stamped 'HUBBARD GRANTHAM' (fl.1841) on rear upper surface of seat.

Single ring and concave turning motif incorporated in all legs; connected by crinoline stretcher. Three long spindles either side of central fretted splat. Stylised fleur-de-lis fretting with unusual upper outward shaping to splat profile. Lower splat with two shaped piercings. Four elliptical shaped underarm spindles and crook shaped underarm supports.

(Courtesy Phillips of Chester)

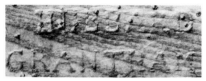

Figure NE25. The stamp of John Hubbard of Northgate, Grantham, taken from the upper seat surface of the chairs shown in Figure NE24. Although numerous name stamped chairs by this maker have been recorded, only one reference to him has been found in public documents. In the 1841 census, he is described as being a wheelwright, aged 40 years.

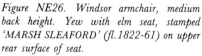

Figure NE26. Windsor armchair, medium back height. Yew with elm seat, stamped 'MARSH SLEAFORD' (fl.1822-61) on upper rear surface of seat.

Single ring and concave turned front legs, plain turned rear legs, connected by crinoline stretcher. Three long spindles either side of central fretted splat. Stylised fleur-de-lis fretting in the upper splat, with four extra frets. Double pierced lower splat. Four elliptical underarm spindles and crook shaped underarm supports. *(Courtesy M. and D. Robinson)*

Figure NE27. Low back Windsor armchair. Yew with elm seat, faintly stamped 'AMOS GRANTHAM' (fl.1814-42) on rear upper surface of seat.

Single ring and concave turning motif on the front legs, plain turned rear legs, connected by crinoline stretcher. Three long spindles either side of central fretted splat. Stylised fleur-de-lis upper splat with petal piercing in the bottom splat. Four elliptical shaped underarm spindles and crook shaped arm supports. *(Collection T.D. Wilson)*

Figure NE28. Windsor armchair, medium back height. Ash with elm splat, stamped 'TAYLORS GRANTHAM' on rear upper surface of seat, c.1813. This stamp was made by William Taylor who worked at 11 Westgate, Grantham in 1813. He advertised his work in the local newspaper and warned that 'none are his works but those marked Taylors. Grantham, on the seat'. The fretting in the upper splat has an unusual flower shaped motif. See Figure NE18 for a similar motif by John Amos.

Single ring and concave turned front legs, plain turned rear legs, connected by H-form stretchers. Central cross stretcher turned in a regional pattern. Three long spindles either side of central fretted splat. Stylised fretting in upper splat. Four elliptical underarm spindles and crook shaped underarm supports

Figure NE29. Low back Windsor armchair. Ash with elm seat, stamped 'MARSH SLEAFORD' (fl.1822-61) on upper rear surface of seat. A similar chair, but with nine long spindles and no central splat is shown in Figure NE133 and illustrates how variations of a particular feature were incorporated to create a new style. A side chair with a similar splat design, also stamped 'MARSH', is shown in Figure NE42.

Single ring and concave turned front legs; plain turned rear legs; legs connected by turned H-form stretchers with cross stretcher turned in a regional pattern. Four long back spindles, each side of a narrow upper and lower fretted splat with central turned roundles. Four elliptical underarm spindles. Underarm supports turned with regional turnery motif. Notch beneath ends of underarm bow.

Figure NE31. Windsor armchair, medium back height. Ash with elm seat, stamped 'TAYLOR GRANTHAM' (fl.1800-43) on rear upper surface of seat.

Single ring and concave turned front legs; plain turned rear legs connected by H-form stretchers. Stylised fleur-de-lis upper splat. Pierced petal motif in lower splat. Three long elliptical spindles each side of splat. Three elliptical underarm spindles. Decoratively turned arm supports showing regional motifs.

Figure NE33. Windsor armchair, medium back height. Yew with elm seat, stamped 'TAYLOR GRANTHAM' (fl.1800-45) on the upper rear surface of seat. This chair has an unusual vase shaped upper splat motif reminiscent of a splat design used in the Camm chair in Figure NE46 and in the Buckinghamshire tradition (see Figure TV77).

Single ring with concave turned front legs; plain turned rear legs with connecting crinoline stretcher. Three long elliptical spindles each side of splat. Three elliptical turned arm spindles. Decoratively turned arm supports showing regional motif. Petal motif in lower splat.

Figure NE32. Probably the stamp of Joseph Taylor of Little Gonerby, Grantham, from the upper rear surface of the chair shown in Figure NE31. Although Joseph is recorded as working from 1841-89, he was aged 30 in 1841, and may have been making chairs from at least 1831. This chair was probably made between 1820 and 1845, and may be the work of John Taylor (fl.1800-41), father of Joseph, although John is known to have used a different stamp (see Figure NE13).

Figure NE34. The stamp of Joseph Taylor, Grantham (fl.1841-89), or John Taylor, Grantham (fl.1800-43) found on rear of upper seat surface of chair shown in Figure NE33. See Figure NE32 for fuller description.

Figure NE30. The stamp of T. or J. Marsh of Sleaford (fl.1822-61) stamped on the upper surface of the chair shown in Figure NE29.

Windsors with turned underarm supports 1835-50

A further range of chairs was made in the Grantham and Sleaford traditions which represents a distinct stylistic group (see Figures NE29-40). These chairs are delicate in construction in the manner of the earliest Lincolnshire crook-arm Windsors. They are distinguished from the first groups illustrated in having a range of decoratively turned arm supports which are distinctive and representative of the earliest group of chairs in this region to be made with this form of support. The splat designs, too, are distinctive, and often incorporate a shield shape as part of the splat outline. In common with the earliest Windsors, all the chairs in this group have either decorative narrow turned rings, or a single ring and concave motif incorporated in the leg design.

119

Figure NE35. Windsor armchair, medium back height. Yew with elm seat, stamped 'BRAND SLEAFORD' (fl.1826-51) on upper rear surface of seat. Decoratively turned front legs similar to those used in Marsh chair, Figure NE38, and Amos chair, Figure NE18. The decoratively turned arm supports show regional motifs, and are similar to those used in the Marsh chair seen in Figure NE40.

Plain turned rear legs; legs connected by shallow curved crinoline stretcher. Three elliptical long back spindles either side of the splat. Four elliptical shaped underarm spindles. Stylised fleur-de-lis fretted upper splat with vase shaped lower profile. Petal motif in lower splat.

(Courtesy National Trust, Llanhydrock, Cornwall)

Figure NE37. High back Windsor armchair. Yew with elm seat. Attributed to Lincolnshire, c.1820-45. Although this chair carries no name stamp, it displays many features of the Sleaford/ Grantham makers, and was clearly a special chair, made to order. This, perhaps, explains why no stamp was needed as it was not publicly sold.

Decoratively turned legs in the manner of Brand and Marsh of Sleaford, and Amos of Grantham. Three tapered long spindles each side of the splat. Three tapered underarm spindles. Decoratively turned arm supports showing regional characteristics. Unusual foliar shaped top and bottom splats.

Figure NE38. High back Windsor armchair. Yew with elm seat, stamped 'MARSH SLEAFORD' (fl.1822-61) on upper rear surface of seat.

Decoratively turned legs with multiple ring turnings, connected by a shallow curved crinoline stretcher. Three tapered long spindles each side of the central splat. Four tapered underarm spindles. Decoratively turned underarm supports. Stylised fleur-de-lis fretted upper splat with two shaped piercings and urn shaped profile below. Two similar shaped piercings in the lower splat.

Figure NE39. The stamp probably used by both Thomas Marsh (fl.1822-26), and his son John (fl.1842-61), taken from the upper rear seat surface of the chair shown in Figure NE38.

Figure NE36. The stamp of John Brand of Southgate, Sleaford, who worked in close proximity to both Thomas and John Marsh of Sleaford between 1826 and 1851. Stamp taken from the upper rear seat surface of the chair in Figure NE35. Note that the Sleaford stamp was struck twice, indicating separate stamps for the name and location. The Sleaford stamp is identical to the one used by the Marshes, but the name stamps are of different sizes.

Figure NE40. High back Windsor armchair. Ash with elm seat and fruitwood splat, stamped 'MARSH SLEAFORD' (fl.1822-61) on upper rear seat surface.

Single ring and concave turned legs connected by H-form stretchers. Multiple turned cross stretcher. Three elliptical long back spindles either side of the splat. Four elliptical underarm spindles; two different decoratively turned underarm supports. Stylised fleur-de-lis fretted splat with lower urn shape with petal motif; petal shaped fret in lower splat.

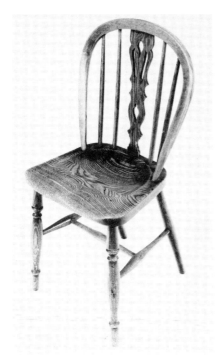

Figure NE41. Hoop back Windsor side chair with splat. Ash with elm seat and splat. Faintly stamped 'TAYLOR GRANTHAM' (fl.1826-43) on upper rear seat surface.

Single ring and concave turning in front legs. Plain turned rear legs connected by H-form stretchers. Two elliptical long spindles each side of the splat. Narrow seat front-to-back. Stylised fleur-de-lis splat with petal motif below.

Figure NE42. Hoop back Windsor side chair with splat. Yew with elm seat and back legs, stamped 'MARSH' (fl.1822-61) on the surface of seat. The 'bell' shaped seat is typical of those used by certain makers in this region. An armchair with this splat design stamped 'MARSH SLEAFORD' is shown in Figure NE29. This form of splat was also utilised by chair makers in Uxbridge, Middlesex. See Figure TV151, Chapter 2 for illustrations.

Single ring and concave turning on all legs, connected by a crinoline stretcher. Three elliptical long back spindles each side of central splat. Pierced splat with central roundel motif.

Figure NE44. Hoop back Windsor side chair with splat. Ash hoop and back legs with elm seat and fruitwood splat, spindles, front legs and cross stretchers. Stamped 'HUBBARD GRANTHAM' (fl.1841) on upper rear seat surface.

Single ring and deep concave turning in front legs; plain turned rear legs; legs connected by H-form stretchers. Central cross stretcher turned with regional turnery device. 'Bell' shaped seat. Two elliptical long back spindles each side of central splat. Unusual pierced splat, typical of this maker's work.

Lincolnshire Side Chairs

Contemporary with early nineteenth century armchairs was the production of side chairs, which were made as both plain stick back styles and also a more elaborate style with pierced splats. Chairs in this group were made in both yew with crinoline stretchers, and ash with H-form leg stretchers. The seats, made in elm or ash, varied in shape according to the maker, and have either a large bell shaped seat, as in Figure NE42, or a shallow seat from front to back, which is typical of many chairs made in this tradition (see Figures NE41 and 48).

A further style of side chair made by the Lincolnshire makers has many characteristics of the later, heavier forms of splat back Windsor armchairs (see Figures NE49-52). These side chairs have three ring turned legs, and a fretted splat which incorporates both the top and bottom splat motifs from a conventional fleur-de-lis splat back Windsor. This design was the last style of chair to develop of the four distinct forms of Windsor side chairs made by the Lincolnshire makers: plain stick

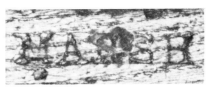

Figure NE43. The stamp of Thomas or James Marsh (fl.1822-61) of Sleaford. Taken from the rear seat upper surface of the chair shown in Figure NE42. Only the name is stamped.

Figure NE45. The stamp of John Hubbard of Northgate, Grantham (fl.1841), taken from rear upper surface of the chair shown in Figure NE44.

backs, those with decorative splats, comb backs, and heavy hoop chairs with fretted splats. However, the chair illustrated in Figure NE50 was made by James Marsh of Sleaford, whose working life ended in the early 1860s; it may be that he was a maker who added this last side chair design to an already extensive repertoire of earlier chairs which he had made.

Interestingly, two virtually identical chairs to the Marsh chair have been recorded, one bearing the label of Benjamin Gilling of Worksop (fl.1841-

51), and the other the stamp of Elizabeth Gabbitass of Worksop (fl.1839-43) (see Figures NE237 and 242). It may be that a transference of design took place between these two centres, but it seems more likely that Gilling and Gabbitass bought this style of chair in Sleaford and fixed their labels and stamps to them, since no other side chairs have been firmly attributed to Worksop makers.

The stick-back side design features chairs which are superficially similar to counterparts made in the Thames

Figure NE46. Hoop back Windsor side chair with splat. Ash with alder seat and fruitwood splat, stamped 'CAMM GRANTHAM' (fl.1830-51) on side edge of seat.

Single ring and concave turned front legs; plain turned rear legs; legs connected by H-form stretchers. Two elliptical long back spindles each side of central splat. Narrow seat front-to-back typical of this region. Pierced splat with urn motif similar to that included in the chair in Figure NE133 made by Taylor of Grantham, and also adopted by some High Wycombe, Buckinghamshire, makers.

Figure NE48. Hoop back Windsor side chair with splat. Ash with elm seat and fruitwood splat. Attributed to Lincolnshire, c.1825-45.

Single ring and concave turned legs, connected by H-form stretchers. Three tapered long back spindles each side of the central splat. Shallow seat front-to-back. Pierced urn shaped splat.

Figure NE49. Hoop back Windsor side chair. Ash with elm seat and fruitwood splat. Attributed to Lincolnshire, c.1840-80.

Two ring turned front legs; plain turned rear legs with vase shaped feet; legs connected by heavy H-form stretcher. Two long elliptical spindles either side of central splat. Stylised fleur-de-lis fretted splat with petal motif in lower half. Shallow seat typical of the region.

(Courtesy Bonsor Pennington)

Figure NE47. The stamp of Thomas Camm of Grantham (fl.1830-51), struck on the side edge of the seat of the chair in Figure NE46. Probably the same stamp was used by father and son, Thomas Senior (fl.1819-51), or Thomas Junior (fl.1842-49), although this chair is probably from the earlier period.

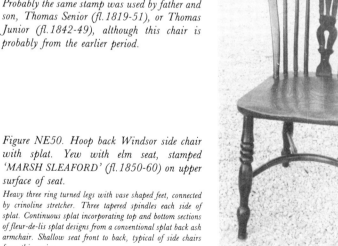

Figure NE50. Hoop back Windsor side chair with splat. Yew with elm seat, stamped 'MARSH SLEAFORD' (fl.1850-60) on upper surface of seat.

Heavy three ring turned legs with vase shaped feet, connected by crinoline stretcher. Three tapered spindles each side of splat. Continuous splat incorporating top and bottom sections of fleur-de-lis splat designs from a conventional splat back ash armchair. Shallow seat front to back, typical of side chairs from this region.

Figure NE52. Hoop back Windsor side chair with splat. Yew with elm seat. Attributed to Lincolnshire, c.1845-65. The splat is typical of those used in high yew tree chairs from this region (see Figures NE22, 26 and 38).

Three ring turned legs with vase feet, connected by crinoline stretcher. Three tapered spindles either side of fretted central splat.

Figure NE51. The stamp of James Marsh of Jermyn Street, Sleaford (fl.1842-61) stamped on the upper rear surface of the seat illustrated in Figure NE50.

Figure NE53. Hoop back Windsor side chair with plain sticks. Ash with elm seat, stamped on upper rear surface of seat, 'SHIRLEY' (fl.1808-43).

Single ring and concave turned front legs; plain turned rear legs connected by a turned stretcher. The four legs joined by H-form stretchers. Six elliptical long back spindles. Narrow seat, front-to-back, typical of side chair designs from the region. (Collection Mr and Mrs H. Watson)

Figure NE54. Stamp of William Shirley located on upper rear surface of the seat of the chair shown in Figure NE53. This refers to either William Shirley senior (fl.1808-43), or his son, also William, who worked in Grantham, 1841-43, before moving to Caistor.

Figure NE55. Hoop back Windsor side chair with plain sticks. Ash with elm seat, stamped 'MARSH SLEAFORD' (fl.1825-60) on upper rear seat surface.

Single ring and concave turned front legs; plain turned rear legs; legs connected by H-form stretchers with central cross stretcher turned with regional turnery form. Seven long elliptical back spindles. Bell shaped seat typical of this maker's chairs.

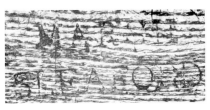

Figure NE56. Stamp of Marsh of Sleaford, probably that of John Marsh (fl.1842-61), of Jermyn Street, Sleaford, stamped at upper rear surface of seat of the chair shown in Figure NE55.

Figure NE57. Hoop back Windsor side chair with plain sticks. Ash with elm seat, stamped 'J. MARCH GEDDINGTON' (fl.1860-76) on rear edge of seat. Seat shape unlike that produced in the North East Midlands, where shallow seats front-to-back are typical in side chairs. This deep, waisted seat shape, combined with the square back and chamfered corners are similar to those produced in Buckinghamshire and surrounding areas. The position of the name stamp on the rear edge of the seat is also a typical practice adopted by makers in the Buckinghamshire tradition. This chair, therefore, reflects the work of a chair maker who was influenced by two regional traditions, and harmoniously blended design features from both. Another design of chair made by John March, which displays many Buckinghamshire features, is shown in Figure NE59.

Single ring and concave turning motif incorporated in front legs; plain turned rear legs; legs connected by H-form stretcher. Six elliptical shaped back spindles supported by the regionally explicit heavy hoop design of the Lincolnshire makers. (Collection Robert Williams)

Figure NE58. The stamp of John March of Queen Street, Geddington, Northamptonshire (fl.1860-76), found on the rear seat edge of the chair shown in Figure NE57.

Valley tradition with simple bow backs and plain sticks in the back. However, the Lincolnshire chairs of this type have qualities which characterise them as chairs of North East Midlands design, including elliptical shaped back sticks, thickened hoop profile, narrow seat back to front, and a generally robust demeanour setting them apart from the structurally lighter chairs produced in Buckinghamshire.

The influence of the Buckinghamshire chairs of this type and those of similar design made in Lincolnshire do, however, find a point of harmonious blending in the work of at least one chair turner, John

March, who worked in the village of Geddington, Northamptonshire, to the South East of Lincolnshire, between 1860 and 1871.[24] This maker produced name stamped chairs, one of which, a stick back side chair, displays features from both regions which are more fully described in Figure NE57. The two further examples of stick back side chairs shown in Figures NE53 and 55 are stamped by their makers, William Shirley of Grantham (fl.1808-43), and James Marsh of Sleaford (fl.1842-61), and illustrate that this form of chair is one of the many regional styles of chairs which compose the extensive repertoire of the Lincolnshire chair

making tradition. Figure NE59 illustrates an unusual scroll back Windsor side chair stamped by John March of Geddington. This chair has features which firmly identify it with chairs made in the Buckinghamshire tradition to the South, including the sawn and scrolled back uprights connected by a plain stay rail, and with cross rails supporting decorative spindles. The seat shape, too, is a common form in Buckinghamshire chairs, and has no parallel in other North East Midlands chairs, where side chairs typically have relatively narrow seats, front to back. The leg forms used in this chair are, however, typical of those used in the North East Midlands, including the two ring motif in the front legs, and plain, elliptical legs to the rear. This chair is, therefore, a stylistic hybrid, uniting elements of two major regional traditions.

Figure NE59. Scroll back Windsor side chair. Beech with fruitwood spindles and elm seat, stamped 'J. MARCH GEDDINGTON' (fl.1860-76) on rear edge of seat. This style of chair is reminiscent of chairs made in the High Wycombe tradition, with the exception of the two ring turned legs which are typical of Lincolnshire made Windsors. This amalgamation of stylistic devices suggests that this maker was working at an interface with the two major regional Windsor traditions from Buckinghamshire and Lincolnshire.

Two ring turned front legs and plain turned rear legs with vase feet. Legs connected by H-form stretchers. Sawn and shaped back uprights with curved stay rail set below top level of back uprights. Two curved narrow cross splats below supporting three turned spindles.

Figure NE60. The stamp of John March of Queen Street, Geddington, Northamptonshire (fl.1860-76), found on the rear seat edge of the chair found in Figure NE59.

Low Back Windsors with Central Splats 1840-1900

The use of crook underarm supports gradually gave way to the use of turned underarm supports. This transition was gradual, and examples of makers using both forms of arm support are recorded. See for example closely similar chairs made by John Amos of Grantham (fl.1814-42), shown in Figures NE27 and 61 which illustrate this use. However, the change to turned underarm supports was irreversible, and as the nineteenth century progressed, more chairs were made with this feature, and by around 1845 the crook arm had been completely abandoned. By this time, the manufacture of the fine medium high back chairs also had ceased, in favour of either distinctly high or low styles.

These chairs, unlike the plain stick back Windsors, have design parallels in chairs made in other areas of the North East, particularly those made by the Nottinghamshire and South Yorkshire makers. However, provenanced chairs from Lincolnshire indicate that regional differences in design distinguished this area's splat back Windsor chairs from those of other regions, particularly in the forms of turnery devices used in underarm supports, leg and cross stretcher turnings, spindle profiles,

Figure NE61. Low back Windsor armchair. Yew with elm seat, stamped 'AMOS GRANTHAM' (fl.1814-42) on rear upper surface of seat.

Single ring with lower concave turned legs, connected by crinoline stretcher. Three tapered long back spindles either side of central splat. Three tapered underarm spindles. Slender, finely turned arm supports. Stylised fleur-de-lis fretted upper splat; petal shape pierced lower splat.

Figure NE62. The stamp of John Amos of Little Gonerby, Grantham (fl.1814-42), found on the rear of the upper seat surface of the chair in Figure NE61.

Figure NE63. Low back Windsor armchair. Ash with elm seat, faintly stamped on side of seat 'T. SIMPSON BOSTON' (fl.1822-60).

Two ring turned front legs with straight foot. Plain turned rear legs, connected by H-form stretchers. Three long spindles, elliptical in the bottom half, either side of central splat. Three elliptical underarm spindles. Regionally explicit underarm support turnings. Stylised fleur-de-lis fretted upper back splat; petal shaped piercing in lower back splat.

Figure NE64. Low back Windsor armchair. Ash with elm seat and splat, stamped twice on rear edge of seat 'WOOD GRANTHAM' (fl.1849-71).

Two ring turned legs connected by crinoline stretcher. Three spindles either side of central back splat. Three elliptical underarm spindles. Turned underarm supports specific to this maker. Stylised fleur-de-lis fretted upper back splat; 'keyhole' motif in lower splat.

Figure NE65. Stamp of Samuel Wood, chair manufacturer, of Manthorpe Road, Little Gonerby, Grantham (fl.1849-71), stamped twice on the back edge of seat of chair in Figure NE64. This maker lived in one of the cottages shown in the plan in the map in Figure NE11 and he may have been the master of the workshop in Manthorpe Road, Grantham.*

---

* The workshop or 'factory' at the side of 50 Manthorpe Road, was organised by a number of owners during the 19th century. The first reference to a chair manufacturer on Manthorpe Road is to Samuel Wood (fl.1849-71) who is referred to as such in the Census of 1851. A name stamped chair by this maker is shown in Figure NE65. James Wilson (fl.1841-76) and his brother George (fl.1841-91) appear to have followed in ownership. George Wilson is noted as employing seven men and three boys in the 1871 Census. James Wilson is described as a chair manufacturer living at 45 Manthorpe Road in 1871, and his wife Elizabeth appears to have taken his place as a manufacturer from 1881-85.

Figure NE66. Low back Windsor armchair. Ash with elm seat and alder splat. Attributed to Lincolnshire, c.1860 (see high back counterpart in Figure NE84).

Two ring leg turning with cup turning below and vase shaped feet; legs connected by H-form stretchers. Three long spindles, elliptical in shape in the lower half, each side of the central splat. Three elliptical underarm spindles. Complex underarm support turnery devices. Unusual 'waisted' profile and fleur-de-lis piercing on upper splat; petal pierced motif in lower splat.

and in some differences in splat designs. Recognition of these regional characteristics has enabled a number of unprovenanced Windsor chairs to be attributed to Lincolnshire, and some of these are illustrated in Figures NE66 and 71-74.

The later nineteenth century splat back Windsors were made in both yew and ash with elm seats, and commonly both forms of chair were made with the stylistically superior crinoline stretcher, but with ash chairs also being made with the more common H-form stretcher. In a similar way to the development of the stick back Windsors, the early nineteenth century splat back Windsors were made with single ring and concave turned legs which are usually, but not always, adopted in the back legs too. The transition in design which took place towards the middle of the nineteenth century altered this feature, when two and three ring legs, and also the rarer ball motif, became the dominant mode of leg turnings throughout the remainder of the nineteenth century.

In viewing the chronology of splat back Windsors illustrated in Figures

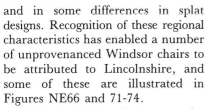

Figure NE68. Stamp of George Wilson (fl.1841-91), chair manufacturer of Manthorpe Road, Little Gonerby, Grantham, found on the chair in Figure NE67. George Wilson probably followed Samuel Wood as the chair master at the Manthorpe Road workshop (see Figure NE11), and also lived in the row of cottages opposite.

Figure NE67. Low back Windsor armchair. Ash with elm seat and alder splat, stamped on rear upper seat surface 'G. WILSON GRANTHAM' (fl.1841-91). The underarm turnings are typical of this maker.

Two ring turned legs with vase shaped feet connected by crinoline stretcher. Three long spindles, elliptical in lower half, either side of central back splat; three elliptical underarm spindles. Stylised fleur-de-lis fretted upper splat; keyhole shaped piercing in lower splat.

Figure NE69. Low back Windsor armchair. Ash with elm seat and alder splat, stamped on rear upper seat surface, 'G. WILSON GRANTHAM' (fl.1841-91).

Two ring turned legs with vase shaped feet, connected by H-form stretcher, with regional turnery signature on central cross stretcher. Three long back spindles, elliptical in lower half, either side of central back splat. Four elliptical underarm spindles, with maker specific turned underarm support (see Figure NE6). Stylised fleur-de-lis fretted top splat; petal shaped piercing in lower splat.

NE18-22 and 61, it is evident that in common with stick backs, the early splat back prototypes adopted a delicacy of form and a structural dynamic which gradually diminished in later chairs, with the result that those Windsors made in the same essential pattern in the second half of the nineteenth century are much heavier in demeanour than those made earlier. The chairs illustrated in Figures NE63-74 exhibit this transition, and show provenanced chairs which were made from about 1835 until around 1890.

It is interesting that although a number of low splat Windsors with makers' stamps have been recorded, illustrating chairs throughout their time of production, only two high Windsors of common design have been recorded with a maker's stamp from this region (see Figures NE79 and 81). This phenomenon also occurred with plain stick back chairs where, similarly, many low chairs have makers' stamps, but in this design no high stick back chair has been recorded with maker identification.

Figure NE70. The exterior of a 'second hand' shop in Grantham, Lincolnshire, photographed in 1938. The Windsor chairs on the pavement show an early crook arm Windsor to the far left with a high back Windsor next to it. The row of four Windsors shows low back splat Windsors with ball turned and single ring turned legs. At this time, Windsor chairs, perhaps bought from local houses, had lost their original cultural position, and become merely 'old fashioned'.

(Courtesy M. Pointer, Grantham)

Figure NE71. Low back Windsor armchair. Ash with elm seat and splat. Attributed to Lincolnshire, c.1840-90. The ball turning in the front leg is a relatively rare form of leg motif. A chair showing this form of leg turning can be seen in Figure NE70.

Legs connected by plain turned H-form stretcher. Three long spindles either side of the central splat, the bottom half elliptical shaped; three elliptical underarm spindles; decoratively turned underarm supports. Conventional fleur-de-lis fretted top splat; keyhole motif in lower splat.

Figure NE72. Low back Windsor armchair. Ash with elm seat and splat. Attributed to Lincolnshire, c.1840-90. The underarm support design is identical to that found on chairs made by G. Wilson of Grantham (see Figures NE67 and 69).

Two ring turned legs with vase shaped feet, connected by H-form stretcher; central cross stretcher showing regional turnery device. Three tapered long back spindles on either side of central splat. Three elliptical shaped underarm spindles. Unusual bulbous shaped fleur-de-lis fretted upper splat; petal shaped motif in bottom splat which is also bulbous in profile.

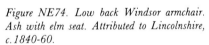

Figure NE73. Low back Windsor armchair. Ash with elm seat. Attributed to Lincolnshire, c.1870-90.

Heavy two ring turned legs with vase shaped feet connected by H-form stretchers. Three long back spindles each side of the central splat, terminating in a tapering section which is a typical feature of a group of Windsors which have been provisionally assigned to the Lincolnshire region. Three parallel underarm spindles; turned underarm supports reminiscent of Nottinghamshire supports. Crude fleur-de-lis fretted top splat; keyhole motif in lower splat.

Figure NE74. Low back Windsor armchair. Ash with elm seat. Attributed to Lincolnshire, c.1840-60.

Unusual three ring turned legs with straight feet, connected by plain turned H-form stretchers. Three tapered long spindles each side of central splat; three tapered underarm spindles. Finely turned underarm supports. Fleur-de-lis fretted top splat; keyhole pierced lower splat.

127

Children's Chairs

Children's low back Windsors were also made in the Lincolnshire tradition as scaled down and simplified versions of adult chairs. These chairs were made in both yew and ash, with elm seats, and embodied both the superior crinoline stretcher, and the H-form stretcher. They were also made, on occasion, as rocking chairs.

Figure NE75. Child's low back Windsor armchair. Ash with elm seat and birch splat. Attributed to Lincolnshire, c.1840-80.

Heavy two ring turned legs with vase shaped feet, connected by crinoline stretcher. Two tapered long back spindles each side of the central splat (top half of left hand spindle missing); two tapered underarm spindles. Turned underarm supports with flattened ball turnings. Fleur-de-lis fretted upper splat; keyhole motif in lower splat.

Figure NE76. Child's low back Windsor armchair. Ash with elm seat. Attributed to Lincolnshire, c.1840-70. Retailer's label glued to underneath of seat. The flattened ball turning of the arm support is typical of the region. See Figures NE75 and 151.

Heavy two ring turned legs with vase shaped feet, connected by plain turned H-form stretchers. Two tapered long spindles each side of the central splat. Two elliptical shaped underarm spindles. Stylised fleur-de-lis fretted upper splat; keyhole motif in lower splat.

Figure NE77. Paper label glued to the underneath of the seat of the child's chair in Figure NE76. S.E. Collison's furniture warehouse (1841-89), Junction Dock Walls, Hull, sold many forms of common household furniture, including a variety of Windsor chairs, which were purchased from suppliers and sold with Collison's label attached.

High Back Windsors with Central Splats

The high back Windsor was the natural alternative to the low back armchair in Lincolnshire, as in other regional traditions in the second half of the nineteenth century. The chairs illustrated in Figures NE78-99 are included because, in each case, some common regional feature found in other provenanced Lincolnshire chairs is repeated in the particular high back chair. These chairs illustrate common variants of the high back style.

Amongst the regional features found in these chairs are elliptically shaped underarm support spindles, whose profile is a strong descriptive feature of the region's Windsors. These particular spindles can hold one of three possible positions — upright, leaning forwards, or leaning backwards. The underarm spindles can all maintain the same angle, or one of the spindles may lean back and mortice into the arm behind the top hoop mortice, and the remainder adopt one of the three positions mentioned above. These differences in angle of mortice form a complex regional stylistic code, particularly since the positioning appears to differ within chairs in the same group, and also in different chairs made by the same maker. Within the high splat Windsor group the most common, but not universal, form of positioning is for the underarm support spindles to lean forward in the same direction as the turned underarm support. This preference may indicate a conscious choice to form a structural opposition to the leverage created by someone leaning back in the chair. The juxtapositioning of different spindles suggests that the makers were aware of the stresses involved in chair use, and attempted to create designs which were made to counter-balance the reclined back; although it appears that a number of solutions to this problem were thought acceptable by the makers.

However, a distinction in design found in the high splat Windsors is the inclusion of both two and three ring leg turnings, which compares with the two ring turnings found alone in low back varieties, with the ball turning occasionally used in both high and low varieties.

In contrast to the common Windsor forms, other much rarer and more

Figure NE78. High back Windsor armchair. Ash with elm seat. Attributed to Lincolnshire, c.1845-85. The underarm support turning is similar to that adopted by G. Wilson of Grantham (see Figures NE67 and 69).

Three long elliptical spindles each side of splat; three elliptical underarm spindles. Heavy two-ring turned front legs with 'vase' feet, plain turned rear legs; legs connected by H-form stretcher. Central cross stretcher showing heavily turned regional motif. Bulbous shaped upper splat with stylised fretted fleur-de-lis; petal shaped fretting in lower splat.

Figure NE79. High back Windsor armchair. Ash with elm seat, stamped 'C. TURNER' on side edge of seat. Maker untraced. Attributed to Lincolnshire, c.1840-90.

Three long elliptical spindles each side of central splat. Three elliptical underarm spindles, with underarm supports showing regional turnery features. Heavy three ring turned legs with 'vase' shaped feet, legs connected by H-form stretcher, with cross stretcher showing regional turnery motif. Waisted profile to upper splat with fleur-de-lis motif; keyhole fret in lower splat.

Figure NE81. High back Windsor armchair. Ash with elm seat, stamped 'G. WILSON GRANTHAM' on rear of top seat surface (fl.1841-91).

Three tapered spindles either side of central fretted splat. Four elliptical underarm spindles and turned underarm supports in the style commonly used by this maker (see Figures NE67 and 69). Decoratively turned front legs and plain turned rear legs connected by H-form stretcher with central cross stretcher showing regional turnery motif, and an extra stretcher connecting rear legs. Unusual fretting in upper splat; petal shaped fret in lower splat.

Figure NE83. High back Windsor armchair. Ash with elm seat and arm bow, fruitwood splat. Attributed to Lincolnshire, c.1860-90.

Three long elliptical spindles each side of splat. Three elliptical underarm spindles; elaborately turned underarm supports. Heavy three ring turned front legs with 'vase' feet; plain turned rear legs, legs connected by H-form stretcher, central cross stretcher displaying regional turnery style. Bulbous shaped splat with stylised fleur-de-lis motif; petal shaped fret in lower splat.

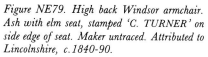

Figure NE80. The stamp of C. Turner impressed on side edge of seat in Figure NE79. C. Turner is untraced. However, the following craftsmen with this surname are recorded working in the Manthorpe Road area of Grantham, Lincolnshire, between 1856 and 1881: Edward Turner, cabinet maker and turner, Little Gonerby (fl.1861-81); Leon Turner, french polisher, Little Gonerby; Mary Turner, turner, Manthorpe Road, Little Gonerby (fl.1856); William Turner, cabinet maker, Wharf Road, Grantham (fl.1871).

Figure NE82. The stamp of George Wilson of Manthorpe Road, Grantham (fl.1841-91) impressed on the rear upper seat surface of the chair shown in Figure NE81.

Figure NE84. High back Windsor armchair. Ash with elm seat and arm bow, fruitwood splat. Attributed to Lincolnshire, c.1860-90. The waisted splat profile with fretted fleur-de-lis exhibits regional form, which has a counterpart in a low back style shown in Figure NE66.

Three long spindles each side of central splat, elliptically shaped in lower half; three elliptical underarm spindles. Underarm supports showing regional turnery feature of flattened ball. Heavy two-ring turned legs connected by plain turned H-form stretchers. Keyhole motif in lower splat.

Figure NE85. High back Windsor armchair. Ash with elm seat. Attributed to Lincolnshire, c.1860-90.

Three long spindles each side of central splat, elliptically shaped in lower half (left upper spindle missing). Three elliptical shaped underarm spindles. Underarm supports showing regional turnery features. Heavy three ring turned legs with vase feet, legs connected by H-form stretcher; central cross stretcher showing regional turnery motif. Waisted profile to upper splat with fleur-de-lis motif; keyhole fret in lower splat.

Figure NE86. High back Windsor armchair. Ash with elm seat and fruitwood splat. Attributed to Lincolnshire, c.1860-90.

Three long spindles each side of central splat, elliptically shaped in lower half; three elliptically shaped underarm spindles. Underarm supports showing regional turnery features. Single ring and concave turned motif incorporated in legs; connected by plain H-form stretcher. Waisted profile to fleur-de-lis fretted upper splat; two shaped frets in lower splat.

Figure NE87. High back Windsor armchair. Ash with elm seat and fruitwood splat. Attributed to Lincolnshire, c.1850-90.

Three long spindles either side of the splat, elliptical in shape in the lower half; three elliptical underarm spindles. Underarm support turning showing regional turnery features. Heavy three ring turned legs with vase feet; legs connected by H-form stretchers; central cross stretcher showing regional turnery feature. Stylised fleur-de-lis in upper splat; keyhole motif in lower splat.

Figure NE88. High back Windsor armchair. Ash with elm seat. Attributed to Lincolnshire, c.1840-90. The waisted splat profile with stylised fleur-de-lis exhibits regional form also shown in Figure NE86 while the underarm support shows regional turnery features.

Three long tapered spindles either side of splat, tapering in shape at point of mortice into seat; three elliptical underarm spindles. Single ring and lower concave motif incorporated into legs, connected by H-form stretcher; central cross stretcher showing regional turnery style. Keyhole motif in lower splat, repeated in upper splat as part of the fleur-de-lis design.

Figure NE89. High back Windsor armchair. Ash with elm seat and fruitwood splat. Attributed to Lincolnshire, c.1860-90. The underarm support turning shows regional turnery features (see Figure NE83 for similar example).

Three long tapered spindles either side of the splat; three elliptical underarm spindles. Heavy three ring turned legs connected by crinoline stretcher. Stylised fleur-de-lis fretted upper splat; keyhole motif in lower splat.

Figure NE90. High back Windsor armchair. Ash with elm seat and fruitwood splat. Attributed to Lincolnshire, c.1860-90. The stretcher design is similar to that shown in Figure NE73.

Three long tapered spindles either side of the splat, tapering in shape at point of entry into the hoop. Three parallel shaped underarm spindles. Underarm support showing regional turnery feature of flattened ball. Heavy three ring turned legs connected by plain turned H-form stretchers, raised in the centre of each stretcher. Waisted splat profile with stylised fleur-de-lis in upper splat; keyhole motif shown in lower splat.

Figure NE91. High back Windsor armchair. Ash with elm seat and fruitwood splat. Attributed to Lincolnshire, c.1860-90.

Three long tapered spindles either side of the splat, tapering as they mortice into the seat. Three tapered underarm spindles. Underarm support turning showing regional turnery features. Heavy three ring turned legs, connected by turned H-form stretchers, raised in their centres. Stylised fleur-de-lis fretted upper splat; keyhole motif in lower splat.

highly elaborated high and low back Windsors were also made in this tradition. Typically these chairs were made in yew with elm seats, and have elaborately turned legs and back splat fretting. These chairs were, no doubt, seen as 'best' chairs, and would have been more costly than those made in ash and elm. Examples of these chairs are shown in Figures NE93-95. Decorative yew chairs made in Lincolnshire have only been recorded with the stamp of George Wilson of Grantham (fl.1841-91), and it may be that Lincolnshire chairs of this kind were made by this maker alone.

As Lincolnshire Windsor chairs moved from the dynamic styles of the early nineteenth century tradition, they changed to heavier, more pedestrian designs. The chairs illus-

trated in Figures NE96-99 are from the later tradition, and are linked to the earlier tradition by the upper splat profile which displays a shield shape which was a characteristic of some chairs made in Grantham and Sleaford in the first half of the nineteenth century (see Figures NE26 and 28).

Other later regional design features which are used in these chairs include elliptically turned underarm spindles, specific underarm support turnings, a regional style of cross stretcher in Figure NE96 and the ball turning incorporated in the leg of Figure NE99. These chairs illustrate that the transition of design from one style of chair to another was a process in which incorporation and modification of design elements was as crucial as the replacement of others.

Figure NE92. High back Windsor armchair. Ash with elm seat and arm bow, alder splat. Attributed to Lincolnshire, c.1860-90.

Three long tapered spindles either side of central splat, tapering as they mortice into the seat. Three tapered underarm spindles; underarm support turning showing regional turnery feature of flattened ball motif. Three ring turned legs, connected by plain turned H-form stretchers, with side stretchers raised at their centres. Stylised fleur-de-lis upper splat; keyhole motif in lower splat.

Figure NE93. High decorative Windsor armchair. Yew with elm seat, stamped 'G. WILSON GRANTHAM' (fl.1841-91). The underarm supports are reminiscent of those used by this maker in his ash and elm chairs (see Figures NE67 and 69).

Three tapered spindles each side of central splat. Three elliptical underarm spindles with turned supports. Decoratively turned legs connected by crinoline stretcher. Elaborately fretted upper and lower splats.

Figure NE94. The stamp of George Wilson of Manthorpe Road, Grantham (fl.1841-91), faintly stamped on the rear upper seat surface of the chair shown in Figure NE93.

Figure NE95. Pair of low back Windsors with decorative splats. Yew with elm seats, stamped 'G. WILSON GRANTHAM' (fl.1841-91).

Three long spindles, elliptical in the lower half, either side of the central decoratively fretted splat. Four elliptical underarm spindles with underarm support turnings similar to those used by this maker in his ash and elm low back Windsors. Decoratively turned legs connected by crinoline stretchers.

(Courtesy Aldridges)

Figure NE96. High back Windsor armchair. Ash with elm seat and alder splat. Attributed to Lincolnshire, c.1860-90. Figures NE97-99 have a similar splat design.

Double ring leg turnings. Legs connected by H-form stretchers. Cross central stretcher displaying regional turnery feature. Three elliptical shaped long back spindles each side of the central splat. Three elliptical shaped underarm spindles. Regional style of underarm support. Stylised fleur-de-lis fretted splat with urn shape below with petal motif. Lower splat pierced with a keyhole shaped motif.

Figure NE97. High back Windsor armchair. Elm seat, splat, arm hoop, supports and sticks, ash top bow legs and stretchers. Attributed to Lincolnshire, c.1850-95. In Figure NE70, the left hand Windsor in the right hand group of chairs illustrated outside a Grantham antiques shop (1938) shows a similar chair with the regional feature of the ball turned legs.

Large ball turning incorporated in front legs. Plain turned rear legs connected by plain H-form stretcher. Three elliptical long back spindles either side of the central splat. Three elliptical underarm spindles. Unusual style of underarm support. Stylised fleur-de-lis fretted splat with urn shape below with petal motif. Petal shaped piercing in lower splat.

Figure NE98. High back Windsor armchair. Ash with elm seat and arm bow and alder splat. Attributed to Lincolnshire, c.1845-75. The underarm supports are turned in the manner of the Samuel Wood of Grantham chair in Figure NE64.

Heavy two ring turned front legs. Plain turned rear legs, connected by plain turned H-form stretchers. Three long spindles each side of the central splat, elliptically shaped below arm hoop; three elliptically shaped underarm spindles. Stylised fleur-de-lis fretted splat with urn shape below with petal motif; petal shaped fret in lower splat.

Figure NE99. High back Windsor armchair. Ash with elm seat and splats. Attributed to Lincolnshire, c.1860-95.

Single ball turning incorporated in front legs; plain turned back legs; connected by plain turned H-form stretcher. Three long spindles each side of central splat, elliptically shaped below arm hoop; three elliptically shaped underarm spindles; underarm supports showing regional turnery features. Stylised fleur-de-lis splat with urn shape below with petal motif; petal shaped fret in lower splat. (Courtesy Bonsor Penningtons)

19th Century Comb Back Windsors

Amongst the repertoire of Lincolnshire chairs are two related styles which find no exact parallel elsewhere in the English Windsor chair tradition. These chairs, both arm and side, are characterised by having a plain curved 'comb' rail, supported by either an arrangement of plain spindles or, more rarely, fretted splat designs (see Figures NE103 and 111). Both the arm and the side chairs of this design are uncommon, compared with the bow or hoop back style of Windsor, and it may be that these designs failed to satisfy potential purchasers in the way that more conventional Windsors did. Essentially, the comb back armchairs within this group have many features in common with the bow or hoop back Windsors, but reject the top hoop in favour of a comb stay rail supported on two turned uprights which carry distinctive patterns common to individual chair makers and are like smaller replicas of arm support turnings. Interestingly, no high back Windsors of this type have been recorded, breaking with the general rule for Windsor design which typically accords complementary low and high back styles in each category of armchair style.

Figure NE100. Unidentified young man sitting on a comb back side chair of a type unique to the Lincolnshire region (see Figures NE104-120), at Holton le Moor, Lincolnshire, late 19th century.

(Courtesy Wellholme Galleries and Grimsby Borough Council)

Figure NE101. Low comb back Windsor armchair. Ash with elm seat and birch comb rail, stamped 'CAMM GRANTHAM' (fl.1830-51) on the side edge of seat.

Eight long tapered back spindles. Three elliptical underarm spindles. Turned underarm supports showing regional features. Single ring and concave turned front legs, plain turned back legs; legs supported by turned H-form stretcher. Plain 'hollowed' comb rail supported on two turned outer spindles.

Figure NE102. Stamp of Camm of Grantham from the side seat edge of the chair illustrated in Figure NE101. This stamp was probably used by father and son, both named Thomas. Thomas the elder worked between 1828 and 1851; Thomas junior between 1842 and 1849. A further junior Camm named Richard is also recorded as a chair maker in 1851, aged 17.[25] Unusually in the Lincolnshire tradition, this stamp is located on the side edge of the seat rather than on the more typical upper seat surface.

Figure NE103. Low comb back Windsor armchair with fretted splat. Ash with elm seat and birch comb rail, stamped 'G. WILSON GRANTHAM' (fl.1841-92) very faintly on upper rear seat surface.

Six long back spindles typical of ash hoop back Windsors. The upper fretted splat is modified to fit a horizontal rather than a crescent shaped hoop. Plain hollow comb rail raised on two turned supports. Unconventional fleur-de-lis fretting in top splat; petal motif in lower splat. Three elliptical underarm spindles; underarm support typical of this maker. Two ring turned front legs; plain turned rear legs; legs supported by plain turned H-form stretchers.

133

Figure NE104. Comb back Windsor side chair. Ash with elm seat, stamped 'J. HILL' on side edge of seat. The location of this maker is currently untraced, but attributed to Lincolnshire, c.1835-70.

Plain comb rail supported by two outer decoratively turned back supports. Six elliptical back spindles. Single ring and concave turned front legs with straight feet and plain turned back legs; legs connected by turned H-form stretchers.

(Courtesy B. Howard)

Figure NE105. Stamp of J. Hill impressed on the side seat edge of the chair in Figure NE104.

Figure NE106. Comb back side chair. Ash with elm seat and birch comb rail, stamped 'MARSH SLEAFORD' (fl.1822-61) on upper rear seat.

Plain comb rail. Five elliptical long back spindles. Decoratively turned outer supports. Single ring turned front legs with straight feet. Plain turned rear legs, connected by H-form stretcher. Central cross stretcher showing regional turnery design. *(Courtesy H. Watson)*

Figure NE107. Stamp of Marsh of Sleaford found on the upper rear seat of chair in Figure NE106. Probably the mark of James Marsh (fl.1842-61). *(Courtesy H. Watson)*

Figure NE108. Comb back Windsor side chair. Ash with elm seat, stamped 'MARSH SLEAFORD' (fl.1822-61) on rear of top seat surface. This chair has identical characteristics to the chair shown in Figure NE106, with the exception that this chair incorporates six elliptical long back spindles in the back design.
(Courtesy H. Watson)

Figure NE109. Comb back Windsor side chair. Ash with elm seat; beech back uprights and comb rail. Stamped 'TAYLOR GRANTHAM' (fl.1800-91) on rear of seat surface.

Plain stay rail supported by two outer decoratively turned uprights. Six elliptical long back spindles. Single ring and concave turned front legs; plain turned rear legs; legs connected by plain turned H-form stretchers.

Figure NE110. Stamp of Taylor of Grantham found on the rear top surface of the seat of the chair shown in Figure NE109. It is possible that both John senior (fl.1800-41), and Joseph (fl.1841-89), adopted the same identification stamp. Two other J. Taylors, James and John (junior) are recorded as chair makers in Grantham in 1841 only.[26]

Figure NE111. Comb back Windsor side chair with fretted splat. Ash cross stretcher and three legs, with elm seat and splat; comb rail, left back leg and turned outer uprights in beech. Stamped 'TAYLOR GRANTHAM' (fl.1800-91), on rear of seat top surface.

Plain comb rail supported by two outer decoratively turned supports. Two elliptical back spindles either side of central splat. Central fretted splat with urn motif. Single ring turned front legs; plain turned rear legs connected by plain turned H-form stretchers.

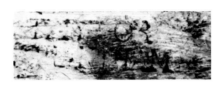

Figure NE112. Stamp of John or Joseph Taylor of Grantham (fl.1800-91) taken from the upper rear seat of chair shown in Figure NE111.

Figure NE113. Low comb back Windsor armchair. Ash with elm seat and birch comb rail. Attributed to Lincolnshire, c.1840-60. Central cross stretcher turned in a manner similar to the Marsh cross stretcher shown in Figure NE40. Underarm supports similar to examples by J. Marsh of Sleaford, and J. Taylor of Grantham (see Figures NE6, 31 and 38).

Eight long tapered back spindles. Three elliptical underarm spindles. Single ring and concave turned front legs; plain turned rear legs; legs connected by H-form stretchers.

Figure NE114. Comb back Windsor armchair. Ash and fruitwood with elm seat. Stamped 'W. ROWE' (fl.1840-43) on side edge of seat. Attributed to Hallaton, Leicestershire. This chair is unusual in being provenanced to a Leicestershire maker, a tradition where a number of chair makers are known to have worked, but for which this chair style alone has been firmly attributed. The large bell shaped seat is typical of many Windsors made in the nearby Lincolnshire tradition.

This large chair has twelve rear spindles and two outer decoratively turned spindles supporting a deeply curved comb rail. The large arm bow supported by crook shaped underarm supports, and four underarm spindles. Legs turned with single ring and shallow concave turning, supported by H-form stretchers. *(Courtesy Key Antiques)*

Figure NE115. The stamp of William Rowe, chair maker, of Hallaton and Medbourne, Leicestershire (fl.1840-43), impressed on the side seat edge of the chair shown in Figure NE114.

Figure NE116. Comb back Windsor side chair. Ash with elm seat and birch comb rail. Attributed to Lincolnshire, c.1840-90.

Plain comb rail supported by two outer decoratively turned uprights, very similar to those found in the Taylor chair in Figure NE109. Six elliptical long back spindles. Pronounced ball turned front legs with vase shaped feet. Plain turned rear legs with vase feet. Legs connected by plain turned H-form stretchers.

Figure NE117. Comb back Windsor side chair. Ash with elm seat and comb rail. Attributed to Lincolnshire, c.1835-70.

Plain comb rail with lower scribe mark decoration supported by two decoratively turned back supports. Six elliptical back spindles. Pronounced ball turned front legs with vase shaped feet. Plain turned rear legs with vase feet. Legs connected by plain turned H-form stretchers.

Figure NE118. Comb back Windsor side chair. Ash with elm seat. Attributed to Lincolnshire, c.1835-70.

Plain comb rail with lower scribe mark decoration supported by two outer decoratively turned back supports. Six elliptical back spindles. Pronounced ball turned front legs with straight feet; plain turned back legs; legs connected by plain turned H-form stretchers.

Figure NE119. Comb back Windsor side chair. Ash with elm seat and alder comb rail. Attributed to Lincolnshire, c.1835-70.

Plain comb rail supported by two outer decoratively turned back supports. Six elliptical back spindles. Three ring turned front legs with straight feet. Plain turned back legs; legs supported by plain turned H-form stretchers.

Figure NE120. Comb back Windsor side chair. Ash with elm seat and beech comb rail. Attributed to Lincolnshire, c.1825-91.

Plain comb rail supported by two outer decoratively turned supports. Six elliptical long back spindles. Unusual three ring turned legs with narrower ring above and below; legs connected by plain turned H-form stretchers.

Figure NE121. Pencil drawing of a low stick back Windsor. From the workshop notebook of John Shadford (fl.1843-81), chair maker, Caistor, Lincolnshire.[27] This chair displays seven long spindles in the back design and two ring leg turnings.   (Courtesy Lincoln Archive Office)

Figure NE122. Pencil drawing of a high stick back Windsor chair from the notebook of John Shadford (fl.1843-81), chair maker, Caistor, Lincolnshire. This chair displays a deep seat and seven long back spindles. The juxtaposition of angles between the turned arm supports and the underarm and back spindles indicates an acute awareness of the supporting tensions of Windsor chair design.

(Courtesy Lincoln Archive Office)

Figure NE123. Low stick back Windsor armchair. Ash with elm seat. Stamped at the rear of the upper seat surface, 'TAYLOR GRANTHAM' (John Taylor, fl.1800-43, Joseph Taylor, fl.1841-91).

Single ring and concave turned front legs. Plain turned rear legs. Legs connected by plain H-form stretchers. Eight long back spindles. Three elliptical underarm spindles. Flattened arm shape. Turned arm supports typical of the region's patterns.

Stick Hoop Back Windsors

The earlier forms of stick back Windsors with crook arm supports gradually gave way to those with turned arm supports around 1840. The resulting stick back chair designs continued to be made in virtually unchanged form throughout the remainder of the nineteenth century.

Within the stick back Windsor group, the crinoline stretcher, typical of the earlier nineteenth century stick backs, was abandoned after about 1840 in all but the rarest examples and the turned H-form stretcher was widely used. Similarly, the turned arm support was adopted in place of the crook underarm support at about this time. These two factors, and the typical use of plain turned back legs and back spindles, suggest that the place of the stick back style in the range of Lincolnshire Windsor chairs was that of the most basic and utilitarian.

It may be significant, too, that the chairs in this group which have been recorded with the maker's name stamp are all chairs made by the early nineteenth century group of Grantham, Sleaford and Boston

makers who were involved in the transition of design which took place in the second quarter of the nineteenth century. In every case, these provenanced chairs have the earlier single ring turned front legs; whereas no stamped chairs have been recorded amongst later stick back chairs, both high and low back forms, which have two or three ring turned legs, perhaps indicating that these chairs were marketed differently by the middle of the nineteenth century, and that the need to name and place stamp products had declined.

This form of stick back Windsor represents a truly Lincolnshire regional Windsor style and, with the exception of only two other known places of manufacture,* all provenanced chairs of this type were made by Lincolnshire makers. The anthology of unstamped low and high stick back chairs illustrated in Figures NE145-163 is, therefore, suggested as Lincolnshire in origin.

Although no name stamped stick back chairs have so far been recorded other than those made by the Grantham, Sleaford and Boston

Figure NE124. The stamp of John or Joseph Taylor of Grantham (fl.1800-91), taken from the chair shown in Figure NE123 on the rear of the upper seat surface.

chair makers, it is clear that an awareness of both the low and high back stick Windsors existed outside these centres, since John Shadford, who was a chair maker in the North Lincolnshire town of Caistor (fl.1843-81) drew simple pencil drawings of the Windsor chairs which he made, in his workshop notebook. Two of these drawings (see Figures NE121 and 122) show respectively a low back stick Windsor with seven long

* There is a stick back Windsor child's chair stamped 'Wheatland. Rockley' (Notts.), (see Figure NE287) and an illustration in a late 19th century catalogue of turned wares and Windsor chairs produced by William Brear, chair manufacturer, of Addingham, nr. Leeds (Figure NE420).

137

Figure NE125. Low stick back Windsor armchair. Ash with elm seat. Stamped twice 'N. ALLEN BOSTON' (fl.1790-1829), on the side edge of the seat. Note similar character to the chair stamped Camm of Grantham shown in Figure NE139. Underarm turnings display regional turnery features.

Single ring and concave turning on front legs; rear legs plain turned with ring turning at base of leg. H-form stretchers connecting legs with central cross stretcher showing regional turnery device. Nine parallel long back spindles. Four elliptical underarm spindles. Unusually deep 'bell' shaped seat. Flattened arm shape.

Figure NE126. The stamp of Nicholas Allen of Boston (fl.1790-1828), struck twice on the side edge of the seat of the chair shown in Figure NE125. This craftsman is one of the earliest chair makers to be recorded for this region, and he combined the turnery trades of pin and spinning wheel manufacturer with that of chair maker.

Figure NE127. Low stick back Windsor armchair. Ash with elm seat. Branded 'S A' on underside of seat, perhaps the mark of Samuel Atkin (fl.1826-41), chair maker, Boston.

Two ring turned front legs; plain turned rear legs; legs connected by a plain, turned H-form stretchers. Eight long back spindles, three elliptical underarm spindles. Flattened arm shape. Underarm supports turned with regional characteristics.

Figure NE128. The mark 'S A' found under the seat of the chair in Figure NE127, possibly that of Samuel Atkin, chair maker, Boston, Lincolnshire (fl.1826-41).

Figure NE129. Low stick back Windsor armchair. Yew with elm seat. Stamped 'T. SIMPSON BOSTON' (fl.1819-56) on side edge of seat. The crinoline stretcher is rare on this type of chair.

Single ring and concave turned front legs; rear legs plain turned. Nine long back spindles and four elliptical underarm spindles. Flattened arm shape. Underarm spindles turned with regional characteristics. (Courtesy Tom Crispin)

Figure NE130. The stamp of Thomas Simpson of Boston (fl.1819-56), impressed on the side edge of the seat of the chair illustrated in Figure NE129.

Figure NE131. Low stick back Windsor armchair. Yew, with elm seat. Stamped 'AMOS GRANTHAM' (fl.1814-42), on top rear surface of seat. The crinoline stretcher is extremely rare in this style of chair. This chair is closely similar in design to the example made by T. Simpson of Boston shown in Figure NE129.

Single ring and concave turned front legs; rear legs plain turned. Nine long back spindles and four elliptical underarm spindles. Underarm spindles turned with regional characteristics. (Courtesy Mrs and Miss Berry, Nottingham)

Figure NE132. The stamp of John Amos of Little Gonerby (fl.1814-42), found on top rear surface of seat of chair in Figure NE131.

spindles in the back and two ring turning in the front legs, and a high stick back Windsor with a deep seat and seven spindles in the back design. The evidence that these chairs were incorporated into the Caistor chair makers' repertoire is, perhaps, not surprising, since the owner of the workshop in which John Shadford worked for some time, was William Shirley junior, who had learned his craft in Grantham, where his father, also William Shirley, was a chair maker, and presumably William junior carried with him to Caistor the chair designs of the Grantham region. Other insights into the working practices of a Lincolnshire chair maker which John Shadford's diary provides are described more fully in pp.144-147.

Figure NE133. Stick back Windsor armchair. Ash with elm seat. Medium back height. Stamped 'MARSH SLEAFORD' (fl.1822-61), on upper rear surface of seat. A similar chair, but with only eight long spindles, is shown in Figure NE135.

Single ring and concave turned front legs; plain turned rear legs; legs connected by turned H-form stretchers with cross stretchers turned in a regional pattern. Nine long back spindles, four elliptical underarm spindles. Flattened arm shape. Underarm supports turned with regional turnery characteristics. Notch beneath ends of arm bow.

Figure NE134. The stamp probably used by both Thomas Marsh (fl.1822-26) and his son John (fl.1842-61), taken from the upper surface of the chair shown in Figure NE133.

Figure NE135. Low stick back Windsor armchair. Ash with elm seat. Stamped 'MARSH' (fl.1822-61), on upper rear surface of the seat.

Single ring and concave turning on front legs; rear legs plain turned; connected by H-form stretcher. Centre cross stretcher showing multiple ball turnings. Eight elliptical long back spindles and three underarm spindles. Flattened arm shape. Underarm turned support style typical of this maker.

Figure NE136. The identification stamp of Thomas or James Marsh of Sleaford (fl.1822-61), taken from Figure NE135, located on the rear of the upper surface of the seat. This stamp is usually combined with the stamp of 'Sleaford' below (see Figure NE138).

Figure NE137. Stool. Yew legs and stretchers with elm seat. Stamped 'MARSH SLEAFORD' (fl.1822-61).

Elm seat, with yew legs and stretchers. Single ring and concave turned motif incorporated in legs. H-form connecting stretchers with central cross stretcher showing regional turnery style.

Figure NE138. The stamp of Thomas or James Marsh of Sleaford (fl.1822-61), on the edge of the seat of the stool shown in Figure NE137.

Figure NE139. Low stick back Windsor armchair. Ash with elm seat. Stamped 'CAMM GRANTHAM' on upper rear surface of seat. Probably the stamp of Thomas Camm, Senior (fl.1828-51). This chair shows distinct design similarities to those of the chair made by Nicholas Allen of Boston shown in Figure NE125.

Single ring and concave turning on front and rear legs. H-form connecting stretchers. Central cross stretcher showing regional turnery style.

Figure NE140. Stamp of Thomas Camm of Grantham (fl.1828-51), found on the upper rear surface of the seat of the chair shown in Figure NE139.

Figure NE141. Low stick back Windsor armchair. Ash with elm seat. Stamped 'CAMM GRANTHAM' (fl.1828-51) on edge of seat. The underarm spindles and supports are produced in an identical fashion in the chair shown in Figure NE61, made by John Amos of Grantham (fl.1814-42). Amos and Camm were contemporaries, and worked within a mile of each other at Little Gonerby, Grantham. It is, perhaps, not surprising, therefore, that design features should be shared amongst makers, and the Grantham Windsors demonstrate many design cross-references between the work of different makers.

Single ring turned front legs; plain turned rear legs; legs connected by H-form stretchers; central cross stretcher turned with regional motif. Eight tapered long back spindles; three elliptical underarm spindles, leaned obliquely backwards; decoratively turned underarm supports.

Figure NE142. Stamp of Thomas Camm of Westgate, Grantham (fl.1828-51), impressed unusually on side edge of seat of chair shown in Figure NE141.

Figure NE143. Low stick back Windsor armchair. Ash with elm seat. Stamped 'G. WILSON GRANTHAM' (fl.1841-92), on rear of seat.

Eight elliptical long spindles composing the back design with three upright elliptical spindles supporting each arm. Underarm support turned with regional characteristics. Flattened arm shape. Single ring and concave turned front legs; plain turned rear legs; legs connected by plain H-form stretchers.

Figure NE144. Stamp of George Wilson (fl.1841-92) located on the chair shown in Figure NE143. This maker lived at 35 Manthorpe Road, and was probably joint owner of the workshop adjoining 50 Manthorpe Road (see footnote to Figure NE65).

Figure NE146. Low stick back Windsor armchair. Ash with elm seat. Attributed to Lincolnshire, c.1850-90.

Seven long elliptical back spindles. Three short elliptical underarm spindles; underarm supports showing regional characteristics. Two ring turned front legs. Plain turned back legs and connecting H-form stretchers.

Figure NE145. Low back stick Windsor armchair. Ash with elm seat. Attributed to Lincolnshire, c.1840-50.

Eight long back spindles. Three short elliptical spindles supporting each arm. Front arm support turned in a mode similar to many Nottinghamshire Windsor arm turnings. Single ring and concave turned front legs; plain turned rear legs; legs connected by plain H-form stretchers. Flattened arm bow profile.

Figure NE147. Low back stick Windsor armchair. Ash with elm seat. Attributed to Lincolnshire, c.1840-80. Legs with this form of ball turning device are shown in the right hand front group of chairs shown in Figure NE70 and appear to be a minority regional leg turning style not found outside the North East Midlands region.

Seven elliptical long back spindles. Flattened arm bow shape. Three sloping elliptical underarm spindles; unusual underarm turnings including a ball device which is reflected in the pronounced ball turning in leg. Plain turned back legs and H-form stretchers.

Figure NE150. Low stick back Windsor armchair. Ash with elm seat. Attributed to Lincolnshire, c.1850-90.

Seven long back spindles. Three elliptical underarm supports. Turned arm support similar to that shown in Figure NE67. Two ring turned front and back legs. Plain turned connecting H-form stretchers.

Figure NE148. Low stick back Windsor armchair. Ash with elm seat. Attributed to Lincolnshire, c.1850-90.

Seven long tapered back spindles. Three tapered underarm supports. Underarm support turning shows certain similarities with those shown in Figure NE161. Three ring turned front legs with vase feet. Plain turned rear legs, connected by a stretcher between the rear legs, as well as the typically plain turned H-form stretcher connecting all legs.

Figure NE149. Low stick back Windsor armchair. Ash with elm seat. Attributed to Lincolnshire, c.1850-80.

Seven long back spindles. Three underarm spindles. Turned underarm supports similar to those typical of Nottinghamshire tradition Windsors. Heavy three ring turned front legs with vase feet. Plain turned rear legs, connected by plain turned H-form stretchers.

Figure NE153. High stick back Windsor armchair. Ash with elm seat. Attributed to Lincolnshire, c.1750-1800. This chair displays many characteristics of primitive Windsors of the mid to late 18th century. There is no provenance for this example, but many of its design features, including nine long back spindles and elliptical underarm support spindles, articulate with later designs from the Lincolnshire tradition. In the later high stick back Windsors, the front plain elliptical arm support is replaced with an elaborately turned spindle. The legs are decoratively turned in the 19th century examples, and are connected by stretchers. Given these alterations in design, the possibility of transition from progenitors of heavier 18th century primitive Windsors, to the more elaborated 19th century form seems credible.

Figure NE151. Child's stick back Windsor armchair. Ash with elm seat, c.1850-80. This chair has been used by successive generations of the Stothard family of Brigg, Lincolnshire.

Five back spindles with two underarm spindles. Ball turning in arm supports. Two ring turned front legs, plain turned back legs supported by H-form stretchers.

(Courtesy Mrs Lingard, née Stothard, Lincoln)

Figure NE152. Child's stick back Windsor armchair. Ash with elm seat. Attributed to Lincolnshire, c.1840-60. The design of this chair has similarities to those shown by the adult sized chair shown in Figure NE154.

Five long back spindles. Two underarm spindles. Two ring turned legs with no interconnecting stretchers.

141

Figure NE154. High stick back Windsor armchair. Ash with elm seat. Attributed to Lincolnshire, c.1800-60. The back hoop is similar to that in Figure NE153, and the turnery devices and demeanour to the child's chair in Figure NE152.

Nine long back spindles. Two elliptical underarm support spindles; heavily turned arm supports. Flattened arm shape. Back hoop sloping forward into the arm bow. Heavy two ring turned legs with vase feet; legs connected by plain H-form stretcher.

Figure NE155. High stick back Windsor armchair. Ash with elm seat. Attributed to Lincolnshire, c.1840-80. The unusual underarm supports are similar to that found in the low stick back Windsor shown in Figure NE147.

Seven long elliptical back spindles. Three elliptical underarm supports. Repair visible to arm hoop. Pronounced single ball turning in front legs with vase feet. Plain turned back legs; legs connected by plain H-form stretchers.

Figure NE156. High stick back Windsor armchair. Ash with elm seat. Attributed to Lincolnshire, c.1840-60. The underarm support is similar to that in Figure NE141.

Eight long elliptical back spindles. Three elliptical underarm spindles. Single ring and incised concave turned front legs; plain turned rear legs; legs connected by H-form stretchers.

Figure NE157. High stick back Windsor armchair. Ash with elm seat. Attributed to Lincolnshire, c.1840. The turned arm supports show a combination of turnery features of both the Nottinghamshire makers and, in the lower ball turning, of the Lincolnshire makers. The feature of sharply tapering tenons appears to be a feature of certain stick and splat back Windsors from Lincolnshire (see Figure NE90 for related example).

Nine long back spindles, tapered at point of entry into hoop. Hoop similarly tapered into arm hoop. Narrow arm and top hoop bows. Four parallel underarm spindles. Turned arm supports. Three ring turned legs with vase feet; legs connected by H-form stretchers which show raised parallel turnings in the centre of the stretchers.

Figure NE158. High stick back Windsor armchair. Ash with elm seat. Attributed to Lincolnshire, c.1850-90. The underarm spindle turning is similar to that in Figure NE160.

Seven long elliptical back spindles. Three tapered underarm spindles. Heavy two ring leg turnings with vase feet; legs connected by plain H-form stretchers.

Figure NE159. High stick back Windsor armchair. Ash with elm seat. Attributed to Lincolnshire, c.1840-85.

Seven tapered long back spindles; three tapered underarm spindles. Heavily turned underarm supports. Two ring turned legs with vase feet; legs connected by plain turned H-form stretchers.

Figure NE160. High stick back Windsor armchair. Ash with elm seat. Attributed to Lincolnshire, c.1850-80.

Seven tapered long back spindles; three elliptical underarm spindles. Heavily turned underarm supports. Heavy two ring turned legs with vase feet; legs connected by H-form stretchers; two side stretchers raised in the centres.

Figure NE161. High stick back Windsor armchair. Ash with elm seat. Attributed to Lincolnshire, c.1840-90. The turned underarm supports are similar to those used by G. Wilson of Grantham (see Figure NE67).

Seven long back spindles, three elliptical underarm spindles. Turned underarm supports. Heavy two ring turned legs, with vase feet; legs connected by H-form stretchers. Central cross stretcher showing regional turnery device.

Figure NE162. High stick back Windsor armchair. Ash with elm seat. Attributed to Lincolnshire, c.1850-80.

Seven long tapered back spindles. Three tapered underarm support spindles. Front underarm support turnings showing features of many Nottinghamshire Windsors. Two ring turned legs with straight feet; legs connected by plain H-form stretchers.

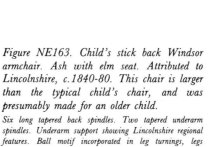

Figure NE163. Child's stick back Windsor armchair. Ash with elm seat. Attributed to Lincolnshire, c.1840-80. This chair is larger than the typical child's chair, and was presumably made for an older child.

Six long tapered back spindles. Two tapered underarm spindles. Underarm support showing Lincolnshire regional features. Ball motif incorporated in leg turnings, legs connected by plain turned H-form stretchers.

143

The Caistor Tradition

If the towns of Grantham, Sleaford and Boston were the homes of many chair makers who identified their chairs by name and place stamping them, a further chair maker, John William Shadford, who lived in the small North Lincolnshire town of Caistor, also left a graphic legacy of his work and the workings of a Lincolnshire chair maker's workshop, in the form of an illustrated notebook. In this book, he made delightfully naïve drawings of the chairs which he produced, as well as the tools and devices which he used, recipes for stains and polishes and evidence of his ambitions in the form of descriptive trade card designs and letters which proposed himself as the owner of his own workshop on leaving the employ of his master.[28]

John Shadford (fl.1843-81), spent his entire working life in Caistor as a chair maker and wood turner, living and working in the same street. Towards the middle of the nineteenth century, he entered the trade which had been established at least as early as the first quarter of the nineteenth century, and which was carried on until about 1890 by a small group of turners and chair makers, numbering three men in 1841, and seven at its peak in 1861. Many of these craftsmen, including John Shadford, appear to have worked in the same workshop in Fountain or Duck Street which was owned from about 1843 until 1890 by William Shirley junior,* who had learned his trade in Grantham, where his father, William Shirley senior,[29] was also a chair maker. William Shirley junior left Grantham in 1843 when he was in his early twenties, to work in Caistor.[30] The workshop which he came to own[31] was unusual in this region in that it was powered by an overshot water wheel, for Fountain Street was well named in having a constant spring which poured water down the steep incline of the street. A photograph taken in the mid-nineteenth century shows that Shirley's workshop utilised a wooden aqueduct to carry the water from the spring to the water wheel (see Figure NE165), and the energy so produced would have been used to power the wood turning lathes and other machinery used in the manufacture of chairs.

It may be expected that William Shirley would have brought knowledge of chair designs with him from Grantham, and that he might have

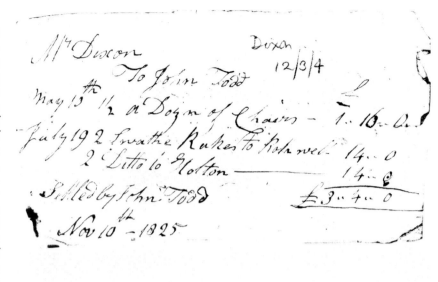

Figure NE164. Invoice dated 13 May, 1825, supplied by John Todd (fl.1825-56), chair maker of Westgate, Caistor, itemising the provision of 'half a dozen chairs' at £1. 16s. 0d. as well as swathe (hay) rakes.
(Courtesy Lincolnshire Archives Office)

carried on making these designs in Caistor. However, this appears to have been only partly true, for the repertoire of chair designs drawn by his employee, John Shadford, shows that in addition to being aware of the high and low stick back Windsor, typical of the Grantham, Sleaford and Boston makers (see Figures NE121 and 122), other chair designs, which have not been recorded from other centres, were made in Caistor. Amongst the chairs which Shadford recorded are stick back children's chairs with food and foot rests and a hole in the seat for a chamber pot (see Figure NE174); a form of Roman side chair (see Figure NE173) which is similar to the design shown on the I. Allsop trade card from Worksop, Notts. (see Figure NE270), a decorative splat high back Windsor with crinoline stretcher, and an important design which may be unique to Caistor which embodies highly decorative turnery design in the back spindles as well as in other turned parts (see Figures NE168 and 169).

Of the latter two designs, a rocking chair with a decoratively fretted splat has been recorded with the name 'Shirley' struck on the edge of the seat (see Figures NE166 and 167). This chair dates from around 1850, and would, therefore, have been the product of William Shirley's workshop at Caistor. The slight differences which this chair shows from the similar one illustrated in Shadford's

drawing (see Figure NE169) indicates that variations on a particular design were made, and that chairs were made as rocking chairs, as well as conventional armchairs.

The design made with two rows of decorative spindles (see Figure NE168) may be a chair that was designed by John Shadford himself. He clearly had a strong sense of this chair, drawing it twice in his diary, once as a counterpart to the decorative splat high back Windsor shown in Figure NE169, as well as a whole page drawing produced in a delicate and ethereal way (see Figure NE172).

Chairs of Caistor design are typically low in the seat, and being fitted to rockers, were clearly made as easy or fireside chairs. These chairs were originally stained with red lead to simulate mahogany. John Shadford confirmed this staining practice in drawing a large container of red lead in the left hand corner of his workshop content drawing shown in the introductory chapter.

The contents of John Shadford's notebook indicate that he was a literate and intelligent man, and it is

---

* A reference to Shirley's workshop in Fountain Street, Caistor, is indicated by the note written on the back of the photograph of his workshop shown in Figure NE165 which reads, 'Shirley's wood-yard, Caistor'.

Figure NE165. William Shirley's wood yard and chair making workshop in Fountain Street, Caistor, Lincolnshire, c.1860. Water from a spring at the top of the street was carried in an aqueduct to drive an overshot wheel which drove the wood turning lathes and other machinery used in the craft.

(Courtesy W.G. Hallgarth Collection, Wellholme Galleries, and the Grimsby Borough Council)

possible that his deafness from birth did not handicap him, as he became a workshop owner in his own right in 1858.

John Shadford's ambitions to own his own chair making business, are revealed in his writings, when at the age of twenty-nine, he designed a personal trade card (see Figure NE170), and wrote a letter in his notebook making claims for his experience in the work of turning and chair making, and soliciting orders (see Figure NE171). Evidence that Shadford successfully continued as a self-employed chair maker is indicated in a letter drafted in his notebook dated 13 June, 1857, to a Mr Day confirming an order for chairs in the following way:

'Sir,

Yours of the 12th. inst. came duly to hand, and in reply I beg to say that I can make you half a dozen small chairs at 2/6 each, and one armchair at 4/6 and will send them next week.

Yours respectfully,

W.J. Shadford'[32]

Figure NE166. High back Windsor armchair with decorative splat, made as a rocking chair. Ash with elm seat and fruitwood splat, stamped 'SHIRLEY' (fl.1841-81) on edge of seat. The underarm support turnings are typical of North East and Yorkshire regional styles (see Figure NE362).

Three elliptical long back spindles each side of splat; three elliptical underarm spindles. Heavy single ball and concave turning motif in front legs; legs fitted to rockers by special dowel tenons turned on to feet. Legs connected by H-form stretchers, with heavy central cross stretcher decoratively turned. Decoratively fretted upper and lower splats which are features more commonly found in chairs made of yew.

Figure NE167. The stamp of William Shirley impressed on the side of the seat of the chair shown in Figure NE166. William Shirley worked in Grantham (1841-43), before moving to Caistor, North East Lincolnshire, to continue his trade. He became the owner of the chair making workshop in Fountain Street in 1843 and continued until about 1890.

145

This letter shows how quickly chairs could be made to order, and the relatively low cost of the chair maker's product. The price of 2/6d (12½p) for side chairs, and 4/6d (22½p) for armchairs in 1857 is not greatly different from the price which Caistor chairs commanded earlier in the century. An invoice produced by one of the early nineteenth century Caistor chair makers, John Todd (fl.1825-56) in 1825 indicates that he supplied half a dozen chairs for £1.16/- (£1.80), i.e. 6/- (30p) each. This invoice also indicates that some Caistor chair makers also produced turned agricultural implements, for Todd supplied four swathe (hay-making) rakes with the chairs (see Figure NE164).

The notebook which John Shadford left is important in many ways, not least in that the drawings showing his workshop tools and devices, constitute the only visual statement of the contents of a nineteenth century chair maker's workshop to have been discovered anywhere in England. An analysis of his drawings is discussed more fully in Chapter 1, pp.24 and 27. Various other working design drawings from the notebook also indicate that Shadford was adept at designing turnery work in a precisely measured way. This revelation is significant since it contradicts a commonly held belief that vernacular chair turnery work was the product of an oral tradition or intuitively produced as part of the act of producing the work. The realisation that Shadford was also a designer may indicate the possibility that other chair makers devised their own turnery patterns using formal design techniques. John Shadford's unpretentious record provides a direct and honest sense of the practices which underlay the working life of one Lincolnshire chair maker producing a range of regional chair types and variations of them.

Figure NE168. The 'Caistor' chair. Ash with elm seat, c.1850-90. Stained with red lead. This style of chair is unique to the Lincolnshire tradition and was probably made in Caistor alone. This chair style was illustrated by John Shadford, chair maker and wood turner (fl.1843-89) in his workshop notebook, and it may be that he was both the designer and maker of this chair.

Figure NE169. Drawings from the notebook of John Shadford (fl.1843-89). The left hand drawing illustrates a decorative splat high back Windsor entitled 'Arm Chair'. A similar chair to this, stamped 'SHIRLEY' on the side of the seat, is shown in Figure NE166. The right hand drawing illustrates a chair with elaborate turnery devices, and entitled 'Arm Chair Selpey' or 'Selfrey'. An example of a similar chair is shown in Figure NE168.

(Courtesy Lincolnshire Archives Office)

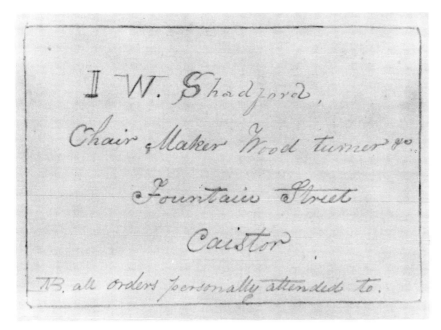

Figure NE170. A trade card designed by John William Shadford in his workshop notebook in 1888, when he was aged about 60. At this time his employer, William Shirley, was nearing the end of his working life and Shadford was preparing to be a self-employed chair maker.

(Courtesy Lincolnshire Archives Office)

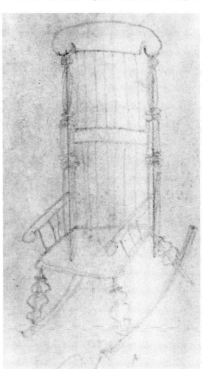

Figure NE172. An evocative drawing of the 'Caistor' chair from the workshop notebook of John Shadford. This unusual chair is unique in the repertoire of Lincolnshire regional styles.

(Courtesy Lincolnshire Archives Office)

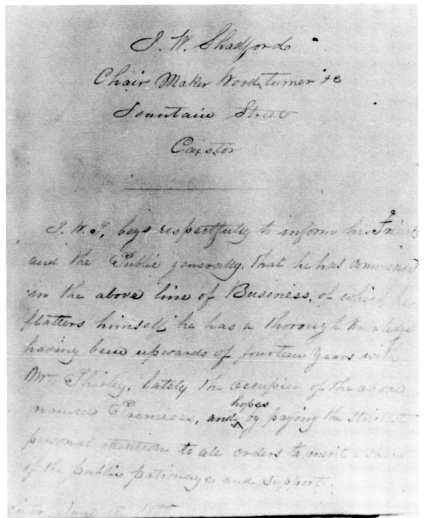

Figure NE171. A letter composed by John William Shadford in 1858, in which he proposes himself as an experienced chair maker in the employment of William Shirley, and who now wished to receive orders for chairs on becoming self-employed. (Courtesy Lincolnshire Archives Office)

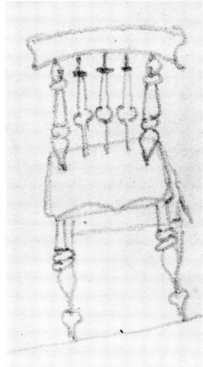

Figure NE173. Drawing of a 'Roman' side chair from the workshop notebook of John Shadford of Fountain Street, Caistor.

(Courtesy Lincolnshire Archives Office)

147

Figure NE174. Drawings from John Shadford's workshop notebook (fl.1843-89), illustrating children's chairs with stick back designs, food trays, foot rests, and a hole cut in the seat to hold a chamber pot. This style of chair was common to a number of North of England chair makers. See the William Brear (of Addingham near Leeds, Yorkshire) design shown in Figure NE420; also the child's high chair made by Hobbs of Newcastle illustrated in Figure NE432 for other examples.

(Courtesy Lincolnshire Archives Office)

Lincolnshire Rush Seated Chairs

Although the Lincolnshire chair making tradition was predominantly concerned with the manufacture of Windsor chairs, hearsay evidence has drawn attention to a Lincolnshire tradition which involved the production of rush seated ladder back chairs. Oral evidence has pointed to a long-standing chair turning trade in the small town of Spilsby, in North East Lincolnshire, which produced a range of ladder back chairs including one variant with square cornered cabriole front legs, a design which is unique within the English tradition. Documentary evidence from the eighteenth and nineteenth centuries extends the oral tradition and confirms that a flourishing and long-lived chair making tradition existed in Spilsby, as well as in the nearby towns of Louth and Alford.[33]

The chair makers working in these towns were largely members of a particular family dynasty, named Ashton, whose earliest known member, Samuel Ashton, was a chair maker in Louth in 1719, and is known to have continued in his trade until 1767. Male descendants continued to make chairs in an unbroken line until about 1890, with a number of related Ashtons making chairs at the same time in the nineteenth century. Other family members who married into the Ashton line were also, in some cases, chair makers, and although no name stamped rush seated chairs have been located to absolutely confirm the styles of chairs made by this extended family, it is clear that there was a rush seat chair making tradition from this area. This is confirmed since in about 1779 William Ashton, chair turner of Louth, left his entire stock-in-trade to his brother-in-law, Robert Green, in trust for his four young children. However, there is no evidence that these children took up the trade, and on his death, Robert Green left his tools and devices, as well as working stock, to his nephew, also Robert Green. His will, a section of which is reproduced in Figure NE175, stipulated that he wished to pass to his nephew 'wrought and unwrought timber', 'wood and planks' and 'rushes' as well as his 'chairs, wheels and turnery ware'. In so doing,

Figure NE175. Extract from the will of Robert Green, dated 1794, chair maker of Louth, Lincolnshire (1729-94), who married Ann Ashton, daughter of Samuel Ashton, chair maker of Louth (fl.1719-91). The will leaves tools, devices and stock in trade to Robert Green's nephew, also Robert Green. This list of chair maker's materials is important since in addition to 'wrought and unwrought timber', 'wood' and 'planks', Green also bequeathed 'rushes' and, in so doing, indicated that the chairs he made were rush seated and not Windsor chairs. Also included in the effects is 'turnery ware' which indicates that Green was a domestic turner, as well as a chair maker.

(Courtesy Lincolnshire Archives Office)

Figure NE176. Left: Ladder back side chair. Ash, c.1800-40. Found in a farm outhouse at Cadney, Lincolnshire. This chair has many regionally specific features including: back leg finial motif; upper front leg turnery motif typical of a group of Lincolnshire chairs (see Figures NE182 and 183); reduced foot turning size typical of other chairs in this group (see Figures NE202-204 for examples); front stretcher turning motif specific to many of this region's chairs (see Figures NE182 and 183 for other examples). Lower right side stretcher missing.

Right: Ladder back side chair. Ash, c.1800-40. Found in a closed church at Cadney, Lincolnshire. This chair has many regionally specific features including: back leg finial turnings; upper front leg turning device typical of a group of Lincolnshire chairs (see Figure NE178); square cornered cabriole legs; front rail turning motif specific to other chairs from this region (see Figures NE187 and 194 for other examples).

Note that the outline shapes of the ladders or splats in these two chairs are closely similar to each other.   *(Courtesy Cadney Churchwarden.)*

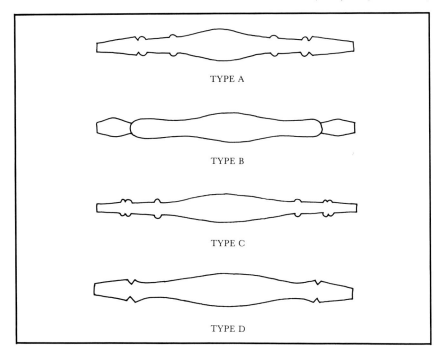

Figure NE177. Front stretcher turning motifs from Lincolnshire rush seated chairs.

Green's will confirmed that he was working in a rush seated chair making tradition.

Robert Green's marriage to a member of the Ashton family was not the only link to chair makers outside the immediate family, for Ann Ashton, daughter of Benjamin Ashton, a chair maker from Boston, married Edward Spikins of Boston around 1820,[34] and in so doing, linked the Ashton family to a further major dynasty of chair turners who had many family members working in the towns of Boston and Spalding throughout the nineteenth century (see Appendix for details). It is not certain that the Spikins family made rush seated chairs, but the evidence of the range of different groups of rush seated chair designs associated with Lincolnshire suggests that a number of different chair makers were probably involved in their production.

A number of characteristic turnery devices and other design features appear to interconnect the Lincolnshire rush seated chairs and the first two chairs shown in Figure NE176 display many of the characteristics associated, by hearsay, to the Spilsby/Louth/Alford makers. The right hand chair shows the pronounced regional feature of square cornered cabriole-shaped front legs, below a turned top section, and joined by a front stretcher which displays one of a small repertoire of specific turnings found in chairs attributed to Lincolnshire (see Figure NE177). This chair has stood in a church in Cadney, Lincolnshire, some thirty-five miles from Spilsby, for many years. Several features of this chair enable other chairs from this region to be identified by design association. These include the finial turning at the top of the back uprights, as well as the particular shape of the top front leg turnings which often, but not invariably, show an acutely angled turned section above a pear-shaped turning. This turnery feature is displayed in many of the region's chairs (see Figures NE179 and 183 for other examples). The turnery device used in the front stretcher of the left hand chair in Figure NE176 is also typical of those adopted in many of this region's chairs (see Figures NE182 and 183 for similar turnery forms). The reduced ankle and indented pad foot of the front legs of this chair is also common to some other chairs attributed to this region (see Figures NE202-204 for other examples). The

149

Plate 22. Ladder back side chair. Ash with rush seat. Lincolnshire, c.1800.

Plate 23. Ladder back side chair. Ash with painted rush seat. Lincolnshire, c.1780.

Plate 24. Ladder back armchair. Ash with rush seat. Lincolnshire, c.1800.

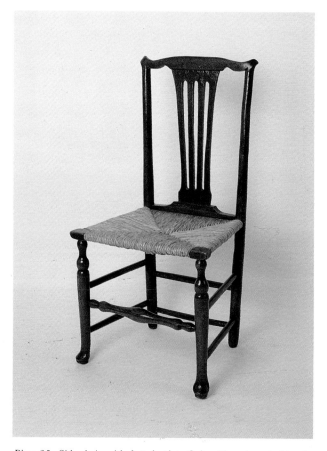

Plate 25. Side chair with fretted splat. Oak with rush seat. Lincolnshire, c.1780.

Plate 26. Comb back Windsor armchair. Elm and ash with black and gold painted decoration. Stamped 'I. TODD 1844'. This stamp refers to James Todd, chair maker, of Caistor, Lincolnshire (fl.1825-56).

Figure NE178. Side chair with vasiform splat. Ash. Attributed to Lincolnshire, c.1780-1820. This unusual style of splat back chair, with a yoke shaped stay rail, represents a rare type of Lincolnshire turned chair, which adopts rudimentary characteristics of some other English 18th century chairs in the inclusion of the solid splat and curved yoke rail. The decoratively turned back uprights show the wide graining pattern typical of segments turned from branches rather than cleft sections of wood. The square cornered cabriole front legs are typical of those attributed to the Spilsby area of Lincolnshire. The front stretcher turnery has parallels in other chairs associated with this region (see Figure NE182 for other examples).

Figure NE179. Side chair with vasiform splat. Maple with tulipwood splat. Attributed to Rhode Island, U.S.A., c.1780-1800. Painted with old brown paint. The design of this chair shows close similarities to the Lincolnshire made chair shown in Figure NE178.

(Courtesy Yale University Art Gallery, The Mabel Brady Garvan Collection)

Figure NE180. Side chair with vasiform splat. Ash. Attributed to Lincolnshire, c.1780-1820. This style of splat back chair with a yoke shaped stay rail represents a rare type of Lincolnshire turned chair where the inclusion of a solid splat and yoke shaped stay rail are reminiscent of 18th century classical chair design. Other design features of this chair are entirely congruent with the early 19th century Spilsby/Alford/Louth group of chairs, including the front stretcher turnery design (see Figure NE176), upper front leg turning devices (see Figure NE183) and straight back uprights terminating in tapered feet.

feature of the plain turned back legs, often terminating at the base in a tapered section, is also a common feature of the chairs in this group. Two plain-turned stretchers join the front to the back legs, and typically two plain stretchers join the back legs. This latter feature is relatively unusual in rush seated chairs, since one rear stretcher is common in other regional traditions.

Further, rare examples from this tradition are made with a plain, vasiform shaped, central splat held by a yoke-shaped crest rail. Examples of this design are illustrated in Figures NE178 and 180. Other designs show influences from classical design, and the example shown in Figure NE181 has a 'wheatsheaf' fretted splat, and a crest rail with terminal ear shapes. These examples are interesting variants and have close similarities with some turned chair

forms made in the American tradition. See an American chair of the plain splat style attributed to Rhode Island, Figure NE179, which has close similarities to the Lincolnshire made chair in Figure NE178. Both examples were made during the period 1790-1830. The possibility of design influences between Lincolnshire and the East Coast of America is strongly supported, since many emigrant movements took place from the North East Midlands, leaving from the port of Boston, during the seventeenth and eighteenth centuries.

This firm identification of some regional design characteristics allows further styles to be related to these first chairs by design association. Enlarging the group of Lincolnshire variants in this way has resulted in the inclusion of distinctly different styles of chairs within the regional group, including those which have

rails connecting the top of the back legs (see Figures NE203-218). These include examples which are decoratively shaped in a similar manner to their ladders (see Figure NE202), as well as those which have plain narrow stay rails and correspondingly plain ladders (see Figure NE206). Others have a thin rounded rail secured by prominent turned buttons to the back uprights (see Figures NE214 and 215). Some examples have parallel turned front legs (see Figure NE218), often with simple turned feet (see Figure NE207), which are less sophisticated in terms of turnery technique than the pad-shaped feet included in other Lincolnshire chairs and this may support the view that different chair makers were involved in their production who were implicitly linked by a common dialect of turnery devices.

Figure NE181. Side chair with fretted splat. Oak. Attributed to Lincolnshire, c.1780-1820. This unusual style of splat back chair represents a rare type of Lincolnshire turned chair where the inclusion of a fretted 'wheatsheaf' motif splat and stay rail are reminiscent of 18th century classical design influences. Other design features of this chair are congruent with ladder back chairs attributed to this region, including the front stretcher turning (see Figure NE177) which is also found in the chairs shown in Figures NE176 and 200.

Figure NE182. Ladder back side chair. Ash with rush seat. Attributed to Spilsby/Alford/ Louth, c.1800-80.

Straight back uprights with tapered feet, terminating in flattened top finials. Four ladders with lower indented shaping; square cornered cabriole front legs morticed into the seat frame and joined by a front stretcher showing regionally specific turnery style (see Figures NE183 and 189 for similar examples). Double plain turned side and rear stretchers.

Figure NE183. Ladder back side chair. Ash with rush seat. Attributed to Spilsby/Alford/ Louth, c.1800-80.

Straight back uprights with tapered feet, terminating in flattened top finials. Four ladders with lower indented shaping; tapered front legs terminating in a graceful pad foot; turned legs morticed into the seat frame and joined by a front stretcher showing regionally specific turnery style (see Figure NE182). Double plain turned side and rear stretchers.

Figure NE184. Ladder back side chair. Ash with rush seat. Attributed to Spilsby/Alford/ Louth, c.1800-80. Figure NE185 has a similar front stretcher.

Straight back uprights with tapered feet, terminating in flattened top finials; five ladders with lower indented shaping; square cornered cabriole shaped front legs morticed into the seat frame, joined by a front stretcher showing regionally specific turnery style. Double plain turned side and rear stretchers.

Figure NE185. Ladder back armchair. Ash with rush seat. Attributed to Spilsby/Alford/ Louth, Figure NE184 has a similar front stretcher.

Straight back uprights terminating in flattened top finials. Five ladders with lower indented shaping. Square cornered cabriole front legs continuing upwards to support the scroll shaped arms, and joined by a front stretcher showing regionally specific turnery style (see Figure NE184 for a similar example). Double plain turned side and rear stretchers.

Figure NE186. Ladder back armchair. Ash with rush seat. Attributed to Spilsby/Alford/ Louth, c.1800-80.

Straight back uprights terminating in flattened top finials. Four ladders with lower indented shaping. Square cornered cabriole front legs morticed into the seat frame and joined by a front stretcher showing regionally specific turnery style; separate arm supports morticed into seat rails and supporting scroll shaped arms. Double plain turned side and rear stretchers.

Figure NE187. Ladder back armchair. Ash with rush seat. Attributed to East Lincolnshire, c.1750-80. Slat or ladder back armchairs are recorded in the Pennsylvania, U.S.A. chair making tradition which incorporate the cabriole leg forms shown in this chair and suggests an awareness of design between these two traditions.

Straight back uprights terminating in flattened top finials. Five ladders with lower indentations. Cabriole shaped front legs, turned above to support the scroll shaped arms, and joined by a front stretcher showing regionally specific turnery style (see Figure NE177, type A). Double plain turned side and rear stretchers. (Collection John Boram)

Figure NE188. Slat back armchair. Probably Lancaster, Pennsylvania, U.S.A., c.1735-80. The style of cabriole leg adopted in this chair is closely similar to those shown in Figures NE178, 185 and 187 made in Lincolnshire.
(Collection Joseph Kindig III
Photograph courtesy Benno M. Forman)

Figure NE189. Ladder back armchair. Ash with rush seat. Attributed to Spilsby/Alford/Louth, c.1800-80. This armchair is the counterpart to the side chair shown in Figure NE183. The front stretcher shows regionally specific turnery style D, Figure NE177 (see Figures NE183 and 192 for similar examples).

Straight back uprights with tapered feet and flattened finials. Four ladders with lower indented shaping. Front legs turned with graceful pad feet and upper turning joining the arms, showing common regional turnery devices. Shaped arms square in section.

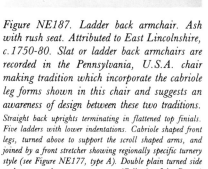

Figure NE190. Photograph of Mrs. Wilmott, aged 102 years, of Kirkby Laythorpe, some 35 miles from Spilsby, c.1890. The ladder back chair in which she sits shows the back leg finial turning typical of many of the Spilsby style chairs (see Figures NE183 and 189). The photograph dates from the late 19th century.
(Courtesy Wellholme Gallery, Grimsby)

154

Figure NE191. Ladder back nursing chair. Ash with rush seat. Attributed to Spilsby/Alford/ Louth, c.1800-80. This chair has a low seat and is fitted with rockers. In other respects it follows the pattern of design features common to this region, including the turnery of the front stretcher (see Figures NE184 and 185).

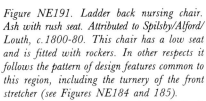

Straight back uprights with tapered feet, terminating in flattened top finials; four ladders with lower indented shaping; straight turned front legs morticed into the seat frame and joined to simple rockers. Double plain turned side and single rear stretchers.

Figure NE192. Ladder back side chair. Ash with rush seat. Attributed to Lincolnshire, c.1780-1820. This chair is larger than the related design made slightly later shown in Figure NE183. The front stretcher shows a specific regional turnery style similar to that in Figures NE176 and 182.

Straight back uprights terminating in flattened top finials. Four ladders with lower indented shaping. Turned front legs with worn feet and upper turning device of regional pattern. Front legs morticed into the seat frame.

Figure NE193. Ladder back side chair. Ash with rush seat. Attributed to Lincolnshire, c.1780-1820. This chair is similar in some respects to that shown in Figure NE192 and has pronounced regional design features including straight back uprights with tapered feet, terminating in finial turnings larger than those in Figure NE192 and similar to those in NE195. The front legs are morticed into the seat frame and end with graceful pad feet, but do not have the typical regional turnings at the top. The front stretcher is similar to Figure NE177, type A. Four ladders with lower indented shaping. Double plain turned side and rear stretchers.

Figure NE194. Ladder back side chair. Ash with rush seat. Attributed to Lincolnshire, c.1770-1820. The front stretcher has a regionally specific turnery style similar to that in Figure NE177, type B, and NE180.

Straight back uprights with tapered feet. Four plain ladders similar in shape to those shown in Figures NE199 and 196. Turned front legs with graceful pad feet and decoratively turned upper section. Legs morticed into the seat frame. Double plain turned side and rear stretchers.

Figure NE195. Ladder back side chair. Ash with rush seat. Attributed to Lincolnshire, c.1780-1820. The front stretcher has a regionally specific turnery motif similar to that in Figures NE177, type B, and NE194.

Straight back uprights with tapered feet, terminating in pronounced top finials similar to those shown in Figure NE193. Four ladders with lower indented shaping, turned front legs with pad feet morticed into the seat frame. Double plain turned side and rear stretchers.

155

Figure NE196. Ladder back armchair. Ash with rush seat. Attributed to Lincolnshire, c.1770-1820.

Straight back uprights joined by five plain ladders common to those in Figures NE197-199. Plain turned front legs morticed into the arms and joined by a front stretcher showing regionally specific turnery devices. (See Figure NE177, type D, and Figures NE198 and 199 for similar examples.) Double plain turned side and rear stretchers. Arm shape similar to that shown in Figure NE215.

Figure NE197. Ladder back armchair. Ash with rush seat. Attributed to Lincolnshire, c.1770-1820.

Straight back uprights; five plain ladders similar to those in Figures NE196 and 198. Plain turned front legs with simple turned feet, morticed into the arms and joined by a front stretcher showing regionally specific turnery type B, Figure NE177. (See Figures NE200 and 195 for similar examples.) Double plain turned side and single rear stretcher.

Figure NE198. Ladder back side chair. Ash with rush seat. Attributed to Lincolnshire, c.1770-1820.

Straight back uprights and pronounced finials similar to examples shown in Figures NE200 and 201. Five plain ladders similar to those in Figures NE196 and 197; plain turned front legs with simple turned foot and joined by a front stretcher showing regionally specific turnery type D, Figure NE177. (See Figures NE196 and 199 for similar examples.) Double plain turned side and single rear stretcher.

Figure NE199. Ladder back armchair. Ash with rush seat. Attributed to Lincolnshire, c.1770-1820.

Straight back uprights; four plain ladders similar to those in Figures NE197 and 198. Back uprights joined by a plain narrow stay rail. Plain turned front legs morticed into the arms and joined by a front stretcher showing regionally specific turnery type D, Figure NE177. (See Figures NE196 and 198 for similar examples.) Double plain turned side and single rear stretcher.

Figure NE200. Ladder back armchair. Ash with rush seat. Attributed to Lincolnshire, c.1770-1820.

Straight back uprights with pronounced finials similar to those in Figures NE201. Five ladders with lower indented shape similar to those in Figures NE189 and 191. Plain turned front legs with simple turned feet and decorative arm support turnings morticed into the arms and joined by a front stretcher showing regionally specific turnery type B, Figure NE177. (See Figures NE181 and 201 for similar examples.) Double plain turned side and single rear stretchers.

Figure NE201. Ladder back armchair. Ash with rush seat. Attributed to Lincolnshire, c.1770-1820.

Straight back uprights; six lower pointed ladders. Plain turned front legs morticed into the arms with lower arm rail connecting back and front legs. Legs joined by a front stretcher showing regionally specific turnery type B, Figure NE177. (See Figures NE181 and 200 for similar examples.) Double plain turned side and rear stretchers.

Figure NE202. Ladder back side chair. Ash with rush seat. Attributed to Lincolnshire, c.1780-1820.

Straight back uprights terminating in a decoratively shaped stay rail with similarly indented design to those shown in Figures NE203 and 204. Front legs morticed into the seat frame and joined by a front stretcher showing regionally specific turnery style. Reduced pad feet turnings. (See Figures NE203 and 204 for other examples.) Double plain turned side and single rear stretcher. One right hand side stretcher missing.

Figure NE203. Ladder back side chair. Ash with rush seat. Attributed to Lincolnshire, c.1780-1820.

Straight back uprights terminating in a plain narrow stay rail. Four ladders with lower indentations. Front legs morticed into the seat frame and joined by a front stretcher showing regionally specific turnery type D, Figure NE177. Reduced pad feet turnings. (See Figures NE202 and 204 for other examples.) Double plain turned side and rear stretchers.

Figure NE204. Ladder back side chair. Ash with rush seat. Attributed to Lincolnshire, c.1780-1820.

Straight back uprights terminating in a decoratively shaped stay rail with similar indented design to the four ladders. Front legs morticed into the seat frame and joined by a front stretcher showing regionally specific turnery type D, Figure NE177. Reduced pad feet turnings. (See Figures NE202 and 206 for other examples.) Double plain turned side and rear stretchers.

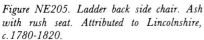

Figure NE205. Ladder back side chair. Ash with rush seat. Attributed to Lincolnshire, c.1780-1820.

Straight back uprights terminating in a decoratively shaped stay rail with similar indented design to the three ladders. Decoratively turned front legs morticed into the seat frame and joined by a front stretcher showing regionally specific turnery style. Double plain turned side and rear stretchers.

Figure NE206. Ladder back armchair and side chair of compatible style. Ash with rush seats. Attributed to Lincolnshire, c.1780-1820.

Armchair with straight back uprights terminating in a plain narrow stay rail with similar design to the four plain ladders as those shown in Figure NE208. Front legs morticed into the arms and joined by a front stretcher showing regionally specific turnery type C, Figure NE177. Reduced pad feet turnings. (See Figures NE202-204 for other examples.) Double plain turned side and rear stretchers. Side chair with straight back uprights terminating in a plain narrow stay rail with plain ladders similar to those shown in the accompanying armchair. Front legs morticed into the seat frame and joined by a front stretcher showing regionally specific turnery type D, Figure NE177. Double plain turned side and rear stretchers.

Figure NE207. Ladder back side chair. Ash with rush seat. Attributed to Lincolnshire, c.1780-1820.

Straight back uprights terminating in a plain narrow stay rail with plain ladders similar to those shown in Figures NE206-211. Plain front legs with simple feet turnings morticed into the seat frame and joined by two worn front stretchers showing regionally specific turnery style D, Figure NE177. Double plain turned side and rear stretchers.

Figure NE208. Ladder back armchair. Ash with rush seat. Attributed to Lincolnshire, c.1780-1820.

Straight back uprights terminating in a plain narrow stay rail with four plain ladders. (See Figures NE206 and 211 for other examples.) Front legs displaying three narrow ring turning with simple turned feet, morticed into the arms and joined by a front rail showing regionally specific turnery motif similar to style C, Figure NE177. Double plain turned side and rear stretchers.

Figure NE209. Ladder back side chair. Ash with rush seat. Attributed to Lincolnshire, c.1800-20.

Straight back uprights with tapered feet and terminating in a stay rail with plain ladders common to those shown in Figures NE206 and 211. Front legs morticed into the seat frame showing upper turnery device, similar to that shown in Figure NE183, and pad feet. Legs joined by a front stretcher showing regionally specific turnery style D, Figure NE177. Double plain turned side stretchers. One right hand side stretcher missing.

Figure NE210. Ladder back armchair. Ash with rush seat. Attributed to Lincolnshire, c.1780-1840. This chair is the counterpart of the side chair shown in Figure NE211.

Straight back uprights terminating in a plain narrow stay rail with four plain ladders. Front legs displaying indented 'ankle' and pad feet turning. Front stretcher showing regionally specific turnery motif similar to style C, Figure NE177. Double plain turned side and rear stretchers. Original rush seat with protective edge strips. Curved shaped arms and turned underarm supports.

Figure NE211. Ladder back side chair. Ash with rush seat. Attributed to Lincolnshire, c.1780-1820.

Straight back uprights with tapering feet terminating in a plain narrow shaped stay rail with four plain ladders similar to those shown in Figures NE206-210. Front legs morticed into the seat frame and joined by a front stretcher showing regionally specific turnery style similar to example C, Figure NE177. Reduced pad feet turnings. (See Figures 176 and 206 for other examples.) Double plain turned side and rear stretchers.

Figure NE212. Ladder back side chair. Ash with rush seat. Attributed to Lincolnshire, c.1770-1820. (See Figure NE216 for a further closely related chair design.)

Four domed ladders with downward shaping below. Back uprights with domed terminals. Turned front legs morticing into corners of seat frame, and waisted feet; legs connected by stretcher, type D, Figure NE177.

Figure NE213. Ladder back armchair. Fruit-wood with elm arms and rush seat. Attributed to South Lincolnshire, c.1800-40. The bell shaped turnery motif used in the front legs is a typical device found in many East Anglian turned chairs, and suggests a close regional affinity. (See Chapter 4, Figure EA63.)

Turned back uprights joined by a flattened curved stay rail fixed with prominent 'button' turnings. Three domed ladders with downward shaping below. Straight turned legs terminating in 'tulip' shaped feet joined by front stretcher type D, Figure NE177. Legs joined by double side and rear stretchers. Flat, shaped arms.

Figure NE214. Ladder back side chair. Fruit-wood with rush seat. Attributed to South Lincolnshire, c.1800-40. This side chair is closely affiliated to the armchair shown in Figure NE213.

Turned back uprights joined by a flattened curved stay rail fixed with prominent button turnings. Three plain domed ladders. Straight turned legs morticing into seat frame, terminating in tulip shaped feet, joined by front stretcher type D, Figure NE177, legs joined by double side and one rear stretcher.

Figure NE215. Child's high 'table' chair. Fruitwood with rush seat. Attributed to Lincolnshire, c.1800-40. The fretted flower motif is seen in Lincolnshire Windsor chairs (see Figures NE18 and 28).

Turned back uprights joined by a flattened curved stay rail fixed with prominent button turnings. Three domed ladders below with fretting, including a flower shaped motif. Straight turned legs, splayed outwards to give stability, terminating in tulip shaped feet, joined by front stretcher type D, Figure NE177. Legs joined by single side and rear stretchers. Curved foot rest joining front legs. Flattened shaped arms, square in section, and underarm turnings similar to those used in the Spilsby armchair illustrated in Figure NE189.

(Courtesy Jane Toller)

Figure NE216. Ladder back side chair. Ash with rush seat. Attributed to Lincolnshire, c.1770-1820. (See Figure NE212 for a closely related chair design.)

Four domed ladders with downward shaping below. Back uprights with domed terminals. Round turned front legs with 'waisted' feet and single ring turnery device, connected by a front stretcher showing turnery style D, Figure NE177.

Figure NE217. Ladder back side chair. Ash with rush seat. Attributed to Lincolnshire, c.1800-40. Chairs shown in Figures NE212 and 216 have similar feet turnings.

Straight back uprights terminating in vase shaped turnings, joined by a flattened cross rail, with three domed ladders below. Front legs morticed into seat frame and joined by two front rails showing regionally specific turnery style similar to type C, Figure NE177. Double plain turned side and rear stretchers.

Figure NE218. Ladder back armchair. Ash with rush seat. Attributed to Lincolnshire, c.1800-40. Flattened, shaped arms, square in section, and underarm turnings similar to those used in the Spilsby armchair illustrated in Figure NE189, indicating a close design affiliation.

Turned back uprights joined by a flattened curved stay rail fixed with prominent button turnings. Three plain domed ladders. Front legs joined by stretcher type D, Figure NE177. Legs joined by double side and rear stretchers.

NOTTINGHAMSHIRE

The second regional chair making tradition in the North East Midlands arose in the county of Nottinghamshire which adjoins Lincolnshire to the East. The county lies on grey lias limestone, and in addition to tracts of fine arable farmland, formerly contained the extensive hardwood forest of Sherwood. Other areas of the county have coalmining as a major industry. The chair making tradition which developed here was pre-eminently that of the Windsor chair, although here the trade developed in relatively fewer centres than in Lincolnshire.

The first recorded location for the Nottinghamshire trade was in Retford, and wills show that chair makers were working there from the middle of the eighteenth century.[35] Newark is the next centre to be recorded in 1805[36] with other traditions emerging in the second quarter of the nineteenth century in Worksop, Wellow and Ollerton,[37] as well as in the nearby hamlets of Rockley and Gamston.[38] The most persistent and major of these centres was Worksop, where the trade gradually came to be the predominant tradition of the county, and whose last working member continued working until the 1930s.[39] The bar charts shown in Figures NE220a-e indicate the large number of individual makers working in these centres and the chronology of their known working lives. Many of the workshop owners in Worksop and from the hamlets of Rockley and Gamston identified their work with their name stamps, and in so doing have created a firmly identified typology. However, apart from two provenanced examples of chairs made in Newark (see Figures NE274 and 276) no name stamped examples have been recorded from the other centres of chair making in this region.

The Nottinghamshire chair tradition appears to have been entirely

Figure NE219. A family portrait taken outside a terraced house in Worksop in the 1880s. This group typifies the artisan families in this region during the 19th century. The men wear traditional North Country dress: boots and heavy trousers, waistcoats, neck mufflers and caps. The women are wearing long dresses and the 'badges' of working class women, the pinafore and apron. The man to the right of the picture sits on a typical Worksop 'Office' chair. (See the I. Allsop & Son Trade card shown in Figure NE269 and 270.) A turned toy horse in the right hand corner of the picture illustrates one of the many domestic uses of the turner's craft.

(Courtesy Worksop Central Library)

Figure NE220. Mr Jack Kelk outside his workshop in Shelley Street, Worksop, which he rented from Garside's sawmills prior to 1900, and George Oates, Sawyers, until the 1930s. Kelk was the last Windsor chair maker working in Worksop, and had been an apprentice at Allsop's prior to their closure in 1887. He also made and repaired cricket bats. Kelk is seen with newly made cricket bats and yew Windsor chairs, as well as incomplete bats and those awaiting repair. In the foreground, bent chair hoops awaiting shaping are placed on a pile of yew branches.[40]

concerned with the production of Windsor chairs* which were generally structurally and aesthetically of the highest quality. Firmly identified chairs from this area were made from around 1820 until the end of the nineteenth century with some new designs of chairs being introduced into the repertoire after 1850.

Unlike the Lincolnshire chair making trade, no evidence exists of an early nineteenth century system of prototypes, although a few eighteenth century Windsor chair makers are known to have worked in Retford. It may be that Nottinghamshire regional chair designs originated there and were transmitted to other towns where they were developed, more or less simultaneously, by many makers

and where they continued to be made during the nineteenth century.

Ultimately, after 1850 the Nottinghamshire Windsor chair making trade declined in most centres and gradually became absorbed into the Worksop trade where it continued into the twentieth century.

Worksop

Contributory factors which enabled Worksop to become an important centre of the trade included the nearness to a relatively large railway dispatch centre from which chairs could quickly be supplied to towns in many parts of the country.** Nearby sources of wood must also have been attractive to the chair makers since Worksop was the centre for a number

of large sawmills whose owners felled hardwood timbers in nearby Sherwood

---

* A chair making trade of considerable size arose in the adjoining villages of Wellow and Ollerton between 1830 and 1845, employing 33 men at its peak in 1841.[41] Inexplicably, this trade died out in the 1850s and at least one of the major employers, John Goodwin Jnr., moved to work in Worksop by 1871 with his son. Interestingly, this maker was born in the chair making centre of High Wycombe, Buckinghamshire, and had moved to Wellow with his father, John senior, before 1830. Since the High Wycombe trade was predominantly that of Windsor chair making, it may be that the Goodwins had some knowledge of the trade, and adapted their skills to making local Windsor styles.

** The link with the railway and the chair trade is illustrated in the account of a latter-day chair maker. Mr A. Pearson, who recorded that in his employment with Bramer's chair making firm that 'Jack Prudence was varnisher and polisher, me and Bill Knowles also had all the chairs to wrap, legs, arms, and backs, with straw. They sent chairs all over the country. Great Central, Midland, Great Northern (railways) drays called for them.'[42]

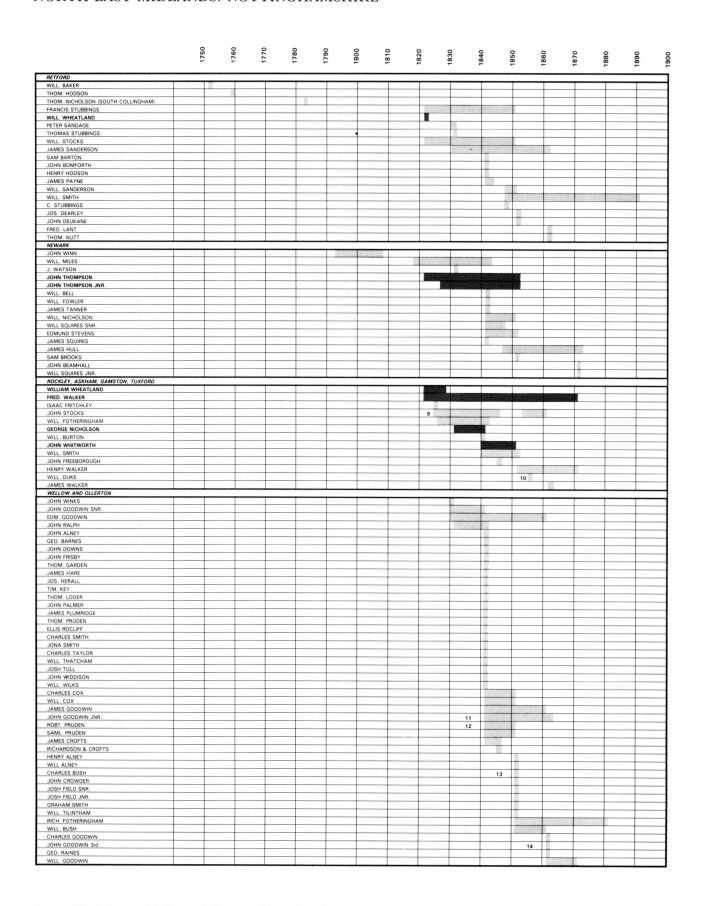

Figure NE221. Bar graph indicating the known working periods of the chair makers in the Nottinghamshire centres of Worksop, Retford, Newark, Rockley, Wellow and Ollerton, 1750-1900. Those makers whose names and working times are more heavily shaded are those for whom provenanced work has been identified.

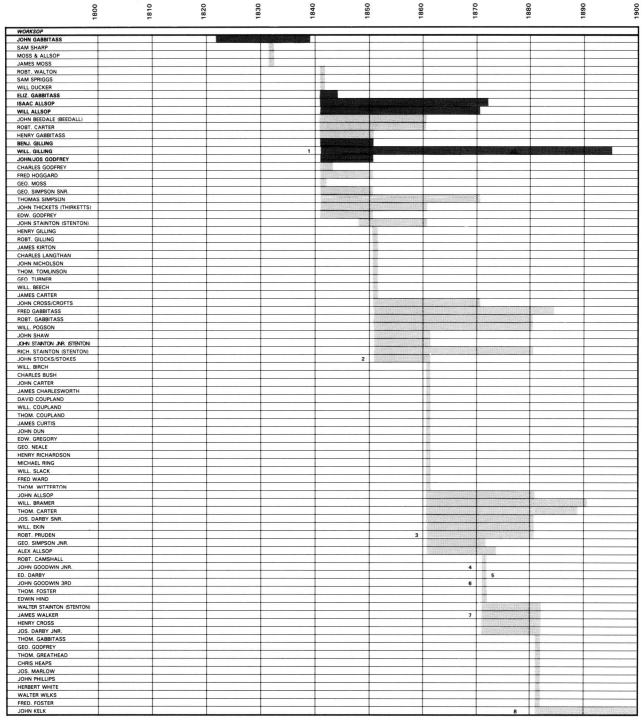

WORKSOP	1800	1810	1820	1830	1840	1850	1860	1870	1880	1890	1900
JOHN GABBITASS											
SAM SHARP											
MOSS & ALLSOP											
JAMES MOSS											
ROBT. WALTON											
SAM SPRIGGS											
WILL DUCKER											
ELIZ. GABBITASS											
ISAAC ALLSOP											
WILL ALLSOP											
JOHN BEEDALE (BEEDALL)											
ROBT. CARTER											
HENRY GABBITASS											
BENJ. GILLING											
WILL. GILLING				1							
JOHN/JOS GODFREY											
CHARLES GODFREY											
FRED HOGGARD											
GEO. MOSS											
GEO. SIMPSON SNR.											
THOMAS SIMPSON											
JOHN THICKETS (THIRKETTS)											
EDW. GODFREY											
JOHN STAINTON (STENTON)											
HENRY GILLING											
ROBT. GILLING											
JAMES KIRTON											
CHARLES LANGTHAN											
JOHN NICHOLSON											
THOM. TOMLINSON											
GEO. TURNER											
WILL. BEECH											
JAMES CARTER											
JOHN CROSS/CROFTS											
FRED GABBITASS											
ROBT. GABBITASS											
WILL. POGSON											
JOHN SHAW											
JOHN STAINTON JNR. (STENTON)											
RICH. STAINTON (STENTON)											
JOHN STOCKS/STOKES					2						
WILL. BIRCH											
CHARLES BUSH											
JOHN CARTER											
JAMES CHARLESWORTH											
DAVID COUPLAND											
WILL. COUPLAND											
THOM. COUPLAND											
JAMES CURTIS											
JOHN DUN											
EDW. GREGORY											
GEO. NEALE											
HENRY RICHARDSON											
MICHAEL RING											
WILL. SLACK											
FRED WARD											
THOM. WITTERTON											
JOHN ALLSOP											
WILL. BRAMER											
THOM. CARTER											
JOS. DARBY SNR.											
WILL. EKIN											
ROBT. PRUDEN						3					
GEO. SIMPSON JNR.											
ALEX ALLSOP											
ROBT. CAMSHALL											
JOHN GOODWIN JNR.								4			
ED. DARBY									5		
JOHN GOODWIN 3RD								6			
THOM. FOSTER											
EDWIN HIND											
WALTER STAINTON (STENTON)											
JAMES WALKER								7			
HENRY CROSS											
JOS. DARBY JNR.											
THOM. GABBITASS											
GEO. GODFREY											
THOM. GREATHEAD											
CHRIS HEAPS											
JOS. MARLOW											
JOHN PHILLIPS											
HERBERT WHITE											
WALTER WILKS											
FRED. FOSTER											
JOHN KELK									8		

1. NOT RECORDED AT WORKSOP BETWEEN 1841 AND 1881
2. FROM ROCKLEY
3. FROM WELLOW
4. FROM WELLOW
5. TO BRIGHOUSE, YORKS.
6. FROM WELLOW
7. FROM TUXFORD
8. DIED 1948
9. TO WORKSOP, c.1851
10. TO WORKSOP
11. TO WORKSOP, 1871
12. TO WORKSOP, 1861
13. TO WORKSOP, 1861
14. TO WORKSOP, 1871

Figure NE222. Aerial view of Godley and Golding's woodyard and sawmills in Worksop in 1930, showing the large stocks of wood awaiting conversion, and the steam rising from the engines housed in the rear building which powered machinery. The Windsor chair making firm of William Bramer were tenants of Godley and Golding, and rented 'space and power' in an upstairs room measuring some 56ft x 28ft. Here they produced chairs until 1887, when varnished Windsor chairs left over night to dry by a wood-burning stove, caused a fire which led to their being ejected from the building. The firm of Bramers then moved to Priory Mill, Worksop, a chair making factory where they worked until about 1912, when a further fire closed them down.[43]   (Courtesy D.H. Godley)

Forest and on large estates in Nottinghamshire,* and supplied many trades.[44] These large timber yards, founded at least as early as 1790,[45] gradually changed in the early nineteenth century from using pit saws to using steam powered engines and belt-driven machinery. The chair makers of the town were eventually also to adopt steam engines to power their saws and lathes, but this did not come about until the last quarter of the nineteenth century and, as late as 1874, the large Windsor chair making firm of I. Allsop & Son bought their timber in both plank and coppiced form from local wood merchants and largely relied on a specialist firm of local wood turners for turned parts.** The chair makers reserved their own

skills for making chair bottoms and bannister splats as well as shaping and bending the hooped parts, and sawing and shaping segments for the three-part arm found in the smoking high and office chairs. The most highly skilled craft was probably seen as that of morticing the correct angles and in assembling the well balanced chairs which are the hallmark of Worksop chairs.

Although coppice ash and elm for legs, hoops, underarm turnings, spindles and stretchers, and sawn planked elm for seats were the most common woods used by the chair makers, a survey of woods found in Worksop made chairs indicates that other woods were used, apparently on a random basis. These secondary

woods included alder and birch, and were used particularly for splats,

---

* A Worksop Windsor chair maker, Mr Joseph Darby, who had been apprenticed to his father, also Joseph Darby, at the firm of I. Allsop & Son in the 1870s, recalled in a local newspaper interview in 1936 that 'Sandbeck Park and Scratta Wood were prominent in the supply of raw materials.'[46]

** The list of devices and machinery at I. Allsop & Son's Chair Manufactory in 1876 indicates that the firm had only one wood turning lathe.[47] This firm, and possibly other chair makers in the town, appear to have preferred to buy their turned parts from a specialist firm of wood turners, owned by William Caudwell, who worked in Canal Street, close to Allsop's, and employed twenty-eight turners in 1871,[48] and forty in 1881.[49] It is recorded that by the early 1880s, Allsop's had a steam engine, and were producing their own turned parts on machine driven lathes.[50] This is reinforced in an interview in the *Worksop Guardian* in 1936 with Mr Joseph Darby, Junior, which quotes '...Premises at the rear of the site of the White Swan were in use in the early days and turning was done at Mr Caudwell's on the Canal Side. The firm of Allsop's eventually secured their own place for turning in premises alongside.'

Figure NE223. Priory Mill, Worksop, in the early 1900s. William Bramer set up his Windsor chair manufactory here after 1887 when he left rented premises at Godley and Golding's sawmill. Bramer's employed a group of men and boys here, and continued at Priory Mill as the last major producer of Windsor chairs in Worksop until 1912. (Courtesy M. Jackson)

and wild cherry available, and the price list for chairs in alternative woods given on I. Allsop & Son's trade card, 1871-87, indicates that chairs made of cherry were seen as superior to those made in ash and elm, but definitely inferior to chairs made in yew. Comparative prices show that smoking high chairs were priced at 18/- (90p) in yew, 14/- (70p) in cherry, and 13/- (65p) in elm. Yew was universally adopted by chair makers for use in their finest quality chairs and 'best' high chairs at 14/- each and best low at 13/- were only quoted in this wood [52] (see Figure NE269).

In these chairs the yew hoops for the back, arm, and crinoline stretcher were steamed and bent to shape after rough shaping of the branches, and planks of yew were converted to produce the legs, arm supports and spindles. The use of both sawn wood in making turned parts and branches in making hoops was a creative use of materials by the makers since it resulted in a distinctive variegation of colour with the yellow outer sapwood typically bordering the rich, dark colour of the heartwood. In time, yew typically darkens to a rich red-brown colour which has a particularly attractive warmth and lustre.

underarm supports and spindle turnings. Elm and ash for turned parts and hoops were used about equally, and a combination of an elm arm hoop and an ash top hoop is not uncommon in Worksop chairs. It is interesting to note, however, that a list of the timbers in I. Allsop & Son's well stocked wood yard in 1876,[51] included elm, yew, cherry and walnut only; no ash or minority timbers were recorded.

The sawyers' access to ornamentally grown timbers on estates made yew

The Worksop chair makers usually

Figure NE224. Apprenticeship indenture, witnessed on 2 August 1830, between John and Edmund Goodwin, Chair-Masters of Wellow near Worksop, Nottinghamshire, and John Winks. This document itemises three stages of apprenticeship training including turnery, bench-work and framing, to be undertaken for various periods of time over a four year period. For such work the apprentice was to receive 6/- (30p) per week for the first year, and after that, he would receive half of a journeyman's wages for the work he did. (Courtesy Roy Wells)

165

Figure NE225. A pair of small 'dresser' stools, c.1850-80. Attributed to Worksop. Height 5½ in. (14cm), top 6¼ in. (16cm) x 4¾ in. (12cm). Yew legs, elm tops with highly figured grain, and concave shaped edges and corners. These stools were probably produced by the chair makers for use in their homes, and not as generally saleable items. Their intended purpose was to stand on a dresser or sideboard, perhaps to display pottery, a use unique to the region.

Figure NE226. A small dresser stool, 'scratch' dated underneath the top '1792'. Attributed to Worksop. Height 6¾ in. (17cm), top 9¼ in. (23.5cm) x 6¼ in. (16cm). Unusually, made entirely in yew with ornately turned legs, chamfered edge to top and turned roundel in its centre.

bought their wood from the local wood merchants, storing it adjacent to their workshops,* or they rented space in sawyers' buildings to carry on their craft in close proximity to the raw material. For example, the last of the Worksop chair makers, John Kelk, first worked in wooden premises owned by the Garside sawmills in Lister's Yard off Kilton Street which was taken over by George Oates, Sawyer, in 1900. John Kelk was one of the last apprentices trained by I. Allsop & Son before their closure in 1887.[53] In addition to being a chair maker, he also made cricket bats. Kelk carried on his trade from the end of the nineteenth century until the 1930s and the photograph taken in 1929 shown in Figure NE221 shows Kelk with completed low back Windsors and cricket bats outside his workshop in Shelley Street, with bent hoop segments and yew coppice poles in the foreground.[54]

A further Worksop chair making enterprise, the firm of William Bramer's, rented an upstairs workshop at Godley and Golding's sawmill, measuring some 56ft. by 28ft. in which they are reported to have produced some fifty to sixty chairs a week.[55] A photograph of this sawmill, taken in 1930, is shown in Figure NE222; the chair workshop was to the rear of the timber yard.

This association of chair workshops

and sawmills was fraught with difficulties; the chair making trade in general suffered from periodic fires in premises where varnished chairs were carelessly left to dry overnight around woodburning stoves. William Bramer's were forced to leave their workshop after such a fire, as the last owner of Godley and Golding's sawmills, Mr D.H. Godley describes: 'I was in the timber trade and dealt with many of the chair makers. One of them, Bramer's, were let space and power in a room over our sawmill until 1887 when a fire destroyed the lot and my grandfather blamed them for their habit of drying the varnish round a big fire at night and cleared them out.'[56]

On leaving the premises of Godley and Golding, William Bramer's moved to other premises at Priory Mill, Worksop (see Figure NE223). These premises offered both water and steam power which could be employed to power lathes and saws. Records show that this was a highly productive business with William Bramer employing six men and three boys in 1881.[57] Unfortunately for Bramer's, there was a fire at the new premises and, as a result, the firm finally gave up chair making in about 1912.[58]

The Windsor trade in Worksop was highly productive, with demand for its durable and comfortable

products coming from many parts of the Midlands and the North of England. However, the saleability of their products did not ensure great wealth for the excellent craftsmen who made them, as is evidenced by the sale of the stock-in-trade of one of the most productive of the Worksop firms, I. Allsop & Son in 1876 on the death of Alexander (Allick) Hill Allsop. The Allsops worked in mortgaged premises and the total revenue from the sale amounted to only £430.10.2d.[59] (See the detailed description on pp.174-178). A tradesman at his peak earnings received only eightpence (3p) an hour in 1902 and apprentices taking up the trade for four years of training could expect to earn even lower wages. Although no records of Worksop chair making apprentices have been found, the evidence of the indenture of a chair making apprentice from Wellow, some twelve miles from Worksop, indicates the lowly pay rates which a person entering the trade earned in 1830.[60] This document, shown in Figure NE224, which was a contract between chair makers John and Edmund Goodwin, and an apprentice named Thomas Winks,

---

* For example, the wood yard of I. Allsop & Son was opposite to their Windsor chair manufactory which was adjacent to the White Swan public house at Cheapside, Worksop. Here, in 1876[61] a large amount of planked timbers, including yew, elm, cherry and walnut was stored, as well as coppice elm poles and yew branches.

Figure NE227. Examples of small scale Windsor chairs produced in Worksop, c.1840-90. Left: height 6in. (15cm), width 3½in. (9cm), depth 3¾in. (9.25cm). Right: height 6¼in. (16cm), width 6in. (15.25cm), depth 3¾ (9.25cm). The chairs are made entirely in yew. The side chair is a replica of the Worksop 'Roman' chair, and the armchair is an 'Office' chair. See the Allsop trade card, Figure NE270. These attractive miniatures were probably made as household ornaments or as apprentice pieces, and were not intended for sale. (Collection B. Morley)

Figure NE228. An example of a miniature Windsor chair, produced in Worksop, c.1850-80. Height 10¾in. (27cm), width 5¼in. (14cm). Made in yew with an unusual turned back spindle replacing the typical fretted splat of Worksop chairs. The arm turnings are particularly characteristic of Worksop made chairs. The hoop segments are extremely small, and much skill must have been involved in their bending. (Courtesy John Dench Antiques)

indicates that in his first year of training, the apprentice would receive six shillings weekly. This would perhaps represent one (old) penny an hour for a sixty hour working week. The trainee would then receive half the journeyman's wage for work done during the subsequent three years of his apprenticeship. In return, the apprentice was offered a comprehensive training at his trade, and the stages of training which the apprentice was to undertake illustrates the hierarchy of skills of which the craft was composed. These include three separate 'branches' of the trade, within each of which the apprentice spent different periods of instruction.

During the first two years, the 'turning' branch of the trade was taught. This indicates that turning was seen as a trade requiring relatively long training, and that unlike the practice in the nearby Worksop trade, turning of parts was undertaken by the Wellow chair makers. The next eighteen months of training was spent at the 'bench' branch of the work. This would have principally involved the fretting of decoratively pierced splats, as well as steaming and bending 'hooped' parts. The final six months training was to be spent at 'the art of framing'. The phrasing of the last part of the training

process clearly indicates that assembling chairs was seen as sufficiently complex to be considered an 'art' form, and probably indicates that the skilled process of boring different angles of mortice to receive legs, stretchers, and back spindles, as well as the ultimate assembling was seen as the most skilled task. Making the seats or 'bottoming' is not specifically mentioned, and it is not clear at which point this skill was taught.

The continuity of the chair making trade in Worksop says much about the entrepreneurial and craft skills of the workshop owners and their employees, for the trade was consistently productive over a sixty year period.* The ultimate decline of the industry coincided with greater competition from mass produced Windsor chairs. This competition came particularly from the Leeds and Sheffield areas of Yorkshire and Addingham, near Leeds, during the last twenty years of the nineteenth century, where previously the Windsor chair making trade had been relatively undeveloped. The mass produced chairs from these centres have the essential features of North Country Windsors, including the production of both high and low back varieties, and are characterised by a general heaviness of design, the use of alder in many of the seats, the typical use

of the H-form stretcher, and broad fleur-de-lis and fir tree fretted design back splats. These highly standardised chairs were sold widely in Yorkshire, often through the agency of household furnishing stores, and were also hired out for social gatherings. Examples of these chair styles with trade labels are shown in Figures NE386-390. The late development of the Yorkshire Windsor trade did, no doubt, have a severe effect on the viability of the Nottinghamshire trade which would have relied to a large degree on retailing outlets in other Northern centres, as the trade customers from Yorkshire towns and cities named in the list of creditors at the sale of assets of I. Allsop & Son of Worksop, in 1876 illustrates.[62]

* The trade reached its peak in 1851, when thirty-two chair makers were engaged in the trade, and by the 1870s the trade was declining slightly in numbers with twenty-two chair makers working. This number of chair makers remained static until the beginning of the 20th century when the trade went into rapid decline. At this time, one manufacturer remained, the firm of William Bramer's, who continued to make chairs at Priory Mill until about 1912 when a fire caused the closing of their business. John Kelk continued as the last of the Worksop makers in his workshop at Lister's Yard, until his death in the 1930s.

The manufacture of other styles of mass produced chairs in Yorkshire, particularly the simple kitchen varieties, would also have reduced sales for the superior Windsors made in Worksop, and gradually the viability of the trade seems to have diminished. However, the demise of the Nottinghamshire Windsor craft was probably the result of a number of influences and events which corporately undermined the continuance of the trade, rather than one overwhelming reason being responsible. For example, one major firm, that of I. Allsop and Son, ultimately failed to create enough wealth, under the management of the late Alexander Allsop's wife and her husband, to replace worn out machinery.[63] Another chair maker failed to recruit his sons to the trade to ensure continuance* and as mentioned above, a fire put the firm of Bramer's out of business.[64]

The concentration of chair makers and wood turners in Worksop also resulted in the production of a range of small turned items which were familiar to the townspeople, but which were probably not intended for sale outside the area. Amongst these items were many variations of miniature four-legged stools which were sometimes made with roundel turnings and with shaped edges to the top. These were usually made in the same woods as Windsor chairs, with elm tops and yew legs, although those made entirely in yew, as well as plainer stools in elm with ash legs, were also made (see Figures NE225 and 226). The use to which these stools were put was unusual; they were intended to be either purely ornamental or to stand on a dresser or sideboard to display a prized piece of pottery. This use appears to be unique to the Worksop region. Small and miniature Windsor chairs were also made, and provide fascinating examples of the dexterity of the craftsmen (see Figures NE227 and 228) and were probably intended as ornaments for the chair makers' homes.

The Gabbitass Family of Chair Makers

Records show that the Worksop Windsor chair making trade began to develop in the first quarter of the nineteenth century and between 1820 and 1841, about twenty Windsor chair makers came into the trade. Amongst these were craftsmen who were to form family dynasties of

Figure NE229. Low decorative splat back Windsor armchair. Yew with elm seat. Branded underneath the seat, 'J. GABBITASS' (fl.1822-39). This chair is an example of the most elaborate and decorative form of Windsor produced in the Nottinghamshire tradition, and was probably the most expensive. Other similar examples of the same general style are shown in Figures NE240, 250 and 255.

Single ring turned legs with elongated bell shaped turning below, leading to ball shaped feet; legs connected by crinoline stretcher. Four tapered spindles either side of central back splat. Three tapered underarm spindles with regional style of turned underarm support on left hand side, right hand arm support replaced. Arm bow terminating in notches on under surface. Elaborately fretted top and lower splats.

(Courtesy T. Crispin)

Figure NE230. Stamp of John Gabbitass of Worksop (fl.1822-39), branded underneath the seat of chair shown in Figure NE229. This maker came from Retford and was the first member of the Worksop chair making trade to be recorded, and may have the distinction of being the originator of the trade in this town.

Figure NE231. Low splat back Windsor armchair. Yew with elm seat. Stamped on side edge of seat, 'E. GABBITASS WORKSOP' (1839-44).

Three ring turned legs with vase feet connected by crinoline stretcher. Three long tapered spindles either side of central back splat. Three tapered underarm spindles with regional style of turned underarm support. Stylised fleur-de-lis fretted top splat with two extra piercings. Two shaped frets in lower splat.

Figure NE232. Stamp of Elizabeth Gabbitass of Eastgate, Worksop (fl.1839-44), impressed on side seat edge of chair shown in Figure NE231. The widow of John Gabbitass, Elizabeth, carried on the business until her death in the 1840s,[66] when Henry, younger brother of John Gabbitass, carried on the business employing a large workforce until the 1850s.[67] The firm continued after this point under the ownership of Frederick and Robert Gabbitass until the 1880s.[68]

Windsor chair makers, including members of the Gabbitass, Gilling, Godfrey and Allsop families. These makers employed other craftsmen, and raised substantial businesses making a range of high quality Windsors, both arm and side chairs, in yew and cherry as well as in ash and elm.

The first recorded chair maker working in Worksop was John Gabbitass who, in 1822, worked 'on the common' on the edge of the town.[65] It is possible that this maker

was the first member of the trade in Worksop and that he and his younger brother, Henry, also a chair maker who probably worked for John, brought knowledge of local chair making skills and designs with them from Retford.[69] Few chairs carrying the name of John or Henry Gabbitass have been recorded. However, an example branded J. Gabbitass beneath

---

* For example, the last owner of the Gabbitass firm of Windsor chair makers, Robert Gabbitass, had six sons. All of these failed to enter the trade, and five of them became coal miners in local collieries.[70]

Figure NE233. Low splat back Windsor armchair. Ash with elm seat and fruitwood splats. Stamped on side edge of seat 'E. GABBITASS WORKSOP.' (fl.1839-44).

Three ring turned legs with vase feet connected by crinoline stretcher. Three long tapered spindles either side of central back splat. Three tapered underarm spindles with regional style of turned underarm support. Stylised fleur-de-lis fretted top splat. Keyhole shaped fret in lower splat.

Figure NE235. High splat back Windsor armchair. Ash with elm seat, arm hoop, under-arm supports, splats and legs. Stamped on side edge of seat, 'E. GABBITASS WORKSOP.'

Three ring turned legs with vase shaped feet connected by crinoline stretcher. Three long tapered spindles either side of central back splat. Three tapered underarm spindles with regional style of turned underarm support. Stylised fleur-de-lis fretted top splat. Keyhole shaped fret in lower splat.

Figure NE237. Windsor side chair. Yew with elm seat, stamped 'E. GABBITASS WORKSOP' on side edge of seat. Nottinghamshire (fl.1839-44). This chair is virtually identical to that recorded with the maker's stamp of James Marsh of Sleaford (Lincolnshire) shown in Figure NE50 and it may be that chairs of this type were purchased from the Lincolnshire makers and sold under the name of Worksop manufacturers.

Heavily turned three ring legs with vase feet, connected by crinoline stretcher. Three tapered spindles either side of central back splat. Stylised fleur-de-lis fretted splat with two shaped frets below.   *(Courtesy M. Legg Antiques)*

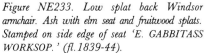

Figure NE234. Stamp of Elizabeth Gabbitass of Worksop (fl.1839-44), impressed on the side seat of chair shown in Figure NE233.

Figure NE236. Stamp of Elizabeth Gabbitass of Worksop (fl.1839-44), impressed on the side seat edge of the chair shown in Figure NE235.

Figure NE238. The stamp of Elizabeth Gabbitass of Worksop (fl.1839-44), widow of John Gabbitass. This mark is impressed on the side seat edge of the chair in Figure NE237.

the seat is shown in Figure NE229. It is elaborately made in yew of the best regional quality.

On the death of John Gabbitass in 1839,[71] his business passed to his wife, Elizabeth, who carried on as proprietress until her death in the 1840s.* Henry Gabbitass then carried on the business as a master chair maker employing a large work force including his nephew, Frederick and his son Robert, as well as nine men, three boys and three apprentices. After Henry's death in the 1850s, the business passed to Frederick and Robert who continued the business until the 1880s. The chair making trade at this point was in serious decline and no further members of the family joined the business, which closed on the retirement of Robert from the trade.

Figure NE239. High decorative splat back Windsor armchair. Yew with elm seat. Attributed to Nottinghamshire, c.1820-80. Leg turnings peculiar to the Worksop region. This style of chair, although not stamped, is entirely congruent with other identified Worksop made chairs. See Figures NE229, 250 and 255.

Single ring turned legs with elongated bell shaped turning leading to ball feet, connected by crinoline stretcher. Four long tapered spindles either side of central back splat. Three tapered underarm spindles with regional style of turned underarm support. Elaborately fretted top and lower splats.

---

* After the death of John Gabbitass, only Elizabeth appears to have identified her chairs with the family name stamp, and many examples bearing her stamp have been recorded. Given the short period of her ownership, and the large number of recorded chairs stamped with her name, it may be that under Henry's, and later Frederick and Robert's owner-ship, the business continued to use her stamp.

Figure NE240. Low decorative splat back Windsor armchair. Yew with elm seat, ash back legs and crinoline stretcher. Pasted paper label underneath the seat of 'Benjamin Gilling. Windsor chair maker. Worksop.' (fl.1841-51).

Three ring heavily turned legs more reminiscent of the Yorkshire tradition, with vase shaped feet, connected by crinoline stretcher. Three long tapered spindles either side of central back splat. Three tapered underarm spindles, turned underarm supports in a style peculiar to this maker. Decoratively fretted top and lower splats in a simplified form of the Nottinghamshire elaborately fretted splat. *(Courtesy C. Gilbert)*

Figure NE242. Windsor side chair. Yew with elm seat of typical Lincolnshire design. Paper label of Benjamin Gilling of Worksop (fl.1841-51), pasted beneath the seat. This chair is virtually identical to a chair recorded with the maker's stamp of James Marsh of Sleaford, Lincolnshire, shown in Figure NE50.

Heavily turned three ring legs with vase shaped feet, connected by crinoline stretcher. Three tapered spindles either side of central back splat. Stylised fleur-de-lis fretted splat with keyhole shaped fret below.

Figure NE244. Best high smoking chair. Yew with elm seat. Made by William Gilling of Bridge Place, Worksop, c.1860-90. Paper identification label fixed underneath the seat.

Elaborately turned legs with cup and vase shaped feet. H-stretcher with two cross stretchers with central ball motif. Four turned spindles either side of central fir tree fretted splat above the arms, two turned spindles either side of central fir tree motif fretted splat below the arms and turned underarm supports. *(Courtesy Wingetts)*

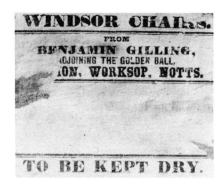  

Figure NE241. Paper label of Benjamin Gilling (fl.1841-51), affixed under the seat of the chair shown in Figure NE240. This maker came to Worksop in about 1841 from Yorkshire.[72] By 1851 he had become a chair master at premises adjoining the Golden Ball public house employing six men.[73] Unaccountably, he is last recorded in Worksop aged 33 in 1851. Possibly he left with two other younger relatives to join William Gilling in the U.S.A.

Figure NE243. Trade label of Benjamin Gilling of the Golden Ball, Worksop (fl.1841-51), affixed under the seat of the chair shown in Figure NE242.

Figure NE245. Trade label of William Gilling (fl.1841-98), of Worksop, Nottinghamshire, affixed to the underneath of the seat of the high smoking chair shown in Figure NE244. This maker had left Worksop at some time between 1841 and 1851 to work in America, and on his return in the 1860s, set up a cabinet and chair making business which continued into the 20th century. The chair label shows the styles which were made by William Gilling, and these are similar to those shown on the Allsop trade card, Figure NE270. The faded writing on the label reads: 'Mr. J. Bingham, Bury Station, Lancashire. 5 chairs. March 4th. Carriage Paid.'

The Gilling Family

Of the many other Windsor chair makers to be attracted to Worksop between 1823 and 1841, Benjamin Gilling was to establish himself as a significant workshop owner employing other chair makers. In 1841, at the age of twenty, Benjamin, who was born in Yorkshire, had come to live in Carlton Road and was probably employed in the chair making trade.[74] Benjamin's relation, William Gilling who was aged twenty-four in 1841, also worked in Worksop as a cabinet maker, having been apprenticed to John Wright of the White Hart Yard.[75] At some time between 1841 and 1851 William left for the U.S.A., returning in the early 1860s[76] with his two sons, Charles and Frederick, who were born in Buffalo Falls, Ohio, U.S.A.[77] Benjamin, who had remained in Worksop, prospered, and by 1851 was described as a chair master with premises adjoining the Golden Ball public house and employing six men.[78] Unaccountably, Benjamin appears to have given up his business after 1851 when it was flourishing. Two other Gillings, Robert and Henry, aged twenty-seven and eighteen respectively, both chair makers, also left the Worksop trade at about this time. Whether William was joined by one or more of these relatives in the U.S.A. and whether they made Windsor chairs there is not known.

On his return to Worksop, after an absence of some years, William Gilling re-entered the cabinet making trade in which he had been trained, and ultimately raised a substantial chair making business which, in 1881, employed thirteen men and two boys, including his two sons.[79] The chair making business continued until 1898, when William died, and thereafter the business continued as a general builders and cabinet makers manufacturing some Windsor chairs.[80]

Of the two distinct phases of the Gillings' business, provenanced chairs from both the first and later periods have been recorded with paper labels pasted underneath their seats (see Figures NE240-245). These labels show Benjamin Gilling as a maker of Windsor chairs adjoining the 'Golden Ball' at the Common, Worksop, Notts. A space below the title was left for the customer's address to be added.

Of the two chairs so labelled, a low back and a Windsor side chair, several distinctive features in their design differentiate them from those

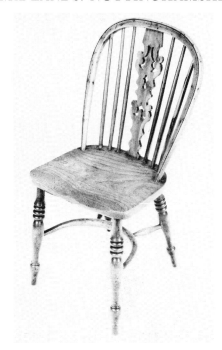

Figure NE246. Windsor side chair. Yew with elm seat of typical Lincolnshire shape, c.1840-60. The scribe mark on the hoop is typical of that found on Worksop smoking high chairs, and the hoop would be interchangeable with that found on a smoking high chair. The splat is fretted in the manner of the Benjamin Gilling chair shown in NE240.

Heavily turned three ring legs with vase shaped feet, connected by crinoline stretcher. Three long slightly elliptical back spindles either side of the central fretted back splat.

Figure NE247. High splat back Windsor armchair. Yew with elm seat. Attributed to Worksop, c.1840-60. The underarm turning style and the upper and lower decorative splat fretting are similar in design to those shown in the Benjamin Gilling chair in Figure NE240.

Heavy three ring turned legs with vase shaped feet, connected by a crinoline stretcher. Four long tapered spindles either side of central back splat. Three tapered underarm spindles and turned underarm supports.

of other identified Worksop makers. Amongst these are the use of very heavily turned three ring legs, more typical of Yorkshire Windsors than those made in Nottinghamshire, and also the use of seat shapes typical of those found in Lincolnshire Windsor chairs. The decorative splat design, shown in the low Windsor chair in Figure NE240 is unlike any other chair recorded from Worksop. These two features are combined with a distinctive underarm turning design which is also unlike typical Worksop styles, and may indicate that Benjamin's origin in Yorkshire resulted in an importation of design characteristics which were incorporated into the local tradition. These features are found in a number of other Windsors which do not carry identifying makers' labels and which may therefore be associated with the Gilling chair shown in Figure NE240. These chairs are shown in Figures NE246-249.

The second chair, shown in Figure NE242, which carries Benjamin Gilling's label, is a side chair made of yew with a fleur-de-lis splat, heavy

three ring turned legs and a crinoline stretcher. This chair style appears to have been a rare design in the Worksop tradition. Similar chair styles were, however, made in Lincolnshire and an example made by Marsh of Sleaford is shown in Figure NE50 and may indicate that Gilling imported chairs from Sleaford and affixed his own label to them.

A chair made by William Gilling in the later period of chair making, c.1860-80, is shown in Figure NE244. This high smoking chair is made in yew with an elm seat, a style made by other Worksop makers during the second half of the nineteenth century. This chair has a label fixed to the underneath of the seat, Figure NE245, which illustrates other chairs made by this maker, including the office or smoker's bow chair, a best low chair, and a Grecian side chair, below which is the text, 'From William Gilling, Bridge Place, Worksop, Notts.'. The purpose of this label was clearly both to advertise this maker's products, as well as to give instructions for the delivery of the chair, and faded writing below reads: 'Mr. J. Bingham, Bury Station, Lancashire. 5 chairs. March 4th. Carriage paid.' The illustrated chairs on this label show that William Gilling was producing a similar repertoire of designs to I. Allsop & Sons, another major manufacturer in Worksop, who showed similar designs on their trade card illustrated in Figure NE270. These designs also indicate that by the 1880s, William Gilling was producing a different range of chair designs from those made by Benjamin Gilling in the first half of the nineteenth century.

Figure NE248. High splat back Windsor armchair. Yew with elm seat. Attributed to Worksop, c.1840-60. The underarm turning style and upper and lower decorative splat fretting are similar in design to those shown in the Benjamin Gilling chair in Figure NE240.
Heavy three ring turned legs with vase shaped feet especially turned to fit rockers. Legs connected by a crinoline stretcher. Four long tapered spindles either side of central back splat. Four tapered underarm spindles and turned underarm supports.

Figure NE249. Medium height decorative splat back Windsor armchair. Yew with elm seat. Attributed to Worksop, c.1840-60. The underarm turning style and upper and lower decorative splat frettings are similar in design to those shown in the Benjamin Gilling chair in Figure NE240.
Heavy double ring turned legs terminating in ball feet, legs connected by crinoline stretcher. Three long tapered spindles either side of central back splat. Three tapered underarm spindles with turned arm supports. Arm bow terminating in notches on under surface.

The Godfrey and Darby Families

A further chair maker, Joseph Godfrey, who name stamped his chairs, had moved to Worksop by 1841 to work in the developing Windsor chair making trade. Godfrey was born in about 1797 in the small parish of Gamston,[81] a few miles from Worksop, and it was here that he and a contemporary, John Whitworth, probably received instruction in Windsor chair making from William Wheatland who came to live and work there in about 1822.[82] Their instruction may have continued at Rockley, some half a mile from their homes. Here William Wheatland, Frederick Walker, John Stocks (Stokes) and Isaac Fritchley were working in Wheatland's newly established workshop.[83] Both Wheatland[84] and Stocks[85] had come here from Retford to establish their craft, and their movement serves to reinforce the belief that the Nottinghamshire Windsor designs may have originated in Retford before being transferred by makers moving to other centres.

Joseph Godfrey, however, moved to Worksop at some time between 1823 and 1841 where he worked at Eastgate[86] and may have worked with, or for, the first of the recorded Worksop chair makers, John and Henry Gabbitass, who also worked in Eastgate.[87] However, by 1841 a relative of Joseph Godfrey, Charles Godfrey aged twenty-five years, was also working in Eastgate as a chair maker and may have been employed by Joseph.[88] A further relative, Edward Godfrey, moved from Scrooby in Lincolnshire, where he had been a chair maker, to work with his relatives.[89] In 1851, Joseph Godfrey

Figure NE250. High decorative splat Windsor armchair. Yew with elm seat. Stamped 'J. GODFREY MAKER WORKSOP.' twice on side edge of seat (fl.1841-51). The turning of the legs is typical of the region (see Figures NE229 and 300).
Four long tapered spindles either side of central decorative splat. Three tapered underarm spindles (one of left hand set missing). Underarm supports replaced. Single ring turned legs with elongated bell shaped turning below. Feet missing. Legs connected by crinoline stretcher. Elaborately fretted upper and lower splats; lower splat damaged.

Figure NE251. Stamps of Joseph Godfrey of Worksop (fl.1841-51), impressed on the side edge of the chair seat in Figure NE250. Godfrey was born about 1797 at Gamston near Rockley, Nottinghamshire, and was a contemporary of John Whitworth, also a chair maker of that hamlet. He probably received instruction in Windsor chair making from William Wheatland who came to live in Gamston in 1822. Godfrey moved to Worksop between 1823 and 1841, and ultimately set up his own workshop in Eastgate.

Figure NE252. Low splat back Windsor armchair. Yew with elm seat, stamped on side edge of seat, 'J. GODFREY MAKER WORKSOP'.

Three ring turned legs with vase feet, connected by crinoline stretcher. Three long tapered spindles either side of central back splat. Three tapered underarm spindles with regional style of turned underarm supports. Stylised fleur-de-lis fretted top splat with two extra piercings above. Two shaped frets in lower splat.

Figure NE253. Stamp of Joseph Godfrey of Worksop (fl.1841-51), impressed on the side seat edge of the chair shown in Figure NE252.

Figure NE254. Joseph Darby junior in 1936. The chairs included in this photograph show a child's chair made by Darby senior, and a smoking high chair, made by Joseph Darby junior, both made whilst they were working, in the late 19th century, at the Allsop chair manufactory at Cheapside, Worksop.

also employed a 'chair maker's labourer' who was his stepson.[90] The joining together of relatives following a common trade was not unusual in the Worksop chair making tradition, but in the case of the Godfrey business, no makers other than relatives were employed. The business continued until 1861, when the first three original chair making Godfreys had ceased working.[91] The family's last chair making member, George Godfrey, was recorded as an unemployed chair maker at Cheapside, Worksop, in 1881,[92] perhaps indicating that he had worked for Isaac Allsop & Son of Cheapside after the closure of his family's business.

A further chair maker, Joseph Darby, extends the connection with the Retford Windsor trade for he, too, was born in that town, around 1829,[93] and moved to Worksop at some time between 1855 and 1861.[94] This craftsman was employed by I. Allsop & Son, where he probably remained until the firm closed in 1887. At some time during the mid-1870s Joseph Darby's son, also Joseph, joined him as his apprentice at Allsop's,[95] and after training as a skilled tradesman he also worked at Allsop's until the closure of the firm, when he went to work for William Bramer's at Priory Mill, Worksop[96] where he remained until he became a postman in 1906. A further son, Edward Darby, who was also born in Retford in 1855[97] and probably trained under his father at Allsop's, is believed to be responsible for transmitting chair design from Worksop to Dewsbury, near to Brighouse in Yorkshire, where he is recorded as working, in an 1881 trade directory.[98] His younger brother, in an interview in 1936,[99] emphasised Edward Darby's role in introducing Worksop style chairs into Yorkshire.

The Darby family were probably typical of this region's highly skilled chair makers, men who worked over many years producing chairs within the distinguished Worksop tradition, but whose chairs cannot usually be identified as the work of a particular individual. However, in the case of Joseph Darby and his son Joseph, we can identify two chairs as made by them. A photograph (Figure NE254), taken in 1936, shows Joseph junior, aged seventy-eight, with a child's chair of typical Worksop design made by his father, and a smoking high chair made by himself.

The Allsop Family

Of the many Windsor chair makers who were to develop their skills in Worksop during the early nineteenth century, probably none were to play a more significant part than the Allsop family. Originally, the Allsops came from Morley in Derbyshire to Wellow near to Worksop in 1819, where Robert Allsop, a wheelwright, worked as a carpenter.[100] In 1824[101] he moved to Worksop with his family which included two sons, Isaac and William, who were ultimately to found one of the most important Windsor chair manufactories in the whole of the North East of England. On arriving in Worksop at the age of thirteen years, Isaac may have been apprenticed to one of the few chair makers working there at that time, James Moss, who worked in Gateford Road.[102] Later Isaac appears to have become his partner, for in 1832, when Isaac was twenty-one, a trade directory lists 'Moss and Allsop' as chair makers in Potter Street.[103] Isaac's entrepreneurial skills enabled him to branch out on his own, however, and by 1841 he had set up a business at Cheapside next to the White Swan public house in premises which were owned by his brother-in-law, Allick Hill. The timber used in the chair manufactory was stored in a wood yard on the opposite side of the road to the workshop.[104]

By 1841 Isaac's brother, William, now aged fifteen, had joined him as an apprentice,[105] and was probably part of a team of workers making Windsors. However, it appears that William occasionally stamped his own chairs, for one chair, made in yew with a decorative splat, has been recorded with his name stamp impressed on the edge of the seat (see Figures NE255 and 256).

The firm of Isaac Allsop continued to grow, and in 1851 employed eight men,[106] as well as using the services of the nearby turnery firm of William Caudwell's in Canal Street, who produced turned parts for Allsop's and perhaps other chair makers in the town at this period.[107] Later Allsop's did their own turning, and it is known that the firm had a 'Cornish steam engine' to power their lathes and saws.[108]

By 1861 Isaac's son, Alexander, had joined the business and worked with Isaac, William and another relative, John Allsop.[109] It appears that during the next decade, the health of both Isaac and William had

Figure NE255. High decorative splat back Windsor armchair of medium overall proportions. Yew with elm seat, stamped twice on side edge of seat, 'W. ALLSOP' (fl.1841-71).

Highly decoratively turned legs connected by crinoline stretcher. Crinoline supports also decoratively turned. Three long tapered spindles either side of central back splat. Three tapered underarm spindles with regional style of underarm support. Arm bow terminates in notches on the under surface. Decoratively fretted upper and lower splats with damage to upper splat. Scribe marks around upper hoop.

(Courtesy Timothy D. Wilson Antiques)

Figure NE256. Stamps of William Allsop, younger brother and apprentice to Isaac Allsop of Worksop (fl.1841-71), impressed on side seat edge of the chair shown in Figure NE255.

Figure NE257. 'Best' low decorative splat back Windsor armchair. Yew with elm seat, stencilled beneath the seat, 'ALLSOP Maker Worksop NOTTS.' (fl.1841-71). Retailer's paper label of R. Gresham pasted above.

Highly elaborately turned legs with ball feet, connected by crinoline stretcher. Three long tapered back spindles either side of central back splat. Three tapered underarm spindles with regional style of turned underarm supports. Arm bow terminates in notches on under surface. Highly decorative fretted top and lower splats, similar to those included in the John Gabbitass chair shown in Figure NE229.

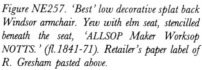

Figure NE258. Stencilled label from beneath the seat of the chair shown in Figure NE257. After 1871 and until 1887, the firm was styled I. Allsop & Son. This form of identification was an unusual device for makers to use, and one of three methods used by the Allsop firm, which also included paper labels and name branding. The paper label affixed above Allsop's stencil refers to a firm of pawnbrokers in Mansfield, Nottinghamshire, who apparently purchased Allsop's chairs for resale.

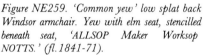

Figure NE259. 'Common yew' low splat back Windsor armchair. Yew with elm seat, stencilled beneath seat, 'ALLSOP Maker Worksop NOTTS.' (fl.1841-71).

Three ring turned legs with vase shaped feet, connected by crinoline stretcher. Three tapered spindles either side of central back splat. Three tapered underarm spindles with regional style of turned underarm supports. Stylised fleur-de-lis fretted top splat with two extra piercings. Two shaped frets in lower splat.

Figure NE260. 'Roman' kitchen chair. Yew with stained elm seat. Paper label fixed to underneath of seat; 'I. ALLSOP & SON, WINDSOR CHAIR MANUFACTURERS. WORKSOP, NOTTS.' (fl.1871-87). Variegation in colour of the heart wood and sap wood can be seen in the stay rail.

Heavy, elaborately turned legs joined by heavy H-stretcher, centre stretcher with central ball motif. Broad shaped seat similar to those used in the 'Best Smoking High' chairs. Top stay rail or 'head' supported by shaped and turned outer supports, and three turned central spindles.

(Courtesy John Dench Antiques)

Figure NE262. 'Smoking high' broad armed chair. Cherry with elm seat. Branded underneath the seat, 'I. ALLSOP & SON.' (fl.1871-87). See Allsop's trade card, Figure NE269, for details of similar chair. The basic chair, made in cherry, cost 14/- (70p). The addition of rockers was 1/- (5p) extra.

Elaborately turned legs with vase shaped feet, especially turned to fit into rockers. H-stretcher with back legs connected by a further cross stretcher. Central ball motif in cross stretchers. Four tapered spindles either side of central decoratively fretted splat above the arms. Two turned spindles either side of central decoratively fretted splat below the arms, and turned underarm supports typical of regional style.

failed, and by 1871 Isaac, though called a chair manufacturer, had become blind[110] and William, who still worked as a chair maker, was deaf.[111] Isaac's health continued to deteriorate and he died in 1873 aged sixty-five years,[112] but before his death in 1871 he had passed the business to his son, Alexander, who was married to his cousin, Elizabeth, daughter of Allick Hill.[113] At the point of takeover the firm was renamed I. Allsop & Son, and was employing ten men.[114] Fortunately a number of chairs bearing identification marks of I. Allsop and Son have been recorded and are illustrated in Figures NE257-263.

The firm continued under Alexander's management until his untimely death on 5th November, 1874, at the age of thirty-three.[115] He died intestate and the day to day running of the firm passed to his wife, Elizabeth, who appears to have run the business successfully for an interim period of about two years, prior to the business premises and its goodwill and stock-in-trade being sold by public auction in 1876. At

Figure NE261. Paper label affixed beneath seat of the chair shown in Figure NE260 bearing the name of 'I. Allsop & Son, Worksop, Notts.' (fl.1871-87). The capital letters AB await interpretation. See Allsop trade card in Figure NE269 which refers to 'Roman' chairs in yew costing 10/- (50p) each.

this sale, Elizabeth, who borrowed money from her father, Allick Hill, on the issuing of a promissory note, purchased the business in her own right in two parts: lot 1, the land together with the White Swan public house, a row of small houses, workshops and wood yard for £525; lot 2, good-will, stock-in-trade, and the plant of a Windsor chair making manufactory, for £169.[116] She continued to run the business under the name of I. Allsop & Son, perhaps

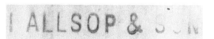

Figure NE263. Brand of Isaac Allsop & Son of Worksop Notts. (fl.1871-87), from beneath the seat of the chair shown in Figure NE262.

intending that her infant son, Tom, would in due course inherit it.

The contents of the stock-in-trade and plant which were listed at the death of Alexander in 1874,[117] show that the firm held a substantial stock of its principal woods which included yew, cherry, elm and some walnut in a variety of forms such as branches, poles and sawn planks. There were also considerable holdings of chair parts.

The 1,544 chair bottoms in stock, for example, illustrate the confidence with which the firm was trading, and indicate that the elm seats may have been made in 'green' form and then

Figure NE264. 'Office' or smoker's bow chair. Yew with stained elm seat. Identified beneath the seat with stencil which reads: 'FROM W. SNELL CABINET MAKERS LINCOLN'. There is no evidence to suggest that this style of chair was made in Lincolnshire, and this chair was probably bought from makers in Worksop and sold with the supplier's label affixed. This chair is identical to the Nottinghamshire 'Office' chair illustrated in Figure NE273 and to the drawing on the Allsop trade card Figure NE270.

Elaborately turned legs with vase shaped feet, connected by H-stretcher with central ball motif typical of Allsop chairs. Six turned spindles, and Nottinghamshire regionally typical arm supports.

Figure NE265. Painted stencil beneath the seat of the chairs shown in Figures NE264 and 266 of William Snell, Master Cabinet Maker of the Black Swan Yard, Lincoln (fl.1851-56). Snell appears to have imported chairs from Nottinghamshire to sell as part of his repertoire of furniture.

Figure NE266. 'Best High' armchair. Yew with elm seat. Identified underneath the seat with stencil which reads: 'FROM W. SNELL CABINET MAKERS LINCOLN.' There is no evidence to suggest that this style of chair was made in Lincolnshire, and this chair was probably bought from makers in Worksop and sold with the supplier's label affixed. This chair is similar to the 'Best High' chair shown in Figure NE271, and to the drawing on the Allsop trade card shown in Figure NE270.

Elaborately turned legs similar to the Allsop chair illustrated in Figure NE255 (feet missing). Legs connected by crinoline stretcher. Four tapered long back spindles either side of central decoratively fretted top and lower splats with fir tree motif. Four tapered underarm spindles, and Worksop style of turned underarm supports.

Figure NE267. Low splat back Windsor armchair. Yew with elm seat. Paper label affixed to underneath of seat of W. Keeling, cabinet maker, 6, Poultry, Nottingham (fl.1860-64).

Three ring turned legs with vase shaped feet, connected by crinoline stretcher. Three tapered spindles either side of central back splat. Three tapered underarm spindles, with Worksop style of turned underarm support. Stylised fleur-de-lis fretted top splat with two extra piercings. Two shaped frets in lower splat.

Figure NE268. Paper label of W. Keeling affixed under the seat of the chair shown in Figure NE267. William Keeling is recorded as a cabinet maker trading at 6, Poultry, Nottingham, between 1860 and 1864.

left to dry before assembly. A reference is made to '50 yew arms and crooks'. The term 'crook' may have been given to the crinoline stretcher connecting the legs in some chair designs.[118] The '6 dozen Elm and Cherry arms and tops' probably refer to the sawn-out arms and the supporting top section which were used in the construction of 'smoking high' and 'office' chair arms.

The Allsop inventory also records '75 dozen bannisters ready for use'[119] which were probably the turned back spindles of kitchen chairs, and indicates the large numbers of Worksop chairs which could be assembled at that point. The supply of '6 dozen Grecians sawn and ready for use', may refer to two plain horizontal splats, or to the back uprights of Allsop's Grecian chair (see Figure NE270).

The low value (only £7) of chairs in stock may indicate that the majority of Allsop's chairs were being made to order, and that making parts in anticipation of orders, rather than assembling from finished parts, was a high priority in the organisation of this business.

The Allsop inventory of 1874 also itemises '9 pair of vice', indicating that bench work, including the making of splats and sawn arm parts used in 'smoking high' and 'office chairs', as well as sawn parts for 'Roman' and 'Grecian' style chairs were predominant tasks in this workshop; whereas the presence of only one turning lathe indicates that the task of producing turned parts was not undertaken on a major scale, and thus supports the view that specialist turnery firms undertook this work.

The provision of 'metal steam box, etc.' emphasises the central place of steaming and bending of hooped parts in the chair making process and the reference to a 'dog cart' and a 'heavy cart' indicates the manner in

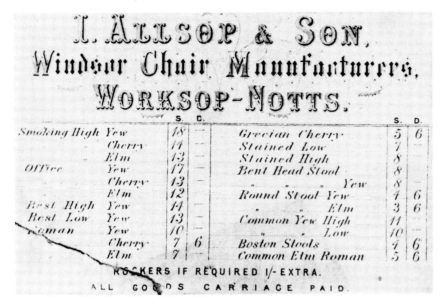

Smoking High Yew	18	—	Grecian Cherry	5	6
Cherry	14	—	Stained Low	7	—
Elm	13	—	Stained High	8	—
Office Yew	17	—	Bent Head Stool	8	—
Cherry	13	—	„ „ Yew	8	—
Elm	12	—	Round Stool Yew	4	6
Best High Yew	14	—	„ „ Elm	3	6
Best Low Yew	13	—	Common Yew High	11	—
Roman Yew	10	—	„ „ Low	10	—
Cherry	7	6	Boston Stools	4	6
Elm	7	—	Common Elm Roman	5	6

ROCKERS IF REQUIRED 1/- EXTRA.

ALL GOODS CARRIAGE PAID.

Figure NE269. I. Allsop & Son, Worksop, Nottinghamshire (fl.1871-87). Price card indicating ten varieties of Windsors offered for sale, both arm and side chairs, as well as four stool patterns.

(Courtesy Worksop Library)

Figure NE271. 'Best High' chair. Yew with elm seat. Attributed to Nottinghamshire, c.1840-87. See illustration of similar chair on Allsop's trade card shown in Figure NE270. This chair was originally priced at 14/- (70p).

Heavy, two ring turned legs terminating in ball shaped foot, connected by crinoline stretcher. Four tapered long back spindles either side of central decoratively fretted splat. Fir tree motif fretted in upper and lower splats. Three tapered underarm spindles and regional design of underarm supports similar to the left hand support on the John Gabbitass chair in Figure NE229.

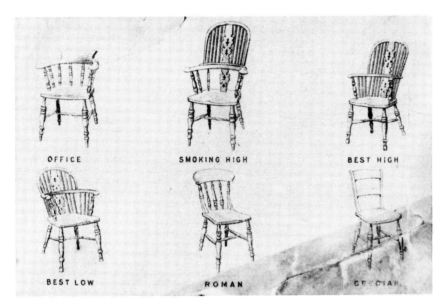

OFFICE SMOKING HIGH BEST HIGH

BEST LOW ROMAN GRECIAN

Figure NE270. I. Allsop & Son, Worksop, Nottinghamshire (fl.1871-87). Illustrations printed on reverse of price list of some of the chairs listed on the price card. Some common forms of Worksop chairs are not illustrated, including 'stained low', 'stained high', and 'common yew, high and low Windsors', as well as Windsors with multiple pierced splats.

(Courtesy Worksop Library)

Figure NE272. 'Best Low' chair. Yew with elm seat. Attributed to Nottinghamshire, c.1840-87. See illustration of similar chair on Allsop's trade card shown in Figure NE270. This chair was originally priced at 13/- (65p).

Heavy, two ring turned legs terminating in ball foot, connected by crinoline stretcher. Three tapered spindles either side of decorative central back splat with fir tree motif in fretting. Three tapered underarm spindles and regional design of underarm supports similar to the left hand support in the John Gabbitass chair in Figure NE229.

which the finished chairs were taken to the railway station.

The business of I. Allsop and Son appears to have been well managed by Elizabeth Allsop, and this is perhaps evidenced in the schedules produced at the death of her husband, Alexander Allsop in 1874. This inventory shows that the firm at that time had twenty-six accounts owing money to them for goods supplied,[120] whereas in 1876, when an affidavit relating to the firm's assets and liabilities was given by Elizabeth Allsop, the number of accounts increased to thirty-nine

without more money being owed.[121] The majority of these accounts were from cabinet makers who no doubt sold Allsop's chairs as part of their furniture stock, probably with their own labels attached. Examples of this practice are shown in Figures NE264-268 illustrating Windsor chairs which show characteristics of Worksop made chairs. Two of these carry stencils of a Lincoln cabinet maker and the third that of a Nottingham cabinet maker. Other accounts mentioned in the inventory are from chair makers, and these may have been for

177

Figure 273. 'Office' or smoker's bow chair. Yew with stained elm seat. Attributed to Nottinghamshire, c.1851-87. See illustration of similar chair on Allsop's trade card in Figure NE270.

Elaborately turned legs with vase shaped feet, connected by H-stretcher with central ball motif typical of Allsop chairs. Six turned spindles and two regionally typical arm supports. Sawn and shaped arms with raised central back section attached.

chair parts or complete chairs to enhance their own range of products. The locations of these sales outlets show a wide distribution including Bingley, Bradford, Cleckheaton, Doncaster, Glossop, Huddersfield, Manchester, Oldham, Stalybridge and Wakefield.

A trade card produced by I. Allsop & Son, dated between 1871 and 1887, has also survived, partially illustrating the range of chairs which they made, and giving the names and details of the prices for each type. These chairs were available in a hierarchy of woods, with yew being the most valuable, cherry the second, and elm the least expensive, each made with elm seats. The price card also indicates that any of the chairs could be fitted with rockers for one shilling extra, and that stools were also offered in the three principal woods. See Figures NE269 and 270. Figures NE271-273 illustrate chairs very similar to those on the card but which are not stamped with Allsop's mark.

The illustrations shown on the trade card do not, however, portray the whole range of chairs made by this firm since, for example, no drawings are shown of the 'stained low', 'stained high' or 'common yew, high and low' Windsor styles which were amongst the most common Worksop patterns. Nor is there an illustration of one of the best high yew chairs with the highly decorative splat fretting shown in Figure NE255, and it may be, therefore, that other trade cards were also produced illustrating additional chairs.

However, I. Allsop's range of chairs is more extensive than that recorded for any other North East Midlands chair maker. The essential form of the majority of this region's Windsors incorporates a narrow bow bent arm and Allsop's use of the three part sawn arm in producing 'smoking high' and 'office' chairs, is an unusual form in chairs recorded for this region, and is more typical of those made in the industrial towns in South Yorkshire, as well as in the far North East of England. The form and construction of the three part sawn arm shape is illustrated in Chapter 5, Figures SW5-16.

At some time between 1876 and 1880, Alexander Allsop's widow Elizabeth married a saddler in the town, named George Johnson, who took over the day-to-day running of the firm.[122] Johnson may have merged his saddlery business with the chair manufactory since his accounts did not distinguish between the two businesses at the point of the ultimate bankruptcy of the firm.[123] His position as head of the concern over several years[124] coincided with a gradual decline in the viability of I. Allsop & Son and the firm was placed in bankruptcy in 1887 for the sum of £1,574.6s.3d. The reasons for an excess of liabilities over assets were described at the hearing. The largest sum to be claimed was the recall of a personal loan of £925 owing to Allick Hill. The 'collapse of the engine and boiler' (£85) was described, 'Depreciation of machinery (£10.11s.3½d.)' and 'building a drying shed' (£67.17s. 6d.)'[125] accounted for further liabilities.

The firm of I. Allsop & Son thus came to an abrupt end and the local newspaper reported that: 'The failure of one of the oldest chair-making firms in Worksop caused a considerable stir among the members of the chairmaking trades of Worksop'.[126] The passing of this firm marked the end of one of the most productive and skilled of the Windsor chair manufacturers in the North Eastern tradition.

Chair making in Retford and Newark

The town of Retford, in which the Nottinghamshire Windsor chair making tradition probably began, has left no recorded name stamped chairs. However, the trade here, which is known to have existed at least as early as the middle of the eighteenth century,[127] continued to attract new chair makers who were born in the late eighteenth century. At least two of these makers were to continue as chair makers until 1851,[128] and a further maker, James Saunderson, born in about 1794, continued as a chair maker until at least 1861.[129] This maker was a master wood turner and chair maker working at Beardsall Row, and may have trained William Wheatland who had also worked at Beardsall Row in 1822,[130] prior to moving to Gamston and Rockley.

The trade in Retford had also attracted at least nine young men between 1830 and 1850, but these did not continue beyond the middle of the century. The last of the Retford Windsor chair makers was William Smith who had been apprenticed to George Nicholson in Rockley, and later also worked there for Frederick Walker, leaving his employment at some time before 1848. Smith moved to Retford where he worked as part of what was at that time an ageing community of some ten chair makers, all of whom had retired by 1864, leaving Smith as the last Windsor chair maker in this town where he

Figure NE274. Low splat back Windsor armchair. Ash with elm seat and splats. Stamped on seat edge 'J. THOMPSON' (fl.1832-53). The adoption of the two ring turned legs in this chair is atypical of the Nottinghamshire tradition, but common in the Lincolnshire tradition, and reflects design influences from two adjoining traditions.

Two ring turned legs with vase feet connected by H-stretcher. Three long back spindles either side of central splat. Three tapered underarm spindles with turned underarm supports. Stylised fleur-de-lis fretted top splat; keyhole shaped piercing in lower splat.

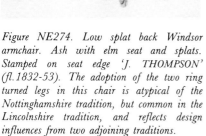

Figure NE275. The stamp of John Thompson found on the side seat edge of the chair shown in Figure NE274. A father and son of this name were working in Kirkgate and Guildhall Street, Newark, Nottinghamshire, between 1832 and 1853.

Figure NE276. Slat back or kitchen armchair. Ash legs and stretchers, beech stay rail and slats, alder back uprights, elm seat, arms and arm supports. Stamped 'WILKINSON BROS. NEWARK' on back edge of seat. This style of chair is typical of many made in chair making factories in other parts of the country, particularly in High Wycombe, Buckinghamshire. However, the 'ball' turning in the front legs and plain turned rear legs are features of Lincolnshire Windsor chairs, while the arcaded shaping in the stay rail, between the slats, is more typically found in North Country Windsors of this type, than in the Buckinghamshire tradition.

Figure NE277. Stamp of Wilkinson Bros. of Newark, Nottinghamshire, impressed on rear seat edge of chair shown in Figure NE276. This firm, first recorded in 1879 at Church Street, Newark, continued trading until 1961.

and son named John Thompson who are recorded in 1832, the father working in Kirkgate and the son working as a cabinet maker in Guildhall Street. By 1841 they were both recorded as chair turners and they seem to have continued in their trade until 1853 when their business is last noted.[133] The evidence of the chair design shown in Figure NE274, stamped with their name, illustrates that they were working within the tradition of the regional Nottinghamshire Windsor chair styles, with influences detectable in their work from the Lincolnshire tradition. Amongst these, the form of the underarm turning has a parallel in the turnings used by some makers from Grantham (see Figure NE141, p.140). The use of two ring turned legs is also typical of Windsors made in the Lincolnshire tradition rather than those made in Worksop, where three ring turnings were usual. This merging of influences from the Lincolnshire and Nottinghamshire traditions is perhaps understandable since Newark is located at about the same distance from Worksop and the major Lincolnshire chair making centre of Grantham.

The second chair to have been recorded with a Newark maker's stamp is shown in Figures NE276 and NE277. This chair was probably made by a firm of cabinet makers, Wilkinson Brothers, and may be described as a lath back or kitchen chair design. This style is typical of others made in this general style in various parts of England, and particularly in the chair making factories of High Wycombe and the West Country. However, specific design details within this example identify it as being made in the North of England, amongst which are the underarm turnings which are typical of those found in certain Worksop best yew chairs. The ball turned motif in the front legs, combined with plain turned rear legs is a feature of many Windsors made in Lincolnshire. See Figures NE71 and NE155 for examples, both features indicating the joint influence of the Lincolnshire and Nottinghamshire chair designs on the Newark tradition. The arcaded shaping in the stay rail between the slats also locates this chair as a North Country variety.

continued his trade until 1891.[131] His presence virtually confirms that the Retford Windsor chairs were made in the regional style of the Worksop/Rockley tradition. (A discussion of possible Windsor styles made in

Retford is given on p.183.)

A further centre, the town of Newark on Trent, lies some eight miles south of Retford, and in 1841 had a community of eleven chair makers,[132] amongst whom was a father

Figure NE278. The row of cottages, built in red brick with pantile roofs at Rockley, c.1820, to house the agricultural workers of William Calvert, Esq. (Photograph 1984.) In 1822 William Wheatland bought a piece of land behind the right hand house, and built a low, red brick workshop on the site. He was joined here by other chair makers, and in 1840 five of the thirteen cottages were lived in by these craftsmen.[134] He gave a small plot of land adjoining the right hand cottage for a Wesleyan Chapel to be built on.

Chair Making in Rockley

Amongst the local chair making centres which lay outside Worksop, perhaps the most significant arose in the hamlets of Rockley and Gamston which lie close to each other on the old Great North Road between Retford and West Markham, some eight miles from Worksop. The three chair makers who, at different times, owned the workshop at Rockley, and another maker who worked at Gamston, habitually stamped their products, and in so doing, have provided evidence of chairs which can be attributed to these craftsmen, and to the North East Midlands regional tradition in which they worked.

Interestingly, the styles of provenanced Windsor chairs which have been recorded from Rockley are, with a few exceptions, all armchair varieties, where the arm is a continuous narrow bow. The Rockley makers appear to have retained their essentially rural chair making techniques of steaming and bending the

Figure NE279. Plaque commemorating the building of the Wesleyan Chapel at Rockley, where the chair maker, William Wheatland was the first class leader and local preacher. The chapel has now been converted to a garage, and only vestigial remains of it exist.

arm and top bow segments, and not to have extended their repertoire of designs to include those Windsors which have the three part sawn arm.

As was the case in the Worksop tradition, the original maker to come to this area was a chair maker from nearby Retford, named William

Figure NE280. Low splat back Windsor armchair. Ash with elm seat. Stamped on side edge of seat 'WHEATLAND ROCKLEY' (fl. 1822-28).

Single ring turned legs with straight feet connected by crinoline stretcher. Three long tapered spindles either side of central back splat. Three tapered underarm spindles with regional style of turned underarm supports. Stylised fleur-de-lis fretted top splat. Keyhole shaped fret in lower splat with added rear support covering fret.

Figure NE281. Low splat back Windsor armchair. Yew with elm seat and back legs. Stamped on side edge of seat 'WHEATLAND ROCKLEY' (fl. 1822-28).

Single ring turned legs with straight feet connected by crinoline stretcher. Three long tapered spindles either side of central back splat. Unusually in the Nottinghamshire tradition, the back spindles pass right through the seat (see Figure NE283). Three tapered underarm spindles with regional style of turned underarm supports. Stylised fleur-de-lis fretted top splat with two additional piercings. Two shaped frets in lower splat.

Figure NE282. The stamp of William Wheatland of Rockley (fl. 1822-28), impressed on the side seat edge of the chair shown in Figure NE281.

Figure NE283. View of the underside of the seat of William Wheatland's chair illustrated in Figure NE281 showing that the spindles mortice through the seat and were cut level. This constructional device was commonly used in 18th century Windsor chairs.

Figure NE284. View of the left front leg of the chair in Figure NE281 illustrating the precise and refined turnery forms typical of the Rockley makers. The single ring and concave leg turning motif was used by this group until about 1835 when multiple ring leg turnings were adopted.

Wheatland, who had been a chair maker in Beardsall Row in East Retford in 1822[135] before he moved to the small parish of Gamston, to revive a lapsed Methodist class of some half dozen members. Here he worked as a chair maker and local Methodist leader and preacher. Within two years Wheatland's class had grown to fourteen members,[136] and the need for a chapel had become evident. Land for this purpose was not available from the major local landowner, the Duke of Newcastle,[137] but a new hamlet was about to be constructed between the nearby Great North Road and the River Idle. This parish was to be called Rockley, by the landowner, William Calvert Esq., since there were prominent rocks overhanging the banks of the river.[138] The location of this hamlet is two miles from the parish centre of Askham, and situated in a totally isolated setting, surrounded today by large tracts of arable land. Here some fourteen simple red brick and flint cottages under red clay tile roofs were built in a single row at right angles to the main road, in Mill Lane. The cottages, although originally built to house agricultural workers, were occupied by five chair makers and their families.[139] Each house was designed with large gardens to the front, fuel stores, privies and wash houses to the rear, as well as a row of pigsties, one for each household.

It was to this newly formed community that William Wheatland came to live at some time between 1822 and 1827. Here he was able to buy some land adjoining the Great North Road, to the rear of the cottages, and on this land he built a single storey red brick workshop. Wheatland was joined by another Retford chair maker, John Stocks, who was an Anglican, and William Fotheringham, who lived next door to Stocks in Mill Lane, and was a practising Methodist.[140] In about 1827, a further chair maker, Isaac Fritchley, joined them for a short time.[141] In 1823, another chair maker, Frederick Walker from Thornhill near Huddersfield, Yorkshire, joined the Gamston Methodist class and in 1828 joined Wheatland at his workshop.[142] This maker was to spend the rest of his working life here in Rockley, and was ultimately to become the last and the most productive workshop owner.

John Whitworth of Gamston, a contemporary of Joseph Godfrey's (see Figures NE250-253) may also have been trained in Wheatland's workshop, since although he is recorded as a wheelwright in Gamston,[143] yew chairs made in the local style have been recorded with his name stamp (see Figures NE291-294), and he appears to have made chairs as part of his occupation only.

In 1827, William Wheatland was able to offer his class a small piece of land facing the front door of his workshop and adjoining the last cottage in the row, on which a chapel was to be built. The new chapel was well received, and the membership grew to twenty-four in 1828.[144] Wheatland's finances appear to have been stretched to the full however, and in February 1830 he was made bankrupt. The liquidation of Wheatland's business, although a rare event amongst chair makers, was perhaps caused by a general decline in prosperity amongst those relying on agriculture for their living, for in the late 1820s and early 1830s, a number of bad harvests occurred in succession, and unemployment and suffering amongst the poor was widespread.[145]

The disgrace of bankruptcy apparently caused Wheatland to resign as class leader and local preacher, and he is not recorded as a Windsor chair maker in Nottinghamshire again. His employee, Frederick Walker, who was a committed Methodist, took over the position of Rockley class leader and local preacher, and carried on in the role of giving spiritual and moral guidance to the community. His wife was also involved in this work, and ran a second class for a short time.[146]

Wheatland's contribution to the chair making history of the region was highly significant, since he learned his trade from the early Retford makers before passing on his skills to others, who were to continue making fine quality chairs long after his disappearance. Name stamped chairs made by Wheatland are rare relative to those stamped by later Rockley makers, and examples of those that have been located are illustrated in Figures NE280-287, and show a mixture of regional styles of conventional construction and beauty. Amongst the chairs recorded bearing Wheatland's stamp, however, is a child's chair without a splat, and with sticks only composing the back design (see Figure NE287). This style of chair is common to the Lincolnshire Windsor tradition, but not to Nottinghamshire. A further high back Windsor made by Wheatland, shown in Figure NE285, has flattened crook shaped arm supports which are atypical of the nineteenth century Nottinghamshire Windsors, which have

Figure NE285. High splat back Windsor armchair. Yew with elm seat. Stamped on side edge of seat 'WHEATLAND ROCKLEY' (fl.1822-28). The use of the flattened underarm support is unusual in the Nottinghamshire Windsor tradition, but is found in early chairs attributed to the Retford makers. See Figures NE288 and 289. This form of underarm support is also found in the single hoop armchairs of High Wycombe Windsor tradition. See Chapter 2, Figures TV71 and 73.

Single ring and concave turned legs. Single ring and straight feet. Legs connected by crinoline stretcher. Four long tapered spindles either side of central back splat. Three tapered underarm spindles with shaped and flattened underarm supports, notched and screwed into side edge of seat. Stylised fleur-de-lis fretted top splat with two extra piercings. Two shaped frets in lower splat. (Courtesy A. Jones Antiques)

Figure NE286. The stamp of William Wheatland (fl.1822-28), impressed on the side seat edge of the chair in Figure NE285. This chair unusually has shaped and flattened arm supports morticed into the seat edge, and in so doing, has cut through the maker's stamp, indicating that the maker stamped this seat prior to assembling the chair.

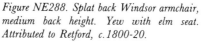

Figure NE288. Splat back Windsor armchair, medium back height. Yew with elm seat. Attributed to Retford, c.1800-20.

Single ring and concave turning motif incorporated in all legs, connected by a shallow curved crinoline stretcher. Bell shaped seat with scribe line around the edge. Shaped and flattened underarm support morticed into the edge of the seat in the manner of many Buckinghamshire Windsors. Three tapered underarm support spindles, eight long tapered back spindles. Stylised fleur-de-lis upper splat with two shaped piercings in lower splat.

Figure NE287. Child's Windsor armchair. Ash with elm seat and back legs, fruitwood arm supports, front legs, and stretcher. Stamped 'WHEATLAND ROCKLEY' (fl.1822-28). This style of chair is common in the Lincolnshire tradition and no other chairs of this style have been provenanced to Nottinghamshire, suggesting that Wheatland was influenced by this Lincolnshire chair design, although the majority of his work is firmly centred in the Nottinghamshire regional styles.

Six tapered sticks composing back design (back hoop loosened away from back sticks). Two tapered underarm spindles and turned underarm support (right underarm support missing). Single ring turned legs (feet missing).

(Courtesy Bradford City Museums and Art Gallery)

Figure NE289. Low splat back Windsor armchair. Yew with elm seat. Attributed to Retford, c.1800-20.

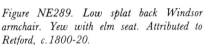

Single ring and indented turning motif incorporated in all legs, connected by shallow curved crinoline stretcher. Bell shaped seat with scribe line around the edge. Shaped and flattened underarm support morticed into the edge of the seat. Three tapered underarm support spindles, eight long tapered back spindles. Stylised fleur-de-lis upper splat with two shaped piercings in lower splat.

Figure NE290. Low splat back Windsor armchair. Yew with elm seat. Attributed to Retford, c.1820-40. This chair has close stylistic similarities with the chair shown in NE289. The use of turned arm supports suggests a slightly later date of production however and this example may represent a point in design transition. The paper label from the underneath of the seat of this chair reads 'From Luke Swallow, . . . '.

Single ring and indented turning motif incorporated in all legs, connected by shallow curved crinoline stretcher. Bell shaped seat with scribe line around the edge. Turned arm supports. Three tapered underarm support spindles, eight long tapered back spindles. Stylised fleur-de-lis upper splat with two shaped piercings in lower splat.

Figure NE291. Low splat back Windsor armchair. Yew with elm seat. Stamped on side edge of seat 'WHITWORTH GAMSTON.' (fl.1841-51).

Single ring turned legs with straight feet connected by crinoline stretcher. Three long tapered spindles either side of central back splat. Three tapered underarm spindles, with regional style of turned underarm support. Stylised fleur-de-lis fretted top splat. Two shaped frets in lower splat.

Figure NE292. Stamp of John Whitworth (fl.1841-51), wheelwright and chair maker of Gamston near Rockley, impressed on the side seat edge of the chair shown in Figure NE291. This maker probably trained in William Wheatland's workshop in Rockley, and evidently made chairs as a part time occupation, combined with that of village wheelwright.

turned arm supports.

The use of the flattened arm supports in some of Wheatland's chairs is combined with a further structural feature, that of the back spindles morticing through the seat, and being sawn off after hammering through (see Figure NE283). These characteristics are not found in other chairs made by known Nottinghamshire makers, where turned underarm supports and spindles morticing into, but not through the seat, are usual. However, the use of the flattened crook arm support was occasionally used by George Nicholson, who took over the Rockley workshop after Wheatland's departure in 1830, and this design feature is also common to certain chair designs from the Thames Valley tradition and demonstrates a link between it and the North East Midlands tradition.

Although the stylistic features of morticed through spindles combined with flattened underarm supports were uncommon in chairs from the Nottinghamshire centres which have provided name stamped examples, a further group of chairs, as yet not firmly attributed to a place of manu-

facture, also show these features (see Figures NE288-289). These chairs are sufficiently dissimilar to the Grantham and Boston styles, from Lincolnshire, to suggest that they were not made in these centres, nor indeed, for similar reasons, in the Windsor chair making centres of nearby Nottinghamshire.

Examples were made as both high and low Windsors, and are usually made in yew with elm seats, and typically appear to have greater age and less uniformity in their manufacture than examples which have turned arm supports. Given that Wheatland was trained as a Windsor chair maker in Retford, it may be therefore, that this design was the precursor to those that were made later in Rockley, Worksop, Newark, and perhaps in Wellow and Ollerton, and reflects the originating design of the Nottinghamshire Windsor style, made in Retford.

Around the time of Wheatland's bankruptcy in 1830, George Nicholson, also a Methodist, came to the Rockley workshop from Cresswell in Derbyshire, some ten miles from Rockley. This maker possibly purchased the workshop and continued to employ the three incumbent chair makers, Frederick Walker, William Fotheringham and John Stocks, who had worked for Wheatland. Isaac Fritchley appears to have left by this time.

Nicholson followed his trade in Rockley for at least ten years with the same employees as Wheatland, with the addition of one apprentice,

Figure NE293. High splat back Windsor armchair. Yew with elm seat. Stamped on side edge of seat, 'WHITWORTH GAMSTON' (fl.1841-51). The fine quality of this chair is typical of this maker's work, and epitomises the best features of this region's Windsor chair tradition.

Single ring turned legs with straight feet, connected by crinoline stretcher. Three long tapered spindles either side of central back splat. Three tapered underarm spindles, with regional style of turned underarm support. Stylised fleur-de-lis fretted top splat. Two shaped frets in lower splat.

Figure NE295. Low splat back Windsor armchair. Ash with elm seat, fruitwood left front leg and splats. Stamped on side edge of seat 'NICHOLSON ROCKLEY' (fl.1831-41).

Single ring turned legs with straight feet connected by crinoline stretcher. Three long tapered spindles either side of central back splat. Three tapered underarm spindles with regional style of turned underarm support. Stylised fleur-de-lis fretted top splat. Keyhole fret in lower splat.

Figure NE297. Child's splat back Windsor armchair. Ash with elm seat, fruitwood arm supports and splats. Stamped on side edge of seat 'NICHOLSON ROCKLEY' (fl.1831-41).

Single ring turned legs with straight feet connected by crinoline stretcher. Two long tapered spindles either side of central back splat. Two tapered underarm spindles with regional style of turned underarm support. Stylised fleur-de-lis fretted top splat. Keyhole shaped fret in lower splat. Arm support turning similar to that found in William Wheatland's child's chair shown in Figure NE287.

(Courtesy H.C. Chapman & Son)

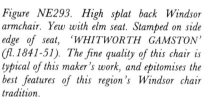

Figure NE294. The stamp of John Whitworth (fl.1841-51), wheelwright and chair maker of Gamston near Rockley, impressed on the side seat edge of the chair in Figure NE293.

Figure NE296. Stamp of George Nicholson of Rockley (fl.1831-41), impressed on side seat edge of chair shown in Figure NE295. This maker took over the Rockley workshop from William Wheatland around 1830. George Nicholson came from Cresswell in Derbyshire, ten miles from Rockley. He continued to work here for at least ten years and to employ the same men who had worked for Wheatland.

longer recorded as chair makers in Nottinghamshire. The reason why the workshop came to be virtually disbanded is not clear. Possibly the distance of the workshop from the market place and railway distribution points of Retford and Worksop presented too great a strain on the business resources, or perhaps disagreement arose amongst the men. However, of the original makers, Frederick Walker alone decided to take over the workshop and continue working there. He immediately employed a chair maker, William Burton, to assist him, but this maker seems to have been employed for only a short time. William Smith, who had been apprenticed under George Nicholson, also decided to stay at Rockley for a short time before moving to Retford around 1848[150] where he continued in his trade until 1891.[151]

Frederick Walker, who was to be the longest serving of all the Rockley makers, and was to leave the largest legacy of name stamped chairs, appears to have worked through a

William Smith.[147] Nicholson lived in one of the cottages in Mill Lane, and raised a family who were baptised between 1831 and 1836 in the chapel which was central to the lives of the community. Amongst his children, his son John was to be trained as a chair maker, but he moved to Worksop to work, lodging with John Stocks who had also moved to Lowtown, Worksop by 1851.[148]

The Rockley business seems to have prospered, and many chairs of the highest quality bearing Nicholson's stamp have been recorded (see Figures NE295-304). Although the majority of these chairs show close affiliation with local regional styles, a chair has

been recorded bearing Nicholson's stamp, shown in Figure NE298, which embodies the flattened crook arm exhibited in the Wheatland chair shown in Figure NE285.

The final record of George Nicholson as a chair maker in Rockley is in 1841 when he was aged forty. Shortly after the departure of this maker from Rockley, William Fotheringham and John Stocks also left. But whereas Stocks is known to have moved to carry on as a chair maker in Worksop,[149] Nicholson and Fotheringham are no

Figure NE298. Low splat back Windsor armchair. Yew with elm seat. Stamped on side edge of seat 'NICHOLSON ROCKLEY' (fl.1831-41).

Single ring and decoratively turned legs with straight shaped feet. Legs connected by crinoline stretcher. Three long tapered spindles either side of central back splat. Three tapered underarm spindles with shaped and flattened underarm support morticed and screwed into seat edge. Stylised fleur-de-lis fretted top splat with two extra piercings. Two shaped frets in lower splat.

Figure NE300. Pair of low decorative splat back Windsor armchairs. Yew, with elm seats, stamped on side edge of seat 'NICHOLSON ROCKLEY' (fl.1831-41). These elegant chairs produced in the Rockley workshop show a high awareness of the achievement of dynamic style by the juxtaposition of elaborate and simple turnery devices and complex splat fretting.

Double ring turned front legs with elongated bell shaped turning below. Narrow lower leg leading to pear shaped foot. Back legs similarly turned to front legs but without the bell turning. Legs connected by crinoline stretchers. Three long tapered spindles either side of central back splat. (Usually best yew wood chairs have four spindles either side of the central splat.) Three tapered underarm spindles and turned underarm supports in the regional style, similar to those found in Worksop-made chairs shown in Figures NE229 and 255, and identical to the Walker chair shown in Figure NE315. Arm bow terminating in notches on under surfaces. This feature was usually reserved for chairs made with elaborately decorative splats. Elaborately fretted top splat with this design reflected in lower splat.

(Courtesy Timothy D. Wilson Antiques)

Figure NE301. The stamp of George Nicholson of Rockley (fl.1831-41), impressed on the side seat edge of the chairs in Figure NE300. This maker took over the Rockley workshop from William Wheatland around 1830.

Figure NE299. Stamp of George Nicholson of Rockley (fl.1831-41), impressed on side seat edge of chair shown in Figure NE298. This maker took over the Rockley workshop from William Wheatland around 1830.

Figure NE302. Side view of central section of chair shown in Figure NE300 showing the profile of the underarm notch and the use of square pegs to hold the arm bow to the top hoop and underarm turning. The three underarm spindles are inclined backwards to form a reciprocal tension with the forward inclined underarm support.

Figure NE303. Left hand front leg in yew from chair in Figure NE300 showing detail of this elaborate regional style of leg turnery used by Nottinghamshire chair makers in some decorative splat 'Best' Yew Windsors.

Figure NE305. Stamp of George Nicholson of Rockley (fl.1831-41), impressed on the side edge of the seat of the chair shown in Figure NE304.

Figure NE304. High splat back Windsor armchair. Yew with elm seat. Stamped on side edge of seat 'NICHOLSON ROCKLEY' (fl.1831-41).

Two ring decoratively turned legs similar to rear legs found on the chair shown in Figure NE300. Pear shaped feet. Legs connected by crinoline stretcher. Unusual turned connecting supports to crinoline with bell shaped motif. Four long tapered spindles either side of central back splat. Three tapered underarm spindles with unusual style of multiple turned underarm supports. Arm bow terminates in notches on under surface. Stylised fleur-de-lis fretted top splat with two extra piercings. Two shaped frets in lower splat.

(Courtesy T. Crispin)

Figure NE307. Stamp of Frederick Walker of Rockley impressed on the side seat edge of the chair shown in Figure NE306. Walker was the longest serving of the Rockley chair makers. He began working with William Wheatland in Rockley in 1823, and continued under the ownership of George Nicholson, and he became workshop owner some time between 1841 and 1848. Frederick Walker continued working with his son, Henry, until about 1871 when the Rockley tradition came to an end.

Figure NE306. High splat back Windsor armchair. Ash with elm seat and splats. Stamped on side edge of seat 'F. WALKER ROCKLEY' (fl.1823-71).

Three ring turned legs with vase feet, connected by crinoline stretcher. Three long tapered spindles either side of central back splat. Three tapered underarm spindles with regional style of turned underarm supports. Stylised fleur-de-lis fretted top splat. Keyhole shaped fret in lower splat.

difficult time, for after William Burton left he continued for the next ten years with only William Smith to assist him for a short time, with one further chair maker, John Freeborough joining him for about a year in 1847.

By the early 1850s, Frederick Walker's son Henry had joined him,[152] probably from 1841 onwards, and for about two years Frederick and Henry Walker worked together with William Smith. In about 1848 Smith moved away and the Walkers evidently tried to replace him with a new chair maker, William Duke.[153] This maker stayed only for a short time, and Frederick and Henry worked together

for the next seventeen years, with Frederick's younger son, James, joining them for about three years between 1861 and 1863, at which point he, too, moved to Worksop to work for I. Allsop.[154]

The Rockley Windsor tradition continued until about 1871 when we have the last record of Frederick Walker, now aged seventy-three, and Henry, aged forty-eight, working together at the trade.[155] With the passing of these two makers this highly significant centre of Windsor chair making came to a close.

The history of this community and the excellent craftsmen who worked

there, epitomises the difficulties of the nineteenth century makers of these beautifully crafted products, whose markets were often subject to the vagaries of economic and social fortunes and, as in the case of the Rockley workshop, to their geographic isolation which made supplying or finding new markets difficult. Even with these factors against them the Rockley workshops continued for about fifty years, producing work of the highest quality and integrity, many examples of which remain as a legacy to the Rockley craftsmen.

Figure NE308. High splat back Windsor rocking chair. Ash with elm seat and splats. Stamped on side edge of seat 'F. WALKER ROCKLEY' (fl.1823-71).

Two ring turned legs with straight feet connected by crinoline stretcher. Feet turned to tenon into rockers. Three long tapered spindles either side of central back splat. Three tapered underarm spindles with regional style of turned underarm supports. (Right hand arm support replaced.) Stylised fleur-de-lis fretted top splat. Keyhole shaped fret in lower splat.

Figure NE310. Low splat back Windsor armchair. Ash with elm seat and splats. Stamped on side edge of seat 'F. WALKER ROCKLEY' (fl.1823-71).

Two ring turned legs more typical of Lincolnshire Windsors than those made in Nottinghamshire. Vase shaped feet. Legs connected by crinoline stretcher. Three long tapered spindles either side of central back splat. Three tapered underarm spindles with regional style of turned underarm supports. Stylised fleur-de-lis fretted top splat. Keyhole shaped fret in lower splat.

Figure NE312. Low splat back Windsor armchair. Yew with elm seat. Stamped on side edge of seat 'F. WALKER ROCKLEY' (fl.1823-71).

Three ring turned legs with vase feet connected by crinoline stretcher. Three long tapered spindles either side of central back splat. Three tapered underarm spindles with regional style of turned underarm supports. Stylised fleur-de-lis fretted top splat with two extra piercings. Two shaped frets in lower splat.

Figure NE309. Stamp of Frederick Walker of Rockley (fl.1823-71), impressed on the side seat edge of the chair shown in Figure NE308.

Figure NE311. Stamp of Frederick Walker of Rockley (fl.1823-71). Impressed on the side edge of the seat of the chair shown in Figure NE310.

Figure NE313. Stamp of Frederick Walker of Rockley (fl.1823-71), impressed on the side seat edge of the chair shown in Figure NE312.

Figure NE314. Low splat back Windsor armchair. Yew with elm seat. Stamped on side edge of seat 'F. WALKER ROCKLEY' (fl.1823-71).

Single ring turned legs with straight feet more typical of early 19th century Lincolnshire tradition than that of Nottinghamshire. Legs connected by crinoline stretcher. Three long tapered spindles either side of central back splat. Three tapered underarm spindles with regional style of turned underarm supports. Stylised fleur-de-lis fretted top splat with two extra piercings. Two shaped frets in lower splat.

Figure NE315. High decorative splat back Windsor armchair. Yew with elm seat. Stamped on side edge of seat 'F. WALKER ROCKLEY'. This chair has moved no more than five miles from its point of origin in Rockley to the nearby village of West Markham, and has remained in the same family since it was made to date (1985).

Double ring turned legs with elongated bell shaped turning below. Narrow lower leg leading to pear shaped foot. Legs connected by crinoline stretcher. Four long tapered spindles either side of central back splat. Three tapered underarm spindles with turned underarm supports similar in design to those used by George Nicholson (see Figure NE300). Arm bow terminating in notches on under surface. Decorative fretted top and bottom splats.   (Courtesy Dr B. Biggs)

Figure NE316. Low decorative splat back Windsor armchair. Yew with elm seat. Stamped 'F. WALKER ROCKLEY' (fl.1823-71), on side edge of seat. This chair is an example of the most elaborate and decorative form of Windsor produced in the Nottinghamshire tradition. Another similar example, made by this maker, but in the high back form, is shown in Figure NE315.

Double ring turned legs with elongated bell shaped turning below, leading to ball shaped feet; legs connected by crinoline stretcher. Three long tapered spindles either side of central back splat. Three tapered underarm spindles with regional style of turned underarm supports. Elaborately fretted top and lower splats. *(Courtesy Timothy D. Wilson, Bawtry)*

Figure NE318. Low splat back Windsor armchair. Yew with elm seat and ash back legs. Stamped on side edge of seat 'F. WALKER ROCKLEY' (fl.1823-71).

Two ring turned legs with vase shaped feet connected by crinoline stretcher. Three long tapered spindles either side of central back splat. Three tapered underarm spindles with regional style of turned underarm supports. Stylised fleur-de-lis fretted top splat with two extra piercings. Keyhole shaped frets in lower splat.

Figure NE320. Low splat back Windsor child's chair. Yew with elm seat and ash back legs. Stamped on side edge of seat 'F. WALKER ROCKLEY' (fl.1823-71).

Two ring turned legs with straight feet connected by crinoline stretcher. Two long tapered spindles either side of central back splat. Two tapered underarm spindles with regional style of turned underarm supports in the same style as those found on the Wheatland and Nicholson children's chairs illustrated in Figures NE287 and 297. Stylised fleur-de-lis fretted top splat. Keyhole shaped fret in lower splat.

Figure NE319. Stamp of Frederick Walker (fl.1823-71), of Rockley, impressed on the side seat edge of the chair illustrated in Figure NE318.

Figure NE321. Stamp of Frederick Walker (fl.1823-71), of Rockley, impressed on the side seat edge of the child's chair shown in Figure NE320.

Figure NE317. The stamp of Frederick Walker (fl.1823-71), of Rockley, impressed on the side seat edge of the chair shown in Figure NE316.

Figure NE322. Two children's high or table chairs. Ash with elm seats and alder splats. Attributed to Rockley, c.1820-60. The chair to the right has the initials 'I.H.' fretted in the top splat, which probably referred to the child for whom the chair was made.

(Courtesy Timothy D. Wilson Antiques)

188

Figure NE323. Low splat back Windsor armchair. Ash with fruitwood splat and elm seat, stamped on side edge of seat 'J. SPENCER', a maker who is believed to have worked in Nottinghamshire, c.1840-70.

Three ring turned legs with vase shaped feet, legs connected by a crinoline stretcher. Three long tapered spindles either side of central back splat. Three tapered underarm spindles with turned underarm supports typical of Nottinghamshire Windsors. Stylised fleur-de-lis fretted top splat. Keyhole shaped fret in lower splat.

Figure NE325. Low splat back Windsor armchair. Yew with elm seat. Attributed to Nottinghamshire, c.1840-80 (see Figure NE323). Stamped on side edge of seat 'J. SPENCER.'

Three ring turned legs with vase shaped feet connected by crinoline stretcher. Three long tapered spindles either side of central back splat. Three tapered underarm spindles with turned underarm support typical of Nottinghamshire Windsor styles. Stylised fleur-de-lis fretted top splat with two extra piercings. Two shaped frets in lower splat.

Figure NE327. High splat back Windsor armchair. Ash with fruitwood splat and elm seat. Stamped twice on side of seat, 'J. SPENCER', c.1840-70.

Three ring turned legs with unusual parallel turned feet. Legs connected by a crinoline stretcher. Three tapered spindles either side of central stylised fleur-de-lis fretted upper splat. Keyhole shaped fret in lower splat. Three tapered underarm spindles. Turned underarm supports which reflect the Nottinghamshire tradition.

Figure NE324. The stamp of J. Spencer (fl.c.1840-70), impressed on the side seat edge of the chair shown in Figure NE323. This maker was probably working in Nottinghamshire c.1840-70, producing chairs which reflected the Nottinghamshire design tradition.

Figure NE326. The stamp of J. Spencer, impressed on side edge of seat of the chair shown in Figure NE325. This maker, who made a range of different Windsor styles in the manner of the Nottinghamshire makers, has not been firmly located.

Figure NE328. The stamp of J. Spencer impressed on the side seat edge of the chair shown in Figure NE327.

J. Spencer

One chair maker whose output was prolific, and who consistently stamped his work, was J. Spencer. This maker remains an enigma; the style of his chairs show that he clearly worked in the Nottinghamshire regional tradition, producing a wide range of different designs, but his location remains a mystery. As he is not recorded working in, or near to, the known centres of chair production, it seems that his workshop was situated in a community not included in the trade directories of the region. Examples of his work are shown, therefore, in Figures NE323-334 as suggested evidence of this maker's regional style.

Figure NE329. High splat back Windsor armchair. Yew with elm seat. Stamped on side edge of seat 'SPENCER', c.1840-70.

Heavy three ring turned legs with unusual original tapered feet. Legs connected by crinoline stretcher. Four long tapered spindles either side of central back splat. Three tapered underarm spindles. Turned underarm supports, typical of the Nottinghamshire Windsor chairs. Stylised fleur-de-lis fretted top splat with two extra piercings. Two shaped frets in lower splat.

Figure NE331. High splat back Windsor armchair. Yew with elm seat. Attributed to Nottinghamshire, c.1840-80. Stamped on each side edge of seat 'J. SPENCER'. This chair is typical of the 'best' yew high Windsors from this region, which are illustrated on the Allsop trade card shown in Figure NE270.

Ornately turned legs with cup and ball foot. Legs connected by crinoline stretcher. Four tapered spindles each side of central fir tree motif fretted upper and lower splats. Three tapered underarm spindles, and regionally specific underarm turnings. Arm notched beneath ends of arm hoop.

Figure NE333. Child's splat back Windsor armchair. Elm with yew splat and oak legs. Attributed to Nottinghamshire, c.1840-70. Stamped twice on side edge of seat 'J. SPENCER'.

Two ring turned legs with vase and parallel turned shaped feet, a crinoline stretcher connecting legs. Two parallel shaped spindles either side of stylised fleur-de-lis fretted upper splat. Keyhole shaped fret in lower splat. Two parallel shaped underarm spindles. Turned underarm supports. Height 26in. (66cm).

Figure NE330. The stamp of J. Spencer impressed twice on side edge of chair in Figure NE329.

Figure NE332. The stamp of J. Spencer impressed twice on each side seat edge of the chair shown in Figure NE331.

Figure NE334. The stamp of J. Spencer impressed twice on the side seat edge of the chair shown in Figure NE333. This chair has been owned for 'many generations' by the same family who acquired it when resident in Elland, near Halifax, Yorkshire.

Epilogue

* * * * * * *

The history of the Nottinghamshire Windsor chair making trade is that of a truly native tradition, whose designs and manufacturers owed nothing to classical influences. The makers who worked in this craft were highly skilled, and retained the economy of materials and balanced construction throughout a repertoire of styles. These designs were dynamic, yet simple in concept, and although new styles were introduced into the range after 1850 in the Worksop trade, the quality of construction was retained at the highest level. Their products were made in large quantities, and exported to markets throughout the North of England and the Midlands. With the demise of the Windsor trade in Nottinghamshire in the late nineteenth century, an important tradition of English vernacular furniture disappeared in the wake of inferior, mass-produced seating.

Figure NE335. A resident of Brighouse, Yorkshire, late 19th century, sitting in a Windsor chair with Nottinghamshire characteristics including the arm and leg turnings, and the narrow arm typical of that region. Edward Darby, who trained in Worksop, moved to Brighouse around 1880 to carry on his trade as a chair maker and this may account for the Nottinghamshire characteristics.[157] (See p.173 for a further description.)

YORKSHIRE

Yorkshire was the largest county in the North East Region, and was divided into three administrative areas, the North, East and West Ridings. Its population during the nineteenth century was far in excess of any other county in the North East Midlands and the North East (see table on p.102 for comparative figures), and

of the three areas of Yorkshire, the West Riding contained the largest population of working people, who were employed in the many industrial towns and cities throughout the South West of the county. These cities were centres for the textile industry, as well as for those industrial traditions based on the metal trades, including

smelting and the production of cutlery, and included Halifax, Huddersfield, Barnsley, Wakefield, Rotherham, Sheffield and Leeds.

With the exception of the major seaport city of Kingston upon Hull, situated on the River Humber, on the southern edge of the East Riding, the remainder of Yorkshire was essentially a rural county with towns of mercantile importance, but essentially serving an agriculturally based community, rather than an industrial one. Nowhere else in England could one region claim the diversification of terrain which Yorkshire had, from sparsely populated tracts of moorland in the Dales, to the North and West of the county, productive agricultural lands in the centre, and the densely populated communities in the industrial region to the South with important mercantile and shipping interests in the East.

Given this geographical and cultural diversity, it is, perhaps, not surprising that the chair makers who served this county directly reflected the population differences which were present. Consequently the chair making trade was a sparsely populated trade in the rural areas, and more highly developed where the population was greatest. At the beginning of the nineteenth century, chair makers were recorded working only in the large, relatively prosperous cities of Sheffield and Leeds to the West, and Hull to the East.[156] Even in these centres, only a few people were employed in the trade (see Figure NE2 for details). By the 1840s, other chair makers were recorded working in rural centres, for example, in Kirkbymoorside to the North East, Easingwold, Doncaster and Selby in the centre and the South, and Skipton and later Addingham to the West. (See the distribution map in Figure NE2.)

Given the high population density, it seems surprising that the chair making tradition in Yorkshire was so poorly developed relative to that which arose in the adjoining counties of Nottinghamshire and Lincolnshire. However, it is probable that the chair trade was so productive in these Midlands counties that many common chairs were exported to Yorkshire, as a matter of convenience.*

---

* It is recorded, for example, in the list of creditors in 1876 of I. Allsop & Son, Windsor chair manufacturers of Worksop, that clients for their Windsor chairs were in many of the industrial towns of South Yorkshire including Bradford, Cleckheaton, Doncaster and Huddersfield.

Figure NE336. The hearth of Salters' Gate Inn, in Pickering, North Yorkshire, where the peat fire was reputed to have burned for one hundred years, photographed in the late 19th century. The Windsor chair on the left is typical of Yorkshire Windsors, with the broad fleur-de-lis fretted splat produced in South Yorkshire during the 19th century.

The Yorkshire 'common' chair making tradition which did develop, however, was primarily involved in making Windsor chairs which are typically much heavier and less refined in design than the forms of chairs made in the Nottinghamshire and Lincolnshire regions. There were exceptions to this rule, and a few chair makers adopted the lighter, more dynamic styles of the Nottinghamshire makers (see Figure NE358 for an example). In general, however, Yorkshire Windsors which have been recorded with their makers' stamps or with retailers' labels attached to them, indicate a tradition which produced a limited repertoire of robust chair designs, amongst which the Smoking High or broad arm Windsor was a predominant style, with the related Office or Smoker's Bow chairs less in evidence. Low and high backed Windsors of heavier styles than those made in the other North East Midlands counties were also made, as were different styles of kitchen Windsors, and stools which were commonly used as alternatives

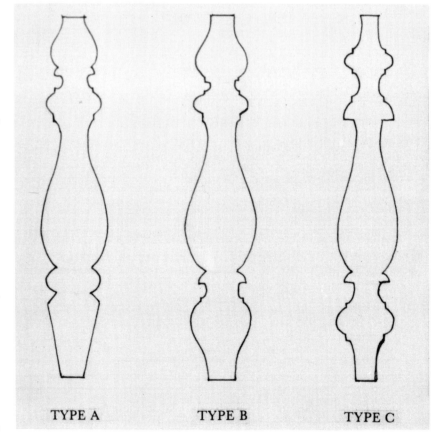

TYPE A   TYPE B   TYPE C

Figure NE337. Profiles of the most commonly found Yorkshire Windsor chair underarm support turnings.

192

Figure NE338. A best high back smoker or broad arm Windsor chair. Yew with elm seat. Stamped 'W. TURNER' (fl.1817-43), on inner side of right arm. This chair is an extremely well balanced example of the regional style and owes much to the skill of the maker's ability in 'framing' (assembling), the chair.

Elaborately turned legs with vase shaped feet. H-stretchers, with back legs connected by a further cross stretcher. Central ball motif in cross stretchers. Four parallel shaped spindles either side of central fir tree motif fretted splat above arms. Two turned spindles either side of central fir tree motif fretted splat below the arms, with heavily turned underarm supports.

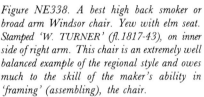

Figure NE339. The stamp of William Turner impressed on the inner side of the right hand arm of the chair shown in Figure NE338. This maker's stamp is the only one recorded in this unusual position in the English tradition, and seems to have been made more as an inventory record for its producer, rather than as an act of advertising. Three William Turners are recorded amongst the group of early 19th century makers in the North East (see Appendix) and the early working periods of these makers support the belief that the broad arm Windsor was known and made in the first part of the 19th century in Yorkshire.

Figure NE340. Best high back smoker or broad arm Windsor chair. Ash with elm seat. Stamped on rear edge of seat 'FROM T. RHODES HALIFAX' (fl.1866-1908).

Heavy single ball motif in turned legs with vase shaped feet. H-stretcher connected by two cross stretchers. Two turned ring motif in cross stretchers. Four tapered long back spindles, with further taper at arm mortice. Central fir tree motif fretted splat above arms. Two turned spindles either side of central fir tree motif fretted splat below the arms. Heavily turned underarm supports.

Figure NE341. The stamp of T. Rhodes of Halifax (fl.1866-1908), impressed on the rear seat edge of the chair shown in Figure NE341. This furnishing business was described in 1890 as 'one of the largest concerns in its line in Western Yorkshire'.

range of interesting but uncommon varieties attributed to Yorkshire is shown in Figures NE367-382.

Other Yorkshire chairs show a general demeanour similar to the refined North East Midlands made chairs, but in these examples, a tendency towards heavy structure, and the use of the Yorkshire regional styles of arm turnings (see Figure NE337) are clearly in evidence, as is the inclusion of heavy leg turnings, including the use of two ring turned legs and cup and pear shaped feet. See Figures NE360-365.

High back smokers

The following group of chairs is typical of Yorkshire chairs made from the 1830s until about 1900, particularly in the major centres of Leeds, Sheffield and Hull. These are the high back splat Windsors which are characterised in having a sawn and shaped three-part arm (see Chapter 1, p.22 for structural details) and are the largest of all the English Windsor chairs, made with heavy individual parts and large seats. These Windsors were called 'smoking high' chairs by the Nottinghamshire makers,[158] and 'best high back smokers' by the Yorkshire makers.[159] In recent years, 'broad arm' Windsor has become common as a descriptive term, since it focuses on the relative distinction between the continuous bent narrow arm bow, typical of many Windsors, and the broad flattened shape utilised in the smoking high chairs.

The relatively large number of these chairs which has been recorded with makers' stamps probably indicates both the popularity of this design, and the strong competition which existed between makers in the industrial towns of the West Riding of Yorkshire.*

This style of chair was made in a hierarchy of woods in the same way

majority of recorded Yorkshire tradition Windsors and examples may be seen in Figures NE373, 377 and 398. However, other less common underarm turnings also appear, showing great individuality of style.

Although the majority of Yorkshire chair designs conform within their individual stylistic group, this region's makers experimented with alternative splat designs, spindle and splat arrangements, as well as moving leg styles from one chair design to another. The merging of parts of the best high back smoker chair designs with narrow arm Windsor styles was also a feature of this tradition. A

to chairs in many places of work, education and recreation in the North of England.

Throughout the Yorkshire Windsor system of designs, stylistically unifying features are found in the forms of underarm support turnings, three of which appear most commonly, and are shown in Figure NE337. These three variants occur as options in the

* Of the many long-standing chair makers to work in Sheffield, some were family businesses which continued over several generations, and probably built up concerns which were capable of producing a large quantity of chairs. For example, the Barton family of Sheffield worked from 1854 until 1898 at the Soho Saw Mills in Water Street under the ownership of four members of the family in turn. They explicitly advertised as Windsor chair makers. The Leeds chair makers included many family dynasties too, for example the Longbotham family who worked from 1842 until 1881 at Silsden, Leeds. Amongst the chair makers in Hull were a number of highly productive businesses who advertised themselves as Windsor, lath and Grecian chair makers. Amongst these, the firm of William and, later, S.J. Russell & Sons of Prospect Street, continued working until the end of the 19th century.

193

Figure NE342. Best high back smoker or broad arm Windsor chair. Ash hoop, top spindles, legs and stretchers; alder arm segments, lower spindles, arm supports and splats; elm seat. Stamped on rear edge of seat 'S. SHAW' (fl.1879-87).

Elaborately turned legs with pear shaped feet. H-stretcher connected by two cross stretchers. Central ball motif in cross stretchers. Four tapered spindles either side of central fir tree motif fretted splat above arms. Two turned spindles either side of central fir tree fretted splat below the arms. Heavily turned underarm supports.

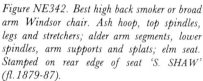

Figure NE343. The stamp of Scaife Shaw impressed on the rear seat edge of the chair shown in Figure NE342. This maker worked at 16 Neville Street and Trafalgar Row in Meadow Lane, Leeds (fl.1879-87).

Figure NE344. Best high back smoker or broad arm Windsor chair. Elm with ash top hoop and alder splats. Attributed to Yorkshire, c.1840-70. Stamped 'F. HALL' on rear edge of seat.

Turned legs with cup and tulip shaped feet. H-stretcher with two cross stretchers with central ball motif. Four tapered spindles either side of central fir tree motif fretted splat above arms. Two turned spindles either side of central fir tree fretted splat below the arms. Turned underarm support in regional style type C, Figure NE337.

Figure NE345. The stamp of F. Hall impressed on the rear seat edge of the chair shown in Figure NE344. No record has been found of F. Hall, although he was probably related to a family of that surname who had members working as turners and chair makers in Meadow Lane, Leeds from 1816 until the 1830s. John Hall was making chairs in Sheffield between 1845 and 1857. Much later in the century, Thomas Hall was working as a chair maker in Hull between 1885 and 1900.

Figure NE346. Best high back smoker or broad arm Windsor chair. Ash with fruitwood splats and upper arm section, and elm seat. Stamped on rear edge of seat 'J. WATSON' (fl.1828-75). Regional style of turned underarm support type A, Figure NE337, commonly found on narrow arm Windsors from this area. See Figures NE360 and 371 for examples.

Similar turned three ring legs to those on chair in Figure NE340. Vase shaped feet. H-stretcher, connecting legs. Central gouge turned motif in cross stretcher. Four tapered spindles either side of central fir tree motif fretted splat above arms. Two turned spindles either side of central fir tree fretted splat below the arms.

Figure NE347. The stamp of John Watson, impressed on the rear seat edge of the chair shown in Figure NE346. A father and son of the same Christian name are recorded at Swadforth Street, and Cross Hills, Skipton, Yorkshire (fl.1828-75).

as those made in the Worksop, Nottinghamshire tradition where yew was the most prestigious wood, with cherry or alder next, and ash and elm being the least expensive option.

The 'best high back smokers' illustrated in Figures NE338-351 conform in general stylistic terms for this type of chair. However, Yorkshire makers experimented with the basic design, and examples are shown below in which arrangements of turned spindles are incorporated into the back design in place of plain spindles (see Figure NE353). A further style has a square back design with a stay rail and cross rail incorporating rows of short and long elaborately turned spindles (see Figure NE354), and a further version is shown with an upholstered back in Figure NE355. These styles are uncommon, but their existence is interesting in indicating how traditional Windsor chair makers did, on occasion, attempt to cause a design 'shift', perhaps to modernise their products. Other variants of best high back smokers are shown in relation to narrow armed Windsors in Figures NE371, 372, 375 and 376, where amalgamations of different chair designs were attempted.

Figure NE348. Best high back smoker or broad arm Windsor rocking chair. Fruitwood with elm seat. Stamped 'J. WATSON' on rear edge of seat (fl.1828-75).

Three ring turned legs with vase shaped feet turned to fit rockers. H-stretcher with central ball motif in cross stretcher. Four parallel shaped spindles either side of central fretted splat with fir tree motif above arms. Two turned spindles either side of central fir tree fretted splat below the arms. Ornately turned underarm support.

Figure NE349. The stamp of John Watson (fl.1828-75), of Cross Hills, Skipton, Yorkshire, impressed on the rear seat edge of the chair shown in Figure NE348. John Watson was a cabinet and chair maker who lived at Cross Hills, Skipton, and who had his workshop at Swadforth Street.

Figure NE350. Stamp beneath the seat of chair shown in Figure NE348 which reads, 'HIRED FROM MAXEY & CO., 26 & 32 MEADOW STREET, SHEFFIELD'. The hiring of Windsor chairs for gatherings was probably not uncommon (see Figure NE388 for further example); however, for what event a rocking chair would be hired is not clear.

Figure NE351. Best high back smoker or broad arm Windsor chair. Yew with elm seat. Stencil beneath the seat reads, 'FROM S.E. COLLISON. Cabinet Maker &c., 12 & 15 JUNCTION DOCK WALLS, HULL.' (fl.1841-89).

Three ring turned legs similar in design to those shown on the J. Watson chairs, Figures NE346 and 348 with cup and vase shaped feet. H-stretcher form with two cross stretchers.

Figure NE352. Stencil of S.E. Collison (fl.1841-89), cabinet maker, of 12 and 15 Junction Dock Walls, Hull, found beneath the seat of the chair shown in Figure NE351.

Figure NE353. Best high back smoker or broad arm chair. Alder seat, arms and splats; remainder elm. Attributed to Yorkshire, c.1840-80. The use of decoratively turned upper back spindles is very uncommon, and indicates the Yorkshire makers' tendency for design alteration.

Heavy, elaborately turned legs with cup and vase shaped feet. H-stretcher, with two cross stretchers. Ball motif in cross stretchers. Three decoratively turned spindles either side of central fir tree motif fretted splat above arms. Two turned spindles either side of central fir tree motif fretted splat below the arms. Elaborately turned underarm supports.

Figure NE354. Best high back smoker or broad arm chair. Yew with elm seat. Attributed to Yorkshire, c.1870-1900. This very unusual style of chair may have been made for a special order, and is a reflection of a move for greater comfort than conventional Windsors allowed. A hanging padded cushion may have been placed over the spindle arrangement when the chair was in use.

Turned legs with cup and vase shaped feet. H-stretcher with two cross stretchers. Central ball motif in cross stretchers. The back design embodies a row of short turned spindles, supported between the stay rail and cross rail, below which, six long elaborately turned back spindles are supported between the arm support section and the upper cross rail. The sawn and turned back uprights terminate with decorative finials. Five turned spindles below the arm similar in design to the upper back spindles, with arm supports turned in a regional style, type C, Figure 337.

Figure NE355. Best high back smoker or broad arm Windsor chair. Yew with elm seat. Attributed to Yorkshire, c.1880-1900, and stamped 'L.L.' on rear edge of seat. The use of upholstery as an adaption of a traditional Windsor chair is very unusual, and indicates that the maker attempted to create a more comfortable and 'modern' chair design from the earlier style.

Elaborately turned legs with cup and vase shaped feet. H-stretcher with two cross stretchers with central ball motif. Curved back uprights with shaped stay rail. Six turned short spindles supported between stay rail and cross bar. The back upholstered and covered with 'leatherette' (imitation leather fabric) in a 'buttoned' pattern. The arms made in the manner of a broad arm Windsor style with two turned spindles, and arm supports similar in style to type C, Figure NE337.

Figure NE356. Office or smoker's bow Windsor chair. Elm with alder arms and stay rail. Attributed to Yorkshire, c.1840-80.

Elaborately turned legs with vase shaped feet. H-stretcher with central ball motif in cross stretcher. Six turned spindles connecting the arm to the seat, and two turned underarm supports. Both spindles and underarm supports turned in the regional style.

Figure NE357. Office or smoker's bow Windsor chair. Alder seat, splats, arms, and stay rail, remainder elm. Attributed to Yorkshire, c.1840-80. The stylistic variation of three fir tree splats is very uncommon and indicates the Yorkshire makers' tendency to vary elements within a particular conventional design to create a new style of chair.

Elaborately turned legs with cup and vase shaped feet. H-stretcher with two cross stretchers with central ball motif. Three fir tree fretted splats connecting the arm to the seat. Underarm supports turned in a regional style, type C, Figure NE337.

Office or low back smokers

A further low backed chair, made in Yorkshire, reflects many of the basic characteristics of the best high back smoker chair. This is a chair named the 'office' chair by the Nottinghamshire makers,[160] and a 'best low back smoker' by the Yorkshire makers.[161] This style of chair was commonly used literally as an office chair as well as in many other settings such as working men's clubs and public houses. The chair has the general heaviness of structure and style which typified the best high back smoker, but does not have the top hoop, spindles, and fretted splat which the high variety has. Rather, a shaped cresting rail is incorporated across the arm joint to fit the shape of the user's lower back. No short splat is typically included in the lower arcade between the arms and seat, and six turned spindles and two arm supports are the most common form. No maker or retailer identified chair of this type has been recorded from Yorkshire, but a chair which embodies the spindle turnery features of the region is shown in Figure NE356.

In common with the best high smoking chair, variations and elaborations in this style of chair were occasionally attempted, and an example of an unconventional 'smoker' chair design is shown in Figure NE357. This design has clearly borrowed the fir tree motif fretted splats used in the lower half of a best high back smoker.

Figure NE358. Low splat back Windsor armchair. Ash with elm seat. Stamped twice on front top corners of seat 'J. BANKS J. BANKS SELBY' (fl.1841-61).

Heavy three ring turned legs. Legs connected by an H-form stretcher. Three long tapered spindles either side of central back splat. Slightly elliptical underarm spindles with underarm support turning typical of the Nottinghamshire tradition. Stylised fleur-de-lis fretted top splat. Keyhole shaped fret in lower splat.

Bent Arm Windsors

In addition to the best high back smoker chairs, Yorkshire chair makers also made Windsor chairs with narrow bent arm bows which include a wide range of different splats and leg turning styles, forms of leg stretchers, underarm turnings and numbers of back spindles. Examples in the group shown in Figures NE358-364 have been recorded with makers' identification. Other examples assigned to this group show a degree of conformity in terms of exhibiting underarm support turning devices which affirm their regional origin.

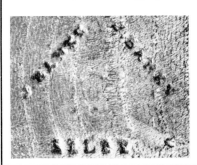

Figure NE359. The stamp of James Banks (fl.1841-61), impressed, in a triangulated form, with 'J. Banks' stamped twice, and 'Selby' forming the base line. The stamps are made on the front of the seat above the front leg positions. This maker worked at Broad Gate, Selby, as a chair maker and turner, and later moved to Gowthorpe, Selby, where he is last recorded in 1861. He was a member of a large family of chair makers, wood turners and cabinet makers, all working in Yorkshire towns and villages, two of whom worked as chair makers in Easingwold, and another worked as a chair maker in Kirkbymoorside. Other family members worked as wood turners in York, Thirsk, Tadcaster and Hull.

Figure NE362. Low splat back Windsor armchair. Ash with elm seat and splat. Stamped on side edge of seat 'A. BOOTH'. Untraced, but believed to be from Yorkshire, c.1850-70. The style of arm support turning is regionally specific, and represents one of the major turnery signatures forms incorporated in the late 19th century Windsors shown in Figures NE386-395.

Heavy three ring turned legs with vase shaped feet connected by a crinoline stretcher. Three long spindles tapering above the arm, either side of central back splat. Elliptical shaped underarm spindles. Stylised fleur-de-lis fretted top splat. Keyhole shaped fret in lower splat.

Figure NE360. Low splat back Windsor armchair. Ash with birch splat and elm seat, stamped on side edge of seat 'A. WILSON' (fl.1871-79). The design of the underarm turning on this chair is regionally specific and is one of the major turnery forms incorporated in the mass produced Windsors shown in Figures NE386-395.

Three ring turned legs with vase shaped feet connected by H-stretchers. Three long parallel shaped spindles either side of central back splat. Three tapered underarm spindles. Stylised fleur-de-lis fretted top splat. Keyhole shaped fret in lower splat.

Figure NE363. The stamp of A. Booth impressed on the rear seat edge of the chair in Figure NE362. This maker has not been firmly located, but records show that four members of a Booth family were wood turners and cabinet makers in Sheffield during the first half of the 19th century, and it may be that A. Booth was related to this family. Other Booths were recorded working as individual turners and cabinet makers in other towns in Yorkshire. See Appendix for details.

Figure NE361. The stamp of A. Wilson impressed on the side seat edge of the chair shown in Figure NE360. Two A. Wilsons are recorded as chair makers in Yorkshire. Alfred Wilson worked at Grafton Street, Leeds (fl.1871-77); Arthur Wilson worked at Nawton, York, in 1879.

Figure NE364. Low splat back Windsor armchair. Ash with alder splat and seat. Attributed to Yorkshire, c.1840-80.

Heavy three ring turned legs with vase shaped feet. H-stretchers connecting legs, central cross stretcher having ring shaped motif. Three tapered spindles either side of broad stylised fleur-de-lis fretted upper splat. Keyhole shaped fret in lower splat. Three tapered underarm spindles, turned underarm supports which embody regional design type B, Figure 337.

Figure NE365. Low splat back Windsor armchair. Ash with elm seat and splats. Attributed to Yorkshire, c.1830-70.

Heavy two ring turned legs with pear shaped feet in a regional style. Legs connected by crinoline stretcher. Three tapered spindles either side of central back splat. Three tapered underarm spindles with regional style of turned underarm support which embodies flattened sections. Stylised fleur-de-lis fretted top splat. Keyhole shaped fret in lower splat.

Figure NE366. Self portrait in watercolour by the artist, Mary Ellen Best, born Eastergate, York, 1809. The interior of the artist's room in Yorkshire shows three low-back splat Windsors. The splats of these chairs are unusual, and similar in design to the chair illustrated in Figure NE367 made by S. Shaw, of Leeds.

(Courtesy Sotheby's New York)

Figure NE367. High splat back Windsor armchair. Yew with elm seat. Stamped 'S. SHAW' on side edge of seat (fl.1879-87).

Two ring turned legs with vase shaped feet, connected by crinoline stretcher. Four tapered long spindles each side of an unusual fretted upper splat. Lower splat with keyhole shaped fret. Four elliptical shaped underarm spindles. The underarm support is turned in a regional style type B, Figure NE337.

Figure NE368. Stamp of Scaife Shaw impressed on side seat edge of the chair shown in Figure NE367. Scaife Shaw worked at Neville Street and Trafalgar Row, Meadow Lane, Leeds, in 1879-87.

Chairs with experimental designs

A number of examples (Figures NE367-382) illustrate the propensity of the Yorkshire makers to experiment with design. Their ability to amalgamate features between certain narrow and broad arm styles of Windsors is characterised in this group, as well as chairs which display similar features within the framework of essentially different types of chairs. In each case, however, the underarm turning device acts as a sign of regional origin.

Figure NE369. Low splat back Windsor armchair. Ash with alder splat and elm seat. Attributed to Yorkshire, c.1840-80. The fret motif in the splats is found in other varieties of chair. See Figures NE370-372 for other examples.

Three ring turned legs with vase shaped feet. H-stretcher connecting legs. Three parallel spindles either side of heart shaped fretted upper splat. Heart shaped fret in lower splat. Three tapered underarm spindles. Turned underarm supports which embody regional design type B, Figure NE377.

Figure NE370. High splat back Windsor armchair. Ash with alder splat and seat. Attributed to Yorkshire, c.1840-80.

Two ring turned legs with pear shaped feet. H-stretcher connecting legs. Three tapering spindles either side of heart shape fretted upper splat. Heart shaped fret in lower splat. Three tapered underarm spindles. Turned underarm supports which embody regional design type B, Figure NE337. This fret design is also shown in different styles of chairs shown in Figures NE369, 371 and 372. This form of leg is typical of Yorkshire Windsors, and other examples are shown in Figures NE372 and 378.

Figure NE371. High splat back Windsor armchair. Ash with alder splats and seat. Attributed to Yorkshire, c.1840-80. See Figures NE369, 370 and 372 for other chairs using this style of splat. The style of single ring turned leg is shown in the stool design in Figure NE414.

Single ring turned legs with vase shaped feet. H-stretchers connecting legs. Three elliptical spindles either side of heart shaped fretted upper splat. Heart shaped fret in lower splat. Three elliptical shaped underarm spindles. Turned underarm supports which embody regional design type A, Figure NE337.

199

Figure NE372. Best high back smoker or broad arm Windsor chair. Elm with alder sawn arm parts and splats. Attributed to Yorkshire, c.1840-80. The fretting motif of the splats is probably particular to the Yorkshire makers, and was used in a number of Windsor designs. See Figures NE369-371 for other examples.

Heavy two ring turned legs with pear shaped feet. H-form stretchers with central ball motif in cross stretcher. Four tapered spindles either side of central heart shaped fretted splat above arms. Two turned spindles either side of central heart shaped fretted splat below the arms, and turned underarm support of type A, Figure NE337.

Figure NE373. High splat back Windsor armchair. Elm with alder splats. Attributed to Yorkshire, c.1840-80. The unusual style of splat is also adopted, in a reduced size, in the chair shown in Figure NE374 and indicates the willingness of the Yorkshire makers to introduce different devices into their chairs.

Heavy two ring turned legs with vase shaped feet. H-form stretchers connecting legs. Four tapered spindles either side of broad clover motif fretted upper and lower splat motif. Three tapered underarm spindles. Turned underarm supports of regional design type A, Figure NE337.

Figure NE374. Best high back smoker or broad arm Windsor chair. Elm seat, top hoop, back spindles and arms, alder splat, legs and stretchers. Attributed to Yorkshire, c.1840-80. The lack of a splat below the arms, and the fretting in the upper splat are unusual. Both spindles and arm turnery patterns are similar to those used in the 'F. Hall' chair in Figure NE344.

Elaborately turned legs with cup and vase shaped feet. H-form stretcher, with central ball motif. Three tapered spindles above arms either side of central fretted splat with clover motif. Six turned spindles below the arms, and turned underarm supports, type C, Figure NE337.

Figure NE375. High splat back Windsor armchair. Ash with alder splats and seat. Attributed to Yorkshire, c.1840-60.

Heavy three ring turned legs; vase shaped turning with cup shape feet. Crinoline stretcher connecting legs. Three elliptical underarm spindles, turned underarm supports which embody regional design type B, Figure NE337.

Figure NE376. Best high back smoker or broad arm Windsor chair. Ash with alder splats and elm seat. Attributed to Yorkshire, c.1840-1900.

Elaborately turned legs with cup and vase shaped feet. H-form stretchers with central ball motif in cross stretcher. Four tapered spindles either side of central decoratively fretted splat above arms. See Figure NE375 for similar fretting device. Two turned spindles either side of central decoratively fretted splat below the arms. Turned underarm supports in regional style type A, Figure NE337.

Figure NE377. High splat back Windsor armchair. Ash with alder splat and elm seat. Attributed to Yorkshire, c.1840-80.

Three ring turned legs with vase shaped feet. H-form stretcher connecting legs. Three tapered spindles either side of broad upper splat with flame motif fret. Keyhole shaped fret in lower splat. Three tapered underarm spindles. Turned underarm supports which embody regional design type B, Figure NE337.

Figure NE378. High splat back Windsor armchair. Elm with alder splats and seat. Attributed to Yorkshire, c.1840-80. This uncommon chair embodies design characteristics from the high splat back Windsors with narrow arms, and the feature of turned spindles below the arm which is typical of the best high back smoker or broad arm Windsor. This chair indicates the tendency for Yorkshire Windsors to cross design boundaries, and amalgamate features from different chairs.

Heavy two ring turned legs with cup and vase shaped feet typical of a Yorkshire regional leg style. H-form stretchers connecting legs. Multiple ring turnings on central cross stretcher, ring turnings on side stretchers. Three spindles either side of broad fretted upper splat with flame and keyhole motifs. Petal shaped fret in lower splat. Two turned underarm spindles. Turned underarm supports which embody regional design type B, Figure NE337.

Figure NE379. High splat back Windsor armchair. Ash with alder splat and elm seat. Attributed to Yorkshire, c.1840-80.

Elaborately turned legs with vase shaped feet. H-form stretcher connecting legs. Three tapered spindles either side of broad upper splat with uncommon flame shaped motif. Flame shaped fret in lower splat. Three tapered underarm spindles. Turned underarm supports which embody regional design type B, Figure NE337.

Figure NE380. High splat back Windsor armchair. Ash top hoop, and remainder of chair in elm. Stamped 'A. ISAAC' on rear edge of seat. Attributed to Yorkshire, c.1840-70.

Two ring turned legs with ball shaped feet in regional style. Crinoline stretcher connecting legs. Three tapered spindles either side of broad stylised fir tree fretted upper splat. Fir tree shaped fret in lower splat. Three tapered underarm spindles, turned underarm support which embodies regional design type C, Figure NE337.

Figure NE381. Stamp of A. Isaac impressed on the rear seat edge of the chair in Figure NE380. This maker is untraced. The chair embodies the Yorkshire regional features of leg and underarm turning style, suggesting a date of manufacture between 1840 and 1870.

Figure NE382. A turned rocking armchair. Yew with elm seat. Stamped 'A. WILSON MAKER' (fl.1871-79), on rear edge of seat. The use of yew was typically associated with 'best' chairs, and this, combined with an unusual design, probably means that this was a specially designed chair.

Heavy, ornately turned legs with feet turned to fit rockers, legs connected by H-form stretcher, the central cross stretcher having multiple middle turnings. Two heavy outer ring turned uprights, supporting a curved stay rail similar in design to those used in Allsop kitchen chairs (see Figures NE260). Three multiple turned back spindles connecting the stay rail and seat. Grecian style swept arm shape with heavy multiple ring turned arm supports.

Figure NE383. The stamp of A. Wilson impressed on the side seat edge of the chair shown in Figure NE382. Two A. Wilsons are recorded as chair makers in Yorkshire. Alfred Wilson worked at Grafton Street, Leeds, 1871-77; and Arthur Wilson worked at Nawton, York, in 1879.

Side chairs

Windsor bow back side chairs also appear to have been made in this tradition, but probably not in large numbers. An example of this type of Yorkshire chair is shown in Figure NE384 which exhibits the general heaviness of construction and a leg turning form which are common to this region's chairs.

Late 19th century chairs

The majority of existing Windsor chairs produced in Yorkshire were probably made late in the nineteenth century when records show that as the Windsor chair making trade was declining in other areas, the chair making trade in Yorkshire, particularly in the towns of Leeds and Sheffield, was increasing. The trade in the third major centre, Hull, remained undiminished until the end of the nineteenth century, whereas the rurally based Yorkshire chair makers had largely disappeared by the third quarter of the nineteenth century. See Figure NE2 which shows in graph form the relative numbers of chair makers recorded in trade directories for all the counties of the North East region.

The numerically predominant style of late nineteenth century Yorkshire Windsor chairs is typically of the high back variety, with a standardisation of design and materials which suggests that they were the product of an essentially industrial manufacturing process, and were evidently produced in large numbers, and sold widely to wholesale customers, house furnishers, cabinet makers, and those who hired chairs for social events. Examples of these late nineteenth century chairs are shown in Figures NE385-399. No chairs of this type have been recorded with maker's marks, but all those illustrated here have retailers' identification, from many parts of the county. The wide dispersal of these 'common' chairs suggests that the chair manufacturers may have produced a form of catalogue similar to that illustrated in Figures NE413 and 419 which are taken from the 1920 catalogue of William Brear & Sons, chair makers of Addingham, and that the practice of retailers ordering chairs from wholesale sources in the county became common. The evidence of mass-production in Yorkshire also suggests competitive pricing, which may have contributed to the decline of the chair trade in Nottinghamshire and perhaps Lincolnshire

Figure NE384. Windsor side chair. Yew with yellow stained elm seat. Attributed to Yorkshire, c.1835-80. The leg design, large seat, and overall robust design suggest that this is a Yorkshire style of Windsor.

Heavy two ring turned legs with ball shaped feet. Elaborately shaped back splat with two fir tree motif frets, similar in design to splats commonly used in the upper part of smokers high or broad arm Windsors. Robust hoop with scribed edge. Three parallel spindles each side of central splat.

Figure NE385. High splat back Windsor armchair. Elm with alder splats. Attributed to Yorkshire, c.1860-1900. The turned underarm supports embody regional design similar to that shown in the 'high back mock-smoker' chair illustrated in the catalogue of William Brear & Sons of Addingham.

Three ring turned legs with vase shaped feet. H-form stretcher connecting legs. Three tapered spindles either side of fir tree fretted upper and lower splats. Three tapered underarm spindles.

Figure NE386. High splat back Windsor armchair. Ash with fruitwood splat and elm seat. Paper label pasted beneath the seat reads, 'JOHN EASTEN & SONS. MARKET PLACE. HULL.' (fl.1872-1901). This style of chair is typical of those made in large numbers during the late 19th century in Yorkshire.

Three ring turned legs with vase shaped feet. H-form stretchers connecting legs. Three spindles either side of broad stylised fleur-de-lis fretted upper splat. Keyhole shaped fret in lower splat. Three elliptical shaped underarm spindles. Turned underarm supports type B, Figure NE337.

Figure NE387. Paper label pasted beneath the seat of the chair shown in Figure NE386 advertising the large firm of household furnishers, John Easten & Sons of Market Place, Hull. This firm (fl.1872-1901), both bought in and made furniture for sale. The Windsor chair shown in Figure NE386 was probably bought from a specialist maker, and resold as part of the Easten stock-in-trade.

Figure NE388. High splat back Windsor armchair. Ash with alder splat and elm seat, c.1880-1900. Stamped 'J. DUKE ON HIRE' on rear edge of seat. This chair is an example of a common style of late 19th century Yorkshire Windsors, which were hired out for gatherings by firms who specialised in this trade.

Three ring turned legs with vase shaped feet. H-form stretchers connecting legs. Three spindles either side of broad stylised fleur-de-lis fretted upper splat. Keyhole shaped fret in lower splat. Three tapered underarm spindles. Turned underarm supports of regional type B, Figure NE337.

Figure NE390. High splat back Windsor armchair. Ash with alder splat and elm seat. Stencilled beneath the seat 'FROM G. WHARTON & SON. CABINET MAKERS, UPHOLSTERERS, &C. NORTHALLERTON' (fl.1840-79). This style of chair is one of a range of mass-produced Windsors made in Yorkshire, probably during the last quarter of the 19th century.

Three ring turned legs with vase shaped feet. H-form stretchers connecting legs. Three parallel turned spindles either side of broad stylised fleur-de-lis fretted upper splat. Keyhole shaped fret in lower splat. Three tapered underarm spindles. Turned underarm supports which embody regional design type A, Figure NE337.

Figure NE392. High splat back Windsor armchair. Fruitwood with ash arm and top, hoop, and elm seat, stamped on rear edge of seat 'J. & W. HASTINGS ROTHERHAM' (fl.1870-present day).

Three ring turned legs with vase shaped feet. H-form stretchers with central ball motif in cross stretcher. Three parallel shaped spindles either side of central fir tree fretted splat. Three tapered underarm spindles and regional turned underarm support type C, Figure NE337, similar to those shown in Figures NE380 and 394.

Figure NE389. The stamp of J. Duke impressed on the rear seat edge of the chair shown in Figure NE388. This unidentified owner evidently hired out chairs, and stamped them for purposes of recognition. The evidence of hiring indicates that this style of chair was of relatively lowly value, and supports the view that these were inexpensive, mass-produced Windsors.

Figure NE391. Stencil from beneath the seat of the chair shown in Figure NE390 advertising the firm of G. Wharton & Son, cabinet makers of Northallerton, Yorkshire (fl.1840-79). This firm supplied general household furnishings, and appears to have purchased chairs from specialist makers, and to have applied their own retailing stencil.

Figure NE393. Stamp of J.W. Hastings of Rotherham (fl.1870-present day (1987)), impressed on the rear edge of the chair shown in Figure NE392. This firm of house furnishers had a cabinet making department in the 19th century, but they probably bought chairs from specialist makers, and sold them with their own stamp attached.

in the second half of the nineteenth century, since makers in these regions had previously sold many chairs to the North Eastern counties.

The repertoire of Yorkshire high back styles from the late nineteenth century group of chairs includes a number of variants, the most common of which have broad splats with fleur-de-lis fretting and three ring turned legs with vase shaped feet, connected by H-stretchers. These chairs are typically made in ash with alder splats, and often have alder seats, although seats in elm are recorded, but less commonly so. Low back Windsors of this variety have also been recorded, but they appear to be less common, and none have been discovered with identification labels. Further styles from this late tradition include chairs with a fir tree fretted motif in the splat (see Figures NE385 and 392), and include those with three ring turned legs and vase shaped feet (see Figure NE385) as well as the leg style common in other Yorkshire chairs, which have two heavy ring turnings and a ball shaped foot (see Figure NE398). This style has been recorded with both three and four spindles each side of the back splat.

Figure NE394. High splat back Windsor armchair. Fruitwood with ash arm bow and top hoop, and elm seat. Brass plate fixed on rear edge of seat which reads 'SUMMERS BROS HOUSE FURNISHERS, NORTH STREET SCARBOROUGH' (fl.1889). This chair appears to be a larger and more robust version of the chair shown in Figure NE392.

Three ring turned legs with vase shaped feet. H-form stretchers with back legs connected by a further cross stretcher. Central ball motif in cross stretchers. Four tapered spindles sharply tapering into the seat, either side of central fir tree motif fretted upper and lower splats. Four turned underarm spindles, and regionally specific design of turned underarm support type B, Figure NE337.

Figure NE396. High splat back Windsor armchair. Yew with elm seat. Stencil beneath seat reads, 'From S.E. COLLISON, Cabinet Maker &c., 12, JUNCTION DOCK WALLS, HULL' (fl.1841-89). This chair is typical of the 'best' yew high Windsor chairs from this region.

Ornately turned legs with ball feet. Legs connected by crinoline stretcher. Four tapered spindles each side of central fir tree motif fretted upper and lower splats. Three tapered underarm spindles, and regionally specific underarm turnings. Arm notched beneath ends of arm hoop.

Figure NE398. High splat back Windsor armchair. Yew with elm seat. Applied paper label reads 'FROM R. ODDY, CABINET MAKER, 60 KING STREET, HUDDERSFIELD'. Ralph Oddy was, no doubt, the supplier of this chair rather than the maker. The inclusion of this example, which is closely similar to chairs made by the firm of I. Allsop & Son of Worksop, Nottinghamshire, and by J. Spencer, who is also believed to have worked in Nottinghamshire, reinforces the view that some Yorkshire furniture suppliers imported the high quality Windsors from elsewhere, and sold them under their own name.

Heavy three ring turned legs with ball shaped feet. Legs connected by crinoline stretcher. Four long tapered spindles either side of central back splat. Three tapered underarm spindles with turned underarm support, typical of Nottinghamshire Windsor chairs. Fir tree fretted motifs in top and lower splats.

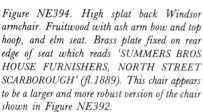

Figure NE395. Brass plate of Summers Bros of North Street, Scarborough, Yorkshire, 1889, attached to the rear of the chair shown in Figure NE394. This firm probably bought chairs from specialist suppliers, and attached their own retailing labels to them.

Figure NE397. Stencil beneath seat of the chair shown in Figure NE396. S. Collison appears to have been both a chair and cabinet maker. However, the North Eastern design features which this chair exhibits could also be the product of other Yorkshire makers, or perhaps from Worksop in Nottinghamshire. Collison evidently sold chairs from other regions. See Figure NE76 for example.

Figure NE399. The paper label of Ralph Oddy of King Street, Huddersfield, under the seat of the chair in Figure NE398. Ralph Oddy, a cabinet maker and upholsterer, is first recorded in Sheepridge, Huddersfield, in 1841 and in King Street in 1875. Cabinet makers commonly bought Windsor chairs from specialist makers and sold them as part of their repertoire of furniture, and this example came from a Nottinghamshire maker (see Figure NE271).

Imported chairs from other regions

In addition to purchasing locally made chairs, it seems probable that some Yorkshire cabinet makers also imported Windsors from Nottinghamshire and sold them under their own name. This is illustrated by a chair stamped by Bunning of Doncaster shown in Figure NE400. The chair has identical features to those which would be expected of chairs made at Rockley in Nottinghamshire and it may be that as George and James Bunning were cabinet makers and not chair makers, this chair was imported from there. Other chairs have also been recorded bearing Yorkshire cabinet makers' labels or stencils, but having the characteristics of Nottinghamshire chairs. Examples of these are illustrated in Figures NE396 and 398, which in both cases show best high chairs made in yew and elm which are closely similar to those made by the firm of I. Allsop & Son of Worksop, and by J. Spencer, who is also believed to have worked in Nottinghamshire.

Figure NE400. High splat back Windsor armchair. Ash with fruitwood splat and elm seat. Stamped on side edge of seat 'BUNNING, DONCASTER' (fl.1837-58).

Single ring turned legs with straight feet. Legs connected by a crinoline stretcher. Three long slightly tapered spindles either side of central back splat. Three tapered underarm spindles with turned underarm support typical of those found in Nottinghamshire Windsor chairs. Stylised fleur-de-lis fretted top splat. Keyhole shaped fret in lower splat. This chair has the stylistic qualities of Nottinghamshire Windsor chairs of the ordinary ash and elm variety, particularly made by the Rockley makers, and was probably imported from Rockley, since the Bunnings were cabinet makers and upholsterers rather than chair makers, and sold under this name.

Figure NE401. The stamp of James or George Bunning, impressed on the side seat edge of the chair shown in Figure NE400. James Bunning worked at Frenchgate, Doncaster in 1837. George Bunning also worked at 4, Frenchgate in 1858.

Kitchen Windsors

Amongst the chairs produced in the late nineteenth century, a range of kitchen Windsor styles was also made, with variations of laths, turned spindles and large fretted splats composing the back designs. These chairs are typically robust in style, and made in a mixture of hard and semi-hard woods which were typically stained in 'walnut, mahogany or light colour'[162] and varnished. These were mass-produced chairs which were evidently intended as cheap utilitarian products with little craft quality (see Figures NE402-410).

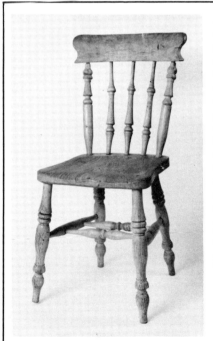

Figure NE402. Roman style kitchen chair. Ash legs; birch connecting stretchers, back supports and spindles; beech stay rail; and elm seat. Stamped 'J. & W. HASTINGS ROTHERHAM' (fl.1870), on back rear edge of seat. This style of heavy kitchen chair is typical of a range of mass-produced kitchen Windsors, made in many parts of the North of England during the second half of the 19th century. The production of inexpensive utilitarian chairs of this kind which, although less stylistically pleasing and well made than the Nottinghamshire chairs, nevertheless reduced the market availability and probably hastened the demise of the Worksop, Nottinghamshire kitchen Windsor trade.

Heavy two ring turned legs connected by H-form stretchers with two central cross stretchers with ball motif. Stay rail similar in design to those illustrated in the Allsop trade card Roman chair, see Figure NE270. Two turned outer supports. Three turned spindles connecting the stay rail to the seat.

Figure NE403. The stamp of J. & W. Hastings, house furnishers of Rotherham (fl.1870-present day (1987)), impressed on the rear edge of seat of the chair shown in Figure NE402.

Figure NE404. *Kitchen spindle back chair or spindle balloon back chair. Ash with beech back uprights and stay rail, and elm seat. Stamped 'W. BREAR MAKER ADDINGHAM VIA LEEDS' on rear edge of seat. The large seat and strong construction of this chair are typical of chairs made in Yorkshire.*

Elaborately turned legs and vase shaped feet of a type commonly found on smoker's bow Windsors from this region. See Figure NE356 for example. Side leg stretchers connected by two cross stretchers. Sawn and turned back uprights supporting a curved stay rail. Four turned spindles composing the back design.

Figure NE406. *Lath back or kitchen Windsor. Beech stay rail, sycamore laths, ash, with elm seat. Attributed to Yorkshire, c.1870-1900. Branded '7. W. YORK. R' on rear edge of seat, possibly West Yorkshire Riding.*

Turned legs with vase shaped feet, connected by H-form stretchers. Two elaborately turned back uprights, shaped stay rail, and five bent narrow laths, tapered at point of mortice into the seat and stay rail. The laths of this chair are similar to those included in the chair by G. Shaw of Leeds shown in Figure NE407 and suggest that the chair was, perhaps, bought by a local authority in Yorkshire and identified for inventory purposes.

Figure NE407. *Lath back or kitchen chair. Ash hoop, legs, and stretcher, sycamore laths and alder seat. Stamped on rear edge of seat 'G. SHAW LEEDS' (fl.1871-77). The design of this chair is atypical of the region's chair tradition, and may represent this maker's attempt to produce a new style.*

Plain elliptical legs joined by H-form stretchers. A further cross stretcher joins the rear legs. The hoop is linked to the seat by five bent, narrow laths which taper to a round tenon section at the upper and lower ends. Two rear supports connect the hoop to a wedge at the rear of the seat.

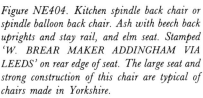

Figure NE405. *The stamp of William Brear, chair maker and wood turner of Addingham near Leeds. This maker, born 1813, son of a master chair maker, owned a large firm which made many varieties of chairs both for adults and children, as well as making a wide range of domestic and other turnery wares. He is recorded working between 1871 and 1881, but the firm of William Brear & Sons continued to produce chairs into the 1930s.*

Figure NE408. *The stamp of George Shaw impressed on the rear of seat edge of the chair shown in Figure NE407. This maker worked variously at Water Lane, Holbeck, Leeds; Neville Street, and 39 Middle Row, Campfield, Leeds, between 1871 and 1877.*

Figure NE409. *Bannister balloon back Windsor chair. Beech stay rail, birch back supports and spindles, alder splats and elm seat. Branded beneath the seat, 'T. HOGG & CO' (fl.1837-75). This style of chair, with variations of splat fretting was common in many parts of the North of England. This particular example has been stripped with a solution of caustic soda; originally it would have been stained with a 'mahogany, walnut, or light coloured' stain and varnished.*

Heavily turned three ring legs with vase shaped feet and straight feet on the rear. H-form stretchers with back legs connected by a further stretcher. Sawn and turned back uprights supporting a shaped stay rail. One turned spindle either side of a broad shaped splat with two frets.

Figure NE410. *The brand of Thomas Hogg & Co, found beneath the seat of the chair in Figure NE409. Thomas Hogg is first recorded working in Sheep Street, Skipton, Yorkshire, in 1837, and by 1875, the firm, now under the name of J & W Hogg, was working in High Street, Skipton. Since Thomas Hogg was a cabinet maker, it is possible that this chair was purchased from a chair maker and identified by Hogg as the retailer.*

Figure NE411. Primitive high elm topped stool with crudely turned elm legs morticed and wedged through the seat. This type of seating was the most basic form available and was made to serve the many work places which required people to sit at machines or benches. It gave such little comfort to the user, that it may be considered to be more of a perch than a seat.

Figure NE412. An illustration of Sheffield cutlers at work in the early 20th century. They sit on primitive three-legged stools of a kind which was used throughout the industrial North where workers had to sit at bench or machine work (see Figure NE411).

Figure NE413. An extract from the catalogue of Wm. Brear & Sons of Addingham, Yorkshire, showing two of the many forms of stools which this firm of chair and domestic turnery ware makers produced until 1930.

Stools and children's furniture

Many styles of stools were also made by the Yorkshire chair makers for use as foot stools, children's stools, occasional stools for the home and places of recreation, and particularly for use in the many factories found in the industrial north of England. The stools which were made in this region vary greatly in the quality of their production, and include crudely made examples with three roughly turned legs, morticed into a block of elm (see Figure NE411). These were widely used in factories involved in the metal trades and are illustrated in use in a cutlery works in Sheffield in Figure NE412. Stools with greater refinement were made by the Windsor makers with the general leg forms used in Windsors, made in elm or ash, with turned, round alder or elm tops. The legs were connected either by box form stretchers or cross stretchers of both wood and metal braces. See Figures NE415 and 416 for common examples.

Figure NE414. A low or nursery stool. Alder top, birch legs and stretchers, c.1880-1920. Similar in design to the stool advertised on page 25 of the William Brear & Sons catalogue, 1920, priced at 24/- a dozen.

Turned circular top with single ring turned legs and vase shaped feet. Cross form of stretchers with one thin stretcher morticed through a thicker one.

Figure NE415. A stool in the style of that in the William Brear & Sons catalogue 1920, priced at 40/- a dozen. Elm circular turned top, ash legs and stretchers, c.1880-1920.

Four legs turned with a ball shaped motif and vase shaped feet. Cross stretchers constructed with one piercing the other.

Figure NE416. Round top stool. Elm top, ash legs and stretchers. Attributed to Yorkshire, c.1840-1920.

This universal form of stool was made widely in Yorkshire as alternative seating to a chair. The Brear catalogue illustration in Figure NE413 shows a similar stool which is described as a piano stool and is no doubt one of the uses to which the stool could be put.

Figure NE417. Stool. Oak. Stamped underneath the seat 'G. WELLS' (fl.1822-34).

Two ring turned legs with cup and vase feet. Turned cross stretchers with central connecting block form.

Figure NE418. The stamp of George Wells who was a chair maker and turner working at Queen Street, Hull, between 1822 and 1834. This maker also advertised himself in 1826 as a 'fancy chair and cane worker'.

Amongst the chair makers producing Windsors in Yorkshire, William Brear & Sons, chair makers and turners of Addingham, near Leeds, illustrated a range of stools for sale at '44/- a dozen', in their early twentieth century catalogue (Figure NE413), and three examples of stools probably made by this firm are shown in Figures NE414-416. This firm also made standard Windsor side and armchairs as well as children's chairs, and an example of one of these designs is shown in Figure NE422. Another priced at 30/- a dozen, and advertised 'as supplied in hundreds to council schools' is shown in Figure NE421.

Very few stools apparently warranted makers' impressed name stamps, but one which did is shown in Figure NE417 stamped G. Wells (fl.1822-34), who worked as a chair maker and turner in Queen Street, Hull. This example is made in oak with an elm top.

Figure NE419. A street market scene at Colne, Lancashire, showing children's rocking chairs, and washing dollies being sold as part of locally produced domestic ware, in the 1890s. These wares were probably produced by Wm. Brear & Sons, chair and domestic turnery makers of Addingham, Yorkshire, whose business was a few miles from Colne. Chairs of this type were still being made by Brear in 1920, as the illustration in Figure NE422 shows.

Figure NE420. 'Second size babies' chair', attributed to Wm. Brear & Sons, Addingham, Yorkshire, c.1880. Alder back uprights and stay rail, oak back spindles and right arm. Ash legs and stretchers and left arm. Alder rockers. Height 22½in. (57cm), width 15in. (38cm), depth 11½in. (29cm).

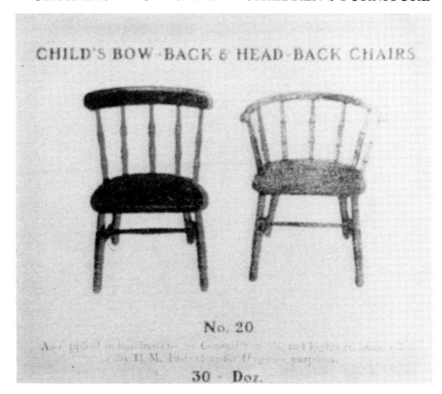

Figure NE421. An extract from the 1920 catalogue of William Brear & Sons of Addingham, Yorkshire, which shows two of the styles of children's chairs which they made. The catalogue claims that these 'Are supplied in hundreds to the Council Schools and highly recommended by His Majesty's Inspectors for hygiene purposes'.

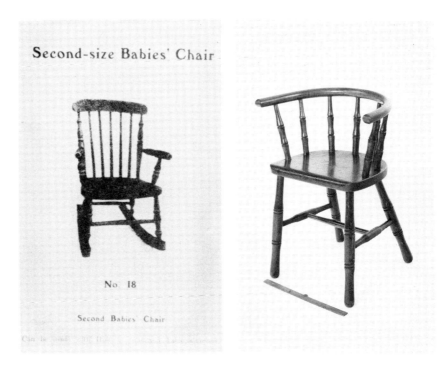

Figure NE422. An extract from the catalogue of Wm. Brear & Sons of Addingham, Yorkshire, 1920, showing a second size babies' chair similar to the one shown in Figure NE420. This chair was advertised with the possibility of being made with a hole in the seat, and table attached.

Figure NE423. Child's 'bow-back' chair. Alder arm hoop, elm spindles and seat, pine legs and stretchers, c.1880. Illustrated in William Brear & Sons' catalogue at 30/- a dozen. This chair was stained bright yellow and varnished. The eclectic use of materials is typical of the Yorkshire mass-produced chairs, where staining removed the need for the graining of the wood to be part of the design of the chair.

209

Figure NE424. High splat back Windsor. Ash with alder splat and seat. Stamped on rear edge of seat 'T. HERDMAN MAKER' (fl.1853-71). This chair has many of the general characteristics of the heavy Yorkshire Windsors. The detail of the splat design is, however, peculiar to this maker.

Two ring turned legs with vase shaped feet. H-form stretchers connecting legs. Four tapered spindles either side of broad stylised fir tree fretted upper splat, with plain wavy edge below. Fir tree shaped fret in lower splat. Three tapered underarm spindles, and turned underarm supports which embody regional design typical of Yorkshire Windsor chairs. See type A, Figure NE337.

Figure NE426. High splat back Windsor. Ash with alder seat, legs and splat. Stamped on rear edge of seat 'T. HERDMAN' (fl.1853-71). This chair has characteristics typical of Yorkshire Windsors, particularly in its underarm turning style. The leg turnings, however, are typical of certain Windsors found in the North West Midlands tradition. The Wilkinson chair, see Figure NE276, indicates that design similarities between regions did occur with, as in this case, two distinct traditions being merged into a third regional style.

Figure NE428. High back smoker or broad arm Windsor chair. Fruitwood with elm raised arm section and seat. Stamped on rear edge of seat 'HOBBS MAKER NEWCASTLE' (fl.1879).

Heavy, elaborately turned legs with vase shaped feet. H-form stretchers with two cross stretchers. Central ball motif in cross stretchers. Four parallel shaped spindles either side of central decoratively fretted splat above arms. Two turned spindles either side of decoratively fretted splat below the arms. Simple turned underarm support.

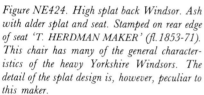

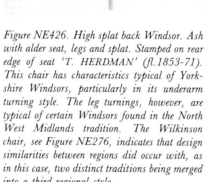

Figure NE425. The stamp of Thomas Herdman of Westgate Road, Newcastle upon Tyne (fl.1853-71), stamped on the rear edge of the seat of the chair shown in Figure NE424. This maker followed various trades and is recorded as a cabinet maker, joiner, furniture broker, funeral furnisher, marble merchant, newsagent and chair maker.

Figure NE427. The stamp of Thomas Herdman of Westgate Road, Newcastle upon Tyne (fl.1853-71), stamped on the rear edge of seat of chair shown in Figure NE426.

Figure NE429. The stamp of Walter Hobbs, impressed on the rear edge of the seat of the chair shown in Figure NE428. This chair maker is recorded in 1879, working in Ridley's Yard, Newcastle upon Tyne, Northumberland.

DURHAM AND NORTHUMBERLAND

To the North of Yorkshire lie the adjoining counties of Durham and Northumberland, bordering on to the Scottish Lowlands. These two counties formed a region in the early nineteenth century which was extremely remote from the rest of England, and whose economy relied mainly on agriculture and forestry to the far north, and fishing from the many small ports on the East coast. The region had few major inland towns, except for the county town of Durham, Stockton on Tees, and Darlington, to the south of the county. The city of Newcastle upon Tyne, in Northumberland, was the centre of trade for the entire northern region.

The numbers of chair makers in this region were very small, and it seems possible that the majority of common chairs and stools found in this area were imported from Yorkshire and the North East Midlands. However, there were a few chair makers, and it seems clear from the evidence of the few provenanced chairs which have been recorded, that these makers, too, were working in a similar Windsor chair tradition to that of the North East region.

Chair making was first noted as a specialist craft in 1801,[163] in the only consistently recorded location of chair making, Newcastle upon Tyne, when there was one chair maker recorded, in contrast with thirty-two cabinet makers. Two chair makers are recorded here in 1824,[164] but the numbers did not rise above three at any point during the nineteenth century. In County Durham, an occasional chair maker is recorded; one maker in Durham in 1834,[165] and one in Sunderland in 1873.[166] The only prominent maker in the whole area was a Windsor and fancy chair maker, Benjamin Lacey, who worked in Stockton on Tees between 1873 and 1894.

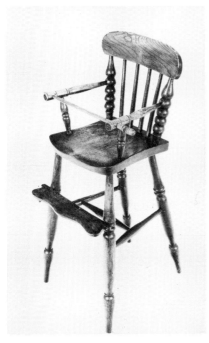

Figure NE430. Child's high Windsor chair. Ash with alder seat and elm back uprights and stay rail. Stamped on rear edge of seat 'HOBBS MAKER NEWCASTLE' (fl.1879).

Four turned legs with vase shaped feet. Legs connected by H-form stretchers. Shaped foot-rest attached to front legs. Multiple ball shaped turnings in back uprights, shaped stay rail supported by four plain back spindles. Round turned arms supported by turned arm supports. Detachable turned spindle connects arms to secure the seated child.

Figure NE432. Child's high or table Windsor chair. Ash with alder seat and elm uprights and stay rail. Stamped on rear edge of seat 'HOBBS MAKER NEWCASTLE' (fl.1879).

Two ring turned legs with vase shaped feet. Legs connected by H-form stretchers. Shaped foot rest attached to front legs. Plain turned back uprights, shaped stay rail supported by four plain turned back spindles. Round turned arms supported by turned arm supports. Detachable turned spindle to secure seated child missing.

Figure NE434. Office or smoker's bow chair. Beech with elm seat and arms. Stamped on rear edge of seat 'C. IVES CHAIR MAKER NEWCASTLE' (fl.1858-79).

Heavy ball motif turned legs with vase shaped feet. H-form stretchers with two cross stretchers with central ball motif. Six simple back spindles, and two heavy turned arm supports supporting a three part arm with raised back support.

Figure NE431. The stamp of Walter Hobbs, chair maker of Ridley's Yard, Newcastle upon Tyne (fl.1879), impressed on the back seat edge of the chair shown in Figure NE430.

Figure NE433. The stamp of Walter Hobbs (fl.1879), chair maker of Ridley's Yard, Newcastle upon Tyne, impressed on the back edge of the seat of the chair in Figure NE432.

Figure NE435. The stamp of Charles Ives impressed on the rear edge of the seat of the chair shown in Figure NE434. This maker is recorded working at Victoria Market, in 1858, and at Pottery Lane, Newcastle in 1879. This simple version of a well known chair has the distinction that the maker's stamp is the only recorded one which shows him explicitly to be a 'chair maker' as opposed to the more common title of 'maker'.

Of the makers who worked in Newcastle upon Tyne, examples of the work of three men have been recorded and are shown below. The first of these makers, Thomas Herdman, who worked at Westgate Hill, Newcastle, between 1853 and 1871, practised many trades including cabinet maker, joiner, furniture broker, newsagent, funeral furnisher, and chair maker. Two chairs stamped by Herdman explicitly as the maker have been recorded, and are shown in Figures NE424 and 426. These chairs have the general demeanour of the robust Windsors typically made in Yorkshire, and both have fir tree motif fretted splats in a style peculiar to this maker. The underarm support turnings are similar to the Yorkshire turning type A, Figure NE337, and

the two ring turned legs incorporated in the chair in Figure NE424 are also typical of the heavy Yorkshire turned legs of this style. The leg turnings of the chair in Figure NE426, however, are closely similar to the single ball turned front legs and plain turned rear legs from the North West Midlands tradition. See the Wilkinson Newark chair in Figure NE276 p.179 for an example, indicating an occurrence of design similarity between two distinct geographic areas.

Three examples are shown here of a further Newastle chair maker's work. These include a best high back smoker chair (Figure NE428) with a decorative splat, and two children's high chairs, (Figures NE430-432) made by Walter Hobbs, who is recorded working after Herdman's

time at Ridley's Yard, Newcastle, in 1879.[167] A chair by another maker, Charles Ives, who worked in Victoria Market in 1858, and in Pottery Lane, Newcastle in 1879, is shown in Figure NE434 and is an example of a smoker's bow chair[168].

The few makers who worked in the far North East areas contrast dramatically with the busy trade found in the Lincolnshire and Nottinghamshire areas to the south, and serve to emphasise the dominance which these epicentres had in the North East region's history of 'common' chair making.

The East Anglian counties of Norfolk, Suffolk and Essex form a tract of land protruding into the North Sea. This region is enclosed on its northern boundary by The Wash, and in the south by the Thames, and the metropolitan area of London. To the west, the county of Cambridgeshire completes this large rural area, where the fertile fenland, which links Norfolk and Cambridgeshire, joins the grassland wolds and woodlands to the south in Suffolk and Essex.

East Anglia has traditionally held a reputation for being isolated from the rest of England and probably the inferiority of East/West road systems prevented easy movement of people and goods into and out of the area.

The physical isolation was reduced with the coming of the railways in the first half of the nineteenth century. This extension of communication brought opportunities not only for greater movement of the population, but also allowed products from other areas to be brought into the region, creating competitive forces which challenged the previous autonomy of locally made goods. East Anglian chair makers were unevenly dispersed throughout the region, with relatively few cabinet and chair makers recorded in either Cambridgeshire or Suffolk during the first half of the nineteenth century,[1] contrasting with a widely distributed and populous trade in Norfolk and Essex. Figures EA1-3 show the pattern of distribution within the counties of East Anglia during the first major periods of recorded development.

The concentration of chair and cabinet makers in Norfolk and Essex may be accounted for in terms of trade domination, rather than in terms of great differences in population densities (see table right). The

products of the Norfolk and Essex trade satisfied the needs of the whole region and, in so doing, suppressed the need for local chair making in the surrounding counties. This notion of trade supremacy certainly occurred in other areas, for example in the Thames Valley chair making tradition, where a highly competitive and productive trade in Buckinghamshire, and High Wycombe in particular, reduced the need for alternative traditions to arise, to any significant degree, in virtually all of the surrounding counties.

A series of chair designs was produced throughout the East Anglian area, forming a regional group of styles rather than a single style, which, although diverse in the range of individual designs, follows strict rules of stylistic conventions.

Although the city of Norwich provided a distinct cultural centre for the region, the close proximity of London no doubt brought metropolitan

influence to bear on this rural area and London fashions are clearly reflected in the styles of seating furniture. The work of classical eighteenth century and Regency designers, notably Chippendale, Hepplewhite and Sheraton, as well as neoclassical Regency designs, widely known through the design books of the period, were often transposed and adapted. The East Anglian 'common' chair designs are, however, significantly different from the classical forms, in that the level of technical quality, as well as the physical scale of the work, was rudimentary and generally of an unsophisticated form.

Craft practices were also subject to the metropolitan influence and the chair making tradition which developed in East Anglia has no parallel in other regions of England. Here the chair making craft came firmly within the domain of woodworkers who were described jointly as both cabinet and chair makers as a separate

---

Table of Population for East Anglia

	1801	1831
Cambridgeshire	89,346 (.16 p.p.a.)	143,962 (.26 p.p.a.)
Essex	227,682 (.23 p.p.a.)	317,507 (.32 p.p.a.)
Norfolk	273,479 (.20 p.p.a.)	390,054 (.29 p.p.a.)
Suffolk	214,404 (.19 p.p.a.)	296,317 (.31 p.p.a.)

Comparative population figures for the East Anglian Counties from the 1921 Census Report which shows that population densities grew in all areas between 1801 and 1831, and were roughly similar in population densities per acre. (p.p.a.)

These figures compare with the industrially based and more densely populated county of Lancashire, for example, which recorded .56 and 1.11 persons per acre in 1801 and 1821 respectively.

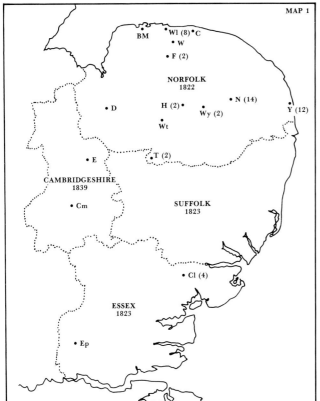

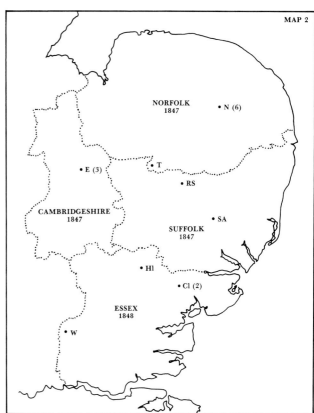

KEY

Cambs.
Cm = Cambridge
E = Ely

Essex
Cl = Colchester
Ep = Epping
Hl = Halstead
W = Waltham Abbey

Norfolk
BM	= Burnham Market	T	= Thetford
C	= Cley	W	= Walsingham
D	= Downham	Wt	= Watton
F	= Fakenham	Wl	= Wells
H	= Hingham	Wy	= Wymondham
N	= Norwich	Y	= Yarmouth

Suffolk
RS = Rickinghall Superior
SA = Stonham Aspal
I = Ipswich

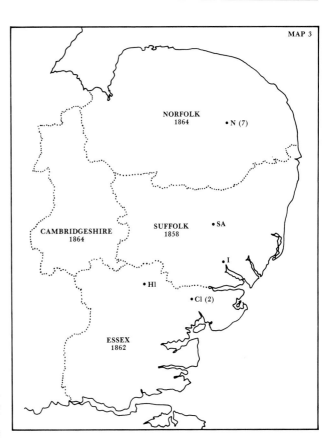

Figures EA1-3. Maps of the East Anglian region showing the distribution of chair makers only recorded in trade directories, 1822-1864.
Cabinet and chair makers in this period are found in twenty-two Norfolk towns with the greatest numbers working in Norwich, Yarmouth and Wells.[2] In Suffolk they were found in relatively small numbers in seven centres, of which Woodbridge was the most important.[3] Cabinet and chair makers were recorded in seven towns in Cambridgeshire with most in Cambridge and Wisbech.[4] In Essex, Colchester was the main chair making centre, with cabinet makers in twenty-four other towns.[5] However, trade directory sources typically record only owners of established businesses, rather than numbers of persons employed in the craft, so it may be assumed that the actual number of chair makers was larger than those expressed in trade records. For example, a trade directory records three chair makers working in Colchester in 1839[6] whereas the 1841 Census shows twenty-four people working in the chair making trade.

category from cabinet makers alone (trade directories for other regions separate the two crafts even where cabinet makers also made chairs), or from the 'turner' chairmakers. Wood turners were involved in chair making but in an ancillary role, producing front legs, 'buttons' for back decoration, and short underarm turnings. A few transitional styles of chairs have been recorded where more turned parts are included than usual, and some where complete turnery is involved, resulting in either spindle or ladder back styles with rush seats. However, examples of these are relatively rare, and illustrations may be seen in Figures EA84-89.

The manufacture of chairs by 'cabinet and chair makers' resulted in the chairs in this tradition being almost entirely constructed in the form of cabinet furniture, with planed sections of seasoned wood being used rather than turned segments, and with conventional mortise and tenon joints rather than dowel jointing. This crucial distinction in the construction of East Anglian chairs resulted in a regional tradition which was both productive and varied within a strictly ordered system of conventions, which owed much to the forms available to cabinet making, and where turned parts were often included purely as decorative devices.

As in other regions, the chairs are typically made with locally grown woods, principally elm, fruitwood, oak and, occasionally, walnut, during the late eighteenth and early nineteenth centuries, rather than the mahogany and walnut adopted in the classical designers' work. However, mahogany was used in the manufacture of some of the later nineteenth century East Anglian common chairs.

Classical chair designs were amended by the mixing of parts from different styles. This occurred particularly in the design of chair backs, where vertical and horizontal splats, including plain, shaped and fretted varieties, were used. (The *Norwich Chair-makers' Book of Prices*, 1801, uses the terms 'bannister' and 'splat' to refer to vertical segments contained in the back design. The term 'splat' only is used here to refer to both horizontal and vertical segments). Other designs included arrangements of turned 'buttons' or balls, supported between horizontal splats. Front legs are tapered and square in section in the

Figure EA4. The underneath of a hollow or concave wooden seat, showing supporting blocks and the use of hessian strips glued on to the seat with Scotch glue as a support against the seat splitting.

INTRODUCTION.

AS a guide to the following prices, it will be neceſſary to notice, that Chairs, Sofas, &c. of all kinds, are ſtarted as plain as poſſible, that any pattern of back, top, &c. may be introduced in the ſame.

Articles that generally occur in the Chair are mentioned in the Extras of the ſame.

Figure EA5. Introduction to the Norwich Chair-makers' *Book of Prices, 1801.*

(Courtesy Norfolk Library Service)

earlier chairs, with turned legs being used increasingly as the nineteenth century proceeded.

Three different methods of seat construction were most commonly used. The first type of seat was made from flat sections of thin wood, usually in elm, but also made in oak, mahogany, and fruitwood, nailed to the seat frame. This was a feature of late eighteenth and early nineteenth century East Anglian chairs (see the Forehoe Union chair shown in Figure EA8).

As the nineteenth century progressed, the form of seating which gradually became most common within the region, and one distinctive to it, was the 'hollow' or concave seat. This was formed from one, or occasionally two thin sections of wood, with the grain running from the front to the back of the seat, bent and nailed to a shaped seat frame. See Figures EA4, 14, 41 and 67 for examples of chairs showing this construction. Within this form of seat, the underneath surface is typically supported and strengthened by wooden blocks glued to the seat and the outside framing, and supported either across the grain of the seat, or following the joints in the seating sections, with broad hessian strips, glued on to the seat with Scotch glue (see Figure EA4).

The third, much less common form, was a removable wooden frame, woven with rush, which fitted into the rebated seat frame. It is, perhaps, surprising that rush seating was apparently so uncommon in this regional tradition, since freshwater rushes grew in abundance on the many inland waterways and rivers of Norfolk and Suffolk. However, rush seating is typically found in combination with turned chairs in the English tradition, and it may be that rush seating seemed an inappropriate technique or material for the cabinet making mode of chair manufacturing in this area. See Figures EA37 and 38 for examples of this seating mode.

East Anglian chairs appear to have generally been made without their maker's stamp or label, though an exception is shown in Figures EA78 and 79, and attribution of regional origin relies, therefore, largely on the evidence of pictorial reference as well as by known association with families, homes, institutions, or places of work.

A number of chairs from this region, and particularly from Norfolk, have been provenanced in these ways, and the documenting of these chairs has supported the design classification given below.

Further evidence particularly concerning manufacturing principles and the rules leading to the variation of basic design is clearly revealed in the introduction to the *Norwich Chair-makers' Book of Prices,* 1801[7] and the ensuing price guide. This significant text makes it clear that the alteration of designs within this region's chairs, was produced from the formalised way in which stylistic variations were presented as a detailed list of design possibilities, as well as giving the prices which journeymen cabinet makers were to be paid for each item of the work. For the many types of the chairs listed, each begins with the basic frame and seat style, which was then embellished according to a list of possible 'extras', whose application effectively led to design differences in

chairs occurring within each major group. This organisation of choice was clearly seen as a desirable way to approach chair making in this regional tradition, as the opening paragraphs of the introduction to the *Norwich Chair-makers' Book of Prices,* 1801, makes clear. See Figure EA5, where the basic chair frame and seat was priced separately from the list of 'extras'.

The creation of this wide variation in design possibilities was presumably the product of competition between the makers, and the consequent need to produce different and new products for sale. However, the breadth of design innovation found in this region's chairs is dissimilar to that found in most, but not all, other regional vernacular chair traditions, and may illustrate a distinction between the relatively conservative continuity of the turner/chair makers' work, typically found in other rural regions of England, and that of the cabinet maker/chair maker. The

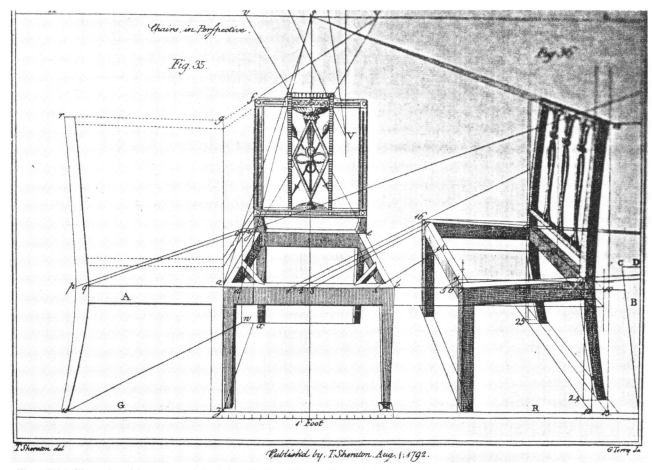

Figure EA6. Illustration of the geometry of the chair, taken from Thomas Sheraton's Cabinet Maker and Upholsterer's Drawing Book, *1802,[8] showing two different chairs. The square back and perpendicular splats, as well as raised stay rail are all features found in certain groups of East Anglian 'common' chairs. See Figures EA8-27.*

latter was, perhaps, more concerned with issues of fashion and change in furniture design, and was expected to produce a variety of products which in some sense reflected current metropolitan modes, albeit in a highly modified form.

A significant exception to this is the style of chair attributed by hearsay evidence, to Mendlesham in Suffolk, where fine quality chairs of distinctive and regionally unique design were reputedly made by a cabinet and chair maker named Richard Day, during the first third of the nineteenth century. This refined and enigmatic chair style owes more to a unity of design between features of the Buckinghamshire made Windsors, and certain influences from classical chair design, than to typical East Anglian styles, and is considered more fully later in this chapter, pp.230-246.

The Sheraton Influence

The East Anglian chairs illustrated here are placed into groups which have design associations in common. The first groups are typical of the chair varieties which show some design relationship with certain chair styles designed by Thomas Sheraton (1751-1806). Figure EA6, taken from Sheraton's *Cabinet Maker and Upholsterer's Drawing Book,* 1802, indicates this designer's interest in the geometry of the chair, as well as illustrating possible relationships between his designs and the first three groups of 'common' East Anglian chairs shown below. Within these groups, variations of size and arrangement of stay rails and splats are found within a framework of a square back, or with a shaped top rail. The seats may be 'hollow' or flat, or with a loose drop-in rush-woven seat, as well as being constructed as a commode or child's chair.

The *Norwich Chair-makers' Book of Prices,* 1801 [9] makes it clear that flat seated square back 'kitchen chairs' were seen as being more rudimentary than the 'hollow' seated or 'loose seat chairs', in that they were priced at 2/- (10p) for the basic frame, compared with 2/6d. (12½p) for the more elaborate hollow seat chair variety, and 2/8d. 'for loose seat chairs'.[10] The design features and price description given for 'square back kitchen chairs, No.II.', included in Figure EA7, show that elm, ash, beech or walnut were available woods. However, the majority of

A SQUARE BACK KITCHEN CHAIR, No. II.

FOR framing a fquare back Kitchen Chair, elm, afh, beech, or walnut-tree, with ftraight top, and ftay rail; fingle pitch-back feet, plain tapered above the feat; flat feat, with two rails of a fide; plain Marlbro' feet, without banifter, or fplats - - - £.0 2 0

EXTRAS.

For a top, hollow in front, not exceeding one inch in hollow - - - -	0 0	2
Stay rail, the fame hollow in front - -	0 0	1
If top be more than inch in the hollow, not exceeding inch and half - - -	0 0	3
Stay rail, the fame hollow in front - -	0 0	1½
So on in proportion to the hollow of each top and ftay rail		
Double pitch-back feet, each chair - -	0 0	2
Top with one plain fweep - - -	0 0	4
Top with a plain fweep and break at the corners - - - - -	0 0	5
Top with hollow corners, and ftraight in the middle - - - - - -	0 0	5
Stay rail, with one plain fweep - - -	0 0	2
Round upper ends to back feet, each chair -	0 0	1
Cutting up ditto, with a hollow under ftay rail, each chair - - - - -	0 0	2
Framing ftraight fplats, not exceeding one inch in joint, each fplat - -	0 0	1½
If fplats are more than one inch in joint, not exceeding two inches in ditto -	0 0	2
And fo on in proportion, according to the width of each fplat.		
If fplats are round in front, each fplat extra from ftraight ones - - -	0 0	0¼
Cutting holes in fplats, each hole - -	0 0	1
Outfides of ditto to be charged for according to the work there is in them.		-
If thefe chairs are made of cherry-tree, charge extra from other common wood, in each fhilling - - - -	0 0	1½
For other extras—*See tables.*		

Figure EA7. Price list for costing the 'Square Back Kitchen Chairs', Norwich Chair-makers' Book of Prices, *1801, pp.1 and 2.* (Courtesy Norfolk Library Service)

Plate 27. Reclining armchair with 'hollow' seat. (Cross stretcher missing.) Elm. East Anglia, c.1810.

Figure EA8. Example of a 'Square Back Kitchen Chair'. Elm. Attributed to East Anglia, c.1780-1830. This chair was owned by the Forehoe Union, Wicklewood House of Industry, Wymondham, Norfolk.[11]

(Courtesy Norfolk Museums Service)

Figure EA9. The institutional brand indicating ownership by the Forehoe Union applied to the rear seating strip of the chair shown in Figure EA8.

Figure EA10. Square back kitchen chair. Elm. Attributed to East Anglia, c.1790-1830.

Flat seat and square tapered front legs. Box stretchers. Narrow stay rail fitted across top of back uprights. Two plain splats supported between the stay rail and narrow lower cross splat and a pierced central splat.

Figure EA11. Square back kitchen armchair. Fruitwood. Attributed to East Anglia, c.1790-1830.

Flat seat with square tapered front legs. Side stretchers united by central cross stretcher. Narrow stay rail fitted across top of back uprights. Two plain back splats with central pierced splat supported between the stay rail and a narrow lower cross splat. Shaped arms with curved arm supports in the Hepplewhite manner (see Figure EA29).

chairs from this tradition, in common with other types of East Anglian vernacular furniture, are typically made in elm. No price difference was given for the varieties of woods listed above, but cherrywood was offered at the additional cost of 1½ old pence in the shilling.[12]

Included in the detailed variations in design given for the 'kitchen chair' shown in Figure EA7, is a price given for both plain splats at 1½d. and 2d. each according to size.[13] Clearly some preference is indicated in the chairs illustrated, for the adoption of four back splats, but the option of cutting holes in the splats for a further penny[14] may have been a minority demand, since few recorded chairs show this feature.

Examples of the flat seated style of square backed kitchen chairs are shown in Figures EA8-13. The chair shown in Figure EA8 came from the Forehoe Union House of Industry, Norfolk, and is branded on the rear seating strip with the name 'Forehoe Union' (see Figure EA9).

The Journeymen's prices quoted in the *Norwich Chair-makers' Book of Prices*[15] indicate that even the simplest styles of chairs would cost around 2/2d. to produce, rising to 4/- for the more elaborate styles. These prices raise questions related to the group of people who would have purchased the chairs. Given that agriculture was the principal employment for the region, agricultural labourers' wages were precariously fixed at 9/- per week for the married man, and 6/- for single men, throughout the first half of the nineteenth century.[16] It would, therefore, seem doubtful that workers following this employment were the typical purchasers of the East Anglian 'common' chairs. It would appear more likely that the market for the chairs would have been from occupational groups which produced more income than the basic agricultural wage, indicating purchasers who were, perhaps, shopkeepers, merchants of a modest scale, artisans, clerks, and other occupational groups included in the 'lower middle' class.*

Examples of the second group of

chairs described in the Norwich chair makers' pattern book are illustrated in Figures EA14-27. The descriptive title given to chairs in this group, 'A Square Back Elm Chair' indicates that this style was considered superior to the 'Kitchen' chair in being given a personal name, rather than a use name only. Within this design, the inclusion of a 'hollow' seat, splayed back uprights, scribed splats and shaped top rails combine to create a slightly more elegant and comfortable style than the 'Kitchen' chair. Although a choice of woods was offered, elm again is typically the most commonly used wood in this group of chairs. Certain 'extras' are listed for this chair, too, which are not included for the 'kitchen' chair, for example, the possibility of a 'top

* The unlikely possibility that agricultural workers were the purchasers of much of the cabinet makers' work is underlined in the evidence of many contemporary accounts of nineteenth century rural life, including the graphic autobiographical account of Sir George Edwards (1850-1933) *From crow scaring to Westminster*, which records the poverty of the farm workers.

Figure EA12. Square back kitchen armchair. Elm. Attributed to East Anglia, c.1790-1830. Note the reeded button turnings, typical of this region, which form the top of the underarm turnings.

Flat seat. Square tapered front legs. Box stretchers (right stretcher missing). Narrow stay rail fitted across back uprights. Four long vertical splats between stay rail and lower cross splat. Regency style arms on short, turned arm supports.

Figure EA13. Square back kitchen chair. Fruitwood. Attributed to East Anglia, c.1790-1830.

Flat seat. Square tapered front legs. Box stretchers. Stay rail described as 'top with hollow corners, straight in the middle, 5 pence (extra).'[17] Back decoratively interpreted with four scribed vertical splats and three horizontal splats separated by turned buttons.

Figure EA14. Square back chair. Elm. Attributed to East Anglia, c.1790-1830.

Hollow seat. Square tapered front legs. Box stretchers. Top stay rail fitted across back uprights. Three reeded vertical splats, supported between stay rail and cross splat.

Figure EA15. Square back armchair. Elm. Attributed to East Anglia, c.1790-1830.

Hollow seat. Square tapered front legs. Box stretchers. Narrow stay rail fitted across back uprights. Three long vertical splats supported between stay rail and lower cross splat. Swept arms and arm supports in the Hepplewhite manner (see Figure EA29).

Figure EA16. Square back chair. Elm. Attributed to East Anglia, c.1790-1830.

Hollow seat. Square tapered front legs. Box stretchers. Top stay rail fitted across back uprights. Four reeded vertical splats, supported between stay rail and cross splat.

Figure EA17. Square back chair. Elm. Attributed to East Anglia, c.1790-1830.

Hollow seat. Square tapered front legs. Box stretchers. Top stay rail extending over the line of the back uprights. Four reeded vertical splats, supported between stay rail and cross splat.

219

Plate 28. 'Square back elm chair' with 'hollow' seat. Elm. East Anglia, c.1820.

Plate 29. 'Square back elm' armchair with 'French' elbows (arms). Elm. East Anglia, c.1810.

Plate 30. 'Loose seat chair' with wide top and 'French' elbows. A commode chair with loose rush seated cover. Alder. East Anglia, c.1840.

Plate 31. 'Wide top' side chair with 'hollow' seat and turned front legs. Elm, stained to simulate mahogany. East Anglia, c.1870.

Plate 32. 'Square back kitchen chair' with flat seat. Alder. East Anglia, c.1810.

Figure EA18. Square back chair. Elm. Attributed to East Anglia, c.1790-1830.

Hollow seat. Square tapered front legs. Box stretchers. 'Top with hollow corners and straight in the middle'. Four splayed vertical splats supported between stay rail and cross splat.

Figure EA19. Square back chair. Elm. Attributed to East Anglia, c.1790-1830.

Hollow seat. Square tapered front legs. Box stretchers. Scrolled stay rail and back uprights. The back uprights are thickened in section from the seat level to the floor. Four reeded vertical splats, supported between stay rail and cross splat.

Figure EA20. Square back armchair, the natural counterpart to the side chair in Figure EA18. Elm. Attributed to East Anglia, c.1790-1830. This chair has been in the same family ownership for at least four generations, initially at Old Hunstanton, Norfolk, used by the great-grandmother of the present owner (1984).

Hollow seat. Square tapered front legs. Box stretchers. 'Top with hollow corners and straight in the middle'. Four vertical splats supported between stay rail and cross splat. Shaped arms and curved arm supports.

(Courtesy Mrs M. Fann, Norwich)

Figure EA21. Square back chair. Elm. Attributed to East Anglia, c.1790-1830.

Hollow seat. Square tapered front legs. Box stretchers. Arched stay rail. Four vertical splats supported between stay rail and lower cross splat.

Figure EA22. Square back chair. Elm. Attributed to East Anglia, c.1790-1830.

Hollow seat. Square tapered front legs. Box stretchers. Arched stay rail. Four reeded splayed vertical splats supported between stay rail and lower cross splat.

Figure EA23. Square back child's chair. Elm. Attributed to East Anglia, c.1790-1830. Height 23¾ in. (60cm); width 12in. (30cm); depth 9¾ in. (25cm). This chair has been used by children in the same Norfolk family for seven generations. The present user (1983) is two years old.

Flat seat. Square tapered legs. Box stretchers. Arched stay rail with three reeded splats and lower cross splat. Heavy applied arms and arm supports.

(Courtesy Mrs Mary Harvey, nr. Norwich)

Figure EA24. Square back chair. Elm. Attributed to East Anglia, c.1790-1840. Unusually tall in the back, perhaps intended as a fireside chair.

Hollow seat. Square tapered front legs. Box stretchers. Arched top stay rail. Four vertical reeded splats. Two reeded lower cross splats. Shaped arms supported on two turned arm supports.

with one sweep and breaks at the corner', and 'ditto with hollow corners, straight in the middle, 5 [old] pence',[18] provides extra possible embellishment. See Figure EA20 for an example of this latter feature.

A further design closely related to the 'Square Back Elm Chair' is described in the *Norwich Chair-makers' Book of Prices,* 1801, as an 'Elm loose seat chair',[19] an example of which is shown below in Figure EA27. A description for producing the basic frame is shown in Figure EA28. This style of chair was perhaps considered somewhat superior to the previous two groups of wooden-seated chairs, and although following certain essential design features of these groups, was made to hold a loose seat of woven rush. Certainly the basic frame of this chair was more costly to make than the wooden-seated varieties discussed above, and it may be that the extra cost of producing the rushed frame design dissuaded many from

choosing this seating style, since chairs recorded from this region suggest that this option is least commonly found. However, it may be that since rush seating was less durable than wood, on falling into disrepair, many chairs with this form of seat were discarded, rather than repaired.

The Hepplewhite Influence

The influence of a further classical furniture designer's work, George Hepplewhite (d.1786), is found in another group of East Anglian 'common' chairs. Figure EA29 illustrates a graceful example of Hepplewhite's renowned 'shield back' chair with 'wheat sheaf' splat, and evidences the origins of the East Anglian chairs reflecting this designer's work[20] (see Figures EA30-34). These chairs typically display an arched stay rail as a prominent stylistic feature of the group, as well as incorporating shaped

Figure EA25. Square back chair. Elm. Attributed to East Anglia, c.1790-1830.

Hollow seat. Square tapered front legs. Side stretchers united by central cross stretcher. Four long, splayed, vertical splats, mitred into the rear support rail, rather than into a lower cross splat.

Figure EA26. Square back commode kitchen chair. Elm. Attributed to East Anglia, c.1790-1830.

Flat lift-off seat. Square tapered front legs joined by shaped frieze which discreetly conceals the chamber pot. Scrolled over stay rail. Four vertical splats between stay rail and lower cross splat. Regency style arms supported on short, turned arm supports.

Figure EA27. Elm loose seat chair. Attributed to East Anglia, c.1790-1840.

Loose rush seat. Square tapered front legs. Side stretchers united by central cross stretcher. Arched stay rail. Four plain, long, vertical splats supported between stay rail and lower cross splat.

223

Plate 33. A Mendlesham area chair, showing characteristic features of chairs in this tradition, c.1800-60. Fruitwood with elm seat. Unusual arched stay rail with double-turned buttons joining first cross rail. A central 'ripple' shaped splat divided by plain turned spindles from two half splats, with two further spindles, complete the central back decoration. A lower 'crinoline' stretcher is joined to the lower cross rail by two turned buttons or balls. The back uprights above the arm mortices, the stay rail, and first cross rail, as well as joining points in the fretted splats are inlaid with a thin line of sycamore. Scribe lines are made as a further decorative feature on both front edges of the back uprights, stay rail, first cross rail, and around the edge of the seat. (See Figure EA105 for a further significant example of non-decorative scribing on this region's chairs.) The legs are decoratively turned and are one of many different variations found in this tradition. The central cross stretcher shows a prominent barrel shaped turning which is typically found in chairs from both major groups A and C (see pp.246-52). Note the very pronounced angles of leg mortices which are peculiar to this tradition's chairs. The curved and shaped arms and arm supports show a refinement uncommon in Windsor chairs from other traditions which use this design. This chair is also shown as EA140, as part of the study.

AN ELM LOOSE-SEAT CHAIR.

FRAMING and fweeping a loofe-feat banifter-back chair, elm, afh, beech, or walnut-tree, ftraight joint in top, top ftraight in front, fingle pitch back feet, with two rails on a fide, ftraight feat rails, plain banifter and pedeftal, plain Maribro' feet, with blocks in front corners   -   -   -   -   £.0   2   8

EXTRAS.

Figure EA28. Description for producing the basic frame for the drop-in rush seat variety of East Anglian chair, taken from the Norwich Chair-makers' Book of Prices, *1801.*

(Courtesy Norfolk Library Service)

and fretted splats, albeit in an unsophisticated form, and a suggestion of the shaped and 'waisted' feature found in Hepplewhite's chair back designs. The swept arms and arm supports, typical of Hepplewhite's chairs, are also reflected in the armchair designs. Interestingly, the turned legs which are illustrated as part of the Hepplewhite chair design are not typically found in this group of 'common' chairs.

Figure EA29. Illustration taken from Hepplewhite's Cabinet Maker and Upholsterer's Guide, *1788, showing a 'shield back' chair displaying the arched stay rail, 'wheat-sheaf' back splat design, waisted back shape, swept arms and arm supports, and turned front legs. This chair exhibits many features incorporated within a group of East Anglian 'common' chair designs (see Figures EA30-34).*

Figure EA30. Armchair. Fruitwood. Attributed to East Anglia, c.1790-1840.

Hollow seat. Square tapered front legs. Side stretchers joined by central cross stretcher. Shaped arms and curved arm supports. Arched stay rail supporting fretted splat which is mortised into the rear seat rail. Waisted shaped back uprights showing influence of Hepplewhite chair styles.

Figure EA31. Armchair. Fruitwood. Attributed to East Anglia, c.1790-1830.

Hollow seat. Square tapered front legs. Box stretchers. Shaped arms and curved arm supports. Arched stay rail supporting fretted splat which is mortised into the rear seat rail. Waisted shaped back uprights showing influence of Hepplewhite's chair styles.

Figure EA32. Armchair. Fruitwood. Attributed to East Anglia, c.1790-1840.

Hollow seat with square tapered front legs. Side stretchers joined by central cross stretcher. Straight stay rail supporting wheat-sheaf design fretted splat which mortises into the rear seat rail. Refined shaped arms and arm supports showing influence of Hepplewhite's chair styles.

Figure EA33. Side chair. Fruitwood. Attributed to East Anglia, c.1790-1840.

Flat seat. Square tapered front legs. Side stretchers joined by central cross stretcher. Arched stay rail. Fretted splat which mortises into the stay rail, as well as the pedestal at rear of seat. Waisted back uprights showing influence of Hepplewhite's chair styles.

The Chippendale Influence

Within this regional tradition, a further group of sturdy, simple chair designs shows an awareness of another major classical furniture maker, Thomas Chippendale (1718-1779). Figure EA35 shows an example of a mahogany chair in the style of Thomas Chippendale which exhibits typical features of this designer's work.[21] The essential design features of the group of chairs shown in Figures EA36-41, particularly suggest a sense of Chippendale's influence in the adoption of the shaped top stay rail, which terminates in the characteristic 'eared' shaping, as well as in the adoption of a fretted, but not carved, splat. The graceful shaping of Chippendale chair backs is suggested, too, in the 'waisted' shape of the back uprights, which splay out to meet the top rail. The arrangement of the lower cross-stretcher was apparently constructed in the optional positions of being mortised to join the side stretchers or to join the front legs.

Chairs with unfretted splats were also made which accord with this group's generic design features. In these cases, the splats may be thought to reflect those typically found in walnut 'spoon' back chairs, made in the first half of the eighteenth century, rather than the later eighteenth century fretted splat design; although in most other respects, reflecting the influences of later classical design.

The influence of Chippendale's designs on provincial chair makers was not restricted to the East Anglian tradition, however, and modified forms of so called 'country' Chippendale chairs are found in other areas of the English common chair tradition. They are often incorporated as part of vernacular designs, so that amalgamations of local origin and classical designers' work were created (see Chapter 7, Figures NW163 and 166, which show Lancashire rush seated chairs but which have Chippendale or Hepplewhite influence in the design of the back).

The dissemination of Chippendale's work throughout the English tradition makes regional attribution of vernacular chairs showing this designer's influence difficult to assign. However, examination of primary design 'signatures' helps identification in certain cases. Within the East Anglian tradition, for example, the use of the curved underarm supports shown in Figures EA38, 40 and 41 is typical of this group's regional design, whereas turned arm supports, found in other regions' chairs, are not.

Where turned arm supports do appear (see Figures EA68, 69 and 75), the form is regionally specific, and typically shows a separate turned support, fixed by a block to the side seat rail. In other English chair traditions, the turned arm support tends to be a continuous part of the front leg, and this appears to be true, too, for the 'country' Chippendale chairs produced in other regions.

Figure EA34. Commode chair. Fruitwood. Attributed to East Anglia, c.1790-1830.

Lift seat with deep frieze which conceals the chamber pot. Square legs with no supporting stretchers. Elegant swept arms and arm supports. Arched stay rail. Fretted splat mortising into stay rail and pedestal at rear of seat. Waisted back uprights showing influence of Hepplewhite's chair styles.

Figure EA35. 'Ribbon back' chair in the manner of Thomas Chippendale. Mahogany, c.1760. Upholstered seat. Certain styles of East Anglian chairs reflect the features of the classical styles including the adoption of a shaped stay rail supporting a shaped and fretted splat which mortises into a cross support at seat level. The waisted shape of the back uprights occurs too, in combination with the square sectioned front legs; swept back feet and either box stretchers or side stretchers joined by a central cross stretcher.

Figure EA36. Side chair. Elm. Attributed to East Anglia, c.1790-1840.

Shaped top stay rail, fretted splat, splayed and waisted back uprights. Flat seat.

(Courtesy Strangers' Hall Museum, Norwich. Photograph courtesy Norfolk Museums Service)

Figure EA37. Side chair. Elm. Attributed to East Anglia, c.1790-1840.

Shaped top stay rail. Fretted splat. Splayed and waisted back uprights. Loose rush-woven seat. Square legs. Cross stretcher uniting side stretchers.

Figure EA38. Commode chair. Elm. Attributed to East Anglia, c.1790-1830. (Similar arm forms can be seen in Figures EA40, 53 and 60).

Shaped stay rail, fretted splat, elegantly shaped arms with curved arm supports, showing influence of Chippendale's chair designs. Loose rush-woven seat. Shaped frieze which discreetly hides the removable chamber pot.

Figure EA39. Side chair. Fruitwood. Attributed to East Anglia, c.1780-1830. This chair was found at Beech House, Gressenhall, the former House of Industry, Mitford and Launditch Union, opened in 1777.

Shaped top stay rail. Unfretted vasiform splat. Waisted, splayed back uprights and flat seat.

(Courtesy Norfolk Rural Life Museum. Photograph courtesy Norfolk Museums Service)

Figure EA40. Commode chair. Fruitwood. Attributed to East Anglia, c.1780-1830. (Arm forms similar to Figures EA38, 53 and 60).

Shaped top stay rail. Unfretted, vasiform splat. Elegantly shaped arms, and curved arm supports, showing influence of Chippendale's chair designs. Loose rush-woven seat. The shaped seat frieze discreetly hides the removable chamber pot.

Figure EA41. Child's armchair. Elm. Attributed to East Anglia, c.1790-1840. Given to Strangers' Hall Museum, Norwich, by a Norwich resident in 1927.

Shaped top stay rail. Unfretted, vasiform splat. Refined arm shape and curved arm supports (see Figures EA30-32 for similar design feature). Hollow seat.

(Courtesy of Strangers' Hall Museum, Norwich. Photograph courtesy Norfolk Museums Service)

East Anglian 'Button' Backs

A further group of chairs contains many commonly found examples in this regional tradition, and is characterised by the presence of turned wooden 'buttons' (balls), or short spindles, incorporated as a decorative feature of the back design. The single or multiple turnings are held between two, or occasionally three (see Figure EA13) horizontal splats at a mid-point in the back, with two or three turnings being most commonly found.*

Chairs with this stylistic feature have commonly been attributed as 'Essex or Suffolk Ball Backs', and in Figure EA43, a late nineteenth century photograph of the kitchen of Priory Farm, Nacton, Suffolk,** we see such a chair in situ.

Rose Tenent, writing on English country chairs, comments that 'The Essex chair is usually made of elm or fruitwood. It is a pretty chair with a square back and hollowed out seat. A double rail runs across the back at waist level, joined together in the

middle by two or more small balls. The legs are straight with straight stretchers. There are several variants of this chair... Some of them have narrow strips of wood joining the top to the waist rail. Others have rush seats and four rails across the back. None of them have any pretensions to grandeur, but they are ideal for the small house or cottage...'[22]

However, there seems little reason to suppose that this style was not made throughout the East Anglian tradition. Certainly the principal

*The feature of the back turnings is significant since it indicates that turners were employed in the chair making trade, albeit in a minor role, to supply 'buttons' and spindles, as well as the turned arm supports and front legs. Indeed, the *Norwich Chair Makers' Price Book*, 1801, makes the presence of turners explicit in quoting the 'extras' price description for turned parts thus; 'Round buttons between splats prepared by the turners, ½d.' and 'turned spindles, each spindle one penny'.[23]

**According to legend, this kitchen was the scene of the harvest supper on the eve of Margaret Catchpole's adventure with Will Laud recounted by Revd. Richard Cobbold in *The History of Margaret Catchpole, a Suffolk Girl*.

Figure EA42. Square back side chair. Fruitwood. Attributed to East Anglia, c.1790-1840. From a former three room dwelling at Doll's Hole, Beetley, Norfolk.

Plain stay rail set level with the back uprights. Three narrow splats, the centre two joined with two wooden buttons. Hollow seat, square tapered front legs.

(Courtesy Norfolk Rural Life Museum. Photograph courtesy Norfolk Museums Service)

Figure EA43. The farmhouse kitchen at Priory Farm, Nacton, nr. Ipswich, Suffolk; late 19th century, showing on the right two variations of East Anglian chairs. These display typical back arrangements of horizontal splats and turned buttons (balls) in the right hand example; hollow wooden seats, and both turned and square tapered front legs. The armchair on the left of the scene is typical of those made in large numbers by the Buckinghamshire (Wycombe) chair makers.

(Courtesy Suffolk Records Office, Ipswich)

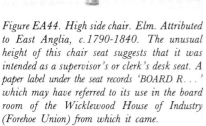

Figure EA44. High side chair. Elm. Attributed to East Anglia, c.1790-1840. The unusual height of this chair seat suggests that it was intended as a supervisor's or clerk's desk seat. A paper label under the seat records 'BOARD R . . .' which may have referred to its use in the board room of the Wicklewood House of Industry (Forehoe Union) from which it came.

Wide plain stay rail set below the top of the back uprights. The middle two cross splats united with three round and two half round wooden buttons. Hollow seat and square tapered front legs. Box stretchers.
(Courtesy Norfolk Museum of Rural Life. Photograph courtesy Norfolk Museums Service)

Figure EA45. Side chair. Fruitwood. Attributed to East Anglia, c.1790-1840.

Hollow seat, and square tapered front legs. Box stretchers. Plain, wide stay rail, set below the top of the back uprights. Two middle narrow cross splats joined by two turned wooden buttons.

Figure EA46. Side chair. Fruitwood. Attributed to East Anglia, c.1830-50.

Hollow seat. Turned front legs. Plain, wide stay rail set level with the top of the back uprights. Two narrow cross splats joined by three turned spindles.

Figure EA47. Side chair. Elm. Attributed to East Anglia, c.1790-1840.

Hollow seat and square tapered front legs. Box stretchers. Plain stay rail set below the top of the two back uprights. Two narrow cross splats joined by three turned spindles.

Figure EA48. Side chair. Elm. Attributed to East Anglia, c.1830-50.

Hollow seat. Turned front legs. Plain wide stay rail set below the top of the back uprights. Two narrow cross splats joined by three turned spindles.

Figure EA49. Armchair. Fruitwood. Attributed to East Anglia, c.1790-1840.

Hollow seat. Square tapered front legs. Square back of side chair dimensions. Plain wide stay rail set at the height of the two back uprights. Three narrow cross splats; the upper two joined by three wooden buttons. Regency style arms with short turned arm supports. Box stretchers.

aspects of this group's design conform to the common features of the regional style including the adoption of 'hollow' and flat wooden seats as well as loose seats, turned as well as square tapered front legs, square backs and neoclassical arm shapes supported by turned as well as flattened and curved arm supports, with elm and fruitwood as the most commonly used woods.

The basic frame shape of this group of chairs is composed of the simple square back form seen in the first group of 'kitchen' and 'elm square back chairs' shown in Figures EA8-28 with the buttons and spindles being the only purely decorative embellishment to the most basic form of back design. Indeed a sense of the simplicity of construction of these chairs is heightened in that some armchair designs are made by merely adding arms and their supports to a

basic side chair. See Figures EA49 and 51 for examples of this adaptation.

Where the arm supports are turned as part of the front leg, as in Figures EA50 and 55, then clearly these were constructed as armchairs, but even in these cases, the back and seat sizes are interchangeable with the comparable side chairs. Only in Figure EA53 does the back height suggest specific armchair design measurements.

In common with many other styles of East Anglian chairs illustrated here, the top stay rail in this group of chairs may be either level with the back uprights, or set below the top level, and the cross stretcher may be set between the side rail stretchers or between the front legs. These two features appear to have been used as further uniform discretionary conventions of this region's chairs.

Figure EA50. Armchair. Elm. Attributed to East Anglia, c.1790-1840.

Hollow seat. Displaying square back of side chair dimensions. Wide stay rail set below top level of back uprights. Two narrow cross splats joined by two turned buttons. Regency style arm shape joined to turned and Regency style sabre shaped front legs. Scribed line embellishment to front legs, arms, and back surfaces, in the mode of Regency styles.

Figure EA51. Armchair. Elm. Attributed to East Anglia, c.1790-1840.

Hollow seat. Square tapered front legs. Box stretchers. Square back design of side chair dimensions. Plain, wide stay rail set below top level of back uprights. Two narrow cross splats, joined by two turned buttons. Regency style shaped arms dowelled to back uprights rather than, morticed and supported by short turned arm supports

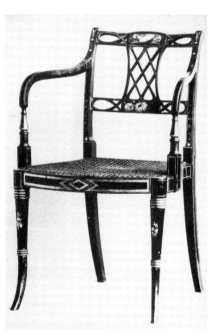

Figure EA52. Regency armchair. Beechwood, japanned and gilded. Attributed to East Anglia, c.1800. This chair exhibits neoclassical forms, many of which were directly adapted in East Anglian common chair styles. These include the swept arm shape supported by short, turned arm supports pegged to the side seat rails; fine ring turnings on the front legs; swept back legs which were sometimes wider and stepped at seat level; and the essential feature of a stay rail supporting a vertical splat between itself and a lower cross splat. (Courtesy Victoria and Albert Museum)

Figure EA53. Armchair. Fruitwood with mahogany seat. Attributed to East Anglia, c.1800-40.

Hollow seat. Square tapered front legs. Box stretchers. Square back with plain stay rail set below the top of the back uprights. Two narrow cross splats joined with two round and two halved turned buttons. Curved flat arms, with curved, flattened supports.

Chairs with reclining backs

East Anglian common chairs, although clearly made to be robust and withstand the rigours of daily use, were not necessarily constructed with bodily comfort as a high priority. However, rare examples of high backed chairs made to create ease of resting are shown in Figures EA56-60. These unusual chairs combine the features of the hollow seat with a high back which was made to recline, with a metal racking device to control the angle of the back.

Figure EA54. Armchair. Elm, with drop-in rush seat. Attributed to East Anglia, c.1800-40. This chair belonged to the present owner's grandmother, born in 1848, and remains in the region of its manufacture, Wisbech, Cambridgeshire.

Square back with reeded stay rail set below the top of the back uprights. Two narrow reeded cross splats joined with three round turned buttons. Curved flat arms with curved flattened supports.

Figure EA55. Commode chair. Elm. Attributed to East Anglia, c.1790-1840.

Square back of side chair dimensions. Plain stay rail set below the top of the back uprights. Two cross splats joined by two turned buttons. Regency style arm shape supported by turned and square tapered legs. The seat lifts off to reveal the chamber pot which the deep frieze discreetly hides.

Figure EA56. Reclining chair. Elm seat and seat stretchers, remainder in fruitwood. Attributed to East Anglia, c.1790-1840. Height 47½in. (121cm); width 25¼in. (64cm); depth 18in. (46cm). This chair shows an unusual constructional combination of turned and square parts. The specific decorative turnery devices offer significant regional design signatures which suggest associations with those found in the group of turned chairs shown in Figures EA84 and 85.

Hollow seat. Turned front legs. Turned box stretchers. (See Figures EA84 and EA85 for regional turnery associations.) The back is hinged at seat level, and supported in upright and reclining position by metal racking devices attached to each arm and the back uprights. The stay rail is curved and extends beyond the width of the back uprights. (See Figure EA69 for similar style.) The cross splats are reeded and the middle two are joined by three turned wooden spindles.

(Collection Lionel Reynolds)

Figure EA57. Reclining chair. Elm with rush seat. Attributed to East Anglia, c.1790-1840. The style of this chair has design parallels with the side chairs shown in Figures EA16 and 17 which display characteristics of the 'Square Back Elm Chairs', described in the Norwich Chair-makers' *Book of Prices, 1801, including the vertical reeded splats composing the back design and square legs connected by box form stretchers. The back is hinged at seat level, and supported in the upright and reclined positions by metal racking devices. This chair is unusual in having a rush seat which is an uncommon seating form in East Anglian chairs.*

(Courtesy Simon Carter Gallery)

Figure EA58. Reclining commode armchair. Fruitwood with elm seat board. Attributed to East Anglia, c.1790-1840. The seat board has a circular hole in which to place a chamber pot, which was probably covered originally with a removable upholstered seat, now missing. The back is hinged at seat level, and supported in upright and reclining positions by adjustable metal racking devices attached to each arm and the back uprights. (See photographic detail in Figure EA59.) The back design includes a stay rail which supports three splayed vertical reeded splats in a manner which unites this chair with

the 'Square Back' side and armchairs illustrated in Figures EA14 and 25, as do the square legs joined by box form stretchers. The flattened and scrolled arms, supported on turned supports, are typical of this form of chair. See Figures EA56 and 57 for other examples. (Private Collection)

Figure EA59. Detail of the metal adjusting device used to support the hinged back of the chair shown in Figure EA58. Reclining chairs are rare amongst English 'common' chairs, and were probably restricted in the 19th century, to those made in the East Anglian tradition.

Figure EA60. Reclining chair. Oak seat and cross splats, elm arms and supports, fruitwood legs, stay rail and back uprights. Attributed to East Anglia, c.1790-1840. Height 44in. (112cm); width 22¾in. (58cm); depth 16¼in. (41.3cm).

Hollow seat. Straight tapered front legs. Box stretchers. The back hinged at seat level, and supported in reclining position by metal racking devices attached to each arm and back uprights. *(Collection Lionel Reynolds)*

Cross Splat Chairs

The following group of chairs displays the regional features typical of those shown in the preceding major group, with the exception that a range of cross splat designs was produced with varying degrees of plainness or decoration, including the use of plain curved splats, turned splats, and carved splats. The *Norfolk Chairmakers' Book of Prices*, 1801, makes it clear that the provision of costs for these variations had to be paid for according to time.[24] Wood turners' work is again found in one of the back designs in this group (see Figures EA66-69), where a curved, decoratively turned splat is used, similar to that found in many of the simpler forms of chairs made in the Thames Valley (see Chapter 2, Figures TV175 and 181).

If the late eighteenth century and early nineteenth century chairs shown here indicate that the East Anglian

Figure EA61. Child's chair. Elm. Attributed to East Anglia, c.1780-1820. This chair was used by a farming family at Limpenhoe, near Norwich, from about 1850.

Hollow seat. Square tapered front legs; some loss of leg length and side stretchers missing. Plain, wide stay rail overlapping the back uprights, and single narrow cross splat. Curved arms on curved arm supports.

(Courtesy Norfolk Rural Life Museum. Photograph courtesy Norfolk Museums Service)

Figure EA62. Child's chair. Elm. Attributed to East Anglia, c.1800-50. This chair has been in the present family ownership since about 1875, and was originally owned by Mr Gooch, the blacksmith at Wymondham, Norfolk.

Hollow seat with stay rail set below top of back uprights. Single, plain cross splat. Regency style arms on short turned arm supports. Square tapered front legs and box form stretchers.

Figure EA63. Child's chair. Elm. Attributed to East Anglia, c.1820-50. The chair belonged to the Fox family of Hoe, Dereham, Norfolk. Mr H.W. Fox was the last Chairman of the Mitford and Launditch Union Board of Guardians.

Hollow seat with stay rail set below top of back uprights. Single plain cross splat. Regency style arms on short, turned arm supports. Turned front legs. Interestingly, the flagon shaped turnings which form part of the arm supports and the front leg turnings are similar to the front leg turnings of the ladder back chair shown in Figure EA89.

(*Courtesy Norfolk Rural Life Museum. Photograph courtesy Norfolk Museums Service*)

Figure EA64. Side chair. Fruitwood. Attributed to East Anglia, c.1790-1830.

Hollow seat with square tapered front legs. Box stretchers. Stay rail set below the top of back uprights. Single, plain curved splat. Decorative reeding on back legs and cross splats.

Figure EA65. Side chair. Elm. Attributed to East Anglia, c.1790-1840. Possibly the simplest and least elaborate version of this region's chairs.

Hollow seat with square tapered front legs and box stretchers. Stay rail set below top of back uprights. Single, curved splat.

Figure EA66. Arm and side chair. Elm. Attributed to East Anglia, c.1810-50. Narrow ring turnings incorporated in underarm supports are a typical turnery signature from this region. These chairs have been in the ownership of the same Norfolk family since the turn of the century, and were used 'in our living room, by four children and in turn were buses, trains, pulpits and horses when not used for sitting round the meal table. Mother also stood them near the fire with clothing on them to air.'

Hollow seat, square tapered front legs, and box stretchers. Wide stay rail set below the top of the back uprights. Single, turned cross splat reminiscent of similar Regency styles, and also a dominant design feature in certain kitchen chair types from Buckinghamshire and Oxfordshire. See Chapter 2, Figures TV175 and 181. Regency style arms on turned arm supports.

(*Courtesy Miss M. Green, Bury St. Edmunds, Suffolk*)

common chair tradition of this period was influenced by the classical eighteenth century and neoclassical chair designs of the Regency period, the resulting chairs, although simplified and modified, often achieved a pleasing economy of design and materials. However, as chair designs became increasingly time-distanced from this initial period of production, so cabinet makers' chair designs gradually came to reflect the heavier, more ornate taste, typical of much later nineteenth century furniture. For example, the front legs, made in a relatively refined form during the initial period, and which may have represented attempts to emulate the delicately carved and turned legs typical of the Hepplewhite chair styles, as well as the delicate turned legs of some Regency styles, gave

233

Figure EA67. Side chair. Elm with mahogany seat. Attributed to East Anglia, c.1840-60. A very simple design with minimal decoration.

Hollow seat, turned front legs, and wide stay rail set below the top of the back uprights. Single turned cross splat.

Figure EA68. Armchair. Elm. Attributed to East Anglia, c.1820-50. See ladder back chair, Figure EA89 for similar flagon shaped turning device in legs.

Hollow seat and turned front legs. Regency style arms supported by short, turned supports. Wide stay rail set below top of back uprights. Single turned and curved cross splat.

Figure EA69. Armchair. Fruitwood. Attributed to East Anglia, c.1830-50. Note multiples of narrow ring turnings typical of turnery devices in this region.

Hollow seat, and turned front legs. An attempt at producing greater refinement and decoration than is typical in this style, with wide, curved stay rail with reeded decoration overlapping the back uprights. A curved, turned cross splat, and a narrow, reeded cross splat. Regency style arms on short, turned arm supports.

Figure EA70. Side chair. Fruitwood. Attributed to East Anglia, c.1790-1830.

Hollow seat with square tapered front legs. Box stretchers. Wide stay rail set below top of back uprights. A plain chair relieved with a broad, decoratively carved cross splat exhibiting scroll motif.

Figure EA71. Side chair. Elm. Attributed to East Anglia, c.1800-30.

Hollow seat with square tapered front legs. Box stretchers. Wide stay rail set below the top of back uprights. Reeded decoration on back uprights and stay rail. Decorative carved back splat with tablet shaped motif.

Figure EA72. Side chair. Fruitwood. Attributed to East Anglia, c.1820-50.

Hollow seat and turned front legs. A more refined chair than others in this group, with elegantly shaped back legs, a wide, reeded stay rail set below back uprights, and carved cross splat with scroll motif.

234

Figure EA73. Side chair. Fruitwood. Attributed to East Anglia, c.1830-50.

Hollow seat, heavily turned front legs. Attempted refinement of design in shaped Regency style, reeded back uprights. Wide, reeded stay rail set below top of back uprights. Shaped cross splat with central tablet.

Figure EA74. Side chair. Elm. Attributed to East Anglia, c.1830-50.

Hollow set and heavily turned front legs. Wide stay rail inlaid with a band of mahogany veneer. Shaped cross splat with central tablet inlaid with mahogany veneer.

Figure EA75. Commode chair. Elm. Attributed to East Anglia, c.1830-50.

Lift off seat and deep frieze to conceal presence of chamber pot. Scrolled back uprights. Plain stay rail set slightly below top of back uprights. Fretted and shaped cross splat with central tablet. Regency style arm shape, supported by short, turned arm supports.

Figure EA76. The rear of artisan housing at Stiffkey, Norfolk, following the great flood of August, 1912. The inhabitants have brought their more portable possessions outside to be cleaned and dried. The rear and middle distance contains many lath and spindle back arm and side chairs typical of the chairs made in the Thames Valley tradition, the products of which were sent to areas throughout Southern England, following the development of railway transport. The side and armchairs in the foreground of the scene are typical East Anglian chairs, and examples of similar chairs are shown in Figures EA77 and 78.

(Courtesy Mrs M. Dowsing)

way to much heavier and less elegant turned legs as the century progressed beyond about 1840. The use of square tapered legs, too, which were typical of the chairs from the initial period, were gradually discontinued beyond this time. The elegance of classical arm design disappeared too, and exaggerated scrolled arms, reminiscent of certain chair styles from the Regency period, were typically adopted (see Figure EA77). The general size of construction increased as the nineteenth century progressed, and chairs which were made after about 1840 are characterised by a heaviness of demeanour and lack the earlier simplicity of style.

Chairs from the later period were no doubt made in large numbers for an increasing and perhaps more affluent population than had been the case in the first quarter of the nineteenth century. However, the opportunities created by the expansion of railway transport provided the means for the import of inexpensive chairs which must have created a considerable challenge to locally made goods. This point is illustrated in Figure EA76 which shows the rear area of a row of cottages in Stiffkey, Norfolk, in 1912,

Figure EA77. Arm and side chair. Elm. Attributed to East Anglia, c.1860-90. These chairs were rescued by the present owners from a deserted Norfolk cottage where 'they had been used as perches for invading birds for some twenty years'.

Hollow seats and heavily turned front legs. Wide, rounded stay rails overlapping the shaped back uprights. Simple, curved, cross splats. Regency style scrolled arms. Similar chairs to these are included in the domestic scene shown in Figure EA76.

following a flood which forced the inhabitants to carry out their more portable ground-floor possessions. The image shows many Wycombe made chairs to the rear of the picture, including both arm and side chairs of the lath-back as well as spindle-back variety. A Wycombe style child's

Figure EA78. Armchair. Elm with mahogany seat. Attributed to East Anglia, c.1880-1900. The chair was originally supplied by J.J. Harvey & Son, North Walsham, Norfolk (1883-1904). See Figure EA79.

Hollow seat with heavily turned legs with feet turnings missing. Wide shaped stay rail extending beyond the back uprights. Single narrow plain cross splat. Exaggerated Regency style scrolled arms on short supports.

(Courtesy Mr R.W. Edwards)

Figure EA79. Illustrated paper label glued to the underneath surface of the seat of the chair shown in Figure EA78. J.J. Harvey & Son are recorded in trade directories as cabinet makers of Market St., North Walsham, Norfolk, between 1883 and 1904,[25] although James John Harvey is recorded as cabinet maker in North Walsham as early as 1861, aged 39.[26] From 1908 onwards, no trade directory entry has been found for this firm. (Courtesy Mr R.W. Edwards)

Figure EA80. Armchair. Wood not identified. Attributed to East Anglia, c.1815-50. The chair was found at Beech House, Gressenhall, former House of Industry, Mitford & Launditch Union.

Hollow seat and turned legs. Wide stay rail extending beyond the back uprights. Single plain cross splat. Regency style arms with short, turned supports.

(Courtesy Norfolk Rural Life Museum. Photograph courtesy Norfolk Museums Service)

table chair also appears to the left of the scene. In the foreground are situated two typical late nineteenth century East Anglian chairs. Coincidentally, the only chair recorded to date from this region which has a supplier's, and possibly the maker's label attached to it, is similar in design to the East Anglian armchair shown in this domestic scene. This chair is shown in Figure EA78 and the supplier's label which is glued to the underneath of the seat is shown in Figure EA79 and refers to J.J. Harvey & Son of North Walsham, Norfolk.

The firm of J.J. Harvey & Son were makers of furniture, and are listed in trade directories in the form presented on the label as J.J. Harvey & Son. Cabinet Makers, Market St.,

North Walsham, Norfolk, between 1883 and 1904.[27] However, James John Harvey is recorded as a cabinet maker prior to this time. The chairs portrayed on this label are characteristic of those made in the High Wycombe tradition, and not those of East Anglia. This label dates from between 1880 and 1900, and illustrates that the price of 'sitting room chairs' was 18/- for six chairs; a price for each chair which was less than suggested as a construction price for each complete chair for journeymen cabinet makers in 1801.[28] The lath back chair is priced at 6/9d. (39p) and the side chairs at 2/6d. (13p). Both of these prices are comparable with the early nineteenth century prices for equivalent chairs.

Figure EA81. Side chair. Mahogany. Attributed to East Anglia, c.1850-80.

Hollow seat and heavily turned front legs. Shaped back legs. Broad shaped stay rail extending beyond the back uprights. Ornately carved cross splat.

Figure EA82. Side chair. Elm. Attributed to East Anglia, c.1860-1900.

Hollow seat and heavily turned legs. Unusual shaped front seat support. Shaped back legs. Wide rounded stay rail extending beyond the back uprights. Shaped, cross splat with tablet motif.

Figure EA83. Side chair. Mahogany. Attributed to East Anglia, c.1850-60. This simple, unembellished form of chair was bought as part of a set of six at a sale at Bungay, Suffolk, in 1914 for £2. The present owner bought them for £2.50, to store until she married, in 1922. They remain in this lady's possession in Bungay.

Hollow seat and heavily turned front legs. Shaped back legs. Stay rail extending beyond back uprights. Single undecorated cross splat.

Turner made chairs

Although the East Anglian common chair tradition is firmly located within the province of the cabinet maker, a small number of turner made chairs, both rush and wooden seated, is attributable, by design association, to East Anglia. Within this group are found chairs with back designs which incorporate turned spindles and turned buttons, those with turned spindles alone, and chairs with 'ladder' or cross splats.

The spindle back chairs illustrated in Figures EA84-89 display different adaptations within the typical form of the East Anglian chair, and indicate strong regional affiliation, even when alternative modes of decoration are employed in the same chair.

Figure EA86. Side chair. Fruitwood. Attributed to East Anglia, c.1790-1830. A transitional style in which the turned spindles, retaining the feature of the ball or button turning, form a significant part of the chair's decoration, but where the essential design features remain conventionally East Anglian.

Hollow seat. Square tapered front legs (centre cross stretcher missing). Plain stay rail extending beyond the square back uprights. Four long, turned spindles supported between the stay rail and a central cross splat. Narrow plain splat below spindles.

Figure EA84. Side chair. Fruitwood, rush seat. Attributed to East Anglia, c.1790-1830. This chair exhibits true turner's work, whilst still retaining its regional identity in the signature of the turned buttons or balls, and in the ring turnings of the front legs and front stretcher.

Turned front legs and front rail displaying ring turning typical of this regional turnery style. Wide stay rail. Four long spindles retaining the regional feature of the ball or button turning, supported between the top rail and the middle cross splat. Lower narrow cross splats joined by three turned buttons. (See Figures EA45 and 47 for stylistic similarities.)

Figure EA85. Armchair. Fruitwood. Attributed to East Anglia, c.1790-1830. This chair is the armed counterpart to the side chair shown in Figure EA84, and embodies similar design features. The arms and arm supports are also turned to include the typical fine ring turnings of this region.

Figure EA87. Side chair. Fruitwood. Attributed to East Anglia, c.1790-1830. A completely turned chair with rush seat. This chair is speculatively associated with the East Anglian group in exhibiting the pronounced regional design signatures of ball turnings in the spindles, as well as fine double ring turnings in the front leg and front stretcher.

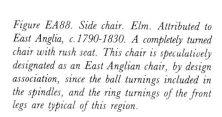

Figure EA88. Side chair. Elm. Attributed to East Anglia, c.1790-1830. A completely turned chair with rush seat. This chair is speculatively designated as an East Anglian chair, by design association, since the ball turnings included in the spindles, and the ring turnings of the front legs are typical of this region.

Figure EA89. Armchair. Fruitwood and elm. Attributed to East Anglia, c.1800-40. A turned chair with three bent cross splats or ladders. This chair is speculatively designated as East Anglian/Lincolnshire in origin by virtue of the use of elm, which is common to the East Anglian chair tradition. The fine double turnings of the arm supports, and the shaped bell turnings included as part of the front legs are regionally indicative (see Figures EA63 and 68 for similar turnery devices), as are the 'buttons' which occur as a decorative feature at the top of the back uprights. Similar chairs are attributed to Lincolnshire (see Chapter 3, Figure NE213).

Gout Cradle

Amongst the ancillary objects made by the East Anglian chair makers was a cradle to hold the foot of someone suffering with gout. This affliction was presumably common enough in the eighteenth and nineteenth centuries to warrant a description for journeymen cabinet makers, since the *Norwich Chair-makers' Book of Prices* [29] gives a separate heading for a 'Gouty Cradle' (see Figure EA90).

It is clear from this description that elaborately made cradles were designed to be raised on a wooden rack to ease placing the foot into the cradle. The term 'hollow' seat presumably refers to a 'seat' for the foot. Although the gout cradle shown in Figure EA91 is not as sophisticated in construction as the description in the *Norwich Chair-makers' Book of Prices*,[30] it is, perhaps, not difficult to imagine a country cabinet maker who made

Figure EA91. 'Gouty Cradle'. Elm. Attributed to East Anglia, c.1790-1840, made for the relief of those suffering from gout.
(Courtesy Strangers' Hall Museum, Norwich. Photograph courtesy Norwich Museums Service)

hollow seat chairs adapting this technique to make the simpler form of gout cradle shown in Figure EA91.

GOUTY CRADLE.

	£	s	d
FOR making a gouty cradle; ftraight feat, framed in two parts, hung with hinges	0	7	6
If framed in three parts	0	9	6

EXTRAS.

If with knuckle joints, each joint	0	0	10
For a hollow feat to ditto	0	1	0
If only one of thefe at one time, extra	0	0	6

Figure EA90. Description and price estimate for a 'Gouty Cradle' from the Norwich Chairmakers' Book of Prices, *1801.* *(Courtesy Norfolk Library Service)*

Stool designs

As well as chairs, stools of various uses and designs formed part of the East Anglian chair makers' repertoire. These included those which acted as tables, with the option of having a drawer in the frieze, possibly intended for children who sat at them in children's chairs (see Figure EA96); foot stools, including square, oval and octagonal designs (see Figure EA99); night (commode) stools; window stools; camp stools; 'nail-seat' stools (see Figure EA93); and shop or compting (counting) house stools (see Figure EA94). They are most commonly made in elm, although occasionally in mahogany (see Figure EA93), or yew (see Figure

EA98), or pine was used. Within this range, a wide variety of uses is seen, in which both utilitarian and personal comfort needs were simply provided for. The construction of stools in this region follows the general design principles of the chairs proper, and may have hollow and flat seats, as well as rush or upholstered loose seats. They may have square tapered as well as turned legs, the former having the option of 'box' stretchers or two side and one central stretcher. Stools intended for institutions or counting houses are typically taller than the normal low stool (see Figure EA94) and sometimes these are created as 'back stools', having a distinctive back support (see Figure EA95).

Figure EA92. Stool. Elm. Attributed to East Anglia, c.1790-1840.
Hollow seat, square tapered legs with H-design stretchers.

Figure EA93. Stool. Mahogany. Attributed to East Anglia, c.1820-50.

Hollow seat, turned legs. The form of the leg turnings with minor variations, is a typical design 'signature' of East Anglian chairs and stools. Other examples of related turnings can be seen in Figures EA85 and 98.

Figure EA96. An elm stool or a child's table. Elm. Attributed to East Anglia, c.1790-1840. The basic stool was made for 2/-; with the embellishment of a drawer which may be 'scratch-beaded, for a further 1/3d.'[32] This design of stool would perhaps have been used by a child for eating from, as well as writing or drawing on. The drawer would probably have been used to keep writing materials or playthings in.

Flat top. Straight tapered legs, and H-frame stretchers.

Figure EA97. An upholstered loose seat stool. Elm. Attributed to East Anglia, c.1790-1840.

Straight legs, supported by an H-shaped stretcher. Rebated frame to hold loose upholstered seat.

Figure EA94. Compting (counting) house or shop stool. Elm seat, pine legs. Attributed to East Anglia, c.1840-80. The production cost of the basic stool without embellishment was 2/2d. in 1801.[31] This form of simple framed stool would have been in common use in commercial premises for clerks to sit at desks. The stool illustrated here was used in the Norwich Co-operative Society's premises.

Hollow elm seat. Straight tapered pine legs. Box stretchers. (Courtesy Strangers' Hall Museum, Norwich. Photograph courtesy Norfolk Museums Service.)

Figure EA98. Oval top stool. Figured yew. Attributed to East Anglia, c.1820-40.

Oval top with shaped hand grip. Turned legs exhibiting typical East Anglian turnery signatures. See Figures EA84 and 93 for other similar turnery examples.

Figure EA95. Compting (counting) house or shop stool. Elm. Attributed to East Anglia, c.1840-80.

Stuffed over flat seat. Simple raised back with curved stay rail and two broad splats. Square tapered legs and box stretchers.

In addition to the stools made by cabinet makers and turners, other forms of stools and domestic objects were made, probably by general wood-turners* and village carpenters, which were unsophisticated and intended as utilitarian objects and which would have been inexpensively made. These stools would have provided domestic seating in the poorer cottage, as well as providing foot stools, spinning stools, and milking stools. Figure EA100 shows the kitchen interior of a poor East Anglian farm house in which a tall, primitive stool is seen to the left of the photograph, and a lower stool to the right.

*The trade of turning domestic objects of all kinds was a developed and ancient trade in the Norfolk town of Wymondham. Mosby and Agar[33] comment: 'It was probably in Tudor times that Wymondham became noted for its wood-turning industry which flourished for more than three centuries and still survives, though in a different form in the brush and wood turning factories. The crude carvings of wooden tops, spindles, spoons and skewers on the pillars and beams of the Market Cross furnish evidence that by the early seventeenth century it was regarded as the staple trade of the place. The arms of the town are a wooden spoon, crossed by a spigot, and the name of a neighbouring hamlet, Spooner Row, also undoubtedly originated with this ancient occupation.' Blomefield in 1739 wrote: 'Men, women and children are continually employed in this work'. About a century later, another writer stated that the poorer inhabitants were chiefly engaged in making spigots and fassets, spindles, spoons and other small wares, or in weaving'.

240

The 'Mendlesham' chair

Oral tradition insists that within the East Anglian chair making tradition, a distinctive and graceful style of Windsor chair, unlike any other of the region's chairs, was made in the Suffolk village of Mendlesham, by members of the Day family, possibly father and son, Daniel (Dan) Day and Richard Day, during the late eighteenth and early nineteenth centuries. Many written references have also appeared which have commented on the enigmatic status of the Mendlesham chair, and its mythological place in the folklore of East Anglia.[34]

Although no positive evidence has been found firmly linking the creation of the so-called Mendlesham chair with the village of that name and with the Day family, the strong evidence of long standing local ownership of these chairs, and a consistent belief that their origin was from Mendlesham, creates a sufficiently plausible framework to warrant exploration of the basis for this belief, and to examine records of surrounding parishes for evidence of an extended tradition outside Mendlesham.

Records show that families with the surname Day were found in Mendlesham and the nearby villages and towns of Stonham Aspal, Stonham Parva, Oakley, Walsham Le Willows, Budsdale (part of Rickinghall Superior), and Eye, from at least the middle of the eighteenth century[35] until the late 1830s.[36] Days from the last four locations were involved in the woodworking trades as carpenters, joiners and builders, and wheelwrights. The only reference to a Daniel Day in this region is that of a Day with that Christian name living in Eye, some miles from Mendlesham, between 1844 and 1855, where he was described as a joiner and builder.[37]

The first record of Days in Mendlesham shows that Robert Day married Susan Ottowell on 17 August, 1756,[38] and that Robert's father was named George. Robert and Susan are probably the grandparents of Richard Day, since a Richard and Mary Day (née Potter) are recorded at the baptism of their daughter Mary in 1791,[39] and given the birth date of 1783 for the last Richard Day in Mendlesham,[40] these may well be his parents too. The latter Richard Day is unrecorded until 1830 when he is listed in trade directory sources,[41] as a cabinet and chair maker, living in Mendlesham.

Figure EA99. A group of sitting and foot stools with elm tops and ash legs. Attributed to East Anglia, early 19th century. (Collected in the Wymondham area of Norfolk.) The ash washing dolly, in the centre, is a further example of the turners' products, and was part of a wide repertoire of turned goods.
(Courtesy Mr R. Standley)

Figure EA100. Photograph of a farmhouse kitchen on the Norfolk/Suffolk border, c.1890. The contents of this scene indicate a poor household, and furniture is virtually absent except for primitive stools*.
(Courtesy Norfolk Museums Service)

* The group of stools shown in Figure EA99 is accompanied by another turners' product, the washing dolly. This was used to agitate the washing in a large boiling copper, a typical example of which is seen in the kitchen scene shown in Figure EA100, with a pottery jug shown on its wooden lid.

This single reference confirms the belief that chair making was undertaken in the village. However, no other record is found until Richard's burial is recorded in the Mendlesham Parish Register on 14 December, 1838 when he was fifty-five years of age.[42]

Given that the style of Mendlesham chairs suggests that they originated around the late eighteenth or early nineteenth centuries, the first of these chairs could have been made by Richard Day the latter, as he would have been twenty years of age in 1803, and perhaps at this stage able to produce chairs of the grace and detail typical of the Mendlesham chair. Since Richard is described as a cabinet maker as well as chair maker, he no doubt made case furniture for local use, as well as his 'special' chairs, and may have continued to do so throughout his working life of about thirty-five years. During this time, there is some indication that Day may have had assistance in his work for at least part of this time,

Figure EA101. Interior of a farmhouse near Lowestoft, Suffolk, showing 'Mendlesham' chairs which have been in this farming family for some five generations. (Courtesy Mr and Mrs J. Oldrin)

Figure EA102. Fore Street, Mendlesham, c.1900, showing a well kept village with cobbled footpaths and neat houses. Tradition suggests that Richard Day, cabinet maker and chair maker, lived at 16 Front (Fore) Street, which is near the far end of the street on the right hand side.

(Courtesy Suffolk Photographic Archive, Suffolk County Council)

Figure EA103. Main Street, Rickinghall Superior, seven miles north of Mendlesham in 1908. Here, Jonathan Blowers and his son Jonathan worked as chair makers, following the death of Richard Day in 1838. (*Courtesy Suffolk Photographic Survey, Suffolk County Council*)

since a member of the nearby village of Earl Stonham named Samuel Ling is recorded at the baptism of his son in 1818 to be a chair maker.[43] He is later recorded at his burial in Mendlesham churchyard on 28 August, 1820 to be a rake-maker.[44]

The recorded presence of Richard Day and Samuel Ling as chair makers only serves to heighten the enigma of the Mendlesham chair. Since no other chair makers are recorded in any other parish in the surrounding area of Mendlesham in the eighteenth or early nineteenth centuries, this evidence seems to support the view that if the origin of the Mendlesham chair was in this village, then Richard Day was probably the original designer. In any event the designer of these chairs had clearly been influenced by Thomas Sheraton's chair designs[45] as well as the arm styles of George Hepplewhite's chairs, and interpreted them within the 'Mendlesham' style. These

influences are often found in other East Anglian common chairs, but typically not in such a refined and distinctive manner as that found in the Mendlesham chair.

These regionally congruent features, however, are combined with aspects of chair design which originate outside this region, those of the Windsor chair makers whose products embody turned legs and H-form stretchers, and a shaped elm seat into which the legs, back, and arm supports were morticed. The style of the Mendlesham chair therefore embodies two traditions; one which reflects the region's reliance on interpretations of classical design, and the other which reflects the Windsor chair makers' techniques and styles typically found in Buckinghamshire and Oxfordshire to the west, Lincolnshire to the north, and the Windsor chair makers of London and the Home Counties to the south. This wide awareness of chair styles from both within and outside East

Anglia suggests that if Richard Day was the designer of the Mendlesham chair, he was an original and innovative craftsman, whose knowledge extended beyond his immediate village, indicating, perhaps, that he had travelled to metropolitan areas, or perhaps to the chair making centre of High Wycombe, where chairs of a somewhat similar stature to the Mendlesham chairs were made.

The unexplained nature of the 'Mendlesham chair' is further extended since the wide detailed design differences found in this group are such that the purpose or purposes for which the chair was made is brought into question. Since few side chairs of this style have been recorded,[46] and relatively few of the armchairs are precisely identical in design detail to each other, except where pairs are found, it may be that these chairs were intended, not for daily domestic use, but rather made for special occasions as gifts, perhaps for a

243

Figure EA104. A gathering of Mendlesham area chairs at Elm Farm, Mendlesham, 27 June, 1984, courtesy of Mr Roy Clement-Smith, showing the collection of chairs loaned by owners throughout East Anglia. Some of the many people who came from the surrounding district to see the chairs are included in the photograph. Left to right Mr Denton-Cardew, cabinet maker and chair maker; Mrs G. Cotton; Dr B. Cotton; M. Robinson, research assistant; Mr Godart-Brown, owner; Mrs L. Reynolds, owner; Mr Roy Clement-Smith, cabinet and·Mendlesham chair maker; Mrs M. Maundrell, turner; Mr L. Reynolds, furniture historian; Mrs R. Clement-Smith; Mr W. Clement-Smith.

wedding or baptism. Certainly such fine and delicate chairs were seen as 'special' rather than 'every day'.

Oral histories given by owners with long family associations with this style of chair, support the view that these chairs were used primarily on special occasions. An oral transcript from one owner describing the place of the Mendlesham chair in the tradition of his East Anglian farming family is given in Appendix B, p.259, and illustrates the sense of occasion in which Mendlesham chairs were involved.

The village of Mendlesham itself is typical of those found in the Suffolk Wolds, with well made brick houses, some plastered, under red clay tile roofs, or the occasional thatched roof. The early twentieth century photograph of Fore Street, Mendlesham (see Figure EA102), portrays a quiet, well maintained village with sub-

Figure EA105. Cabinet maker's marks made prior to cutting the dovetail mortice into which the arm support fits. These marks were noted on the majority of measured chairs; four further chairs had one mark only, and three had no marks. Since these marks are so consistently found within the group, and are apparently not intended for decorative purposes, they constitute unconscious makers' signatures and indicate the application of a disciplined learned procedure, and perhaps suggest that if other chair makers who arose around Mendlesham did make this local style of chair, then they may have received training from the same chair maker.

stantial cottages, wide cobblestone footways, and clean streets, engendering a sense of husbandry and quiet prosperity. During the nineteenth century, the village was a thriving community, with a wide variety of trades and occupations, and as early as 1830 blacksmiths, painters and glaziers, butchers, glovers, bricklayers, boot and shoemakers, coopers, millers, a watch and clock maker, a cabinet and chair maker, a saddler, carpenters, shopkeepers, and a mason are all noted working in the village.[47]

Nevertheless, the creation of such superior chairs from a typical small pastoral village in rural Suffolk is a remarkable event in the history of English craft work; one which seems to have held such an important place in the region's cultural life, that following the death of Richard Day in 1838, other chair makers followed in his footsteps and continued making chairs from the early 1840s until at least the 1860s, and cabinet and chair makers are recorded working in parishes within walking distance of Mendlesham.

In 1841 Jonathan Blowers and his son, also Jonathan, were recorded as chair makers in Rickinghall Superior some seven miles north of Mendlesham.[48] Although Jonathan the younger is only recorded at this time, his father continued as a chair maker and is last recorded as such in 1851. Figure EA103 shows a street scene in Rickinghall Superior taken in 1908. The village perhaps looks less prosperous than Mendlesham, but has the same essential characteristics of cobbled footways and red brick houses.

At about the same distance from Mendlesham to the south east, a further chair maker, Thomas Blowers, is first recorded as working at Stonham Aspal in 1847,[49] where he continued in his trade for many years, employing at least one apprentice,[50] and was last recorded as working as a cabinet maker in 1861,[51] and finally on the event of his death in 1889.[52] Even nearer to Mendlesham is the village of Old Newton, where a further chair maker, Edmund Wicks, is recorded working in 1844,[53] although he is also recorded as a rake-maker.[54]

The evidence suggests, therefore, that although Richard Day may have been the originator of the Mendlesham chair, he was not the only maker, since others appear to have arisen to continue in the craft. However, since

Figure EA106. The four most common splats found in Mendlesham chairs. The wheel fretted motif is the least common of the four.

little documentary evidence has emerged to link specific chairs within the Mendlesham group with these individual makers, a research programme has been specially designed to examine the existing evidence and to combine the detailed record searches with extensive field research; a project which has ultimately resulted in photographically recording and measuring a sample of chairs, the data from which was presented for statistical analysis.

Illustrated advertisements were placed in the East Anglian regional press for owners of so-called Mendlesham chairs to come forward and offer them, as well as oral evidence, for examination. As a result many chairs were offered by owners throughout East Anglia, and some sixty chairs were collected together at Elm Farm, near to the centre of Mendlesham where interested people, including owners, chair and cabinet makers, local historians, as well as others from the village and surrounding regions, were invited to see the gathering of these beautifully made chairs. A few of those who attended are shown with the collection of chairs in Figure EA104.

Each chair was photographed and an oral history taken; thirty-two measurements were taken related to observable structure and thirty-one other observations were coded, to

include such elements as woods used and decorative devices. Appendix A, pp.257-8 gives details of the measurements and other codes which were noted for each chair.

Given that the chairs made available to the study included, in addition to the typical low back armchair, smaller numbers of high backed chairs, children's chairs, and some non-standard designs, it was decided to include only the standard armchairs, and to exclude any of these which appeared to have replacement parts. This enabled a statistically acceptable sample of forty-five chairs to be included within the analysis. The object of this investigation was to examine the inter-relationships between the individual measurements and qualitative codes of each chair, with all other chairs in the sample, in order to establish degrees of similarity and dissimilarity between them. Ultimately, the complex matrix of correlations was interrogated to display individual chairs according to nearness/distance of similarity from other chairs in the group. The resulting dendrogram shown in Figure EA167, Appendix A, indicates groups of chairs which were linked by statistical similarity to each other, according to a nearness/distance profile, and where the greater the distance at which chairs meet the base-line 'X', the greater their dissimilarity from

GROUP A

Figure EA107. Group A, case 1. Fruitwood with elm seat, heart splat, unusual pierced cresting rail. Back height 46cm (18in.); seat depth 37.2cm (14¾in.); width 46.4cm (18¼in.). (Courtesy the Goodwin Family, Ipswich)

Figure EA108. Group A, case 5. Fruitwood with elm seat, heart splat. Back height 43.8cm (17¼in.); seat depth 37.5cm (14¾in.); width 46.4cm (18¼in.).
(Courtesy the Goodwin Family, Ipswich)

Figure EA109. Group A, case 12. Fruitwood with elm seat, heart splat. Back height 44cm (17¼in.); seat depth 38.6cm (15¼in.); width 45.2cm (17⅞in.).
(Courtesy the Vicar of Mendlesham)

the primary group A. In this way, five groups of chairs were distinguished as significantly separate from each other in the sample; their differences sufficiently pronounced as to suggest that the notion that all of these chairs were made in one workshop is unlikely.

However, since there is no preexisting evidence to deny the basic belief in the origin of this chair group to the village of Mendlesham, the results of this statistical analysis might therefore suggest three alternative explanatory propositions which require examination:

(a) That there was more than one maker at work producing these chairs, not working in the same workshop, but working within the same cultural tradition.

(b) That the groups represent changes in design at a relatively unobservable, but nevertheless significant level; which may have occurred over time, and the groups therefore represent a chronology of chairs produced by one craftsman.

(c) That the chairs were made in the same workshop by different people either concurrently or consecutively.

Of these options, the last seems the weakest, since records show little evidence to support this, and in any event, it would seem improbable that

workers in the same workshop, making essentially the same product, would have used templates which measured differently. Option (b) is possible, except that this is rendered less probable by evidence of the number of chair makers being located in the immediate area of Mendlesham over an extended period of time. Given this information, the likelihood of option (a) being the most probable origin of this group of chairs is discussed below.

The statistical evidence distinguishing significantly separate sub-groups of chairs tends to support the documentary implications that the Mendlesham chair may have been made by people working in the same cultural tradition, adopting similar, but not precisely identical measurements. This is evidenced since the numerical correlations record differences which would seem to suggest more than those endemic in producing non-standard 'hand made' work. It would appear that either different sets of templates were used or that the makers' approach to measurement varied significantly. There are also distinct groupings of splat variations (Figure EA106) and arrangements of plain spindles.

Figure EA110. Group A, case 31. Fruitwood with elm seat and birch arms, heart splat. Back height 44.2cm (17½in.); seat depth 39.7cm (15¾in.); width 45.3cm (17⅞in.).
(Courtesy Mr Baker, Mendlesham)

Figure EA111. Group A, case 14. Fruitwood with sycamore seat, heart splat. Back height 44cm (17¼in.); seat depth 37.2cm (14¾in.); width 47cm (18½in.).

Figure EA112. Group A, case 22. Fruitwood with elm seat, heart splat. Back height 43.3cm (17in.); seat depth 38cm (15in.); width 46.8cm (18½in.).

Figure EA113. Group A, case 23. Fruitwood with elm seat, heart splat. Back height 42.6cm (16¾in.); seat depth 38.3cm (15in.); width 46.6cm (18¼in.).

The illustrations of Mendlesham chairs shown are those used in the analysis. They are illustrated in order of their appearance on the dendrogram shown in Figure EA167, which shows the grouping of chairs with the chairs most similar to themselves.

In examining the visual images of the chairs which the analysis grouped together as being statistically different from other groups, it is important to note that the codings supplied for analysis did not include details of splat design, merely the presence or absence of one or more splats. Consequently, it is significant that in grouping the chairs, the two major Groups A and C included chairs which contain respectively a predominance in Group A of 'heart' motif splats, with only one exception which incorporates a 'ripple' splat (see Figure EA122), whereas Group C contains a majority of ripple and 'wheatsheaf' motif splats, with the exception of one heart splat motif shown in Figure EA129, and one chair which contains a 'wheel' motif in its splat (see Figure EA138). Group E also reflected distinct back design differences from A and C in grouping the chairs made totally in elm and made without a splat. The one exception in this group has a splat of a uniquely elaborate fretted design (see Figure EA151).

The three chairs which form Group B display two heart splat motif chairs, one of which, Figure EA127, is located with unusual decoratively turned spindles: a further chair displays a wheel motif splat similar to the chair in Figure EA138. Statistically, these chairs are closer to Group A than Group C. The three chairs in Group D show two chairs with ripple shaped splats, and one displaying the heart motif. Statistically, these chairs are shown to be closer in design terms to those included in Group C, and are as close to Group C as those in Group B are to Group A.

The groupings achieved from the sample used suggest, therefore, two major groups, A and C, with two small related sub-groups, B and D. Group E appears to be very dissimilar to all the other groups.

Group A	EA107-125
Group B	EA126-128
Group C	EA129-142
Group D	EA143-145
Group E	EA146-151
Others	EA152-165

The evidence supplied by the documentary information, and the

Figure EA114. Group A, case 27. Fruitwood with elm seat, heart splat. Back height 43.9cm (17¼in.); seat depth 39cm (15¼in.); width 46.5cm (18¼in.).

247

statistical grouping, would therefore seem to support the view that the Mendlesham chair was probably made between about 1800 and 1860, with several makers working in the tradition. Following on from Richard Day, who worked from about 1800 to 1838, at least four chair makers are recorded working in the Mendlesham area, working within what they may have believed were the conventions of this style, adding only their own innovations of different splat designs or, indeed, absence of a splat.

However, the work of the various makers was, if relatively similar to each other, evidently sufficiently divergent from some other chairs in the group for detailed comparisons of all the measurements to highlight significant differences in their making.

From this evidence, it is not possible to say which group of chairs was made by which maker. However, the existence of a number of makers and distinct groups of chairs creates the possibility that the Mendlesham area chair was the focus of a significant tradition of English regional chair making, rather than the exclusive 'child' of one craftsman/designer.

GROUP A continued

Figure EA115. Group A, case 10. Fruitwood with elm seat and walnut arms, heart splat. Back height 43.9cm (17¼ in.); seat depth 39.8cm (15¾ in.); width 45.9cm (18in.).

(Courtesy Mr A. Alston, Mendlesham)

Figure EA116. Group A, case 21. Fruitwood with elm seat, heart splat. Back height 43.5cm (17in.); seat depth 38.5cm (15¼ in.); width 47.2cm (18½ in.).

Figure EA117. Group A, case 13. Fruitwood with elm seat, heart splat. Back height 45.4cm (18in.); seat depth 39.9cm (15¾ in.); width 44.9cm (17⅞ in.).

Figure EA118. Group A, case 15. Fruitwood with elm seat and legs, yew 'cowhorn' back stretcher, heart splat. Back height 44.4cm (17½ in.); seat depth 39.4cm (15½ in.); width 45.7cm (18in.).

Figure EA119. Group A, case 9. Elm with birch seat, fruitwood spindles, splat and turned buttons, walnut back cowhorn, heart splat. Back height 43.5cm (17in.); seat depth 36.5cm (14½ in.); width 46cm (18in.).

(Courtesy Mr A. Alston, Mendlesham)

Figure EA120. Group A, case 42. Fruitwood with elm seat, heart splat. Back height 43.2cm (17in.); seat depth 35.8cm (14in.); width 47cm (18½in.).

(Courtesy Christchurch Museum, Ipswich, Suffolk)

Figure EA121. Group A, case 29. Fruitwood with elm seat, legs, and centre stretcher, heart splat. Back height 41cm (16¼in.); seat depth 38.6cm (15¼in.); width 47.1cm (18½in.). Purchased 1970 from Kettlebaston Church, Suffolk (now closed).

(Courtesy Mrs Payne, Mendlesham area)

Figure EA122. Group A, case 11. Fruitwood with elm seat, ripple splat, unusual arched cresting rail. Back height 44cm (17¼in.); seat depth 37.4cm (14¾in.); width 45.5cm (18in.).

(Courtesy the Vicar of Mendlesham)

Figure EA123. Group A, case 34. Fruitwood with elm seat, arms, arm supports, and back uprights, heart splat. Back height 41.8cm (16½in.); seat depth 38.8cm (15¼in.); width 41.1cm (16¼in.).

(Courtesy Mr Baker, Mendlesham area)

Figure EA124. Group A, case 41. Fruitwood with elm seat, legs, and stretchers, heart splat. Back height 44.1cm (17¼in.); seat depth 40cm (15¾in.); width 47cm (18½in.).

(Courtesy Christchurch Museum, Ipswich, Suffolk)

Figure EA125. Group A, case 40. Yew with elm seat, and fruitwood legs, cross stretchers, bottom back cross rail, spindles, and splat. Heart splat, unusual decoratively turned back spindles. Back height 43cm (17in.); seat depth 39cm (15¼in.); width 43.3cm (17in.).

(Courtesy Christchurch Museum, Ipswich, Suffolk)

Figure EA126. Group B, case 19. Fruitwood with elm seat, unusual wheel splat. Back height 43.7cm (17¼ in.); seat depth 39.5cm (15½ in.); width 45.2cm (17¾ in.).

Figure EA127. Group B, case 35. Fruitwood with elm seat, walnut back cowhorn, heart splat, unusual turned spindles. Back height 43.3cm (17in.); seat depth 39.1cm (15½ in.); width 46.8cm (18½ in.).

Figure EA128. Group B, case 3. Fruitwood with elm seat, heart splat. Back height 43cm (17in.); seat depth 38.2cm (15in.); width 46.4cm (18¼ in.).

(Courtesy the Goodwin Family, Ipswich, Suffolk)

GROUP C

Figure EA129. Group C, case 2. Fruitwood with elm seat, heart splat. Back height 43.5cm (17in.); seat depth 38cm (15in.); width 47cm (18½ in.).

(Courtesy the Goodwin Family, Ipswich, Suffolk)

Figure EA130. Group C, case 30. Elm with fruitwood turned buttons, wheatsheaf splat. Back height 44.7cm (17½ in.); seat depth 40cm (15¾ in.); width 43.5cm (17in.).

(Courtesy Mr Godart-Brown, Mendlesham area)

Figure EA131. Group C, case 7. Fruitwood with elm seat, ripple splat. Back height 43cm (17in.); seat depth 40.5cm (16in.); width 45cm (17¾ in.).

Figure EA132. Group C, case 8. Fruitwood with elm seat, ripple splat. Back height 42.5cm (16¾in.); seat depth 39.6cm (15½in.); width 44.7cm (17½in.).

Figure EA133. Group C, case 37. Elm throughout, wheatsheaf splat. Back height 42.3cm (16¾in.); seat depth 40.5cm (16in.); width 44cm (17¼in.).

(Courtesy Christchurch Museum, Ipswich, Suffolk)

Figure EA134. Group C, case 25. Fruitwood with elm seat, ripple splat, unusual turned spindles. Back height 42.5cm (16¾in.); seat depth 40.5cm (16in.); width 45.7cm (18in.).

Figure EA135. Group C, case 28. Fruitwood with elm seat, ripple splat. Back height 43cm (17in.); seat depth 38.5cm (15¼in.); width 46cm (18in.).
(Courtesy Mr L. Reynolds)

Figure EA136. Group C, case 39. Elm throughout, ripple splat. Back height 43cm (17in.); seat depth 37.2cm (14½in.); width 46cm (18in.).
(Courtesy Christchurch Museum, Ipswich, Suffolk)

Figure EA137. Group C, case 38. Fruitwood with elm splat, ripple splat. Back height 42cm (16½in.); seat depth 37.7cm (14¾in.); width 47cm (18½in.).
(Courtesy Christchurch Museum, Ipswich, Suffolk)

GROUP C continued

Figure EA138. Group C, case 20. Fruitwood with elm seat. Unusual wheel splat. Back height 43.5cm (17¼ in.); seat depth 38.2cm (15in.); width 47.1cm (18½ in.).

Figure EA139. Group C, case 16. Fruitwood with elm seat, three ripple splats. Back height 43.8cm (17¼ in.); seat depth 38.9cm (15¼ in.); width 44cm (17¼ in.).

Figure EA140. Group C, case 43. Fruitwood with elm seat, three ripple splats, curved top back rail. Back height 44.2cm (17½ in.); seat depth 40.5cm (16in.); width 44.5cm (17½ in.).

Figure EA141. Group C, case 21. Fruitwood with elm seat, laburnum back uprights, three back cross rails, three wheatsheaf splats. Back height 42.9cm (16¾ in.); seat depth 40.3cm (15¾ in.); width 44.7cm (17½ in.).

(Courtesy Mr Bourlay, Mendlesham area)

Figure EA142. Group C, case 36. Elm throughout, three wheatsheaf splats. Back height 43.1cm (17in.); seat depth 41.1cm (16¼ in.); width 44.7cm (17½ in.).

(Courtesy Norfolk Museums Service, Strangers' Hall, Norwich)

GROUP D

Figure EA143. Group D, case 4. Fruitwood with elm seat, three ripple splats. Back height 43.5cm (17in.); seat depth 35.5cm (14in.); width 47.2cm (18½in.).

(Courtesy the Goodwin Family, Ipswich, Suffolk)

Figure EA144. Group D, case 33. Fruitwood with elm seat, ripple splat, curved cresting rail. Back height 43.9cm (17¼in.); seat depth 40.1cm (15¾in.); width 44.3cm (17½in.).

(Courtesy Mr Baker, Mendlesham area)

Figure EA145. Group D, case 32. Fruitwood with walnut seat, heart splat. Back height 44.2cm (17½in.); seat depth 33.6cm (13¼in.); width 46.5cm (18¼in.).

(Courtesy Mr Baker, Mendlesham area)

GROUP E

Figure EA146. Group E, case 6. Elm with six fruitwood back spindles, no splat. Back height 42.8cm (16¾in.); seat depth 39.9cm (15¾in.); width 44.6cm (17½in.).

Figure EA147. Group E, case 18. Elm with sycamore arms and arm supports; fruitwood back uprights, middle and bottom back cross rails, back cowhorn, spindles, and buttons. Unusually, eight back spindles, no splat. Back height 43.3cm (17in.); seat depth 43.5cm (17in.); width 47.1cm (18½in.).

(Courtesy the Goodwin Family, Ipswich, Suffolk)

Figure EA148. Group E, case 17. Elm with fruitwood back uprights, top and middle cross rails, spindles, and turned buttons. One walnut side stretcher and cross stretcher, six back spindles, no splat. Back height 43.2cm (17in.); seat depth 39.8cm (15¾in.); width 46.7cm (18¼in.).

GROUP E continued

Figure EA149. Group E, case 44. Elm throughout, six back spindles, no splat. Back height 44.2cm (17½in.); seat depth 39.1cm (15½in.); width 45cm (17¾in.).

Figure EA150. Group E, case 45. Elm with fruitwood back uprights, three cross rails, and turned buttons, six spindles, no splat. Back height 43.9cm (17¼in.); seat depth 39.8cm (15¾in.); width 43.1cm (17in.).

Figure EA151. Group E, case 26. Fruitwood with elm seat, unusually decorative splat, six hexagonal spindles (two bottom buttons missing). Back height 44.3cm (17½in.); seat depth 39.3cm (15½in.); width 44cm (17¼in.).

(Courtesy Mr A.J. Gower, Suffolk)

MENDLESHAM CHAIR VARIANTS

Figure EA152. Child's chair. Fruitwood with elm seat, ripple splat. Attributed to East Anglia. Similar to adult sized chairs shown in Figures EA135 and 137.

(Courtesy the Goodwin Family, Ipswich, Suffolk)

Figure EA153. Child's chair. Fruitwood with elm seat, ripple splat. Attributed to East Anglia.

(Courtesy the Goodwin Family, Ipswich, Suffolk)

Figure EA154. Child's chair. Fruitwood with elm seat, ripple splat. Attributed to East Anglia. Similar to chairs shown in Figure EA131 and EA132, but with turned arm supports, not noted in adult chair models.

(Courtesy Christchurch Museum, Ipswich, Suffolk)

Figure EA155. 'Fireside' chair. Fruitwood with elm seat. Attributed to East Anglia. Unusually high back (104.5cm (41¼ in.) to floor) with a double row of decoratively turned spindles. Upper splat with 'draught' motif. The double turned buttons held between stay rail and first cross rail. Cowhorn stretcher absent in back design.

(Courtesy Christchurch Museum, Ipswich, Suffolk)

Figure EA156. Fireside chair. Fruitwood with burr elm seat. Attributed to East Anglia. Unusually high back (127.5cm (50¼ in.) to floor) with a double row of decoratively turned spindles, splayed outwards from the centre. Upper splat with draught motif. Single turned buttons held between the stay rail and the first cross rail. Cowhorn stretcher incorporated in back design.

(Courtesy the Goodwin family, Ipswich, Suffolk)

Figure EA157. Fireside chair. Fruitwood with elm seat. Attributed to East Anglia. Unusually high back, with two rows of plain spindles. Continuous splat with wheatsheaf design. The single turned buttons held between stay rail and first cross rail. Cowhorn stretcher incorporated in back design.

Figure EA158. Fireside chair. Fruitwood with elm seat. Attributed to East Anglia. Unusually tall back with one row of plain spindles and one ripple shaped splat. Three single turned buttons held between stay rail and first cross rail. Two lower cross rails. Cowhorn stretcher absent.

(Courtesy the Goodwin Family, Ipswich, Suffolk)

Figure EA159. Fireside chair. Fruitwood with elm seat. Attributed to East Anglia. Unusually tall back with a double row of plain spindles. Continuous 'flame' shaped splat. Three single buttons held between the top stay rail and upper cross rail. Cowhorn stretcher incorporated into back design.

(Courtesy Christchurch Museum, Ipswich, Suffolk)

Figure EA160. Side chair. Fruitwood with elm seat. Attributed to East Anglia. Ripple splat; back supported by two supporting rods. Side chairs of the Mendlesham type are extremely rare. This example forms part of a set of four.

(Courtesy Christchurch Museum, Ipswich, Suffolk)

255

Figure EA161. Low backed armchair. Fruitwood with elm seat. Attributed to East Anglia. Unusual flame shaped splats.

Figure EA162. Armchair. Birch seat, beech elsewhere. Attributed to East Anglia. A rustic version of the Mendlesham area chair. Found in Wymondham, Norfolk. This chair may represent a crude attempt to copy the chair style proper.

(Courtesy Mr R. Standley, Wymondham, Norfolk)

Figure EA163. Armchair. Elm with fruitwood splat, spindles, and turned buttons. Attributed to East Anglia. Incorporating typical features of the East Anglian chair, including square back, neoclassical arm shape, square tapered legs, supported by cross stretchers; as well as including aspects of the Mendlesham group back design. This chair has the same provenance as that given for the chair in Figure EA164.

(Courtesy Mr A. Alston, Mendlesham area)

Figure EA164. Side chair. Elm with fruitwood splat, spindles and turned buttons. Attributed to East Anglia. This chair incorporates typical features of the East Anglian chair, as well as a sense of the back design of the Mendlesham group of chairs. This chair may have been made by the Mendlesham area chair makers, and was presented as a gift of thanks to a Home Guard Commanding Officer in the Mendlesham area.

(Courtesy Mr A. Alston, Mendlesham area)

Figure EA165. Armchair. Elm seat and splat, ash hoop and sticks, fruitwood legs and stretchers. Attributed to East Anglia. Typical Windsor chair configuration, but showing leg turning detail typical of that found in some Mendlesham chairs. The wheatsheaf splat is similar to those employed in certain of the Mendlesham group chairs. The manufacturing detail in the chair indicates a close relationship with the Mendlesham area chairs, and it may be that this style of chair formed part of the repertoire of this generic chair group.

(Courtesy the Goodwin Family, Ipswich, Suffolk)

Appendix A. Summary of statistical programme employed in the investigation of the 'Mendlesham' chair groups

AIM

To investigate the belief, held as part of the folklore of East Anglia, that the Mendlesham style chair was the product of one, or possibly two chair makers. Oral history holds that this group of chairs was made by a father and son, surnamed Day, during the late eighteenth century until the late 1830s. The research programme described here sought to examine whether or not a statistical examination of the primary structural measurements and other qualitative codes, including materials used, as well as decorative devices, supported or denied this hypothesis.

SAMPLE

Sixty chairs of various designs were borrowed from owners throughout East Anglia following an appeal for help with this project in the *Eastern Daily Press*. Of this sample, forty-five chairs were finally selected as both in 'original' condition, and conforming to the group style chosen for the analysis.

DATA COLLECTION

An instrument was designed which would account for thirty-two numeric variables and thirty-one qualitative variables (see Figure EA166). The measurements were taken with woodworking callipers and a solid metric rule.

STATISTICAL PROGRAMME

Cluster analysis was seen as the most useful form of approach to investigate the problem.[55] This mode offers a technique for producing classifications from previously unclassified data; to search for natural groupings within the data; to simplify the descriptions of a large set of data; and to generate hypotheses. This form of analysis is particularly applicable to the project's needs, since its primary function is to devise a classification scheme for grouping a number of objects into a number of classes, where the objects within classes are similar in some respects, and unlike those from other classes. The reasons for producing such data clustering analyses may include the following possibilities:

(i)   Finding a true typology.
(ii)   Model fitting.
(iii)   Prediction based on groups.
(iv)   Hypothesis testing.
(v)   Data exploration.
(vi)   Hypothesis generating.
(vii)   Data reduction.[56]

Of these options, the project described here essentially sought to produce the elements of (i) a true typology of chairs, according to difference/similarity, and (iv) test the hypothesis that is it more or less likely that the group of sampled chairs were made by one or more makers.

Given these procedural aims, the cluster analysis was programmed to investigate the inter-relationships between the individual structure measurements and qualitative codes noted for each chair, and to compare these with all other chairs in the sample. These comparisons were

Figure EA166. Example of a completed pro-forma used to list information related to quantative and qualitative data for chair No.43. Each chair was analysed in this way to provide details for the statistical analysis.

sought in order to establish degrees of similarity and dissimilarity between them, and to illustrate the levels of significance of difference/similarity. Ultimately, the complex matrix of correlations was interrogated to display individual chairs according to nearness/distance of similarity from other chairs in the group. The results of this were represented within different forms of analysis, including cluster diagnosis of: means, standard deviations and F ratios; variable correlation matrices; tests of association for numerical and non-numeric categories; histograms; scatterplots and dendrograms.

RESULTS

The data representation given in the dendrogram shown in Figure EA167 indicates groupings of chairs which were grouped by statistical similarity to each other, according to a nearness/distance profile, and where the greater the distance at which the chairs meet the base line 'X', the greater their dissimilarity from the primary group A. The results indicate that five groups of chairs were distinguished as significantly separate from each other in the sample; and that their differences were sufficiently pronounced as to suggest that the notion that all of these chairs were made in one workshop is unlikely. (See text p.248 for a discussion of the implications of this result.)

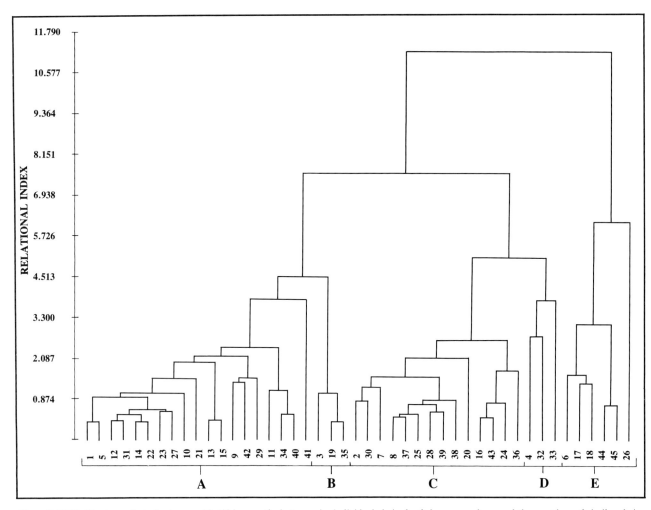

Figure EA167. Cluster analysis dendrogram identifying, on the bottom axis, individual chairs by their case numbers, and the groupings of similar chairs.

"My name is John Oldrin and I live near Lowestoft, East Suffolk.

My mother had two Mendlesham chairs that she brought with her when she was married to my father and they lived on his farm, Rushmere. These chairs were kept in the parlour or drawing room and I think that my father called it the 'keeping room'. They were used at tea parties and on several occasions, mostly by the very young, the grandchildren, when they came to meals, to tea, to lunch. They were tied into the Mendlesham chair with a scarf and they had a cushion, a special cushion of course. There's many children have been fed and sat up in those chairs at the table rather by using them in the place of a high chair.

These chairs were always respected and were used, and had to be used, with visitors. I always remember them being used when there was any tennis on the lawn in front of the house when my sisters used to have tennis parties. We had the local vet come to us and he used to come to us and play tennis. The visitors used to sit on these Mendlesham chairs as well as on a very old, hard, very ornamental seat. He (the vet) had four chairs, Mendlesham chairs which he had left to him by his father. He and my mother had quite a good nature because he said he would like to buy her two chairs to make them up to half a dozen, and she said if you sell me one, then we could have three each.

Well, in 1967, I went to his sale after he died, and these chairs were for sale. They were not in the catalogue, and I spoke to the auctioneer who was quite a good friend of mine. He told me that the family were not interested in them. So at the sale, I was right at the back of the tent and when the lot 144 came up, Sam Flick said there was quite a number of dealers there. 'Now then you lot, who's going to be the spokesman for you? How do you want them sold? Singly or together?' They agreed they should be sold the lot, the four of them, and he put them up. The bidding went from about £20 slowly up to £160 plus. He was going to knock them down and I started bidding. I think it was about £160 or £170 and I bid up to £180, £185, £190, £200, and they were knocked down by me. There was a dispute. There was a lady there who said she bid that, and Sam, Mr Sam Flick, the auctioneer said 'No, they were knocked down to John Oldrin'. I was delighted. The lady then came to me and said would I take a profit on these chairs, and I said 'No, I certainly won't.' I said 'I've been waiting over forty years to buy these chairs and I'm afraid I'm not going to sell now.'

That night I had a phone call from a friend of mine living near Diss, and he said 'John, you've bought the chairs I wanted.' Then we had a good laugh and we are still very good friends.

The four chairs that I bought were not anything like the ones that were Granny's chairs. Granny's chairs, to me are a very delicate, light, and I think they are the best that I have seen. This is only my opinion, of course. They are extremely delicate and I am glad to say that I have two reproductions of those which were made by Mr Clement Smith. He made a wonderfully good job of them and these two reproductions I have given to my two grandsons, who are six and eight years old. Granny's chairs, of course, I have given to my daughter, Bridget ......, so they certainly will have four very nice chairs. But I'm using them for the time being.

The legs of these two chairs have been made from walnut wood that was grown on our land, in the next door garden, and that was dried, and rightly or wrongly they are a very special job.

About fifteen or twenty years ago, I saw two Mendlesham chairs in a shop at Lavenham, and I did ask a friend of mine to have a look at them. He was quite happy that they were reasonably well. He did have to restore them quite a bit.

So during that time I have collected just a few chairs. That's been one of the pleasures in my life. That, and to restore a thatched house, and living in it, where my great great grandfather lived. Its given me quite a boost. Last year, in April, I went to an auction at Norwich, the Blackfriars' Hall, and there was lot 136, antique Mendlesham fruit wood elbow chair, new leg with stretcher rail, that made £200. That was a very heavy, not a balanced chair at all. I have seen Mendlesham chairs at the Norwich Castle Museum. One or two, I believe, are there. Also at the Christchurch Museum at Ipswich, I believe there are four or five there on view at most times."

J.O. 1984

Postscript

Since making this transcript, Mr John Oldrin has died and his chairs are now at the Norfolk Rural Life Museum, Gressenhall, Norfolk.

Figure SW1. 'Polishing Day' by Harold Harvey (1874-1941). *(Courtesy Bearnes, Torquay)*

Chapter 5
SOUTH WEST REGION
CORNWALL,
DEVON AND SOMERSET

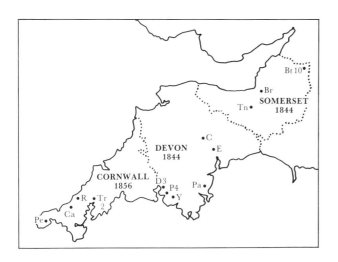

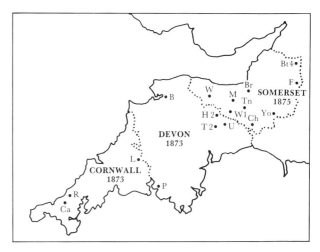

Key:

Somerset	Devon	Cornwall
Bath = Bt	Crediton = C	Camborne = Ca
Bridgwater = Br	Devonport = D	Launceston = L
Taunton = Tn	Exeter = E	Penzance = Pe
Wiveliscombe = W	Paignton = Pa	Redruth = R
Frome = F	Plymouth = P	Truro = Tr
Milverton = M	Yealmpton = Y	
Yeovil = Yo	Barnstaple = B	
Chard = Ch	Uffculme = U	
Wellington = Wl	Tiverton = T	
Burnham = Bn	Holcombe Rogus = H	
	Bideford = Bi	

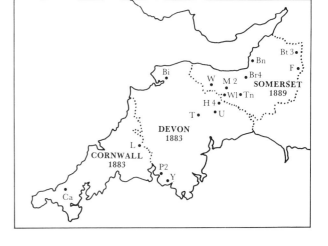

Figures SW2-4. Recorded chair makers in the West Country showing the development of the trade from the mid to late 19th century. The different dates shown coincide with trade directory publications for each county.

The counties of Cornwall, Devon and Somerset compose the South West peninsula of England, where the close proximity of the land to the sea on both the North and South coasts has had profound effects on the climate and cultural life of the region.

Within the southern part of the West Country, the mining of tin, copper, and lead formed important industries for several centuries. These mining communities, as well as the small agricultural and fishing villages of Devon and Cornwall, were isolated from each other, and from the rest of England by poor roads, as well as the difficulty, in parts, of traversing tracts of largely uninhabited moorland areas. The coastline was rocky and treacherous to shipping, creating conditions in which hardy communities of fishermen and seafarers arose who travelled the known world. Indeed, it was from the coastal towns and villages of Devon and Cornwall that many early emigrants left to colonise the coast of New England,[1] and in Figures SW50 and 58 we see examples of New World chairs closely related to those of this region. The thriving city of Bristol was not only the major West Country port, but was the home of many crafts, including that of cabinet and chair making.

During the eighteenth century, the making of furniture for the cottage

261

Figure SW5. Primitive comb back Windsor chair. Ash with elm seat, legs and spindles. Attributed to West Country, c.1750. This primitive chair exhibits the prototype form of the three-part arm which developed in the West Country, but not in other regions. Later chairs showing the development of this form are shown in Figures SW11-13, 25 and 27.

Broad elm seat with four hand-shaped legs, through morticed and wedged. Five hand-shaped back spindles supporting a plain comb rail. Arms supported by three tapered spindles. Arm made of three shaped sections, the outer two being thinner than the back section, lapped over and nailed to form the joint, and pierced by outer back spindles.

(Courtesy Torquay Natural History Museum, Devon)

Figure SW6. Primitive comb back Windsor chair. Sycamore with elm seat, legs and spindles. Attributed to West Country, c.1750. This primitive chair exhibits an alternative prototype form to the three-part arm which developed in the West Country. This style was abandoned in favour of the single bent arm and the three-part arm types which developed in the late 18th and early 19th centuries.

Broad elm seat with four hand-shaped legs, through morticed and wedged. Five turned back spindles supporting a plain comb rail. Arms supported by three spindles. Arms made of two sections, shaped to form the arms and half the back section, lapped over and pierced by central back spindle.

(Collection Torquay Natural History Museum, Devon)

Figure SW7. Primitive comb back Windsor chair. Elm with oak seat. Attributed to West Country, c.1770. This primitive chair has an unusual prototype form of the three-part arm which developed in the West Country.

Broad seat with two square legs to the rear, and two rudimentary cabriole legs with hoof shaped feet, through morticed and wedged to the front. Eight turned back spindles supporting a plain comb rail. Arms supported by six tapered spindles. Arms made of three shaped sections, butted at the back corners to form the joint, and pierced by back spindles.

(Courtesy Sotheby's)

Figure SW8. Primitive comb back Windsor chair. Made entirely in elm. Attributed to West Country, c.1800. This chair is a variant of the three-part arm form of Windsor construction which developed in the West Country.

Broad elm seat with four octagonal shaped legs through morticed and wedged. Six turned back spindles supporting a shaped stay rail. Arms supported by two tapered spindles and flat shaped arm supports morticed into the seat edge, in a manner similar to many High Wycombe low back Windsor forms. Arms made of three shaped sections, the outer two being thinner than the back section, and a thicker middle section which overlaps and unites the two arms. These three sections are glued and screwed together, and pierced by the back spindles.

(Courtesy Sotheby's)

Figure SW9. Comb back Windsor chair. Ash with elm seat, original blue paint surface removed. Attributed to West Country, c.1780. This is an unusual chair which exhibits many commonly found features of West Country chairs, in an exaggerated form.

Shaped and waisted elm seat with egg and reel turned legs, joined by H-form stretchers. Seven hand-shaped elliptical back spindles, the outer two splayed outwards, supporting a shaped stay rail with decorative scribe line below. Arms supported by exaggerated flattened crook shaped arm supports and decorative ribbed turnings behind. Arms made of three shaped sections, the outer two being thicker than the back section which is thinner and overlaps and unites the two arms. The sections are glued and screwed together and pierced by the back spindles.

and farmhouse homes of the region probably fell within the domain of the village carpenter. Cabinet makers appear to have been restricted to the major towns, and chair making as a separate craft is not recorded in trade directory sources in Cornwall until 1856,[2] and within Devon, it awaits directory records of 1844[3] before chair makers are noted in significant numbers. It does not of course follow that there were no chair makers in this early period, but may indicate a lack of detail in the survey of occupations made by directory compilers. Figures SW2-4 show the presence of recorded chair makers in the West Country during the nineteenth century, although because of the difference in the date of production of trade directories for Devon and Cornwall, identical time comparisons are not given in every case.

Three-part arm Windsors

Within this region, several distinct Windsor chair styles were developed, with two distinct prototype forms emerging in the eighteenth century. These had either an arm form made of three shaped sections, or a single arm bow. In each of these essential styles, chairs with both hoops and 'comb' back rails were made. Of these two major variants, those made in the eighteenth century with three-part arms show that in the emerging form, three roughly shaped sections of similar length were made, the two outer pieces being thinner in section, and simply lapped over and nailed to a thicker middle segment to form the arm. Figure SW5 shows an example of the three-part arm. It has a large, shaped seat and is supported by four round turned legs which pierce the seat and are wedged through their ends in a manner typical of this region's eighteenth century Windsors. This chair is surmounted by a plain comb or stay rail supported on hand drawn spindles.

Alternative forms of arm construction used in eighteenth century Windsors from the region included two shaped segments joined at a central point, or three sections, the outer sections forming butted joints with the middle section. Examples are shown in Figures SW6 and 7.

In addition to primitive three-part arm Windsors with comb or plain stay rails, others were made with bent hoops in the upper back section.

Figure SW10. Primitive hoop back Windsor chair. Ash with elm seat, legs and spindles, original dark green paint surface. Attributed to West Country, c.1780. This primitive chair is a prototype form of the three-part arm hoop Windsors which developed in the West Country, but not in other regions. Later chairs showing the development of this form are shown in Figures SW18 and 19.

Broad elm seat with four hand-shaped legs, through morticed and wedged, and one turned front leg. Five turned back spindles tapered and morticed through a lath shaped hoop. Arms supported by crude underarm supports. Arms made of three shaped sections, the outer two being thinner than the back section, lapped over and pierced by a short spindle and five long back spindles.

Figure SW11. Hoop back Windsor chair. Ash with elm seat, legs and spindles, original dark blue paint. Attributed to West Country, c.1780. This chair is a developmental form of the three-part arm which developed in the West Country.

Broad elm seat. Legs turned with a concave turning device, morticed and wedged through the seat and joined by a plain H-form stretcher. Turned back spindles morticed through a round hoop made from an ash sapling. Arms supported by two decoratively turned spindles. Arms made of three shaped sections, the outer two being thinner than the back section, lapped over and glued to form a joint which is pierced by a short spindle and the long back spindles.

(Collection Key Antiques, Chipping Norton)

Two forms of hoop were used; one which was cleft into a lath shape, and the other which was round in section and made from a sapling. Many chairs made with hoops had round or octagonal shaped legs which were not united by cross stretchers, in a similar manner to those made with comb or plain stay rails. Other examples were made with decoratively turned legs which were united by H-form stretchers, as well as with varying forms of regional seat shapes. See Figures SW10-14 and 18-27 for examples of different interpretations of the bow back style which utilised the three-part arm form.

In addition to the three-part armchair, Windsor settees were also occasionally made. These are extremely rare items of seating furniture within the English tradition, and an example is shown in Figure SW15. This settee embodies many of the features of West Country Windsor chairs, including the form of three-part arm common

to this region where the arm sections are united to the long back section by lap joints which are pierced by a long back spindle. The other back spindles mortice through the hoop and are pegged through the front to secure them.

The three-part arm structure became a defining feature of a major group of West Country Windsor chairs which were made during the greater part of the nineteenth century across a wide area which extended from Penzance in Cornwall in the south, to Bristol in the north of the region. However, as the nineteenth century forms of this style emerged, those with comb or stay rails were abandoned, and the bow back became the permanent form.

The use of three sections to form the arm bow is not in itself unusual within the English tradition, but the particular form adopted in the West Country chair is peculiar to this region. In other English Windsor chairs adopting the three-part arm

Figure SW13. Hoop back Windsor chair. Ash with elm seat, legs and spindles, and traces of original blue/green paint. Attributed to West Country, c.1800. This chair is a developmental form of the three-part arm West Country Windsor.

Shaped elm seat. Front legs turned with egg and reel motif; plain rear legs, joined by H-form stretchers. Seven turned back spindles, the outer two splaying outwards, morticed through a round hoop made from an ash sapling. Arms made of three shaped sections, the outer two being thinner and narrower than the back section, lapped over and glued to form the joint, and pierced by two short spindles and the long back spindles, with crook shaped underarm supports.

Figure SW14. A detail of the top hoop of the chair in Figure SW13 showing the through morticing and pegging of the back spindles, a common constructional feature of many West Country chairs, but rarely found in the later 19th century West Country three-part arm Windsor variety.

Figure SW12. Hoop back Windsor chair. Ash with elm seat and arms, and traces of original blue paint. Attributed to West Country, c.1800. This chair exhibits an unusual form of the three-part arm which developed in the West Country, with many commonly found features in an exaggerated form.

Shaped and waisted elm seat with egg and reel turned legs, joined by H-form stretchers. Seven turned back spindles. Arms supported by exaggerated flattened crook shaped arm supports. Arms made of three shaped sections, the outer two being thinner and flattened; the back section which is thicker, overlaps and unites the two arms. The sections are glued together and pierced through the joints by the back spindles.

Figure SW15. Windsor settee, 87in. (221cm) wide. Elm with beech legs. This rare example of an English Windsor seat embodies many of the commonly found features of West Country Windsors, including an arm made of three sections, where the sawn, shaped arms are overlapped by a back section which is glued, and pierced by a long back spindle to secure the joint. In common with other West Country Windsor furniture, the back spindles mortice through the hoop, and the two outer ones splay outwards. The underarm supports are decoratively turned in a similar manner to those shown in the chair in Figure SW11, and exhibit a regional arm turnery form. The heavily turned legs mortice through the seat, which is square fronted in the manner of many West Country Windsors.

(Courtesy Christie's)

design, notably the high smoking chairs and smokers' bow or office chairs made in Yorkshire, Nottinghamshire and High Wycombe, the raised back arm section lies on top of the two outer arm sections, which meet in the middle. In this construction, the middle section effectively acts as a supporting and strengthening device, rather than a link between the two separated segments, as is the case in the West Country design of the three-part arm. Figure SW16 illustrates the structural differences between these regional modes. It is interesting to note that both forms of three-part arm construction occur within the New England Windsor chair tradition, with the method of manufacture shown for the West Country Windsor being the most common form of arm construction in New England bow back Windsors, and with the alternative North Country mode being

found in bow back Windsors from Rhode Island.[4]

Of the three-part arm bow back Windsors to develop in the first half of the nineteenth century, two secondary forms were made. The first of these has the three-part arm where the arms are supported by two or

three decoratively turned underarm spindles. The hoops are lath shaped, supported by five or six hand shaped elliptical spindles which are splayed outwards. The legs typically terminate in an egg and reel turning, and the seats are straight across the front. In common with other West Country

Plate 34. High comb back Windsor. Ash with elm seat. Original blue/green paint. West Country, c.1760.

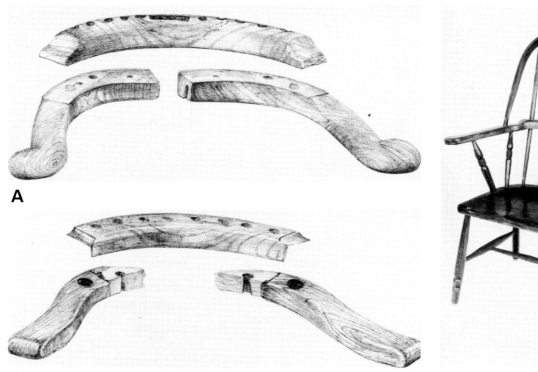

A

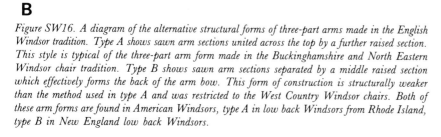

B

Figure SW16. A diagram of the alternative structural forms of three-part arms made in the English Windsor tradition. Type A shows sawn arm sections united across the top by a further raised section. This style is typical of the three-part arm form made in the Buckinghamshire and North Eastern Windsor chair tradition. Type B shows sawn arm sections separated by a middle raised section which effectively forms the back of the arm bow. This form of construction is structurally weaker than the method used in type A and was restricted to the West Country Windsor chairs. Both of these arm forms are found in American Windsors, type A in low back Windsors from Rhode Island, type B in New England low back Windsors.

Figure SW18. Primitive three-part arm Windsor chair. Ash with sycamore seat. Attributed to West Country, c.1790-1810.

Egg and reel turned leg with H-form supporting stretcher. Hand-drawn spindles morticed through hoop. Two pairs of turned spindle arm supports. Square front to seat. See Figure SW17 for similar chair.

Figure SW17. The interior of a Cornish house painted by Walter Langley in 1885 entitled 'Memories'. The primitive three-part arm Windsor chair with turned underarm supports to the left of the picture is similar to the one shown in Figure SW18 and the side chair similar to that shown in Figure SW64.

(Courtesy Birmingham Museums and Art Gallery)

Figure SW19. Three-part arm Windsor. Elm with sycamore seat, stamped 'EATHORNE MAKER PENZANCE' on rear seat edge (fl.1847-56). This chair is important in firmly placing this design to Cornish manufacture.

Shaped seat straight on front edge. Turned front legs with lower egg and reel turning. Plain turned back legs and H-form stretchers. Six long turned back spindles, splayed outwards and morticed through the hoop. Decoratively turned underarm spindles.

Figure SW21. High back three-part arm Windsor chair. Elm. Attributed to West Country, c.1830

Shaped seat straight on the front. Turned front legs with lower egg and reel turning. Plain turned back legs and H-form stretchers. Six long back spindles morticing through the hoop. Three decoratively turned underarm spindles.

Figure SW22. Three-part arm Windsor. Ash with elm seat, residual blue paint. Attributed to West Country, c.1850-75.

Three ring turned leg with H-form connecting frame. Turned arm supports. Both leg and underarm turnings were also produced in High Wycombe, Buckinghamshire, chairs (see Chapter 2). Turned spindles not morticing through the hoop.

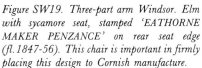

Figure SW20. The stamp of J. Eathorne, chair maker, of North Street, Penzance (fl.1847-56), impressed on the rear seat edge of the chair in Figure SW19.

Windsors, they were originally covered with blue, green or red paint.

A number of chairs of this design have been recorded by artists of the Cornish Newlyn school of painters, in cottage interior scenes. For example a painting by Walter Langley entitled 'Memories', shown in Figure SW17, portrays a Cornish cottage interior showing a primitive painted Windsor armchair which employs the precise turnery and construction detail of the chair shown in Figure SW18. A further example of a chair of this general type, showing the unusual feature of three decorative underarm supports is shown in Figure SW21.

The Cornish three-part arm Windsor style is exemplified by the chair shown in Figure SW19 which has similar features to those Windsors shown in Figures SW18 and 21 and has the maker's name 'Eathorne' stamped on the rear seat edge with its place of manufacture given as Penzance in south Cornwall. Whether this style was made further north, in Devon and Somerset, is not certain. However, it seems unlikely, since a second common form of the three-part arm Windsor has been positively identified to centres in these counties. This form does not have the two or three turned underarm spindles, but rather the early nineteenth century form of crook underarm supports (see Figures SW23-28), later examples having single, turned underarm supports (see Figure SW22).

A number of design variants have been recorded within the three-part arm group and changing forms of design detail indicate that this style of chair was made by the late eighteenth century and over a long period during the nineteenth. The earlier chairs in this group are finely constructed, and were typically painted blue or green. The front seat edge is distinctive in being straight along the front and square at the corners.

As the nineteenth century progressed, the finer form of this chair was superseded by a heavier mass-produced design which incorporated single ring and concave motif turned legs and rounded fronts to the seat. In the second half of the nineteenth century, examples of the three-part arm Windsors have larger seats with rounded fronts, and typically incorporate heavy three ring turned legs and single turned underarm supports (see Figure SW22). Although this group of nineteenth century Windsors has some features typically found in other chairs from this region, for example, painted surfaces, and the occasional morticing of the back spindles through the top hoop, in general the three-part arm Windsors made from the second quarter of the nineteenth century have features of chairs more common to other regions. These include the use of turned rather than hand drawn back spindles, single ring and concave as well as triple ring turned leg motifs, and the use of both crook and single, turned underarm supports.

Plate 35. High back Windsor chair. Ash with elm arm sections and sycamore seat. Original blue/green paint with later coats of black varnish. Impressed 'EATHORNE MAKER PENZANCE' on rear edge of seat (fl.1841-56).

Plate 36. Continuous arm Windsor. Ash with elm seat. Painted in original yellow paint with black painted nodes on spindles and legs. West Country, probably Yealmpton, c.1815.

Figure SW23. High back three-part arm Windsor chair. Birch spindles, underarm supports, legs and stretchers, ash hoop, and elm arms and seat. Stamped 'R. FROST' on rear seat edge (fl.1823-41).

Heavy single ring and concave turned front legs and plain elliptical turned rear legs, with lower ring and straight turned feet, and H-form stretchers. Eight long back spindles, two short underarm spindles and crook arm supports.

Figure SW24. The stamp of Richard Frost, cabinet maker, of Fore Street, Cullompton, Devon (fl.1823-41), impressed on the rear seat edge of the chair illustrated in Figure SW23.

Figure SW25. High back three-part arm Windsor chair. Elm with birch spindles, legs and stretchers. Stamped 'W. JENKINS' on rear edge of seat. Attributed to the Cullompton, Devon, area, c.1830. This chair is closely similar to the Richard Frost chair in Figure SW23, suggesting that there may have been a close working relationship between these makers.

Shaped seat, heavily turned single ring and concave turned front legs and plain elliptical turned rear legs with lower ring and straight turned feet and H-form stretchers. Eight long back spindles. Two short underarm supports and crook shaped arm supports.

Figure SW26. The stamp of W. Jenkins impressed on the rear seat edge of the chair in Figure SW25. This maker is untraced. James Jenkins, probably a relative, is recorded working as a cabinet maker in The Square, Axbridge, Somerset, in 1839 and 1840. Other cabinet makers named Jenkins include John Jenkins of Fore Street, Exeter, 1830, and Joseph Jenkins of Lostwithiel, Cornwall, 1830.

Figure SW27. High back three-part arm Windsor chair. Elm, stamped 'U. ALSOP' on rear edge of seat (fl.1851-1900). Attributed to West Country. This chair is closely similar to the chairs made by Richard Frost and W. Jenkins, and confirms this style as the product of many West Country chair makers in the 19th century.

Heavily turned single ring and concave turned front legs and plain elliptical turned rear legs with lower ring and straight turned feet and H-form stretchers. Eight long back spindles. Two short underarm spindles and crook shaped arm supports.
(Courtesy Torquay Natural History Museum, Devon)

Figure SW28. The stamp of Uriah Alsop impressed on the rear seat edge of the chair in Figure SW27. A father and son of this name are recorded as cabinet makers in Broadmead, Bristol, between 1851 and 1900.

Stamped chairs

Few West Country chair makers stamped their work, but examples of those who did have confirmed the distinctive three-part arm design as part of the repertoire of common chairs from this region. For example, the chair shown in Figure SW23 is stamped by Richard Frost who was a cabinet maker working in Cullompton, Devon, between 1823 and 1841, and apparently made chairs as part of his work. His brother, Samuel Frost, was also a chair maker, working in West Street, Wiveliscombe, in 1839. A second name stamped chair, shown in Figure SW25, is stamped by W. Jenkins. This maker has not been traced, but a James Jenkins, who was probably a relative of W. Jenkins, worked as a cabinet maker at Axbridge in Somerset between 1839 and 1840, and other Jenkins, cabinet makers, worked in Exeter and Lostwithiel in 1830, as well as in Bristol in 1833. The chairs made by Frost and Jenkins are so similar in design that it seems probable that Jenkins was working in the same workshop or locality as Frost.

A further example of this style bears the stamp of Uriah Alsop who was a cabinet maker and furniture broker who had extensive premises in Bristol between 1852 and 1900. The chair stamped by this maker is shown in Figure SW27 and shows a close similarity to those made by both Jenkins and Frost. Other chairs of the smoker's bow design have been recorded with this maker's stamp (see Figure SW29).

Figure SW29. Smoker's bow chair. Elm, stamped 'U. ALSOP' (fl.1851-1900), on rear edge of seat. Attributed to West Country. This style of chair was made in chair making centres in many parts of England in the second half of the 19th century, including the West Country centre of Holcombe Rogus (see Figure SW76).

Figure SW30. The stamp of Uriah Alsop impressed on the rear seat edge of the chair in Figure SW29. A father and son of this name are recorded as cabinet makers in Broadmead, Bristol, between 1851 and 1900.

Figure SW31. Comb back Windsor chair. Ash with elm seat, legs and spindles. Attributed to West Country, c.1750. The use of faux bamboo motifs in this chair (see Figure SW32) indicates that this device was an earlier feature of Windsor turnery than the commonly found form in Yealmpton made chairs (see Figures SW47, 54 and 57) and probably means the form originated in the West Country. The comb also has regional features found in other chairs in the area (see Figures SW9 and 33). The chair has some features of Windsor chairs made in the Thames Valley tradition and is evidence that

many design features were common to several regions; each region, however, adapted such features in its own manner.

Broad elm seat. Two rudimentary cabriole legs to the front connected by H-form stretchers to simulated bamboo turned legs (lower 2¾ in. (7cm) replaced). Single bent arm pierced by six hand-shaped back spindles supporting a shaped comb rail with terminal ear forms shaved to the rear to create a sharpened edge. Central urn shaped splat morticed into comb, front of arm bow and seat. Arms supported by four spindles and a flattened front support.

Figure SW32. Back view of the comb back Windsor chair shown in Figure SW31 illustrating the simulated bamboo turnings on the back legs.

Single bow arms

Contemporary with the development of the three-part arm form of construction during the eighteenth century was the second major Windsor form which was made with a single bow arm. This conventional mode of construction was common in the Windsor chair making traditions in other parts of England, and both comb back and hoop back varieties were made in a similar way. However, many other constructional and surface decoration features adopted by West Country Windsor chair makers have a closer relationship with Windsor styles made in New England than elsewhere in the British traditions.

In common with the West Country three-part arm Windsor, the single arm bow varieties were made with round turned or octagonal shaped legs which morticed and wedged through the seat, and which were not connected by stretchers. A second leg form, made with decoratively turned legs connected by H-form stretchers, was also made in the hoop back varieties. The use of primitive cabriole legs is also not unknown in this tradition, and an example of a West Country comb back Windsor with that leg form is shown in Figure SW31. Interestingly the rear legs (Figure SW32) show the use of simulated bamboo turnings. This decorative device is found in early nineteenth century chairs made in the Yealmpton

tradition and occasionally in other chairs from the West Country as well.

Both comb and hoop back designs were painted in blue or green, in common with other West Country Windsors. The back spindles were hand drawn rather than turned, and, in the hoop back varieties, were morticed and wedged through the arm bow sections. A further distinguishing feature of the single bent arm bow West Country Windsor was the use of thin, bent cleft sections to support the front underarm supports, and also occasionally used to support the outer long back spindles, in the comb back varieties (see Figures SW33-35 for examples).

Plate 37. Windsor side chair. Ash with sycamore seat. Painted in original yellow paint with petallate decoration around hoop; border on seat and nodes accentuated in black paint. (Left hand stretcher missing.) West Country, probably Yealmpton, c.1820.

Figure SW33. Comb back Windsor chair. Ash with elm seat, legs and spindles, traces of original light blue paint. Attributed to West Country, c.1770. The cleft curved section of ash on the outer arm is a regional feature of 18th century bent arm Windsors from the West Country. This comb back form of the bent arm Windsor was discontinued in the 19th century in favour of the bow back form.

Broad elm seat with four hand-shaped legs, through morticed and wedged. Eight hand-shaped back spindles supporting a decoratively shaped comb rail with terminal ear forms shaved to the rear to create a sharpened edge. Single bent arm supported by four tapered spindles, the outer one supported by a cleft curved section of ash.

Figure SW34. Hoop back Windsor chair. Ash with elm seat, legs and spindles, pine hoop and arm bow, original dark green paint. Attributed to West Country, c.1780. The cleft ash arm support section is a device typical of 18th century West Country bent arm Windsors. This chair is a prototype form of hoop back which was developed in the West Country in the 19th century (see Figures SW37-40).

Broad elm seat with decoratively turned front legs, plain turned rear legs, connected by H-form stretcher, morticed and wedged through the seat. Seven hand-shaped elliptical long back spindles piercing bent arm hoop, round hoop made from pine branch. Arms supported by three elliptical spindles with a decoratively turned underarm spindle which is supported by a curved cleft ash section (the right hand one missing).

Figure SW35. Hoop back Windsor chair. Sycamore with elm seat, legs and spindles, stripped of original blue paint. Attributed to West Country, c.1770. This primitive chair is an unusual prototype form of the bent arm Windsor which developed in the West Country.

Broad elm seat with four hand-shaped legs, through morticed and wedged. Seven hand-shaped back spindles, the outer two splaying outwards, morticed through a round hoop made from an ash sapling. Single bent arm supported by three spindles supported by a curved cleft ash section to the front. Two outer spindles support flat arm sections which are nailed to these and the top of the arm.

Figure SW36. A photograph taken in the early 20th century of a Cornish interior showing the simple furnishings of the traditional farmhouse. The elderly man sits on a settle, and wears the gaiters and boots of farmers' dress. To the right of the picture is a desk, perhaps where the farm accounting was done. The primitive high back Windsor in the foreground is a typical form of this region's Windsor chairs, and other examples are shown in Figures SW38 and 39.

The bent arm bow Windsors continued to be made during the nineteenth century, but in common with the three-part arm style, the comb back variety was gradually abandoned in favour of hoop back varieties, and the visual evidence given in paintings and photographs of nineteenth century Cornish life clearly portrays the presence of these consistent and specific forms of West Country Windsor chairs which display features not found in other English Windsor chairs (see Figures SW36 and 52). The high back Windsor chairs shown in these interiors have bent top hoops and arm bows, and often appear more crudely constructed than their eighteenth century ancestors, although they typically embody many similar structural details. These include the use of hand drawn spindles which are morticed through the hoop (see

Figure SW37. Mid-19th century double bow Windsor chair. Ash, with sycamore seat. Attributed to West Country, c.1850.

The seat is shaped and square to the front. Painted with later black paint. Plain elliptical turned legs and H-form stretchers. Six hand-drawn long back spindles, morticing through the hoop. Three short underarm spindles, and plain elliptical turned arm supports.

Figure SW38. Early 19th century double bow Windsor chair. Ash with sycamore seat. Attributed to West Country, c.1820.

The seat is square to the front. Plain elliptical turned legs and H-form stretchers with decorative ball motif in cross stretcher. Seven hand-drawn long back spindles splayed outwards from the arm bow, morticed through the hoop and pegged to the front. Two short underarm spindles and plain elliptical turned arm supports.

Figure SW39. Early 19th century double bow Windsor chair. Ash with sycamore seat. Attributed to West Country, c.1820. This chair is similar to the one shown in the farmhouse interior illustrated in Figure SW36.

The seat is square to the front. Plain elliptical turned legs and H-form stretchers. Six hand-drawn long back spindles splayed from the arm hoop, morticed through the top hoop but not pegged. Two plain elliptical underarm spindles and turned underarm supports morticing through the arm bow.
(Courtesy The National Trust, Lanhydrock, Bodmin, Cornwall)

Figure SW41), legs and stretchers which are often plain turned, although others have a form of egg and reel turning to the base of the legs. The seats of these chairs are typically made from semi-hardwoods, including sycamore and lime, and shaped straight across the front, with elm becoming widely used in the second half of the nineteenth century for seats and other parts. Some of these later chairs have painted surfaces, but others are stained with a mahogany stain and varnished over, in the manner of many inexpensive Windsor chairs from other English regions. This practice was the hallmark of utility chairs which were stained, in an attempt to enhance their fashionable qualities. Their construction is often primitive, and they contain a minimum of turned parts, suggesting that they were made by carpenters rather than chair makers.

Stools

In common with other English regions, stools made in the nineteenth century form a minor but often regionally specific form of seating design, and this remains true for those made in the West Country. In

Figure SW40. Early 19th century double bow Windsor chair. Ash with sycamore seat. Attributed to West Country, c.1800. A primitive Windsor with similar leg turnings is shown in the cottage interior shown in Figure SW17.

Turned legs with lower egg and reel turning and elliptical H-form stretchers. Seven hand-drawn long back spindles splayed from the arm bow, morticing through the top hoop. Alternate spindles pegged through the front of the arm bow. Two underarm spindles and turned decorative arm support morticing through the arm bow.
(Courtesy The National Trust, Lanhydrock, Bodmin, Cornwall)

Figure SW41. The hand-drawn spindles morticed and wedged through the hoop of the chair shown in Figure SW40. This feature is found in the construction of many chairs from this region, but occurs infrequently in the 19th century three-part arm chairs from this area.

Figure SW42. Stool. Elm top, ash leg and stretchers. Attributed to West Country, c.1840.
Legs octagonal in shape, morticed and wedged through the plain stool top.

Figure SW44. A 19th century photograph of Yealmpton, Devon, the home of an important centre of chair making in the West Country.   *(Courtesy P. Holloway, Yealmpton)*

Figure SW43. Stool. Elm top with pine legs. Attributed to West Country, c.1840. Top displays regional decorative gouged edge pattern.
Legs octagonal in shape, morticed and wedged through the top.
(Courtesy Michael Legg, Dorcester)

this region, many stools had tops made from a rectangular piece of elm which is often, but not invariably, gouge carved in a serrated pattern on the ends (see Figure SW42). The legs used for stools are typically made in ash, but other woods, including pine, were used (Figure SW43), and they are usually octagonal in shape. These are morticed through the stool top and wedged to secure them. In addition to stools, benches of identical construction were made to accompany the farmhouse dining tables.

Yealmpton chair makers

In addition to the three-part arm and single bent arm Windsors made throughout the West Country, further styles were made which were probably unique to a small community of chair makers who worked in the village of Yealmpton, at the head of the River Yealm, some six miles from the port of Plymouth. The village of Yealmpton emerged in the nineteenth century as a small agri-culturally based community of one thousand people, living in 181 houses.[5] The many trades listed within the village indicate a community which was substantially self-sufficient in craft skills, and which had the benefit of receiving goods by merchant ships which sailed up the Yealm estuary to the nearby Kitley Quay.[6] The photograph of Yealmpton shown in Figure SW44, taken in the 1880s, evokes something of the essential character of the village in the nineteenth century.

The earliest origins of chair making in Yealmpton are unclear, since parish records between 1754 and 1812[7] show no villager mentioned as a chair maker, although eight carpenters are recorded during this time.[8] However, it is clear from parish records that the first period when Yealmpton chair makers were identified as such was between 1812 and 1832, when the following four chair makers are recorded at different dates, on the occasion of the baptism of a child:[9] 1812, William Milman; 1815, Thomas Chambers; 1817, William Selley; 1832, Henry Chambers.

By 1841, this group of chair makers had declined to only one, Thomas Chambers, who was then aged sixty, and was presumably nearing the end of his working life.[10]

It is unclear why the chair making craft disappeared from this village at this time, since the chairs which these early makers created were successfully integrated into the regional character of West Country furniture. However, the lack of family continuity in the craft indicates that the chair making trade in this village had reached a crisis in its viability, since none of the original craftsmen's sons entered the trade: the sons of William Milman, Frederick and John, became wheel-wrights in the nearby parishes of Kington and Holberton respectively,[11] and John Chambers, son of Thomas, became a carpenter at Newton Ferrers.[12] This decline may have occurred since large firms of chair makers and household furnishers were working in Plymouth and Exeter throughout the greater part of the nineteenth century, producing a range of fashionable 'fancy' chairs which probably usurped the hand-made rural chair makers' products.*

---

* The port of Plymouth, near to Yealmpton, was a thriving centre of trade and commerce, and the following chair makers are recorded working there and in Exeter: **Snawdon**, recorded as chair makers in Plymouth, 1862-1897, 46, Union St., Stonehouse, Yealmpton Sawmills, 41, Bedford St. and 10, East St. Place;[13] **Lavers**, recorded as chair makers in Plymouth, 1873-1902, 58, Richmond St. and 10, Russell St.;[14] **Toms (Thoms)**, recorded as chair makers in Exeter, 1796-1846, North St. and 148, Fore St. Hill.[15]

Figure SW45. The interior of a Yealmpton farmhouse kitchen (1983), showing chairs made in the village, and in use in this house since the 1840s.

Continuous arm Windsors

Although no early nineteenth century name stamped chairs have been identified to confirm the Yealmpton makers' products, many chairs reputed to have been made in the village have been located. All are 'Windsor' chairs, with two essential armchair types and a variety of side chair designs. A number of distinct design variants were produced within each of these basic designs. Of the two distinct styles of armchairs made in Yealmpton, the first has no parallel elsewhere in the English tradition, but does have close similarities with designs of chairs made in the New York region during the eighteenth and nineteenth centuries. This design is described within the American tradition as the 'continuous arm Windsor', since the arms and back are made from a single cleft segment of wood, bent to form an attractive flowing line, resulting in a style of great elegance. An example of an American Windsor of this type is shown in Figure SW50 and may be compared with those attributed to Yealmpton shown in Figures SW42-49.

The belief that the continuous arm Windsor and compatible side chairs were made in Yealmpton exists in a

widely held local awareness of these chair styles, many of which have been owned for several generations by local families. A photograph taken in 1983 (Figure SW45) shows the interior of a farmhouse near to Yealmpton which has been owned by the same family for three generations, and where the chairs shown in the photograph of the kitchen have been in daily use from around 1840 when the owner's grandfather was in occupation. A larger illustration of the continuous armchair illustrated in this interior is shown in Figure SW49. Such evidence of continuous ownership is sufficiently common in the immediate area around Yealmpton to provide substantial confirmation for the existence of the chair making tradition in this village, and those held in local ownership have enabled a pictorial anthology of design variants to be made.

The reasons which limited the production of continuous arm English Windsors to one centre are not clear. However, a disadvantage of the design, in practical terms, lay in the need to curve the wood on two axes, one to form the back hoop, and the other to form the forward bend of

Figure SW46. Continuous arm Windsor. Ash with sycamore seat. Attributed to West Country, c.1840. Found in the Gatehouse, Lanhydrock, Bodmin, Cornwall.

Egg and reel turned legs. H-form leg stretcher. Hand-drawn spindles. Stripped of original paint.

(Courtesy The National Trust)

276

Figure SW47. Continuous arm Windsor. Ash with sycamore seat. Attributed to West Country, c.1820.

Exaggerated simulated bamboo turned legs (shortened). H-form leg stretcher. Painted black over original green paint.

Figure SW48. Continuous arm Windsor. Ash with elm seat. Attributed to West Country, c.1820.

Simulated bamboo turned stretchers, legs and spindles. Box framed leg stretchers. Original yellow paint with 'nodes' accentuated in black. Height 33½in. (85cm); width 20¼in. (51.3cm); depth 15¾in. (40cm).
(Collection T. Robinson)

Figure SW49. Continuous arm Windsor (see Figure SW45 for this chair illustrated in situ). Ash with elm seat. Attributed to West Country, c.1820.

Legs, stretchers and arm supports with simulated bamboo turnings. Back spindles hand drawn. Vestiges of original blue paint.

the arms. This would have required a relatively complex bench or frame to allow for the creation of the arm and back shape. This design contrasts with the more common form of Windsor bow which requires a pegging device allowing a semicircle to be made in one plane only, for top hoops, arm hoops, and, in some designs, curved leg stretchers.

Although no other group of English chair makers chose to make their chairs in this way, the continuous arm form Windsor was made in large numbers in the U.S.A., particularly in New York and Rhode Island where a number of branded or labelled examples have been recorded.[16] From New York, this design seems to have filtered out into New England, and the American scholar, Charles Santori, in his excellent account of the American Windsor chair (1981), has been able to produce a system of distinctions which typify New York made chairs, from those made by Connecticut makers.[17] However, the view proposed by some American

scholars that the continuous arm chair is exclusively an American product clearly fails to recognise the existence of the West Country tradition, and the obvious possibility for design transmission between New England craftsmen and the chair makers of Devon. Certainly inhabitants of the village of Yealmpton, in common with people from other coastal towns in the West Country, were amongst the earliest emigrants to leave for the new lands in America.[18] The nineteenth century photograph of a merchant sailing ship at Kitley Quay on the River Yealm some five miles from Yealmpton, shown in Figure SW51, illustrates the proximity of the sea, and the possibilities it held for trade and contact with other lands. Indeed, the Devonian and Cornish sailors particularly exploited the resources of the American seaboard from earliest seafaring times.*

The awareness of the close relationship between the people of the West Country and New Englanders does

not, however, clarify who may have influenced whom in the design of the continuous arm Windsors, for although early American furniture design was influenced by various immigrant workers,[19] the dating of these West Country chairs to the late eighteenth and early nineteenth centuries is more or less contemporary with those made in America. However, the manufacture of this style of chair in America seems to have finished in the first quarter of the nineteenth century,[20] whereas the group of chair makers recorded as working in Yealmpton continued until at least 1832.[21] The continuous arm Windsor tradition, therefore, continued a little later in England than in New England.

* R.D. Brown in his history of Devon emigration, *Devonians and New England Settlements*, records the familiarity which West Country sailors had with the New England coastal waters in writing that: 'Hundreds of West countrymen, led by Devonians, had been fishing regularly in North American coastal waters since the 1580s. By 1626, Devon ports alone were sending more than 150 ships across the Atlantic annually... More than 95% of emigrants from the West Country came from coastal villages, or from parishes near a coastal town.'[22]

277

Figure SW50. Continuous arm Windsor. Oak arm spindles, supports and stretchers, chestnut seat, maple legs, traces of old blue/green paint. Branded 'E.P. TRACY' (fl.1780-1803), Lisbon, Connecticut, U.S.A. This style of chair has similarities with those made in the Yealmpton area (see Figures SW46-49).

(Courtesy Los Angeles County Museum of Art)

Figure SW51. A 19th century photograph of a merchant sailing ship at Kitley Quay on the River Yealm, some five miles from Yealmpton, illustrating the possibilities which this region had for trade and travel across the Atlantic Ocean. *(Courtesy P. Holloway, Yealmpton)*

Figure SW52. The kitchens of Compton Castle, near Paignton, South Devon, showing locally made chairs including a bent arm Windsor, as well as a double bow West Country Windsor to the right (see Figures SW37-40 and 54-56). *(Courtesy Mrs W.R. Gilbert, Compton Castle)*

Applied bent arm Windsors

The second form of Windsor armchair attributed to Yealmpton manufacture may be termed an applied 'bent arm' Windsor, since the arms are fashioned from a steamed and bent section of ash, which is shaved thinner at the point at which the right angle bend was made.* The method of creating the arm embodied the simple cleaving and shaping techniques found in many other coppice crafts including spale basket making and hurdle making, and it is, perhaps, surprising that this feature was confined to this regional chair. This style embodies many of the essential construction features of the English continuous arm Windsor and related side chairs. These similarities occur

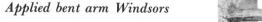

Figure SW53. A hand-drawn ash spindle.

particularly in relation to seat shapes, leg and stretcher turnings, and the oval shaping, through morticing and wedging of the hand drawn back spindles (see Figure SW53). This design has no counterpart in either New England or elsewhere in the English Windsor chair tradition although a chair using this arm device has been recorded from the lower Canadian Provinces.[23] Figures SW54 and 55 show examples of the

bent arm Windsor which illustrate their similarity with the continuous arm Windsor in using simulated bamboo leg turnings, with H-frame and box stretchers respectively, as well as the egg and reel form of leg turning, an example of which is shown in Figure SW56.

---

* In effect, the armchair design is simply a development of the compatible side chair, in that the armchair seat is only slightly larger than the side chair seats, and the bent arms have been added.

278

Figure SW54. Applied bent arm Windsor. Ash with elm seat. Attributed to West Country, c.1820.

Simulated bamboo turned legs and H-form stretchers, with three nodal turnings on each segment. Hand-drawn spindles and back brace. Original green paint. Height 34 ¾ in. (88cm); width 21 ¼ in. (54.2cm); depth 17 ¼ in. (43.6cm).

Figure SW55. Applied bent arm Windsor. Ash with elm seat. Attributed to West Country, c.1820.

Simulated bamboo turned legs and box stretcher with two node turnings on each segment. Hand-drawn spindles. No back brace. Original green paint. Height 33 ¾ in. (86cm); width 19 ¾ in. (50cm); depth 15 ½ in. (39.1cm).

Figure SW56. Applied bent arm Windsor. Ash with elm seat. Attributed to West Country, c.1820.

Egg and reel leg turnings with H-form stretchers. Hand-drawn spindles and back brace. Black paint over red, over original green.

Side chairs

In addition to the four distinct styles of armchair attributed to the West Country, a range of side chairs was also made. Of these, a number of styles are closely related to the continuous and applied bent arm Windsors in their general configuration. Similarities between them occur particularly in the seat shapes which adopted more or less exaggerated forms of shaping to create waisted profiles (see Figure SW61). This mode of seat shaping, although not used elsewhere in the English Windsor tradition, has close similarities to seat shapes used in some American Windsors. The leg turnings in both traditions use simulated bamboo and egg and reel turnings, with similar conventions of both box and H-form stretchers used with faux bamboo turned legs, and an H-form stretcher only used with egg and reel turned legs in both side and armchairs.

Side chairs which are related to the continuous and bent arm chairs are also comparable in having hand drawn back spindles which mortice through the hoop; although rarely, more elaborate chairs were produced

Figure SW57. Side chair. Painted in yellow ochre with nodes painted in black. Attributed to West Country, c.1800.

Seat chamfered below. Seven spindles turned to simulate bamboo. Legs turned with prominent bamboo simulation, joined by H-form stretchers, also simulated. Gouge marks made above each nodal turning to accentuate imitation bamboo.

(Collection James Ayres)

Figure SW58. New England side chair showing simulated bamboo turned legs with plain H-form leg supports. The unpegged back spindles have protruded through the hoop as the hoop has 'settled', showing the through morticed spindle form of construction.

(Courtesy Old Sturbridge Village. Photograph Henry E. Peach)

279

Figure SW59. West of England side chair painted in yellow with foliate decoration and nodes painted in black. The simulated bamboo legs are joined by a box form of leg support, typical of this style (left hand stretcher missing). The unpegged spindles can be seen to be slightly protruding above the hoop, showing this form of through morticing. (Collection G. Olive)

Figure SW60. Side chair. Ash with sycamore seat. Attributed to West Country, c.1820.
Waisted seat shape. Seven hand-shaped elliptical spindles through morticing the hoop. Legs with egg and reel turning, connected by H-form stretchers. Painted blue. Height 33¾ in. (86cm); width 13¾ in. (35cm); depth 14¼ in. (36cm).

Figure SW61. Seat profile of a West Country side chair illustrating the waisted shaping typical of chairs attributed to Yealmpton manufacture.

Figure SW62. Side chair. Ash with elm seat. Attributed to West Country, c.1810.
Painted yellow ochre base, over-painted brown, and rubbed out on the front of the turned parts to simulate bamboo colouring. Nodes painted in red with a thin black line. Egg and reel turned legs to the front, plain turned legs to the rear, joined by plain H-form stretchers. Waisted seat shape at front and sides, with rear wedge and back spindle supports. Seven hand-drawn spindles morticed and wedged through the hoop.

Figure SW63. Side chair. Ash with elm seat. Attributed to West Country, c.1810.
Painted yellow ochre base, over-painted brown and rubbed out on the front of turned parts to simulate bamboo colouring. Nodes painted in red with a thin black line. Simulated bamboo legs joined by plain H-form stretchers. Waisted seat shape at front and sides, with rear wedge and back spindle supports. Five hand-drawn spindles morticed and wedged through the hoop.

which have simulated bamboo turnings in the manner of the example shown in Figure SW57. The spindles in this chair have the added refinement of small gouge marks above the nodal turnings to accentuate the bamboo effect.

Side chairs were painted in the manner of the armchairs in an overall colour, with either blue or green as the most common colour, and yellow used much less frequently. Although a single colour was usual, some side chairs were decorated over the base colour. This usually took the form of rings painted in red with an inner ring of black, to simulate nodes on both back spindles and legs; and occasionally this decorative device was used to form an internal border on the seat surface (see Figures SW63 and 64 for examples). A further side chair has been recorded with foliar designs painted in black over the yellow base colour (see Figure SW59).

Side chairs made and decorated in these ways are entirely compatible with the continuous and applied bent arm chairs attributed to Yealmpton manufacture in the first half of the nineteenth century, and as with the continuous arm design, have close similarities with some forms of bow back side chairs made in the American tradition. See Figures SW57 and 58 for a comparison of these forms which reinforces the belief that transmission of chair design between the West Country and North America was an important catalyst in the development of these significant designs.

Other forms of side chairs which were made in the West Country form a stylistically distinct group in having close similarities with the three-part arm Windsors attributed to Cornwall (see Figure SW64). Side chairs in this group typically have lath shaped hoops, hand drawn back spindles

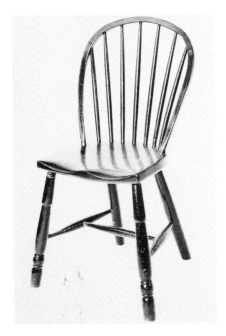

Figure SW64. Side chair. Ash with sycamore seat. Attributed to Cornwall, c.1810.

Painted black over red lead finish. Egg and reel turned front legs, plain turned rear legs, joined by plain H-form stretchers. Straight front to seat, shallow front to back. Slight chamfer to under edges of seat.

Figure SW65. A Cornish cottage interior painted by Legthe Suthers (1856-1924), entitled 'Finery'. This interior shows typical 'common' furniture of the region including a dresser, gate-leg table, and two Windsor chairs of West Country design. The man sits in an armchair similar to those shown in Figures SW38 and 39. A side chair similar to that shown in Figure SW60 stands by the window. (Courtesy Atkinson Art Gallery, Southport)

which are elliptical in profile and mortice through the hoop. Seats in these varieties are distinguished in being straight along the front, and not waisted in the manner of those attributed to Yealmpton manufacture, and the legs have the egg and reel turning device. As well as having closely similar design details to the armchairs attributed to Cornish origin, many examples of these side chairs appear as 'innocent' props in paintings by members of the Newlyn School of painters who illustrated many scenes of vernacular home life in Cornwall in the nineteenth century.

An example of such a cottage interior entitled 'Finery' by Legthe Suthers, shown in Figure SW65, records both a common regional style of Windsor armchair, as well as a side chair of compatible design.

Figure SW66. A 19th century photograph showing a team of horses transporting coppiced ash to Snawdon's sawmills and chair making factory, Yealmpton, Devon.

(Courtesy Mr and Mrs F. Snawdon, Yealmpton)

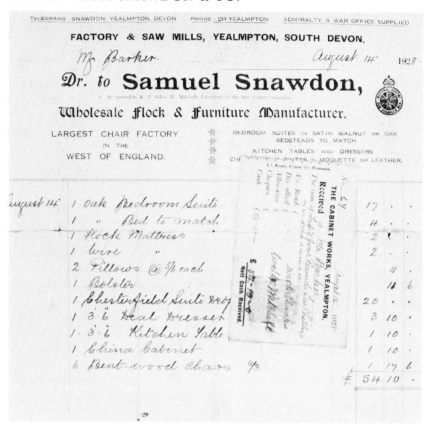

Figure SW67. An invoice dated 1928 from Samuel Snawdon, Yealmpton. In addition to chairs, Snawdon's clearly made a complete range of household furnishings, and although the firm still described themselves as the 'largest chair factory in the West of England', this invoice indicates that in the 1920s they made a large repertoire of household furniture, including dressers and tables.

(Courtesy Mr and Mrs F. Snawdon)

Figure SW68. Stick back Windsor side chair. Beech with plain elm seat, stamped 'S. SNAWDON MAKER YEALMPTON' on rear edge of seat (fl.1890-1930). This style of chair was widely made in the High Wycombe chair manufacturing tradition, and a closely similar chair, made by the High Wycombe firm of Gibbons can be seen in Chapter 2, Figure TV201. However, the seat shape used in the Snawdon chair is closely similar to the side chairs made in Yealmpton during the late 18th and early 19th centuries, and represents a continuity of this motif.

Heavy three ring turned legs with lower ring and tulip shaped feet. Legs connected by turned stretchers. Turned back uprights incorporating a three ring turning similar to the leg turnings, with curved shaped stay rail passing over the back uprights. Four plain spindles connecting the seat and stay rail.

Snawdon & Co.

The first period of chair making in Yealmpton, in which the continuous arm and applied bent arm Windsor designs, as well as side chairs were made, continued until about 1851, when the last of the original group of known chair makers, Thomas Chambers, now seventy-three years of age, was recorded for the last time.[24] The indigenous Windsor chair craft in Yealmpton seems to have died out with this maker. However, the chair making trade was to be resurrected in Yealmpton by a firm of chair and cabinet makers, Snawdon & Co., who were established in Stonehouse, Plymouth by the mid-nineteenth century.[25] In around 1880 Snawdons purchased the sawmills at Yealmpton, where they began making the Windsor chairs which they advertised and sold at their Plymouth premises as 'Specialitie: Windsor chairs own make 14/- the dozen'.[26]

In setting up their chair making business in Yealmpton, the Snawdons took advantage of the water power which had been harnessed by the construction of a canal leading from the River Yealm. This water flow drove an overshot wheel which operated the existing sawmill, and the power source was extended to operate belt driven wood turning lathes, on three floors. This facility, combined with local timber sources, enabled the firm to rapidly expand its chair production, and for the owners to make the claim, written on a large sign on the roadside leading to the mill, that this was 'The largest chair making factory in the West of England'.[27]

At the point at which Snawdon's moved to Yealmpton, there may have been no skilled chair makers left in the village from the earlier period, since it appears that workers were brought into the village who had learned their skills in other areas. In 1881 there were four chair makers and cabinet makers, and three apprentices living in Yealmpton, of whom two were born in the Buckinghamshire chair making towns of Stokenchurch and High Wycombe, and one was born into a chair making

Figure SW69. The stamp of Samuel Snawdon, chair manufacturers of Yealmpton in Devon. This family firm, still in existence today, was first recorded in the mid-19th century in Plymouth, and had moved their business to Yealmpton by about 1880.

family in Birmingham.*

The firm of Snawdon's prospered, and after closing their Plymouth business around 1897, the total

---

* The Snawdons employed the following chair makers in 1881, who had been trained in High Wycombe: Charles Priest, aged 28, born Birmingham, wife and daughter born High Wycombe, Buckinghamshire; Fane, Edwin, aged 23, born Stokenchurch, Buckinghamshire; Stallwood, James, aged 39, born High Wycombe, Buckinghamshire.[28]

Figure SW70. Display sign of Mr Jack Drake, cabinet maker, who was trained by one of the last chair and cabinet makers in Holcombe Rogus.

Figure SW71. The last remaining chair and cabinet making workshop in Holcombe Rogus.

Holcombe Rogus, Uffculme and Burlescombe

The general difficulties of accurately ascribing specific furniture or chair styles to makers, even when their presence was well documented, is illustrated in the history of another West Country chair making centre which arose in the villages of Holcombe Rogus, Uffculme and Burlescombe. These small agriculturally based communities lie in close proximity to each other in the rich pastureland and wooded countryside of North Devon.* The houses in these villages reflect both the architecture of Devonshire and nearby Somerset, being made of 'cob' walls and thatched roofs, typical of Devon houses, as well as flint stone walls under red pantile roofs, found in Somerset. The location of these three villages appears to offer no special advantage which would have made them obvious places for a chair making industry to have arisen, yet early nineteenth century records show that a flourishing community of chair turners existed here, employing members of many local families.** Indeed, in Holcombe Rogus in 1841, twenty-two chair makers are recorded. Burlescombe provided eight chair makers and there were six chair makers living in Uffculme.[30] These men were generally not newcomers to the area, but belonged to families who had lived in the three villages since at least the early seventeenth century and members of which persisted as chair makers throughout the nineteenth century, finding a consistent, if generally poor, living from the craft.

In the early part of the nineteenth century, these chair makers appear to have worked as separate craftsmen, using their own workshops, built adjacent to their cottage homes.[31] This traditional way of working continued until the third quarter of the nineteenth century, when the trade became centralised in Holcombe Rogus, where two families, the Warrens and Scotts, became chair masters, and by 1871 were employing

production of their cabinet and chair making was centred at the sawmills and workshops at Yealmpton, where around one hundred men were employed by the early 1900s.[29] The photograph shown in Figure SW66, taken in the late nineteenth century, shows coppiced ash, used extensively in making chairs, being brought to the sawmills by teams of horses. Figure SW67 shows an invoice of 1928 indicating that they made a large repertoire of household furniture.

It seems probable that in this second phase of chair making in Yealmpton the local styles made in the early nineteenth century were rejected in favour of what became the more popular and universal designs of inexpensive, mass produced chairs which were made in High Wycombe and the North Midlands Counties, and copied elsewhere. These later chair styles included, for example,

the wheel back chair, smoking or office chairs, which were made in many English chair making centres during the nineteenth century, as well as chairs with flat slats or turned spindles forming the back. An example of this latter style, stamped 'S. Snawdon. Yealmpton' is shown in Figure SW68, which, although similar in design to simple kitchen chairs made in Buckinghamshire and many North Country chair making centres, has retained the seat shape of West Country chairs from the early nineteenth century. A similar range of chairs was also made in the late nineteenth century at the West Country chair making centre of Holcombe Rogus, Burlescombe, and Uffculme in North Devon. The firm of Snawdon's continues today at Yealmpton Sawmills, specialising in the manufacture of furnishings for public houses and hotels.

* *Whites Directory*, 1848, gives the following population figures: Burlescombe, 958; Holcombe Rogus, 843; Uffculme, 2,011.

** Family names of chair makers in the Holcombe Rogus area: Agland, Baxter, Berry (Perry), Bowerman, Cavil, Cotterall, Davey, Evans, Ewins, Frost, Grant, Hawkins, Holley, Horne, Jones, Kerslake, Payne, Poole, Radford, Rice, Scott, Tooze, Trevellian, Twitchings, Wall, Waring, Warren, Wills, Wyatt, Woodbury.

most of the other chair makers and ancillary craftspeople including polishers, caners, and rush-workers.[32] At a time (1871) when the total number of chair workers in the village was twenty-eight, Warren was recorded as employing thirteen men and boys, and Scott as employing four boys and fifteen men. This change in employment reflected a shift in the basis of working, from individual chair makers turning their chair parts on a pole lathe and assembling the complete chair, to one where a division of labour was introduced in what were essentially industrially based workshops. These utilised water from the local stream to power the lathes and other machinery, and specialist trades of turning, seat making, assembling (framing), polishing, and rush or cane seating were employed as separate crafts.

Virtually all traces of the two major workshops have now disappeared from Holcombe Rogus, but one of the last workshops to be created in the village, belonging to the last members of the Warren family, remains. This workshop is situated on the edge of the village, and is owned by the last direct descendant of the chair and cabinet making tradition in Holcombe Rogus, Mr Jack Drake, who was apprenticed to Mr. Bowerman and who bought the business on his retirement in the early part of this century. The workshop and its painted signboard, shown in Figures SW70 and 71, represent the total remaining architectural evidence of the large number of small workshops which existed in the village during the last century.

The output of chairs from these communities was very large, and transporting items to their market was, no doubt, made by barge, since in 1915, the Grand Western Canal terminal was built at Holcolme Rogus, giving access to the nearby market town of Tiverton, and thus developing the chair making trade, as well as that in wool, beer, and flour produced by several mills at Uffculme. However, in the second half of the nineteenth

Figure SW72. Simple rush seated ladder back chair. Beech. Attributed to West Country, c.1860. Chairs of this type were made in thousands by the chair making community which flourished in Holcombe Rogus during the 19th century, for use in churches and cathedrals throughout the west of England. This chair was part of a group bought from Holcombe Rogus for the church of St. Thomas at Ash Thomas, Devon, some seven miles from Holcombe Rogus.
Sawn back uprights, ladders and stay rail. The front legs and connecting stretchers are turned (one cross stretcher is missing).
(Courtesy Church Wardens, Ash Thomas, Halberton, Devon)

Figure SW73. Dining chair. Oak, made in the Bowerman workshop, Holcombe Rogus, late 19th century.

century, reports show that in addition to canal transport the inexpensive Holcombe chairs, sold at 4/6d. a half dozen, were also delivered by horse-drawn vehicles to Exeter, Plymouth, Bristol and South Wales.[33]

The development of the chair making trade in these villages was doubtless further assisted by the railway which was opened in 1844, connecting Burlescombe with Exeter, and it was from the station at Burlescombe, later in the nineteenth century, that the prodigious annual output of chairs, given as '5,000 frames, completed chairs, and couches', was transported to many destinations in Bristol, Exeter, South Wales and the Midlands.[34]

The craftsmen of Holcombe Rogus, Burlescombe and Uffculme formed the largest single group of chair makers in the West Country, yet no evidence of their having made a truly regional chair style for use in domestic settings has been identified, and a survey of homes in the village and surrounding area has revealed no evidence of early nineteenth century chair styles which can be attributed to village manufacture.

The enigma of the chair styles made in these communities is simply explained by reference to an early twentieth century newspaper account of the Holcombe Rogus chair making trade which describes the vast chair contracts obtained by the village chair makers in the late nineteenth century, in the following terms. 'Something like an idea of the character and extent of the industry in the village may be had when we give the following: Chairs for Colston Hall, Bristol, 2,000: Redcliffe Church, Bristol, 600; Temple Church, Bristol, 300; Baptist Church, Bristol, 600; Exeter Cathedral, 1,500; Victoria Hall, Exeter, 600; Bath Abbey, Bath, 500; Malvern Priory, 1,200; Central Hall, Truro, 600; The Parish Church Hall, 600; and Wells Cathedral, 1,000.'[35] This picture of a trade, making chairs for large institutions, both secular and religious, was so

Chair makers recorded by census 1841-1881					
	1841	1851	1861	1871	1881
Holcombe Rogus	22	31	24	28	24
Burlescombe	8	8	2	3	3
Uffculme	6	3	6	4	2

Figure SW74. Roman spindle chair. Beech, elm seat. Made in Holcombe Rogus, Devon, late 19th century. This style is typical of North Midlands kitchen Windsors. See, for example, Chapter 3, Figure NE402.

Figure SW75. Lath-back chair. Beech, elm seat. Made in Holcombe Rogus, Devon, late 19th century. The style is typical of High Wycombe kitchen Windsors (see Chapter 2, Figure TV188).

Figure SW76. Smoker's bow chair. Beech with elm seat. Made in Holcombe Rogus, Devon, late 19th century. The chair has some similarities to those made in many other chair making centres.

vast in the numbers produced, that local oral history records that chairs were left to dry along the edges of the local lanes, since their numbers were too great to store in the workshops.[36] The chairs made and supplied for these large orders were of the simplest ladder back design, with modifications made to create a particular resting rail on the top of the back legs to aid prayer, and in some cases, a service book holder was made behind each chair at seat height. An example of this particular style of chair is illustrated in Figure SW72.

The evidence of so productive and specific a trade in the late nineteenth century may indicate that this tradition, from its earliest times, fulfilled a need for the low cost, simple chairs required in public places, rather than providing chairs for the home. The large and consistent numbers of chair makers working in the villages would seem to support the view of a trade which had regular demand from wholesale agents in a number of recorded centres, including Cardiff in Wales and Malvern in Worcestershire.[37] This demand for chairs outside the immediate area by the last quarter of the nineteenth century was documented in an early twentieth century report in the

Western Enterprise which stated that 'Messrs Scott and Kerslake are also manufacturers on a smaller scale, but next in point of importance is the business of Mr John Scott, whose shop adjoins the village. Here, his father [James] directed affairs before him, and had... a connection with South Wales... Between them, the business has been carried on for three quarters of a century, and during that long period, there have been fluctuations, chiefly through competition. Through a Mr Nash, the Cardiff wholesale agent, contracts of the first importance have been executed, whilst through Messrs Cox and Painter of Malvern, orders from the Midlands have been large and extensive.'[38]

The chair making trade in Holcombe Rogus began to decline in terms of the numbers employed towards the end of the nineteenth century. This may have been caused by the level of competition offered by the highly productive chair making centres of High and West Wycombe in Buckinghamshire, as well as by cheaper imports of chairs from other counties.[39] However, it is evident that by the end of the chair making history in Holcombe Rogus, the chair makers were attempting to combat the competitive challenge of

other centres, making patterns of chairs in a highly competent way, which were typical of both the Buckinghamshire and North Midlands styles of chairs. Examples of these later chairs exist locally, and are illustrated in Figures SW74-76.

Towards the end of the chair making era in Holcombe Rogus, the capacity to produce large numbers of chairs would have radically declined, with a reduction in craftsmen employed,[40] and the last of the chair makers, Francis (Frankie) Tooze, who continued as a chair maker at least until 1919, making typical mahogany and oak chairs of the period.[41]

The complex and varied tradition of West Country chairs epitomises the capacity of the early English chair makers to create new and distinctly different chair designs from other regions. The occurrence of painted Windsor chairs, including the continuous arm and the bent arm Windsors, are unique forms in the English tradition. The three-part arm Windsors are, too, fundamentally different from other regional three-part arm Windsors. Yet this disparate group of chairs has a unity of design features which reflects a distinctive regional tradition.

Figure WM1. 'For what we are about to receive', by the Worcestershire artist, Edward Thompson Davis, c.1880. The scene shows the interior of a West Midlands cottage with simple furnishings. The woman sits on a wooden seated chair from the West Midlands tradition, similar to the one shown in Figure WM54.

(Courtesy Phillips, London)

Chapter 6
WEST MIDLANDS

Figure WM2. An ash seat side rail articulating with the chamfered edge of an elm seat panel, a construction feature typical of chairs from the West Midlands region.

Figure WM3. The jointing of the seating rails and the front under-frieze into the front leg, showing the square pegging both to the side and the rear of the leg, a constructional feature universally used in this region's wooden seated chairs.

The chair makers of the rural West Midland counties of Worcestershire, Herefordshire and Shropshire, and their more industrialised neighbour, Staffordshire, produced a diverse repertoire of spindle and ladder back chairs which were refined and economical in design. The majority of chairs were made with a form of wooden seat which is an important constructional signature of this region's distinctive chairs, though some otherwise identical chairs were produced with rush seats.

The chair turners of the region worked in a rural craft tradition where typically the chair frame was made in cleft green ash, turned on a pole or a treadle powered lathe. The wooden seats were made of seasoned elm. Rush seats would, no doubt, have been made from local rushes from the Rivers Severn and Avon and their tributaries in Worcestershire, from the Rivers Wye and Lugg in Herefordshire, and from the Rivers Severn, Teme and Clun in Shropshire.[1]

The construction of the wooden seat, and the way in which the front under-seat frieze and the adjoining seat rails were pegged is so consistent in chairs made by known makers of this region, that unnamed chairs of the same construction can be designated to the West Midlands area with confidence (see Figure WM3).

An elbow chair made by Philip Clissett (1817-1913), of Stanley Hill, Bosbury, is shown in Figure WM18. Made in ash with an elm seat, it clearly demonstrates the form of seating typical of the West Midlands vernacular chair.

The wooden seats were constructed from a panel of dry elm, some 1cm thick, which was chamfered at the edges to slot into a deep groove made in the round side rails. Figure WM2 illustrates the point of union of the seat with a side rail. The jointing of the framework of chairs from this region was typically made without glue, and is square pegged to hold the seat joints secure. Pegging to hold the ladders of the cross rails holding the spindles in position is also commonly

287

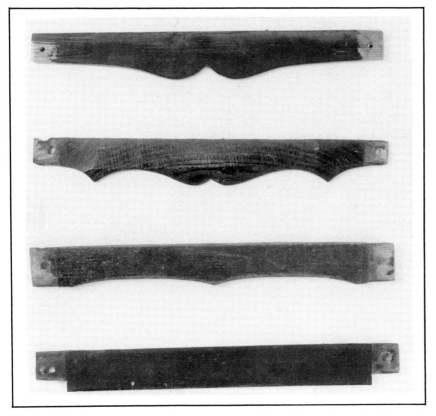

Figure WM4. The front under-seat frieze designs found in West Midlands 'common' chairs provide a regional signature of which the four styles shown above are examples. A wooden frieze is also found below the front rail of some West Midlands rush seated chairs.

used on at least the top back rail. Throughout the West Midlands tradition, wooden seated chairs were made with one of the four shapes of front-seat frieze shown in Figure WM4.

Individual chair styles are firmly identified to examples made in such varied locations as the busy market town of Evesham in Worcestershire, the quiet hamlet of Bosbury in Herefordshire, the village of Clun, remote and virtually self-contained within the Clun Forest of Shropshire, as well as in the busy and expanding town of Oswestry in North Shropshire, where chair makers no doubt served the population of the developing industrial regions of Coalbrookdale and surrounding areas. A further chair style has been identified to Rugeley, Staffordshire, to a maker who worked 'near the foundry' in this highly industrialised area of the Midlands (see Figures WM44 and 45).

The growth and ultimate decline of the native chair making craft in the West Midlands was reflected in the particular social developments of the area where the craftsmen worked.

Throughout the region, there was a general increase in the number of recorded chair makers and turners, a term which was often synonymous with that of chair maker from the late eighteenth century to the second quarter of the nineteenth century. Just after the middle of the nineteenth century, a sharp decline occurred in the number of workers in the trade. In some remote areas, the Clun Forest and central Herefordshire, for example, isolated chair makers are known to have continued making traditional chair designs until the close of the century. However, in general, rural craftsmen producing local designs may have been unable to respond to changes which led to the demand for modern and fashionable furnishing styles which became readily available in smaller towns as a result of the increase in transport facilities emanating from larger towns. It may also be that certain cabinet makers in the major regional towns utilised the work of local turners in producing their own repertoire of chair styles based more on nationally changing fashion than on the native regional styles.

Certainly, the Midlands city of Birmingham, located on the northern boundaries of Worcestershire, and the Black Country towns to the north of this city continued to grow and expand their engineering-based industries. The result of this development was an increase in relatively prosperous communities of factory workers, who were absorbed into industry from the surrounding agricultural areas. Their changing culture had needs based on fashion rather than tradition, and in response to this, furniture makers, in common with other producers of consumer goods, attempted to make items which would appeal to this new market. Chair makers were not excluded from the change, and the growth in 'fancy' styles of mahogany, upholstered, inlaid, painted, and simulated bamboo turned chairs, for example, proliferated. The work of one Black Country chair maker was advertised in 1832, and provides an illustration of the styles which were made in contrast to the vernacular styles (see Figure WM5).

The recorded history of chair making in the West Midlands provides clear evidence of the development and ultimate decline of the regional chair maker. The maps shown in Figures WM6-8, illustrate this decline in the county of Worcestershire.

The Kerry Family

From extant chairs it would appear that few West Midlands makers identified their work with a stamped signature. One exception, within the county of Worcestershire, is the chairs made and stamped by the Kerrys of Evesham. The range of these chairs demonstrates a varied repertoire, including a rush seated elbow chair, wicker seated nursing chairs, rush seat pad foot side chairs, and wooden seated side chairs. In all of the examples illustrated in Figures WM10-16 the name Kerry is stamped at least once, and often twice, on the front and back of the back legs above seat level. In the case of the chair shown in Figure WM10 the name Evesham is also stamped below that of Kerry (see Figure WM11). All recorded examples of their work are of ladder back design, and are usually distinguished by a special stylistic signature, in that only the top ladder in each chair has an upward shaped, flowing indentation on the bottom edge of the ladder, whereas the others are straight on the lower edge.

Plate 38. Ladder back armchair. Ash with rush seat. Stamped 'KERRY EVESHAM' on back uprights. This stamp refers to John Kerry, chair maker of Evesham, Worcestershire (fl.1819-61).

Exceptions to this rule include the chair shown in Figure WM16 in which all the ladders are shaped with upward indentations underneath. Interestingly, this chair is made entirely of fruitwood and is of exceptionally fine quality; presumably a special or 'best' chair. A further chair, made and stamped by Kerry, is shown in Figure WM14. This is of considerable importance in relation to the development of chair design within the Arts and Crafts Movement's interpretation of chair styles in the late nineteenth and early twentieth centuries, and a further discussion of its significance is given on pp.297-300.

The same name stamp appears to have been used for all the illustrated chairs. Three of them are also stamped 'Evesham' (Figures WM10, 13 and 14) and as the trade directories record Kerrys in Evesham between 1820 and 1861, we may assume the chairs were made within that period. Two chairs (WM12 and 16) do not bear the Evesham stamp and though stylistically they too would appear to have been made at the same period, it is possible that Kerrys worked as chair makers in the eighteenth century. They had moved from Offenham, a village near Evesham, and when John Kerry senior is first recorded as a wood turner and furniture broker in 1820 at High Street,[2] Evesham, he was already seventy-five years of age. At the same time his nephew, John Kerry, aged thirty-seven, is recorded as a wood turner working nearby in the Market Place. By 1829,

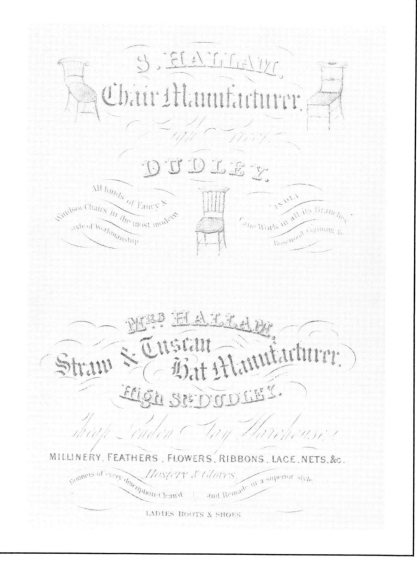

Figure WM5. An advertisement of the Black Country chair maker, S. Hallam, Dudley, 1832. The chairs illustrated by this maker show designs of 'fancy' chairs. The production of fashionable furnishings, such as these, and the extension of the railway into rural areas, led to the decline of local chair makers.

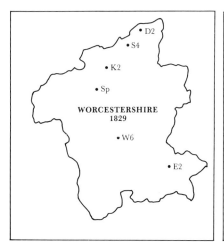

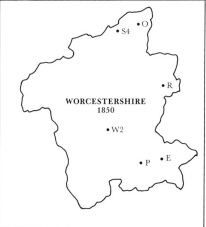

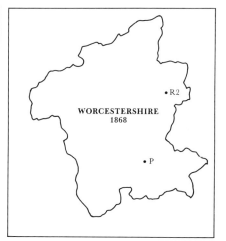

Key: D = Dudley   E = Evesham   K = Kidderminster   O = Oldbury   P = Pershore   R = Redditch   S = Stourbridge   Sp = Stourport   W = Worcester

Figures WM6-8. Maps showing the distribution of chair makers and turners in Worcestershire in 1829, 1850 and 1868.

Figure WM9. The High Street, Evesham, Worcestershire, c.1900. It has remained largely unchanged since John Kerry junior was recorded working here in 1829.
(Courtesy Worcestershire Local Studies Library)

Figure WM10. Ladder back armchair. Ash, stamped 'KERRY EVESHAM' on the rear and front of the back uprights (fl.1820-61). The incorporation of the shaped and upper indentation to the lower edge of the top ladder is a signature of Kerry made chairs. See Figures WM12 and 13 for other examples.

Round front legs joined by turned stretcher. Round turned back legs connected by double stretchers; double side stretchers. Rush seat with edge protective strips missing. Round back uprights with six ladders, graduated in size, with a large dome topped curved ladder at the top shaped and indented below. Five lower domed ladders, straight underneath. Curved shaped arms supported by underarm turnings which are half of the front stretcher turning. Height 113cm, width 60cm; depth 40cm.

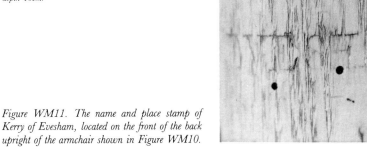

Figure WM11. The name and place stamp of Kerry of Evesham, located on the front of the back upright of the armchair shown in Figure WM10.

291

Plate 39. Ladder back side chair. Ash with elm seat. Impressed 'KERRY EVESHAM' on back uprights, c.1840.

Plate 40. Ladder back low fireside chair. Ash with willow seat. Impressed 'KERRY EVESHAM' on back uprights, c.1840.

Plate 41. Side chair with vasiform splat. Ash with elm seat. Impressed 'CROS' on top of both front legs. This stamp refers to Thomas Cross, chair turner, recorded working 'near the foundry' at Rugeley, Staffordshire, in 1818.

Plate 42. 'Corner' or 'smoking' chair. Ash with rush seat. West Midlands region, c.1840.

Plate 43. Spindle back armchair. Ash with elm seat. Impressed 'P C' on top of back uprights. This stamp refers to Phillip Clisset (fl.1837-1913), chair turner, who lived and worked at Stanley Hill, Bosbury, near Ledbury, Herefordshire.

John Kerry the younger was working at the address given for his uncle nine years before,[3] in the High Street, Evesham. His uncle, William Kerry, the brother of John Kerry senior, aged seventy-eight, is also recorded at this address.[4] John Kerry senior's name does not appear, and by 1841 William Kerry, too, is no longer in the directories.[5]

John Kerry the younger was alone working as a wood turner in the Market Square in 1841.[6] In the Evesham town census of 1851, he is recorded as being aged sixty-four years, and to have become a master cabinet maker and furniture broker, employing two men. He is last recorded working in the town in 1854.[7] However, the family connection with furniture was continued beyond this point, since William Kerry Chambers, a grandson of John Kerry the younger, is recorded as a cabinet maker and wood turner in 1861, but not beyond this point.[8]

The general development and ultimate demise of the Kerry tradition thus accords with a general decline in chair making in other Worcestershire towns during the mid-nineteenth century.

Figure WM12. Ladder back side chair. Ash, stamped 'KERRY' on the front of the back uprights (fl.1820-61).

Round front legs, terminating in vase shaped feet, joined by turned stretcher. Round turned back legs connected by single stretcher, double side stretchers. Thin elm seat morticed into side and rear stretchers, and nailed to a shaped cross frieze at the front. Round back uprights with four ladders, graduated in size, with a larger curved ladder at the top, shaped and upwards indented below, and three lower domed ladders, straight underneath. Height 96cm; width 47cm; depth 33cm.

Figure WM13. Ladder back low side chair. Ash, stamped 'KERRY. EVESHAM.' on the front of both back uprights (fl.1820-61).

Short round front legs terminating in ring shaped feet, joined by turned stretcher. Round turned back legs connected by single stretcher; double side stretchers. Original wicker seat. Round back uprights with five ladders, graduated in size, with a large curved ladder at the top, shaped and upwards indented below, and four lower domed ladders straight underneath. Height 91cm; width 47cm; depth 36cm.

Figure WM14. Low ladder back armchair. Ash, stamped 'KERRY EVESHAM' (fl.1820-61). This chair is interesting in that it illustrates stylistic features of chairs made by Philip Clissett of Bosbury, Herefordshire, and in chairs designed by Ernest Gimson, a leading member of the Arts and Crafts Movement during the latter part of the 19th century. This Kerry chair may, therefore, represent a vernacular prototype, and a further discussion of this point is given on pp.297-300.

Curved back uprights joined by three graduated ladders, shaped and flattened at the top, and straight below. Straight front legs joined by two parallel (replaced) stretchers. Two side stretchers; the upper one shaped and morticed to accommodate flattened arm supports. Refined turned and shaped arm supports (replaced: pattern taken from original fragments) morticing through the side seat rails. Rush replaced.

Figure WM16. Ladder back side chair. Fruitwood, stamped 'KERRY' on the front of both back uprights (fl.1820-61). This is an elaborate form of chair which exhibits stylistic refinements, including the pad feet of the front legs and the shaping of all the ladders.

Turned front legs terminating in pad feet, legs morticing into square corners of seat frame and joined by turned stretcher. Round turned back legs connected by single stretcher; double side stretchers. Replaced rush seat with edge protective strips missing. Round back uprights with five ladders, graduated in size, domed at the top and shaped and upwards indented below.

Figure WM15. The stamp of the Kerry family of Evesham, Worcestershire (fl.1820-61), impressed on the back upright of the chair shown in Figure WM14.

Figure WM17. A view of the Vale of Evesham, Worcestershire in the early 20th century, looking from Castlemorton on the edge of the Malvern Hills, towards Bredon Hill in the distance. The Clissett family of chair makers lived in the village of Birtsmorton in the first quarter of the 19th century, close to Castlemorton, and this was the rural environment in which they worked and found markets for their chairs in the local towns of Malvern, Pershore, Evesham and Ledbury.

(Courtesy Worcestershire Local Studies Library)

The Clissett Family

Contemporary with John Kerry the elder, a further chair maker, Moses Clissett, was born in the Worcestershire town of Pershore, some twelve miles from Evesham, in 1768.[9] Although it is not known whether Clissett's and Kerry's fathers were chair makers before them, it is certain that both of these craftsmen lived within a sufficiently close proximity to have been familiar with each other's chairs, which might well have been sold in local town markets. Moses is known to have left his birthplace, and to have moved some eight miles away to the tiny parish of Birtsmorton,[10] which lies under the eastern scarp of the Malvern Hills, overlooking the fertile plain of the Vale of Evesham. The Vale has a long history of growing fruit and

vegetables, as well as providing abundant grazing, resulting from the equitable climate and rich loam soil. Figure WM17 gives an impression of the Vale of Evesham looking from the Malvern Hills, creating a sense of place, similar to that which the Clissetts must have experienced.

It may be assumed that the village of Birtsmorton became a significant centre of rural chair making in the nineteenth century, for in addition to Moses, his two sons, Cyrus, born 1805,[11] and Philip, born 1817,[12] both became chair makers. The former had his own chair making workshop at nearby Berrow, and his son, also Cyrus, born 1829,[13] and a daughter Mary, born 1837, also became chair makers, and are known to have been working with their father in 1851.

Since Cyrus junior and Mary were only twenty-two years and fifteen years respectively at this time, it may be that these later Clissetts continued as chair makers for a longer time than this. However, their lives probably exhibited the difficulties of making a consistent living, common amongst rural workers during this period, and Moses appears to have carried on his craft until at least his eighty-third year, when he had moved to live with his daughter, Hannah, at nearby Eastnor, and is recorded as a pauper chair maker relying on Parish relief in 1851.[14]

No name or initial stamped chairs from the Birtsmorton Clissetts have been recorded. However, we may assume that this group made chairs similar to those known to have been

295

Plate 44. Spindle back side chair. Ash with elm seat, c.1860. Stamped 'W C' on top of both uprights. This stamp refers to William Cole (fl.1851-71), chair maker and brother-in-law of Phillip Clisset, who also worked at Bosbury, Herefordshire.

Plate 45. Spindle back side chair. Ash with elm seat, c.1860. Stamped 'P C' on top of both back uprights.

Plate 46. Spindle back side chair. Ash with elm seat, c.1860. Impressed 'W C' on top of both back uprights.

Plate 47. Spindle back side chair. Ash with elm seat, c.1860. Impressed 'P C' on top of both back uprights.

Figure WM18. A typical armchair of the type made by Philip Clissett (fl.1841-1913), of Stanley Hill, Bosbury, near Hereford. His chairs represent a true regional style, and were made from locally grown ash, with elm for the seats. Clissett typically stamped his work with his initials on the top of the back uprights (see Figure WM19).

Figure WM20. The stamp used by the Bosbury chair maker, William Cole (fl.1841-71), located on the top of one of the back legs of the chair shown in Figure WM21.

Figure WM21. A view of a chair bearing the initial stamp of William Cole (fl.1841-71), impressed on the top of a rear upright. The placing of this form of identity is unusual and was practiced particularly by makers in this region.

Figure WM19. The mark of Philip Clissett, (fl.1841-1913), stamped on the top of the back uprights of the chair shown in Figure WM18.

produced later by Philip Clissett, who stamped his initials 'P.C.' on the top of the back uprights of his chairs (see Figure WM19). He moved from Birtsmorton some time between 1841 and 1843[15] to Stanley Hill, an outlying part of his wife's home village of Bosbury, some eight miles away on the western side of the Malvern Hills in the county of Herefordshire.* Here he was to carry out his craft during the rest of his long life, and his work was ultimately to assure him a part in influencing national developments in furniture design.

Philip Clissett's life as a chair maker appears to have epitomised the idealised simplicity and economy of his craft, and he became a model of the rural craftsman, untainted by the vicissitudes of fashion. Within this tradition, the green coppiced ash used in turning the framework for his chairs was felled in the autumn, and brought home by cart from the nearby Childer Wood at Cannon Frome,[16] some half a mile away.

Clissett adopted the classic techniques of the green chair making craft in cleaving his sawn lengths of wood into segments before shaping them with a side axe and draw knife, then turning them on his pole lathe which was erected to operate in the small workshop attached to his cottage home, situated on the roadside at Stanley Hill. Here he was within constant sight of the small blue and yellow brick Wesleyan Chapel, standing within a few hundred yards of his home, towards the top of the hill, where he was Steward for many years.[17]

Throughout the major part of his life, Clissett seems to have made chairs which embodied a simplicity of design and an economy of materials which satisfied the needs of the local community as well as the sensibilities of significant designers associated with the Arts and Crafts Movement later in the nineteenth century. Clissett's wooden seated chairs reflect the general design conventions of the West Midlands chair group, and they appear to have remained consistent in design throughout his life. The wooden seat design and seat pegging

* Of all the West Midlands counties, Herefordshire was, perhaps, the least touched by the industrial revolution, and remained an essentially agriculturally based county, famous for its cider and beef cattle throughout the 19th century. The absence of industrial development is clearly reflected in the county's relatively low population figures for the early 19th century,[18] compared with both Worcestershire and Shropshire, where there were some industrial communities.

Population figures for 1831	
Shropshire	170,000
Worcestershire	146,000
Herefordshire	111,000

Figure WM22. Single row spindle back side chair. Ash with elm seat, stamped 'P C' on top of back uprights. This chair illustrates the simplest style made by Philip Clissett (fl.1841-1913). A more elaborate design of this maker's work is shown in Figure WM23.

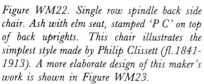

Round turned front legs terminating in vase shaped feet, connected by two plain turned stretchers. Swept round back legs connected by two stretchers. Double side stretchers. Swept back uprights connected by round turned top rail with two round turned cross rails below connected by four spindles. Thin elm seat morticed into round rails at side and rear, and nailed to shaped frieze rail at front.

Figure WM23. Single row spindle back side chair. Ash with elm seat, stamped 'P C' on top of back uprights.

Turned front legs with indented turning and terminating in vase shaped feet, connected by two plain turned stretchers. Swept round back legs connected by two stretchers. Double side stretchers. Swept back uprights connected by plain stay rail, two round turned cross rails below. Stay rail connected by four spindles to lower cross rails. Thin elm seat morticed into round rails at side and rear, and nailed to shaped frieze rail at front.

Figure WM24. Single row spindle back side chair. Ash with elm seat.

Round turned front legs, terminating in vase shaped feet, connected by two plain turned stretchers. Swept round back legs connected by two stretchers. Double side stretchers. Swept back uprights connected by a round turned top rail with two round turned cross rails below connected by three spindles. Thin elm seat morticed into round rails at side and rear, and nailed to a shaped frieze rail at front.

are compatible with other West Midlands regional styles (see Figures WM2 and 3).

Clissett's wooden seated chairs differ from other chairs in the West Midlands regional group in a number of significant ways, however. These include the utilisation of two plain dowels instead of the elaborate front rail turning which was typically adopted throughout the region. The back spindle turnings constitute specific 'signatures', with two styles being produced. The typical Clissett side chairs in Figures WM22 and 23 clearly show the precise nature of his chair composition, and the attractive graining of the ash and elm which was untouched, in manufacture, by stains or paints.

Clissett was also a teacher, and passed on his craft to others, and it is likely that during the second quarter of the century, he taught his chair turning skills to his son William, who

died at the early age of twenty-one years, when he was about to be married.[19]

Philip also taught the craft to his wife Mary's brother, William Cole, a native of Bosbury and eight years younger than Philip, having been born in 1825.[20] Subsequently, William Cole became a craftsman who produced chairs of similar design and equal quality to that of Clissett, and he, too, stamped his chairs with his initials, W.C., on the top of the back legs (see Figures WM20 and 21). Figures WM24 and 25 show typical chairs made by Cole. He continued working at Briarcroft, Bosbury, at least until 1871;[21] but by 1881 he had become a farmer with eight acres at Foxhill, Bosbury, and was no longer a chair maker.[22]

Both Cole and Clissett also made similar elbow and side chairs to each other. Figures WM22-25 show side chairs made by Clissett and Cole

Figure WM25. Single row spindle back side chair. Ash with elm seat, stamped 'W C' on top of back uprights.

Decorative ring turned front legs terminating in vase shaped feet, connected by two plain turned stretchers. Swept back uprights connected by plain stay rail, with two round turned cross rails below. Stay rail connected by four spindles to lower round cross rail. Thin elm seat morticed into round rails at side and rear, and nailed to shaped frieze at front.

Figure WM26. The interior of a farmhouse at Bosbury, Herefordshire, c.1930. This farm stands within sight of Philip Clissett's cottage, and the armchair is a typical Clissett chair, but has six long vertical spindles in the back rather than the more usual four spindles (see Figure WM18). A six spindle chair of the type shown in this scene, stamped 'P C' on the top of each back upright, is shown in Figure WM27.

(Courtesy The Countryman, *Burford)*

respectively, and it is clear that each made both a simpler and a more elaborate model. Indeed, the difference in elaboration is reflected in the prices charged. Clissett is recorded [23] as selling his side chairs for 2/6d. (12½p) and 4/- (20p) and his armchairs for 8/6d. (42½p).*

A further chair maker, Richard Edwardes, is recorded in Bosbury and in 1851 he was a lodger in Philip Clissett's house,[24] as was Elizabeth Cole, sister of Mary Clissett and William Cole. By 1861, Richard Edwardes had married Elizabeth, and had apparently learned the chair making craft from Clissett since he too is recorded as a chair maker, living now at 65, The Village, Bosbury.[25] He remained as a chair maker for at least ten years, but by 1881 he had returned to agricultural labouring, and was living with his brother-in-law, William Cole, at Fox Hill.[26] No work by Edwardes has

been found with an initial or name stamp, and it may be that some of the chairs of the Clissett/Cole style which occur without identification marks may have been made by this maker.

Although Clissett is reputed in many writings to have made rush seated ladder back chairs, no initial stamped chairs made by him of this style have been recorded, whereas numerous wooden seated spindle back chairs have. There can be little doubt, however, that towards the end of the nineteenth century, Clissett did make rush seated ladder back chairs, as well as the occasional rush seated spindle back armchair.[27] In the photograph in Figure WM28, which shows Clissett as an old man with a grandchild on his knee, he is sitting in a ladder back armchair. However, it is not clear whether Clissett had knowledge of this style from earlier times, or was introduced to it by members of the London

based Art Workers' Guild, who visited him towards the end of his working life. At this time Philip Clissett and his craft entered, quite accidentally, into the history of design through the awareness of indigenous crafts evoked by the Arts and Crafts Movement during the late nineteenth century. Prominent amongst this movement was the architect, Ernest Gimson, who, whilst experimenting in London during the early 1890s with chair designs and plasterwork for housing, was inspired,

---

* It may be assumed that Philip Clissett was of some standing in his community, both as a self employed craftsman, and Steward at the Stanley Hill Wesleyan Chapel. He was, too, a well known Liberal, and took great interest in Parliamentary elections. His obituary in the *Hereford Journal* of 25 January 1913, noted that the local Liberal candidate is reported to have taken Clissett on his first motor car journey to register his vote in his 93rd year.

Figure WM27. Single row spindle back armchair. Ash with elm seat, stamped 'P C' on top of back uprights (fl. 1841-1913). A chair similar in design is shown in the farmhouse interior in Figure WM26.

Round turned front legs terminating in vase shaped feet, connected by two plain turned stretchers. Swept round back legs connected by two stretchers. Double side stretchers. Swept back uprights connected by plain stay rail with three round turned cross rails below. Stay rail connected by six spindles to a lower cross rail. Thin elm seat morticed into round rails at side and rear, and nailed to shaped frieze rail at front. Curved shaped arms supported by turned underarm supports.

(Courtesy G. Olive)

Figure WM28. Photograph of Philip Clissett with his grandchild, outside his cottage at Stanley Hill, Bosbury, taken early this century. Clissett is shown seated in one of his rush seated ladder back chairs similar to the chair shown in Figure WM29.

(Courtesy The Archivist, The Old Barracks, Hereford)

Figure WM29. A ladder back armchair. Ash, c.1880-1913. Attributed to Philip Clissett, Bosbury, near Hereford, who is seen nursing his grandchild in Figure WM28.

Round front legs tapering towards foot, joined by two plain turned front stretchers. Rush seat, with edge protective strips missing. Reclined round back uprights with five cross splats or ladders, graduated in size, shaped and flattened at the top and straight below. Curved arms supported by simple turned arm supports.

it is believed, by rush seated chairs which had been bought for 10/6d. (52½p) each, by James Maclaren of the Art Workers' Guild, from Philip Clissett. However, the low ladder back chair made by Kerry of Evesham (fl. 1820-1861), shown in Figure WM14, indicates that the origin of this primary design could have emanated from this source rather than from Clissett himself, since no further evidence exists to suggest that Clissett made ladder back chairs until the end of the nineteenth century. In this event, it may be that the 'Clissett' ladder back chair, with its characteristic ladder shape and elegant high back, was introduced to Clissett by Maclaren as a 'new' design (see Figure WM29). Certainly a number of the chair designs made in Gimson's workshop at Sapperton, near Cirencester, included low back forms which have the ladder shape and number, the arm fixing device and the straight turned legs and stretchers

which are all included as features of the earlier Kerry chair. Although no attribution to a vernacular origin for their chair designs was given by Gimson or his followers, it seems clear that members of the group were aware of the 'common' tradition illustrated by Kerry's work, and transposed it in similar form into their chairs. However, Maclaren's relationship with Clissett was undoubtedly a seminal point in the subsequent development of the Arts and Crafts Movement, and their first meeting was graphically described by the journalist and painter, D.S. McColl:
'Shortly before the first Arts and Crafts Exhibition, I think, the late James Maclaren, an architect whom many of my readers will remember, had some work to do at Ledbury, and in a walk we took one day we found in a little Worcestershire [sic] village, a real survival of village industry; an old man who made rush bottomed

chairs with no other apparatus than his cottage oven for bending the wood. Maclaren made him one or two drawings improving a little upon his designs, which he was quite content to do at eight shillings apiece. When the Art Workers' Guild was formed, these chairs, known to some of its members, were adopted and passed from that into many houses.'[28]

Gimson was so attracted by the essentially romantic notion of Clissett's craft being carried on as a rural idyll that he travelled to Bosbury during 1890 and spent some time working with Clissett, being taught the fundamental skills of the chair maker's craft by him. The competence which Clissett displayed, using his pole lathe, was later described by Gimson to his workshop foreman, Edward Gardiner, who was employed to make chairs at Sapperton. Gardiner reported:
'Mr. Gimson told me how quickly Clissett could turn out his work from cleft ash poles on his pole lathe,

300

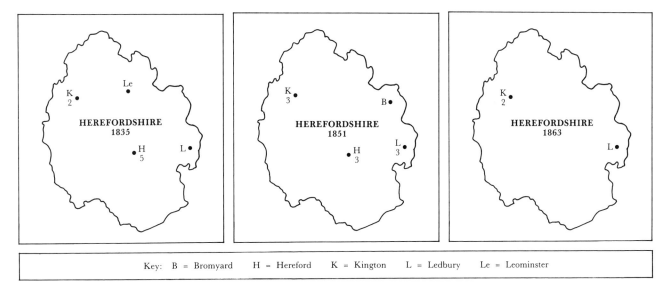

Key: B = Bromyard   H = Hereford   K = Kington   L = Ledbury   Le = Leominster

Figures WM30-32. Maps showing the location of Hereford chair makers in 1835, 1851 and 1863.

steam, bend and all the rest. He seems to have made a chair a day for 6/6d. and rushed it in his cottage kitchen, singing as he worked. According to old Philip Clissett, if you were not singing, you were not happy.'[29]

Local hearsay confirms that Philip Clissett continued to make chairs beyond his ninetieth year, and the last two chairs which he turned were made at the request of a Miss Price of Leominster. R.C. Morgan records this event, and noted:

'Both are armchairs of good design: the first (now in the Museum) was found to be too high for Miss Price who therefore induced Clissett to make one a little lower.'[30]

The Clissett chair making tradition continued beyond Philip with his two grandsons, John and William, sons of Philip John, making chairs at the Old Smithy, at the nearby village of Taplow. It is reported that they used Philip's old pole lathe.[31] It may be that these last Clissett chair makers continued until the onset of the First World War, since Clissetts are shown to have fallen or to have been wounded, on the War Memorial at nearby Lugwardine.

How far the Bosbury made chairs were typical of those made by other makers in Herefordshire and Worcestershire is not clear. Certainly other chair makers worked in a number of Hereford towns during the first half of the nineteenth century. Figures WM30-32 indicate the development and ultimate decline of the Herefordshire tradition.

Figure WM33. Side chair attributed to John Warander, Bransford, Worcestershire, c.1841. This maker typically stamped his work with his initials, 'I. [J.] W.' on the top of the back uprights. Note that is identical in design to the elaborate side chairs made by Philip Clissett, indicating that the chair makers in this region were working with a common code of design and craft practice.

Figure WM34. The mark of John Warander (fl.1841), on the top of the back uprights of the chair shown in Figure WM33.

The Waranders

At least one further chair making family produced work which was identical to the more elaborate of the Clissett/Cole designs. These makers, father and son, were both named John Warander. They produced chairs at Gilberts Lane, Bransford,[32] a Worcestershire village lying between Worcester and the Malvern Hills, some eight miles from Bosbury, and ten miles from Birtsmorton. These makers typically initial stamped their work on top of the back legs, and an example of their work and their stamp is shown in Figures WM33 and 34. Comparison of this chair with the Clissett made chair illustrated in Figure WM23 shows virtually the same design.

Shropshire and Staffordshire chairs

The possibility of direct transmission of design by one maker observing the chairs made by another is clear. Equally, it may be that similar design developments arose in a number of places spontaneously and independently. The identification of regional designs is often further complicated by the existence of a number of parallel design systems within a given area. Such diversity is typified in the Shropshire and North West Midlands chair making tradition, where distinctions in design and productivity may be assumed between the work of the relatively isolated rural chair makers, working, for example, in South Shropshire in the Clun Forest, who produced simple forms of chair (see Figure WM52), and the chair makers who worked in the generally more urbanised and prosperous towns of North Shropshire, where strong, industrially based communities developed, particularly in the districts of Wellington, Telford, Coalbrookdale and Ironbridge. Indeed, design ideas from other regions may well have been imported into the area through the movement of chair makers. In the developing town of Wellington, makers were recorded in the 1861 census, with places of birth as diverse as Liverpool, Ireland, London, Manchester, Lincoln and Nailsworth (Glos.).

Although no illustrations of the earliest Shropshire chairs have been identified, it is clear from the probate inventories made in the areas of Wellington, Telford and Coalbrookdale[33] during the late seventeenth and early eighteenth centuries, that by the late seventeenth century rush seated chairs were found conjointly with 'joyned' stools, chairs and benches, as well as chairs made with cane and leather seats and backs. For example, the probate inventory of Richard Stainer,[34] gentleman, of Aston, Wellington, made in 1711, shows that with other items, the parlour contained 'Eight leather chairs. Two Elbowe segg chairs'.* The parlour chamber contained 'Two Elbowe caine chairs and ten other caine chairs'. Whereas the hall chamber contained, in addition to a bedstead, a close stool and a small dressing table, 'Six segg chairs', valued at 6d. The hall itself contained 'Six joyned chairs', valued at 12/-, and 'Four leather chairs', valued at 10/-. No mention of the typical thin elm seated chairs is made

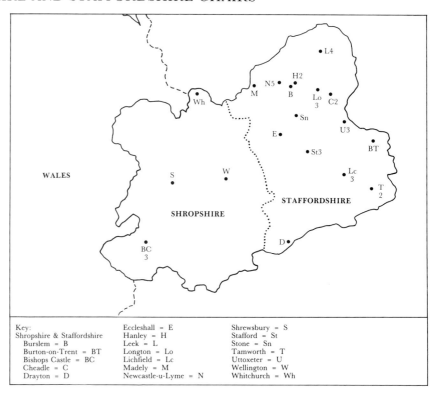

Figure WM35. Map showing the distribution of chair makers in Shropshire and Staffordshire in 1841.

Key: Shropshire & Staffordshire		
Burslem = B	Eccleshall = E	Shrewsbury = S
Burton-on-Trent = BT	Hanley = H	Stafford = St
Bishops Castle = BC	Leek = L	Stone = Sn
Cheadle = C	Longton = Lo	Tamworth = T
Drayton = D	Lichfield = Lc	Uttoxeter = U
	Madely = M	Wellington = W
	Newcastle-u-Lyme = N	Whitchurch = Wh

Figure WM36. New Street, Wellington, Shropshire. This street, as well as nearby King Street and Walker Street, was a centre of the chair making trade, and by 1841, ten chair makers are recorded working here. The town of Wellington is situated on the borders of Shropshire and Staffordshire, and no doubt the chairs made here supplied both counties.   (Courtesy Local Studies Library, Wellington)

in Shropshire inventories of the seventeenth and eighteenth centuries, indicating that the typical wooden seated chair of the early nineteenth century was a later innovation.

In making the existence of rush seated chairs clear, eighteenth century records give little indication of the distribution of chair makers or wood turners in Shropshire and Stafford-

shire, and it is the evidence of the earliest census records made in 1841, and entries in Trade Directories from 1790, which enable a pattern of chair making to emerge. It is clear that at around 1840, those tradesmen who

---

* The term 'segg' is used to described rush in the early inventories, presumably derived from the term sedge.

Figure WM37. A shoe making factory in Stafford, photographed in the late 19th century. A single row spindle back chair, typical of those made in the West Midlands region, is shown on the right. The common chairs of the region were made for hard use in homes, institutions and places of work, and it says much for the robustness of their design that they were able to withstand daily use in places of work such as this.

(Courtesy Stafford Museum and Art Gallery)

described themselves as chair makers and wood turners, or as wood turners, were found in the places indicated in Figure WM35. It is not in itself surprising to find a high concentration of ten chair makers in 1841, in Wellington,[35] since this town, situated on the Shropshire/Staffordshire border, was the centre of trade for the whole region, supplying goods to the relatively large and prosperous population, involved particularly in mining, steel and iron smelting, and industrial manufacturing, as well as farming.

The photograph of New Street, Wellington (see Figure WM36) in the 1880s shows that New Street was a busy trading area of the town, and would have been an attractive area for artisans of many kinds, including chair makers.

It may be that this period was the time when chair making as a specific native craft was at its most productive in the North West Midlands, since by 1861 only one chair maker is explicitly recorded in the Wellington

census, although seventeen wood turners and fifteen cabinet makers are named.[36] It is suggested by these records, that by this time, in a similar way to other regions of the West Midlands, chair making had largely lost its independent status, and that chair production had become part of the cabinet makers' repertoire, with wood turners supplying chair parts to large manufacturers who assembled and supplied the finished chairs.

In terms of styles, photographic records of vernacular chairs found in the Shropshire and Staffordshire area indicate that a number of clear generic design signatures exist which may enable a typology of styles to be formed. Amongst these appears a major design feature, not found in this precise form amongst other English chairs; that of a shaped wooden top rail supporting the back legs.*

Although few early illustrations of household interiors in this area have so far been located, a photograph[37] taken in a shoe making factory in

Stafford in the late nineteenth century (see Figure WM37) shows a chair to the right of the picture which is similar to the chairs shown in Figures WM38 and 39. This illustration is interesting in indicating that the common chairs of this region were perhaps seen as suitable for places of work as well as at home.

A further photograph taken in the 1950s at Lightmoor, near to Coalbrookdale and Wellington, showing the interior of a traditional ironstone miner's home, portrays a chair of the type attributed by hearsay evidence to Shropshire, which displays the feature of the top rail (see Figure WM40). Figures WM41-43 illustrate the wide range of chairs which adopt this critical stylistic signature which designates these North West Midlands chairs as distinct from those illus-

* It is the case that a generic group within the Lancashire tradition also exhibits variations of shaped top rails across the top of the back legs, but these are significantly heavier in design than the West Midlands version (see Chapter 7, Figures NW203-251).

trated from the South West Midlands areas.

Within this group of chairs, several common design features may also be identified, including back designs, composed of ladders, turned spindles, or a single urn shaped splat. Common to this group, too, is the pad or turned foot of the front legs, which, given the complex turnery techniques involved in producing this feature, would have designated these chairs as a relatively sophisticated product.*

Certain designs were also made without the feature of the top rail, but which were similar in other respects (see Figures WM38, 39, 46 and 54). As with chairs made in Worcestershire and Herefordshire, certain of the designs illustrated here occur with either rush or wooden seats, although the majority of designs appear to have been made with wooden seats.**

The West Midlands cottage interior painted by the nineteenth century Worcester artist,[38] Edward Thompson Davis, shown in Figure WM1, shows two chairs of the West Midlands type: one similar to that shown in Figure WM54 but with a rush seat, and the second shows a shaped top rail chair which may be assumed to have held a central splat similar to the chair shown in Figure WM44.

If the Northern Shropshire/ Staffordshire towns may be thought to represent relatively sophisticated communities, other parts of Shropshire underwent relatively little social development between the eighteenth and nineteenth centuries. In consequence, the poorer and more isolated communities retained their traditional crafts and way of life well into this century. The village of Clun represents such a community, and here lived what was probably the longest continuing family of truly vernacular chair makers in the county, the Owens, who pursued their craft over several generations, from at least the early nineteenth century and probably much before this, until about 1910.[39] Elderly villagers recall that the last

Figure WM38. Single row spindle back side chair. Ash with elm seat. Attributed to Shropshire/ Staffordshire, c.1820-60.

Round turned front legs with pear shaped turning motif, terminating in round feet, connected by turned stretchers. Round back legs connected by single stretcher. Double side stretchers. Straight back uprights connected by round turned top rail with two round turned cross rails below connected by three spindles. Thin elm seat morticed into round rails at side and rear, and nailed to shaped frieze rail at front.

Figure WM39. Single row spindle back side chair. Ash with elm seat. Attributed to Shropshire/ Staffordshire, c.1820-60.

Turned front legs with concave turning motif terminating in pad shaped feet, connected by turned stretcher. Round back legs connected by single stretcher. Double side stretchers. Straight back uprights connected by curved round turned top rail with two curved round turned cross rails below, connected by four spindles. Thin elm seat morticed into round rails at side and rear, and nailed to shaped frieze rail at front.

Figure WM40. Interior of an ironstone miner's cottage at Lightmore, near Coalbrookdale and Wellington, North Shropshire, showing a chair style attributed to the North West Midlands tradition of chair making, and similar to the chair illustrated in Figure WM41.

(Photograph Edwin Smith)

---

* The pad foot found as part of the front leg design on many vernacular chairs was a refinement requiring the leg to be centred on the lathe twice during the turning operation in order to produce the offset shape of the foot. The straight leg which is also commonly found in turner's chairs, required only one centring on the lathe, and was thus a less costly form of leg to produce.

** This latter feature may be assumed to be a later eighteenth or early 19th century innovation, since no clearly identifiable reference to wooden seated chairs is recorded concurrent with rush or 'segg' chairs in the early 18th century probate records.

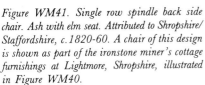

Figure WM41. Single row spindle back side chair. Ash with elm seat. Attributed to Shropshire/ Staffordshire, c.1820-60. A chair of this design is shown as part of the ironstone miner's cottage furnishings at Lightmore, Shropshire, illustrated in Figure WM40.

Turned front legs with single ring and concave turned motif, terminating in pad shaped feet, connected by a turned stretcher. Straight round back legs connected by one stretcher. Double side stretchers. Straight back uprights connected by curved thin stay rail with two round turned cross rails below connected by three spindles. Thin elm seat morticed into round rails at side and rear, and nailed to shaped frieze rail at front.

Figure WM42. Ladder back side chair. Ash with rush seat. Attributed to Shropshire/ Staffordshire, c.1820-60. The front stretcher turning design found in this chair is incorporated in many chairs from the West Midlands region (see Figures WM10, 12, 13, 16 and 51 for examples), as well as from chairs made in the Cheshire/Lancashire tradition (see Chapter 7, Figure NW289, type J).

Turned front legs with concave turned motif terminating in pad shaped feet, joined by turned stretcher. Round back legs connected by two stretchers; double side stretchers, right stretchers missing. Replaced rush seat with edge protective strips missing. Round back uprights with four ladders, graduated in size, domed on top with shaped and upward indentation below. Uprights connected by a curved shaped stay rail.

Figure WM43. Ladder back single chair. Ash with elm seat. Attributed to Shropshire/ Staffordshire, c.1820-60.

Turned front legs with concave and inverted cup turning motif terminating in pad shaped feet, joined by turned stretcher. Round back legs connected by two stretchers, and double side stretchers. Thin elm seat morticed into round rails at side and rear, and nailed to shaped frieze rail at front. Round back uprights with four ladders, graduated in size, domed on top with shaped and upwards indentation below. Back uprights connected across the top by a thin shaped stay rail.

Figure WM44. Splat back side chair. Ash with elm seat. Stamped 'CROS' on front top of front legs (fl.1818-34). Attributed to Staffordshire. The front leg connecting stretcher design is particularly resonant of this region's common chair designs and other examples can be seen in Figures WM39, 43 and 46.

Turned front legs with concave and cup turned motif terminating in pad shaped feet, joined by turned stretcher. Round turned back legs connected by two stretchers (now missing); double side stretchers. Thin elm seat morticed into round rails at side and rear, and nailed to shaped frieze at front. Straight back upright tapering to a curved and shaped stay rail. Shaped splat connecting stay rail and seat.

Figure WM45. The stamp of 'Cros' impressed on the top of both front legs. This stamp may refer to the more conventional surname of 'Cross', and to a Thomas Cross, who is recorded working as a chair maker and turner, 'rear of the Foundry' at Rugeley, Staffordshire. Ralph Cross, a turner is also recorded in 1834, working in Albion St, Rugeley.

Figure WM46. Single row spindle back side chair. Ash with elm seat. Attributed to Shropshire/ Staffordshire, c.1820-60.

Turned front legs with concave and inverted cup motif terminating in pad shaped feet, connected by a turned stretcher. Round back legs connected by two stretchers. Double side stretchers. Straight back uprights connected by plain stay rail, with thin cross rail below connected by three spindles. Thin elm seat morticed into round rails at side and rear, and nailed to plain frieze rail at front.

Figure WM47. Ladder back armchair. Ash. Attributed to Shropshire/Staffordshire, c.1820-60.

Front legs with concave and ring turning terminating in pad shaped feet, joined by turned stretcher. Back legs connected by two stretchers; double side stretchers. Replaced rush seat with edge protective strips missing. Round back uprights with six ladders, graduated in size, with a large 'dished' ladder at the top, and five domed ladders below, all with shaped upper indentations below. Flattened and scrolled arms supported by turned arm supports.

Figure WM48. Ladder back armchair. Ash. Attributed to Shropshire/Staffordshire, c.1820-60.

Front legs with single ring turning terminating in cup shaped feet, joined by turned stretcher. Back legs connected by stretchers showing regional turnery device. Rush seat with edge protective strips missing. Round back uprights with six ladders, graduated in size, with a large dished ladder at the top, and five domed ladders below, all with shaped upper indentations. Flattened and shaped arms supported by turned arm supports.

Figure WM49. Ladder back armchair. Ash. Attributed to Shropshire/Staffordshire, c.1820-60. This armchair is the natural counterpart to the side chair shown in Figure WM54.

Round front legs joined by turned stretcher. Back legs connected by single stretcher; double side stretchers. Rush seat, with edge protective strips missing. Round back uprights with five ladders, graduated in size, with domed tops and straight below. Shaped arms supported by turned underarm supports.

Figure WM50. Single row spindle back armchair. Ash. Attributed to Shropshire/Staffordshire, c.1820-60.

Turned front legs with concave and inverted cup turning terminating in pad shaped feet, connected by a turned stretcher. Round back legs connected by two stretchers; double side stretchers. Straight back uprights connected by a plain stay rail, with two flattened cross splats below. The stay rail connected by four spindles to a narrow cross splat. Rush seat with edge strips missing.

Figure WM51. Ladder back armchair. Ash. Attributed to Shropshire/Staffordshire, c.1820-60. This armchair is the natural counterpart to the side chair shown in Figure WM43.

Round front legs terminating in shaped feet, joined by turned stretcher. Back legs connected by two stretchers; double side stretchers. Thin elm seat morticed into round rails at side and rear, and nailed to shaped frieze rail at front. Round back uprights with four ladders, graduated in size, domed on top and shaped and upward indented below. The tapered back uprights are connected by a thin curved stay rail.

Figure WM52. Single row spindle back side chair. Ash with elm seat. Attributed to the Owen family of chair makers of Clun village in Shropshire (fl.1820-1900).

Round turned front legs terminating in tapered feet, connected by two turned stretchers. Straight round back legs connected by single stretcher; double side stretchers. Straight back uprights connected by round turned top rail with two round turned cross rails below connected by three spindles, with the centre one decoratively turned. The elm seat morticed into round rails at side and rear, and nailed to plain frieze rail at front.

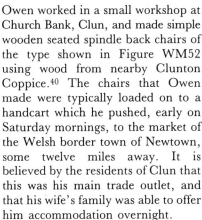

Owen worked in a small workshop at Church Bank, Clun, and made simple wooden seated spindle back chairs of the type shown in Figure WM52 using wood from nearby Clunton Coppice.[40] The chairs that Owen made were typically loaded on to a handcart which he pushed, early on Saturday mornings, to the market of the Welsh border town of Newtown, some twelve miles away. It is believed by the residents of Clun that this was his main trade outlet, and that his wife's family was able to offer him accommodation overnight.

J. Owen proved to be the last of the Clun line of chair makers, however, since Clunton Coppice was sold in 1898 by the Clun Burgesses, depriving Owen of his source of wood.[41] Local remembrance of Owen chairs indicates that his designs were confined to variations of spindle back chairs. However, given that numerous examples of simple ladder back chairs have been recorded which have a similar general demeanour to the Owen chairs, it may be that a nearby group of four chair makers, Richard Green, Samuel Medlicott, and Thomas and William Richards, who worked about eight miles away

Figure WM53. Single row spindle child's high chair. Ash with elm seat. Attributed to Shropshire/Staffordshire, c.1820-60. The spindle designs are similar to the side chair shown in Figure WM52 and suggest the same local manufacturer for these chairs.

Round turned front legs terminating in vase shaped feet, connected by two plain turned stretchers. Straight round back legs connected by round turned top rail with two round turned cross rails below connected by three spindles, the centre one decoratively turned. Thin elm seat morticed into round rails at side and rear, and nailed to shaped frieze rail at front. Round turned arms supported by turned arm supports.

Figure WM54. Ladder back side chair. Ash. Attributed to Shropshire/Staffordshire, c.1820-60. A chair of this design is shown as part of the cottage interior illustrated in Figure WM1 which portrays the kind of home for which these chairs were made.

Round front legs tapering towards foot, joined by turned stretcher. Back legs connected by single stretcher; double side stretchers. Thin elm seat morticed into round rails at side and rear, and nailed to plain frieze rail at front. Round back uprights with four simple graduated ladders, domed on top and straight below.

(Collection M. and D. Harding Hill)

Figure WM56. Detail of the T. Beard name stamp which appears on the front of the seat frieze of the chair illustrated in Figure WM55.

Figure WM55. A spindle back armchair. Ash with thin elm seat. Stamped 'T. BEARD' on the front under-seat frieze. Attributed to West Midlands. The 'bell' and 'collar' turnings shown in Figures WM57 and 58 constitute regional turnery signatures which may help to provide an identification key for unnamed chairs carrying similar signatures.

Figure WM57. Detail of the bell turning of the front leg of the Beard chair in Figure WM55.

Figure WM58. Detail of collar turning of the back leg of the Beard chair in Figure WM55.

Figure WM59. Ladder back chair. Ash with rush seat. Attributed to Shropshire/Staffordshire, c.1820-60. This chair exhibits a front seat frieze typical of those found on the wooden seated variety of this chair. The turnery details shown in Figures WM60 and 61 are closely similar to those found on the chairs illustrated in Figures WM55 and 62.

Figure WM62. Ladder back side chair. Ash with elm seat. Attributed to Shropshire/ Staffordshire, c.1820-60. This chair shows similar turnery details to the Beard chair shown in Figure WM55.

Figure WM60. Detail of the bell turning from the front leg of the chair shown in Figure WM59.

Figure WM63. Detail of the bell turning from the front leg of the chair shown in Figure WM62.

Figure WM61. Detail of the collar turning from the rear leg of the chair shown in Figure WM59.

Figure WM64. Detail of the collar turning from the rear leg of the chair shown in Figure WM62.

on the edge of the Clun Forest at Church Street, Bishop's Castle,[42] between 1840 and 1870, may have produced a more extensive repertoire of designs, possibly including ladder back chairs of the type shown in Figure WM54.

Only one name stamped chair attributed to the Shropshire/Staffordshire tradition has so far been identified, that of T. Beard impressed on the front under-frieze of the chair in Figure WM55. This chair was made in the first half of the 19th century, but no Beard with the initial T has been traced as a chair maker during this time. However, it may be that this maker was a relative of the Beard family of cabinet makers who worked in Willow Street, Oswestry (1826-1909).

The Beard chair is interesting, not only because it is typical of a group of Shropshire chairs, but also because the chair exhibits at least two precise turnery signatures (see Figures WM57 and 58) which have been identified in some other chairs believed to be made in the West Midlands.

Figures WM59 and 62 show two ladder back chairs which have similar features to each other apart from a difference in seating mode. The specific turnery 'signs' mentioned above are located in the bell turning of the mid front leg (see Figures WM60 and 63) and the graduated back leg which exhibits a single ring turning a short way up from seat level (see Figures WM61 and 64). These two features seem to represent positive individual stylistic differences from other chairs in the regional group. Following the view proposed in Chapter 7, that at least two orders of production signature may be employed by makers: those general to the regional group, and those personal to the maker or his workshop, the turnery features illustrated here may serve to provide evidence which supports this position. In this event, the two unnamed chairs shown in Figures WM59 and 62 may achieve at least regional recognition by association of design with the identical design features found as parts of the known Beard chair.

The West Midlands chair making tradition is clearly an example of a diverse regional tradition produced to provide basic utilitarian furniture and their simple elegance assures them a clearly identifiable place in the history of English furniture craft and design.

Figure WM65. Philip Clissett sat in his workshop, at Stanley Hill, Bosbury, Herefordshire, c.1904. See Figures WM18, 19, 22, 23, 27 and 29 for examples of chairs by this maker.

Chapter 7
THE NORTH WEST REGION

The North West regional chair making tradition is drawn from a large geographic area which includes the county of Cheshire to the South, Lancashire in the central area, and the Dales areas of Lancashire, Cumberland and Westmorland (Cumbria) to the north. To the east of Cheshire, the county of Derbyshire is known to have had chair makers too, but firm evidence of this area's products is much less certain than in the other counties of this area.

Culturally, this region spanned very different forms of terrain and ways of life during the nineteenth century. The southern part of Cheshire, for example, was dairying country, with lush pasture and prosperous farms. Towards the north east of the county, many towns, including Macclesfield, Stockport, Hyde, Sandbach and Altrincham, came under the influence of the industrial revolution which developed in England from the middle of the eighteenth century, and into the nineteenth century. It was in North Cheshire and many areas of Lancashire, including Manchester and other towns in central Lancashire, that the textile industry developed, on which much of England's industrial wealth was based during the nineteenth century. The transition from a rurally based economy to an industrial one resulted in the formation of rapidly expanding conurbations throughout the central North West area, and it was to the towns of Manchester, Salford, Rochdale, Bury, Bolton, Preston, Oldham, and many others, that country people flocked to the new found work of the cotton mills. Many of these new workers had been hand spinners and weavers and had

been impoverished by the invention of machines which were able to do the work faster. These included the invention of the 'Spinning Jenny' by James Hargreaves in 1769. Arkwright invented the Water Frame in 1769, and Crompton improved both of these inventions to produce the spinning mule which revolutionised the textile industry, for with this machine the spinning of cotton became a factory based activity, utilising either water or steam power. By the 1780s the cotton spinning industry was firmly established in both Lancashire and Derbyshire. In the North West, weavers worked on a cottage industry basis, and it was during the second quarter of the nineteenth century that weaving, too, was brought within the confines of the factory system, with the consequent decline of the home based weaving industry.

Other country workers who moved to the towns had been smallholders and farmers, and as they moved to find a higher income, their land was taken over by larger farmers who needed greater production to feed the rapidly expanding populations of the textile towns. Such was the influx of these workers that the population of Lancashire rose from about 674,000 to 1,400,000 in the thirty years between 1801 and 1831,[1] and thus provided a massive market for producers of all kinds of goods (see the table below).

However, if the possibility of higher wages attracted people to the new towns, the housing and working conditions they encountered must have been discouraging in the extreme, for the quality of housing was both poor and scarce. Rows of back-to-back houses were hurriedly and cheaply built close to the factories to house the immigrants. These were quickly overcrowded, and families lived in cellars and garrets, often with whole families living in one room. The conditions were insanitary, with a few outside lavatories serving many households. Water was typically collected from outside stand-pipes, and the only means of heating water for washing was over the small open fire, or in a washing 'copper' or boiler which served many households on a rotational basis. Work began early in the morning, and continued until evening, and a twelve hour working day was typical. Child labour was common, and many committees of enquiry set up to consider the conditions of work, deplored the cruel and harmful conditions under which children and adults worked.[2]

Improvements in housing came

Comparative population figures for the counties within the north west region, taken from H.M.S.O. census report, 1921		
	1831	**1861**
Derbyshire	237,181	339,327
Cheshire	334,391	505,428
Lancashire	1,336,854	2,429,440
Cumberland	169,262	205,276
Westmorland	55,041	60,817

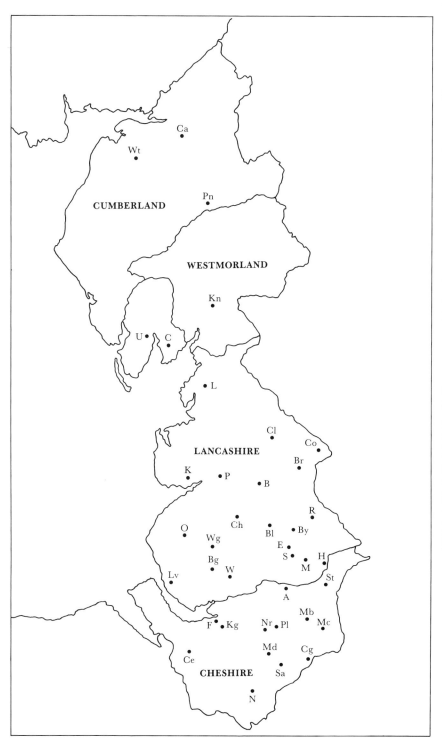

Figure NW1. Location of chairmakers in the North West between 1825 and 1850.

KEY:

CUMBERLAND
Carlisle	= Ca
Penrith	= Pn
Wigton	= Wt

WESTMORLAND
Kendal	= Kn

LANCASHIRE
Blackburn	= B
Bolton	= Bl
Burnley	= Br
Bury	= By
Cartmel	= C
Chorley	= Ch
Clitheroe	= Cl
Colne	= Co
Eccles	= E
Kirkham	= K
Lancaster	= L
Preston	= P
Rochdale	= R
Warrington	= W
Wigan	= Wg
Manchester	= M
Liverpool	= Lv
Ulverston	= U
Billinge	= Bg
Salford	= S
Hyde	= H
Ormskirk	= O

CHESHIRE
Frodsham	= F
Kingsley	= Kg
Macclesfield	= Me
Nantwich	= N
Sandbach	= Sa
Middlewich	= Md
Plumley	= Pl
Mobberley	= Mb
Stockport	= St
Northwich	= Nr
Altrincham	= A
Chester	= Ce
Congleton	= Cg

gradually. The development of water-borne sewage systems relieved the insanitary conditions, and allowed for indoor lavatories to be fitted in some new housing, although outdoor lavatories continued to be used in terraced industrial housing until well into the twentieth century. House plans were also improved, and the two storey cottage was doubled in size. A basic house plan was repro-duced for use in the industrial north, and, with the help of standardised bricks which were made possible by the invention of the Hoffman Kiln, a similar style of working class housing was built throughout the industrial areas of England.[3]

It was principally for this kind of industrial community that the chair makers of north east Cheshire and Lancashire were making their products, and it is not by accident that many of the known chair makers and chair making centres were either located around Manchester, or within other industrially based towns in north Cheshire. Chair makers worked too, in and around Liverpool, which also had a thriving commercial base, in industry, merchandising and shipping. Other chair makers worked in agricultural or mining villages, but

311

Figure NW2. Spindle back side chair. Ash. Attributed to the North West, c.1740-80.

Round turned front legs joined by two turned stretchers similar to front rail type A, Figure NW26. Back legs connected by single stretcher, second stretcher missing; triple side stretchers. Seat replaced with later seagrass with edge protective strips missing. Round back uprights with single row of three plain turned spindles supported between two elliptical cross rails, with additional turned cross rail above, similar to front stretcher.

Figure NW3. Spindle back side chair. Ash. Attributed to the North West, c.1740-80.

Straight round front legs with decayed feet, joined by two stretchers, type D, Figure NW26. Back legs connected by two stretchers and triple side stretchers. Replaced rush seat with three edge protective strips missing. Round back uprights with single row of three elliptical turned spindles similar to those shown in type k, Figure NW27, supported between two round cross rails with additional turned cross rail above.

Figure NW4. Spindle back side chair. Ash. Attributed to the North West, c.1740-80.

Round front legs with single ring turnings, joined by two elliptical stretchers with central double ring turning. Back legs connected by two stretchers and triple side stretchers. Painted rush seat with rear edge protective strip missing. Round back uprights with single row of four elliptical turned spindles with two ring central motif similar to front stretcher motif supported between two round straight cross rails with additional cross rail above, decoratively turned at ends.

in these cases, the development of the extensive canal system, particularly the Bridgewater and Sankey canals, and the various regional railway systems, enabled the rural chair makers to supply orders from urban retailers in the same way that other producers moved their products around the north of England. See Figure NW1 for details of the distribution of chair makers in the region.

In the north of Lancashire, in the Fylde to the west, and the forested Trough of Bowland to the north, Lancashire remained agriculturally based, and chairs common to the industrialised towns were no doubt equally familiar in the farmhouses, cottages and inns in this part of the country, as they were throughout the rural areas of Cheshire and Derbyshire to the south. To the north of these areas, however, in the Lancashire, Westmorland and Cumberland Dales, the terrain was that of hills and mountains, with many streams and lakes. The valleys were fit for limited cultivation only, and sheep farming was the principal form of agriculture. In this wildly beautiful,

but inhospitable area, the population was relatively small, with few principal towns.

Further chair styles developed here which were lighter in construction than the Lancashire and Cheshire varieties, and both spindle and ladder back styles were made. The general demeanour of these chairs is that of simplicity which seems to reflect a less industrialised form of production. The variation of design in the spindle back style is very marked, and examples are shown in Figures NW22-56. The ladder back style is of a particular design which has an unsophisticated elegance, examples of which are shown in Figures NW57-64. Interestingly, ash was the universal wood used in these chairs, and the rush seats were often painted black or blue, as original decoration.

A further style of armchair was made for use in the farmhouses and cottages of the Lancashire and Yorkshire Dales areas, which is unlike any other form of chair in the English tradition, and seems to be a distinct regional style attributable to

the north of England. This chair has a 'box' form construction with a panelled back and winged projections to keep out draughts. The chair is typically panelled and enclosed below the arm, and the legs are usually boxed in with panels. A drawer is sometimes included in the frieze. See Figures NW431-437.

Early Eighteenth Century Chairs

The chairs which were made in the late eighteenth and nineteenth centuries to supply the large industrial population of central Lancashire, and the rural communities to the north and south of this area had antecedents in earlier eighteenth century forms of turned spindle and ladder back chairs. These earlier chairs were probably much heavier and more naïve in style than the later chairs, with thick front leg posts and back uprights which, in some cases had pronounced finial turnings. The adoption of ladders, or spindles in the back design seems to have been the option which created one style of chair or the other, since the remainder

Plate 48. Wavy ladder back armchair. Ash with rush seat. North West region, c.1780.

Figure NW5. Spindle back side chair. Ash. Attributed to the North West, c.1760-80. The turnery devices adopted in the back uprights and front stretcher turnings of this chair are paralleled in the chair shown in Figure NW6. The ring turnings incorporated in the front legs are similar to those adopted in the early 18th century ladder back chairs from this region. See Figures NW10 and 12 for examples.

Round turned front legs joined by turned stretchers. Back legs connected by two stretchers and triple side stretchers. Decoratively turned back legs with pronounced finials. Rush seat with edge protective strips missing. Round back uprights with single row of three turned spindles supported between two straight turned cross rails with additional elaborately turned cross rail above.

Figure NW6. Spindle back side chair. Ash. Attributed to the North West, c.1760-1800. This style of chair is similar to 18th century chair designs found in both the English and American traditions[4] (see also Figure NW7).

Round turned front legs with pear motif in leg and turned foot. Front legs joined by turned stretcher. Back legs connected by single stretcher, double side stretchers. Replaced rush seat with edge protective strips missing. Round back uprights with single row of four turned spindles similar to front rail turnings found in many Lancashire chairs (see type A, Figure NW26), supported between two round cross rails with additional elaborately turned cross rail above with similar turnery design to front stretcher.

Figure NW7. Spindle back side chair. Ash. Newhaven, Connecticut, U.S.A., c.1700-50. The pear shaped turnery devices in the back uprights are similar to those in the front legs of the chair in Figure NW6. The front legs and connecting stretchers are similar to those adopted in the chair shown in Figure NW8. The identification of turnery modalities and general demeanour of this chair strongly suggest design transmission between the North West of England chairs and the corresponding American designs.

Round turned front legs joined by two turned plain stretchers. Back legs connected by single stretcher; double side stretchers. Replaced rush seat with edge protective strips missing. Round back uprights with pronounced finials, connected by a single row of three turned spindles supported between two round straight cross rails.

(Courtesy Yale University Museum and Art Gallery)

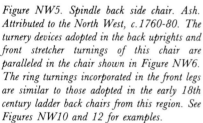

of the chair was made with similar turnings and construction. These relatively crude chairs gradually became more refined and lighter in structure as the eighteenth century proceeded. Finial turnings disappeared, and in the second half of the century, a great proliferation of styles of ladder back and spindle back chairs arose which continued to be made until at least the middle of the nineteenth century.

The number of progenitors was probably relatively small, the spindle back forms of which are the clear product of the wood turner, and are made entirely without sawn, square sectioned parts. Chairs from this tradition are much heavier in construction than the late eighteenth and nineteenth century counterparts. Shown in Figures NW2-9, they have

thick back uprights which are typically connected by three turned back cross rails, alternatively supporting three or four spindles. The heavily turned front legs are usually connected to the back legs by three turned stretchers, a strengthening feature which was continued in a number of nineteenth century Lancashire chairs. See Figures NW290 and 292 for examples.

The front legs are usually connected by two stretchers, which is also a design feature included in some nineteenth century chairs from this region. Other turnery features included in these chairs may be traced in nineteenth century chairs as well, for example the bulbous vertical back spindles of the chair in Figure NW6, and the front leg stretcher design shown in Figure NW3 is often used in the front stretchers of double row

spindle back chairs, as well as in early eighteenth century examples of ladder back and shaped splat back chairs, examples of which are shown in Figures NW11 and 15. Similarly, the front stretchers included in Figure NW2 as well as the vertical back spindles shown in Figure NW3, are both design forms found in nineteenth century single row spindle back chairs from Lancashire and the Cumbrian Dales.

Other variations of eighteenth century spindle back chairs have been recorded with pronounced finials on the back uprights, and with ring turnings in both back and front legs. These features have been recorded in both early eighteenth century ladder and spindle back chairs attributed to the north west of England. An example of an English chair which

Figure NW8. Spindle back side chair. Ash. Attributed to the North West, c.1780-1800.

Round turned front legs joined by two plain turned stretchers. Back legs connected by two stretchers; double side stretchers. Rush seat with edge protective strips missing. Round back uprights with single row of three elliptical turned spindles supported between two round straight cross rails with additional turned cross rail above with central ring turning.

incorporates these features is shown in Figure NW5. This chair has similar turnings in the back uprights to the chair shown in Figure NW6, which is attributed to the North West, and has similar leg turnings to those shown in the early eighteenth century ladder back chair shown in Figure NW12 from the same region, which suggests a sense of historical continuity between these designs.

Styles similar to this latter design were made, too, in the eastern states of the U.S.A. during the eighteenth century, an example of which is shown in Figure NW7. This chair has striking similarities in its turnery devices with Lancashire examples, including the 'pear' shaped turnings in the back uprights, which are also similar to the front leg turnings shown in Figure NW6. The front legs and connecting stretchers of the American chair are similar too, to those shown in Figure NW8. The common features which are found in the design of eighteenth century North West England spindle back chairs, and comparable American chair designs, present exciting evidence

of the transmission of regional style between these cultures.

Examples of ladder back chairs from the first half of the eighteenth century which exhibit North West regional design characteristics have also been recorded. In a similar way to the spindle back chairs shown in Figure NW9, these examples (Figures NW10-12) have simple thick front legs and back uprights which are connected by shaped ladders. These chairs were originally rush seated, but the example shown in Figure NW12 probably had a thin wooden seat. All were originally painted either blue or green, and have received several coats of darker paint overlaying this. It may be that the rush seats of these chairs were originally painted too, and that the practice of painting seats, shown particularly in the the nineteenth century Dales chairs had antecedents in this earlier tradition.

The chair illustrated in Figure NW10 shows the use of turned finials in a manner similar to that often found on carved chairs from the Charles II period. It has crescent

Figure NW9. A group of turned chairs photographed in Bakewell, De: ' shire. Attributed to the North West, c.1760-1800. These chairs are typical of the 18th century turned chairs which contained no square sawn parts and were made throughout the North West Midlands and the North West counties of England. Variations in the number of spindles and spindle shapes as well as front stretcher turnings are shown, but the essential design is similar, with heavy front legs and straight back uprights connected by three turned cross rails joined by a row of simple spindles. These designs were gradually refined and 19th century heirs to the tradition show a wide variety of turnery differences and juxtapositions of back cross rails. Examples are shown in Figures NW22-56.
(Courtesy M. Goldstone Antiques)

315

Plate 49. Elaborate bar top ladder back armchair. Ash with rush seat. North West region, c.1830.

*Plate 50. Bar top ladder back side chair. Alder and ash with rush seat.
Stamped 'P. LEICESTER' on rear of both legs. Peter Leicester was the
half brother of Charles Leicester, also a chair maker, of Macclesfield,
Cheshire (see Plate 51), and is recorded working in Plumley near to
Macclesfield, 1841-74.*

*Plate 51. Low ladder back nursing or fireside chair. Ash with rush seat,
originally stained black and varnished. Stamped 'C. LEICESTER' on
rear of both legs. Charles Leicester and his three sons variously worked
as chair makers at Chestergate, Macclesfield, 1816-80.*

*Plate 52. Standard ladder back side chair. Fruitwood with rush seat.
Decorated with gouge carving on both front legs. North West region,
c.1780.*

*Plate 53. Wavy ladder back side chair. Ash with rush seat. Stamped
'T. CLAYTON' on both back legs. Thomas Clayton is recorded as a
chair turner at Stockport in 1829.*

Figure NW10. Standard ladder back side chair. Ash. Attributed to Lancashire/Cheshire, c.1700-40. This is an early form of Lancashire/Cheshire ladder back chair which shows the massive turned uprights and legs often found in early vernacular chair examples, and has turned finials reminiscent of those incorporated in Carolean chairs. The ladder shape and front rail turning are found in late 18th and early 19th century examples of chairs from this region (see Figures NW268 and NW159).

Round turned front legs with single ring turning. Front legs joined by turned stretcher type c3, Figure NW289. Round back legs connected by single stretcher; double side stretchers. Original rush seat replaced by upholstered seat. Straight round turned back uprights terminating in pronounced turned finials. Five graduated crescent shaped ladders. Original blue/green paint covered by later layers of black paint.

Figure NW11. Standard ladder back side chair. Ash. Attributed to Lancashire/Cheshire, c.1740-80. This mid-18th century example of a Lancashire/Cheshire rush seated ladder back chair exhibits massive uprights and front legs, as well as incorporating ladder shapes which are found in examples of later 18th and 19th century ladder back chairs. The front stretcher turning is commonly found in double row spindle back chairs from this region.

Plain round turned front legs with decorative scribed ring turnings on the top, terminating in cup shaped feet. Front legs joined by two turned stretchers, type V, Figure NW70. Round back legs, connected by double stretchers; double side stretchers. Rush seat replaced by wooden seat. Straight round turned back uprights terminating in scribed ring and nipple finials. Four heavy graduated crescent shaped ladders. (top ladder damaged) Original blue/green paint covered by later layers of black paint.

Figure NW12. Standard ladder back side chair. Ash. Attributed to Lancashire/Cheshire, c.1720-60. Heavy uprights and legs. The ladder shape in this chair is found in some 19th century varieties of Lancashire/Cheshire ladder back chairs (see Figure NW344).

Round turned front legs with three decorative single ring turnings (replacement feet). Front legs joined by two plain turned stretchers. Round back legs connected by single stretcher. Double side stretchers. Straight round turned back uprights terminating in domed finials. Five graduated ladders shaped above and below with downward tip. Side stretchers rebated to hold a thin wooden seat. Layers of black paint covering original blue/green paint.

shaped ladders which are found in a number of later ladder back chairs from the region (see Figures NW314-324), as is the front stretcher turning which is found in the chair shown in Figure NW159, for example. The chair shown in Figure NW11 also has crescent shaped ladders, but has no pronounced finials. In this chair the use of the double stretcher, type v, Figure NW69, is interesting, since this is a common form utilised in many double row spindle back chairs from this region. (See Figure NW78 for example.)

The chair shown in Figure NW12 has thick turned front legs which are decorated with three ring turnings. This mode of decoration is a feature of certain styles of early eighteenth century northern European, as well

as American chairs. The use of two plain front leg stretchers is also typical of some early American and North West region ladder back chairs. The ladder shape adopted in this chair is found in some styles of late eighteenth and early nineteenth century ladder back chairs from the North West and is particularly similar to the style shown in Figure NW344 suggesting a design continuity between them. This chair had a wooden seat originally, since its side stretchers, now covered by later upholstery, are rebated to receive the wooden seat. This seat style has no counterpart in the later rush seated chair tradition from this area, and suggests a design relationship with the seventeenth century wooden seated chair design.

A further prototype has been recorded from this region which shows a number of design features found in other, later styles of chairs (NW13 and 14). This chair has a shaped splat rather than ladders or spindles, offering a completely different back design which was not adopted as a common form in this tradition. This chair has a complex system of design motifs, since its front legs are typical of type b (Figure NW351) found in the wavy-line ladder back group (Figures NW351-368); the side stretchers are type V (Figure NW70), typically found in double row spindle back chairs; the back leg style is typical of some Dales ladder back chair designs (see Figure NW60). The shaped stay rail and splat display a turner's attempts to emulate the

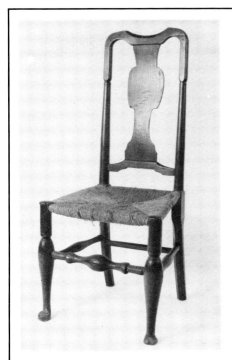

Figure NW13. Side chair. Ash. Attributed to the North West, c.1740-80. This chair is an attempt by a chair turner from the North West to produce a style which embodies a fashionable back design, reminiscent of chairs from the Queen Anne period, in combination with other features from this region's 'common' chairs. This chair contains a number of design motifs found in late 18th and early 19th century chairs from this region, including the front leg design which is typically found as leg type B in wavy line ladder back chairs (see Figure NW351); side stretchers which are commonly found in double row spindle back chairs from this region (see Figure NW70, type V), and swept,

chamfered back legs found in some Dales chairs (see Figures NW58 and 60).

Round turned upper front legs, bulbous turning below, terminating in pad feet. Front legs joined by turned stretcher. Square and lower chamfered swept back legs, connected by single stretcher. Rush seat with wooden edge protective strips missing. Round turned back uprights tapered to square section, which continues into a yoke shaped stay rail which joins a thin, shaped splat to a shaped lower cross rail.

Figure NW14. Side view of the chair shown in Figure NW13 illustrating the incorporation of regional design features, including the swept and chamfered back legs, side stretchers, and front legs.

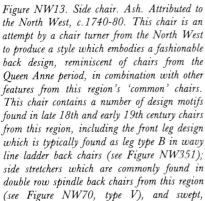

Figure NW15. Side chair. Ash. Attributed to Lancashire/Cheshire, c.1780-1800. This is a late 18th century example of a turner's attempt to produce a design which is influenced by chairs from the Queen Anne tradition. It adopts many design features of the Dales spindle back chairs, including the front legs and front rail, which are also shown in Figures NW29 and 31; and a painted rush seat which is commonly found in the Dales chair tradition.

Plain round turned tapered front legs, joined by turned stretcher, type A, Figure NW26. Round tapered back legs, connected by single stretcher. Double side stretchers. Painted rush seat with wooden edge protective strips. Round turned back uprights, tapered to round section, morticed into shaped stay rail terminating in ear shaped motifs. Thin, shaped central splat connected to lower stay rail which is similar in design to that shown in Figure NW13.

elegant style of some Queen Anne chairs. This unusual chair is included as an illustration of the extremely naïve stylistic results which can emerge from attempts to incorporate classicism within a vernacular style. Although few of the region's chair makers chose to produce such opposed unions of style, a few attempted to incorporate splats as back designs, and an example is shown in Figure NW15 which shows a basic Dales chair design which incorporates a shaped stay rail and splat, as well as type D, Figure NW26, front stretcher. The rush is also painted with original black paint.

Workshop organisation and chair makers' tools

The exact location of the early eighteenth century turner chair makers in the North West is unclear, but they were probably few in number, and scattered throughout the region. This is evidenced in that only twenty-five chair making workshops were recorded in this region at the end of the eighteenth century, at a time when the population was undergoing rapid expansion.[5] The makers who worked in this area probably shared related codes of design, and produced simple, regionally identifiable styles of spindle and ladder back chairs, which were used as common chairs throughout the North West, from Cumberland in the north, the Lancashire and Yorkshire Dales in the mid-region, and Cheshire and Derbyshire in the south. An illustration (Figure NW16) of a farmhouse kitchen

interior at Brinsley, near Nottingham, two miles from the Derbyshire border, in 1861, for example, shows two chairs of the eighteenth century spindle back type, similar to those shown in Figure NW2 included in a context with an armchair of a later Lancashire type (see Figure NW208). Examples of eighteenth century spindle back chairs from the North West are shown in Figures NW2-9 with a comparative example made in the U.S.A. Ladder back prototypes from the region are shown in Figures NW10-12.

The nature of the wood working trades, created partly by the qualities of the raw materials used, produced a different working environment from that of the textile and metal manufacturing trades which surrounded

Plate 54. Spindle back armchair. Ash with rush seat. North West region, c.1800.

Plate 55. Ladder back armchair. Ash with rush seat. Stamped 'SANDE...' on top of back left upright. Joseph Sanderson was recorded as a chair maker 1829-48, in Penrith, Cumberland.

Plate 56. Spindle back armchair. Ash with rush seat. Lancashire/Westmorland Dales area of the North West, c.1820.

Plate 57. Spindle back side chair. Ash with rush seat. North West region, c.1750.

Figure NW16. A watercolour of the kitchen interior of Mr. Hurst's Farm at Brinsley, near Nottingham, painted and dated 1861 by William Egley (1826-1916). Two examples of 18th century North West spindle back chairs and a slightly later armchair from Lancashire may be seen, illustrating the territorial movement which some chairs from the North West made by the mid-19th century and that different types of rush seated chairs were often found in the same setting. *(Courtesy Victoria and Albert Museum)*

them, and superficially produced an impression of a less mechanistic approach to the production of goods. However, the chair makers, particularly in the industrialised parts of Lancashire and North East Cheshire, probably organised their craft with similar principles to those of other manufacturing processes around them, and for whose workers the chairs were intended. This form of industrial organisation believed in mechanisation, a division of specialised labour, standardised and generally high qualities in the products they made, and, as a response to competition, a belief in diversification and the production of different designs.

Chair making was a widely dispersed craft in the North West by the second quarter of the nineteenth century, particularly in the counties of Lancashire and Cheshire, and makers' workshops were located in diverse social settings, which ranged from small agriculturally based and mining villages, textile and silk weaving towns, to the industrially based suburbs of Manchester, and

the dockland area of Liverpool. This diversity of location might be expected to have led to differences in the production techniques, and, in turn, to the kinds of chair qualities produced. The evidence of the chairs suggests, however, that although great diversity of chair design was produced, the manufacturing techniques were generally similar for the majority of the designs. These qualities significantly include the use of circular sawn timber to produce segments for turnery, as opposed to the cleaving of segments more commonly found in rural chair making traditions. The evidence of generally similar production techniques, and a recognisable system of regional patterns suggests that a common code of both design and manufacturing practice existed, of which evidently many of the chair makers were aware and observed in their working lives. Very little information has been found which refers directly to the workshop organisation of chair makers in the North West. However, two records which have come to light

are very explicit and allow an insight into the working practices[6] and the hand tools used by Lancashire chair makers.[7]

The first account refers to the itemising of stock and equipment of a chair and bobbin turner's workshop in the village of Aighton Bailey and Chaigley in north east Lancashire in the first quarter of the nineteenth century.[8] The contents of this workshop were listed following a fire which entirely destroyed the stock, machinery and fabric of the workshop (Figure NW17). The owner, Mark Chippindale, made representations to the parish for public money to restore the workshop, in the form of a deposition which laid out the precise contents which were destroyed, including details of the machinery, tools and devices, completed bobbins, baskets to store them in, woods, completed chairs and chair parts, as well as their values. Details of the affidavits given by witnesses of the fire, and the statements given by supporters of the petition are published in verbatim form in the

[A] The Schedule of Inventory of Stock in Trade Timber Machinery Tools Utensils and Effects and the value of each Article set opposite thereto herein before referred unto — viz.

		£	s	d
One Drum and pit-wheel	valued at	9	15	8
One press	Do	3	"	"
Two Grind Stones	Do	"	10	"
One circular Saw and Fixture	Do	5	"	"
One pair of Bellows and Articles belonging to the Smithy	Do	8	15	"
Vice, Boards and Benches	Do	2	10	"
Two Boreing Lathes and Fixtures	Do	6	17	"
Three Turning Benches and Fixtures	Do	15	3	"
One press Drill and Drawery	Do	2	9	"
carried to paper annexed		£53	19	8

	£	s	d
Brought from paper annexed	53	19	8
[B] Drums and Shafts	11	10	"
Do	6	"	2
Gallowses and Fixtures	2	"	"
Turning Bench and Fixtures	3	3	"
Belts and Straps	20	"	"
Tools of all Descriptions used in the Business	24	"	"
Stocks and Benches	2	"	"
Baskets and packsheets	4	16	"
Bobbins ready for sale viz.			

	£	s	d		£	s	d
Four Gross of Stublin [?] Bobbins at 3 per Gross	12:	"	"				
Seven Do of large roving Do at 2/5 per Do	15:	15	—				
15 —— Do of —— Do —— Do at 28s/per Do	21:	"	—				
24 —— Do of spinning. Do at 9s/per Do	70:	16:	—				
20 Do of Barrels in the Rough at 5s pr Do	5:	"	"				
6 Do of Do —— at 6s per Do	1:	16:					
27 Do of Ends and Barrels for spinning	6:	15:	"				
Bobbins at 5s per Gross					73	2	"
24 Gross of Bushes for bobbins in the rough at 4/5 per Gross					5	6	"
4080 feet of Deal Boards					42	10	"
188½ feet of Ash and Eder Boards					4	10	"
133¼ Do feet of Birch Boards					6	13	4
Bobbin wood					8	"	"
Joists ffellies and Door Steads					5	4	"
Ash wood					1	"	"
Crab and Alder Boards					4	10	"
Training Benches					2	1	"
Shelving Boards					2	11	4
Chair Backs and Chairs finished					46	10	"
					329	6	6

Figure NW17. An extract showing the workshop contents from the deposition made in 1815 by Mark Chippindale, chair maker and bobbin turner of Aighton Bailey and Chaigley, Lancashire, to his parish authorities for financial assistance to reinstate his workshop and contents destroyed by fire. The details of the circumstances of the fire are given as an Appendix on pp.438 and 439.

(Courtesy County Archivist of the Lancashire County Record Office. Cat No. QSP 1813)

Appendix to this chapter on pp.438 and 439.

Here was a workshop with a high degree of mechanisation. Section B of Figure NW17 includes 'Drums and Shafts' and 'Belts and Straps' which were probably used to drive the many pieces of equipment that the workshop contained, including those in Section A which lists two grind stones, one circular saw, two boring lathes, three turning benches in Section A and a further one in Section B, and one press drill. A further unidentified piece of equipment 'Gallowses and Fixtures' is also included in Section B, and may have required belt driven power. The source of power for the ten or eleven pieces of equipment was undoubtedly water, since the witnesses's affidavits claimed that 'The said Mark Chippindale, the rest of his family, and diverse others endeavoured as

Figure NW18. A rear and side view of the front leg of a Lancashire/Cheshire spindle back chair illustrating the circular saw marks made in creating the blank segment for turning.

Figure NW19. A late 19th century photograph of an itinerant rush seat worker in the north of England replacing rush in a removable seat frame. Such a worker did his work wherever he could, carrying his materials with him. The rushes he is using are freshwater rushes, Scirpus Lacustris, *which have a larger stem than the saltwater variety.*

much in them lay to save and preserve the said stock, tools, utensils, and machines from being burnt and destroyed by the said fire, they were utterly unable to save any part thereof except one large water wheel which was very much injured by the fire, and its being hastily thrown down and removed.'[9]

We know that the roof was thatched from the comment that 'The dryness of the weather, and the building being wholly thatched, the building was completely destroyed,'[10] and it is probable that if the destruction was complete, the walls were wooden.

Given the large number of pieces of machinery, wood stocks and saleable turned goods which the workshop held, the building must have been large, and the overall impression created is an image of a thatched roofed workshop situated on the banks of a stream, with its turning water wheel. Inside the workshop, this scene of rural tranquillity must have been diminished amongst the clatter and noise of belt driven lathes, circular saw and post drill. This industrious and bustling image is certainly confirmed in the long list of turned parts produced for the textile industry which included 'bobbins, barrels, ends and barrels for spinning, and bushes for bobbins completed and ready for sale',[11] as

well as the large number of chairs and chair parts which must have taken up a considerable storage area, for the inventory ends with a reference to chair backs and chairs finished, valued at £46.10.0d. Given that the average man's wage would probably have been between 5/- (25p) and 9/- (45p) per week at that time,[12] and a rush seated chair perhaps cost 2/6d. (12½p),[13] the stock of chairs must have been in excess of 300, representing a considerable capital investment.

Since Chippindale was conversant with turning bobbins for the textile trade, it seems reasonable to assume that he may have also turned spindles for the backs of at least some, if not all, of his chairs. The price of his individual chairs is not exactly known, but a reference to spindle back chairs being sold by a retailer as part of a list of household furnishings in Preston in 1857 is shown in Figure NW67. This itemises '6 Spindle chairs' at 18/- (3/- each). Since inflation rose little during the eighteenth century, this probably confirms the approximate value of Chippindale's chairs in 1815.

The quantity and value of the workshop contents indicates that Chippindale had developed a business containing a considerable investment in saleable stock, and the means of

producing the work, although he evidently had little money for re-instating his workshop outside of his stock holding. He leased his workshop rather than owned it, since the petition states (Appendix, p.438 and 439) '. . . the petitioner being also obliged by his lease to rebuild the workshop'.[14]

It may also be that Chippindale sublet part of his workshop, since other tradesmen, described as 'neighbours' had detailed knowledge of the workshop (see section B of Appendix), which includes mention of John Emmott, cordwainer, John Kendrick, joiner, Robert Coulthurst, carpenter and millwright, who all swore on oath as witnesses and supporters of Mark Chippindale's deposition. These men may have used the workshop for their own trades, particularly of joinery and carpentry, since entries on the schedule of contents 'B' (Figure NW17) include 'joists, ffellies and door steads', and '4080 feet of deal boards', and 'shelving boards'. Another entry itemises 'one pair of bellows and articles belonging to the smithy'.[15] Whether the smithy constituted part of the workshop, or if the equipment was present for repair, is not stated.

If the Chippindale chair making workshop was typical of those in the North West, it is not surprising that so many turned chairs were produced there, since at this early date, the workshop was operating an essentially industrial process which allowed for the rapid production, on the circular saw, of blank sections for turning. An example of the use of the circular saw in preparing blank sections is shown in Figure NW18, which illustrates saw marks on two sides of the chair leg, allowing only the bare material necessary to produce the turned part.

The belt driven lathes would have reduced the back-breaking labour needed to treadle both pole and fly-wheel powered lathes, and made a longer working day possible, as well as increasing output. The presence of a press drill would no doubt have been used to make the round mortises for the legs and stretchers.

Unfortunately, the inventory gives only a general description of 'tools of all descriptions used in the business',[16] although the value at £24 was high in relation to other items, and indicates that many tools were present. However, a further document, the will of James Tomlinson, turner and chair maker of Lancaster, who died in 1848, provides insight into the hand tools used by a chair turner from the region. This text gives a detailed list of the tools and other effects which Tomlinson left to his two sons who followed him as chair makers, and who were evidently left part of his stock in trade sufficient for them to make a living at the craft, provided that they combined their resources. The part of the will which deals with Tomlinson's bequests to his sons reads as follows:

To my eldest son Thomas my watch, metal Tankard, my longer cramp, Bed brace, Hand screws, Holdfast, large Glue kettle, two mortice chisels, one pair of pinchers, one Trying Plane, a Turning saw, a Dancing Saw, a wood Square, Six chair bows, one Bench, a Mattrefs making box, a Drawing knife, a pair of Shears, five Saw files, one Screw Cutter and one Bed brace, and my Vice.

To my Son John my lesser cramp, Iron Brace and bits, two handsaws, and dovetail saw, Axe, Adze, two Trying Planes, all my smoothing planes, one Turning Saw, my Bevil, two Screw cutters, one Drawing knife, two wood Braces, six mortice chisels, one pair of Plyers, one Holdfast, a Bench, two pinchers, all my hammers, my oilstone, all my paring chisels, two spoke shaves, a Dancing Saw, a wood square and

Figure NW20. The Uppermill, Lancashire, rush cart in 1896, showing the skill in producing the tightly packed bundles of rush, on top of which a man, dressed as a green 'imp', sat. The decoration was made with flowers and coloured papers, and each village or neighbourhood vied with each other to produce the most decorative cart.

four Saw files.'[17]

The tools may be placed into categories of use in the following ways: *Holding devices:* One lesser and one longer cramp, several handscrews, two holdfasts, two benches, one vice, one pair of plyers; *Cutting tools:* Eight mortice chisels, three trying planes, two draw knives, one pair of shears, three pairs of pinchers, three screw cutters, one axe, one adze, two + smoothing planes, two + paring chisels; *Marking tools:* Two wood squares, one bevil; *Boring tools:* Iron brace and bits, two wood braces;

Saws: Two turning saws, two dancing saws, two handsaws, one dovetail saw; *Miscellaneous:* Glue kettle, fourteen saw files, two + hammers, oilstone, bed brace, six chair bows, mattress making box.

The list of tools and devices is certainly as comprehensive as would be used by a cabinet maker, and would have been more than extensive for a turner chair maker.

Interestingly, no lathe is mentioned, and since Tomlinson is described in his will explicitly as a 'turner chair-maker', this creates an enigma. This inventory, and the prominence given to the bequest, serves to indicate the importance of tools in a working craftsman's life, and the necessity of passing them on for the livelihood of the next generation.

The use of alder and other woods

Vernacular craftsmen, typified by Chippindale and Tomlinson, worked with locally grown timbers rather than with mahogany and other imported woods. However, Lancashire was not particularly well provided with woodland which could have supplied the chair and general turnery trade, and John Holt commented in 1795, 'There are no natural woods [in Lancashire] of any consequence to merit attention. The plantations are in general intended as embellishments for gentlemen's seats, cover for game, or shelter from the blast, rather than with a view of supplying the country with timber, and preventing importation.'[18] Holt's general lack of enthusiasm for this region's timber growing capabilities was emphasised in his description of stunted trees and hedgerows to the east of Lancashire, bent to the east under the constant battering of the Atlantic winds. To the west of the county, however, he reported that Scots fir, sycamore, platanus and ash thrived, and 'seem most congenial to the soil'.[19] Holt also mentioned that in the north, many acres of coppice were cut down each year.

Above all, however, Lancashire developed the use of alder as an important wood for many trades, and alder, in conjunction with the ubiquitous ash, became the predominant woods in the chair making trade. Alder is an unusual choice of material, for this wood is not extensively used elsewhere in the English chair making tradition, and is, therefore, often useful in providing a key to the origin of a particular chair design to the North West.

Alder grows where other trees will not, and it particularly favours swampy areas. Holt noted, 'The alder has of late years become an article of great consequence, for the demand for its wood, which makes the best poles whereon to hang cotton yarn to dry, that wood acquiring a fine polish by frequent use, nor does it splinter by exposure to the weather, and its bark also sells at nearly a penny per pound as an article for dye'.[20] The cultivation of this tree variety was initially undertaken in the late

eighteenth century as a way of supporting the edges of rivers and canal banks, with its fine network of roots; as well as for a fabric dye which was produced from the stripped, boiled bark. Many uses for the tree appear to have developed from the early nineteenth century, and alder, grown as a coppice wood, gradually became used as an important turnery wood. Edlin, in his survey of woodland crafts in Britain, comments that 'Alder is soft, weak and perishable... But softness in timber may sometimes be an advantage from the economic point of view. The turners of every day household goods prefer a soft wood that can be cut with the minimum of effort and therefore produced cheaply.'[21]

The twentieth century survey which Edlin produced included uses for the bark of alder as an historically important agent in tanning leather, until the late nineteenth century. The wood was also used to turn broom heads and, importantly, to make hat blocks for the hat makers of London, Luton, and south east Lancashire, who needed a soft wood which could be recarved to suit the different shapes required by changing fashions.

Alder was best known in the North West, however, for its use in the manufacture of the traditional clogs*. They were made by travelling bands of clog makers who moved from one estate to another, felling the alder coppice, and making the outline sole shapes from the cleft green wood, with a specially adapted clogging knife. Footwear was made from this wood since, as well as its soft cutting properties, it has a natural resistance to water, which made it ideal for this purpose. The clog gave this area one of its distinctive qualities, for the sound of the metal shod clogs clattering on cobbled streets in the early morning, as hundreds of textile and other workers went to work, and the silence which followed, was an evocative part of industrial town life which heralded the start of every working day.

However, it was not for reasons of water resistance that alder was used as a major wood in the chair making trade, second only to ash. The more probable reason is that on cutting the surface of the wood, oxidation occurs, and the surface attains a pinkish-brown colour, which, particularly when enhanced with a mahogany stain, achieves an appearance similar

to mahogany in both grain and colour. The simulation of a wood normally reserved for more fashionable furniture no doubt seemed an advantageous use of materials to the makers, and, as well as producing chairs entirely in this wood, they commonly incorporated it in parts of chairs, particularly the back uprights and stay rails, in chairs otherwise made in ash. The use of alder as a substitute for mahogany was known in other areas, too, and Edlin comments that 'In the Highlands, where few other timbers were available, alder logs were sometimes immersed in peat bogs after felling, when they assumed an attractive reddish stain. This "Scots mahogany" was then used for furniture making.'[22]

Occasionally fruitwood was also used in this region's chairs, and the Mark Chippindale's workshop inventory itemises his woods,[23] and provides an insight into the material used by this Lancashire chair maker. This record shows that the workshop had large quantities of deal boards which were probably used by the carpenters who also used his workshop, as well as birch and 'Eder' (willow),** which were typically used for small items of turnery, and were probably used for making bobbins. A further unexplained wood named as 'bobbin' wood is also included, valued at 8/-. In addition to these woods, 188½ ft. of ash and eder boards, are itemised valued at £4.10s.0d. Ash wood valued at £1.0s.0d., and crab (apple) and alder boards valued at £4.10s.0d. were also included. (See the complete schedule presented in Figure NW17 for further details.) The inclusion of ash and crab/alder at about the same values indicates that at this time, Chippindale was possibly incorporating ash and alder in his chairs, with some fruitwood.

The use of rushes

Rushes were clearly needed in some quantity for seating the chairs. No reference was made to rushes being

---

* These cheap and hard-wearing articles of footwear were peculiar to the North West and consisted of a wooden sole and leather uppers, with metal strips nailed below (Figure NW57 illustrates this form of footwear being worn by a hand-knitter from the Dales area of north Lancashire) and are distinct from the Dutch clogs or French sabots which are entirely made from carved wood.

**The word 'Eder' is probably a mis-spelling of the archaic term, 'Edder', which the Oxford Dictionary gives as an early term for Osier or Willow. (Salix.)

destroyed in the Chippindale work-shop fire, although 'Chair backs and chairs finished'[24] valued at £46.10.0d. indicate that a large quantity of chairs was either seated or about to be rushed. This perhaps indicates that rush 'matting' or seating was undertaken as a separate trade, probably by local villagers, who were usually men, since this craft requires much physical strength to twist the rush.

The rushes used were of two species: freshwater rush (*Scirpus Lacustris*) and saltwater rush (*Scirpus Maritimus*) and both species, as well as other species of *Scirpus,* were recorded growing widely in both Lancashire and Cheshire.[25]* These were harvested and dried by rush workers in early July, for use throughout the year. However, rush is a bulky material, and would have required a large dry storage building to hold the amount of material needed by a person engaged in the trade as a full time worker, and harvesting would have meant a considerable commitment of time and resources. Given that rush seating was considered a lowly trade, one which became the domain of itinerant workers during the latter part of the nineteenth century, it perhaps seems unlikely that all of the rush used in this region's chairs was harvested in this way. See Figure NW19 which shows a travelling rush seat worker in the north of England, replacing the rush in a removable framed chair seat). There were rush merchants and dealers in many Lancashire towns, with Preston alone, for example, having three merchants dealing in rush in 1854.[26] These merchants were dealing in rushes imported from Holland, where saltwater rush was an important economic crop. This importation of rushes is also evidenced in the Port of Liverpool tariffs which, in 1813, listed the dockage rates for importing consignments as 'Rushes, load of 63 bundles, 1 shilling'.[27]

However, the North West had a special relationship with rushes emanating from archaic times, which may help to explain the prolific manufacture of rush seated chairs in the area. Rushes are known to have been used throughout the British Isles for many centuries as a floor covering for the earthen or flag stoned floors of houses and churches. Floors were typically unswept, and were strewn with fresh rushes, some-times mixed with herbs or flowers,

which provided a warm and soft floor covering, collecting the dirt and dust below it, and was cleared out once a year when new rushes were available.**

The custom was commonly noted in churchwardens' accounts in many parts of England from the fifteenth to the eighteenth centuries, and the event of 'rushbearing' was clearly an important day. At Wilmslow, for example, in 1625, 7/6 was paid for sweeping out the church, polishing the pews and bringing in new rushes.[28] Earlier, at Congleton, Cheshire, in 1607, such events were attended by the ringing of the church bells, at the cost of one penny; and wine, ale and cakes were bought to refresh the rushbearers at a cost of sixpence.[29]

If churches seem to have been fastidious in their ritual of cleaning out the old rushes and replacing them with new, many private houses were not so particular, and many contemporary accounts from the sixteenth century indicate that the old rushes were often allowed to remain, and new rushes merely spread upon the surface.[30]

With the advent of the eighteenth century, improvement in building practices and the production of alterna-tive flooring materials became common, and, with increased understanding of hygiene this led to the general abandonment of rushes as a floor covering. However, although the original practice of spreading rushes ceased throughout most of England, the tradition of bearing rushes to the local church was continued as a ritual throughout the late eighteenth century and the whole of the nineteenth century in the North West, as well as in the Yorkshire Dales.[31]

Originally the rushes were brought to the church on sledges. This gradually changed to the use of a cart. The villages, particularly in south east Lancashire, vied with each other to produce the most decorative cart (see Figure NW20). The rush was neatly stacked to produce a tall structure which was plaited on the corners, decorated with flowers and coloured paper, and terminated with a bough from a tree. The rush was accompanied by a man dressed as a green 'imp' or demon, who sat on the top of the rushes, and who would be 'exorcised' and driven out on the arrival of the cart at the church. The building of these carts accompanied the 'wakes' or summer holiday times in the north of England, and

gradually this festival took the form of a pageant accompanied by music and Morris dancing, and often a fair. Alfred Burton, who observed and wrote about ancient folk customs in Lancashire and the Dales, wrote in the late nineteenth century that 'South East Lancashire was the home of the rush cart. Almost every village had one, and the rivalry between the people sometimes rose to such a pitch that bloodshed occurred.'[32]

The general secularisation of the rush bearing ritual was indicated in an account given by the author of a 'Pictorial account of Lancashire', in 1844, who commented that in Roch-dale, eight or nine carts paraded for this event, each having its own band. The rushes, however, were not strewn in the church, although the procession made its way around the town before eventually meeting at the church. The rushes were sold after the event, and it was noted of the Rochdale event that 'instead of men, horses now draw the cart, and in most places, the rushes are sold after the festivity, which, from having no small portion of a religious character, has degenerated into a mere holiday making'.[33]

Since the main use for rushes in the nineteenth century, apart from occasional bedding for cattle, was for seating chairs, it seems probable that the rushes were sold for that purpose after the ceremony. Since the men who built the cart probably also cut and dried the freshwater rush from local meres and water courses, they no doubt directly benefited from the sale of the rush. Given the wide-spread practice of the rush bearing

*Joseph Dickinson in his *Flora of Liverpool*, 1850, states that *Scirpus Lacustris* was 'Abundant in ditches on Bidston Marsh. Walton. Crosby Marsh. Plentiful in a pond near Car Lane, West Derby. Southport'. *Scirpus Maritimus* was to be found in abundance 'on Bidston Marsh, in ditches. Bootle shore near the Rimrose brook. Tranmere Pool, Scarce'.

In his *Flora of Cheshire*, 1899, Lord de Tabley states that *Scirpus Lacustris* could be found on the 'Edges of Radnor Mere, Alderley Park. The North West borders of Rostherne Mere. In Booth mill-dam near Knutsford; it grows in a pit 200 yds. due South of Tabley House; Also copiously at Budworth Mere and at Pickmere; In a pit by the Cheshire Midland Railway between Knutsford and Mobberley. Margin of a pit between Great Meols Station and Newton. Near Middle Trafford. Marbury Small Mere; The margin of Qoisley Big Mere, near Marbury; Marbury Mere; Combermere Mere. Brereton Mere, Congleton.' He added, 'I have seen but little of this in Cheshire'. The *Scirpus Maritimus* was 'generally diffused on the three coasts', but could be found at 'Norton Marsh; Extends to the extreme East of Richmond Marsh. Ditches off 'The Rake Lane' near Helsby Station; Ince Marsh.'

** In medieval times, this practice took place each summer, and Thomas Newton, for example, writing in his *Herball to the Bible* in 1587 commented that 'Sedge and rushes, with which many in the country do use in sommer time to strawe their parlours and churches, as well for coolness and pleasant smell.'

Figure NW21. These men worked in the old established woollen firm of J.B. Moore & Sons, Drapers and Woollen Manufacturers. They were photographed, sitting outside the carding mill at Hallthwaites Green, near Millom, Cumberland, in 1872. The owner of the firm is on the left. The chair to his left is of the style shown in Figure NW41, with the spindle turning shown in type n, Figure NW27.

Figure NW22. 'Dales' or single row spindle back armchair. Ash. Attributed to the North West, c.1800-70.

Round front legs, joined by turned stretcher, type B, Figure NW26. Back legs connected by single stretcher; double side stretchers. Chamfered back legs. Replaced rush seat with edge protective strips missing. Round back uprights inclined backwards with single row of four decoratively turned spindles, type A, Figure NW27, supported between two round curved cross rails with additional cross rail, below. Curved shaped arms, typical of this group, which mortice into back uprights with turned tenons. Arms supported by decoratively turned underarm supports, similar to those found in the Dales ladder back chair shown in Figure NW58.

Figure NW23. Chamfered back leg from the chair illustrated in Figure NW22. This design feature is unusual in the single row spindle design, but is commonly found in a range of North West ladder back chairs (see Figures NW248 and 269).

ceremony in all the North West counties throughout the nineteenth century, it may well be that a productive relationship was developed between the chair making trade and this ritual use of rush, one which mutually supported the existence of the other, until the ceremonies largely died out towards the end of the nineteenth century.

'Dales' or single row spindle backs and ladder backs

Of the many styles of rush seat chairs to develop in the North West from the beginning of the nineteenth century, a group of single row spindle back chairs, provides the widest repertoire of turnery devices of any group of chairs from this region. These chairs are constructed in a similar way to the earlier group shown in Figures NW2-NW9, and are made of turned parts only. They depart from their antecedents in being more refined in style, with lighter back uprights and front legs. Greater invention of design is shown, too, in the wide range of front stretchers and back spindle turning devices which are incorporated. However, they retain the essential simplicity of design which typifies the earlier styles.

The later single row spindle back

327

Figure NW24. A late 19th century painting of the interior of a traditional Lakeland cottage. The furnishings include a corner cupboard, table, and two simple Dales chairs; a similar one to the right hand chair is shown in Figure NW25. *(Photograph courtesy Museum of Lakeland Life and Industry)*

Figure NW25. Dales or single row spindle back side chair. Ash. Attributed to the North West, c.1800-70.

Round front legs joined by turned stretcher, type B, Figure NW26. Back legs connected by single stretcher; double side stretchers. Round turned back legs. Rush seat with edge protective strips missing. Round back uprights with single row of three decoratively turned spindles, type c, Figure NW27, supported between two round curved cross rails with additional turned cross rail above.

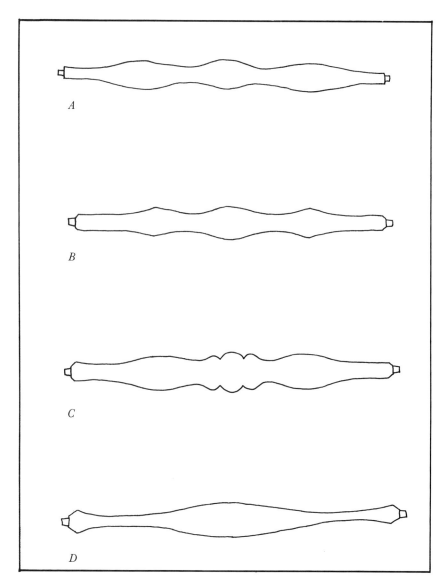

A

B

C

D

Figure NW26. Front stretcher turnings incorporated in Dales or single row spindle back chairs. Types A, B and D are also included in Dales ladder back varieties.

chairs are dissimilar to the early prototypes in not having three side leg connecting stretchers or two front stretchers. Some examples also depart from the simple, straight back uprights typical of the early group, and have backs which are reclined from the seat to give extra comfort. These chairs have chamfered back legs, or a square block at seat level, and are round turned below, in the manner of some double row spindle back chairs from the North West.

The later Dales chairs have a natural counterpart in a simple ladder back chair, which has a similar frame to the spindle back, but instead of spindles, includes four simple ladders in the back design, with a large curved ladder at the top, and three domed ladders below. Unlike the spindle back chairs, little design variation was made, and the essential form of the armchair shown in Figure NW58 and the side chair shown in Figure NW60 are the most common varieties.

Hearsay evidence suggests that both the spindle and ladder back chairs were made for use in areas north of the Lancashire industrial conurbations, and were essentially a

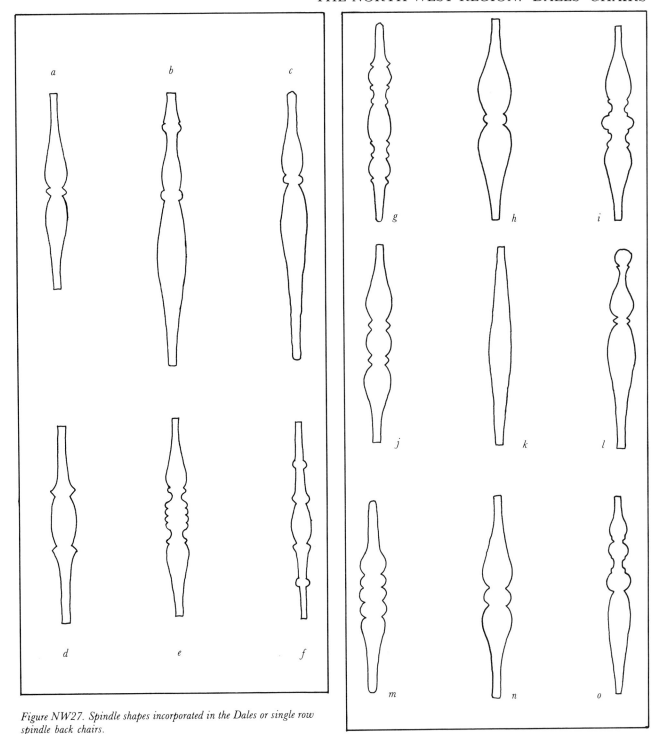

Figure NW27. Spindle shapes incorporated in the Dales or single row spindle back chairs.

common chair for the rural population of Lancashire and West Yorkshire, and as far north as the Cumberland and Westmorland Dales. This is supported by pictorial evidence (see Figures NW21, 24 and 40).

The only name stamped chair to be recorded from this group is a common form of Dales ladder back armchair, attributed to Joseph Sanderson, chair maker, of Castlegate, Penrith, Cumberland (fl.1829-48) (see Figures NW58 and 59). This maker was one of a number of chair makers from Westmorland and Cumberland who were centred in the major regional towns of Kendal and Penrith in Cumberland, and Carlisle and Wigton in Westmorland. These towns provided the major trade centres for a large and sparsely populated region, and no doubt household chairs, in common with other goods, would have been supplied from these few centres of trade.

Interestingly, many chairs in this group have painted seats which appear to be original. If this is so, it would seem to be a distinctive regional way of 'finishing' the seats.

The light structure of the Dales chairs also suggests a marked difference in design from the relatively heavy forms of double row spindle back chairs and heavy ladder back styles associated with the industrial areas of Lancashire and Cheshire, and as such, they are compatible in style with other single row spindle back chairs which were made in the rural areas of Herefordshire and Shropshire on the Welsh border, and those made in north Staffordshire on the Cheshire border. See Chapter 6, pp.297-307 for examples.

Figure NW28. Dales or single row spindle back armchair. Ash. Attributed to the North West, c.1800-70. This chair is a 'hybrid' of two regional styles; single, and double row spindle backs. The curved shaped arms which mortice into back uprights with turned terminal tenons, are supported by turned underarm supports with urn motifs. The front legs, front stretcher turning, arm design and back leg design are all typical of those found in two and three row spindle back armchairs from this region (see Figures NW106 and 118), suggesting that the makers of the single row spindle back chairs were probably also making other spindle back chairs.

Turned front legs terminating in pad feet, joined by turned stretcher. Back legs connected by single stretcher; double side stretchers. Chamfered lower back legs. Rush seat with edge protective strips. Round back uprights with single row of four turned spindles, supported between two broad flattened cross rails, with two additional cross rails above and below.

Figure NW29. Dales or single row spindle back armchair. Ash, c.1800-70. The incorporation of square tapered front legs, typical of those found in the first group of rush seat kitchen chairs (see Figures NW373 and 374 for example), is an interesting amalgamation of regional styles, and further illustrates the community of chair designs which were made, as contemporaries, by the North West chair turners, and their willingness, on occasion, to experiment with the transference of chair parts to other styles. *(Courtesy Mrs J. Eddy)*

Square tapered front legs joined by stretcher typical of those found in many double row spindle back chairs. Back legs connected by single stretcher; double side stretchers. Chamfered lower back legs. Replaced rush seat with edge protective strips missing. Round back uprights with two flattened cross splats connected by three spindles turning type b; Figure NW27. Further flattened rail above. Typical curved shaped arms which mortice into back uprights with tapered terminal tenons, supported by turned underarm supports. The back uprights have two turned projecting wings which were used as supports for hanging a padded cushion or back support.

Figure NW30. Dales or single row spindle back armchair. Ash. Attributed to the North West, c.1800-70.

Round front legs tapering towards foot, joined by turned stretcher, type A, Figure NW26. Chamfered back legs ocnnected by single stretcher; double side stretchers. Replaced rush seat with three edge protective strips missing. Round back uprights with single row of three turned spindles supported between two broad flattened cross rails. Typical curved shaped arms which mortice into back upright with turned terminal tenon, supported by turned underarm supports.

Figure NW31. Dales or single row spindle back side chair. Ash. Attributed to the North West, c.1800-70. This side chair is the generic counterpart to the armchair illustrated in Figure NW32.

Round front legs tapering towards foot, joined by turned stretcher, type D, Figure NW26. Round turned back legs, tapering towards foot, connected by single stretcher; double side stretchers. Painted rush seat with edge protective strips missing. Round back uprights with single row of three turned long spindles, type b, Figure NW27, supported between two flattened cross rails.

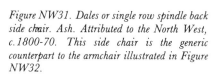

Figure NW32. Dales or single row spindle back armchair. Ash. Attributed to the North West, c.1800-70.

Round front legs tapering towards feet, joined by eliptical turned stretcher. Back legs connected by single stretcher; double side stretchers. Chamfered lower back legs. Painted rush seat with edge protective strips. Round back uprights with single row of three turned spindles supported between two broad flattened cross rails. Curved shaped arms which mortice into back upright supported by turned underarm supports.

Figure NW33. Dales or single row spindle back side rocking chair. Ash. Attributed to the North West, c.1800-70. The back uprights have similar turnings to the arms in the child's chair illustrated in Figure NW56.

Round front legs tapering towards foot to mortice into rockers, joined by turned stretcher, type A, Figure NW26. Round turned back legs connected by single stretcher; double side stretchers. Plywood replacement seat. Round back uprights, decoratively turned at top, with single row of three splayed decoratively turned spindles type a, Figure NW27, supported between two flattened cross rails.

Figure NW34. Dales or single row spindle back armchair. Ash. Attributed to the North West, c.1800-70.

Round front legs with quarter round blocks at seat level, tapering towards foot, joined by turned stretchers, type C, Figure NW26, back legs connected by single stretcher; double side stretchers. Chamfered back legs. Replacement plywood seat. Round back uprights inclined backwards with single row of four decoratively turned spindles, type e, Figure NW27, supported between two round curved cross rails with additional turned cross rail below. Curved shaped arms, typical of the style, which mortice into back upright with turned terminal tenon, supported by turned underarm supports.

Figure NW35. Dales or single row spindle back side chair. Ash. Attributed to the North West, c.1840-70.

Multiple ring turned front legs morticing into seat frame, terminating in vase shaped feet, joined by decoratively turned stretcher with multiple rings. Back legs connected by single stretcher; double side stretchers. Round turned back legs. Rush seat with edge protective strips missing. Round back uprights with single row of three multiple turned spindles, type e, Figure NW27, supported between two curved cross rails with additional cross rail above.

Figure NW36. Dales or single row spindle back armchair. Ash. Attributed to the North West, c.1800-70. This chair is similar in demeanour to that shown in Figure NW22 except that the back legs are not chamfered and the spindle design is different.

Round front legs joined by turned stretcher, type B, Figure NW26, back legs connected by single stretcher; double side stretchers. Chamfered lower back legs. Damaged rush seat, with edge protective strips. Round back uprights inclined backwards with single row of four decoratively turned spindles, type d, Figure NW27, supported between two round curved cross rails with additional cross rail below. Curved shaped arms which mortice into back upright with turned tenons, with decoratively turned underarm support, similar to turned underarm supports in Figure NW22.

Figure NW37. Dales or single row spindle back side chair. Ash. Attributed to the North West, c.1800-70. This side chair is the generic counterpart to the armchair shown in Figure NW36.

Round front legs joined by turned stretcher, type B, Figure NW26, round turned back legs connected by single stretcher; double side stretchers. Painted rush seat with wooden edge protective strips. Round back uprights with single row of four decoratively turned spindles, type d, Figure NW27, supported between two round curved cross rails with additional cross rail below.

Figure NW38. Dales or single row spindle back armchair. Ash. Attributed to the North West, c.1800-70.

Round front legs joined by turned stretcher, type C, Figure NW26, back legs connected by single stretcher; double side stretchers. Chamfered lower back legs. Rush seat with edge protective strips missing. Round back uprights with single row of three decoratively turned spindles supported between two round curved cross rails with additional elaborately turned cross rail above. Curved shaped arms which mortice into back upright with turned terminal tenons, supported by turned underarm supports.

Figure NW39. Dales or single row spindle back side chair. Ash. Attributed to the North West, c.1800-70. This side chair is the generic counterpart to the armchair shown in Figure NW38.

Round turned legs with quarter round turning above, tapering towards feet, joined by turned stretcher, type C, Figure NW26. Chamfered back legs connected by single stretcher; double side stretchers. Rush seat with three edge protective strips missing. Round back uprights, inclined backwards, with single row of three decoratively turned spindles, type f, Figure NW27, supported between two round curved cross rails with additional elaborately turned and curved cross rail above.

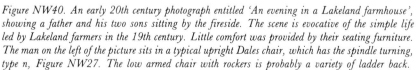

Figure NW40. An early 20th century photograph entitled 'An evening in a Lakeland farmhouse', showing a father and his two sons sitting by the fireside. The scene is evocative of the simple life led by Lakeland farmers in the 19th century. Little comfort was provided by their seating furniture. The man on the left of the picture sits in a typical upright Dales chair, which has the spindle turning, type n, Figure NW27. The low armed chair with rockers is probably a variety of ladder back.

Figure NW41. Dales or single row spindle back side chair. Ash. Attributed to the North West, c.1800-70.

Round front legs tapering towards feet, joined by turned stretcher, type B, Figure NW26. Round turned tapered back legs connected by single stretcher; double side stretchers. Replaced rush seat with edge protective strips missing. Round back uprights with single row of four decoratively turned spindles, type i, Figure NW27, supported between two round curved cross rails with additional cross rail below.

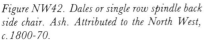

Figure NW42. Dales or single row spindle back side chair. Ash. Attributed to the North West, c.1800-70.

Round front legs tapering towards feet, with top of front leg turnery design similar to that found in other Lancashire chairs. Front legs joined by turned stretcher, type D, Figure NW26. Round turned back legs, tapered at feet, connected by single stretcher; double side stretchers. Rush seat with wooden edge protective strips. Round back uprights with single row of four turned spindles, type h, Figure NW27, supported between two round curved cross rails with additional cross rail below.

Figure NW43. Dales or single row spindle back side chair. Ash. Attributed to the North West, c.1800-70.

Round turned front legs with quarter round turning above, joined by turned stretcher, type B, Figure NW26. Chamfered back legs connected by single stretcher; double side stretchers. Rush seat with protective strips missing. Round back uprights inclined backwards, with single row of four decoratively turned spindles, supported between two round curved cross rails with additional cross rail below.

Figure NW44. Dales or single row spindle back side chair. Ash. Attributed to the North West, c.1800-70.

Quarter round upper front legs, round turned below, joined by turned stretcher, type A, Figure NW26. Chamfered back legs connected by single stretcher; double side stretchers. Seat replaced with seagrass. Round back uprights inclined backwards, with single row of four decoratively turned spindles, type l, Figure NW27, supported between two round curved cross rails with additional cross rail below.

Figure NW45. Dales or single row spindle back side chair. Ash. Attributed to the North West, c.1800-70.

Round front legs terminating in vase shaped feet, joined by turned stetcher, type B, Figure NW26. Chamfered lower back legs connected by single stretcher; double side stretchers. Painted rush seat with edge protective strips. Round back uprights with single row of three decoratively turned spindles, type c, Figure NW27, supported between two round curved cross rails with additional cross rail below.

Figure NW46. Dales or single row spindle back side chair. Ash. Attributed to the North West, c.1800-70.

Round front legs terminating in vase shaped feet, joined by unusual turned stretcher. Round turned back legs connected by single stretcher; double side stretchers. Rush seat with three edge protective strips missing. Round back uprights with single row of three decoratively turned spindles supported between two round curved cross rails with additional cross rail above.

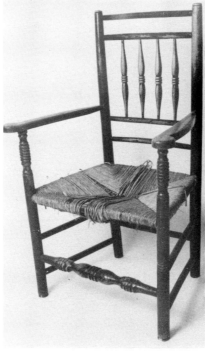

Figure NW47. Dales or single row spindle back side chair. Ash. Attributed to the North West, c.1800-70.

Round front legs terminating in cup shaped and tapered feet, joined by unusual turned stretcher. Round turned back legs, tapered at feet, connected by single stretcher; double side stretchers. Rush seat with three edge protective strips missing. Round back uprights with single row of three elliptical turned spindles, type k, Figure NW27, similar to those found in Figure NW4, supported between two round curved cross rails with additional cross rail above.

Figure NW48. Dales or single row spindle back armchair. Ash. Attributed to the North West, c.1800-70.

Round front legs with multiple ring turnings. Round turned back legs connected by single stretcher; double side stretchers. Damaged rush seat, with edge protective strips missing. Round back uprights with single row of four decoratively turned spindles, type e, Figure NW27, supported between two round curved cross rails with additional turned cross rails above and below. Flattened scroll shaped arms which mortice into back upright with tapered tenon.

Figure NW49. Dales or single row spindle back armchair. Ash. Attributed to the North West, c.1800-70.

Round front legs with square blocks at seat level, joined by turned stretcher, type B, Figure NW26. Back legs connected by single stretcher; double side stretchers. Round turned back legs. Rush seat with edge protective strips. Round back uprights inclined backwards with single row of four turned spindles, type m, Figure NW27, supported between two round curved cross rails with additional cross rail below. Curved shaped arms which mortice into back upright with decoratively turned terminal tenons.

Figure NW50. Dales spindle back armchair. Ash. Attributed to the North West, c.1800-70.

Round front legs joined by turned stretcher, type B, Figure NW26. Chamfered lower back legs connected by single stretcher. Double side stretchers. Rush seat, with wooden edge strips. Round back uprights inclined backwards with upper and lower galleries of four turned long spindles separated by a row of five shorter turned spindles supported between four curved round cross rails, with additional elaborately turned cross rail above. Curved shaped arms which mortice into back upright with turned tenon, supported by turned underarm supports with urn shaped motifs.

Figure NW51. Dales or single row spindle back side chair. Ash. Attributed to the North West, c.1800-70.

Round front legs terminating in vase shaped feet, joined by turned stretcher, type i, Figure NW70, typical of those found in many double row spindle back chairs. Back legs connected by single stretcher; double side stretchers. Round turned back legs. Rush seat with edge protective strips missing. Curved round back uprights with single row of three decoratively turned spindles, type a, Figure NW27, supported by two round curved cross rails with additional cross rail above.

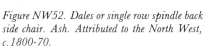

Figure NW52. Dales or single row spindle back side chair. Ash. Attributed to the North West, c.1800-70.

Warped round turned front legs with quarter round turning above, joined by turned stretcher, type B, Figure NW26. Chamfered lower back legs connected by single stretcher; double side stretchers. Painted rush seat with edge protective strips. Round back uprights with single row of five decoratively turned spindles, type h, Figure NW27, supported between two round curved cross rails with additional cross rail below.

Figure NW53. Dales or single row spindle back armchair. Ash. Attributed to the North West, c.1800-70.

Round front legs with quarter round blocks at seat level joined by turned stretcher, type B, Figure NW26. Back legs connected by single stretcher; double side stretchers. Chamfered lower back legs. Replaced sea grass seat. Round back uprights inclined backwards with single row of five turned spindles, type d, Figure NW27, supported between two round curved cross rails with additional cross rail below. Curved shaped arms, typical of the style, which mortice into back upright with turned terminal tenons, plain turned underarm supports.

Figure NW54. Dales or single row spindle back side rocking chair. Ash. Attributed to the North West, c.1800-70.

Round front legs tapering towards feet to mortice into rockers, joined by turned stretcher, type B, Figure NW26. Round turned tapering back legs connected by single stretcher; double side stretchers. Replacement fabric seat. Round back uprights with single row of four decoratively turned spindles, type n, Figure NW27, supported between two round curved cross rails with two additional cross rails below.

Figure NW55. Child's Dales or single row spindle back armchair. Ash. Attributed to the North West, c.1800-70.

Round front legs tapering towards feet, turned to fit into rockers, joined by plain turned stretcher. Back legs connected by single stretcher; no side stretchers. Round turned back legs. Painted rush seat with edge protective strips. Round back uprights with single row of three turned spindles, type n, Figure NW27, supported between two round straight cross rails. Round turned arms with slots cut to hold tray, which is missing. Turned underarm supports.

Figure NW56. Child's Dales or single row spindle back armchair. Ash. Attributed to the North West, c.1800-70.

Round front legs tapering towards feet, joined by decoratively turned stretcher. Round turned back legs connected by single stretcher; double side stretchers. Willow seat. Round back uprights with single row of three decoratively turned spindles, type o, Figure NW27, supported between two round curved cross rails with additional elaborately turned cross rail above. Round turned arms supported by turned underarm supports.

335

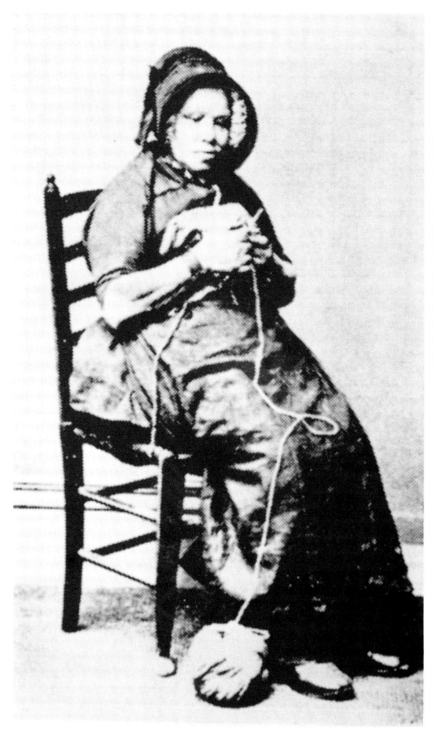

Figure NW58. Ladder back armchair. Ash. Cumberland, c.1820-50. Stamped 'J SANDERSON' on top of back upright (see Figure NW59).

Round front legs joined by turned stretcher type A, Figure NW26. Chamfered back legs connected by single stretcher; double side stretchers. Rush seat, with three edge protective strips missing. Round back uprights with four ladders, graduated in size, with a large curved ladder at the top, and three domed ladders below. Curved shaped arms which mortice into back upright with turned terminal tenons, supported by turned underarm supports.

Figure NW59. The stamp of Joseph Sanderson who was a chair maker working between 1829 and 1848 at Castlegate, Penrith. This stamp is in an extremely unusual place on the top upright of the chair shown in Figure NW58. The stamp has not completed its impression but sufficient is identifiable to strongly suggest that it is this maker's stamp.

Figure NW57. There was a very strong local tradition of hand knitting at Garsdale, close to the chair making centre of Kendal in Cumberland. The chair is typical of the Dales ladder back chairs shown in Figures NW58-64, except that pronounced finials are shown in this example. A cushion is used to provide greater comfort to the sitter, who wears the traditional regional footwear of wooden clogs.[34]
(Courtesy Dalesman Publishing Co.)

Figure NW60. Ladder back side chair. Ash. Attributed to the North West, c.1800-70. This chair is similar to the one in which Mally Gibson, a Dales knitter sits, in Figure NW57, except that this chair has less pronounced finials.

Round front legs tapering towards feet, joined by turned stretcher type B, Figure NW26. Back legs connected by single stretcher; double side stretchers. Chamfered steamed and bent back legs. Rush seat with three edge protective strips missing. Round back uprights inclined backwards with four ladders, graduated in size, with a large curved ladder at the top, and three domed ladders below.

Figure NW61. Unusually tall ladder back armchair. Ash. Attributed to the North West, c.1800-50.

Round front legs, joined by turned stretcher type B, Figure NW26. Chamfered back legs connected by single stretcher; double side stretchers. Replaced rush seat, with edge protective strips missing. Round back uprights inclined backwards with seven ladders, graduated in size, with a large curved ladder at the top, and six domed ladders below. Curved shaped arms which mortice into back upright with turned tenons, supported by turned underarm supports, similar to the turnings on the single row spindle armchair shown in Figure NW30.

Figure NW62. Ladder back side chair. Ash. Attributed to the North West, c.1800-70.

Round front legs joined by turned stretcher type A, Figure NW26. Round turned back legs connected by single stretcher; double side stretchers. Rush seat, with three edge protective strips missing. Round back uprights with four ladders, graduated in size, with a large curved ladder at the top, and three domed ladders below.

Figure NW63. Ladder back side chair. Ash. Attributed to the North West, c.1780-1840. The use of two front stretchers was typical of 18th century single row spindle back chairs (see Figure NW8).

Round front legs with cup shaped feet, partly missing, joined by two plain turned stretchers. Round turned back legs connected by single stretcher; double side stretchers. Replaced rush seat with edge protective strips missing. Round back uprights with four ladders, graduated in size, with a large curved ladder at the top, and three domed ladders below.

Figure NW64. Unusually large ladder back armchair. Ash. Attributed to the North West, c.1770-1820.

Round front legs, joined by two plain turned stretchers. Back legs connected by two plain turned stretchers; double side stretchers. Chamfered back legs. Repaired rush seat, with edge protective strips missing. Reclined round back uprights with five ladders, graduated in size, terminating in prominent dome and nipple finials. Flattened scroll shaped arms which mortice into back upright with tapered terminal tenon, supported by turned underarm supports.

337

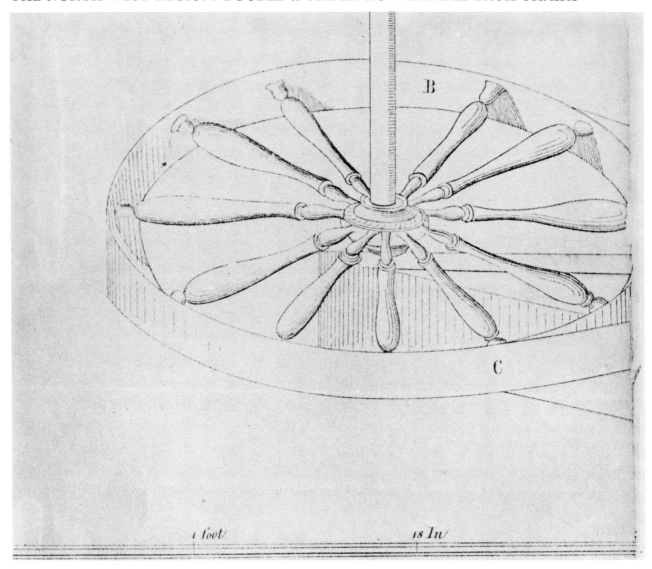

Figure NW65. Part of the original drawing produced by Richard Arkwright in 1769, of his spinning machine, showing the decorative spindles used as spokes in the belt driven wheel. These are similar in style to those used in certain of the double row spindle back chairs from this region, illustrating the close regional relationship between the textile industry and the chair designs, since turners were often producing parts for both trades.

Double and triple row spindle backs

Perhaps the most clearly regionally identified of all the Lancashire and Cheshire rush seated chairs are the spindle back chairs which typically have two rows of spindles in the side chairs, and three rows in the armchairs. The particular form of spindle used in this style of chair was probably adopted from pre-existing turnery motifs which were incorporated in various types of industrial machinery, used particularly in the textile industry. For example, turned spindles were used by Richard Arkwright in his spinning machine, patented in 1769, as spokes in a belt driven wheel (see Figure NW65). The adoption of this shape by the turner chairmakers, who were, no doubt, often turning bobbins and other parts for the textile

industry, implies a closely linked code of design which was deeply and cogently related within the regional culture.

This relationship extends to other aspects of turnery found in regional textile machinery prototypes, which were of mid-eighteenth century origin. The frame of Arkwright's spinning machine, for example, shown in Figure NW66, illustrates vase shaped turnings in the corner uprights, which have direct parallels in underarm supports in both spindle back chairs and ladder back chairs from this region. See Figures NW98 and 58 for examples.

There were probably more chairs made of this general type than any other single variety in the region, and

their sturdy, well designed structure has protected them against indifference and hard use. This broad group of chairs is composed of a number of distinct design categories which, in turn, exhibit stylistic sub-groups. The first major group, which has been entitled 'standard' spindle backs here, is the most numerous, and the chairs are characterised in being made from a combination of turned parts, including the use of turned back uprights, front legs, leg stretchers, and spindles; and sawn and shaped cross rails in the back, and, in many examples, sawn and often chamfered back leg sections.

Although ash is a commonly used wood in these chairs, alder is extensively used, either for making

338

Figure NW66. The turned wooden frame of Arkwright's spinning machine, 1769, showing regional turnery devices in the corner uprights which are also included in the arm supports of late 18th and early 19th century ladder and spindle back chairs from this region (e.g. Figure NW98).

(Courtesy Science Museum)

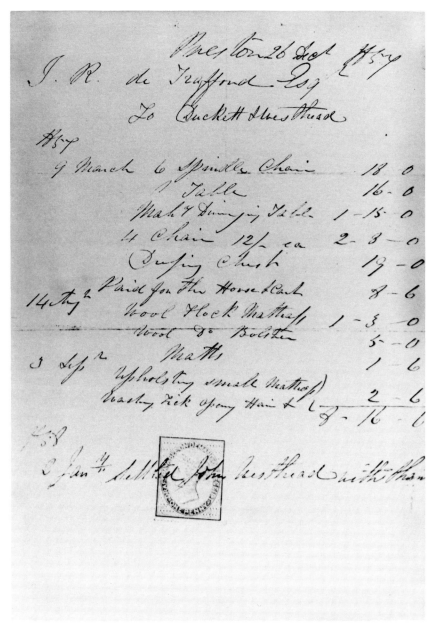

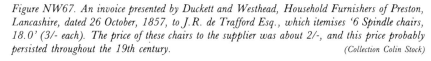

Figure NW67. *An invoice presented by Duckett and Westhead, Household Furnishers of Preston, Lancashire, dated 26 October, 1857, to J.R. de Trafford Esq., which itemises '6 Spindle chairs, 18.0' (3/- each). The price of these chairs to the supplier was about 2/-, and this price probably persisted throughout the 19th century.* (Collection Colin Stock)

Figure NW68. *A photograph taken in the last quarter of the 19th century, of Mrs. A. Hope, of Cross Farm, Styal, Cheshire, saying grace before a meal. She wears the traditional dress of this region, including crossed over woollen scarf, bonnet, apron and pinafore. The chair on which she sits is a double row spindle back side chair which has spindles, type g, Figure NW69, examples of which are shown in Figures NW104-111.* (Courtesy Styal Museum)

the entire chair, or for providing parts in otherwise ash chairs. The intention in using alder was to simulate mahogany, since on sawing, this wood undergoes surface oxidation which produces a reddish colour. This simulation of mahogany was presumably considered a more sophisticated presentation than that produced by indigenous hard woods, and was accentuated by staining the chairs with mahogany stain. Chairs which are now distanced in time from their original manufacture typically show the red base colour below later accumulations of polish and surface detritus, but the original impression of these chairs would have been that of a 'mahogany' finish.

Within the broad group of standard spindle back chairs, a range of specific styles is found which are sufficiently consistent in design to suggest strong local traditions. These sub-groups are designated, for example, by their specific spindle profile, front stretcher turnings, front and back leg designs, chamfering devices and terminal turnings in the back uprights, and distinctions in the general physical weight of the chair, which may be regarded as dividing the group into heavy, medium and light styles of chairs. A persistent belief has held that these features, especially that of the spindle turning, designated the manufacture of these chairs on a north/south axis throughout the region, with longer and thinner spindles being made in North Lancashire, thicker and bolder spindles being made towards the south of the area, and those with a double collar turning, type g, Figure NW69, being made exclusively in North Cheshire and to the south of Manchester. However, the evidence brought by the documenting of maker-stamped chairs indicates that a number of more or less 'pure' sub-group styles were preferred by individual makers and perhaps by groups of makers in a particular locality, and that these could vary from one maker to another in a given area as an issue of personal choice.

This is shown, for example, in comparing the similarly heavy styles

340

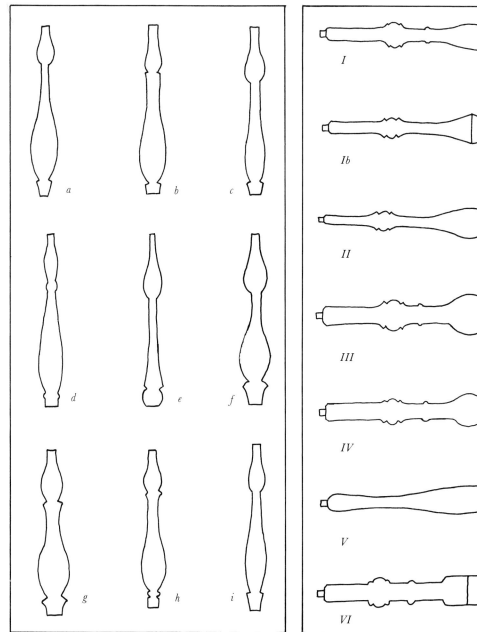

Figure NW69. Back spindle turnings incorporated in two and three row spindle back chairs.

Figure NW70. Front stretcher turnings incorporated in two and three row spindle back chairs.

of spindle back chairs made by John Allen* of Mobberley, Cheshire[35] (see Figure NW72), and D. Neild**[36], who probably also worked in North Cheshire (see Figure NW74).

Another Cheshire chair maker, Charles Leicester of Macclesfield, used a different turning in his 'fan' spindle back chair shown in Figure NW138, which has pronounced shaping to the lower swelling of the spindle, similar to those employed by John Shackleton, who lived at a considerable distance from Macclesfield, in his chair shown in Figure NW93. A further chair stamped by

G.F. Brennand of Huyton near Liverpool, shown in Figure NW153, also exhibits spindle turnings similar to those used by Charles Leicester and John Shackleton, which further

---

* John Allen, born in Macclesfield in 1805, worked as a chair maker and wood turner at Pepper Street in the small village of Mobberley, some ten miles from the chair making centre of Macclesfield, in the mid-nineteenth century.[37] There appears to have been a tradition of chair making in this village for William Sherriff and James Boswell were recorded as chair turners working in the village around the middle of the 19th century. A further wood turner, Simon Brace-girdle, lodged with John Allen, and probably worked for him.[38] A chair bottomer, Timothy Bailey[39] is also recorded working in the village as late as 1872.

** The name stamp of 'D. Neild. R.' has been recorded stamped on the top of the front legs of two

varieties of rush seated chairs, a rush seat kitchen chair (see Figure NW385) and a two row spindle back chair (see Figure NW74). This maker has not been firmly traced, but cabinet makers with this surname are recorded working in two Cheshire towns. George Neild (Nield) worked at Flat Lane and Wheelock Road in Sandbach between 1851 and 1860[40] and Edward Neild worked at Moss Lane, Altrincham, in 1860[41]. Members of the Neild family with various occupations have been recorded in this area of north eastern Cheshire. Given the pronounced tendency of certain of the north eastern Cheshire chair makers to name stamp their work, and given the close design similarity between D. Neild's spindle back and the example stamped by J. Allen of Mobberley, Cheshire, it is most probable that D. Neild was related to the Sandbach and Altrincham Neilds, and worked in this area. An alternative spelling to this name is Nield, and a Daniel Nield is recorded working as a cabinet maker at 145, Yorkshire Street, Rochdale, 1851-64[42]. However, although this location would provide an explanation for the inclusion of the letter 'R', it seems more probable that D. Neild was a member of the Cheshire family of that name.

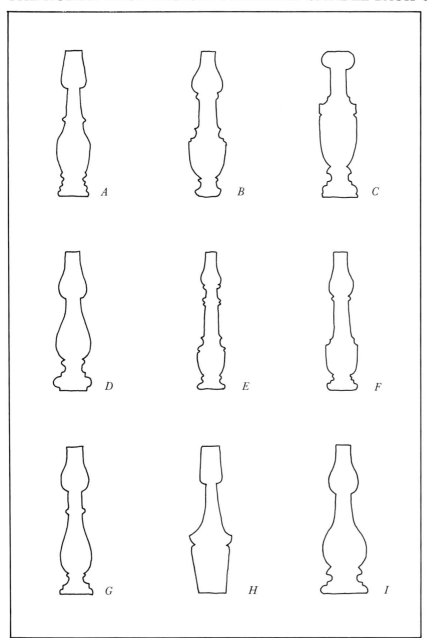

Figure NW71. Underarm turnings incorporated in two and three row spindle and ladder back chairs.

Figure NW72. Standard spindle back side chair. Ash, c.1800-60. Stamped 'J. ALLEN' on side of rear leg. There is a marked similarity between this chair and that shown in Figure NW74.

Quarter round top to the front legs, round turned leg below, terminating in pad foot, joined by turned stretcher, type VI, Figure NW70. Square back legs, chamfered at bottom of legs. Legs connected by box-form stretchers. One stretcher connecting rear legs. Replaced rush seat with wooden edge strips missing. Round back uprights with two rows of five turned spindles, type f, Figure NW69, supported between two curved plain cross rails, and an upper curved shaped stay rail.

Figure NW73. The stamp of John Allen (see footnote p.341), Wood Turner, of Pepper Street, Mobberley, Cheshire (fl.1850-51), impressed on the side of the back leg of the chair illustrated in Figure NW72. This maker worked in a small rural community which had at least two other chair makers and a chair bottomer.

extends the designation of this spindle type to three dispersed centres within the region.

The adoption of different spindle styles made in one region is shown in comparing the lightly constructed spindle back chairs made by John and David Bancroft (fl.1808-13), of Salford, Manchester, which have thin spindle turnings (see Figure NW84), with the completely different style of the double row spindle back armchair made in William Worsley's** workshop at Hanging Ditch, also of Manchester (1772) (see Figure NW106), which has the double collar form of

spindle turning. This latter chair also has a similar spindle turning to the chair attributed to John Steele of Middlewich, in North Cheshire, some fifteen miles south of the Manchester area (see Figure NW113).

It may also be that makers used different spindle turning profiles as well as front stretchers, to extend their own repertoire of designs. This is evidenced in the two different styles of spindle back chairs recorded by J. Shackleton, which show turnery

** One of the earliest known maker's stamps on a rush seated chair is that of William Worsley (see Figure NW106). He was recorded as a chair maker

in Hanging Ditch, Manchester in 1772[43]. However, this maker was a member of a dynasty of chair makers who worked in a number of chair making centres in North Cheshire. These include: Micaiah Worsley, who worked as a chair maker in Altrincham in 1790[44]; Richard Worsley, who worked in Lower Town, Altrincham in 1824, and John Worsley, who worked at the same address 1834-41[45].

John's son, also John, worked with his father in Lower Town in 1841 when he was aged twenty-five years. Further Worsleys worked as cabinet makers and turners in Cheshire and the Manchester area, including Samuel Worsley, who worked in Salford in 1804[46]; James, who was also a chair maker in Northwich in 1860,[47] and a further John who worked as a cabinet maker in Commercial Road, Macclesfield[48]. Another stamp, 'W.L.', is also found on the chair shown in Figure NW109. It occurs commonly on double row spindle back armchairs of this design, and on side chairs of this style. However, no maker with these initials is recorded in trade directories working in the Manchester area as a contemporary of William Worsley, but it is unlikely that as an employee he would have been recorded in these sources.

Figure NW74. Standard spindle back side chair. Alder with ash spindles and stretchers. Stamped 'D. NEILD. R.' on top of both front legs. Attributed to Lancashire/Cheshire, c.1800-60 (see footnote ** p.341 and also Figure NW386 for illustration of a rush seat kitchen chair stamped by this maker).

Quarter round top to the front legs, round turned leg below, terminating in pad foot, joined by turned stretcher type VI, Figure NW70. Square back legs. Legs connected by box-form stretchers. One stretcher connecting rear legs. Replaced rush seat with protective wooden edge strips. Round back uprights with two rows of five turned spindles, type f, Figure NW69 supported between two curved plain cross rails and an upper curved shaped stay rail. Straight back uprights terminating in nipple shaped finial.

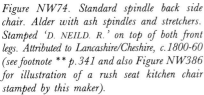

Figure NW75. The stamp of D. Neild impressed on the top of both front legs of the chair shown in Figure NW74.

Figure NW76. Standard spindle back armchair. Alder with ash spindles and stretchers. Attributed to Lancashire/Cheshire, c.1800-60. This armchair is the natural counterpart to the side chairs shown in Figures NW72, 74 and 77.

Quarter round turned front legs terminating in pad feet, joined by turned stretcher, type III, Figure NW70. Square lower chamfered back legs. Legs connected by box-form stretchers. One stretcher connecting rear legs. Rush seat with wooden edge protective strips. Round back uprights with upper and lower galleries of five turned spindles, type f, Figure NW69, separated by a row of seven short turned spindles, supported between three curved plain cross rails, and an upper curved shaped stay rail. Straight back uprights. Curved shaped arms which mortice into back uprights with tapered terminal tenons. Underarm turning similar to type B, Figure NW71.

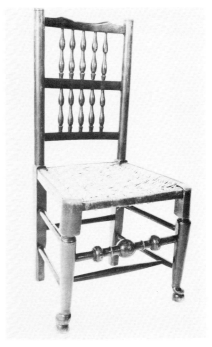

Figure NW77. Standard spindle back side chair. Ash. Attributed to Lancashire/Cheshire, c.1800-60. This chair is similar in design to those shown in Figures NW72 and 74 except that it exhibits the feature of the lower cross stretcher which is common in this group. The seat is made from wicker, which was occasionally used as an alternative to rush.

Quarter round front legs terminating in pad feet, joined by turned stretcher type III, Figure NW70. Square back legs, chamfered towards the base in a similar manner to the J. Allen chair shown in Figure NW72. Legs connected by box-form stretchers. Lower side stretchers connected by elliptical turned cross stretcher. One stretcher connecting rear legs. Split willow woven seat with wooden edge protective strips. Round back uprights with two rows of five turned spindles, type f, Figure NW69, supported between two curved plain cross rails, and an upper curved shaped stay rail.

and overall stylistic differences (see Figures NW93 and 100).

However, given the range of theoretical possibilities for altering the design of this style of chair, it appears that chair makers preferred to work within the conventions of an acceptable design for a particular sub-group, and rarely attempted to alter completely the design by adding unusual front stretcher turnings, or altering the front leg shape. This conservatism has the consequence that the acceptable differences allowed for the group are shown to fall into relatively few sub-groups.

Figure NW78. Standard spindle back armchair. Ash with alder cross rails. Attributed to Lancashire/Cheshire, c.1800-60.

Quarter round front legs, turned legs below, terminating in pad feet, joined by turned stretcher, type V, Figure NW70. Square and lower chamfered back legs. Legs connected by box-form stretchers. One stretcher connecting rear legs. Rush seat with wooden edge protective strips. Round back uprights with upper and lower galleries of five turned spindles, type f, Figure NW69, separated by a row of five short turned spindles, supported between three curved plain cross rails, and an upper curved shaped stay rail. Back uprights terminating in pronounced nipple shaped finials. Curved shaped arms which mortice into back uprights with tapered terminal tenons. Right hand arm replaced. Underarm support turning, type H, Figure NW71.

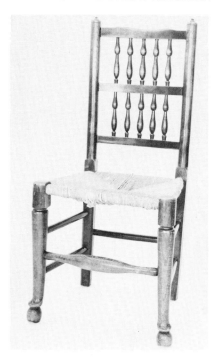

Figure NW79. Standard spindle back side chair. Ash with alder stay rail. Attributed to Lancashire/ Cheshire, c.1800-60.

Quarter round top to the front legs, round turned legs below, terminating in pad feet, joined by turned stretcher, type V, Figure NW70. Square and lower chamfered back legs. Legs connected by box-form stretchers. One stretcher connecting rear legs. Rush seat with wooden edge strips missing. Round back uprights with two rows of five turned spindles, type f, Figure NW69, supported between two curved plain cross rails, and an upper curved shaped stay rail. Straight back uprights terminating in pronounced nipple shaped finials.

Figure NW80. Standard spindle back side chair. Ash with alder cross rails. Attributed to Lancashire/ Cheshire, c.1800-60.

Quarter round top with scribed line to front legs, turned legs below, terminating in pad feet, joined by turned stretcher, type V, Figure NW70. Square back legs, chamfered below. Legs connected by box-form stretchers. One stretcher connecting rear legs. Rush seat with wooden edge protective strips missing. Reclined round back uprights with two rows of five spindles, type i, Figure NW69, supported between two curved plain cross rails, and an upper curved shaped stay rail. Back uprights terminating in pronounced nipple shaped finials.

Figure NW81. Heavy standard spindle back armchair. Ash. Attributed to Lancashire/Cheshire, c.1800-60.

Quarter round turned front legs, terminating in pad feet, joined by turned stretcher, type V, Figure NW70. Square and lower chamfered back legs. Legs connected by box-form stretchers. One stretcher connecting rear legs. Damaged rush seat with wooden edge protective strips. Round back uprights with upper and lower galleries of five turned spindles, type i, Figure NW69, separated by a row of seven short turned spindles, supported between three curved shaped stay rails. Back uprights terminating in pronounced nipple shaped finials. Curved shaped arms which mortice into back uprights with tapered terminal tenons. Underarm support turning, type H, Figure NW71.

Figure NW82. Standard spindle back side chair. Alder. Attributed to Lancashire/Cheshire, c.1800-80.

Quarter round turned legs terminating in pad feet, joined by turned stretcher, type V, Figure NW70. Square back legs chamfered below. Legs connected by box-form stretchers. One stretcher connecting rear legs. Rush seat with wooden edge protective strips missing. Round back uprights with two rows of five turned spindles, type i, Figure NW69, supported between two curved plain cross rails, and an upper curved shaped stay rail. Back uprights terminating in dome shaped finials with pronounced nipple turnings.

Figure NW83. Child's spindle back rocking armchair. Ash with alder front legs and stay rail. Attributed to Lancashire/Cheshire, c.1800-50.

Short round turned front legs, terminating in ring turned feet fitted to original iron rockers. Legs joined by turned stretcher, type V, Figure NW70. Square and lower chamfered back legs. Legs connected by single box-form stretchers. Rush seat with wooden edge protective strips. Round back uprights with two rows of four turned spindles, type i, Figure NW69, supported between two curved plain cross rails, and an upper curved shaped stay rail. Back uprights terminating in nipple shaped finials. Turned arms, similar to those found in other children's chairs from this region, see Figures NW55 and 368.

Figure NW84. Standard spindle back side chair. Ash. Stamped 'J. & D. BANCROFT' on rear of back leg, Salford, Manchester, Lancs. (fl.1808-13). See Figures NW163 and 161 for other styles of spindle back chairs made by John and David Bancroft.

Quarter round top with scribe line to the front legs, turned legs below, terminating in pad feet. Legs joined by turned stretcher, type IV, Figure NW70. Round turned back legs. Legs connected by box-form stretchers. Lower side stretcher connected by elliptically turned cross stretcher. Two stretchers connecting rear legs. Replaced rush seat with wooden edge protective strips missing. Round back uprights with two rows of five turned spindles, type c, Figure NW69, supported between two curved plain cross rails, and an upper curved shaped stay rail. Reclined back uprights.

Figure NW85. The stamp of John and David Bancroft, impressed on the rear leg of the chair in Figure NW84. These makers, father and son, are recorded working at 126 Chapel Street, Salford, in 1808, when they advertised themselves as having a 'Fancy Chair Warehouse'. They are recorded in 1813 working at 141, Chapel Street, Salford. See footnote p.365 for a description of this significant chair making family.

Figure NW86. Two row spindle back armchair. Ash. Attributed to Lancashire/Cheshire, c.1800-60. The use of two rows of spindles instead of the more conventional three rows in this style of armchair is uncommon. See Figure NW106 for a further example.

Quarter round top to the front legs, round turned legs below, terminating in pad feet, joined by turned stretcher, type IV, Figure NW70. Round turned back legs with square block at seat level. Legs connected by box-form stretchers. One stretcher connecting rear legs. Replaced rush seat with wooden edge protective strips missing. Round back uprights with two rows of five turned spindles, type c, Figure NW69, supported between two curved plain cross rails, and an upper curved shaped stay rail. Back uprights terminating in nipple shaped finials. Curved shaped arms which mortice into back uprights with turned terminal tenons. Underarm support turning similar to type B, Figure NW71.

Figure NW87. Standard spindle back armchair. Ash with alder back legs and stay rail. Attributed to Lancashire/Cheshire, c.1800-50.

Quarter round turned front legs, round turned legs below, terminating in pad feet, joined by turned stretcher, type IV, Figure NW70. Round turned back legs with square section at seat level. Legs connected by box-form stretchers. One stretcher connecting rear legs. Replaced rush seat with wooden edge protective strips. Round back uprights with upper and lower galleries of five long spindles, type c, Figure NW69, separated by a row of seven shorter turned spindles, supported between three curved plain cross rails, and an upper curved shaped stay rail. Straight back uprights terminating in nipple shaped finials. Curved shaped arms which mortice into back uprights with decoratively turned terminal tenons. Underarm support turning, type B, Figure NW71.

Figure NW88. Standard spindle back armchair. Ash. Attributed to Lancashire/Cheshire, c.1800-50.

Quarter round top to the front legs, round turned legs below, terminating in pad feet, joined by turned stretcher, type IV, Figure NW70. Square and lower chamfered back legs. Legs connected by box-form stretchers. One stretcher connecting rear legs. Rush seat with wooden edge protective strips missing. Round back uprights with upper and lower galleries of five turned spindles, type c, Figure NW69, separated by a row of seven shorter turned spindles, supported between three curved plain cross rails, and an upper curved shaped stay rail. Back uprights terminating in nipple shaped finials. Curved shaped arms, notched underneath, which mortice into back uprights with tapered terminal tenons. Underarm support turning, type B, Figure NW71.

Figure NW89. Standard spindle back side chair. Alder with ash spindles. Attributed to Lancashire/Cheshire, c.1800-50.

Quarter round top with scribed line to the front legs, round turned legs below, terminating in pad feet, joined by turned stretcher, type IV, Figure NW70. Round turned back legs with square section at seat level. Legs connected by box-form stretchers. One stretcher connecting rear legs. Rush seat with wooden edge protective strips missing. Round back uprights with two rows of five turned spindles, type a, Figure NW69, supported between two curved plain cross rails, and an upper curved shaped stay rail. Back uprights terminating in nipple shaped finials.

Figure NW90. Standard spindle back side chair. Ash with alder cross and stay rails. Attributed to Lancashire/Cheshire, c.1800-50.

Quarter round top with scribed line to the front legs, round turned legs below, terminating in pad feet, joined by turned stretcher, type IB, Figure NW70. Square back legs with pronounced lower chamfer. Legs connected by box-form stretchers. One stretcher connecting rear legs. Replaced rush seat with one wooden edge protective strip missing. Round back uprights with two rows of five turned spindles, type c, Figure NW69, supported between two curved plain cross rails, and an upper curved shaped stay rail. Reclined back uprights terminating in nipple shaped finials.

Figure NW91. Standard spindle back side chair. Ash. Attributed to Lancashire/Cheshire, c.1800-50.

Quarter round top with scribed line to the front legs, turned legs below, terminating in pad feet, joined by turned stretcher, type IB, Figure NW70. Square back legs with pronounced lower chamfer. Legs connected by box-form stretchers. Lower side stretchers connected by elliptically turned cross stretcher. Rush seat with wooden edge protective strips. Round back uprights with two rows of five turned spindles, type h, Figure NW79, supported between two curved plain cross rails, and an upper curved shaped stay rail. Back uprights terminating in pronounced nipple shaped finials.

Figure NW92. Standard spindle back side chair. Ash with alder middle cross rail. Attributed to Lancashire/Cheshire, c.1800-50.

Quarter round top to the front legs, turned legs below, terminating in pad feet, joined by turned stretcher, type V, Figure NW70. Square back legs with pronounced lower chamfer. Legs connected by box-form stretchers. One stretcher connecting rear legs. Rush seat with wooden edge protective strips missing. Round back uprights with two rows of five turned spindles, type c, Figure NW69, supported between two curved plain cross rails, and an upper curved shaped stay rail. Reclined back uprights terminating in nipple shaped finials.

Figure NW93. Standard spindle back side chair. Ash with alder cross stretchers and stay rail. Stamped 'J. SHACKLETON', from Todmorden, Yorkshire, on rear of back leg, c.1820-60.

Quarter round top to the front legs, turned legs below, terminating in pad feet, joined by turned stretcher, type III, Figure NW70. Square back legs with pronounced chamfer. Legs connected by box-form stretchers. One stretcher connecting rear legs. Rush seat with wooden edge protective strips missing. Reclined round back uprights with two rows of five turned spindles, type a, Figure NW69 (top and bottom right hand spindles replaced), supported between two curved plain cross rails, and an upper curved shaped stay rail. Back uprights terminating in pronounced nipple shaped finials.

Figure NW94. The stamp of John Shackleton of Todmorden, Yorkshire, 1861[49]. impressed on rear leg of chair in Figure NW93. Todmorden is a few miles inside the Yorkshire border with Lancashire. However, this maker, who worked at the timber yard and sawmill at Todmorden, was working within the Lancashire chair making tradition.

Figure NW95. Standard spindle back side chair. Ash with alder back uprights, cross and stay rails, attributed to Lancashire/Cheshire, c.1800-60.

Quarter round top with scribed line to the front legs, turned legs below, terminating in pad feet, joined by turned stretcher, type IV, Figure NW70. Square back legs with pronounced chamfer. Legs connected by box-form stretchers. Lower side stretchers connected by elliptically turned cross stretcher. One stretcher connecting rear legs. Replaced rush seat with wooden edge protective strips. Round back uprights with two rows of five turned spindles, type a, Figure NW69, supported between two curved plain cross rails, and an upper curved shaped stay rail. Reclined back uprights terminating in dome shaped finial.

Figure NW96. Standard spindle back side chair. Ash with alder stay rail, attributed to Lancashire/ Cheshire, c.1800-60.

Quarter round top with scribed line to the front legs, turned legs below, terminating in pad feet, joined by turned stretcher, type V, Figure NW70. Square back legs with pronounced chamfer. Legs connected by box-form stretchers. Lower side stretchers connected by elliptically turned cross stretcher. One stretcher connecting rear legs. Rush seat with wooden edge protective strips missing. Round back uprights with two rows of five turned spindles, type a, Figure NW69, supported between two curved plain cross rails, and an upper curved shaped stay rail. Reclined back uprights terminating in domed and nipple shaped finials.

Figure NW97. Standard spindle back side chair. Ash, attributed to Lancashire/Cheshire, c.1800-60. The front leg turning on this chair is unusual in a spindle back chair, and is more commonly found in the ladder back chairs shown in Figures NW355-65, and illustrates the tendency of chair makers in this region to integrate design features of one chair with another.

Round turned front legs terminating in pad feet, joined by turned stretcher, type V, Figure NW70. Square back legs with lower chamfer. Legs connected by box-form stretchers. One stretcher connecting rear legs. Rush seat with wooden edge protective strips missing. Round back uprights with two rows of five turned spindles, type a, Figure NW69, supported between two curved plain cross rails, and an upper curved shaped stay rail. Reclined back uprights terminating in domed and nipple shaped finials.

Figure NW98. Standard spindle back armchair. Ash. Attributed to Lancashire/Cheshire, c.1800-60.

Round turned front legs, terminating in pad feet, joined by turned stretcher, type V, Figure NW70. Square back legs with pronounced chamfer. Legs connected by box-form stretchers. Lower side stretchers connected by elliptically turned cross stretcher. One stretcher connecting rear legs. Replaced rush seat with wooden edge protective strips. Round back uprights with upper and lower galleries of five turned spindles, type i, Figure NW69, separated by a row of seven short turned spindles, supported between three curved plain cross rails, and an upper curved shaped stay rail. Reclined back uprights terminating in domed and nipple shaped finials. Curved shaped arms with notch underneath which mortice into back uprights with tapered terminal tenons. Underarm turning, type G, Figure NW71.

Figure NW99. Standard spindle back rocking armchair. Ash with alder cross rails. Attributed to Lancashire/Cheshire, c.1800-60.

Round turned front legs terminating in pad feet, joined by turned stretcher, type V, Figure NW70. Square back legs with pronounced chamfer. Legs connected by box-form stretchers. One stretcher connecting rear legs. Rush seat with wooden edge protective strips. Round back uprights with upper and lower galleries of five turned spindles, type a, Figure NW69, separated by a row of seven short turned spindles, supported between three curved plain cross rails, and an upper curved shaped stay rail. Back uprights terminating in nipple shaped finials. Curved shaped arms which mortice into back uprights with tapered terminal tenons. Underarm support turning similar to type D, Figure NW71.

Figure NW100. Standard spindle back nursing rocking armchair. Ash. Stamped 'J. SHACKLETON', (from Todmorden, Yorkshire), on rear leg, c.1800-60.

Quarter round top to the short front legs, round turned legs below, terminating in pad feet, joined by turned stretcher, type V, Figure NW70. Square and lower chamfered back legs. Legs connected by box-form stretchers. One stretcher connecting rear legs. Rush seat with wooden edge protective strips. Round back uprights with upper and lower galleries of five turned spindles, type a, Figure NW69, separated by a row of seven short turned spindles, supported between three curved plain cross rails, and an upper curved shaped stay rail. Back uprights terminating in nipple shaped finials. Curved shaped arms which mortice into back uprights with tapered terminal tenons. Underarm support turning similar to type G, Figure NW71.

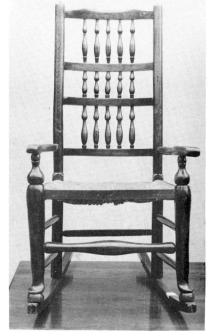

Figure NW101. The stamp of John Shackleton of the Saw Mills, Todmorden, Yorkshire (fl.1861), impressed on rear leg of chair in Figure NW100. Although this maker lived and worked in Yorkshire, a few miles from Lancashire, his chairs are allied with the Lancashire chair making style.

Figure NW102. Standard spindle back armchair. Ash. Attributed to Lancashire/Cheshire, c.1800-60. The stay rail shape is evocative of that typically found as part of the 'ear' back spindle variety stay rail. See Figures NW127 and 129.

Quarter round and turned front legs, terminating in pad feet, joined by turned stretcher, type III, Figure NW70. Square back legs with pronounced chamfer. Legs connected by box-form stretchers. Lower side stretchers connected by eliptically turned cross stretcher. One stretcher connecting rear legs. Rush seat with wooden edge protective strips. Round back uprights with upper and lower galleries of five turned spindles, type a, Figure NW69 (one spindle in lower row missing) separated by a row of seven short turned spindles, supported between three curved plain cross rails, and an upper curved shaped stay rail. Reclined back uprights terminating in nipple shaped finials. Curved shaped arms which mortice into back uprights with tapered terminal tenons. Underarm support turning similar to type g, Figure NW71.

Figure NW103. Standard spindle back armchair. Ash. Attributed to Lancashire/Cheshire, c.1800-60.

Quarter round top to the front legs, turned legs below, terminating in pad feet, joined by turned stretcher, type IV, Figure NW70. Square and lower chamfered back legs. Legs connected by box-form stretchers. One stretcher connecting rear legs. Replaced rush seat with wooden edge protective strips. Round back uprights with upper and lower galleries of five turned spindles, type g, Figure NW69, separated by a row of seven shorter turned spindles, supported between three curved plain shaped cross rails and upper shaped stay rail. Straight back uprights terminating in nipple shaped finials. Curved shaped arms which mortice into back uprights with turned terminal tenons. Underarm support turning, type B, Figure NW71.

Figure NW104. Standard spindle back side chair. Ash. Stamped 'J.S.' on top of front leg, attributed to John Steele of Middlewich, Cheshire, c.1780-1840. The front leg and front stretcher design of this chair are similar to those shown for the chairs in Figures NW72 and NW74 made by J. Allen and D. Nield of Cheshire, and suggest a design affinity between these makers.

Quarter round turned front legs, terminating in pad feet, joined by turned stretcher, type VI, Figure NW70. Square back legs. Legs connected by box-form stretchers. One stretcher connecting rear legs. Rush seat with wooden edge protective strips. Straight round back uprights with two rows of five turned spindles, type g, Figure NW69, supported between two curved plain cross rails, and an upper curved shaped stay rail. Back uprights terminating in nipple shaped finials.

Figure NW105. The stamp of 'J.S.' impressed on the top of the front leg of the chair shown in Figure NW104. This may refer to John Steele, chair maker, of Hawk Street, Sandbach, Cheshire, 1841; or to his uncle, also John Steele, of Lewin Street, Middlewich, Cheshire, 1824 (see footnote, p.352).

Figure NW106. Standard spindle back arm-chair. Ash. Stamped 'W.L.' on rear of back leg. Untraced. Also stamped 'W. WORSLEY' (from Manchester, 1772), on inside rear left hand leg.

Quarter round front legs, terminating in pad feet, joined by turned stretcher, type IV, Figure NW70. Square back legs. Legs connected by box-form stretchers. One stretcher connecting rear legs. Rush seat with wooden edge protective strips. Round back uprights with two rows of five turned spindles, type g, Figure NW69, supported between two curved plain decorative cross rails, and an upper curved shaped stay rail. Reclined back uprights terminating in nipple shaped finials. Curved shaped arms which mortice into back uprights with tapered turned tenons. Underarm support turning, type B, Figure NW71.

Figure NW107. The stamp of William Worsley, impressed on the inside of the left hand back leg of the chair shown in Figure NW106. This is the name of a chair maker recorded working at Hanging Ditch, Manchester in 1772[50]. Other Worsleys are recorded working as chair makers in Macclesfield, Altrincham and Northwich in Cheshire during the mid-19th century.

Figure NW108. The initials W.L. stamped on the rear of the back leg of the chair illustrated in Figure NW106. This stamp has been recorded frequently on both arm and side chairs of this variety and on a ladder back armchair. See Figures NW109 and 284.

Figure NW109. Standard spindle back side chair. Ash. Stamped 'W.L.' on the back of the back leg (see Figure NW110). Attributed to Manchester, c.1780-1820.

Quarter round top to the front legs, turned legs below, terminating in pad feet, joined by turned stretcher, type VI, Figure NW70. Square back legs. Legs connected by box-form stretchers. One stretcher connecting rear legs. Rush seat with wooden edge protective strips. Straight round back uprights with two rows of five turned spindles, type g, Figure NW69, supported between two curved plain cross rails, and an upper curved shaped stay rail. Back uprights terminating in nipple shaped finials.

Figure NW110. The initials 'W.L.' stamped on the rear of back leg of the chair illustrated in Figure NW109. This stamp occurs commonly and has been recorded on both arm and side chairs of this variety, as well as on a ladder back armchair. See Figures NW106 and 284. The maker of this chair is untraced, but the chair in Figure NW106 combines this stamp with that of W. Worsley who worked in Manchester in 1772.

Figure NW111. Standard spindle back side rocking chair. Ash. Attributed to Lancashire/Cheshire, c.1800-60. This chair is an alternative form of nursing rocker to those made with low set arms. See Figures NW100 and 128.

Quarter round top to the front legs, short turned legs below, terminating in ball feet fitted to rockers, joined by turned stretcher, type VI, Figure NW70. Square back legs. Legs connected by box-form stretchers. One stretcher connecting rear legs. Rush seat with wooden edge protective strips. Straight round back uprights with two rows of five turned spindles, type g, Figure NW69, supported between two curved plain cross rails, and an upper curved shaped stay rail. Back uprights terminating in nipple shaped finials.

Figure NW112. Standard spindle back side chair. Ash with alder back legs and cross rails. Attributed to Lancashire/Cheshire, c.1800-60.

Quarter round top with scribed line to the front legs, turned legs below, terminating in pad feet, joined by turned stretcher, type IV, Figure NW70. Square back legs. Legs connected by box-form stretchers. Lower side stretchers connected by elliptically turned cross stretcher. One stretcher connecting rear legs. Rush seat with wooden edge protective strips missing. Straight round back uprights with two rows of five turned spindles, type g, Figure NW69, supported between two curved plain cross rails, and an upper curved shaped stay rail.

'Ear' spindle back chairs

The second group of spindle back chairs shown here are those in which the design of the stay rail is shaped and terminates in ear projections, passing over the back uprights and creating a style which is suggestive of classical chair designs of Thomas Chippendale. However, this similarity is rudimentary, and since the direction of the flow of stylistic influence between vernacular and metropolitan designers' work is unclear, no definite relationship can be assumed.

Chairs in this group are also typified in having many sawn and shaped parts, including the back leg uprights, cross rails, and stay rails. The back uprights are square in section, waisted, and typically chamfered to lighten them in the upper sections. In some instances they are cut so that they recline backwards from the seat. The great majority, however, have straight back uprights.

The remainder of this style of chair is composed of turned parts which are typical of the standard style of spindle back chairs, except that the plain front leg stretcher (see type V, Figure NW70), found in a number of standard spindle back designs (see Figures NW96-100), was rarely made to fit chairs of the eared style. This group of chairs contains a number of sub-groups, but not as many as found in the standard spindle back chairs, and chairs of this type appear to have been made in rather smaller quantities than the standard designs.

The most common variety in the group has the spindle turning, type f or g, Figure NW69, which is found in combination with front leg stretcher, type IV, Figure NW70.

Chairs in this major sub-group are of a typically sturdy design, and were probably made by the same makers who made the equivalent form of standard chair. This is evidenced in that both eared and standard varieties stamped 'J.S.' on the top of the front legs have been recorded (see Figures NW105 and 113). This stamp is

Figure NW113. Ear spindle back side chair. Ash with alder back uprights, stay rail and cross rail, c.1800-1840. Stamped 'J.S.' on the top of each front leg (see Figure NW104). Attributed to John Steele, chair maker, of Cheshire (see footnote p.352).

Quarter round section at seat level and turned leg below, terminating in pad foot, joined by turned stretcher, type iv, Figure NW70. Square back legs. Legs connected by box-form stretchers. One stretcher connecting rear legs. Replaced rush seat and wooden edge strips. Back uprights square in section, waisted, and chamfered to the rear upper section with upper and lower galleries of five spindles, type g, Figure NW69. Shaped stay rail passing over back uprights, terminating in ear motifs, lower surface of stay rail shaped to emphasise the flow of the upper shaping.

Figure NW114. The stamp of 'J.S.' impressed on the top of the front leg of the chair shown in Figure NW113. This may refer to John Steele, chair maker of Hawk Street, Sandbach, Cheshire, 1841[51] or to his uncle, also John Steele, of Lewin Street, Middlewich, Cheshire, 1824[52].

Figure NW115. Ear spindle back armchair. Alder with ash spindles. Attributed to Lancashire/Cheshire, c.1800-1840. This armchair is the counterpart to the side chair shown in Figure NW113 and incorporates spindle turnings which are characterised by having two sharply indented turnings.

Quarter round top to the front legs, turned leg below, terminating in pad feet, joined by turned stretcher, type III, Figure NW70. Square back legs. Legs connected by box-form stretchers. One stretcher connecting rear legs. Rush seat with wooden edge strips. Straight back uprights square in section, waisted, and chamfered to rear of upper section with upper and lower galleries of five turned long spindles, type g, Figure NW69, separated by a row of seven short turned spindles, supported between three curved plain cross rails. Shaped stay rail passing over back uprights, terminating in ear motifs. Lower surface of stay rail shaped to emphasise the flow of the upper shaping. Shaped arms, which mortice into back uprights with turned tenons. Decorative underarm turnings, type C, Figure NW71.

Figure NW116. Ear spindle back armchair. Ash with alder back legs and stay rail. Attributed to Lancashire/Cheshire, c.1800-1840. The side chair shown in Figure NW117 is the stylistic counterpart to this chair, and is the most heavily made type in this group.

Quarter round section at seat level, round turned leg below, terminating in pad feet, joined by turned stretcher, type III, Figure NW70. Square back legs. Legs connected by box-form stretchers. One stretcher connecting rear legs. Rush seat with wooden edge strips. Straight back uprights square in section, waisted, and chamfered to rear of upper section with upper and lower galleries of five turned long spindles, type f, Figure NW69, separated by a row of seven short turned spindles, supported between three plain cross rails. Shaped stay rail passing over back uprights, terminating in ear motifs. Shaped arms with shaped terminal tenons morticing into back uprights. Turned underarm supports, type D, Figure NW71.

Figure NW117. Ear spindle back side chair. Alder stained. Attributed to Lancashire/Cheshire, c.1800-1840. The armchair, shown in Figure NW116, is the stylistic counterpart to this chair, and is the most heavily made type in this group.

Long quarter round top to the front legs, turned leg below, terminating in pad feet, joined by turned stretcher, type III, Figure NW70. Square back legs. Legs connected by box-form stretchers. One stretcher connecting rear legs. Rush seat with wooden edge strips missing. Back uprights square in section, waisted, and chamfered to the rear with upper and lower galleries of five spindles, type f, Figure NW69. Shaped stay rail passing over back uprights, terminating in ear motifs, lower surface of stay rail shaped to emphasise the flow of the upper shaping.

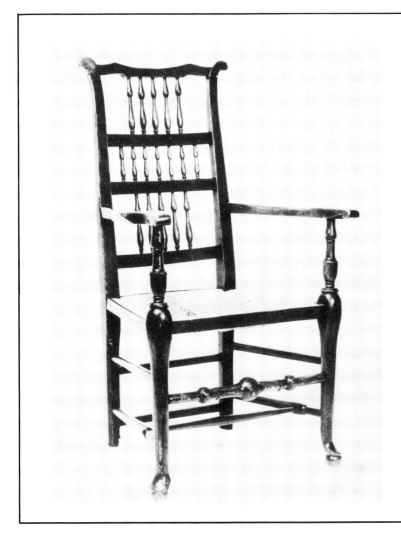

Figure NW118. Ear spindle back armchair. Ash with beech arms and cross rails, and alder stay rail. Stamped 'J & D BANCROFT' on rear of leg (fl.1808-13), of Salford, Manchester (see Figure NW84). This chair exhibits many of the finest characteristics of the English common chair, in that it employs a harmonious union of stylistic devices, to create a comfortable and design-conscious chair.

Quarter round section at seat level, round turned leg below, terminating in pad feet, joined by turned stretcher, type IV, Figure NW70. Square chamfered lower back legs. Legs connected by box-form stretchers. Lower side stretchers connected by plain turned cross stretcher. Two stretchers connecting rear legs. Replaced rush seat and wooden edge strips. Back uprights, inclined backwards, square in section, waisted, and chamfered with upper and lower galleries of five turned long spindles, type c, Figure NW69, separated by a row of seven short turned spindles, supported between three curved plain cross rails. Shaped stay rail passing over back uprights, terminating in ear motifs, lower surface of stay rail shaped to emphasise the flow of the upper shaping. Shaped arms, square morticed into back uprights, type B, Figure NW71.

Figure NW119. The stamp of John and David Bancroft, impressed on the rear leg of the chair in Figure NW118. These makers, father and son, are recorded working at 126 Chapel Street, Salford, in 1808[53] when they advertised themselves as having a 'Fancy Chair Warehouse'. They are recorded in 1813, working at 141 Chapel Street, Salford[54]. See footnote, p.365 for a description of this significant chair making family.

351

Figure NW120. Ear spindle back armchair. Ash with alder back uprights and stay rail. Attributed to Lancashire/Cheshire, c.1800-1840.

Quarter round section at seat level, round turned leg below, terminating in pad feet, joined by turned stretcher, type V, Figure NW70. Square chamfered lower back legs. Legs connected by box stretchers. One stretcher connecting rear legs. Lower side stretchers connected by plain turned cross stretcher. Two stretchers connecting rear legs. Rush seat with wooden edge strips missing. Reclined back uprights, square in section, waisted, and chamfered on rear surface, with upper and lower galleries of five long turned spindles, type b, Figure NW69, separated by a row of seven short turned spindles, supported between three curved plain cross rails. Shaped stay rail passing over back uprights, terminating in ear motifs, lower surface of stay rail shaped to emphasise the flow of the upper shaping. Shaped arms with square mortice into back uprights. Turned underarm supports, type E, Figure NW71.

Figure NW121. Ear spindle back side chair. Ash. Attributed to Lancashire/Cheshire, c.1800-1840. This chair is uncommon, and has been attributed by hearsay evidence to the Liverpool chair makers.

Short quarter round top to the front legs, turned leg below, terminating in pad feet, one foot damaged, joined by turned stretcher, type IV, Figure NW70. Round turned back legs. Legs connected by box form stretchers. One stretcher connecting rear legs. Rush seat with wooden edge strips. Lower side stretchers connected by plain turned stretcher. Back uprights square in section, waisted, and chamfered to the rear, with upper and lower galleries of five long turned spindles, type h, Figure NW69, separated by a row of seven short spindles supported between three straight cross rails. Shaped stay rail passing over back uprights, terminating in incised ear motifs, lower surface of stay rail shaped to emphasise the flow of the upper shaping.

Figure NW122. Ear spindle back side chair. Ash. Attributed to Lancashire/Cheshire, c.1800-1840.

Quarter round top to the front legs, turned legs below, terminating in pad feet, joined by turned stretcher, type I, Figure NW70. Round back legs. Legs connected by box-form stretchers. One stretcher connecting rear legs. Lower side stretchers connected by elliptical turned stretcher. Rush seat with wooden edge strips. Reclined back uprights square in section, waisted, and chamfered to the rear, with upper and lower galleries of five turned spindles, type h, Figure NW69, supported between two plain curved cross rails. Shaped stay rail passing over back uprights, terminating in ear motifs, lower surface of stay rail shaped to emphasise the flow of the upper shaping.

believed to apply to either John Steele of Middlewich[55], or John Steele[56] of Sandbach, Cheshire*. A compatible armchair of this style is also shown in Figure NW115.

A further sub-group which has clearly related arm and side chairs, has many of the features shown in the heavy styles of standard spindle back chairs, made, for example, by J. Allen of Mobberley, Cheshire, and D. Neild of north Cheshire (see Figures NW72 and 74), including the heavy style of front leg, connecting stretcher (type III, Figure NW70), and the attendant spindle turning type f, Figure NW69. An arm and side chair from this sub-group are shown in Figures NW116 and 117.

Two further examples of eared armchair varieties which have been provenanced may not have had natural side chair counterparts, but

were probably intended as easy or fireside chairs and were made by John and David Bancroft (fl.1808-13), of Salford, Manchester[57] (see Figures NW118 and NW125). These are designs which have sweeping back uprights which hold the three galleries of spindles between the elegantly shaped stay rail and the cross rails, creating an effect of compelling stylistic detail. The two chairs shown by these makers are distinguished from each other in that one has

* The Steele family of chair makers from Cheshire and Lancashire formed a dynasty of chair turners who worked during the first half of the nineteenth century in a number of centres. Thomas Steele of Sandbach is recorded as a turner in 1772[58], and George Steele is the first member recorded working as a chair maker between 1774 and 1825[59] at Shudehill in Manchester. A further George Steele, born in Middlewich, possibly the son of George, senior, is recorded working as a chair maker, first in Lewin Street, Middlewich in 1834[60] and in 1850-1 in Newton near Middlewich[61]. His brother, Thomas, who was born in Middlewich[62], Cheshire, is recorded as a

chair maker at Scotch Common and Hawk Street, Sandbach, Cheshire, between 1822 and 1851[63]; and another relative, Richard Steele, also a chair maker, worked in Bridge Street, Sandbach, 1828-34.[64] Thomas apparently moved for a while to the chair making centre of Macclesfield, where he is recorded working as a chair maker in 1825 in the same area of the town as the Leicester family at Chestergate[65] (see footnote, p.340). This record suggests that the Steele dynasty of chair makers were aware of the chair styles produced in that town with all the possibilities that this implies for design transmission between this extended group of makers.

However, of the Steele family, only one member appears to have stamped his work with his name initials, and the large initials, 'J.S.' have been recorded stamped clearly on the top of the front legs of both ear and standard spindle back chairs (see Figures NW104 and NW113). This stamp may refer to Thomas's son John, born in 1821[66] and who worked with his father in Hawk Street, Sandbach in 1841;[67] alternatively the stamp may refer to his uncle, a second John Steele who was the brother of George Steele of Middlewich, and worked at Lewin Street, Middlewich, in 1824[68].

The style of both of the chairs shown in Figures NW104 and NW113 has the form of spindle turning attributed to a chair by a provenanced Manchester maker (see Figure NW106), and to certain types of spindle back chairs attributed to Cheshire by hearsay evidence (see Figures NW109 and NW11), evidence which supports the view that John Steele of Cheshire was the maker of these chairs. These name initials do not, however, contribute absolute proof of attribution to John Steele, but few other makers in this region are recorded with these initials.

Figure NW123. Ear spindle back armchair. Ash. Attributed to Lancashire/Cheshire, c.1800-1840.

Quarter round section at seat level, round turned legs below, terminating in pad feet, joined by turned stretcher, type III, Figure NW70. Round turned back legs. Legs connected by box-form stretchers. Two stretchers connecting rear legs. Rush seat with wooden edge strips missing. Reclined back uprights square in section, waisted, and chamfered to rear of upper section with upper and lower galleries of five turned long spindles, type h, NW69, separated by a row of seven short turned spindles, supported between three curved plain cross rails. Shaped stay rail passing over back uprights, terminating in ear motifs, lower surface of stay rail shaped to emphasise the flow of the upper shaping. Shaped arms with tapered terminals morticing into back uprights. Turned underarm supports, type F, Figure NW71.

Figure NW124. Ear spindle back side chair. Ash. Attributed to Lancashire/Cheshire, c.1800-1840. This is a very uncommon variety of chair which hearsay evidence attributes to Liverpool makers.

Quarter round top to the front legs, turned leg below, terminating in pad feet, joined by turned stretcher, type IV, Figure NW70. Round back legs. Legs connected by box-form stretchers. One stretcher connecting rear legs. Rush seat with wooden edge strips. Back uprights square in section, waisted, and chamfered to the rear; upper and lower galleries of five turned spindles, type c, Figure NW69, separated by a row of seven short spindles. Shaped stay rail passing over back uprights, terminating in diminished ear motifs, lower surface of stay rail shaped to emphasise the flow of the upper shaping.

Figure NW125. Ear spindle back armchair. Ash with alder back legs and stay rail. Attributed to Lancashire/Cheshire, 1800-1840.

Quarter round section at seat level, round turned legs below, terminating in pad feet, joined by turned stretcher, type III, Figure NW70. Square back legs. Legs connected by box-form stretchers. Two stretchers connecting rear legs. Lower stretcher connected by plain turned cross stretcher. Rush seat with wooden edge strips. Reclined back uprights, square in section, waisted, and chamfered to rear of upper section with upper and lower galleries of five turned long spindles, type c, Figure NW69, separated by a row of seven short turned spindles, supported between three curved plain cross rails. Shaped stay rail passing over back uprights, terminating in diminished ear motifs, lower surface of stay rail shaped to emphasise the flow of the upper shaping. Curved arms with square tenons morticing into back uprights. Turned underarm supports, type F, Figure NW71.

turned front pad feet, and the other tapered feet.

Three rare sub-groups of the eared style sometimes have turned back legs in combination with the square shaped uprights. This feature is found as part of the rarest of all the spindle back side chair designs (see Figure NW121), that of the side chair which has three rows of spindles in the manner of the armchair counterpart shown in Figure NW120. This finely made design is larger in all dimensions than the typical spindle back side chairs, and hearsay evidence suggests that this style was made in Liverpool, apparently in very small numbers.

A further rare sub-group which has compatible arm and side chairs, also often has round turned back legs and three galleries of spindles as part of the side chair design (see Figure NW124). In both the arm variety (see Figure NW125), and the side chair, an alternative stay rail design is incorporated, where the terminal ears are vestigial, and uncharacteristic of the general group design.

Further rare styles of arm and side chairs are shown in Figures NW122 and 123. In these examples, the side chairs have two rows of spindles typical of the group. The armchair has the normal design specifications for this type, but is lighter in design than the two major sub-groups shown in Figures NW113-16.

Within the eared spindle group, low armed and full sized rocking chairs were also made. Figure NW128 illustrates a small low armed version, and the chair in Figure NW129 shows a magnificently designed chair which is tall in the back, and exhibits all the ebullience which represents the best of the chair turners' craft.

An exceptional chair amongst the ear shaped spindle backs is that shown in Figure NW130. Here the ears are modified by the inclusion of a restrained stay rail shape, and the inclusion of a simple front rail, type V, Figure NW70, which is typically found in some styles of standard spindle back chairs, but not in the eared varieties. Such deviation was apparently limited by design contraints, and this chair is interesting for its rarity.

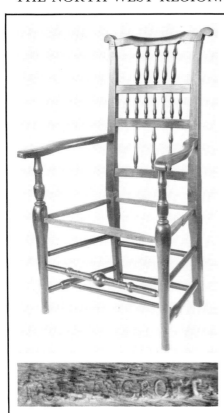

Figure NW126. Ear spindle back armchair. Alder with ash back legs and beech cross rails. Stamped 'J & D BANCROFT' on rear of back legs (fl.1808-13). This chair is similar to the J. & D. Bancroft chair shown in Figure NW118, with the exception of the alternative leg form.

Quarter round section at seat level, round turned legs below. This style was made without the more typical terminal pad foot. Front legs joined by turned stretcher, type IV, Figure NW70. Square chamfered lower back legs. Legs connected by box-form stretchers. Two stretchers connecting rear legs. Rush seat missing. Reclined back uprights square in section, waisted, and chamfered to rear of upper section with upper and lower galleries of five turned long spindles, type c, Figure NW69 (two spindles missing in bottom row), separated by a row of seven shorter turned spindles, supported between three curved plain cross rails. Shaped stay rail passing over uprights, terminating in incised ear motifs, lower surface of stay rail shaped to emphasise the flow of the upper shaping. Curved arms, notched underneath at hand rest, morticed into back uprights. Turned underarm supports, type B, Figure NW71.

Figure NW127. The stamp of John and David Bancroft, impressed on rear leg of the chair in Figure NW123. These makers, father and son, are recorded at 126, Chapel Street, Salford, in 1808[69], when they advertised themselves as having a 'Fancy Chair Warehouse'. They are also recorded in 1813, working at 141 Chapel Street[70]. See footnote p.365 for a description of this chair making family.

Figure NW128. Ear spindle nursing rocking chair. Alder. Attributed to Lancashire/Cheshire, c.1800-60.

Quarter round section at seat level, round turned legs below, terminating in pad feet, fitted to rockers. Legs joined by turned stretcher type III, Figure NW70. Square back legs. Legs connected by box-form stretchers one stretcher connecting back legs. Rush seat with wooden edge strips missing. Straight back uprights, square in section, waisted and chamfered on rear surface, with upper and lower galleries of five turned long spindles, type G, Figure NW69, separated by a row of five shorter spindles, supported between three straight plain cross rails. Shaped stay rail passing over back uprights terminating in ear motifs, lower surface of stay rail shaped to emphasise the flow of the upper shaping. Curved arms with turned terminal tenons, morticing into back uprights. Turned underarm supports.

Figure NW129. Ear spindle back rocking chair. Ash. Attributed to Lancashire/Cheshire, c.1780-1840.

Quarter round section at seat level, round turned legs below, terminating in pad feet, joined by turned stretcher, type IV, Figure NW70. Square chamfered and curved back legs. Legs connected by box stretchers. Two stretchers connecting rear legs. Lower side stretchers connected by decoratively turned cross stretcher. Rush seat with wooden edge strips missing. Straight back uprights, square in section, waisted and chamfered to the rear, with upper and lower galleries of five long turned spindles, type c, Figure NW69, separated by a row of seven long turned spindles, supported between three curved plain cross rails. Shaped stay rail passing over back uprights, terminating in incised ear motifs, lower surface of stay rail shaped to emphasise the flow of the upper shaping. Curved arms, with square lap-around mortice into back uprights. Turned underarm supports similar to type F, Figure NW71.

Figure NW130. Ear spindle back armchair. Ash. Attributed to Lancashire/Cheshire, c.1800-1840. The front rail on this chair is typical of those incorporated in the standard spindle back chairs illustrated in Figures NW96-100.

Quarter round section at seat level, round turned legs below, terminating in pad feet, joined by turned stretcher, type V, Figure NW70. Square chamfered lower back legs. Legs connected by box stretchers. One elliptical spindle connecting rear legs. Lower side stretchers connected by turned cross rail. Rush seat with wooden edge strips missing. Reclined back uprights, square in section, waisted and chamfered to rear, with upper and lower galleries of five long turned spindles, type c, Figure NW69, separated by a row of seven short turned spindles, supported between three curved plain cross rails. Shaped stay rail passing over back uprights, terminating in vestigal ear motifs. Curved arms with tapered terminals morticed in to back uprights. Turned underarm supports, type G, Figure NW71.

354

Figure NW131. Painting of a cottage interior, in the mid-19th century, by William Henry Midwood. Amongst the simple furnishings, a Liverpool or 'fan' chair is shown to the left of the picture.   *(Courtesy Christie's)*

'Fan' or Liverpool spindle backs

The 'fan' or Liverpool spindle back chair is so named because of the fan or shell-shaped motif carved into its stay rail, which is a pivotal decorative device found in a small range of chairs from the North West. In some cases the chair design equates with similar standard spindle backs, and in others is created as an individual style.

The most common design of fan back, shown in Figure NW132, is characterised by its fine turnings, reclined back uprights and cross rail turnings which are round with a turned 'knuckle' at the point of the spindle mortice. This style of chair is shown in a cottage setting in Figure NW131. A similar chair is illustrated in Figure NW132 and an armchair in Figure NW133. Typically well made and dynamic in design, fan back armchairs, although recorded, were

apparently made less frequently than those made for other styles of spindle backs. The reason for this is unclear, but suggests, perhaps, that this style may have been made for social assemblies, rather than for everyday domestic use.

The drawing taken from Gillow's Catalogue of 1801,[71] (see Figure NW134) shows a light framed chair entitled the 'Liverpool' chair. It is similar to the chair shown in Figure NW135 with the exception that it has a front stretcher, type V, Figure NW70, and no inner cross connecting stretcher is included. From the date of the drawing we can assume that this was an established design attributed to Liverpool chair makers by 1801.

A further style which also has knuckle turned cross rails, has a spindle, type e, Figure NW69, which

is unique to this design, and was made with round turned back legs and reclined back uprights (see Figure NW136). In this style, the rare armchairs are turned with many decorative devices, and are typified in having only two rows of spindles (see Figure NW137). The back upright finials are similar to those used in the ladder back shown in Figure NW279, and suggest a stylistic relationship between these design groups.

Although the Gillow's attribution of this chair style to Liverpool[72] may be important in locating the origin of one variation of this style, it is probable that chairs bearing the fan motif were made in many different parts of the North West. For example, two further designs of this chair having the essential characteristics of the group are stamped by Charles

Figure NW132. Liverpool or fan spindle back side chair. Ash with birch top rail. Attributed to Lancashire/Cheshire, c.1790-1840.

Quarter round top to the front legs. Turned legs below, terminating in pad feet, joined by turned stretcher, type I, Figure NW70. Square back legs. Legs connected by box-form stretchers, one stretcher connecting rear legs. Lower side stretchers connected by plain turned cross stretcher. Replaced rush seat with wooden edge strips missing. Round turned spindles, type c, Figure NW69, supported between two straight decoratively turned cross rails, and an upper shaped stay rail with centre shell or fan carved motif. Back uprights terminating in scribed ring and nipple finials.

Figure NW133. Liverpool or fan spindle back armchair. Ash. Attributed to Lancashire/Cheshire, c.1790-1840.

Turned front legs terminating in pad feet, joined by turned stretcher, type II, Figure NW70. Square back legs. Legs connected by box-form stretchers. One stretcher connecting rear legs. Rush seat with wooden edge strips. Round back uprights with upper and lower galleries of five long turned spindles, type c, Figure NW69, separated by a row of seven short turned spindles supported between three straight decorative cross rails, and an upper shaped stay rail with central shell or fan carved motif. Shaped arms which mortice into back upright with turned terminal tenon with underarm turnings of type F, Figure NW71.

Leicester of Macclesfield (fl.1816-60) (Figures NW138 and 140). These chairs were stained black, in common with other chairs made by Leicester. One is a tall back type with bent back uprights and inner cross stretcher below, the other a shorter variety with a similar back design, but lacking the lower cross connecting stretcher, and probably intended as a less expensive version of the taller variety.

Two further fan designs are shown in Figures NW143 and 144 which have the heavy structure typical of the standard spindle backs made, for example, by J. Allen (see Figure NW72) and D. Nield (see Figure NW74), both of North Cheshire. The example shown in Figure NW143 is very similar in demeanour to these chairs, and has been created as a fan back chair simply by the addition of knuckle turned cross rails and a fan carved stay rail. Figure NW144 is also heavy in design, but in this case, the conversion to a fan back chair is simply made by the addition of a 'fan' carved stay rail; the cross rails remain curved and flattened.

The heaviest of all the fan backs are shown in Figures NW146-148. These chairs, which include an arm, side, and low side chair, are characterised by their large dimensions, and the mode of assembling the galleries of spindles between curved, sawn, cross rails. In this design, the spindles are spaced in an equidistant manner, so that the back space is more completely filled by the spindles than in other forms of spindle backs. This is particularly noticeable in the armchairs of this variety (see Figure NW146) where the three galleries of heavy spindles dominate the back design.

Another style of heavy fan back was produced by incorporating cross rails which have round turned ends and a flattened middle section (see Figure NW149). These cross rail shapes are similar to those used in the 'ribbon' ladder back chairs (see Figures NW276-281), and suggest a design relationship between these styles of chairs. A further style of fan back which has similar cross rails to the previous variety, but in other respects is characterised as a Dales chair, is shown in Figures NW150 and 151. Both the arm and the side chairs of this type have two rows of spindles held between two turned and flattened cross rails, and in both cases, the front legs are round turned, terminating in vase-shaped feet in the case of the armchair, and plain tapered feet in the case of the side chair. The stretcher connecting the front legs is typical of those in the Dales spindle and ladder back varieties, and these stylistic features suggest a design relationship between this form of fan back and the far North West chair making tradition.

These very different styles of fan back chairs strongly suggest a series of regional styles in which this design was made with modifications related to local influences, and certainly the areas of Macclesfield (see Figures NW138 and 140), Liverpool (see Figure NW136), and the Dales areas (see Figures NW150 and 151) are strongly suggested as areas of production.

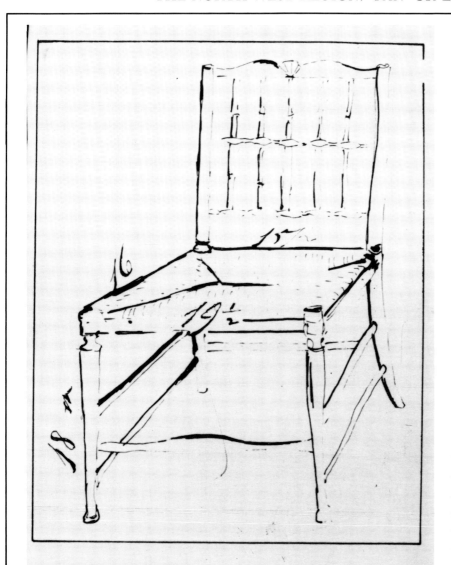

'Liverpool' Chair
Gillows of Lancaster, 1801
Estimate Sketch Book 344/98. p.1620
Inscr: Liverpool chair/Stained red.
Cost analysis:
Liverpool chair

	£	s	d
1 ft of Ash wood 1/8 rush 6d		2	2
Staining Wax and Sprigs 6d			6
Making Jno Harrison		2	3
		4	11

Figure NW134. A chair design and costing from Gillow's of Lancaster, 1801, for a Liverpool chair. The name may indicate that this style was known to be from the Liverpool area and that Gillow's were asked to make a similar style. This drawing shows a front stretcher, type V, Figure NW70, which is atypical for this style. The general design of this chair is very similar to that shown in Figure NW135, except that no lower stretcher connecting rail is shown. The materials costing is interesting in that it indicates that this chair was to be stained red, probably to simulate mahogany. The rushes for the seat were relatively expensive, costing a third as much as the ash with which the chair frame was made, and the cost of making the chair was about the same as the material costs. The separate note of 'sprigs' or small nails indicates that pinning the joints was a sufficiently special practice to warrant separate costing.   (Courtesy Westminster City Libraries Archive Department)

Figure NW135. Liverpool or fan spindle back side chair. Ash with birch stay rail. Attributed to Lancashire/Cheshire, c.1790-1840. The front stretcher is unusual in this style of chair, but is similar to that shown in Figure NW134.

Quarter round top to the front legs. Turned legs below, terminating in pad feet, joined by turned stretcher, type V, Figure NW70. Square chamfered lower back legs. Legs connected by box-form stretchers. Lower side stretchers connected by elliptical turned cross stretcher. Replaced rush seat with edge protective strips missing. Round back uprights with two rows of turned spindles, type e, Figure NW69, supported between two straight decoratively turned cross rails, and an upper curved shaped stay rail with central shell or fan carved motif. Back uprights terminating in scribed line and nipple finials.

Figure NW136. Liverpool or fan spindle back side chair. Ash. Attributed to Lancashire/Cheshire, c.1790-1840.

Quarter round top to the front legs. Turned legs below, terminating in pad feet, joined by turned stretcher, type II, Figure NW70. Round turned back legs. Legs connected by double box-form stretchers. Lower side stretchers connected by plain turned cross stretcher. One stretcher connecting rear legs. Replaced rush seat with wooden edge strips missing. Round back uprights with two rows of five turned spindles, type e, Figure NW69, supported between two straight decoratively turned cross rails, and an upper shaped stay rail with centre shell or fan carved motif. Back uprights terminating in dome shaped finials.

Figure NW137. Liverpool or fan spindle back armchair. Ash with sycamore arms. Attributed to Lancashire/Cheshire, c.1790-1840. This elegant and elaborately turned example shows the finest qualities of the English North West chair turner's art.

Turned front legs, terminating in pad feet, joined by unusual turned stretcher. Round turned back legs with quarter turnings at seat level. Legs connected by box-form stretchers. Lower stretchers connected by decoratively turned cross stretcher. One stretcher connecting rear legs. Rush seat with wooden edge strips. Round back uprights with two rows of five turned spindles, type e, Figure NW69, supported between two straight decorative cross rails, and an upper shaped stay rail with bold central shell or fan carved motif. Back uprights terminating in dome shaped finials. Shaped arms which mortice into back upright with square terminal tenons. Underarm turning design which embodies half the turning of the front rail and the inner cross stretcher.

Figure NW138. Liverpool or fan spindle back side chair. Ash, stained black. Stamped 'C. LEICESTER' on back legs. Macclesfield, Cheshire (fl.1816-60). The stained wood finish of this chair and that in Figure NW140 is typical of that applied by the Leicester family to their chairs.

Quarter round top to the front legs. Turned legs below, terminating in pad feet, joined by turned stretcher, type I, Figure NW70. Lower chamfered square back legs, left hand leg restored. Legs connected by box-form stretchers. Lower side stretchers connected by plain turned cross stretcher. One stretcher connecting rear legs. Rush seat with wooden edge strips. Curved round back uprights with two rows of five turned spindles, type a, Figure NW69, supported between two staight decoratively turned cross rails, and an upper shaped stay rail with central shell or fan carved motif.

Figure NW139. The stamp of Charles Leicester, Macclesfield, Cheshire, impressed on to the back leg of the chair shown in Figure NW138. The stamp may be that of either Charles senior (fl.1816-60), or that of Charles junior (fl.1841-51), who both worked as chair makers at the same address in Chestergate with other members of the Leicester family.

Figure NW140. Liverpool or fan spindle back side chair. Ash, stained black. Stamped 'C. LEICESTER' on back legs (fl.1816-60). This chair is shorter than that shown in Figure NW138 and there is no inner cross stretcher suggesting that this was made as a less expensive version.

Quarter round top to the front legs. Turned legs below, terminating in pad feet, joined by turned stretcher, type I, Figure NW70. Lower chamfered square back legs. Legs connected by box-form stretchers. One stretcher connecting rear legs. Rush seat with three wooden edge strips missing. Curved back uprights with two rows of five turned spindles, type a, Figure NW69, supported between two straight decoratively turned cross rail, and an upper shaped stay rail with central shell or fan carved motif.

Figure NW141. The stamp of Charles Leicester of Macclesfield, Cheshire, impressed on to the back leg of the chair shown in Figure NW140.

Figure NW142. The two versions of the Liverpool or fan spindle back chairs produced by C. Leicester of Macclesfield (fl.1816-60).

Figure NW143. Liverpool or fan spindle back side chair. Ash. Attributed to Lancashire/Cheshire, c.1790-1860. The heavy demeanour of this chair is unusual in a fan back and is more closely allied to the standard spindle back chairs shown in Figures NW72 and 74.

Quarter round top to the front legs. Turned legs below, terminating in pad feet, joined by turned stretcher, type III, Figure NW70. Square chamfered lower back legs. Legs connected by box-form stretchers. Lower side stretchers connected by plain turned cross stretcher. One stretcher connecting rear legs. Replaced rush seat with wooden edge strips missing. Round back uprights with two rows of five turned spindles, type f, Figure NW69, supported between two straight decorative cross rails, and an upper stay rail with central shell or fan carved motif.

Figure NW144. Liverpool or fan spindle back side chair. Ash. Attributed to Lancashire/Cheshire, c.1790-1860.

Quarter round top to the front legs. Turned legs below, terminating in pad feet, joined by turned stretcher, type III, Figure NW70. Square chamfered lower back legs. Legs connected by box-form stretchers. Lower side stretchers connected by plain turned cross stretcher. One stretcher connecting rear legs. Rush seat with wooden edge strips missing. Round back uprights with two rows of five turned spindles, type a, Figure NW69, supported between two curved plain cross rails, and an upper shaped stay rail with carved motif. Back uprights terminating in dome shaped finials.

Figure NW145. Spindle back armchair. Ash. Attributed to Lancashire/Cheshire, c.1780-1840. The incorporation of a standard spindle back stay rail into a chair which has fan back spindles and cross rails indicates the tendency of the North West chair turners to occasionally amalgamate design features from different chairs to create a further design.

Turned front legs terminating in pad feet, joined by turned stretcher, type IB, Figure NW70. Square lower chamfered back legs. Legs connected by box-form stretchers, two stretchers connecting rear legs. Rush seat with wooden edge protective strips. Round back uprights with upper and lower galleries of five turned spindles, type h, Figure NW69, separated by a row of five short turned spindles supported between three straight decorative stay rails, and an upper shaped stay rail without the central shell or fan carved motif typically found in association with this style of back design. Shaped arms which mortice into back upright with turned terminal tenon with underarm turnings, type B, Figure NW71.

Figure NW146. Liverpool or fan spindle back armchair. Ash. Attributed to Lancashire/Cheshire, c.1780-1840. This style has an atypical number of back spindles compared with other styles of Lancashire/Cheshire spindle back arm styles, and is the heaviest of fan spindle back designs. The underarm turning style is similar to that used in the double row spindle back chair stamped 'W. WORSLEY' (see Figure NW106).

Turned front legs terminating in pad feet, joined by turned stretcher, type iii, Figure NW70. Square chamfered lower back legs. Legs connected by box-form stretchers. Lower side stretchers connected by plain turned cross stretcher. One stretcher connecting rear legs. Rush seat with wooden edge strips. Round back uprights with upper and lower galleries of seven long turned spindles, type b, Figure NW69, separated by a row of seven short turned spindles, supported between three slightly curved cross rails, and an upper curved shaped stay rail with central shell or fan carved motif. Back uprights terminating in dome shaped finials. Shaped arms which mortice into back uprights with tapered terminal tenon. Underarm turnings, type B, Figure NW71.

Figure NW147. Liverpool or fan spindle back side chair. Ash. Attributed to Lancashire/ Cheshire, c.1780-1840. This style of fan back with plain back cross rails is typically much heavier in design than those which have turned cross rails.

Quarter round top to the front legs. Turned legs below, terminating in worn pad feet, joined by turned stretcher, type III, Figure NW70. Round turned back legs. Legs connected by box-form stretchers. Lower side stretchers connected by plain turned cross stretcher. One stretcher connecting rear legs. Replaced rush seat and wooden edge strips. Round back uprights with two rows of five turned spindles, type b, Figure NW69, supported between two straight plain curved cross rails, and an upper shaped stay rail with shell or fan carved motif.

Figure NW148. Liverpool or fan low spindle back side chair. Ash. Attributed to Lancashire/ Cheshire, c.1780-1840.

Quarter round top to the front legs. Short turned legs below, terminating in worn pad feet, joined by turned stretcher, type III, Figure NW70. Square chamfered lower back legs. Legs connected by box-form stretchers. Lower side stretchers connected by plain turned cross stretcher. One stretcher connecting rear legs. Woven split cane seat. Round back uprights with two rows of five turned spindles, type b, Figure NW69, supported between two curved plain cross rails, and an upper curved shaped stay rail with shell or fan carved motif.

Figure NW149. Liverpool or fan spindle back side chair. Ash. Attributed to Lancashire/ Cheshire, c.1780-1840. The cross splats are similar to the ladder back splats shown in Figures NW276-281, and illustrate the tendency of the Lancashire chair makers to transfer selected features from one style of chair to another.

Quarter round top to the front legs. Turned legs below, terminating in damaged pad feet, joined by turned stretcher, type III, Figure NW70. Square chamfered lower back legs. Legs connected by box-form stretchers. Lower cross stretcher missing. One stretcher connecting rear legs. Replaced rush seat and wooden edge strips. Round back uprights with two rows of five turned spindles, type c, Figure NW69, supported between two straight cross rails, turned at each end and flattened in the middle, and an upper carved shaped stay rail with central shell or fan carved motif. Back uprights terminating in dome shaped finials.

Figure NW150. Liverpool or fan spindle back armchair. Ash. Attributed to North West, c.1800-40. This chair is the armed counterpart to the side chair shown in Figure NW151 and also includes front leg turnings, front stretcher turnings and underarm turnings, arm style and cross stretcher type found in Dales spindle back chairs (see Figures NW22-56). The cross splat design is more usually found in the ladder back chairs shown in Figures NW276-281.

Round turned front legs with quarter round turning at seat terminating in vase shaped feet, joined by turned stretcher, type A, Figure NW26. Chamfered back legs. Legs connected by box-form stretchers. Rush seat with wooden edge strips. Round back uprights inclined backwards with two rows of five turned spindles, type c, Figure NW69, supported between two straight cross rails, turned at each end and flattened in middle and an upper shaped stay rail with central shell or fan carved motif. Shaped arms which mortice into back upright with tapered terminal tenons.

Figure NW151. Liverpool or fan spindle back side chair. Ash. Attributed to North West, c.1800-40. This chair exemplifies the tendency of the Lancashire chair makers to include design features of one style within another, shown in the leg design, front stretcher, and painted rush seat which are all features of the Dales spindle back chairs. The flattened and turned cross rails are features included as the cross splats in the group of ladder back chairs shown in Figures NW276-281.

Quarter round top to the front legs. Round turned legs below, joined by turned stretcher of the single row spindle, type B, Figure NW26. Chamfered back legs. Legs connected by box-form stretchers. One stretcher connecting rear legs. Painted rush seat with wooden edge strips missing. Round back uprights inclined backwards with two rows of five turned spindles, type c, Figure NW69, supported between two straight cross rails turned at each end with a flattened section in the middle and an upper shaped stay rail with central shell or fan carved motif

'Crested' spindle back chairs

A further group of finely made spindle back chairs has been entitled 'crested' spindle back chairs here, and is denoted by the distinctive presence of a flattened crested stay rail, 'waisted' back uprights terminating in domed finials, spindle turnings type d, Figure NW69, a specific round topped form of front leg turning in the side chairs, and decorative underarm turnings in the armchairs.

These chairs were undoubtedly favoured designs which have many detailed turnery devices, and fine rush weaving for the seats. The most common style of arm and side chairs in this group are shown in Figures NW152 and 155. This style of chair is rare relative to standard spindle back chairs since they evidently required greater attention to detail and design qualities than the less elaborated standard designs. This probably made this style significantly more expensive to produce, and perhaps

rendered them less in demand, as a consequence. It may also be that this style of chair was the product of one workshop, or a limited local tradition, since there is little evidence of design transmission between this style and the standard spindle back chair types.

However, design relationships have been recorded between the crested spindle back chairs and three other regional chair designs. The first, shown in Figure NW153, is stamped by G.F. Brennand of Huyton near Liverpool, and has essentially the form of a standard spindle back chair, but includes the features of waisted back uprights, and a crested stay rail. The second variant chair, shown in Figure NW157, is a crested spindle back chair which, unusually, has a quarter round top to the front legs, on which is carved a 'fan' motif (see Figure NW158 for detail). This carving is a regional feature which is commonly found as part of the stay

rail design in fan or Liverpool spindle back chairs (see Figures NW132-151). Conversely, the chair shown in Figure NW156 is made in a similar style to the chair in Figure NW157, but in this case, the crested rail is replaced with a typical fan carved stay rail. The cross fertilisation of these design features suggests that the makers of the crested rail chairs also made fan spindle back chairs, or vice versa.

The chair shown in Figure NW159 also suggests a relationship with a further group of regional chairs, in incorporating front legs and stretchers of the types associated with the Billinge and surrounding district bar-top ladder back chairs (see Figures NW240-248). This unusual amalgamation suggests an awareness of a specific regional group, but little evidence, so far, confirms this spindle back chair style to the Billinge region.

Figure NW152. 'Crested' spindle back armchair. Elm. Attributed to Lancashire/Cheshire, c.1790-1845. This style of spindle back is a rare design. Great attention to turnery and other detail is employed, which suggests that they were a superior but a relatively expensive type to produce. The illustrations shown in Figures NW156 and 157 indicate that this style was probably also made by the makers of the Liverpool or fan chair.

Quarter round top to the front legs, turned legs below terminating in pad feet, joned by turned stretcher, type IV, Figure NW70. Lower chamfered square back legs. Legs connected by box form stretchers. Lower side stretchers connected by turned cross stretchers. One stretcher connecting rear legs. Rush seat with wooden edge strips. Round back uprights with upper and lower galleries of five turned spindles type d, Figure NW69, separated by a row of seven short turned spindles, supported between three curved, plain cross rails, and an upper crested shaped stay rail. Back uprights waisted and terminating in dome shaped finials. Shaped arms which mortice into back upright with tapered tenons. Decorative underarm turnings.

Figure NW153. Crested spindle back side chair. Ash with alder back uprights, cross stay rails, and front legs. Stamped 'G.F. BRENNAND. HUYTON', c.1800. This design variant is essentially a standard spindle back style, but includes the features of crested spindle back chairs, including the waisted upper back uprights, and a crested stay rail.

Quarter round top to the front legs, turned feet below, terminating in pad feet, joined by turned stretcher type IV, Figure NW70. Square back legs with pronounced chamfer. Legs connected by box-form stretchers. Lower side stretchers connected by elliptically turned cross stretcher. One stretcher connecting rear legs. Replaced rush seat with wooden edge protective strips. Round back uprights, waisted at the top, with two rows of five spindles type a, Figure NW69, supported between two curved plain cross rails, and with an upper crested stay rail.

Figure NW154. The stamp of G.F. Brennand of Huyton.

Figure NW155. Crested spindle back side chair. Ash. Attributed to Lancashire/Cheshire, c.1780-1840. The round turning to the upper front leg is specific to this style. This is the most common form of this chair, and is the natural counterpart to the armchair shown in Figure NW152.

Round tops to the front legs, turned leg below, terminating in pad feet, joined by turned stretcher type IV, Figure NW70. Lower chamfered square back legs. Legs connected by box-form stretchers. Lower side stretchers connected by turned cross stretcher, One stretcher connecting rear legs. Rush seat with wooden edge strips. Round back uprights with two rows of five turned spindles type d, Figure NW69, supported between two straight plain cross rails, and an upper curved crested stay rail. Back uprights, 'waisted' towards top, terminating in dome shaped finials.

Figure NW156. Liverpool or fan spindle back side chair. Ash. Attributed to Lancashire/ Cheshire, c.1780-1840. This chair design embodies features found in a related group of crested spindle back chairs shown in Figures NW152-159, including spindle design, 'waisted' back uprights and domed finials, and pronounced 'knee' turning to front leg. These features indicate the close inter-relationship found in a few designs from the region, which display a merging of two styles, to create a third individual design.

Quarter round top to the front legs, turned leg below, terminating in pad feet, joined by turned stretcher type II, Figure NW70. Square chamfered back legs. Legs connected by box-form stretchers. Lower side stretchers connected by turned cross stretcher. Two stretchers connecting rear legs. Replaced rush seat with protective wooden edge strips. Round back uprights with two rows of five turned spindles, type d, Figure NW69, supported between two curved plain cross rails, and an upper curved shaped stay rail with shell or fan carved motif Back uprights, waisted towards top, terminating in dome shaped finials.

Figure NW157. Crested spindle back side chair. Ash. Attributed to Lancashire/Cheshire, c.1780-1840. This chair has an unusual feature of fan carving on the quarter round top to the front leg, which indicates its affinity to the Liverpool or the fan spindle back design. A similarly designed chair which includes the fan in the stay rail is shown in Figure NW156.

Quarter round top to the front legs with shell or fan carving. Turned leg below, terminating in pad feet, joined by turned stretcher type II, Figure NW70. Lower chamfered square back legs. Legs connected by box-form stretchers. Lower side stretchers connected by turned cross stretcher. Two stretchers connect rear legs. Replaced string seat with one wooden edge strip missing. Round back uprights with two rows of five turned spindles type d, Figure NW69, supported between two straight plain cross rails, and an upper crest shaped stay rail. Back uprights waisted towards top and terminating in dome shaped finials.

Figure NW159. Crested spindle back side chair. Ash. Attributed to Lancashire/Cheshire, c.1780-1840. The form of front leg and connecting cross stretcher is unusual in spindle back chairs, but common in a group of Lancashire ladder back chairs (see Figure NW240). The inclusion of these features in a spindle back chair indicates the tendency of the Lancashire chair turners to occasionally assemble chairs with features which cross reference between major chair styles, and evidence that chair makers were probably producing a repertoire of different generic styles in the same workshop.

Round top to the front legs, turned leg below. Pad feet missing. Legs joined by turned stretcher type C3, Figure NW289. Lower chamfered square back legs. Legs connected by box-form stretchers. One stretcher connecting rear legs. Rush seat with wooden edge strips. Round back uprights with two rows of five turned spindles type d, Figure NW69 (three top row spindles missing), supported between two curved plain cross rails, and an upper crested stay rail. Back uprights waisted towards top and terminating in dome shaped finials.

Figure NW158. Fan carving from the top of the front leg of the crested spindle back chair shown in Figure NW157. The inclusion of this unusual feature, which typically appears as part of the stay rail decoration of Liverpool or fan chairs (see Figure NW156), indicates that makers of the crested rail spindle back chairs probably also made those with the conventional fan motif.

Figure NW160. Fretted splat back rush seat armchair. Ash with birch splat and sycamore stay rail. Attributed to the Bancroft chair makers, Lancashire/Cheshire, c.1770-1830. The back legs and stay rail of this chair are closely similar to those incorporated in the eared spindle back chair made by J. & D. Bancroft shown in Figure NW125, and suggest that this chair was made as part of a repertoire of regional designs.

Turned front legs tapered to feet to fit brass cups or castors now missing. Front legs connected by front stretcher similar to type IV, Figure NW70. Square and lower chamfered back legs. Legs connected by box-form stretchers with two side and rear stretchers. Lower side stretchers connected by elliptically turned cross stretcher. Replaced rush seat with wooden protective edge strips missing. Square back uprights waisted in upper section. Delicately shaped stay rail passing over back uprights, terminating in incised ear shaped terminals. Lower surface of stay rail shaped to emphasise the flow of the upper shaping. Broad fretted wheatsheaf motif central splat showing Chippendale influence, connected to stay rail above and raised pedestal below. Flattened curved arms with notch underneath, morticed into back uprights with tapered tenons. 'Gun barrel' turned underarm supports.

Figure NW161. Fretted splat back rush seat side chair. Ash with birch splat and alder stay rail. Stamped 'BANCROFT' on the top of the front legs. Lancashire/Cheshire, c.1780-1830.

Delicate front leg turnings, terminating in pad feet, connected by front stretcher type IV, Figure NW70. Square and lower chamfered back legs. Legs connected by box-form stretchers with two side and rear stretchers. Lower side stretcher connected by elliptically turned cross stretcher. Replaced rush seat with wooden protective edge strips missing. Square back uprights, 'waisted' and chamfered in upper section. Shaped stay rail passing over back uprights, terminating in ear shaped terminals. Lower surface of stay rail shaped to emphasise the flow of the upper shaping. Broad fretted wheatsheaf central splat showing Chippendale influence, connected to stay rail above and pedestal below.

Figure NW162. The stamp of Bancroft impressed on the top of the front legs of the chair shown in Figure NW161. This refers to a member of the Bancroft dynasty of chair makers from Liverpool, Salford, and Prestbury (fl.1725-1832).

Figure NW163. Fretted splat back rush seat side chair. Ash with sycamore stay rail. Stamped 'BANCROFT' on the top of the front legs. Lancashire/Cheshire, c.1780-1830.

Delicate front leg turnings, terminating in pad feet, connected by front stretcher type IV, Figure NW70. Square and lower chamfered back legs. Legs connected by box-form stretchers with two side and rear stretchers. Lower side stretcher connected by elliptical cross stretcher. Replaced rush seat with wooden protective edge strips. Square back uprights waisted and chamfered in upper section. Shaped stay rail passing over back uprights, terminating in ear shaped terminals. Lower surface of stay rail shaped to emphasise the flow of the upper shaping. Broad decoratively shaped and fretted central splat showing Chippendale influence, connected to stay rail above and raised pedestal below.

Figure NW164. The stamp of Bancroft impressed twice on the top of the front legs of the chair show in Figure NW163. This refers to a member of the Bancroft dynasty of chair makers from Liverpool, Salford, and Prestbury (fl.1725-1832).

The Bancroft Family

The evidence of the late eighteenth and nineteenth century north west tradition of rush seat chair making is that of a dynamic craft, producing many different styles of ladder and spindle back chairs. There is some indication that these styles had progenitors in the eighteenth century styles of chairs, examples of which are shown in Figures NW2-12. However, another chair making tradition arose during the eighteenth century which shows design influences from classical patterns of mahogany chairs produced by George Hepplewhite (d.1786) and Thomas Chippendale (1749-1822).

Examples of these chairs are shown in Figures NW160-168, and illustrate the finesse obtained in combining fretted back splats of interlaced and wheatsheaf motifs, set within a framework of square and waisted back uprights which splay outwards and terminate in either a refined shaped stay rail evocative of the more elaborate designs of Chippendale, or alternatively, the domed shaped rail typified in Hepplewhite's chair designs. The remainder of the chair, however, reflects the construction and design of the regional turned double row spindle back chairs, with a large rush seat, finely turned front legs with pad feet, turned front stretcher, type III, Figure NW70, and the lower side stretchers especially turned and connected by an elliptical cross stretcher.

The woods used in their construction reflect, too, the common purpose for which these chairs were made, being predominantly of ash, but with alder, birch, and sycamore being incorporated in the splats and stay rails.

These styles of chairs appear to

Figure NW165. Fretted splat back rush seat side chair. Fruitwood. Attributed to the Bancroft family of chair makers. Lancashire/Cheshire, c.1780-1830.

Square, sawn, reeded front legs. Square, slightly swept back legs. Legs connected by H-form sawn stretchers, with extra stretcher connecting back legs. Rush seat with wooden edge strips. Square back uprights waisted and chamfered in upper section. Domed shaped stay rail showing Hepplewhite influence, passing over back uprights. Broad decoratively shaped and fretted wheatsheaf motif central splat connected to stay rail above and pedestal below.

Figure NW166. Fretted splat back rush seat side chair. Ash. Attributed to the Bancroft family of chair makers. Lancashire/Cheshire (fl.1780-1830).

Delicate front leg turnings terminating in pad feet, connected by front stretcher type IV, Figure NW70. Round back legs. Legs connected by box-form stretchers with two side and rear stretchers. Lower side stretchers connected by elliptically turned cross stretcher. Replaced rush seat with wooden protective edge strips missing. Square back uprights waisted and chamfered in upper section. Domed shaped stay rail showing Hepplewhite influence, passing over back uprights. Broad central decoratively fretted wheatsheaf motif central splat, connected to stay above and pedestal below.

have been made during the last half of the eighteenth century, and in the first quarter of the nineteenth century, and given their rarity, relative to other styles of North West regional chairs, they appear to have been made by fewer makers than were involved in making other regional styles. Of these makers, the Bancroft family of chair makers have left a legacy of name stamped chairs which display this blending of elements from the classical styles with those of local regional forms. This amalgamation and modification of styles achieves chairs of grace and elegance which are quite unlike the primitive regional prototypes. Other fretted splat back chairs which show the same design characteristics as those made by the Bancrofts have also been recorded, and examples of these are shown in Figures NW165-168.

A small range of chairs of conventional regional spindle back style has been recorded with 'J. & D. Bancroft' stamped on the rear of the back legs. This refers to father and son, John and David Bancroft who, as chair makers, had a partnership in a 'Fancy Chair Warehouse' in

Salford, Manchester, between 1808 and 1813.[73] The Bancroft family of chair makers had a long family history in the trade, with the first recorded member, John Bancroft, born in 1691 in Cheshire, and later worked in Stockport.[74] Two further generations of family members continued in the trade working in Liverpool and Salford,[75] and a further Bancroft, who may have been related, worked at Prestbury, Cheshire.[76] The last chair maker member of the family, John (ii), continued working until 1819 in Salford. The elder son of John (ii), John (iii), also worked as a chair maker in Denbighshire in North Wales,[77] before emigrating to America, some time between 1815 and 1824.[78]*

Since the name stamped chairs included here show only the surname Bancroft, stamped on the top of the front legs, this could refer, therefore, to any family member working from the mid-eighteenth century to approximately 1820.

Lancashire chairs, including eared spindle back chairs, standard spindle back chairs, and a repertoire of graceful chairs which incorporate fretted splats within a chair frame which has typical features of spindle back chairs (see Figures NW155-157). This family had a long history of chair making. The first member recorded working in the trade is John Bancroft of Etchells, near Stockport, Cheshire, who was born in 1691, and was recorded in 1725 in Stockport as a chair maker, at the event of his first marriage.[79] Two of his sons, David, born in 1747, and John (ii) born in 1750, both became chair makers. David married in 1781 in Liverpool, and worked in Dale Street as a chair maker until his death in 1811.[80] John's younger son John (ii) was married in Manchester in 1773,[81] and spent the rest of his working life as a chair maker in Salford, until his death in 1832.[82] John (ii) had two sons, John (iii) born in 1774 [83] and David (ii) born in 1777. John (iii) worked as a chair maker in Salford until the death of his mother in 1806 when he moved to Denbighshire in North Wales,[84] where he carried on his trade, and at some time between 1815 and 1824, he emigrated to America.[85] The younger son of John (ii), David (ii), is first recorded in trade directories as a chair maker at Collier Street, Salford in 1804,[86] and in 1808, he formed a partnership with his father, John (ii) at his father's premises in Chapel Street, Salford, under the title, 'John and David Bancroft. Fancy Chair Warehouse.'[87] However, David (ii) died at the premature age of 39 years in 1816,[88] and his father continued as the last member of this important chair making family until 1819 when he was last recorded.[89] John (ii) died in 1832 aged 82 years.[90] One other Bancroft, named Peter, who was born in Knutsford in 1746, worked as a chair maker at Prestbury near to Macclesfield in Cheshire between 1771 and 1809.[91] However, no connection has been traced between this Bancroft and those from Salford, Stockport and Liverpool.

Two forms of stamps naming Bancroft have been recorded, 'J. & D. Bancroft', which appears on the back legs of chairs shown in Figures NW118 and 125, and the single word 'Bancroft' stamped on the top of the front legs of the chairs shown in Figures NW161 and 163. This implies that the spindle backs stamped J. & D. Bancroft were made in Salford between 1808 and 1816, whereas the chairs stamped 'Bancroft' alone could be the work of any of the five Bancroft makers.[92]

---

* The Bancroft family of chair makers, who were Quakers, produced some of the finest examples of

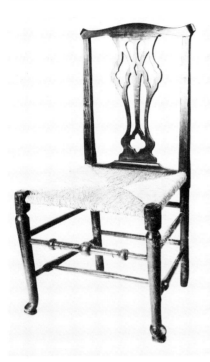

Figure NW167. Fretted splat back rush seat side chair. Ash with birch splat and alder stay rail. Attributed to the Bancroft family of chair makers. Lancashire/Cheshire (fl.1780-1830).

Delicate front leg turnings terminating in pad feet, connected by front stretcher type IV, Figure NW70. Round back legs. Legs connected by box-form stretchers with two side and rear stretchers. Lower side stretchers connected by elliptically turned cross stretcher. Replaced rush seat with wooden protective edge strips missing. Square back uprights waisted in upper section. Shaped stay rail passing over back uprights, terminating in ear shapes. Lower surface of stay rail shaped to emphasise the 'flow' of the upper shaping. Broad decoratively shaped and fretted central splat showing Chippendale influence, connected to stay rail above and pedestal below.

Figure NW168. Fretted splat back rush seat side chair. Ash and alder. Attributed to the Bancroft family of chair makers. Lancashire/ Cheshire (fl.1780-1830). This form of chair is stylistically compatible with other chairs attributed to the Bancroft family of chair makers, which includes those which exhibit both Chippendale and Hepplewhite influences.

Delicate front leg turnings terminating in pad feet, connected by front stretcher type IV, Figure NW70. Square back legs. Legs connected by box-form stretchers with two side and rear stretchers. Lower side stretchers connected by elliptically turned cross stretcher. Rush seat with protective wooden edge strips. Square back uprights, waisted and chamfered in upper section. Dome shaped stay rail showing Hepplewhite influence, passing over back uprights. Broad central decoratively shaped and fretted splat, closely similar to that used in the stamped Bancroft chair shown in Figure NW163, connected to stay rail above and pedestal below.

Figure NW169. Macclesfield ladder back armchair. Ash stained black. Stamped 'C. LEICESTER' on rear of both back legs. Macclesfield, Cheshire (fl.1816-60).

Quarter round front legs at seat, round turned below, terminating in pad feet, joined by turned stretcher type G, Figure NW289. Back legs connected by double stretchers, double side stretchers. Pronounced chamfer to back legs. Rush seat with wooden edge protective strips. Curved edges to seat. Bent round back uprights with double ring turning surmounted by pear shaped finial. Four dome shaped ladders with downward tip below. Curved round turned stay rail passing over back uprights terminating with barrel shaped turnings. Curved shaped arms which mortice into back uprights with turned tenon, supported by decoratively turned underarm supports.

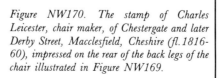

Figure NW170. The stamp of Charles Leicester, chair maker, of Chestergate and later Derby Street, Macclesfield, Cheshire (fl.1816-60), impressed on the rear of the back legs of the chair illustrated in Figure NW169.

The Macclesfield Ladder Back chair
The town of Macclesfield supported a thriving community of chair makers throughout the nineteenth century, and the evidence of the many name stamped chairs produced by a chair making family from this town, the Leicesters, who worked at Chestergate and Derby Street, 1814-81, suggests that this was a dynamic trade in which makers were producing a wide range of regional styles, including two styles of fan back spindle back chairs (see Figures NW138 and 140); rail back chairs (see Figure NW182); rope back rush seat chairs (see Figure NW409); rush seat kitchen chairs (see Figure NW407); and two styles of related ladder back chairs which above all others have been identified with this town through the many recorded examples stamped by Charles Leicester.*

The Macclesfield ladder back chair embodies many of the fine qualities of the English chair turner's craft, and appears to reflect a local design which probably arose in the town of Macclesfield. Chairs of this style are characterised in their refinement of design features, including the bent

Figure NW173. Macclesfield ladder back nursing chair. Ash stained black. Stamped 'C. LEICESTER' on rear of both back legs. Macclesfield, Cheshire (fl. 1816-60).

Quarter round front legs, round turned below, terminating in ball shaped feet, turned with tenons to fit shallow curved rockers, joined by turned stretcher type G, Figure NW289. Back legs connected by single stretcher, double side stretchers. Pronounced chamfer to back legs. Damaged rush seat with wooden edge protective strips. Curved edges to seat. Bent round back uprights with double ring turning surmounted by pear shaped finials. Four dome shaped ladders with downward tip below. Curved round turned stay rail passing over back uprights terminating in barrel shaped turnings. Curved round turned arms with central ring turning and barrel shaped ends, similar to the stay rail turnings.

Figure NW174. The stamp of Charles Leicester, chair maker, of Chestergate, and later Derby Street, Macclesfield, Cheshire (fl. 1816-60), stamped on the rear of the back legs of the chair illustrated in Figure NW173.

Figure NW171. Macclesfield ladder back side chair. Ash stained black. Stamped 'LEICESTER' on rear of both back legs. Macclesfield, Cheshire (fl. 1816-81).

Quarter round top to front legs, round turned below, terminating in pad feet, joined by turned stretcher type F, Figure NW289. Back legs connected by single stretcher, double side stretchers. Pronounced chamfer to back legs. Rush seat with wooden edge protective strips. Curved edges to seat. Bent and waisted round back uprights with single ring turning surmounted by pear shaped finial. Three dome shaped ladders with downward tip below. Curved round turned stay rail passing over back uprights terminating in barrel shaped turnings. This chair is the counterpart of the armchair shown in Figure NW169, and is the most commonly recorded design by this maker.

Figure NW172. The stamp of Leicester of Chestergate and later Derby Street. Macclesfield, Cheshire, impressed on the back leg of the chair in Figure NW171. This stamp is not prefixed by the more commonly found initial 'C' which refers to Charles Leicester, senior (fl. 1816-60). This may indicate that the 'C' was a separate stamp, and was missed out in this case, or, more likely, that the stamp refers to one of his three sons, William, the elder son (1841-81) who took over the workshop after his father's death, Charles junior (fl. 1841-51), or the youngest son, Thomas, recorded working in 1851.

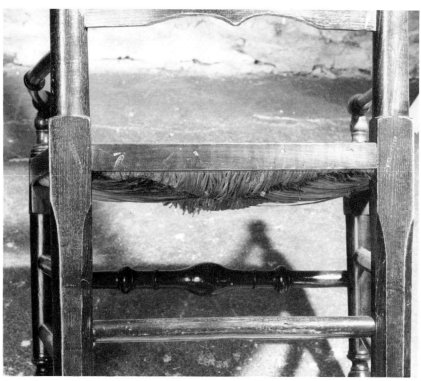

Figure NW175. Rear view of the nursing chair illustrated in Figure NW173, showing the mode of stamping used by the Leicester workshop. Two clear stamps which read 'C. LEICESTER' are impressed diagonally across the back legs at seat level.

---

* The Leicester family of North East Cheshire produced some four members who were chair makers working in the busy silk textile town of Macclesfield, two in the small textile town of Hyde, east of Macclesfield, and at least one further member worked in the village of Plumley some 10 miles west of the town. Other craftsmen named Leicester worked as wood turners elsewhere, including John Leicester who worked as a wood turner in Liverpool in 1882. A further Thomas Leicester worked as a wood turner at 4/6 Thomas Street Works, Mason Street, Manchester in 1858,[93] and a second John Leicester who worked as a wood turner between 1852 and 1871 at Thomas Street, Shudehill, Manchester.[94] The evidence of this John Leicester's advertisement shown in Figure NW184 suggests that the Leicesters who were wood turners, probably did not produce chairs, and were producers of a range of domestic turned ware.

The first member of the chair maker Leicesters recorded in Macclesfield was Charles Leicester who was born in 1784,[95] and recorded working at Chestergate, an area close to the town centre, and later at Derby Street, between 1816 and 1860.[96] This maker had three sons who also worked at the Chestergate address. William, the eldest son was born in 1816, and is recorded working between 1841 and 1887.[97] Charles was born in 1818, and is recorded working between 1841 and 1851.[98] Thomas the youngest son was born in 1830, and is recorded working in 1851.[99] The Leicesters are extremely significant in charting the styles of chairs made in Macclesfield, Hyde and Plumley, and probably in other areas of North East Cheshire and the Greater Manchester area since a large repertoire of different styles of chairs bearing the stamp C. Leicester have

been recorded, and are shown in Figures NW169-183, 407, 409, 138 and 140. A further Leicester worked as a chair maker at Plumley. The first, Peter Leicester, was a nephew of Charles Leicester senior, and was born in 1805. He is recorded working between 1841 and 1874.[100] A chair bearing his name stamp is shown in Figure NW227. Peter's younger brother Samuel, who was born in 1820, was also a chair maker, recorded as such once in 1844 when he returned to Plumley from Hyde to attend a christening.[101] Interestingly, these latter two makers probably did not learn their trade in Plumley, although they were both born there; Peter in 1808, and Samuel in 1820; since records show that both worked as chair makers at Hyde,[102] then a small textile town in North Cheshire, now a south eastern suburb of Manchester. Peter returned to Plumley by 1851 where he worked until 1874.[103]

Figure NW176. Macclesfield ladder back nursing chair. Ash stained black. Stamped 'C. LEICESTER' on rear of both back legs. Macclesfield, Cheshire (fl.1816-60). See Figure NW181 for possible reciprocation of this ladder design with the end supports of the carts used in the Macclesfield silk works during the 19th century.

Quarter round front legs, round turned below, terminating in bell shaped feet, turned with tenons to fit rockers (now missing), joined by turned stretcher type G, Figure NW289. Back legs connected by single stretcher, double side stretchers. Pronounced chamfer to back legs. Damaged rush seat with wooden edge protective strips. Curved edges to seat. Bent round back uprights with double ring turning surmounted by pear shaped finials. Five straight graduated ladders. Curved round turned stay rails passing over back uprights terminating in barrel shaped turnings. Curved round turned arms with central ring turning and barrel shaped ends, similar to the stay rail turnings.

Figure NW178. Macclesfield ladder back side chair. Ash stained black. Stamped 'C. LEICESTER' on rear of both back legs. Macclesfield, Cheshire (fl.1816-60).

Quarter round top to front legs, round turned below, terminating in pad feet, joined by turned stretcher type G, Figure NW289. Back legs connected by single stretcher, double side stretchers. Pronounced chamfer to back legs. Rush seat with wooden edge protective strips missing. Curved edges to seat. Bent and waisted round back uprights with double ring turnings surmounted by pear shaped finials. For plain graduated ladders. Curved round turned stay rail passing over back uprights terminating with barrel shaped turnings.

Figure NW180. Macclesfield ladder back side chair. Ash stained black. Stamped 'C. LEICESTER' on rear of both back legs. Macclesfield, Cheshire (fl.1816-60).

Quarter round front legs, round turned below, terminating in cup shaped feet, joined by turned stretcher type G, Figure NW289. Back legs connected by single stretcher, double side stretchers. Pronounced chamfer to back legs. Rush seat with wooden edge protective strips. Curved edges to seat. Bent and waisted round back uprights with double ring turning surmounted by pear shaped finial. Four plain graduated ladders. Curved round turned stay rail passing over back uprights terminating with barrel shaped turnings.

Figure NW179. The stamp of Charles Leicester of Chestergate, and later Derby Street, Macclesfield, Cheshire (fl.1816-60), stamped on the rear of the back legs of the chair in Figure NW178.

Figure NW177. The stamp of Charles Leicester, chair maker, of Chestergate, and later Derby Street, Macclesfield, Cheshire (fl.1816-60), stamped on the rear of both back legs of the chair illustrated in Figure NW176.

back uprights which curve gracefully from seat level, and are waisted and tapered in the upper section, terminating in distinctive pear shaped turnings.

The round stay rail with barrel shaped ends is a distinctive feature of the chair, and probably reflects the design of a turned wooden device used in the silk manufacturing trade in Macclesfield, called a 'picking stick'

which was used to knock a shuttle along in the warp.

Two alternative front leg styles were used by the Leicesters in their ladder back chairs; the elegantly turned variety with a pad foot, and a less lively design where the leg terminates in a ring and cup shaped turning. Both of these legs were commonly used with the two forms of ladder design, that with a domed top and downward tip below, and the alternative, a plain horizontal splat. This latter ladder design reflects a further industrial design motif, adapted from the carts used to move raw silk

around the silk works in the town. In the cart design, the ends have plain slatted supports, similar to the ladder styles used in the chairs made by Charles Leicester shown in Figures NW178 and NW180. The use of design features adopted in this way, reflect the design codes in which local woodworkers worked, and the common way in which their work was sometimes expressed. The amalgamation of these features in different combinations gives rise to four alternative distinctions of style (see Figures NW171, 188, 178 and 180).

The delicacy and refined structure of these chairs, and the mode of finishing with black stain, suggests that both the ladder and rail back chairs made by the Leicesters, although made in the traditional chair turners' wood of ash, were probably seen as 'fancy' chairs, rather than those for 'common' use. This possibility is reinforced in that the rush seating provided for these chairs is also typically of the highest

Plate 58. Ladder back side chair. Ash with replaced rush seat. Painted with blue/green paint. North West region, c.1740.

Plate 59. 'Ear' spindle back armchair. Ash with rush seat. Impressed 'J. RIDING' on right back leg. John Riding of Chestergate, Macclesfield, was recorded as a chair maker in 1818.

Plate 60. 'Liverpool' or 'fan' back armchair. Ash with replaced rush seat. North West region, c.1800.

Plate 61. 'Crested' spindle back armchair. Ash with rush seat. North West region, c.1800.

Figure NW181. The interior of Brocklehurst's Mill, Macclesfield, c.1890, showing the boiling or de-gumming of the raw silk. The carts used to move the silk have an end design of narrow slats which are similar to those adopted by the Leicester family of Macclesfield chair makers in some ladder back chairs (see Figures NW176-180).

(Photograph courtesy Gordon Campbell)

Figure NW182. Turned rail back side chair. Ash stained black. Stamped 'C. LEICESTER' on rear of both back legs. Macclesfield, Cheshire (fl.1816-60). This style is probably a rare design within the Leicester repertoire, and represents a refined use of turned cross stay rails to create a further style.

Quarter round top to front legs, round turned leg below, terminating in single ring and vase shaped feet, joined by two curved round turned stretchers. Back legs connected by double stretchers, double side stretchers. Round turned back legs with square block at seat level. Rush seat with wooden edge protective strips. Curved edges to seat. Bent and tapered round back uprights. Three upper and two lower curved round turned cross rails.

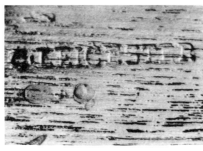

Figure NW183. The stamp of Charles Leicester of Chestergate, and later Derby Road, Macclesfield, Cheshire (fl.1816-60), impressed on the rear of the back legs of the chair illustrated in Figure NW182.

craft quality, with finely woven strands of rush used and, unusually, the seat frame on to which the rush is woven is convex shaped to create a rounded profile to the seat.

This essential design of chair was made by other makers in the north west tradition, and, although similar in design to the Macclesfield made chairs, typically embody other regional turnery features, and lack the elliptical edge shape of the Leicester made chairs. For this reason those chairs from this group, illustrated in Figures NW185-195 have been entitled 'Macclesfield' style chairs.

Figure NW184. An advertisement placed by John Leicester, wood turner of Shudehill, Manchester, in an 18th century Trade Directory. This turner was one of three Leicesters who were all turners and probably related to the Macclesfield Leicesters.

Figure NW185. Macclesfield style ladder back armchair. Ash stained black. Attributed to Lancashire/Cheshire, c.1820-80.

Square top to the front legs, round turned below with triple ring turning, terminating in ball shaped feet, joined by decoratively turned stretcher type C, Figure NW372. Back legs connected by double stretchers, double side stretchers. Square back legs. Wicker seat with curved edges. Bent and waisted round back uprights with single ring turning surmounted by pear shaped finial. Four dome shaped ladders with downward tip below. Curved round turned stay rail passing over back uprights terminating in barrel shaped turnings. Curved shaped arms which mortice into back uprights with turned tenons, supported by decoratively turned underarm supports.

Figure NW186. Macclesfield style ladder back armchair. Ash stained black. Attributed to Lancashire/Cheshire, c.1820-80.

Quarter round front legs at seat, round turned below, terminating in indented pad feet, joined by turned stretcher type D, Figure NW289. Back legs connected by single stretcher, double side stretchers. Pronounced chamfer to back legs. Rush seat with wooden edge protective strips. Bent and 'waisted' round back uprights with double ring turning surmounted by pear shaped finial. Four dome shaped ladders with downward tip below. Curved round turned stay rail passing over back uprights terminating with barrel shaped turnings. Curved shaped arms which mortice into back uprights with turned tenons, supported by decoratively turned underarm supports.

Figure NW187. Macclesfield style ladder back armchair. Ash stained black. Attributed to Lancashire/Cheshire, c.1820-80. This chair represents an unusual variant of the more commonly recorded Macclesfield chair. The front stretcher turning type N, Figure NW289, is also found in a group of tall backed standard ladder back chairs shown in Figures NW314 and 315 and offers an interesting stylistic connection between these dissimilar styles of chairs.

Round front legs with flattened turnings, terminating in pad feet, joined by turned stretcher type N, Figure NW289. Back legs connected by single stretcher, double side stretchers. Rush seat with wooden edge protective strips. Round back uprights with four dome shaped ladders with decorative shaping below. Curved round turned stay rail passing over back uprights terminating with elliptical shaped turnings. Curved shaped arms with notch underneath which mortice into back uprights with tapered tenon, supported by turned underarm supports incorporating an urn motif.

Plate 62. Spindle back armchair. Elm with rush seat. Impressed 'W. WORSLEY' on the lower left hand leg. Incised 'W.L.' on rear of right leg. William Worsley is recorded as a chair maker at Hanging Ditch, Manchester in 1777.

Plate 63. Spindle back armchair. Ash with rush seat. North West region, c.1800.

Plate 64. Low rush seated nursing or fireside chair. Alder with side rails in ash, replaced rush seat. Stamped 'R.H. & J. SIMPSON' on rear of both back legs. R.H. & J. Simpson were cabinet and chair makers at Nicholas Street, Lancaster (fl.1865-90).

Plate 65. Rush seat kitchen side chair. Alder, c.1860. Stamped 'LEICESTER' on rear legs. This stamp probably refers to William Leicester, jnr. (fl.1857-92), of North Street, Macclesfield.

Plate 66. Ladder back side chair. Ash with replaced rush seat. North West region, c.1840.

Plate 67. Child's rush seat kitchen chair. Alder. North West region, c.1860.

Plate 68. Rush seat kitchen chair. Alder with replaced rush seat. North West region, c.1840.

Figure NW188. Macclesfield style ladder back side chair. Ash stained black. Attributed to the Macclesfield chair makers, c.1820-80. This style of chair is similar to the chair shown in Figure NW180, stamped by C. Leicester, but with the addition of downward tip ladders similar to those shown in the Leicester stamped chair in Figure NW171, and probably illustrates that the Macclesfield chair makers amalgamated elements of different chairs to produce a further style.

Quarter round top to the front legs, round turned below, terminating in single ring and ball feet, joined by turned stretcher type G, Figure NW289. Back legs connected by single stretcher, double side stretchers. Pronounced chamfer to back legs. Replaced rush seat and seat rails with wooden edge protective strips missing. Bent and waisted round back uprights with double ring turning surmounted by pear shaped finials. Three dome shaped ladders with downard tip below. Curved round turned stay rail passing over back uprights terminating in barrel shaped turnings.

Figure NW189. Macclesfield style ladder back side chair. Ash stained black. Attributed to North West, c.1820-80.

Square top to the front legs, round turned below, terminating in single ring and cup shaped feet, joined by turned stretcher type C3, Figure NW289. Back legs connected by single stretcher, double side stretchers. Chamfered back legs. Rush seat with wooden edge protective strips. Straight round back uprights with single ring turning surmounted by pear shaped finials. Three dome shaped ladders. Curved round turned stay rail passing over back uprights terminating in barrel shaped turnings.

Figure NW190. Macclesfield style ladder back side chair. Ash stained black. Attributed to Lancashire/Cheshire, c.1820-80.

Turned tip to the front legs morticed into a square on the seat frame, round turned below, terminating in pad feet, joined by turned stretcher type G, Figure NW289. Back legs connected by single stretchers, double side stretchers. Chamfered back legs. Rush seat with wooden edge protective strips. Straight tapered round back uprights with double ring turning surmounted by pear shaped finials. Three dome shaped ladders with downward tip below. Curved round turned stay rail passing over back uprights terminating in barrel shaped turnings.

Figure NW191. Macclesfield style ladder back side chair. Ash stained black. Attributed to Lancashire/Cheshire, c.1820-80. The style of the front legs is found in a range of other North West region ladder back chairs, see Figures NW273, 274 and 302, which indicate that this chair was probably made as part of a repertoire of other styles.

Round front legs with single ring turning below, terminating in indented pad feet, joined by turned stretcher type B2, Figure NW289. Back legs connected by single stretchers, double side stretchers. Pronounced chamfer to back legs. Rush seat with wooden edge protective strips missing. Straight round back uprights with pear shaped finials. Three dome shaped ladders with downward tip below. Curved round turned stay rail passing over back uprights terminating in shaped turnings.

Figure NW192. Macclesfield style ladder back armchair. Ash stained black. Attributed to Lancashire/Cheshire, c.1840-90. This chair represents a variant of the more commonly recorded Macclesfield chair.

Round front legs terminating in pad feet, joined by turned stretcher type C, Figure NW372, which is similar to those found in certain rush seat kitchen chairs, as well as in the kitchen chair made by the Leicester family of Macclesfield, Cheshire (fl.1816-81), shown in Figure NW407. Square back legs connected by single stretcher, double side stretchers. Rush sat with wooden edge protective strips, Round back uprights with four domed ladders shaped with downward tip below. Curved round turned stay rail passing over back uprights terminating in elliptical turnings. Curved shaped arms which mortice into back uprights with tapered tenons, supported by underarm supports incorporating an urn motif type E, Figure NW71.

Figure NW195. Macclesfield style ladder back side chair. Ash stained black. Attributed to Lancashire/Cheshire, c.1820-80. The front leg turnings are similar to those found in a number of other North West ladder back styles (see Figures NW270-272), and indicate that this chair was probably made as part of a repertoire of ladder back designs.

Round front legs terminating in indented pad feet, joined by turned stretcher type F, Figure NW289. Back legs connected by single stretcher, double side stretchers. Pronounced chamfer to back legs. Replaced rush seat with wooden edge protective strips. Straight round back uprights with single ring turning surmounted with pear shaped finials. Three dome shaped ladders. Curved round turned stay rail passing over back uprights terminating in barrel shaped turnings.

Figure NW193. Macclesfield style ladder back armchair. Ash stained black. Attributed to Macclesfield, c.1850-90. The dated inscription (1889), appears to be contemporary with the manufacture of the chair, and it may be that this chair was made especially as a commemorative gift. This places the latest known date of manufacture of this style of chair to the late 19th century.

Brass commemorative plaque dated 1889 fixed to front of top ladder. Round front legs terminating in pad feet, joined by turned stretchers, type M, Figure NW289. Square back legs connected by double stretchers, double side stretchers. Rush seat with wooden edge protective strips. Round back uprights with four domed ladders with shaped downward tip below. Curved round turned stay rail passing over back uprights terminating with elliptical turnings. Curved shaped arms which mortice into back uprights with turned tenon, supported by turned underarm supports.

Figure NW194. The brass commemorative plaque attached to the top ladder of the chair shown in Figure NW193. The Dowager Countess of Airlie of Cortachy Castle, Forfar, was Henrietta Blanche, second daughter of the 2nd Baron Stanley of Alderley, of Alderley Park, Cheshire, some four miles from Macclesfield. Though W. Carnegie was presumably a Scot, it is interesting that nearly forty years after her marriage to the 7th Earl of Airlie in 1851, Henrietta Blanche should choose to present a regional chair from her birthplace as a gift, and in so doing, to have provided circumstantial evidence that this style of chair had continued to be made in the Macclesfield area until near the end of the 19th century, and that it apparently had importance as an artefact of local significance.

Plate 69. Side chair with fretted splat. Ash with rush seat, c.1780. Impressed 'BANCROFT' on top of both front legs. Bancrofts are recorded as chair makers from 1720 to 1819, working variously in Liverpool and Salford in Lancashire, and Prestbury in Cheshire.

Bar top ladder backs

Figure NW196. Bar top ladder back side chair. Ash. Attributed to Macclesfield, c.1800-80. This chair has a ladder and turned foot style in common with that of the Leicester made chair shown in Figure NW180.

Plain round turned front legs terminating in single ring and cup shaped feet. Front legs joined by two turned stretchers type A2, Figure NW289. Square and lower chamfered back legs, connected by single stretcher. Double side stretchers. Replaced sea-grass seat with wooden edge protective strips missing. Straight round turned back uprights terminating in ring and pear shaped turnings. Three plain ladders. Heavy curved bar passing over back uprights.

Figure NW197. Bar top ladder back side chair. Ash. Attributed to Macclesfield, c.1800-80.

Plain round turned front legs terminating in single ring and ball shaped feet. Front legs joined by two turned stretchers type A2, Figure NW289. Square and lower chamfered back legs, connected by two stretchers. Double side stretchers. Rush seat with wooden edge protective strips missing. Straight round turned back uprights terminating in pear shaped turnings. Four graduated plain ladders. Heavy curved chamfered bar passing over back uprights.

It is clear that certain forms of bar top chairs from the north west region too, have a stylistic relationship with the Macclesfield ladder back design, and indeed may have formed part of the Macclesfield makers' tradition. These chairs have round back uprights terminating in pear shaped turnings, but in these cases, a solid curved bar is used as a stay rail, rather than the curved round turned stay rail of the Macclesfield ladder back. Chairs in the bar top group are also not stained black in the same way as the Leicester chairs, and were often stained with mahogany or walnut stain.

Chairs included in the group (see Figures NW196-199 for examples), are clearly aligned with other regional 'common' chairs too, in terms of their heavy design, as well as with the finer Macclesfield chairs. These chairs, in turn, have further design relationships with other bar top ladder backs which do not have terminal pear shaped turnings to the back uprights, and in tracing group relationships by design association, this group of chairs ultimately extends to represent a highly elaborated regional group of designs, one in which the integration of parts from one or more styles into another was more commonly practised than in any other single generic group from this region.

Amongst this group, many of the design features which are included, are also found in other groups of standard ladder back chairs from the North West region, and can be traced as conspicuous associations. These include, for example, the straight front legs found in the bar top ladders shown in Figures NW201-207, which relate these chairs to certain standard ladder back chairs. The square corners to the seat frames shown in bar top chairs in Figures NW209-221 is a common stylistic device found in standard ladder back chairs in Figures NW308-316 for example; and the incorporation of quarter round topped legs and heavy bobbin turned front rails seen in the bar top ladders, Figures NW227-235, as well as the more simply turned front stretcher seen in Figure NW205 are features typical of double and treble

Figure NW198. Bar top ladder back side chair. Ash. Attributed to Lancashire/Cheshire, c.1800-80.

Round turned front legs with single ring turning terminating in pad feet (under pads missing). Front legs joined by turned stretcher type C, Figure NW289. Continuously chamfered back legs, connected by two stretchers. Double side stretchers. Rush seat with wooden edge protective strips missing. Straight round turned back uprights terminating in pear shaped turnings. Three graduated domed ladders, straight underneath. Curved chamfered bar or stay rail passing over back uprights. (See Figures NW273, 274 and 302 for standard ladder back chairs which incorporate this style of leg turning.)

row spindle back chairs from Lancashire and Cheshire, and serve to relate these bar top ladder back chairs to the wider community of North West region chairs.

Although only one provenanced chair of the bar top kind has been recorded, made by Peter Leicester (see Figure NW227), who worked at Hyde near to Manchester, and Plumley, near to Macclesfield,[104] the regional design assocations included in this group suggest that they were made by many makers throughout the Lancashire and Cheshire region, probably as part of different repertoires of spindle and ladder back chairs.

Figure NW199. Bar top ladder back side chair. Ash. Attributed to Lancashire/Cheshire, c.1780-1840.

Plain round turned front legs terminating in pad feet (under pads missing). Front legs joined by two turned stretchers type A3, Figure NW289. Continuously chamfered back legs, connected by double stretchers. Double side stretchers. Replaced sea-grass seat with wooden edge protective strips missing. Straight round turned back uprights terminating in pear shaped turnings. Three graduated domed ladders, straight underneath. Curved chamfered bar or stay rail passing over back uprights.

Figure NW200. Bar top ladder back side chair. Ash. Attributed to Lancashire/Cheshire, c.1780-1840. The design of this chair is similar to those in Figures NW196 and 199, with alternative forms of front leg and stretcher design, indicating the tendency of the North West chair turners to incorporate different design features within the same chair.

Plain round turned front legs terminating in pad feet. Front legs joined by turned stretcher type B2, Figure NW289. Square and lower chamfered back legs, connected by single stretcher. Double side stretchers. Rush seat with wooden edge protective strips. Straight round turned back uprights. Three graduated domed ladders, straight underneath. Curved bar passing over back uprights.

Figure NW201. Bar top ladder back side chair. Ash. Attributed to Lancashire/Cheshire, c.1780-1840.

Plain round turned front legs terminating in pad feet (under pads missing). Front legs joined by turned stretcher type C, Figure NW289. Round back legs, connected by single stretcher. Double side stretchers. Rush seat with wooden edge protective strips. Bent round turned back uprights. Three graduated domed ladders, straight underneath. Heavy curved bar passing over back uprights.

Figure NW202. Bar top ladder back side chair. Ash. Attributed to Lancashire/Cheshire, c.1780-1840. This chair is identical in design to the chair shown in Figure NW200 with the omission of the pear shaped turnings on the back uprights.

Plain round turned front legs terminating in pad feet. Front legs joined by turned stretcher type B2, Figure NW289. Square and lower chamfered back legs, connected by single stretcher. Double side stretchers. Rush seat with wooden edge protective strips. Straight round turned tapering back uprights. Three graduated domed ladders, straight underneath. Curved chamfered bar passing over back uprights.

Figure NW203. Bar top ladder back side chair. Ash. Attributed to Lancashire/Cheshire, c.1800-60. This front leg turning is common to chairs found in the Billinge/Pemberton/Wigan group (see Figures NW240 and 248). The front rail turning is typical of those found in the wavy line ladder group (see Figures NW355 and 358).

Plain round turned top to front legs with indented turning below, turned legs terminating in pad feet. Front legs joined by turned stretcher type H, Figure NW289. Square back legs, connected by single stretcher. Double side stretchers. Damaged rush seat with wooden edge protective strips missing. Straight round turned back uprights. Four graduated domed ladders, straight underneath. Heavy curved chamfered bar passing over back uprights.

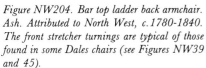

Figure NW204. Bar top ladder back armchair. Ash. Attributed to North West, c.1780-1840. The front stretcher turnings are typical of those found in some Dales chairs (see Figures NW39 and 45).

Plain round turned front legs terminating in pad feet (under pads missing). Front legs joined by three turned stretchers type A3, Figure NW289. Square back legs. Two back stretchers missing. Double side stretchers. Replaced rush seat with wooden edge protective strips missing. Straight round turned back uprights. Four graduated domed ladders, straight underneath. Heavy curved chamfered bar passing over back uprights. Curved shaped arms which mortice into back uprights with turned tenon. Turned underarm supports, type I, Figure NW71.

Figure NW205. Bar top ladder back side chair. Ash. Attributed to North West, c.1780-1840. The front rail stretcher turning is similar to that found in double row spindle back chairs from this region (see Figures NW80-83).

Plain round turned front legs terminating in indented pad feet. Front legs joined by three turned stretchers, type A1, Figure NW289. Continuously chamfered back legs, connected by double stretcher. Triple side stretchers. Rush seat with convex curved seat edges, with wooden edge protective strips. Straight round turned back uprights. Four graduated domed ladders, straight underneath. Heavy curved chamfered bar passing over back uprights.

Figure NW206. Bar top ladder back side chair. Ash. Attributed to North West, c.1780-1840. The use of triple side rails is unusual, and normally found in 18th century single row spindle back chairs from this region (see Figures NW3 and 4).

Plain round turned front legs terminating in pad feet. Front legs joined by two turned stretchers type A2, Figure NW289. Square back legs, connected by double stretchers. Triple side stretchers. Rush seat with wooden edge protective strips. Four graduated domed ladders shaped underneath with downward tip. Heavy curved chamfered bar passing over back uprights.

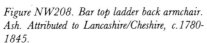

Figure NW207. Bar top ladder back side chair. Ash. Attributed to North West, c.1800-50.

Plain round turned front legs terminating in pad feet. Front legs joined by two turned stretchers type B2, Figure NW289. Square and lower chamfered back legs, connected by double stretchers. Double side stretchers. Rush seat with wooden edge protective strips. Straight round turned back uprights. Four graduated domed ladders, straight underneath. Heavy curved bar passing over back uprights.

Figure NW208. Bar top ladder back armchair. Ash. Attributed to Lancashire/Cheshire, c.1780-1845.

Plain round turned front legs terminating in pad feet. Front legs joined by turned stretcher type D, Figure NW289. Square back legs, connected by single stretcher. Double side stretchers. Damaged rush seat with wooden edge protective strips missing. Reclined round turned back uprights terminating in single ring and pear shaped turnings. Four graduated domed ladders shaped underneath with downward tip. Light curved chamfered bar passing over back uprights. Curved shaped arms which mortice into back uprights with turned tenons. Turned underarm supports type F, Figure NW71.

Figure NW209. Bar top ladder back side chair. Ash. Attributed to Lancashire/Cheshire, c.1800-45. The chairs shown in Figures NW209 and 211 show attempts by their makers to produce greater comfort in steaming and bending the back uprights to recline from seat level. Bending, after turning the uprights, was done over a former or pivot whose indented mark is typically found on the back legs of chairs of this type (see Figure NW210).

Turned tops to the front legs which mortice into the square corners of the seat frame; legs terminating in pad feet. Front legs joined by turned stretcher type E, Figure NW289. Continuously chamfered back legs, connected by single stretcher. Double side stretchers. Rush seat with two wooden edge protective strips missing. Reclined round turned back uprights terminating in pear shaped turnings. Four graduated domed ladders shaped underneath with downward tip. Curved chamfered bar passing over back uprights.

Figure NW210. The 'bruising' mark of the pivot or former over which the back uprights of the chair in Figure NW209 were bent after steaming. The ends of the uprights were probably held by a screw device which was used to bend the segment. This mark is typically found in chair styles shown in Figures NW209-211 and suggests that the style was the product of one maker or local community of makers.

Figure NW211. Bar top ladder back side chair. Ash. Attributed to Lancashire/Cheshire, c.1800-45.

Turned tops to the front legs which mortice into the square corners of the seat frame; legs terminating in pad feet. Front legs joined by turned stretcher type E, Figure NW289. Continuously chamfered back legs, connected by single stretcher. Double side stretchers. Rush seat with wooden edge protective strips. Reclined round turned back uprights terminating in pear shaped turnings. Four graduated domed ladders shaped underneath with upward tip. Curved chamfered bar passing over back uprights.

Figure NW212. Bar top ladder back side chair. Ash. Attributed to Lancashire/Cheshire, c.1800-45. This back leg form is unusual in the design of the bar top ladder chair, and is more usually found in the double row spindle back chair (see Figures NW84, 86 and 87).

Turned tops to the front legs which mortice into the square corners of the seat frame; legs terminating in pad feet. Front legs joined by turned stretcher type E, Figure NW289. Round back legs with square block at seat level, connected by single stretcher. Double side stretchers. Replaced rush seat with wooden edge protective strips missing. Straight round turned back uprights. Four graduated domed laders shaped underneath with downward tip. Thin curved bar passing over back uprights with vestigial ear terminals.

Figures NW213 and 214. The chair on the left is shown as a comparison with a standard ladder back chair, with which it has a close similarity. The back uprights of the right hand chair are taller and lack the pear shaped terminals and an extra ladder is fitted instead of the bar. The production of a different chair style is therefore achieved with the minimum of modification to an existing style.

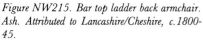

Figure NW215. Bar top ladder back armchair. Ash. Attributed to Lancashire/Cheshire, c.1800-45.

Quarter round top to the front legs, round turned below terminating in pad feet. Front legs joined by turned stretcher type C2, Figure NW289. Continuously chamfered back legs with later additions of flattened turnings, connected by double stretchers. Double side stretchers. Rush seat with wooden edge protective strips missing. Straight round turned back uprights. Four graduated domed ladders shaped underneath with upward tip. Heavy curved bar passing over back uprights. Curved shaped arms which mortice into back uprights with tapered tenons. Turned underarm supports type F, Figure NW71.

Figure NW216. Bar top ladder back side chair. Ash with alder top bar. Attributed to Lancashire/Cheshire, c.1780-1840.

Turned tops to the front legs which mortice into the square corners of the seat frame, terminating in pad feet. Front legs joined by turned stretcher type C2, Figure NW289. Square back legs, connected by single stretcher. Double side stretchers. Rush seat with three wooden edge protective strips missing. Straight round turned back uprights, slightly tapered into bar. Four graduated domed ladders shaped underneath with downward tip. Heavy curved bar passing over back uprights.

Figure NW217. Bar top ladder back side chair. Ash. Attributed to Lancashire/Cheshire, c.1780-1840.

Turned tops to the front legs which mortice into the square corners of the seat frame, terminating in pad feet. Front legs joined by turned stretcher type C2, Figure NW289. Square back legs, connected by double stretchers. Double side stretchers. Rush seat with wooden edge protective strips. Straight round turned back uprights. Four graduated domed ladders shaped underneath with upward tip. Heavy curved bar with vestigial ears passing over back uprights.

381

Figure NW218. Bar top ladder back side chair. Ash. Attributed to Lancashire/Cheshire, c.1780-1840. The back legs of this chair are more typically found in certain double row spindle back chairs (see Figures NW84, 86 and 87).

Turned tops to the front legs which mortice into the square corners of the seat frame, legs terminating in pad feet. Front legs joined by turned stretcher type C2, Figure NW289. Round back legs with square block at seat level, connected by single stretcher. Double side stretchers. Rush seat with wooden edge protective strips missing. Straight round turned back uprights. Four graduated domed ladders shaped underneath with upward tip. Heavy curved bar passing over back uprights.

Figure NW219. Bar top ladder back armchair. Ash. Attributed to Lancashire/Cheshire, c.1770-1840. This chair is the natural counterpart to the side chairs shown in Figures NW220 and 221.

Round turned front legs, with single indented turnings, which mortice into the square corners of the seat frame, legs terminating in indented pad feet (under pads missing). Front legs joined by turned stretcher type C2, Figure NW289. Continuously chamfered back legs, connected by double stretchers. Double side stretchers. Replaced rush seat with wooden edge protective strips missing. Reclined round turned back uprights with upper ring shaped turnings. Five graduated domed ladders shaped underneath with downward tip, top ladder only indented on upper surface. Light, crested chamfered bar passing over back uprights. Flattened scroll shaped arms which mortice into back uprights with tapered tenons. Turned underarm supports type I, Figure NW71, which mortice through the arms and are wedged on top.

Figure NW220. Bar top ladder back side chair. Ash. Attributed to Lancashire/Cheshire, c.1770-1840. The design relationship with Figure NW221, which has a front stretcher type C2, Figure NW289, enables a generic connection to be established between this chair and those in Figures NW215-218.

Turned tops to the front legs which mortice into the square corners of the seat frame. Legs terminating in pad feet. Front legs joined by turned stretcher type E, Figure NW289. Continuously chamfered back legs, connected by single stretcher. Double side stretchers. Rush seat with wooden edge protective strips. Reclined round turned back uprights with upper ring turnings. Four graduated domed ladders shaped underneath with downward tip, top ladder only with upper indentation. Chamfered crested bar passing over back uprights.

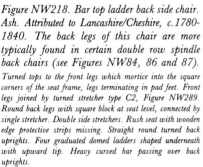

Figure NW221. Bar top ladder back side chair. Ash. Attributed to Lancashire/Cheshire, c.1770-1840. The front rail turnery signature in this chair suggests an association with the chairs shown in Figures NW215-218.

Turned tops to the front legs which mortice into the square corners of the seat frame, legs terminating in pad feet. Front legs joined by turned stretcher type C2, Figure NW289. Continuously chamfered back legs, connected by single stretcher. Double side stretchers. Damaged rush seat with three wooden edge protective strips missing. Straight round turned back uprights with upper indented turnings. Four graduated domed ladders shaped underneath with downward tip, top ladder only indented on upper surface. Light chamfered crested bar passing over back uprights.

Figure NW222. Bar top ladder back side chair. Ash. Attributed to Lancashire/Cheshire, c.1770-1840.

Round turned legs with single indentation, terminating in indented pad feet (pad feet replaced). Front legs joined by turned stretcher type C2, Figure NW289. Continuously chamfered back legs connected by single stretcher. Double side stretchers. Replaced rush seat with wooden edge strips missing. Straight round turned back uprights with upper indented turnings. Four graduated ladders. Top ladder with downward tip underneath; three lower ladders with domed top and straight underneath. Light chamfered crested bar passing over back uprights.

Figure NW223. Bar top ladder back armchair. Alder with ash front rail, stretchers, and ladders. Attributed to Lancashire/Cheshire, c.1780-1820. The ladder design of this chair is also included in standard ladder back chair designs (see Figure NW261). The front rail design included in this chair is also found in ladder back chairs, and Figures NW306 and 307 suggesting a stylistic relationship between them.

Plain round turned front legs terminating in pad feet. Front legs joined by turned stretcher type C3, Figure NW289. Round back legs, connected by single stretcher. Double side stretchers. Rush seat with wooden edge protective strips. Straight round turned back uprights terminating in flattened ball shaped turnings. Five curved graduated domed ladders shaped underneath with downward tip and shallow indentation above. Shaped stay rail passing over back uprights which reflects the design of the ladders. Curved shaped arms which mortice into back uprights with tapered tenons. Turned underarm supports similar to type I, Figure NW71.

Figure NW224. Bar top ladder back side chair. Ash. Attributed to Lancashire/Cheshire, c.1780-1820. This chair is the natural counterpart to the armchair shown in Figure NW223.

Turned top to the front legs which mortice into the square corners of the seat frame, terminating in replaced pad feet. Front legs joined by turned stretcher type M, Figure NW289. Round back legs, connected by single stretcher. Double side stretchers. Rush seat with one wooden edge protective strip missing. Straight round turned back uprights with indented shaped turnings. Four curved graduated domed ladders shaped underneath with downward tip and shaped indentation on top, Curved bar or stay rail passing over back uprights which reflects the shape of the ladders.

Figure NW225. Bar top ladder back armchair. Alder with ash ladders. Attributed to Lancashire/Cheshire, c.1780-1840. The front leg and front rail turnings are typical of those found in wavy line ladder back designs (see Figures NW352 and 368). The ladder shape adopted in this chair is also found in standard ladder back chairs (see Figures NW258-60).

Round turned front legs with ring turning, terminating in pad feet. Front legs joined by turned stretcher type H, Figure NW289. Square back legs, connected by single stretcher. Double side stretchers. Rush seat with wooden edge protective strips. Straight round turned back uprights, tapered into stay rail. Five curved graduated domed ladders, dished on top, straight underneath. Heavy curved chamfered bar with vestigial ears, passing over back uprights. Curved shaped arms which mortice into back uprights with turned tenons. Turned underarm supports type I, Figure NW71.

Figure NW226. Bar top ladder back armchair. Ash. Attributed to Lancashire/Cheshire, c.1770-1820.

Decoratively turned front legs, quarter round at top, terminating in pad feet. Front legs joined by turned stretcher type C2, Figure NW289. Round back legs with square block at seat level, connected by single stretcher. Double side stretchers. Rush seat with wooden edge protective strips missing. Reclined round turned back uprights wih indented turning. Four curved graduated ladder shaped underneath with upward tip. Heavy curved chamfered bar with vestigial ears passing over back uprights. Curved shaped arms which mortice into back uprights with turned tenons. Turned underarm supports type B, Figure NW71.

Figure NW227. Bar top ladder back side chair. Ash. Stamped 'P. LEICESTER' on rear of back legs. Plumley and Hyde, Cheshire (fl.1841-74). The form of front leg turning used in this chair links it with the double row spindle back chair in which this form is more typically found, and suggests that Peter Leicester also made spindle back chairs.

Quarter round top to the front legs, round turned below, terminating in pad feet. Front legs joined by turned stretcher type D, Figure NW289. Square back legs, connected by single stretcher. Double side stretchers. Rush seat with wooden edge protective strips. Slightly reclined round turned back uprights. Four graduated curved domed ladders shaped underneath with upward tip. Heavy curved chamfered bar passing over back uprights.

Figure NW228. The stamp of Peter Leicester of Plumley and Hyde, Cheshire (fl.1841-74), stamped on the side of the right hand leg of chair in Figure NW227. This maker was the nephew of Charles Leicester, senior, chair maker of Macclesfield. Peter was born in 1808, and moved to work near to Manchester at Hyde, Cheshire, with his brother Thomas, also a chair maker. By 1851, Peter had returned to work in Plumley.

Figure NW229. Bar top ladder back armchair. Ash. Attributed to Lancashire/Cheshire, c.1780-1840. The particular form of front stretcher turning links this chair with those shown in Figures NW227 and 230.

Round turned front legs, bulbous at seat level, terminating in pad feet. Front legs joined by turned stretcher type D, Figure NW289. Square back legs, connected by single stretcher. Double side stretchers. Replaced sea-grass seat with wooden edge protective strips missing. Straight round turned back uprights tapered into top bar. Four graduated curved domed ladders shaped underneath with upward tip. Light, curved chamfered bar passing over back uprights. Curved shaped arms which mortice into back uprights with turned tenons. Turned underarm supports type I, Figure NW71, which are half the turning included in the front stretcher.

Figure NW230. Bar top ladder back armchair. Ash. Attributed to Lancashire/Cheshire, c.1780-1840. This chair is similar in design to that shown in Figure NW229, with the exception that the underarm turnings are typical of those found in triple row spindle back chairs.

Plain round turned front legs, terminating in pad feet. Front legs joined by turned stretcher type D, Figure NW289. Square and lower chamfered back legs, connected by single stretcher. Double side stretchers. Rush seat with wooden edge protective strips missing. Straight round turned back uprights. Four slightly graduated curved domed ladder shaped underneath with upward tip. Curved chamfered bar with vestigial ears, passing over back uprights. Curved shaped arms which mortice into back uprights with tapered tenons. Turned underarm supports type B, Figure NW71.

Figure NW231. Bar top ladder back armchair on later rockers. Ash. Attributed to Lancashire/ Cheshire, c.1770-1820. This is an unusual design, of which no side chair version has been recorded.

Round turned front legs with single ring turning terminating in pad feet (left hand foot missing). Front legs joined by two elaborately turned stretchers. Continuously chamfered back legs, connected by single stretcher. Double side stretchers. Damaged rush seat with wooden edge protective strips missing. Reclined round turned back uprights with ring shaped turnings. Five graduated curved ladders with angular shaping above, straight underneath. Light, curved shaped bar passing over back uprights which mortice through the stay rail; back uprights sawn and wedged on top. Curved shaped arms (left hand arm damaged end), which mortice into back uprights with tapered tenons. Turned underarm supports type G, Figure NW71.

Figure NW232. Bar top ladder back armchair. Alder with ash front rail, stretchers and ladders. Attributed to Lancashire/Cheshire, c.1800-50. The underarm support and front rail types are typically found in triple row spindle back armchairs, and link this chair with the spindle back designs The use of alder in the chairs shown in Figures NW232-235 is also typical of many double row spindle back chairs, and suggest that these chairs were perhaps made by the same group of makers.

Heavy quarter round front legs terminating in indented pad feet. Front legs joined by turned stretcher type F, Figure NW289. Square back legs, connected by single stretcher. Double side stretchers. Damaged rush seat with wooden edge protective strips missing. Straight round turned back uprights, tapered into top bar. Four curved graduated domed ladders shaped underneath with downward tip. Heavy curved chamfered bar passing over back uprights. Curved shaped arms which mortice into back uprights with turned tenons. Turned underarm supports type B, Figure NW71.

Figure NW233. Bar top ladder back side chair. Ash with alder back uprights. Attributed to Lancashire/Cheshire, c.1800-50. The front legs and front stretcher turnings are more typically found in double row spindle back chairs.

Plain round turned front legs, terminating in pad feet. Front legs joined by turned stretcher type F, Figure NW289. Square back legs, connected by single stretcher. Double side stretchers. Replaced rush seat with wooden edge protective strips missing. Straight round turned back uprights. Four graduated curved domed ladders shaped underneath with downward tip. Curved chamfered bar passing over back uprights.

Figure NW234. Bar top ladder back armchair. Alder with ash ladders and stretchers. Attributed to Lancashire/Cheshire, c.1800-50. This front stretcher type is typically found in triple row spindle back chairs (see Figure NW102).

Quarter round top to the front legs, turned below, tapering and terminating in pad feet. Front legs joined by turned stretcher type F, Figure NW289. Square back legs connected by single stretcher. Double side stretchers. Rush seat with wooden edge strips. Straight round turned back uprights. Four graduated curved domed ladders with upward tip below. Heavy curved bar passing over back uprights. Flattened scroll shaped arms which mortice into back uprights with tapered tenons. Turned underarm supports type B, Figure NW71.

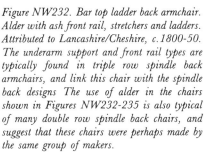

Figure NW235. Bar top ladder back side chair. Alder with ash ladders. Attributed to Lancashire/Cheshire, c.1800-50. This front stretcher type is typically found in the double row spindle back side chairs (see Figure NW109).

Quarter round top to the front legs, round turned below, terminating in pad feet. Front legs joined by turned stretcher type F, Figure NW289. Square back legs connected by single stretcher. Double side stretchers. Rush seat with wooden edge strips missing. Straight round turned back uprights. Four graduated curved domed ladders shaped underneath with upward tip. Heavy curved bar passing over back uprights.

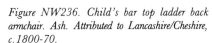

Figure NW236. Child's bar top ladder back armchair. Ash. Attributed to Lancashire/Cheshire, c.1800-70.

Round turned front legs terminating in pad feet. Front legs connected by turned stretcher. Round back legs connected by single stretcher. Double side stretchers. Rush seat with three wooden edge strips missing. Straight round turned back uprights. Three domed ladders shaped underneath with accentuated downward tip. Heavy curved chamfered bar passing over back uprights. Curved shaped arms which mortice into back uprights with turned tenons. Turned heavy underarm supports. Height: 69.6cm. Width: 43cm. Depth: 30cm.

Figure NW238. A photograph of a tableau, taken from the Wigan Advertiser, recording the Wigan Carnival in 1938, which shows the lathe, reputed to have belonged to John Jackson, being used to turn a chair part. The chair styles believed by local tradition to have been made by Jackson in the 1860s are shown to the left of the scene. The chair on the left is a side chair of the type shown in Figure NW240, and the child's chair is shown in Figure NW245.

Figure NW237. Bar top ladder back armchair. Ash. Attributed to the Billinge/Pemberton/Wigan area of Lancashire, c.1800-75. This chair epitomises the strong, well made qualities of the Lancashire/Cheshire chair turners' craft, producing a style of powerful originality within the conventions of an important tradition. See also Plate 49 for a further example.

Quarter round top to the front legs, plain turned below terminating in pad feet. Front legs joined by turned stretcher type I, Figure NW289. Continuously chamfered back legs, connected by single stretcher. Double side stretchers. Rush seat with wooden edge protective strips replaced. Bent round turned back uprights with indented ring and turning above. Five slightly graduated curved domed ladders shaped underneath with downward tip. Curved chamfered bar with prominent crest and downward tip below and vestigial ears, passing over back uprights. Back uprights morticed through the top bar, and secured by domed cap turnings. Flattened curved shaped arms, with prominent spur on outer edge, which mortice into back uprights with tapered tenons. Turned underarm supports similar to type B, Figure NW71.

Figure NW239. The lathe 'bed' believed to be that used by John Jackson. This lathe, now separated from the flywheel and treadle mechanism, was kept in an outhouse in the village of Billinge by a descendant. It is recorded that Jackson hired two labourers to help in the turning of his chairs, and these men probably treadled the lathe as one of their tasks. *Photograph courtesy J.M. Boram*

The Billinge Chair

Both hearsay and documentary evidence suggest that a strong local tradition of chair making developed in the coal mining village of Billinge during the nineteenth century, with one particular style of chair being made. This chair (see Figures NW237 and 240) represents a pinnacle of this region's chair turners' art, and although essentially located within the bar top ladder group, displays forms of detailed turnery and bench work which illustrates the style as an important sub-group, described here as the 'Billinge chair' in recognition of its geographical association.

Of the chair style positively attributed to Billinge, both standard arm and low-armed varieties were made, where the armchairs have elaborate crested stay rails held with decorative buttons to the uprights, and shaped arms with 'spurred' profiles, which are peculiar to this style (see Figures NW237, 246 and 247). The side chairs which accompany these armchairs have a raised domed top bar with a downward tip which reflects the shape of the ladders below, and heavy round topped front legs which are found in a few other regional styles of less elaborate design quality (see Figure NW203). The seat edging strips used for both arm and side chairs are peculiar to this design, and have a concave inside face, made to fit around the rush. This refinement, in combination with the other individually well designed parts, results in a powerfully satisfying local chair style.

However, the notion that this style

Figure NW241. The rear of the left hand back upright of the chair shown in Figure NW240, showing the iron 'sprig' or nail used to fix the top bar in place.

Figure NW240. Bar top ladder back side chair. Ash. Attributed to the Billinge/Pemberton/Wigan area, Lancashire, c.1780-1875.

Plain round turned tip to the front legs, indented turning below; round turned legs, terminating in pad feet. Front legs joined by turned stretcher, type C, Figure NW289. Round turned back legs, connected by single stretcher. Double side stretchers. Rush seat with original wooden edge protective strips. Straight round turned back uprights. Four graduated curved domed ladders, downward projections underneath. Heavy bar with pronounced curved shaping and vestigial ears, passing over back uprights.

Figure NW242. A close-up picture of the indented turning taken from the front leg of the chair shown in Figure NW240, illustrating the precise turnery skills employed by the maker.

Figure NW244. Detail of the top of the left hand front leg of the chair shown in Figure NW240, showing the decorative ring turning often found in this style of chair. This form of decoration is also typically found in wavy line ladder back chairs which have type C legs (see Figures NW362 and 364), and suggests that both of these designs may have been included in the repertoires of the same makers.

Figure NW243. One type of back leg design used in this form of bar top chair which has its corners continuously chamfered to create an octagonal shape. Other versions of this leg are bent at seat level to create greater comfort for the user (see Figure NW247 for an example).

of chair was entirely the province of the Billinge makers is probably erroneous, since although records show that a strong tradition of chair making was carried out in Billinge from around 1790[105] until 1861,[106] other chair makers were also working within a four mile radius of Billinge, including the nearby parish of Lamberhead Green,[107] and in the local textile and mining town of Wigan,[108] as well as the town of Rainford. It may be that this chair style was made in large quantities in other towns too, and the circumstantial evidence of large cabinet and chair making firms working in Ormskirk, points to this town as being a possible place of manufacture.

Within Billinge itself the first recorded maker was possibly Thomas Hunt, who was noted as a chair maker of the Parish of Leigh some eight miles away, at his marriage in Billinge in 1783;[109] or John Holden, who is recorded as a chair maker living in the Parish of Billinge at his marriage in 1796.[110] It remained until the census records of 1841 for another chair maker, John Jackson, aged fifty, to be recorded as a chair maker working at Gorsey Brow, Chapel End, Billinge.

This maker was a member of a large group of chair makers and turners named Jackson, who are recorded working in Lancashire, and in other chair making centres of North Cheshire.* At the same time, another chair maker, Aaron Dixon, aged fifty-five, is also recorded living at and working Chapel End, Billinge.[111] In 1841, James Jackson, son of John, was also recorded, working as a chair weaver,[112] and no doubt rush seated the chairs made by his father and possibly Aaron Dixon. However, by 1851, James had given up his craft and become an agricultural labourer.[113]

By 1851, James Dixon, son of Aaron, who had been a sawyer in Billinge, joined his father as a chair maker,[114] and it may be that at this stage, Aaron Dixon had his own workshop, since he employed Robert Clemison, a chair maker aged thirty-two, as his 'servant'.[115] Another James Dixon, who had a long history as a chair maker working in Byrom Street, Liverpool since 1810,[116] visited Billinge, his birth place, in 1851, when he was aged sixty-one. This maker was probably related to the Dixons who worked in the village, and the record of his visit,[117] confirms the possibility of an aware-

Figure NW245. Photograph of James Fairhurst, aged about seven years, taken in 1931, with the ladder back child's rocking chair which was reputedly made by John Jackson, chair maker of Billinge, Lancashire (fl. 1830-66). Jackson was James Fairhurst's great-great grandfather, and he had made this chair for James's father, Thomas Fairhurst, who was born in 1860. This chair is believed to be the last chair made by Jackson, and was exhibited as such in a local carnival tableau in 1938 (see Figure NW238). However, the chair making tradition continued after Jackson's retirement in Lamberhead Green, near Billinge, until 1881, and in Pemberton until 1909.

Photograph courtesy Betty Gaskell, née Fairhurst.

Figure NW246. Bar top ladder back rocking armchair. Ash. Attributed to the Billinge/Pemberton/Wigan area of Lancashire, c.1780-1875. This chair is the natural counterpart to the chairs shown in Figures NW237 and 240.

Quarter round top to the front legs, round turned below, legs terminating in pad feet fixed to shallow curved wooden rockers. Front legs joined by turned stretcher type J, Figure NW289. Continuously chamfered back legs, connected by single stretcher. Double side stretchers. Rush seat with original wooden edge protective strips. Round turned back uprights with indented ring and turret turning above. Five slightly graduated curved domed ladders, shaped underneath with downward tip. Curved chamfered bar with prominent crest and vestigial ears, passing over back uprights which mortice through the top bar and are secured by domed cap turnings. Low-set flattened curved shaped arms with prominent spur on outer edge, which mortice into back uprights with tapered tenons. Turned underarm supports in a shortened form of type B, Figure NW71.

ness of regional chair styles between Liverpool and the Billinge area makers.

By 1851, a further chair maker, William Preston, aged forty-seven, who was born in Clayton, Lancashire, had set up a workshop at Longshaw End, Billinge.[118] By 1869 he had moved to nearby Lamberhead Green, where he worked for about twelve years,[119] and by 1871, he had been joined by two further chair makers,

father and son, named Jackson and Peter Crousdale, who came from Westmorland.[120] Interestingly, the chair making tradition was continued in Pemberton, later in the nineteenth century, and into the early twentieth century by a chair maker named Harry King who worked as a cabinet and chair maker at Soho Street, Newtown, Pemberton, between 1903 and 1909.[121] This maker, however,

---

* Chair makers and turners with the surname Jackson who are recorded in centres other than Billinge are as follows:

Charles.	1879-1887.	Turner.	Manchester.
George.	1851.	Chairmaker.	Congleton, Cheshire.
George.	1882-1891.	Wood turner.	Blackburn, Lancs.
George.	1882.	Wood turner.	Manchester.
George.	1888.	Chairmaker.	Macclesfield, Cheshire.
Hannah.	1861.	Chairmaker.	Wigan, Lancashire.
John.	1851-1888.	Wood turner.	Congleton, Cheshire.
John.	1874.	Chairmaker.	Altrincham, Cheshire.
John.	1871-1873.	Turner.	Manchester.
Joseph.	1822-1830.	Chairmaker.	Nantwich, Cheshire.
Thomas.	1819.	Chairmaker.	Nantwich, Cheshire.

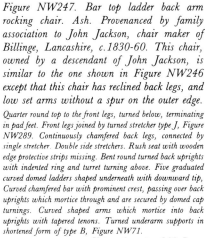

Figure NW247. Bar top ladder back arm rocking chair. Ash. Provenanced by family association to John Jackson, chair maker of Billinge, Lancashire, c.1830-60. This chair, owned by a descendant of John Jackson, is similar to the one shown in Figure NW246 except that this chair has reclined back legs, and low set arms without a spur on the outer edge.

Quarter round top to the front legs, turned below, terminating in pad feet. Front legs joined by turned stretcher type J, Figure NW289. Continuously chamfered back legs, connected by single stretcher. Double side stretchers. Rush seat with wooden edge protective strips missing. Bent round turned back uprights with indented ring and turret turning above. Five graduated curved domed ladders shaped underneath with downward tip, Curved chamfered bar with prominent crest, passing over back uprights which mortice through and are secured by domed cap turnings. Curved shaped arms which mortice into back uprights with tapered tenons. Turned underarm supports in shortened form of type B, Figure NW71.

Photograph courtesy J.M. Boram

Figure NW248. Bar top ladder back side chair. Ash. Attributed to the Billinge/Pemberton/Wigan area of Lancashire, c.1780-1875. The leg and back upright design of this chair is illustrated in detail in Figure NW243 and is similar in form to that shown in Figure NW240.

Plain round turned top to the front legs, indented turning below; round turned legs terminating in pad feet. Front legs joined by turned stretcher type C, Figure NW289. Continuously chamfered back legs, connected by single stretcher. Double side stretchers. Rush seat with replaced wooden edge protective strips. Straight round turned back uprights. Four graduated curved domed ladders, straight underneath. Heavy bar with pronounced curved shaping, with vestigial ears, passing over back uprights.

Figure NW249. Bar top ladder back armchair. Ash with alder. Attributed to the North West, c.1800-50. This armchair is the natural counterpart to the side chair shown in Figure NW248.

Plain round turned front legs terminating in pad feet. Front legs joined by turned stretcher type C, Figure NW289. Square back legs with chamfered corners. One back stretcher; double side stretchers. Straight round turned back uprights. Five graduated domed ladders, straight underneath. Heavy curved chamfered bar passing over back uprights. Curved shaped arms which mortice into back uprights with turned tenons. Turned underarm supports.

was probably making inexpensive Windsor kitchen chairs rather than rush seated chairs, and a kitchen Windsor made by this maker is shown in Figure NW414.

By 1861, John Jackson's son, also John, had joined his father, by now aged seventy-three, as a chair maker's labourer,[122] no doubt carrying out many of the arduous workshop tasks of preparing wood and treadling the lathe. Two further chair makers lived with John Jackson and his son John at this time. Both of these were named William Dixon;[123] the one, aged fifty-one, born in Manchester, the other, aged sixty-two, was born in Ireland, and had been working as a chair maker for the past twenty years in Wigan. Both of these craftsmen probably worked in the

Jackson workshop under the supervision of the now aged owner. It is not clear how long this workshop continued after 1861, but John, senior died, aged seventy-eight, on 14th January, 1866.[124]

In addition to the chair making traditions which arose in the Billinge area, chairs were also made in the nearby town of Wigan. John Holding (Holden) is recorded as a chair maker in Billinge at his marriage in 1796,[125] but by 1816, he had moved to work at Millgate, Wigan,[126] where he remained until 1837.[127] William Dixon also worked in 1841, as a chair maker in Wigan,[128] at Scholar Street and Actons Court, before moving to Billinge around 1861[129] to continue in his trade working for John Jackson.

The existence of chairs attributed to John Jackson, and the evidence of the other makers who were drawn to the village and its environs, as well as to the town of Wigan, indicates that there was a distinct local tradition which probably supplied the nearby industrial town of Wigan with chairs of the kind shown in Figures NW240, 246 and 248. However, given that this region's chair makers typically made a range of chair styles, the Billinge and Wigan chair makers probably also made other designs.

The importance of this local tradition is considerable, since it epitomises a tradition in which craft competence and design innovation combined in the production of chairs of the highest qualities associated with the regional chairs of England.

Figure NW250. Bar top ladder back side chair. Ash. Attributed to the Billinge/Pemberton/ Wigan area of Lancashire, c.1780-1875. This style is similar to that shown in Figure NW248, but is probably a more economically produced chair than other chairs in this group, indicated by straight back legs and uprights, and fewer and simplified ladders.

Round turned top with ring turnings to the front legs, indented turning below; round turned legs terminating in pad feet. Front legs joined by turned stretcher type C, Figure NW289. Round back legs, connected by single stretcher. Double side stretchers. Damaged rush seat with wooden edge protective strips missing. Straight round turned back uprights. Three graduated curved domed ladders, straight underneath. Curved and shaped bar passing over back uprights.

Figure NW251. Bar top ladder back side chair. Ash. Attributed to the Billinge/Pemberton/ Wigan area of Lancashire, c.1780-1875. The front stretcher type shown in this chair is also found in the Dales spindle and ladder back chairs shown in Figure NW45.

Round turned top to the front legs, indented turning below; round turned legs terminating in pad feet. Front legs joined by two turned stretchers, type K, Figure NW289. Round back legs, connected by double stretchers. Double side stretchers. Replaced rush seat with wooden edge protective strips missing. Straight round turned back uprights. Three graduated curved domed ladders, straight underneath. Pronounced curved shaping to bar or stay rail with vestigial ears, passing over back uprights.

Standard ladder back chairs

The great majority of standard ladder back chair styles made in the North West tradition were probably made in local traditions, and tend to be grouped by design association into small repertoires of strongly related styles. The many sub-groups of chairs within this category have been termed standard ladder back chairs. This title is intended merely to designate the basic style, which may be perceived as a chair frame characterised by two back uprights which are connected by a variable number of ladders or splats. This fundamental description serves to distinguish this style of ladder back chair from those which have various forms of top bars, both square in section and round turned, connecting the back uprights. In no other sense is the generic term 'standard ladder backs' intended to be applied.

Individual chairs within these stylistic groups, in turn, show a further tendency to become linked by one or more features to members of other groups, and in this way, a truly rich and diverse network of North West regional styles may be traced. The process of linking design by turnery signatures, particularly that of the front stretcher design, and by ladder shaping, back leg shaping,

finial turnings, and general demeanour, offers a fascinating system which is ultimately codified in a complex manner. This patterning of design features serves to suggest that although individual styles are often superficially quite different from each other, they share a common stylistic code in which the transference of elements from one design to another was open to interpretation and experimentation by their makers.

Some chairs in this diverse group indicate by their condition and design that they have been made from the middle of the late eighteenth century, and it may be that different styles of ladder back chairs underwent great proliferation towards the end of the eighteenth century, before being gradually rejected in favour of more standardised styles which eventually became dominant, for example, in the form of the wavy line ladder back chairs (see Figures NW352 and 355).

In keeping with other forms of regional chair types, this broad group contains physically heavy, medium, and light designs of chairs, and includes those which relate to other major groups of chairs, and those which hold little significant reference to designs outside their own restricted

system. For example, the chairs shown in Figures NW253-261 show a clear relationship with double row spindle back chairs from the region, including the adoption of front leg styles typical of spindle back chairs, and, in the case of chairs shown in Figures NW253 and 254, the front stretcher turning type V, Figure NW70, also connects them to spindle back designs. The ladder shapes shown in the chairs in Figures NW258-262, which have a dished shaped top, also have a stylistic counterpart in a particular design of bar top ladder back chair shown in Figures NW223-225.

The examples shown in Figures NW260 and 263-269, also show a heavy demeanour, but in these cases, the front leg and stretcher turnings refer them to a range of other regional ladder back groups. For example, the front leg and stretcher styles shown in the bar top ladder back chairs in Figures NW209-213 are closely related to them stylistically, and strongly illustrate the tendency in the North West for chair makers to alter one particular aspect of a basic chair design in order to create a new style.

Five other ladder back chairs are illustrated in Figures NW270-274

Figure NW252. *Illustration of Lancashire hand spinners working at home in the early 19th century. On the right a woman sits on a robust ladder back chair which has the general demeanour of those shown in Figures NW253 and 254. This style of chair clearly had strength of structure as a priority, rather than elegance of design.*[130]

Figure NW253. *Heavy standard ladder back side chair. Ash. Attributed to Lancashire, c.1770-1840. This robust style was clearly made as a utilitarian chair, possibly for places of work, and has similarities with the chair shown being used by Lancashire hand spinners in Figure NW252.*

Plain round turned front legs with ring turned feet. Front legs joined by two turned stretchers type A2, Figure NW289. Square and lower chamfered back legs, connected by single stretcher. Double side stretchers. Rush seat with wooden edge protective strips missing. Reclined round turned back uprights terminating in pronounced nipple finials. Three plain ladders, a broad ladder at the top and two narrow ladders below.

Figure NW254. *Heavy standard ladder back side chair. Ash. Attributed to Lancashire, c.1770-1840.*

Plain round turned front legs joined by turned stretcher type A2, Figure NW289. Square and lower chamfered back legs, connected by single stretcher. Double side stretchers. Replaced rush seat with wooden edge protective strips missing. Slightly reclined round turned back uprights terminating in domed nipple finials. Four graduated curved domed ladders, straight underneath.

Figure NW255. *Heavy standard ladder back armchair. Ash. Attributed to Lancashire/Cheshire, c.1800-60. This style of chair is constructed in a similar manner to a typical three row spindle back armchair, but with the incorporation of ladders, and a front rail turning reserved for ladder back chairs.*

Quarter round front legs, turned below, terminating in pad feet. Front legs joined by turned stretcher type D, Figure NW289. Square back legs, connected by single stretcher. Double side stretchers. Rush seat with wooden edge protective strips. Slightly reclined round turned back uprights. Six graduated curved domed ladders. Straight underneath. Curved shaped arms which mortice into back uprights with tapered tenons. Turned underarm supports type I, Figure NW71.

which, although incorporating different styles of ladder shapes, are similar in demeanour, and are further associated in the front leg style which they have. The simple front leg turnings included in the chairs shown in Figures NW270-272, relate these chairs to other styles, including the bar top ladder back, for example, shown in Figure NW207 which also includes the double front stretcher form shown in the standard ladder back chair in Figure NW270. Other standard ladder back chairs made with this front leg style are shown in Figures NW277 and 279. The chairs shown in Figures NW273 and 274 include a round turned front leg which has a prominent ring turning. This style relates these chairs to a community of other designs, including bar top ladder back designs shown in Figure NW196, and to other standard ladder back styles (see Figure NW302).

Figure NW256. Heavy standard ladder back armchair. Ash. Attributed to Lancashire/Cheshire, c.1800-60. The inclusion of ladders within a basic spindle back armchair illustrates the tendency for chair makers to occasionally amalgamate features from two different designs to create a further style; in this case, to produce a rather more powerful design than is typical of the majority of ladder back armchairs.

Heavy quarter round front legs joined by turned stretcher type F, Figure NW289. Square and lower chamfered back legs, connected by single stretcher. Double side stretchers. Original wicker seat with wooden edge protective strips. Slightly reclined round turned back uprights. Seven graduated curved domed ladders, straight underneath. Curved shaped arms which mortice into back uprights with turned tenons. Turned underarm supports type B, Figure NW71.

Figure NW257. Heavy standard ladder back side chair. Ash with alder legs. Attributed to Lancashire/Cheshire, c.1800-60. This chair is similar to the heavy spindle back chairs illustrated in Figures NW72 and 74, made by J. Allen and D. Neild, of Cheshire. This chair, like its armchair counterparts in Figures NW255 and 256, represents an amalgamation of ladders and front rail turnings typical of some ladder back chairs, within a basic heavy spindle back frame, to create a further style.

Quarter round tops to the front legs round turned below, terminating in pad feet. Front legs joined by turned stretcher type S, Figure NW289. Square and lower chamfered back legs, connected by single stretcher. Double side stretchers. Rush seat with wooden edge protective strips. Slightly reclined round turned back uprights. Five graduated curved domed ladders, straight underneath.

Figure NW258. Heavy standard ladder back side chair. Ash. Attributed to Lancashire/Cheshire, c.1800-60. The front legs are typical of that adopted by many heavy double row spindle back chairs (see Figure NW72).

Quarter round tops to the front legs, plain turned below, terminating in pad feet. Heavy front legs joined by turned stretcher type C2, Figure NW289. Square and lower chamfered back legs, connected by single stretcher. Double side stretchers. Rush seat with two broken seat rails and wooden edge strips missing. Straight round turned back uprights. Five graduated curved ladders with shallow indentation above and straight underneath (top of top ladder replaced).

Figure NW259. Heavy standard ladder back armchair. Ash. Attributed to Lancashire/Cheshire, c.1800-60.

Quarter round tops to the front legs, round turned below, terminating in damaged pad feet. Front legs joined by turned stretcher type D, Figure NW289. Square and lower chamfered back legs, connected by single stretcher. Double side stretchers. Rush seat with wooden edge protective strips missing. Straight round turned back uprights terminating in nipple shaped finials. Six graduated curved ladders with shallow indentation above, and straight underneath. Curved shaped arms which mortice into back uprights with tapered tenons. Turned underarm support similar to type D, Figure NW71.

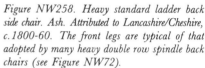

Figure NW260. Standard ladder back side chair. Ash. Attributed to Lancashire/Cheshire, c.1800-60. This front leg style was also incorporated in bar top and Macclesfield style chairs (see Figures NW190 and 218).

Turned tops to the front legs which mortice into the square corners of the seat frame, terminating in pad feet. Front legs joined by turned stretcher type C2, Figure NW289. Square and pronounced lower chamfered back legs, connected by single stretcher. Double side stretchers. Replacement rush seat with wooden edge protective strips missing. Straight round turned back uprights terminating in nipple shaped finials. Five graduated curved ladders with extra large top ladder, dished on upper surface, and straight underneath.

Figure NW261. Heavy standard ladder back side chair on later rockers. Ash. Attributed to Lancashire/Cheshire, c.1800-60. The ladder form in this chair was also adopted in a style of bar top ladder backs. See Figures NW223 and 224. The front leg and stretcher design is typical of that adopted by many double row spindle back chairs (see Figures NW109 and 113).

Quarter round tops to the front legs, plain turned below, pad feet missing. Front legs joined by turned stretcher type F, Figure NW289. Square and lower chamfered back legs, connected by single stetcher. Double side stretchers. Rush seat with two wooden edge protective strips missing. Straight round turned back uprights. Five graduated curved ladders shaped underneath with downward tip, and shallow indentation above.

Figure NW262. Heavy standard ladder back side chair. Ash with alder ladders and back uprights. Attributed to Lancashire/Cheshire, c.1800-60. The leg design of this chair is typically found in bar top ladder back chairs shown in Figures NW240 and 248, particularly from the Billinge area. This particular form of front stretcher turning was also used in some styles of bar top ladder back chairs (see Figures NW217-219).

Round tops to the front legs, turned below, terminating in pad feet. Front legs joined by heavy turned stretcher type C2, Figure NW289. Square back legs, connected by single stretcher. Double side stretchers. Replaced sea-grass seat with wooden edge protective strips missing. Straight round turned back uprights terminating in nipple finials. Five graduated curved ladders (top ladder damaged), with shallow indentation above, and straight underneath.

Figure NW263. Heavy standard ladder back side chair. Ash. Attributed to Lancashire/Cheshire, c.1780-1840. This chair is similar in design to the chair in Figure NW260 which has an alternative form of ladder shape, and to the bar top ladder shown in Figure NW209, which has alternative upright terminals and top bar incorporated to create further styles.

Turned tops to the front legs which mortice into the square corners of the seat frame, terminating in pad feet. Front legs joined by turned stretcher type C2, Figure NW289. Square and lower chamfered back legs, connected by single stretcher. Double side stretchers. Rush seat with wooden edge protective strips missing. Straight round turned bakc uprights terminating in nipple finials. Five graduated curved domed ladders shaped underneath with downward tip.

Figure NW264. Heavy standard ladder back armchair. Alder with ash ladders and stretchers. Attributed to Lancashire, c.1780-1850. This chair has many features of a wavy line ladder back chair (see Figure NW352).

Round turned front legs with indented turning below seat level, terminating in pad feet. Front legs joined by turned stretcher type H, Figure NW289. Square and lowered chamfered back legs, connected by single stretcher. Double side stretchers. Replaced rush seat with wooden edge protective strips. Straight round turned splayed back uprights terminating in domed nipple finials. Six graduated curved domed ladders shaped underneath with downward tip. Curved shaped arms which mortice into back uprights with tapered tenons. Turned underarm supports type I, Figure NW71.

Figure NW265. Heavy standard ladder back side chair. Ash with alder back legs. Attributed to Lancashire/Cheshire, c.1780-1840. This chair is similar in design to the chair shown in Figure NW263 and shows an alternative front stretcher used in this design.

Turned pear shaped tops to the front legs which mortice into the square corners of the seat frame, legs terminating in pad feet. Front legs joined by turned stretcher type F, Figure NW289. Round back legs, connected by single stretcher. Double side stretchers. Replaced sea-grass seat with wooden edge protective strips missing. Straight round turned back uprights terminating in domed finials. Five graduated curved domed ladders shaped underneath with downward tip.

Figure NW266. Heavy standard ladder back side chair. Ash with alder back uprights. Attributed to Lancashire/Cheshire, c.1780-1840. This chair is similar in design to the chairs shown in Figures NW264 and 265 but with the alternative form of upward tipped ladder shape.

Turned pear shaped tops to the front legs which mortice into the square corners of the seat frame, legs terminating in pad feet. Front legs joined by turned stretcher type C2, Figure NW289. Round back legs, connected by single stretcher. Double side stretchers. Rush seat missing. Straight round turned back uprights terminating in nipple finials. Five graduated curved domed ladders shaped underneath with upward tip.

Figure NW267. Heavy standard ladder back side chair. Ash with alder back legs. Attributed to Lancashire, c.1780-1840. The shape of the ladders in this chair is typical of a further group of chairs from this region (see Figures NW299-304).

Turned tops to the front legs which mortice into the square corners of the seat frame, legs terminating in pad feet. Front legs joined by turned stretcher type L, Figure NW289. Round back legs, connected by single stretcher. Double side stretchers. Lower side stretchers connected by elliptically turned cross stretcher. Rush seat with wooden edge protective strips missing. Straight round turned back uprights terminating in scribed ring and nipple finials. Five graduated curved domed ladders shaped underneath with downward tip.

Figure NW268. Heavy standard ladder back side chair. Ash. Attributed to Lancashire/ Cheshire, c.1780-1840. The frame of this chair is identical to that shown in Figure NW267 and illustrates how alternative ladder shapes were used in this tradition to create different styles from essentially the same chair frame.

Turned tops to the front legs which mortice into the square corners of the seat frame, legs terminating in pad feet (damaged). Front legs joined by turned stretcher type L, Figure NW289. Round back legs, connected by single stretcher. Double side stretchers (lower right hand stretcher missing). The cross rail connecting the lower side rails is missing. Rush seat with wooden edge protective strips missing. Straight round turned back uprights terminating in scribed line and nipple finials. Five graduated crescent shaped curved ladders.

Figure NW269. Heavy standard ladder back side chair. Ash. Attributed to Lancashire, c.1780-1840.

Turned pear shaped tops to the front legs which mortice into the square corners of the seat frame. Feet missing. Front legs joined by turned stretcher type C2, Figure NW289. Continuously chamfered back legs, connected by single stretcher. Double side stretchers. Damaged original wicker seat with wooden edge protective strips missing. Reclined round turned back uprights terminating in scribed ring and nipple finials. Four curved domed ladders (top ladder damaged), shaped underneath with downward tip.

Figure NW270. Standard ladder back side chair. Ash. Attributed to the North West, c.1800-60. This shape of ladder was a common form in the Lancashire tradition, and other examples are shown in Figures NW319, 322 and 325. The front stretcher turning is typically found in Dales ladder and spindle back chairs (see Figures NW41 and 49).

Plain round turned front legs terminating in indented pad feet. Front legs joined by turned stretcher type A3, Figure NW289. Round back legs, connected by single stretcher. Double side stretchers. Rush seat with wooden edge protective strips. Straight round turned back uprights terminating in scribed and nipple finials. Four graduated crescent shaped ladders.

Figure NW271. Standard ladder back side chair. Ash. Attributed to the North West, c.1800-60. The front stretcher style is found in other chairs from this region, including the Billinge bar top chair shown in Figure NW240.

Plain round turned front legs terminating in pad feet. Front legs joined by turned stretcher type C, Figure NW289. Square and lower chamfered back legs, connected by single stretcher. Double side stretchers. Replaced rush seat with wooden edge protective strips missing. Reclined round turned back uprights. Four graduated curved ladder shaped underneath with downward tip, indented on top of ladders.

Figure NW272. Standard ladder back side chair. Ash. Attributed to the North West, c.1800-60. This front stretcher form is typically found in double row spindle back chairs from this region. The front leg turning is found in other forms of standard ladder back chairs (see Figures NW270 and 271).

Plain round turned front legs terminating in pad feet. Front legs joined by turned stretcher type A2, Figure NW289. Round tapered back legs, connected by single stretcher. Double side stretchers. Rush seat with three wooden edge protective strips missing. Straight tapered round turned back uprights terminating in domed and nipple finials. Five graduated thin curved domed ladders shaped underneath with downward tip.

Figure NW273. Standard ladder back side chair. Ash. Attributed to Lancashire/Cheshire, c.1800-60. The front leg profile is part of a code of regional turnery styles which characterises a diverse group of chairs from this region (see Figures NW196 and 274).

Round turned front legs with single ring turning, terminating in pad feet. Front legs joined by turned stretcher type F, Figure NW289. Square and lower chamfered back legs, connected by single stretcher. Double side stretchers. Rush seat with wooden edge protective strips. Straight round turned back uprights. Four graduated curved domed ladders (lower ladder damaged), shaped underneath with downward tip and two small indentations.

Figure NW274. Standard ladder back side chair. Ash. Attributed to Lancashire/Cheshire, c.1800-60. The front leg design of this chair is also found in some bar top ladder back chairs (see Figure NW196), and other standard ladder back chairs (see Figures NW273 and 302).

Round turned front legs with single ring turning, terminating in indented pad feet. Front legs joined by turned stretcher type B, Figure NW289. Round tapered back legs, connected by double stretchers. Double side stretchers. Replaced rush seat with wooden edge protective strips missing. Straight tapered round turned back uprights terminating with scribed ring and nipple finials. Four graduated curved domed ladders shaped underneath with two decorative indentations.

The front stretcher styles included in these five chairs are very diverse, and relate the individual chairs to other regional styles. For example, the stretcher type C3, Figure NW271, is also found in the standard ladder back chairs shown in Figures NW306 and 307. The stretcher form type A2, shown in Figure NW272, relates this chair to double row spindle back chairs in which this stretcher commonly appears (see Figure NW80). The stretcher type F, shown in the chair in Figure NW273, is also commonly found in certain double row spindle back designs (see Figure NW91). The stretcher form shown in Figure NW274 is found in other forms of standard ladder back chairs, including those shown in Figures NW288 and 310, for example.

A further distinct group of chairs is shown in Figures NW276-283. These

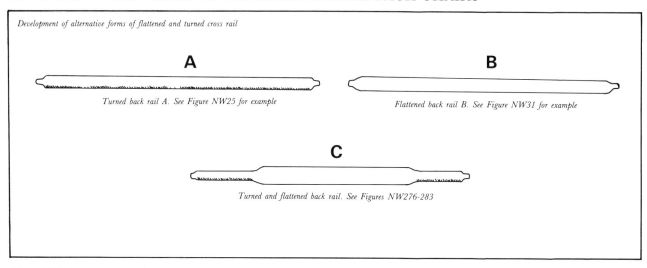

Development of alternative forms of flattened and turned cross rail

A

Turned back rail A. See Figure NW25 for example

B

Flattened back rail B. See Figure NW31 for example

C

Turned and flattened back rail. See Figures NW276-283

Figure NW275. *Two styles of cross rails used in the back design of Dales or single row spindle back chairs, 'A' and 'B' which are unified in 'C', to create a third ladder style incorporated in the associated style of ladder back chairs shown in Figures NW276-283.*

Figure NW276. *Ladder back armchair. Ash, c.1790-1840.*

Round front legs, joined by turned stretchers type A3, Figure NW289, often found in single row spindle back chairs. Continuously chamfered back legs connected by single stretcher. Double side stretchers. Damaged rush seat, with edge protective strips missing. Round back uprights inclined backwards, with five cross splats or ladders. Round turned at each end with a flattened and shaped section in the centre. This ladder shape combines the two alternative cross rail types used in the single row spindle chairs, illustrated in Figure NW275. Flattened scroll shaped arms which mortice into back upright, supported by turned underarm support which is half of the front stretcher style used in a number of chairs from the region (see Figures NW43 and 291).

Figure NW277. *Ladder back side chair. Ash. Attributed to the North West, c.1800-40. This ladder shape combines the two cross rail types used in the single row spindle chairs illustrated in Figure NW275.*

Round front legs terminating in pad feet. This form of leg turning, alternatively joined by one or two stretchers, is found as part of a variety of chairs from the region (see Figures NW206 and 272). Legs joined by turned stretcher similar to type F, Figure NW289, typical of those used in many double row spindle back chairs from the region (see Figures NW93 and 95). Round turned back legs connected by single stretcher. Double side stretchers. Rush seat missing. Round back uprights with four cross splats or ladders, round turned at each end with a flattened and shaped section in the centre.

Figure NW278. *Ladder back armchair. Ash. Attributed to the North West, c.1790-1840. This ladder shape combines the two alternative cross rail types used in the single row spindle chairs, illustrated in Figure NW275.*

Round front legs terminating in indented pad shaped feet, joined by two decoratively turned stretchers similar in design to that used in the rush seat kitchen chairs from the first group, shown in Figure NW381, which illustrates the tendency of this region's chair turners to incorporate turnery devices from one chair style in others. Chamfered back legs connected by single stretcher; double side stretchers. Rush seat, with edge protective strips. Round back uprights inclined backwards, with six cross splats or ladders, round turned at each end with a flattened and shaped section in the centre.

chairs are typified by their unusual ladder shapes which are composed of round turned ends with a flattened section in the middle. This style appears to be an amalgamation between the round and flattened bars which are used as separate devices in Dales chairs (see Figure NW275 for a diagrammatic representation). Chairs included in this group display a number of different design associations with other chairs from the North West, which suggests that this was a universal style made throughout the region. For example, the front stretcher turnings shown in Figues NW276 and 277 are typically incorporated in double row spindle

Figure NW279. Ladder back side chair. Ash. Attributed to the North West, c.1790-1840. This ladder shape combines the two alternative cross rail types as well as the front rail type K, Figure NW289, used in the Dales single row spindle chairs illustrated in Figures NW36-45. See the diagram in Figure NW275 for a fuller visual representation of this union of styles.

Round front legs terminating in pad feet, joined by two turned stretchers. Back legs connected by two stetchers. Double side stretchers. Rush seat, with edge protective strips missing. Round back uprights with four cross splats or ladders, round turned at each end with a flattened and shaped section in the centre.

Figure NW280. Ladder back side chair. Ash. Attributed to the North West, c.1800-40. This ladder shape combines the two alternative cross rail types, round and flattened, used in the single row spindle chairs illustrated in Figure NW275.

Round front legs morticed into seat frame, tapering towards feet, joined by two plain turned stretchers. Back legs connected by single stretcher. Double side stretchers. Round turned back legs. Replaced rush seat with edge protective strips missing. Round back uprights with four cross splats or ladders, round turned at each end with a flattened and shaped section in the centre.

Figure NW281. Ladder back armchair. Ash. Attributed to the North West, c.1790-1850. This ladder shape combines the two alternative cross rail types used in the single row spindle chairs illustrated in Figure NW275.

Round front legs, tapering towards foot, joined by two plain turned stretchers. Back legs connected by single stretcher. Double side stretchers. Round turned back legs. Rush seat, with edge protective strips. Round back uprights with five cross splats or ladders, round turned at each end with a flattened and shaped section in the centre. Curved shaped arms which mortice into back upright with turned terminal tenons, supported by decoratively turned underarm support with urn motif, type B, Figure NW71.

Figure NW282. Unusual ladder spindle back side chair. Ash. Attributed to the North West, c.1790-1840. The feet of the front legs have unusual turnings similar to those used in chairs made by C. Leicester of Macclesfield, Cheshire (see Figure NW173). The merging of two separate systems of turnery devices indicates the close design and manufacturing connection which chairs had with each other in this regional tradition,

Quarter round front legs terminating in cup shaped feet, joined by turned stretcher type G, Figure NW289. Back legs connected by single stretcher. Double side stretchers. Replaced rush seat with wooden edge strips missing. Round back uprights with two central splats or ladders, round turned at each end, with a flattened and shaped section in the centre, connected by three turned spindles. A further cross stay rail above. This chair embodies design features from the double row spindle back chairs, including the spindle and front rail turnings. Collection J. Boram

Figure NW283. Unusual ladder spindle back chair. Ash. Attributed to the North West, c.1790-1840. The front leg design is more usually found in ladder back chairs (see Figures NW270-272). The union of style indicates the tendency for this region's chair turners to occasionally amalgamate separate chair design features to create a further style.

Round front legs terminating in pad feet, joined by turned stretcher. Square back legs connected by single stretcher. Double side stretchers. Rush seat with wooden edge protective strips. Round back uprights with three splats or ladders, round turned at each end, with a flattened, shaped section in the centre, connected by two rows of turned spindles, similar to those typically found in double row spindle back chairs.

Figure NW284. Heavy standard ladder back armchair. Ash. Stamped 'W.L.' on rear of back leg. Attributed to Manchester, c.1770-1840. This style of chair is similar in construction to the two row spindle back armchair stamped by this maker, as well as by William Worsley, chair maker, of Hanging Ditch, Manchester, 1772 (see Figure NW106). The uneven surface of the ladders in this chair indicates that they were cleft rather than sawn. This is a feature of a number of other ladder back chairs which appear to have been made in the same local tradition (see Figures NW286-298).

Quarter round tops to the front legs, turned below, terminating in pad feet. Front legs joined by turned stretcher type F, Figure NW289. Square back legs, connected by single stretcher. Double side stretchers. Rush seat with wooden edge protective strips. Reclined round turned back uprights, terminating in scribed ring and nipple finials. Four curved domed ladder shaped underneath with upward tip. Curved shaped arms which mortice into back uprights with turned tenons. Turned underarm supports type F, Figure NW71.

Figure NW285. The stamp of 'W.L.' impressed into the rear of the chair shown in Figure NW284. This untraced maker is believed to have been an employee of William Worsley of Hanging Ditch, Manchester, in 1772, since his stamp appears on a double row spindle back armchair shown in Figure NW106, which also has the stamp of William Worsley, chair maker, Manchester (1772).

back chairs from this region.

The front legs and stretcher of the armchair shown in Figure NW278 are also regionally specific in their design, and are included in the Macclesfield style armchair shown in Figure NW192, and the front stretcher turning included in the rush seated kitchen chair from the first group of this style shown in Figure NW381. The simple round turned front legs of the chair in Figure NW276 relate this design directly with the standard ladder back chair shown in Figure NW292. The stretcher shape is typically incorporated in Dales chairs, and offers a direct association with this far north west group (see Figures NW22-53).

The amalgamation of spindle back turnery forms with the turned and flattened ladders in this style of chair is shown in Figure NW283, which, in addition to spindle turnings common to this region, also embodies front leg turnings noted in other chairs in the standard ladder and bar top group (see Figures NW270 and 205). The plain leg and connecting stretcher turnings shown in the arm and side chair examples in Figures NW280 and 281 are not common in this regional tradition. However, the underarm turnings shown in the armchair are entirely congruent with type B, Figure NW71, and serve to locate this chair to the North West.

The chairs shown in Figures NW284-298, however, suggest a progenitor amongst their own group, illustrated in the chair shown in Figure NW284, which is similar to the double row spindle back design shown in Figure NW106, and in a similar manner carries the stamp 'W.L.'* This chair is clearly a double row spindle back armchair frame which has been converted to a ladder back chair by the addition of four broad ladders. These ladders hold a pronounced design 'signature' in terms of their shape, as well as in the 'rippling' of the grain, which suggests a particular mode of manufacture, involving cleaving and scraping the sections, rather than sawing and sanding them. The surface condition of the ladders, and the particular domed top and shallow shaping below is reflected in the ladders of a range of further styles shown in Figures NW286-298, and identifies a stylistic and manufacturing association which possibly relates these chairs to a particular maker or number of regionally related makers.

Three other chairs in this group also have an affinity with spindle back chair designs; that in Figure NW287, where the top of the front leg is related to the spindle back form of front leg turning, and those shown in Figures NW296 and 297 which

have similar front legs to those typically used in certain double row spindle back chairs. The other chairs in this category depart from spindle back influence, however, and whilst retaining the common ladder mode, adopt other stylistic references. The chairs in Figures NW288 and 290 have Dales chair influence in their leg stretchers, and Figure NW295 has the front leg turnery device found in primitive spindle back chairs from this region (see Figure NW6). The chairs in Figures NW294-297 form a further association with chairs shown in Figures NW299-303 in adopting pronounced domed finials to the back uprights as a common stylistic feature. This design motif becomes, in turn, a uniting device for a further group of ladders shown in Figures NW299-308 and 312, which combines with particular ladder shapings to form a homogenous sub-group. The ladder shapes include those with accentuated downward tips to the underneath of the ladders (see Figures NW299-304); those with upward indented ladders (see Figures NW305-308); and an unusual variation of this style which has two further ladder indentations (see Figure NW312).

Certain chairs placed within this design group are related to other

---

* See footnote ** on p.342.

Figure NW286. Standard ladder back armchair. Ash with alder back legs. Attributed to Lancashire/Cheshire, c.1780-1840. The ladder shape is similar to that used in the chairs illustrated in Figures NW284 and 287, and shows signs of the 'cleaving', characteristic of the ladders of this chair group.

Plain round turned front legs terminating in vase shaped feet. Front legs joined by turned stretcher type C2, Figure NW289. Square back legs, connected by single stretcher. Double side stretchers. Rush seat with three wooden edge protective strips missing. Straight round turned back uprights terminating in scribed ring and nipple finials. Four curved domed ladders shaped underneath with upward tip. Curved shaped arms which mortice into back uprights with turned tenons. Turned underarm supports type D, Figure NW71.

Figure NW287. Standard ladder back low rocking side chair. Ash. Attributed to Lancashire/Cheshire, c.1780-1840. The cleft ladders and scribed ring and nipple finials unite this chair by design association with the chairs shown in Figures NW284 and 286.

Quarter round tops to the front legs turned below, terminating in vase shaped feet which mortice into shallow wooden rockers. Front legs joined by turned stretcher type C2, Figure NW289 Square back legs tapered into rockers, connected by single stretcher. Double side stretchers. Upholstered over rush seat. Straight round turned back uprights terminating with scribed ring and nipple finials. Four curved domed ladder shaped underneath with upward tip.

Figure NW288. Standard ladder back side chair. Ash. Attributed to the North West, c.1780-1840. The design and appearance of these ladders are closely similar to those shown in Figures NW284-287, but the use of three side and two front stretchers, and the round turned front legs, also suggest a close relationship with the primitive spindle back chairs shown in Figure NW3.

Plain round turned front legs, joined by two turned stretchers, type B, Figure NW289. Round, tapered back legs, connected by double stretchers. Triple side stretchers. Replaced rush seat with wooden edge protective strips, Straight tapered back uprights terminating in scribed ring and nipple finials. Four graduated curved domed ladders shaped underneath with upward tip.

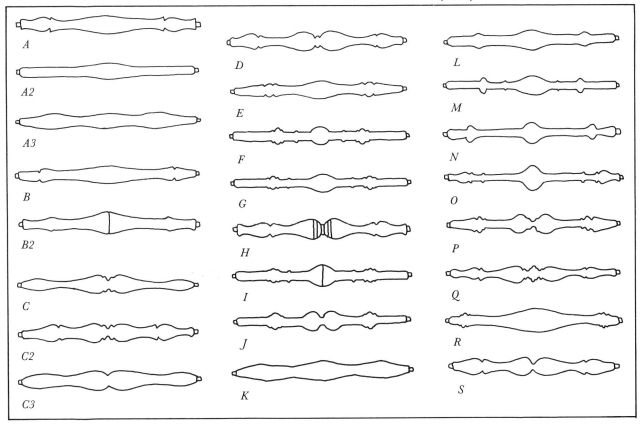

Figure NW289. Ladder back front stretcher turnings.

Figure NW290. Standard ladder back side chair. Ash. Attributed to the North West, c.1800-60. The ladders of this chair have been made from cleft wood, and show a marked similarity with those in the chair shown in Figure NW288, but the use of three side and two front stretchers, and the round turned front legs, also suggest a close relationship with the primitive spindle back chairs shown in Figures NW3 and 4.

Plain round tapered front legs, joined by two turned stretchers type B, Figure NW289. Round, tapered back legs, connected by double stretcher. Triple side stretchers. Rush seat with wooden edge protective strips missing. Straight round turned back uprights terminating in scribed ring and nipple finials. Four graduated curved domed ladders shaped underneath with downward tip.

Figure NW291. Standard ladder back side chair. Ash. Attributed to the North West, c.1800-60. The ladders of this chair have been made from cleft wood, and show a marked similarity with those in the chairs shown in Figures NW288 and 290. The front stretcher turnings are typically found in certain groups of double row spindle back chairs.

Plain round turned front legs, joined by two turned stretchers type A2, Figure NW289. Round, tapered back legs, connected by double stretchers. Double side stretchers. Rush seat with wooden edge protective strips missing. Straight round turned back uprights terminating in scribed ring and nipple finials. Four graduated curved domed ladders shaped underneath with downward tip.

Figure NW292. Standard ladder back armchair. Ash. Attributed to the North West, c.1800-60. The ladder shape of this chair is similar to those shown in Figures NW284-288.

Plain round turned front legs, worn away at the feet, joined by turned stretcher similar to type B2, Figure NW289. Round back legs, connected by double stretchers. Triple side stretchers. Rush seat with wooden edge protective strips missing. Straight round turned splayed back uprights terminating in scribed ring and nipple finials. Five graduated curved domed ladders shaped underneath with upwaard tip. Flattened scroll shaped arms which mortice into back uprights with tapered tenons. Turned underarm supports type I, Figure NW71.

groups by design association, including the chair shown in Figure NW306 which has a front turning stretcher type c, Figure NW289, similar to that typically found in chairs from the Billinge and district group (see Figures NW240 and 248), and the front leg design of many standard and bar top ladder back styles from the region (see Figures NW196, 273 and 274). The chair in Figure NW307 similarly incorporates leg stretcher type C3, which joins the plain round turned front legs, but in this case, two stetchers are included in combination with three plain side stretchers. This mode of construction and the use of the simple leg form, directly refer this chair to the primitive eighteenth century spindle back styles from the North West, and suggest a positive design relationship between them.

The armchair of this group, shown in Figure NW312, has decoratively fretted ladders, a design feature referring this chair to a further style, shown in Figure NW311, which incorporates the same ladder shape. The design of the ladder is the only point of similarity between them, and the side chair adopts a double front stretcher type B, Figure NW289, which, in turn, stylistically relates it to a further chair made with similar front stretchers, the armchair shown in Figure NW310. This chair has links with two further chairs in Figures NW309 and 313. The chair in Figure NW313, which is made in yew, similarly incorporates double front stretchers type B, and suggests a design association which may refer them to a common region of manufacture. The armchair shown in Figure NW310 also refers to the armchair in Figure NW309, where a design link is created between them by their unusual form of arm designs which are specifically similar to each other. These chairs, although not alike in other ways, may nevertheless exhibit alternative forms by the same maker or makers, denoted by the arm design, and serve to alert attention to the importance of design associations between similar individual features as well as those which are more obviously similar, in tracing related designs.

Figure NW293. Standard ladder back side chair. Attributed to the North West, c.1800-60. The ladder shape in this chair is similar to those illustrated in Figures NW284-288 and 292.

Turned pear shaped tops to the front legs which mortice into the square corners of the seat frame, legs terminating in single ring and cup shaped feet. Front legs joined by turned stretcher type B2, Figure NW289. Round back legs, connected by double stretcher. Double side stretchers. Rush seat with wooden edge protective strips missing. Straight round turned back uprights terminating in flattened finials. Five graduated curved domed ladders (bottom ladder damaged), shaped underneath with upward tip.

Figure NW294. Standard ladder back armchair. Ash. Attributed to Lancashire/Cheshire, c.1780-1840. The shallow curved tip to the ladder shaping is closely similar to that found in the ladders of Figures NW293 and 295-297, and suggests a particular local design which stylistically relates this group of chairs.

Plain round turned front legs terminating in single ring and vase shaped feet. Front legs joined by turned stretcher type B, Figure NW289. Round back legs, connected by double stretchers. Double side stretchers. Rush seat missing. Straight round turned tapered back uprights terminating in scribed ring and nipple finials. Four graduated curved domed ladders shaped underneath with upward tip. Flattened scroll shaped arms. Turned underarm supports represented as half the front rail turning.

Figure NW295. Standard ladder back side chair. Ash. Attributed to Lancashire/Cheshire, c.1780-1840. The ball turning device used in the front leg is similar to that found in the 18th century primitive spindle back chairs from this region (see Figures NW5 and 6). The ladder shape and front feet turning device suggests an associated design with the armchair shown in Figure NW294.

Round turned front legs with ball turnings, terminating in single ring and vase shaped feet. Front legs joined by turned stretcher type C2, Figure NW289. Round back legs, connected by single stretcher. Double side stretchers. Rush seat missing. Straight round turned tapered back uprights terminating with scribed line and domed finials. Four graduated curved domed ladders shaped underneath with upward tip.

Figure NW296. Standard ladder back side chair. Ash. Attributed to Lancashire/Cheshire, c.1790-1840. The front leg style is typically found in double row spindle back chairs from this region and the shape of the ladders associates this design with the chairs shown in Figures NW293-295 and 297.

Quarter round tops to the front legs, legs terminating in pad feet. Front legs joined by turned stretcher similar to type C2, Figure NW289. Round back legs, connected by single stretcher. Double side stretchers. Rush seat with wooden edge protective strips missing. Straight round turned tapered back uprights terminating with scribed line and domed finials. Four graduated curved domed ladders shaped underneath with upward tip.

Figure NW297. Standard ladder back side chair. Ash. Attributed to Lancashire/Cheshire, c.1780-1840. The front leg and front stretcher style of this chair are typically found in double row spindle back chairs from this region, and suggest that this chair may have been made as part of a repertoire of regional chairs.

Quarter round tips to the front legs, turned leg below, terminating in pad feet. Front legs joined by turned stretcher type F, Figure NW289. Round back legs, connected by double stretchers. Double side stretchers. Rush seat with wooden edge protective strips. Bent round turned back uprights terminating with scribed line and domed finials. Four graduated curved domed ladders shaped underneath with upward tip.

Figure NW298. Standard ladder back side chair. Ash. Attributed to the North West, c.1780-1840. The ladder shape of this chair is similar to that in the chair shown in Figure NW293.

Plain round turned front legs, worn at feet, joined by turned stretcher typically found in rush seat kitchen chairs (see Figure NW381). Round back legs, connected by double stretchers. Double side stretchers. Rush seat with wooden edge protective strips missing. Straight round turned tapered back uprights. Four curved domed ladders shaped underneath with upward tip.

Figure NW299. Standard ladder back armchair. Ash. Attributed to Lancashire/Cheshire, c.1800-60.

Round turned front legs with single ring turning, terminating in pad feet. Front legs joined by turned stretcher type D, Figure NW289. Round back legs, connected by double stretchers. Double side stretchers. Rush seat with wooden edge protective strips. Straight round turned splayed back uprights terminating in pronounced dome and nipple shaped finials. Five graduated curved domed ladders shaped underneath with accentuated downward tip. Flattened scroll shaped arms which mortice into back uprights with tapered tenons. Turned underarm supports similar to type I, Figure NW71.

Figure NW300. Standard ladder back side chair. Ash. Attributed to Lancashire/Cheshire, c.1800-60. The accentuated shape of the ladders and the domed upright terminals suggest this chair as the natural counterpart to the armchair shown in Figure NW299.

Turned pear shaped tops to the front legs which mortice into the square corners of the seat frame, legs terminating in indented pad feet. Front legs joined by turned stetcher type C2, Figure NW289. Round back legs, tapered at feet, connected by double stretchers. Double side stretchers. Rush seat with wooden edge protective strips. Straight splayed round turned back uprights terminating in pronounced dome and nipple finials. Four graduated curved domed ladders shaped underneath with downward tip.

Figure NW301. Standard ladder back armchair. Ash. Attributed to Lancashire/Cheshire, c.1800-50. The shape of the ladders in this chair is similar to those illustrated in Figures NW299, 300, 302 and 303, suggesting a particular local style where the terminals of the back uprights in each case are conspicuously domed.

Round turned front legs with single ring turning, terminating in indented pad feet. Front legs joined by turned stretcher type C2, Figure NW289. Round back legs, connected by double stretchers. Double side stretchers. Rush seat with wooden edge protective strips missing. Straight round turned back uprights terminating with domed and nipple finials. Five graduated curved domed ladders shaped underneath with accentuated downward tip. Curved shaped arms which mortice into back uprights with tapered tenons. Turned underarm supports similar to type I, Figure NW71.

Figure NW302. Standard ladder back side chair. Ash. Attributed to the North West, c.1800-50. The style of the front leg turning of this chair is incorporated in other examples of standard chairs, including those shown in Figures NW273 and 274, and in bar top ladder back chairs (see Figure NW196), providing a strong regional turnery signature which unites a number of different chair styles.

Round turned front legs with single ring turning, terminating in indented pad feet. Front legs joined by turned stretcher type C2, Figure NW289. Round back legs. Double side stretchers. Rush seat with wooden edge protective strips. Straight tapered round turned back uprights, with single ring turning, terminating in nipple finials. Four graduated curved domed narrow ladders shaped underneath with downward tip.

Figure NW303. Standard ladder back side chair. Ash. Attributed to Lancashire/Cheshire, c.1780-1840. This ladder form is typical of a group of otherwise different styles of regional ladder back chairs (see Figures NW299-302), and offers a design signature for this group.

Turned tops to the front legs which mortice into the square corners of the seat frame, terminating in damaged pad feet. Front legs joined by turned stretcher type B, Figure NW289. Round back legs, connected by double stretchers. Double side stretchers. Rush seat with wooden edge protective strips missing. Straight round turned back uprights with single ring turnings terminating with scribed ring and domed nipple finials. Four graduated curved domed ladders shaped underneath with accentuated downward tip.

Figure NW304. Standard ladder back side chair. Ash. Attributed to the North West, c.1800-50.

Plain round turned front legs terminating in single ring turned feet. Front legs joined by double stretcher type B, Figure NW289. Round back legs, connected by double stretchers. Double side stretchers. Rush seat with wooden edge protective strips missing. Straight round turned back uprights terminating in turned finials. Four graduated curved domed ladders shaped underneath with accentuated downward tip.

Figure NW305. Standard ladder back side chair. Ash. Attributed to Lancashire/Cheshire, c.1800-60.

Turned pear shaped tops to the front legs which mortice into the square corners of the seat frame, terminating in indented pad feet. Front legs joined by turned stretcher type C2, Figure NW289. Round back legs, connected by double stretchers. Double side stretchers. Replaced rush seat with wooden edge protective strips missing. Straight round turned splayed back uprights terminating in pronounced nipple finials. Four curved domed ladders shaped underneath with upward tip.

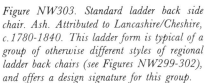

Figure NW306. Standard ladder back side chair. Ash. Attributed to the North West, c.1800-40. The ladder shape in this chair is similar to that in Figure NW305 and suggests an association between these designs.

Round turned front legs with single ring turning, terminating in pad feet. Underpads missing. Front legs joined by worn turned stretcher type C, Figure NW289. Round back legs, connected by double stretchers. Double side stretchers. Rush seat missing. Straight round turned tapered back uprights terminating in domed finials. Four graduated curved domed ladders shaped underneath with upward tip. The front leg turning device incorporated in this chair is located in a number of different chairs from this region, and provides a consistent unifying design signature (see Figures NW196, 273 and 274).

Figure NW307. Standard ladder back side chair. Ash with alder uprights. Attributed to the North West, c.1780-1820. The shape of the ladders joins this chair by design association with those in Figures NW305, 306 and 308.

Plain round turned front legs terminating in single ring and vase shaped feet. Front legs joined by two turned stretchers type C3, Figure NW289. Round back legs, connected by double stretchers. Triple side stretchers. Rush seat with wooden edge protective strips missing. Straight round turned splayed back uprights, terminating in scribed ring domed and pronounced nipple finials. Four graduated domed curved ladders shaped underneath with upward tip. The use of three side connecting stretchers and two front stretchers and the simple round turned front legs suggest this chair as a related design to the 18th century primitive spindle back form shown in Figure NW3.

Figure NW308. Standard ladder back side chair. Ash with alder front legs and back uprights. Attributed to Lancashire/Cheshire, c.1810-50. The decoratively turned front legs and stretcher suggest this chair as an early 19th century design extension of the chair shown in Figure NW307, and perhaps indicates that this style of chair, with modifications, was made continuously from the late 18th to the first half of the 19th century.

Turned tops, with urn motif, to the front legs which mortice into the square corners of the seat frame, terminating in single ring and cup shaped feet. Front legs joined by decoratively turned stretchers. Round back legs, connected by double stretchers. Double side stretchers. Rush seat with wooden edge protective strips missing. Straight round turned splayed back uprights terminating with scribed line and domed finials. Four graduated curved domed ladders (top ladder damaged), shaped underneath with upward tip.

Figure NW309. Standard ladder back armchair. Ash. Attributed to Lancashire/Cheshire, c.1800-40.

Plain round turned front legs terminating in pad feet. Front legs joined by turned stretcher type C2, Figure NW289. Round tapered back legs, connect by single stretcher. Double side stretchers. Replaced rush seat with wooden edge protective strips missing. Round turned tapered back uprights terminating in scribed finial. Five curved domed ladders, middle ladder damaged, shaped underneath with upward tip. Flattened scroll shaped arms which mortice into back uprights with tapered tenons. Turned underarm supports type B, Figure NW71.

Figure NW311. Standard ladder back side chair. Ash. Attributed to Lancashire/Cheshire, c.1800-60. The back uprights and general demeanour of this chair are similar to those shown in the chair in Figure NW274. The stretcher formation in this chair is similar to that adopted in the side chairs shown in Figures NW288 and 290, and the armchair shown in Figure NW310, and suggests a stylistic device common to a small group of chairs. The form of ladder fretting is unusual, and was adopted in a further style of regional chair in Figure NW312.

Turned tops to the front legs incorporating an urn motif, which mortice into the square corners of the seat frame, terminating in single ring and vase shaped feet. Front legs joined by two turned stretchers type B, Figure NW289. Round back legs, connected by double stretchers. Triple side stretchers. Replaced sea-grass seat with wooden edge protective strips missing. Straight round turned back uprights terminating in scribed ring and nipple finials. Four graduated curved domed ladders shaped underneath with upward tip and curved indentation.

Figure NW312. Standard ladder back armchair. Ash. Attributed to Lancashire/Cheshire, c.1780-1840.

Round turned front legs with indented turning; feet missing. Front legs joined by turned stretcher type C2, Figure NW289. Round back legs, tapered at feet, connected by double stretchers. Rush seat missing. Replacement leather seat. Straight round turned back uprights terminating in scribed ring and pronounced nipple finials. Five curved domed ladders decoratively shaped underneath. Flattened scroll shaped arms which mortice into back uprights with tapered tenons. Turned underarm supports type F, Figure NW71.

Figure NW310. Standard ladder back armchair. Ash. Attributed to Lancashire/Cheshire, c.1780-1840. The arm shapes are very similar to those in Figure NW309 and the use of three side stretchers, two back, and two front stretchers, type B, Figure NW289, is identical to that used in the side chair shown in Figure NW311.

Plain round turned front legs with indented turnings, terminating in ring and turned feet. Front legs joined by two turned stretchers type B, Figure NW289. Round, tapered back legs, connected by double stretchers. Triple side stretchers. Rush seat with wooden edge protective strips missing. Straight round turned tapered back uprights terminating with scribed ring and nipple finials. Five graduated curved domed ladders shaped underneath with upward tip. Flattened scroll shaped arms which mortice into back uprights with tapered tenons. Turned underarm supports similar to type I, Figure NW71.

A further group of ladder back chairs adopt a mode of construction which includes the use of taller and often reclined back uprights, creating them as unusually elegant chair styles. The chairs shown in Figures NW314-323 illustrate this design tendency which includes the adoption of crescent shaped ladders. These either describe a flowing line, as in Figures NW314, 316 and 321, or have more acutely shaped curves similar to those shown in Figures NW308 and 323. Chairs in this group also either have straight decoratively turned front legs, or bulbous turned legs with pad feet, which suggests a rudimentary form of the cabriole leg. Within this group, the front stretcher forms, which include types L, M, N, P, and R, Figure NW289, are peculiar to the group. Two other styles from this region also incorporate crescent shaped ladders. These are shown in the armchair in Figure NW324, which also, in turn, relates to a further group of chairs shown in Figures NW346-349 which are associated with each other by the inclusion of pronounced and exaggerated nipple turnings terminating the back uprights. The second chair, shown in Figure NW325, cross relates to Dales chairs in the adoption of front leg and stretcher turnings, as well as the painted rush seat, which occurs commonly in this group.

Other chairs relating to this group are typified by tall back uprights (see Figures NW326-339). These chairs are made with the essential elegance of those with crescent shaped ladders, and commonly incorporate the bulbous form of front leg (see Figures NW326-329, 338 and 339), as well as the simpler form of round turned leg (see Figures NW330-334 and 341). This group, however, includes ladder shapes which have either a downward tip, upward indentation, or are straight across the underneath of the ladders, and also adopts other varieties of front stretcher turnings including types B and E, Figure NW289.

Figure NW313. Standard ladder back armchair. Yew. Attributed to Lancashire/Cheshire. Dated on top ladder '1739'. This chair is, unusually, made in yew, and suggests that it was made as a 'best', or presentation chair. The date, although original to the chair, may reflect a relationship with its owner, perhaps a birth date, rather than the date of manufacture. The front rail turnings are typical of others in this regional group (see Figure NW310 for example), as are the domed finials (Figure NW335). Collection D. Green

Plain round turned front legs; feet missing. Front legs joined by two turned stretchers type B, Figure NW289. Round back legs, connected by double stretcher. Double side stretchers. Rush seat with wooden edge protective strips missing. Reclined round turned back uprights terminating in domed nipple finials. Five graduated curved domed ladders, straight underneath. Flattened shaped arms which mortice into back uprights with tapered tenons. Gun barrel turned underarm supports.

Figure NW314. Standard ladder back armchair. Ash. Attributed to Lancashire, c.1770-1840. This elegant design utilises flowing shapes and a light construction to create a dynamic style of chair which serves to illustrate the rich diversity of styles made in this area. The front stretcher turning style is also found in the Macclesfield style chair in Figures NW187 and 188.

Round turned front legs with indented turning, terminating in pad feet. Front legs joined by turned stretcher type N, Figure NW289. Round back legs, connected by double stretchers. Double side stretchers. Rush seat with wooden edge protective strips missing. Gracefully curved round turned back uprights terminating in slightly domed and pronounced nipple finials. Five graduated curved crescent shaped ladders. Swept, flowing curved arm shapes which mortice into an unusually high position in the back uprights with tapered tenons. Turned underarm supports type I, Figure NW71.

Figure NW315. Standard ladder back side chair. Ash with traces of original black paint. Attributed to Lancashire, c.1770-1840. This side chair is the natural counterpart to the armchair shown in Figure NW314, and with the same number of ladders as the armchair, suggesting an unusual stylistic relationship in a tradition in which the side chairs typically have one less ladder than the armchair of the same style. The front stretcher turning style in this chair is also found in the Macclesfield style chair in Figures NW187 and 188.

Turned tops to the front legs which mortice into the square corners of the seat frame, terminating in pad feet. Front legs joined by turned stretcher type N, Figure NW289. Round back legs, connected by double stretchers. Double side stretchers. Replaced rush seat with wooden edge protective strips missing. Bent round turned back uprights terminating with a slight dome and prominent nipple finials. Five graduated curved crescent shaped ladders.

Figure NW316. Standard ladder back side chair. Ash. Attributed to Lancashire, c.1770-1840. Great elegance is created by the use of tall, curved back uprights, and the flowing line of the ladders. The exaggerated bulbous turned front stretcher provides an attractive device which stimulates visual interest in the lower half of the chair design. This chair relates in style to the chairs in Figures NW314 and 315 and shows them to be a strongly indentified group of chairs with a dynamic sense of design.

Decoratively turned tops to the front legs which mortice into the square corners of the seat frame, terminating in single ring and cup shaped feet. Front legs joined by turned stretcher type O, Figure NW289. Round back legs, connected by single stretcher. Double side stretchers. Rush seat with wooden edge protective strips missing. Bent round turned back uprights terminating with slight dome and nipple finials. Five graduated crescent shaped ladders.

Figure NW317. Rare turned rush seated stool. Fruitwood. Attributed to Lancashire, c.1780-1820. The turned stretchers of this stool are typically found in many Lancashire chair styles (see Figures NW91 and 120). The decorative turnings to the legs are markedly similar to those included in the chairs shown in Figures NW316 and 320, and suggest that this stool was part of the region's chair turners' repertoire.

Four turned legs which mortice into the square corners of the seat frame. Decorative upper leg turnings and ball shaped feet. Two decoratively turned stretchers type F, Figure NW289, on each long side of the stool, and two plain turned stretchers on each short side. Damaged rush seat.

Figure NW318. Standard ladder back armchair. Ash. Attributed to the North West, c.1770-1840. The elegantly turned front legs and sharply curved ladders are effectively used to create a visually exciting chair design. The front stretcher turning has similarities with that used in Dales chairs (see Figure NW48).

Round turned front legs terminating in pad feet. Front legs joined by turned stretcher type Q, Figure NW289. Round back legs connected by single stretcher. Double side stretchers. Rush seat and three rush seat rails missing. Staight round turned splayed back uprights terminating with scribed ring and nipple finials. Six graduated accentuated crescent shaped ladders. Shaped arms, square in section, which mortice into back uprights in a high position. Turned underarm supports type I, Figure NW71, which is half the front stretcher turning.

Figure NW319. Standard ladder back side chair. Ash. Attributed to Lancashire, c.1770-1840. This chair is a simplified version of the crescent ladder style and has back upright finials found in other chairs from this region (see Figures NW313 and 315).

Plain round turned legs terminating in single ring and pear shaped feet. Front legs, joined by turned stretcher type L, Figure NW289. Round back legs, connected by double stretchers (one stretcher missing). Double side stretchers. Rush seat with wooden edge protective strips missing. Straight round turned back uprights terminating in pronounced ring and nipple finials. Four graduated curved crescent shaped ladders.

Figure NW320. Standard ladder back side chair. Ash. Attributed to Lancashire, c.1770-1840. This chair design has similarities to the chair shown in Figure NW316, but without the refinement of reclined back uprights.

Turned tops to the front legs which mortice into the square corners of the seat frame, terminating in single ring and vase shaped feet. Front legs joined by turned stretcher type P, Figure NW289. Round back legs, tapered at feet, connected by double stretchers. Rush seat with wooden edge protective strips missing. Straight round turned back uprights terminating with scribed ring and pronounced nipple finials. Five graduated curved, accentuated, crescent shaped ladders.

Figure NW321. Standard ladder back side chair. Ash. Attributed to Lancashire, c.1770-1840. This chair incorporates a splayed back foot which is a feature of some early 18th century ladder back chairs, and aids stability.

Turned tops to the front legs similar to the central portion of the front rail, which mortice into the square corners of the seat frame, terminating in pad feet. Front legs joined by turned stretcher type P, Figure 289, which is set unusually high between the front legs. Round back legs, connected by double stretchers. Double side stretchers. Rush seat with wooden edge protective strips missing. Curved round turned back uprights terminating in turned finials. Five graduated curved crescent shaped ladders.

Figure NW322. Standard ladder back armchair. Ash. Attributed to Lancashire/Cheshire, c.1770-1840.

Plain round turned tapered front legs terminating in pad feet. Front legs joined by turned stretcher type C2, Figure NW289. Round back legs, curved backwards, connected by double stretchers. Double side stretchers. Rush seat with wooden edge protective strips missing. Reclined, curved back uprights terminating with scribed ring and nipple finials. Five graduated curved crescent shaped ladders. Flattened scroll shaped arms which mortice into back uprights in a high position. Turned underarm supports type I, Figure NW71, which are half the front rail stretcher design.

Figure NW323. Standard ladder back side chair. Ash. Attributed to Lancashire, c.1770-1840. The top ladder design perhaps shows Dutch architectural influence. The leg shape suggests a rudimentary form of the cabriole leg.

Turned pear shaped tops to the front legs which mortice into the square corners of the seat frame, terminating in pad feet. Front legs joined by turned stretcher type R, Figure NW289, set high between the front legs. Round back legs curved backwards, connected by double stretchers. Double side stretchers (two left hand stretchers missing). Replaced rush seat with wooden edge protective strips missing. Curved round turned back uprights terminating with scribed ring and nipple finials. Five graduated curved crescent shaped ladders with accentuated curve below.

Figure NW324. Standard ladder back armchair. Ash. Attributed to the North West, c.1800-40.

Plain round turned front legs joined by turned stretcher. Round back legs, connected by double stretchers. Double side stretchers. Rush seat with wooden edge protective strips missing. Straight round turned back uprights terminating in pronounced nipple finials. Four crescent shaped ladders. Curved shaped arms which mortice into back uprights with turned tenons. Turned underarm supports composed of half of the front stretcher turning.

Figure NW325. Standard ladder back side chair. Ash with alder back uprights and ladders. Attributed to the North West, c.1800-40. The front leg syle, front rail turning, and painted rush seat are common features of Dales spindle and ladder back chairs (see Figures NW42 and 60).

Plain round turned tapering front legs joined by turned stretcher type A2, Figure NW289. Round back legs, connected by single stretchers. Double side stretchers. Painted rush seat with wooden edge protective strips. Straight round turned back uprights. Three graduated curved domed ladders shaped underneath to reflect the upper shaping.

Figure NW326. Standard ladder back side chair. Ash. Attributed to Lancashire, c.1770-1840. The bulbous turned front legs suggest a rudimentary form of the cabriole leg. This chair is similar in design to the chair shown in Figure NW323, with the exception of differently shaped ladders, and indicates the tendency of makers to create alternative designs by changing a particular feature or features of a basic chair type.

Turned pear shaped tops to the front legs which mortice into the square corners of the seat frame, terminating in pad feet. Front legs joined by turned stretcher which is an elaborated form of type R, Figure NW289. Round back legs, curved backwards, connected by single stretcher. Double side stretchers. Replaced rush seat with wooden edge protective strips missing. Curved round turned back uprights terminating with scribed line and nipple finials. Four graduated curved domed ladders with pronounced shaping underneath with upward tip.

Figure NW327. Standard ladder back side chair. Ash. Attributed to Lancashire/Cheshire, c.1770-1840. The turned front legs suggest a rudimentary form of the cabriole leg. The front stretcher turning is similar to those incorporated in the chairs shown in Figures NW329 and 330.

Turned tops to the front legs which mortice into the square corners of the seat frame, terminating in pad feet. Front legs joined by turned stetcher type R, Figure NW289. Round back legs, connected by single stetcher. Double side stretchers. Rush seat with wooden edge protective strips missing. Straight round turned tapered back uprights terminating with scribed ring and nipple finials. Four graduated curved domed ladders shaped underneath with downward tip.

Figure NW328. Standard ladder back armchair. Ash. Attributed to Lancashire, c.1770-1840.

Turned tops to the front legs which mortice into the square corners of the seat frame. Turned front legs (suggesting a rudimentary form of the cabriole leg), terminating in pad feet, connected by turned front stretcher type R, Figure NW289. Round back legs, tapered at feet, connected by double stretchers. Double side stretchers. Rush seat with wooden edge protective strips missing. Straight round turned back uprights terminating in domed nipple finials. Five graduated curved domed ladders shaped underneath with downward tip.

Figure NW329. Standard ladder back side chair. Fruitwood. Attributed to Lancashire, c.1770-1840. The construction of this chair in fruitwood, which is rare in this regional style, suggests that this was considered a superior chair. The shape of the ladders is similar to those shown in Figures NW330-333, and the front stretcher style is found with chairs shown in Figures NW331 and 333.

Turned tops to the front legs which mortice into the square corners of the seat frame, terminating in pad feet. The turned front legs, joined by turned stretcher type R, Figure NW289. Round back legs, connected by single stretcher. Double side stretchers. Lower side stretchers connected by elliptically turned cross stretcher. Rush seat with wooden edge protective strips missing. Staight round turned back uprights terminating in ring and nipple finials. Five graduated curved domed ladders, straight underneath.

Figure NW330. Standard ladder back side chair. Ash. Attributed to Lancashire, c.1770-1840. The front rail turning and ladder shape are similar to those included in the chair in Figure NW329, and suggest that this chair, simpler in design, may have been offered by the same maker, or makers, as a less costly alternative.

Turned tops to the front legs which mortice into the square corners of the seat frame, terminating in cup shaped feet. Front legs joined by turned stretcher type L, Figure NW289. Round back legs, connected by single stretcher. Double side stretchers. Damaged rush seat with wooden edge protective strips missing. Straight round turned back uprights terminating in turned nipple finials. Four graduated curved domed ladders, straight underneath.

Figure NW331. Standard ladder back side chair. Ash. Attributed to Lancashire, c.1770-1840. The decoratively turned straight legs joined by elaborately turned front stretchers is a feature incorporated occasionally in the design code of this region (see Figures NW290, 308 and 311 for other examples of chairs adopting this device).

Turned pear shaped tops to the front legs, which mortice into the square corners of the seat frame terminating in flattened ball shaped feet. Front legs joined by two turned stretchers similar to type M, Figure NW289. Heavy round back legs, connected by single stretcher. Double side stretchers. Damaged rush seat with wooden edge protective strips missing. Heavy, straight round turned back uprights terminating in ring and domed nipple finials. Five graduated curved domed ladders, straight underneath (bottom ladder damaged).

Figure NW332. Low seated standard ladder back rocking side chair. Ash. Attributed to Lancashire, c.1770-1820. This simple design of rocking side chair was probably used by the fireside, and was a less expensive alternative to the rocking armchairs.

Turned tops to the front legs which mortice into the square corners of the seat frame. Plain turned leg below tapered and turned to fit short, shallow rockers. Front legs joined by turned stretcher type P, Figure NW289. Round back legs, tapered at feet, connected by single stretcher. Double side stretchers. Rush seat with wooden edge protective strips missing. Tall, straight round turned tapered back uprights terminating in ring and nipple finials. Five graduated curved domed ladders, straight underneath.

Figure NW333. Standard ladder back side chair. Ash. Attributed to Lancashire, c.1770-1840. This low seated variety of chair is similar to the low rocking chair shown in Figure NW332, and illustrates that social use may have required the construction of chairs which perhaps allowed the user to sit nearer a low set fire.

Plain round turned front legs terminating in cup shaped feet. Front legs joined by turned stretcher type B2, Figure NW289. Round tapered back legs, connected by single stretcher. Double side stretchers. Replaced rush seat with wooden edge protective strips missing. Straight round turned tapered back uprights terminating in turret shaped finials. Four graduated curved domed ladders, straight underneath.

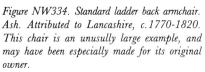

Figure NW334. Standard ladder back armchair. Ash. Attributed to Lancashire, c.1770-1820. This chair is an unusully large example, and may have been especially made for its original owner.

Plain round turned front legs, joined by turned stretcher type P, Figure NW289. Round back legs, connected by single stretcher. Double side stretchers. Replaced rush seat with wooden edge protective strips. Round turned back upright terminating in ring and nipple finials. Six graduated curved domed ladders with downward indentations, shaped underneath with downward tip. Downward curved and shaped arms which mortice into back uprights with tapered tenon. Turned underarm supports type I, Figure NW71.

Figure NW335. Standard ladder back side chair. Ash. Attributed to Lancashire, c.1770-1820.

Turned tops to the front legs which mortice into the square corners of the seat frame, round turned legs below, terminating in pad feet; legs joined by turned stretcher type J, Figure NW289. Round back legs, connected by single stretcher. Double side stretchers. Replaced rush seat with wooden edge protective strips. Straight round turned back uprights terminating in pronounced domed finials. The finials are similar to those shown in the chair in Figure NW313. Five graduated curved domed top ladders with downward indentations, shaped underneath with downward tip, the top ladder with extra embellishment.

Figure NW336. Standard ladder back side chair. Ash. Attributed to Lancashire, c.1770-1820.

Turned tops to the front legs which mortice into the square corners of the seat frame, legs terminating in pad feet, joined by turned stretcher type N, Figure NW289. Round back legs joined by double stretchers. Double side stretchers (one missing). Replaced rush seat with wooden edge protective strips missing. Straight round turned back uprights terminating in scribed ring and nipple finials. Five graduated curved ladders with downward indentations and upward tips on top (tip missing on top ladder), and shaped underneath with downward tip.

Figure NW337. A cottage interior by James Hayllar (1829-1920), entitled 'Gone but not forgotten', which illustrates North Country standard ladder back chairs of the type shown in Figure NW336. This scene shows an interesting combination of vernacular furnishings, including a Windsor and rush seated chairs, a gateleg table, cupboard with drawers below, and a painted dresser with pottery displayed on it.

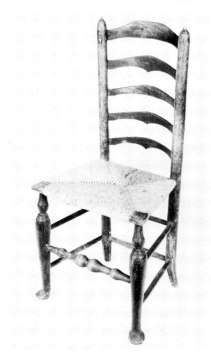

Figure NW338. Standard ladder back side chair. Ash. Attributed to Lancashire, c.1770-1820. The swept back feet in this chair are features more typically found in certain early 18th century chair styles, and were particularly intended to aid stability in tall chairs.

Turned tops to the front legs which mortice into the square corners of the seat frame, terminating in pad feet (the turned front legs suggest a rudimentary form of the cabriole leg). Front legs joined by turned stretcher type C2, Figure NW289. Round back legs, swept and chamfered at feet, connected by double stretchers. Double side stretchers. Replaced rush seat with wooden edge protective strips missing. Straight round turned heavy back uprights terminating in domed nipple finials. Five graduated very curved domed ladders shaped underneath with downward tip (top and middle ladders damaged).

Figure NW339. Standard ladder back side chair. Ash. Attributed to Lancashire, c.1770-1820. Two curved notches appear on the inside of each leg above the stretcher. These appear to be part of the chair design, but are unusual design features, and may represent a use function. The front stretcher turning used in this chair is similar to that shown in Figures NW320, 321 and 332, and serves to associate this chair with a group of elegant chairs from this region.

Turned tops to the front legs which mortice into the square corners of the seat frame, terminating in pad feet. The turned front legs suggest a rudimentary form of the cabriole leg. Front legs joined by turned stretcher type P, Figure NW289. Round back legs, swept and chamfered at feet, connected by single stretcher. Double side stretchers. Rush seat with wooden edge protective strips missing. Curved round turned back uprights terminating in domed and nipple finials. Five graduated domed curved ladders, shaped underneath with upward tip.

A further distinctive group of chairs is shown in Figures NW340-345, which are related, by their general demeanour, to each other, and include examples in which their front leg stretchers are also illustrated as design features of the previous two groups of tall ladder back chairs, but which radically depart from these designs in incorporating shorter straight back uprights which are splayed outwards. These are connected by ladders which have a downward tip, or upward indent. Chairs in this group include those whose front stretcher turnings are found in the previous group including the chairs in Figures NW340 and 341, which have stretcher type N, which is adopted in the ladder back styles with crescent shaped ladders shown in Figures NW314 and 315, and offer a positive design connection between these chairs. Two other chairs in the group, shown in Figures NW342 and 344, have front stretcher turnings similar to types IV and II, Figure NW70, respectively, which are typically included in varieties of double row spindle back chairs, and serve to

relate these examples to a further major group of regional chairs.

The last group of four chairs shown in Figures NW346-349 are associated together because in each case they display the unusual feature of pronounced and exaggerated nipple shaped finials. Two other chairs which have crescent shaped ladders, also have this feature, and are shown in Figures NW324 and 325. Of these chairs, the one shown in Figure NW349 is strongly associated with a number of other ladder back designs, including those in Figures NW314, 315, 340 and 341, which all embody the unusual front stretcher type N, Figure NW289. Two other chairs in this group are closely related to each other, the one in Figure NW348 being a simpler form of the chair in Figure NW347 which, in turn, is associated in terms of its front stretcher turning type B, with the chairs shown in Figures NW336 and 323. The armchair shown in Figure NW346 may be the natural counterpart to the side chairs shown in Figures NW347 and 348.

Figure NW340. Standard ladder back side chair. Ash. Attributed to Lancashire, c.1770-1840. This leg style is incorporated, with slight modifications, in the chairs shown in Figures NW326-329, and provides a positive turnery signature which relates, by association, to a number of chair types, and illustrates how a code of known styles was shared as a dialect of design, and used to create alternative forms.

Turned tops to the front legs which mortice into the square corners of the seat frame, round turned legs below, terminating in pad feet. Front legs connected by turned stretcher similar to type R, Figure NW289. Round tapered back legs connected by double stretchers. Double side stretchers. Rush seat with wooden edge protective strips missing. Staight round turned back uprights terminating with scribed ring and nipple finials. Four curved graduated domed ladders, shaped underneath with upward tip.

Figure NW341. Standard ladder back side chair. Ash. Attributed to Lancashire, c.1770-1840. Many turnery features adopted in this chair relate it to other chair designs. For example, the tops of the front leg turnings are similar to those used in Figures NW316 and 320. The front rail turning is similar to those in Figures NW314 and 315, and the back uprights are similar to those in Figure NW340.

Turned tops to the front legs which mortice into the square corners of the seat frame, terminating in single ring and ball shaped feet. Left hand foot damaged. Front legs joined by turned stretcher type N, Figure NW289. Round, slightly tapered back legs, connected by single stretcher. Double side stretchers. Rush seat with wooden edge protective strips missing. Straight round turned back uprights terminating with scribed ring and nipple finials. Four graduated curved domed ladders shaped underneath with downward tip.

Figure NW342. Standard ladder back side chair. Ash. Attributed to Lancashire, c.1800-60. The wavy shape of the ladders in this chair stylistically relate it to the chair shown in Figure NW343.

Turned tops to the front legs which mortice into the square corners of the seat frame, terminating in pad feet. Front legs joined by turned stretcher type N, Figure NW289. Round back legs, tapered at feet, connected by double stretchers. Double side stretchers. Painted rush seat with wooden edge protective strips. Straight turned back uprights, splayed and terminating in prominent nipple finials. Four graduated curved wavy shaped ladders with downward tip below, and domed on top.

Figure NW343. Standard ladder back side chair. Ash. Attributed to Lancashire/Cheshire, c.1800-50.

Turned tops to the front legs (incorporating a bell shaped motif), which mortice into the square corners of the seat frame, legs terminating in flattened ball shaped feet. Front leg joined by two turned stretchers. Round back legs, connected by double stretchers (both missing). Double side stretchers. Replaced rush seat with wooden edge protective strips missing. Straight round turned splayed back uprights. Four unusual wavy shaped ladders.

Figure NW344. Standard ladder back side chair. Ash. Attributed to the North West, c.1780-1840.

Turned tops to the front legs which mortice into the square corners of the seat frame, terminating in pad feet. Front legs joined by turned stretcher type L, Figure NW289. Round back legs, connected by double stretchers. Double side stretchers. Rush seat with wooden edge protective strips missing. Straight round turned back uprights terminating in exaggerated turned finials. Four graduated curved domed ladders, shaped underneath with downward tips and indented above. The top ladder is fixed by two square wooden pegs to the front.

Figure NW345. Standard ladder back side chair. Ash. Attributed to the North West, c.1800-60. The general demeanour of this chair relates it to those shown in Figures NW341-343, suggesting a small group of stylistically similar chairs.

Turned tops to the front legs which mortice into the square corners of the seat frame, terminating in pad feet. Front legs joined by turned stretcher type B2, Figure NW289. Round back legs, tapered at feet, connected by double stretchers. Double side stretchers. Rush seat with wooden edge protective strips missing. Straight round turned back uprights terminating in scribed line and nipple finials. Four curved domed ladders, shaped underneath with downward tip.

Figure NW346. Standard ladder back armchair. Ash. Attributed to Lancashire/Cheshire, c.1770-1820. The pronounced nipple finials are a prominent feature of some of this region's chairs, which are not necessarily related in other ways (see Figures NW347-349).

Plain round turned front legs, terminating in single ring and cup shaped feet. Front legs joined by turned stretcher type S, Figure NW289. Round back legs, connected by single stretcher. Double side stretchers. Wicker seat. Slightly reclined round turned back uprights terminating with scribed ring and pronounced nipple finials. Five curved domed graduated ladders, straight underneath. Curved shaped top to the arms, square in section, morticed into the back uprights with tapered tenon. Turned underarm supports type i, Figure NW71, which are half of the front stretcher design.

Figure NW347. Standard ladder back side chair. Ash. Attributed to Lancashire/Cheshire, c.1780-1820. This simple style of chair is similar in demeanour to the even simpler design shown in Figure NW348.

Plain round turned front legs terminating in flattened ball feet. Front legs joined by turned stretcher similar to type L, Figure NW289. Round back legs, connected by double stretchers. Double side stretchers. Rush seat with wooden edge protective strips missing. Straight round turned back uprights terminating in domed and pronounced finials. Five graduated curved domed ladders shaped underneath with downward tip.

Figure NW348. Standard ladder back side chair. Ash. Attributed to Lancashire/Cheshire, c.1770-1820. This chair is similar in style to that in Figure NW347, but is a less embellished alternative, which lacks shaping of the ladders and the incorporation of a turned foot and decoratively turned front stretcher. The existence of these two related chairs suggests that chair turners altered their designs to suite their customers' needs.

Plain round turned front legs, joined by turned stretcher type A2, Figure NW289. Round back legs, connected by double stretchers. Replaced rush seat with wooden edge protective strips missing. Straight round turned back uprights terminating in domed and pronounced nipple finials. Five graduated curved domed ladders straight underneath.

Figure NW349. Standard ladder back side chair. Ash. Attributed to Lancashire/Cheshire, c.1780-1820. The style of front stretcher turning associates this chair with a group of other chairs from this region (see Figures NW314, 315, 340 and 341).

Turned tops to the front legs which mortice into the square corners of the seat frame, terminating in pear shaped feet. Front legs joined by turned stretcher type N, Figure NW289. Round back legs, connected by single stretcher. Double side stretchers. Replaced rush seat with wooden edge protective strips missing. Straight round turned back uprights terminating in pronounced nipple finials. Four graduated curved domed ladders shaped underneath with downward tip.

'Wavy' line ladder back chairs

Of the many styles of ladder back chairs made in the North West, one above all seems to have been so stylistically successful that it was made in larger numbers than any other single variety. This style is characterised in having back uprights which terminate in domed nipple shaped finials which are connected by distinctive 'wavy' shaped ladders. These ladders, unusually, were fitted into the back uprights in partially shaped condition, and then finished with a draw knife, a practice which leaves the ladder tenons with a clear 'shoulder' where the slope of the ladder terminates (see Figure NW366 for illustration). The front leg turnings are also peculiar to this style, in having a particular form of round turned top to the front legs with a prominent single ring turning below. Within this basic style of leg are located three distinct leg profiles (see Figure NW351), which combine with two different back leg designs. Those with leg turning B are commonly combined with the straight back uprights. Those with leg turnings A and C commonly combine with square, lower chamfered back legs and with round back uprights, reclined or straight.

Chairs with leg design C which are characterised in having cylindrical rather than barrel shaped under pads to the front legs, typically have decoratively scribed turnery marks on the tops of the front legs (see Figure NW364), and the top ladder is fixed at the back with a square ash peg (see Figure NW363).

The other two leg designs, A and B, have barrel shaped under pads to the front feet. In these cases, their top ladder is either fixed in place with glue alone, or with a 'sprig' or small nail.

The existence of the highly conventionalised chairs with type C legs, and to a less rigidly held degree, those of the other two major subgroups, suggest that these chairs were made in large numbers by a few makers or local traditions of makers, who specialised in their production.

However, the makers of this type of chair, in common with other ladder back chair turners, did not typically stamp the work with their name, and few chairs have been recorded with makers' stamps, including one group of four similar chairs which has been recorded with a name stamp, impressed on the top

Figure NW350. A late 19th century photograph of Adam Houghton of Rose Cottage, Damside, a Non Conformist preacher from the Over Wyre district of the Fylde, West Lancashire (1816-1906). This picture shows Houghton sitting in a wavy line ladder back armchair with cushions provided for extra comfort. Photograph courtesy Catherine Rothwell

of the front legs. The stamp is that of 'W. Slee' whose identity remains untraced (see Figure NW355). A further chair stamped by Thomas Clayton of Stockport, Cheshire (fl.1825) is shown in Plate 53. The 'purity' of design in these chairs seems to emphasise the confidence which the makers had in this style of chair which obviated the need for design alteration, since rarely are modifications created by the incorporation of parts from other chair styles.

Although the style exhibits little inclusion of features from other chairs, some other regional chairs do embody 'borrowed' features from wavy line ladder back chairs, including the adoption of the front leg design incorporated in a form of double row spindle back chairs (see Figure NW97); the incorporation of the back leg design in a related ladder back form (see Figure NW370); and the use of the front stretcher turning in other ladder back styles (see Figure NW263).

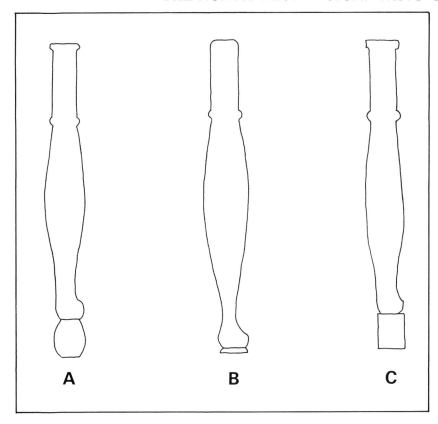

Figure NW351. Front leg turnings included in 'wavy' line ladder back chairs.

Figure NW352. Wavy line ladder back armchair. Ash. Attributed to Lancashire/Cheshire, c.1790-1840. This chair is similar in the form of arm to the chair in which Mr. Houghton sits in Figure NW350.

Round turned front leg type C, Figure NW351, terminating in pad feet, joined by conventional stretcher for this group. Square and lower chamfered back legs. Legs connected by box-form stretchers, one stretcher connecting rear legs. Replaced seat with edge protective strips missing. Reclined back uprights terminating in domed and nipple top finials, connected with six graduated wavy line ladders. Flattened wide arms which mortice into back uprights with tapered tenons. Turned underarm supports morticed and wedged through the arm.

Figure NW354. Wavy line ladder back armchair. Ash. Attributed to Lancashire, c.1790-1840.

Round turned front legs type C, Figure NW351, terminating in pad feet, joined by conventional turned stretcher of this group. Square and lower chamfered back legs. Legs connected by box-form stretchers. One stretcher connecting rear legs. Rush seat with one edge protective strip missing. Straight round back uprights, terminating in domed and nipple top finials, connected with six graduated wavy line ladders. Curved shaped arms which mortice into back uprights with turned tenons. Turned underarm supports of conventional style which is half the turning motif of the front cross stretcher.

Figure NW353. Detail of the fixing method for the flattened arms typical of certain armchairs in this group. In this example, the underarm support has a tenon which passes through the arm, and is secured with a wooden wedge.

Figure NW355. Wavy line ladder back side chair. Ash. Stamped 'W. SLEE.' on top of front legs. Untraced. Attributed to Lancashire, c.1790-1840.

Round turned front legs type A, Figure NW351, terminating in pad feet joined by conventional stretcher of this group. Square and lower chamfered back legs. Legs connected by box-form stretchers, one stretcher connecting rear legs. Replaced rush seat with wooden edge protective strips missing. Straight round back uprights, terminating in domed and nipple finials, connected with five graduated wavy line ladders.

Figure NW356. The stamp of 'W. Slee' impressed on the top of the front leg of the chair shown in Figure NW355. This is probably the maker's stamp, but no maker of this name has been traced.

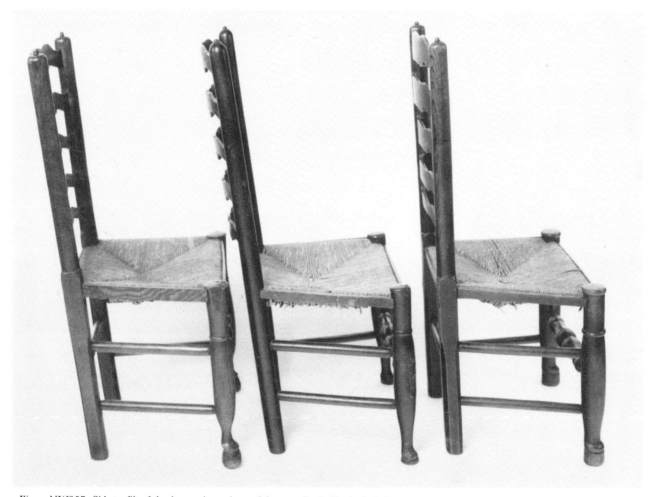

Figure NW357. Side profile of the three major variants of the wavy line ladder back chairs, showing turned front legs type A, B, and C, Figure NW351.

Figure NW358. Wavy line ladder back side chair. Ash. Attributed to Lancashire, c.1790-1840.

Round turned front leg type A, Figure NW351, terminating in pad feet, joined by conventional stretcher for this group. Unusual form of continuous chamfered back legs. Legs connected by box-form stretchers, one stretcher connecting rear legs. Replaced rush seat with wooden edge protective strips missing. Reclined round back uprights terminating in domed and nipple finials, connected with five graduated wavy line ladders.

Figure NW360. Wavy line ladder back side chair. Ash. Attributed to Lancashire, c.1790-1840.

Round turned front legs type B, Figure NW351, terminating in pad feet, joined by conventional stretcher for this group. Round back legs. Legs connected by box-form stretchers, one stretcher connecting rear legs. Rush seat with wooden edge protective strips. Straight round back uprights, terminating in domed and nipple finials, connected with five graduated wavy line ladders.

Figure NW362. Wavy line ladder back side chair. Ash. Attributed to Lancashire, c.1790-1840.

Round turned front legs type C, Figure NW351, terminating in pad feet, joined by conventional stretcher for this group. Square with lower chamfered back legs. Legs connected by box-form stretchers, one stretcher connecting rear legs. Rush seat with wooden edge protective strips. Straight round back uprights with domed and nipple finials, connected with five graduated wavy line ladders.

Figure NW359. The rear of the right hand back upright of the chair in Figure NW358, showing the nailed or sprig form of holding the top ladder in place.

Figure NW361. The rear of the right hand back upright of the chair in Figure NW360, showing the method of fixing the ladder, where glue alone was used to hold the joint secure.

Figure NW363. The rear of the right hand back upright of the chair in Figure NW362, showing the square pegged form of holding the top ladder in place, which is typically found in combination with type C legs which have a decoratively scribed turnery pattern on the top of the front legs (see Figure NW364).

417

Figure NW364. The turned top of the front leg of the chair shown in Figure NW362, this decorative form of turning is typical of those chairs which have type C legs, and the attendant square wood pegging of the top ladder (see Figure NW363).

Figure NW365. Wavy line ladder back side chair. Ash. Attributed to Lancashire, c.1790-1840.

Round turned front legs type C, Figure NW351, terminating in pad feet, joined by conventional stretcher for this group. Unusual form of continuously chamfered back legs. Legs connected by box-form stretchers, one stretcher connecting rear legs. Replaced seat with wooden edge protective strips missing. Reclined round back uprights, terminating in domed and nipple finials, connected with five graduated wavy line ladders.

Figure NW366. An illustration of the ladders morticing into the back uprights of a wavy line ladder back chair, showing evidence of the practice of shaping ladders 'in situ' after fitting in place with a draw knife. This construction practice was commonly used in this style of chair, but was uncommon in other ladder back styles from the region.

Figure NW367. Wavy line ladder back rocking armchair. Ash. Attributed to Lancashire, c.1790-1840.

Round turned front legs type C, Figure NW351, terminating in pad feet, fitted to rockers, joined by turned stretcher more usually found in double row spindle back chairs type V, Figure NW70. Square and lower chamfered back legs. Legs connected by box-form stretchers, one stretcher connecting rear legs. Rush seat with wooden edge protective strips. Reclined round back uprights terminating in domed and nipple finials, connected with six graduated wavy line ladders. Curved shaped arms which mortice into back uprights with turned tenons. Short turned underarm supports of conventional style which are half the usual turning motif of the front stretcher.

Figure NW368. Child's wavy line ladder back rocking armchair. Ash. Attributed to Lancashire, c.1790-1840.

Round turned front legs type V, Figure NW70, terminating in pad feet fitted to rockers, joined by turned stretcher more usually found in double row spindle back chairs type V, Figure NW70. Square and lower chamfered back legs. Legs connected by single box-form stretchers. Rush seat with wooden edge protective strips. Reclined round back uprights terminating in domed and nipple finials connected with five wavy line ladders. Round turned arms, which mortice into back uprights with turned tenons, typical of those used in many children's chairs throughout England (see Figures NW56 and 369). Short turned underarm supports of conventional style which is half the usual turning motif of the front stretcher.

418

Figure NW369. Ladder back child's rocking armchair. Ash. Attributed to Lancashire, c.1790-1840. This chair illustrates the tendency of the chair turners to amalgamate features from different chair styles to create a further style. The back uprights and underarm turning are typical of those found in wavy line ladder backs. The front stretcher is more usually found in some styles of spindle back chairs. The ladders are typically found in some other styles of ladder back chairs from this region (see Figures NW263 and 264).

Round turned front legs fitted to rockers, joined by turned stretcher more usually found in double row spindle back chairs type V, Figure NW70. Round tapered back legs. Legs connected by box-form stretchers. One side stretcher and one connecting rear legs. Rush seat with wooden edge protective strips. Reclined round back uprights terminating in domed and nipple finials, connected with four graduated ladders with domed top and downard tip below. Round turned arms, typical of those found on children's chairs throughout the English regions, with short turned underarm supports typical of those found in wavy line ladder back armchairs.

Figure NW370. Ladder back side chair. Ash. Attributed to Lancashire, c.1790-1840. This style of chair incorporates the back uprights and front rail, and front legs typically found in wavy line ladder back chairs (see Figure NW362). The ladder shape is peculiar to this style of chair and illustrates a chair design which is closely related to the wavy line ladder back chair.

Round turned front legs type B, terminating in pad feet, joined by conventional stretcher of the wavy line group. Round back legs. Legs connected by box-form stretchers, one stretcher connecting rear legs. Replaced rush seat with wooden edge protective strips missing. Straight round back uprights with domed and nipple finials, connected with five graduated bow shaped ladders.

*   *   *   *   *   *   *

Ladder Back Chairs - Epilogue

The anthology of North West standard ladder back chairs illustrated here does not propose itself as exhaustive, but it is presented as reasonably comprehensive and representative, and the brief analysis of design associations given for this large and diverse group of ladder back chairs serves to illustrate something of the common code which links these chairs, sometimes in terms of one detail which links to another, otherwise dissimilar ladder back chair. In other cases, a number of clear features link one group with another ladder back group, or to an entirely different major group of chairs. Some features link to earlier, less sophisticated styles of chairs. The resultant complex of designs offers a cohesive stystem which illustrates both a temporal, as well as a spatial, system in which the chair designs shown here are regionally related.

Rush seated kitchen chairs

Of the many groups of rush seated chairs made in the North West, two forms may be considered to be basic kitchen chair designs. These are distinguished in having sawn back uprights which are products of cabinet makers' work. Of these two groups, the first, above all reflects their origin in classical furniture design. These chairs were made from about 1830 to 1860, and are characterised in having square sawn back uprights connected by a wide variety of turned and shaped stay rails which are joined to a lower plain cross splat by five narrow, curved and square in section, vertical splats. This design echoes chair styles found in both Thomas Sheraton's design books,[131] as well as in later, neo-classical Regency designs which reflected French Empire style furniture's debt to early classical forms.

Typically these chairs were made in stained cherry wood, although examples in ash and elm are not uncommon. The quality of the original rush seating is extremely fine, and the construction of the chairs has considerable refinement in their execution. Two major styles were made; those with turned front legs (see Figures NW378-381), and those with square tapered legs (see Figures NW273 and 274 for examples). Those with turned front legs have elaborately turned front rails which are usually similar to types B and C, Figure NW372, whereas those chairs with square front legs also have narrow, plain rectangular shaped side and back leg stretchers (see Figure NW373 for example).

The North West chair tradition, in which this style is located, is essentially that of the turned chair, and the use of sawn and shaped parts creates this style as the product of the cabinet maker rather than the chair turner. However, chairs of this type have been recorded which incorporate parts from turned chairs, including the legs, front stretcher and inner lower rail assembly, found as part of double row spindle back chairs, as well as turned legs from both side and armchairs of the second group of rush seated kitchen chair designs. Other chairs show combinations of single row Lancashire spindle backs with the square tapered front legs (see Figure NW377), or adopt the arm style of the spindle back chair (see

Figure NW371. *The back of a rush seated kitchen side chair, showing the design influence of Thomas Sheraton. This construction shows evidence of complex turning, sawing and shaping techniques in its execution, work which locates this type of chair within a group which although simple, has a refinement of style and structure which is generally lacking in the second, later group of rush seated kitchen chairs. See Figures NW382-410.*

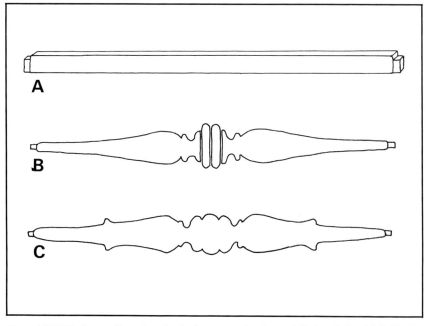

Figure NW372. *Front rail turnings for the first group of rush seated kitchen chairs, 1840-70. See Figures NW371-381.*

Figure NW378). The rare mergers of chair parts shown in Figures NW376-378 have an important function in illustrating the close relationship which these chairs have with other chairs in the North West tradition.

Figure NW373. Rush seated kitchen armchair. Cherry. Attributed to Lancashire, c.1840-60.

Square tapered front legs, joined by plain sawn front rail. Legs connected by box-form plain sawn stretchers, one stretcher connecting rear legs. Rush seat with wooden edge strips missing. Curved sawn back uprights square to the front connected by two plain curved central splats with turned stay rail above, connected to middle cross splat by five narrow vertical splats. Curved arms with turned section morticing into the arms, supported by turned underarm supports.

Figure NW374. Rush seated kitchen side chair. Cherry. Attributed to Lancashire, c.1840-70.

Front legs tapered, joined by plain narrow sawn front stretcher. Legs connected by box-form turned stretcher, one stretcher connecting rear legs. Rush seat with front wooden edge strip missing. Curved back sawn uprights with plain curved narrow splat with turned stay rail above, connected by five narrow vertical splats.

Figure NW375. Rush seated child's kitchen chair. Ash. Attributed to Lancashire, c.1840-70.

Flattened turnings to the front legs, square section at seat level, flattened ring turnings below, short turned leg below with vase shaped feet. Joined by decoratively turned front rail similar to type C, Figure NW372. Legs connected by box-form stretchers, with single stretchers connecting all legs. Replaced rush seat with wooden edge strips missing. Curved sawn back uprights square to the front connected by three plain curved splats with turned stay rail above, connected to middle cross splat by four perpendicular narrow splats, the middle two cross splats connected by two turned balls or buttons.

Figure NW376. Rush seated kitchen side chair. Ash. Attributed to Lancashire, c.1840-60. This chair is a hybrid which embodies features of the first group of rush seated kitchen chairs in the front leg turning and sawn square fronted back uprights. Double row spindle back features are shown in the design of the front stretcher and the incorporation of the side stretchers, turned to incorporate a cross stretcher. The back splats are typical of those found in regional chairs embodying influences from certain designs produced by Thomas Sheraton.

Square tapered front legs joined by turned front rail similar to type V, Figure NW70. Legs connected by box-form stretchers, with the lower rails connected by a cross stretcher and one stretcher connecting rear legs. Rush seat with wooden edge strips missing. Curved back sawn uprights square to the front connected by one plain splat with plain stay rail above, connected by four scribe decorated splats.

Figure NW377. Rush seated kitchen side chair. Alder with ash parts, c.1840-60. This chair represents a merger of rush seated kitchen chairs from this first group and two row spindle back chairs, illustrating the tendency of the North West makers occasionally to merge styles to produce a further design.

Square front legs, joined by plain narrow sawn front rail. Rear legs square with chamfered corners. Legs connected by box-form stretchers, one stretcher connecting rear legs. Rush seat with wooden edge strips. Turned back uprights connected by two plain curved central splats with shaped narrow stay rail above, connected by two rows of spindles type i, Figure NW69. *Collection S. Bourne*

421

Figure NW378. Rush seated kitchen armchair. Cherry. Attributed to Lancashire, c.1840-70.

Quarter round top to the turned front legs; flattened ball and ring turning below, with ball and straight feet. Legs joined by decoratively turned front rail similar to type B, Figure NW372. Legs connected by box-form stretchers, one stretcher connecting rear legs which are swept backwards. Rush seat with wooden edge strips. Curved back sawn uprights, square to the front with narrow lower splat and turned shaped rail above, connected by five plain curved splats. Curved arms similar to those found in examples of single row spindle back chairs. Urn shaped turned underarm supports.

Figure NW379. Rush seated kitchen side chair. Fruitwood. Attributed to Lancashire, c.1840-70.

Square top to the front legs with chamfered corners and flattened ball and ring turning below. Turned legs with ball and straight feet. Legs joined by decoratively turned front rail which represents the top of the leg turning and is similar to type B, Figure NW372. Connected by box-form stretchers. Curved back sawn uprights, square to the front with one plain narrow curved lower splat with turned shaped broad stay rail above, connected by five plain narrow curved splats.

Figure NW380. Rush seated kitchen armchair. Fruitwood. Attributed to Lancashire, c.1850-80. This chair illustrates the merging of characteristics from the two styles of rush kitchen chairs, including the front legs and cross stretcher from group 2 and the back from group 1. The union of these two styles illustrate the willingness of the Lancashire makers to combine two chair styles to create a third.

Front legs, square at seat level with flattened ball and ring turning below; turned legs with pad feet. Legs joined by decoratively turned front rail similar to type C, Figure NW372. Legs connected by box-form stretchers, one stretcher connecting rear legs. Replaced rush seat with wooden edge strips missing. Curved sawn back uprights square to the front with two plain curved splats with turned stay rail above, connected to middle cross splat by five plain curved splats. Curved arms with turned terminal morticing into the back legs, supported by decoratively turned underarm supports with urn motif.

The second group of rush seated kitchen chairs was made rather later than the first, although they probably overlapped in their manufacture around the middle of the nineteenth century. This group of chairs is robustly made, and probably fulfilled the place of the least expensive rush seat utility kitchen chairs. They are typically made from alder, although elm and ash were also used, with the surface of the chairs being stained with walnut or mahogany stain, and finished with varnish. In so far as the back uprights and cross splats of these chairs were produced from sawn rather than turned sections of wood, they have a similar structural relationship with the previous group of rush seated chairs. In other stylistic terms, however, the groups have different characteristics.

The most common of this later group's designs have either one plain curved cross splat in the case of the side chair, or two in the armchair, with a plain shaped stay rail. Alternatively, the back design has two narrow cross splats supporting one row of three short spindles, or two rows in the armchair. In both of these varieties, the front legs are turned with a simple vase shaped foot, or with the more elaborate pad foot.

Other varieties of rush seated kitchen chairs which stylistically affiliate to this group are recorded from Macclesfield, Cheshire, where they were made by members of the Leicester family. The first, illustrated in Figure NW407, has typical features of the chairs from this group's design, but includes an unusual 'rope' carved or 'Trafalgar' back cross rail, typical of some Regency chairs. The second chair, shown in Figure NW409, had the general characteristics of chairs from this group, but in this case, the sawn back uprights are square to the front edge, and joined by a turned and flattened cross rail, typically found in kitchen Windsor chairs from the Oxfordshire and Buckinghamshire tradition, and also found in certain chairs from East Anglia (see Chapter 4, Figures EA68 and 69).

A much rarer type of chair which also belongs to this group, in general design terms, was made with a splat or ladder back, with five domed top ladders, decoratively shaped below (see Figure NW392 for example).

Chairs from the first and second groups were probably made by many chair and cabinet makers throughout the North West. However, examples stamped by their makers have only been recorded for the second group, and examples so identified have been recorded from Lancaster in the north of Lancashire, Blackburn and Ormskirk to the north east of Manchester, and possibly Rochdale in Lancashire or Altrincham in Cheshire, as well as from Macclesfield in Cheshire.

Figure NW381. Rush seated kitchen side chair. Fruitwood. Attributed to Lancashire, c.1840-70. This chair incorporates front leg design typical of that associated with the double row Lancashire spindle back chair, and indicates the close relationship which this chair has with other forms of Lancashire rush seated chairs and the tendency for makers to incorporate elements of one chair design in another.

Turned front legs with pad feet, joined by decoratively turned stretcher similar to type C, Figure NW372. Legs connected by box-form stretchers, one stretcher connecting rear legs. Replaced rush seat with wooden edge strips missing. Curved back sawn uprights square to the front, connected by plain curved narrow lower splat with turned shaped stay rail above, connected by five plain curved splats.

Figure NW382. Rush seated kitchen side chair. Alder. Stamped 'J. SHARPLES' on the back leg (fl.1864-87). This is the plainest of chairs in the group, and was probably the least expensive pattern of the late 19th century Lancashire rush seated chairs. It is similar to the chair stamped 'D. NEILD.R.' illustrated in Figure NW385.

Square top to the front legs, ring turning below, turned leg with vase shaped feet, joined by decoratively turned front rail similar to type C, Figure NW384. Legs connected by box-form stretchers, one stretcher connecting rear legs. Rush seat with wooden edge strips missing. Strips on upper surface of rush intact. Curved sawn back uprights connected by one plain cross splat with plain broad stay rail above.

Figure NW383. The stamp of John Sharples of Blackburn (1864-87), chair maker, cabinet maker, and wood turner, impressed on the rear leg of the chair shown in Figure NW382. John Sharples is recorded as working variously at Fisher Street, Larkhill, and Ainsworth Street, Blackburn, and is also recorded as a Freeman of Hull in 1878.

Examples of common forms of chairs in this group which were not stamped by their makers are illustrated in Figures NW387-392.

Other unusual examples of chairs which fit into this second group are shown in Figures NW400 and 401, illustrating chairs which incorporate design features from other chairs in this regional tradition. For example, the chair shown in Figure NW400 has a front stretcher turning type V, Figure NW70, typically found in double row spindle back chairs. Figure NW401 illustrates a chair which has a typical double row spindle back design, with rush seated kitchen chair front legs and turned stretcher. The chair in Figure NW404, conversely, has a rush seated kitchen chair back, combined with double row spindle back chair front legs and front stretcher type Ib, Figure NW70. This latter group of chairs serves to illustrate the close relationship which the rush seated kitchen chairs have with other chairs in this regional tradition, and to suggest that they were made by the same makers as part of a repertoire of styles.

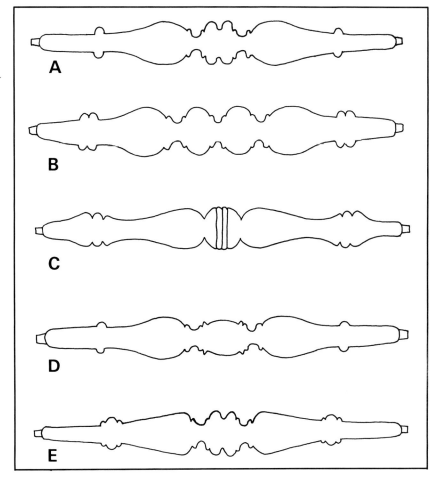

Figure NW384. Front rail turnings incorporated in the second group of rush seated kitchen chairs, 1850-90 in Figures NW382-410.

Figure NW385. Rush seated kitchen side chair. Alder. Stamped 'D. NEILD.R.' on top of both front legs, c.1850-90.

Front legs with square top with chamfered edges, ball and ring turning below, turned legs with ball and vase shaped feet, joined by decoratively turned front rail similar to type D, Figure NW384. Legs connected by box-form stretchers, one stretcher connecting rear legs. Replaced rush seat with wooden edge strips missing. Curved, sawn back uprights, rounded on front surface, connected by plain curved central cross splat, and with broad plain stay rail above, both with single reeding decoration.

Figure NW386. Stamp of D. Neild impressed on the top of both front legs of the chair shown in Figure NW385. Attributed to Lancashire or Cheshire. Members of the Neild family worked as cabinet makers in Altrincham (1860-87), and Sandbach (1860-88), in Cheshire, and a Daniel Nield worked as a cabinet maker at 145 Yorkshire Street, Rochdale, Lancashire in 1851. The 'R' following the stamped 'D. Neild' may refer to Rochdale, but the names are spelt differently, and thus present an ambiguity.

Figure NW387. Rush seated kitchen side chair. Alder. Attributed to Lancashire, c.1860-90.

Front legs with quarter round top, flattened ball and ring turning below, turned legs with pad feet, joined by decoratively turned front rail similar to type B, Figure NW384. Square sawn back legs connected by box-form stretchers, one stretcher joining rear legs. Rush seat with wooden edge strips. Curved sawn back uprights rounded on the front surface connected by plain cross splat with broad stay rail above.

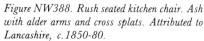

Figure NW388. Rush seated kitchen chair. Ash with alder arms and cross splats. Attributed to Lancashire, c.1850-80.

Turned front legs with square section at seat level, flattened ball and ring turning below; plain turned leg with decoratively turned feet. Legs joined by decoratively turned front rail similar to type A, Figure NW384. Shaped square back legs connected by box-form stretchers, one stretcher connecting rear legs. Rush seat with wooden edge strips. Curved back uprights connected by three plain graduated cross splats with shaped broad stay rail above. Turned underarm supports similar to half the front rail turning. Curved arms morticed into back supports with turned section.

Figure NW389. The interior of a farmhouse kitchen at Ormskirk, Lancashire, 1984. The furniture has been in ths house since the 19th century, and is typical of this region's style. The furniture includes a mahogany cross-banded Lancashire dresser, and settle. The chairs are called 'Ormskirk' chairs in this area, and may be a style specific to this town where a number of chair makers worked in the 19th century. An armchair of this style is shown in Figure NW390. A nursing rocking chair of this type is partly shown in the right hand corner of the kitchen scene, and is illustrated in Figure NW391.*

---

* Chairs in this group have been generically grouped under the title of 'Ormskirk' chairs. The provenanced chairs now recorded within this design category show that these chairs were made in a number of towns in Lancashire and possibly Cheshire. However, hearsay evidence[132] suggests that the style of chair shown in the farmhouse kitchen at Ormskirk, and in Figures NW390 and 391 were a style made in that town by James Banks[133] and Henry Burrows[134] who had a chair making factory in Burscough Street from the mid-nineteenth century, until the early part of the twentieth century.

Figure NW390. Rush seated kitchen chair. Alder. Attributed to Lancashire, c.1880-1920.

Front legs turned with square section at seat level, ball turning below with vase shaped feet. Legs joined by decoratively turned front rail incorporating a ball turning similar to type C, Figure NW384. Square back legs connected by box-form stretchers of sawn rather than turned segments, one stretcher connecting rear legs. Rush seat with wooden edge strips. Curved sawn back uprights connected by two curved cross splats and curved stay rail above, decorated with two rows of double reeding. Curved shaped arm morticing into back uprights with turned tenon (see Figure NW391 for a rocking chair with similar design features).

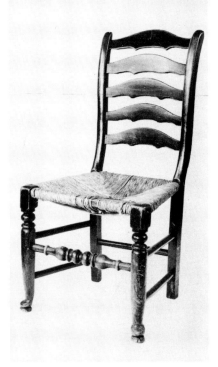

Figure NW393. Rush seated kitchen side chair. Alder. Stamped 'R.H. & J. SIMPSON MAKERS' on top of both front legs (fl.1865-87).

Square top with chamfered corners to the front legs. Flattened ball and ring turning below, with turned leg and vase shaped feet, joined by decoratively turned front stretcher similar to type A, Figure NW384. Legs connected by box-form stretchers, one stretcher connecting rear legs. Replaced rush seat with wooden edge strips. Curved sawn back uprights, ovalled to the front, connected by two plain curved and ovalled cross slats supporting three turned spindles which were stained black. Shaped broad stay rail above. The spindle turnings are also shown in the R.H. & J. Simpson nursing chair shown in Figure NW398.

Figure NW391. Rush seated kitchen rocking armchair. Alder. Attributed to Lancashire, c.1800-1920. The components in this chair are identical to those utilised in the chair shown in Figure NW390, other than the length of the legs and underarm supports, which are shorter in this design.

Front legs turned with square section at seat level and ball turning below. Short turned leg with vase shaped feet morticed into rockers. Legs joined by decoratively turned front rail incorporating ball turning similar to type C, Figure NW384. Sawn back legs connected by box-form stretchers constructed from sawn sections of wood, one stretcher connecting rear legs. Rush seat with wooden edge strips. Curved sawn back uprights connected by two curved cross splats with curved stay rail above, decorated with two rows of double reeding. Short turned underarm supports and curved shaped arms with turned section morticing into back uprights.

Figure NW392. Rush seated splat or ladder back kitchen side chair. Ash. Attributed to Lancashire, c.1850-80. This style of chair embodies many of the features of the more typical rush seated kitchen chairs, but the inclusion of ladders rather than cross splats and spindles creates a further style of chair which properly belongs in this generic group.

Front legs with square top with chamfered edges. Flattened ball and ring turning below; turned legs with pad feet. Legs joined by decoratively turned front rail similar to type B, Figure NW384. Square back legs, connected by box-form stretchers, one stretcher connecting rear legs. Damaged rush seat with wooden edge strips missing. Curved back uprights, rounded to the front, connected by five cross splats or ladders, dome shaped above and decoratively shaped below.

Figure NW394. The stamp of R.H. & J. Simpson, cabinet and chair makers of 18 Nicholas Street, Lancaster (fl.1865-87),[135] impressed on the top of each front leg of the chair shown in NW393. The positioning of this stamp is unusual, and suggests that the Simpsons intended this as an advertising device. Interestingly, this stamp position was used by a further Lancashire maker, D. Neild.R. (see Figure NW386).

Figure NW395. Rush seated kitchen side chair. Alder. Stamped 'R. SIMPSON MAKER' on the top of both front legs (fl.1865-87).

Front legs with square top with chamfered edges. Flattened ball and ring turning below; turned leg with vase shaped feet. Legs joined by decoratively turned front rail similar to type A, Figure NW384. Legs connected by box-form stretchers, one stretcher connecting back legs. Rush seat with one wooden edge strip missing. Curved sawn back uprights ovalled to the front, connected by two plain narrow cross splats, supporting three turned spindles stained black with plain broad stay rail above.

Figure NW396. The stamp of Robert Simpson of Lancaster (fl.1848-87), impressed on the top of the front legs of the chair shown in Figure NW395. This maker worked at St. Nicholas Street, Lancaster, 1848 to 1887,[136] when he formed a partnership with his relative, James Simpson, who had also worked at St. Nicholas Street since 1848. An example of a chair stamped with both of their initials is shown in Figure NW393.

Figure NW397. An elderly lady who was part of the strong tradition of hand-knitters who worked in the Dales area of the North West during the 19th century. She sits in a low armed nursing rush seated rocking chair, which has features in common with those of the chair made by R.H. & J. Simpson[137] of Lancaster, illustrated in Figure NW398. The chair is draped with a hand crocheted cloth, and has a cushion over the worn rush seat to increase the comfort of the chair.

Photograph courtesy Dalesman Publishing Co.

Figure NW398. Nursing rush seated kitchen rocking chair. Alder with elm front legs, front stretchers and rockers. Stamped 'R.H. & J. SIMPSON MAKERS' (fl.1865-90) on back legs. A similar chair to this is shown in Figure NW397.

Short turned underarm supports, square block at seat level. Flattened ball and ring turning above short turned front legs with vase shaped feet below. Decoratively turned front rail similar to type A, Figure NW384. Box-form stretchers, one stretcher connecting rear legs. Chair fitted to rockers. Damaged rush seat with wooden edge strips. Curved sawn back uprights, ovalled on front edge, connected by a plain lower cross splat. Three narrow cross slats above, supporting two rows of three turned spindles. Shaped broad stay rail above. Sloping 'Grecian' style arms.

Figure NW399. The stamp of R.H. & J. Simpson, cabinet and chair makers of 18 Nicholas Street, Lancaster (fl.1865-87) impressed on back upright of chair in Figure NW398. Robert and James Simpson are each recorded as working separately in Nicholas Street from 1848.

427

Figure NW400. Rush seated kitchen side chair. Ash with alder stay rail. Attributed to Lancashire, c.1860-90. The front stretcher style indicates the relationship between these chairs and the makers of the double row Lancashire spindle back chairs from this region.

Front legs with quarter round top, flattened ball and ring turnings, turned leg below with straight feet, joined by plain front rail with similar turning to type V, Figure NW70, which is typically found in double row spindle back chairs. Legs connected by box-form stretchers, one stretcher connecting rear legs. Rush seat with wooden edge strips. Curved sawn back uprights connected by two narrow plain cross splats supporting four elaborately turned spindles; plain stay rail above.

Figure NW401. Spindle back side chair. Ash. Attributed to Lancashire, 1780-1840. The front legs and turned stretcher of this chair are stylistically similar to those found in the rush seated kitchen chairs illustrated in Figures NW382 and 385. However, the back of the chair is typical of double row spindle back chairs illustrated in Figures NW93-97. The union of two styles of Lancashire chairs demonstrates the tendency of the Lancashire makers to merge styles on occasions, as well as illustrating the common tradition in which these chairs were based.

Front legs with quarter round top and flattened ball and ring turning. Plain turned legs below terminating in vase shaped feet and joined by turned stretcher type C, Figure NW384. Chamfered back legs. Legs connected by box-form stretchers, one stretcher connecting rear legs. Damaged rush seat with two wooden edge strips missing. Round back uprights with two rows of five turned spindles, type a, Figure NW69, supported between two curved cross rails and an upper narrow curved shaped stay rail. Back uprights terminating in pronounced nipple shaped finials.

Figure NW402. Rush seated kitchen armchair. Ash with alder back uprights, cross splats, arms and spindles. Attributed to Lancashire, c.1850-80.

Turned front legs with pear shaped underarm turnings, flattened ball and ring turning below, turned legs with pad feet. Legs joined by decoratively front rail similar to type B, Figure NW384. Legs connected by box-form stretchers. One stretcher connecting rear legs. Rush seat missing. Curved sawn back uprights, rounded on front face, connected by plain curved lower splat, three plain narrow cross splats supporting six turned spindles. Shaped broad stay rail above. Sawn shaped arms morticed into back uprights. Turned underarm supports showing similar turnery pattern to half front turning.

Figure NW403. Rush seated kitchen side chair. Alder. Attributed to Lancashire, c.1850-90.

Legs connected by box-form stretchers, one stretcher connecting rear legs. Rush seat with front wooden edge strip missing. Curved sawn back uprights, ovalled to the front, connected by two plain cross splats supporting three turned spindles, with shaped broad stay rail above. *Collection J. Boram*

Figure NW404. Rush seated kitchen side chair. Ash. Attributed to Lancashire, c.1840-80.

Front legs with quarter round top, turned leg below with pad feet, joined by decoratively turned front rail similar to type Ib, Figure NW70. Legs connected by box-form stretchers. One stretcher connecting rear legs. Damaged rush seat with wooden edge strips. Curved sawn back uprights, ovalled on front face connected by two plain cross splats supporting three turned and flattened spindles. Broad shaped stay rail above.

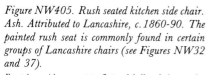

Figure NW405. Rush seated kitchen side chair. Ash. Attributed to Lancashire, c.1860-90. The painted rush seat is commonly found in certain groups of Lancashire chairs (see Figures NW32 and 37).

Front legs with square top, flattened ball and ring turning below, turned leg with vase shaped feet, joined by decoratively turned front rail similar to type B, Figure NW384. Legs connected by box-form stretchers, one stretcher connecting rear legs. Painted rush seat with wooden edge strips. Curved back uprights connected by turned cross splat reminiscent of Regency style, and also a dominant design feature in Buckinghamshire and Oxfordshire kitchen chairs (see Chapter 2, Figure TV181). Broad stay rail and narrow cross splat supporting three ball or button turnings. The adoption of the ball or button turnings and the flattened and turned cross stretcher are similar design features to those used in some East Anglian chairs (see Chapter 4, Figure EA45).

Figure NW406. Rush seated child's kitchen chair. Alder. Attributed to Lancashire, c.1860-90.

Front legs turned with ball and multiple ring motif. Legs joined by box-form stretchers, one stretcher connecting rear legs. Replaced rush seat with wooden edge strips missing. Curved sawn back uprights connected by two plain cross splats supporting three turned balls or buttons, with plain broad stay rail above. Turned arm supports and round turned arms in the style of many English children's armchairs (see Figures NW368 and 369). Collection J. Boram.

Figure NW407. Rush seated kitchen side chair. Fruitwood. Stamped 'LEICESTER' on back leg.

Square top to the front legs, ring turning below. Turned leg with vase shaped feet, joined by decoratively turned front rail. Legs connected by box-form stretchers, one stretcher connecting rear legs. Replacement rush seat with wooden edge strips missing. Curved sawn back uprights, ovalled to the front, connected by a rope patterned or 'Trafalgar' cross splat with plain broad stay rail above.

Figure NW408. The stamp of Leicester of Macclesfield, Cheshire (1816-81), stamped on the rear upright of the chair shown in Figure NW407.

Figure NW409. Rush seated kitchen side chair. Alder. Stamped 'LEICESTER' on back leg. Macclesfield, Cheshire, 1870-81.

Square top to the front legs, ring turning below. Turned legs with vase shaped feet joined by decoratively turned front rail similar to type E, Figure NW384. Legs connected by box-form stretchers, one stretcher connecting rear legs. Rush seat with wooden side edge strips. Curved sawn back uprights connected by a plain broad stay rail above, and turned and shaped central cross rail typical of those found in chairs made in the Oxfordshire and Buckinghamshire tradition, as well as in common chairs from East Anglia.

Figure NW410. The stamp of Leicester of Macclesfield, Cheshire (1816-81), impressed on the rear leg of the chair shown in Figure NW409. This is the stamp of a member of the Leicester family of chair makers who worked in the town (see p.367 for details).

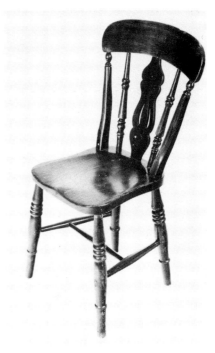

Figure NW412. Bannister balloon-back Windsor chair. Alder with elm seat. Stamped 'HENRY ROBERTS & CO.' on the rear edge of the seat. This style of chair, with variations of splat fretting, was common to many parts of the North of England. This chair has original staining.

Heavily turned three ring legs with straight feet. Legs connected by H-form stretchers. Sawn and turned back uprights supporting a shaped stay rail. One turned spindle either side of a broad shaped splat with two frets.

Figure NW411. A photograph of Mrs Emma Orrett who is sitting and reading in the kitchen of her home at Irlam on the Heights, Manchester, 1911. The chair in which she sits is typical of the North West tradition of kitchen Windsors, and is similar to those illustrated in Figures NW412 and 414. Chairs of this kind were the least expensive of the common chairs, and were found in the majority of artisans' houses in the region. Photograph courtesy Mrs Jessie Peters, née Orrett

Figure NW413. The stamp of Henry Roberts and Co. impressed on the rear edge of the seat of chair shown in Figure NW395. A firm of cabinet makers with this name is recorded working at 7 Berry Street, Liverpool, in 1851, and in Manchester in 1887.[138]

Kitchen Windsors

Although the nineteenth century North West common seating tradition was predominantly that of the rush seated chair, towards the middle of the century, a range of stained kitchen Windsors was made in styles which continued in manufacture until the end of the nineteenth century. These chairs typically have a shaped stay rail, supported by turned spindles and a broad central shaped and fretted bannister splat. Chairs which include shaped laths with a central splat were also made (see Figure NW418 for example).

A mixture of hard and semi-hard woods are found in their construction, including birch, willow, alder, beech, ash, and elm. The mixing of woods probably illustrates that since these chairs were stained in 'mahogany, walnut, or light'[139] that the consistency of wood quality was not important since the makers were primarily producing an inexpensive, utilitarian chair. A number of these chairs, bearing makers' stamps from the North West, including makers in Liverpool, Wigan and Stockport, are shown in Figures NW412-423. These chairs are comfortable to sit in and were found in the great many working class homes in the North of England. The illustrations shown in Figure NW411 shows Mrs. Emma Orrett, sitting on a chair from this group, reading by her fireside at Irlam on the Heights, Manchester, in the early twentieth century.

Stools were also used extensively in the North West, at places of work, clubs, public houses, schools, and in the home. Many of these were made with turned legs, typical of Windsor chairs, and with turned tops in alder and elm. Name stamped stools are rare, and an example of a stool from this region which has the name G. Askew, stamped twice on the edge of the seat is shown in Figure NW427. G. Askew was probably related to Jonathan Askew, who was a chair maker and turner in Cockermouth, Cumberland, between 1820 and 1829,[140] and worked in a regional style of stool making.

430

Figure NW414. Bannister balloon-back Windsor chair. Alder with elm seat, legs and splat. Stamped 'H. KING MAKER WIGAN', on rear edge of seat. This style of chair, with variations of splat fretting was common to many parts of the North of England.

Turned three ring legs with vase shaped feet. H-form stretchers with two cross stretchers. Sawn and turned back uprights supporting a shaped stay rail. One turned spindle either side of a broad shaped splat with two fir tree shaped frets.

Figure NW416. Bannister balloon-back Windsor chair. Alder with ash splat. Stamped 'J. SHARPLES' on the back edge of the seat (fl.1864-87). This style of chair, with variations of splat fretting was common to many parts of the North of England. This chair has been stripped of surface 'finish'. Originally it would have been stained with a 'mahogany, walnut or light coloured stain' and varnished.

Heavily turned three ring legs with vase shaped feet. Legs connected by H-form stretchers. Sawn and turned back uprights supporting a shaped stay rail. One turned spindle either side of a broad shaped splat with a heart shaped fret.

Figure NW418. Splat back rocking armchair. Beech with elm seat. Stamped on rear edge of seat 'J. SHARPLES' (fl.1864-87), who was a chair, cabinet maker and wood turner of Blackburn, Lancashire. This style of chair incorporates many features of the lath back style chairs made in the High Wycombe tradition.

Heavy three ring turned legs with vase shaped feet, turned to fit rockers. Legs connected by heavy H-form stretchers with extra stretcher connecting back legs. Shaped back uprights terminating in turned finials. Shaped stay rail with two shaped laths or splats each side of a shaped central plain splat. Curved arms supported by two decoratively turned supports.

Photograph courtesy C. Gilbert

Figure NW415. The stamp of H. King, chair maker and cabinet maker. Soho Street, Newton, Pemberton, Wigan (fl.1903-9),[141] impressed on rear seat edge of chair in Figure NW414.

Figure NW417. The stamp of John Sharples of Blackburn (fl.1864-87), chair maker, cabinet maker, and wood turner, impressed on the back edge of the seat of the chair shown in Figure NW416. John Sharples is recored as working variously at Fisher Street, Larkhill, and Ainsworth Street, Blackburn. This maker is also recorded as a Freeman of Hull in 1876.[142]

431

Figure NW419. Bannister balloon-back Windsor chair. Birch stay rail, back supports, splat, and spindles, alder seat, ash legs and stretchers. Attributed to Lancashire, c.1850-90. Stamped 'S. NEEDES' on the rear edge of seat. This style of chair, with variations of splat fretting was common to many parts of the North of England. This chair has been stripped with caustic soda, originally it would have been stained with a 'mahogany, walnut or light coloured stain', and finished with varnish.

Heavily turned three ring legs with vase shaped feet and straight feet on rear legs. H-form stretchers with back legs connected by a further stretcher. Sawn and turned back uprights supporting a shaped stay rail. One turned spindle either side of a broad shaped splat which has two curved frets.

Figure NW421. Bannister balloon-back Windsor chair. Birch with alder back uprights and splat, and elm seat. Stamped 'PARKINSON BROS.' on rear edge of seat. Untraced, c.1860-80. This style of chair, with variations of splat fretting, was common to many parts of the North of England. This chair has had its original stain stripped off.

Heavily turned three ring legs with vase shaped feet. Legs connected by H-form stretchers with an additional stretcher connecting rear legs. Sawn and turned back uprights supporting a shaped stay rail. One turned (Roman) spindle either side of a broad shaped splat with two frets.

Figure NW423. Bannister balloon-back Windsor chair. Birch with alder back uprights and seat. Stamped 'G. COWBURN WIGAN WARRANTED' on rear edge of seat (fl.1873-91). This style of chair provided a robust alternative to the rush seated kitchen chair.

Heavy single ring and concave turned legs with vase shaped feet, connected by H-form stretchers. Sawn and turned back uprights supporting a shaped stay rail. Broad shaped central splat with two frets.

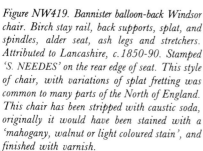

Figure NW420. The stamp of S. Needes on the rear seat edge of the chair shown in Figure NW419. This maker is currently untraced.

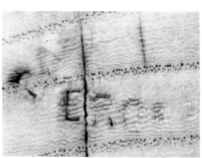

Figure NW422. The stamp of Parkinson Brothers, found on the rear edge of the chair shown in Figure NW421. Although no firm with the name of Parkinson Bros has been traced, John Parkinson is recorded as a chair maker in Chipping, Preston, between 1858 and 1873,[143] and a John Parkinson is also recorded as a furniture broker in Preston in 1877.[144]

Figure NW424. The stamp of George Cowburn, chair maker, of Wigan, Lancashire impressed on the rear edge of the seat of the chair shown in Figure NW423. This chair maker is recorded working at various addresses in Wigan, 1873-91.[145]

Figure NW425. Low splat back Windsor. Ash with alder splat and elm seat. Brass name plate on underside of seat which reads 'URQUART & ADAMSON CABINET MAKERS LIVERPOOL' (1857-87). The manufacture of Windsor chairs was uncommon in Lancashire, and this chair may have been made elsewhere, probably by the firm of Wm. Brear & Sons of Addingham, near Leeds, and sold with a retailer's label affixed.

Two ring turned legs with cup and ball shaped feet. Crinoline stretcher connecting legs. Four graduated spindles either side of fir tree splat. Three tapered underarm spindles. Elaborately turned underarm supports.

Figure NW427. Stool. Alder top, with oak legs and strethcers. Stamped 'G. ASKEW.' twice on edge of seat. Attributed to Cumberland, c.1840-80. No reference has been traced to G. Askew, although Jonathan Askew is recorded as a chair maker in Cockermouth, Cumberland (fl.1820-29),[147] and he may be a relative of G. Askew.

Turned circular top with triple ring turned legs and vase shaped feet. Cross form stretchers with one thin stretcher morticed through a thicker one.

Figure NW429. Spindle back child's rocking armchair, Alder. Stamped on rear edge of seat 'R. SIMPSON MAKER' (fl.1848-87), who was a chair maker, cabinet maker and wood turner of Lancaster, Lancashire. This style of chair was a common form produced for children (see Wm. Brear of Addingham Catalogue, Chapter 3, Figures NE419 and 420).

Single ring turned legs with vase shaped feet, fitted to rockers. Legs connected by H-form stretchers with turned back uprights terminating in turned finials. Shaped curved stay rail connected to four plain turned spindles to the seat. Curved Grecian arms supported by turned supports.

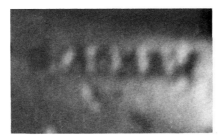

Figure NW426. A brass label affixed to the underside of the seat of the chair shown in Figure NW425 bearing the name of Urquart and Adamson, cabinet makers, Liverpool. This firm is recorded working in Bold Street, Liverpool, 1851-87.[146]

Figure NW428. The stamp of G. Askew, impressed twice on the side of the seat of the stool shown in Figure NW427. Untraced. Attributed to Cumberland, c.1840-80.

Figure NW430. The stamp of Robert Simpson of Lancaster (fl.1848-87), impressed on the top of the front legs of the chair shown in Figure NW429. This maker worked at St. Nicholas Street, Lancaster (fl.1848-87), when he formed a partnership with his relative, James Simpson, who had also worked at St. Nicholas Street since 1848.[148]

Figure NW431. The kitchen of a Lancashire farmhouse in the late 19th century showing a comfortable oak winged armchair by the fireside. The drawer, commonly found in the frieze of chairs of this design, is shown here to contain the family bible.

Winged armchairs

The 'box' form of winged armchair made in the Lancashire and Yorkshire Dales is an extremely diverse and comfortable regional style of chair which is peculiar to this region. Typically these chairs have panelled backs and attached side wings, and are also panelled to enclose the arms and the legs below the seat. Many examples have a drawer in the side or front frieze, and many examples have wooden rockers fitted to the base (see Figure NW433), as well as iron rockers.

Different seat modes are found, including wooden seats (see Figure NW436); rope seats to support a cushion (see Figure NW432); removable upholstered seats (see Figure NW433); and fixed upholstered seats

(see Figure NW434). Oak was the most typical wood for these chairs, but elm and pine with a painted grain finish have also been recorded (see Figures NW435 and 436).

Typically chairs of this style are large, and were probably intended for use by the male head of the household. However, occasional smaller versions of this chair style have been recorded which have the same stylistic connotations as the low armed rush seated chairs from the North West, and were probably made for use by female members of the household. An example of such a chair is shown in Figure NW436, and illustrates a low seated chair made in elm of the box form, which has a drawer in the right hand seat frieze.

The great variety of individual designs found in this group of chairs

suggests that they were made by cabinet makers or carpenters for an individual order, rather than working in the tradition of the turner who made many chairs in the same design. These chairs were, perhaps, the most comfortable and commodious made in the English common chair tradition, and the illustration in Figure NW431 shows the pride of place at the hearth which these chairs traditionally held. Hearsay evidence has claimed that these chairs were 'lambing' chairs, a title which suggests that they were used by shepherds who sat up during the night to oversee their flocks. This belief is probably apocryphal, although by the nature of their regional origins in the sheep farming countryside, they would, no doubt, often have been used at home by shepherds.

Figure NW432. Winged armchair. Oak. Attributed to Lancashire/Yorkshire Dales region, mid-18th century.

Straight sawn front legs with panelled front and saddle shaped seat with interlaced cord seat which would have supported a cushion. Narrow single dome topped panelled back, with corzier shaped back uprights (indicating North Country origins)[149] and side wings. Flattened broad scroll shaped arms. Height 46in.

Collection Roger Warner. Photograph courtesy Christopher Gilbert

Figure NW433. A magnificent large example of a winged armchair provenanced by family ownership to Padiham, near Burnley, Lancashire, c.1800-40. Oak stained to resemble mahogany.

Straight sawn front legs, fitted to rockers, with panelled front. Lift-out seat with later canvas. Two decorative panels in the back with blind 'Gothic' tracery, and upper broad shaped stay rail and side wings. Flattened scroll shaped arms with panel to enclose seat, and lower panel joining front and back legs. Back legs reclined. Height 46½in.
  Photograph courtesy Towneley Hall Art Gallery and Museums, Burnley, Lancashire

Figure NW434. Winged armchair. Originally from the Bay Horse Inn, Clough Bottom, near Whitworth, Lancashire. Oak, c.1750-1800.

Straight sawn front legs, originally fitted to metal rockers, now missing. Enclosed box seat, originally upholstered, with drawer to the front with inset brass handle. Single panelled back with deep dome shaped stay rail and side wings. Flattened scroll shaped arms with single panel below to enclose seat. Lower panel joining back and front legs. Back legs reclined. Height 47½in.
  Photograph courtesy Towneley Hall Art Gallery and Museums, Burnley, Lancashre

Figure NW435. Winged armchair. Pine, painted brown. Provenanced by family ownership to a farmhouse in North Lancashire, c.1750-1850.

Straight sawn front legs with enclosed box seat with drawer to the front and shaped frieze below. Narrow waisted single panelled back with side wings. Flattened scroll shaped arms with panelling which enclosed the seat.   *Private Collection*

Figure NW436. Winged low armchair. Elm. Attributed to Lancashire/ Yorkshire Dales region, c.1750-1840.

Straight sawn front legs with broad straight front frieze and flat wooden seat. Drawer in left hand side of frieze. Single panelled back with yoke shaped stay rail and attached side wings. Flattened scroll shaped arms.

Figure NW437. Winged armchair. Oak. Attributed to Lancashire/ Yorkshire Dales area, c.1750-1800.

Square sawn cabriole shaped front legs, swept rear legs. Interlaced rope seat which would have originally supported a cushion. Single panelled back with shaped stay rail and side wings. Flattened scroll shaped arms with single panel below to enclose seat. Height 121cm.   Collection Keith Hockin

Appendix

Transcript of the deposition* made in 1815, by Mark Chippindale, Chair Maker and Bobbin Turner of Aighton Bailey and Chaigley, Lancashire, to the Parish Authorities for financial assistance in reinstating his workshop which was destroyed by fire.

[A]   The Humble Petition of Mark Chippindale of Aighton Bailey and Chaigley in the parish of Mitton, and County of Lancaster, Bobbin turner and Chair maker.

Sheweth

That on Saturday the nineteenth day of September now last past about three o'clock in the morning a fire was discovered in the petitioners work shops within Aighton Bailey and Chaigley aforesaid, and that from the nature of your petitioners Business, the dryness of the weather, and the Buildings being wholly thatched, your Petitioner was unable either to extinguish the fire, or to save the Building; or any part of the property contained therein, from destruction—

That your petitioner left his workshop about ten o'clock in the Evening, when he said the Fire happened, and that the same then appeared to be perfectly safe, and how or in what manner it happened your petitioner is wholly ignorant, and unable to discover—

That the whole of your petitioners Stock in Trade, together with his Tools, and every other thing requisite for the carrying on of your petitioners Business, except the water wheel used in working his Lathes, having been consumed, and the petitioner being also obliged by his lease to rebuild the workshop, he the petitioner, together with his wife and four children, will, without the aid of charitable assistance, be reduced from a state of comfortable support to indigence and want—

The mark of
Mark Chippindale.

We whose names are hereunder subscribed Housekeepers and neighbours, to the within petitioner do hereby respectively certify that the within statement is true, and we anxiously recommend him as an object of compassion and charity—

Thos. Armitstead Vicar of Mitton
Richd Hall Churchwarden
Thos. Rawcliffe Overseer
Revd. C. Wright of Stonyhurst College
James Wilkinson

[B]   In the Court House of the General quarter Sessions of the peace holden by adjournment at Preston in and for the County palatine of Lancaster the 29th day of April 1815—

John Emmott of Aighton Bailey and Chaigley in the parish of Mitton and County of Lancaster Cordwainer, Edmund Chippindale, Robert Martin [crossed out] and Peter Morris all of the same place Bobbin Turners and Chair Makers, John Kendrick of Aighton Bailey and Chaigley aforesaid Joiner, Robert Coulthurst of Dutton in the same County Carpenter and Millwright and Mark Chippindale of Aighton Bailey and Chaigley aforesaid bobbin turner and Chairmaker severally make oath and say — And first this Deponent John Emmot for himself saith that he has been for some years last past, and still is, a near neighbor to the said Mark Chippindale, and hath often been in the workshop lately used by him, and was well acquainted with the state and condition thereof. And that in the morning of Saturday the nineteenth day of September last past he this Deponent was alarmed by the breaking out of a sudden and terrible fire in the said workshop of the said Mark Chippindale, which entirely destroyed the same, and burnt and consumed the whole of the stock in Trade of him the said Mark Chippindale as a Bobbin Turner and Chair maker, and also all the Tools, Utensils and Machinery therein and though this Deponent with the said Mark Chippindale the rest of his family and divers other persons endeavoured as much in them lay to save and preserve the said stock Tools Utensils and Machinery from being burnt and destroyed by the said fire they were utterly unable to save any part thereof, except one large water wheel which was very much injured by the Fire, and its being hastily thrown down and removed — And these Deponents Edmund Chippindale Robert Martin [crossed out] and Peter Morris for themselves severally say that they were for several years before, and on, the said — nineteenth day of September last past, employed by the said Mark Chippindale in his said Business of a bobbin Turner and Chair maker and that from such employment they were perfectly acquainted with the said Shop, and knew the state and condition thereof and also the nature, description and quantity of the Stock in Trade, Timber, Machinery, Tools Utensils and Effects contained therein and that the Stock in Trade, Timber, Machinery, Tools, Utensils and Effects particularized in the Schedule of Inventory hereunto annexed were in the said shop when the said Fire happened, and were utterly consumed thereby and these Deponents further say that the utmost endeavours were used to save the said property from destruction, but that they were wholly ineffectual. And these Deponents John Kendrick and Robert Coulthurst for themselves say that they were acquainted with the said Workshop of the said Mark Chippindale so burnt and consumed as aforesaid and that they have since the same was so burnt and destroyed viewed the state thereof, and estimated the injury sustained thereby and that they verily believe that upon a reasonable and moderate computation it would cost the sum of Two hundred and thirteen pounds and two shillings at the least to erect and build a workshop of a description similar to that so burnt down and consumed as aforesaid And the Deponents further say that from the description given to them by the said other Deponents Edmund Chippindale, Robert Martin [*crossed out*] and Peter Morris of the Stock in Trade, Timber, Machinery, Tools, Utensils and Effects destroyed by the said Fire and from all other information gained by them, the Deponents, say verily that the same stock in Trade, Timber, Machinery, Tools, Utensils and Effects were really and truly worth the several sums of Money set opposite thereto in the Schedule or Inventory herein before referred to, at the least, and which amount altogether to the sum of three hundred and twenty nine pounds six shillings and sixpence. And this Deponent Mark Chippindale for himself saith that the Depositions of them the said John Emmott, Edmund Chippindale, Robert Martin [*crossed out*], Peter Morris, John Kendrick and Robert Coulthurst herein before contained are true to the full extent thereof — that he the Deponent is bound by lease to rebuild the said Workshop, and that over and beyond the loss which this Deponent has sustained in the manner herein before particularized, and which the Deponents believe to have been considerably underated, he the Deponent hath lost and been deprived of other Benefits and Advantages which he would have enjoyed if the said Workshop had not been burnt down and destroyed: And that unless he the Deponent be relieved by the aid and assistance of the charitable and humane he will be reduced from the state of a comfortable livelihood to poverty and want.

Sworn in open Court

Before [*illegible*]

{ John Emmott
Edmund Chippindale
Peter Morris
John Kendrick
Robert Coulthurst
The mark of Mark Chippindale

---

* The Mark Chippindale deposition was published previously by the author in an article entitled 'The North country chair making tradition: Design, Context, and the Mark Chippindale deposition' in the *Furniture History Society Journal*, Vol.XVII, 1981, pp.42-51. The Mark Chippindale deposition is reproduced by kind permission of the County Archivist of the Lancashire Record Office, Preston (Catalogue No.QSP 1813).

FOOTNOTES

Chapter 2
Thames Valley & The Chilterns

1. High Wycombe Parish Records.
2. Stowe Manuscript, 1798, British Museum.
3. Daniel Defoe, *Tour through the whole Island of Great Britain,* 1724-27.
4. *Universal Directory for Buckinghamshire,* 1790.
5. *Pigot's Directory, Buckinghamshire,* 1830.
6. Ibid.
7. Ivan Sparkes, *The English Country Chair,* Spur 1973.
8. Ibid.
9. L.J. Mayes, *The History of Chair making in High Wycombe,* RKP 1960.
10. *Autobiography of Benjamin North,* 1882.
11. L.J. Mayes, *The History of Chair making in High Wycombe,* RKP 1960.
12. Ibid.
13. Oral transcript, Mr & Mrs W. Stevens, Radnage, Bucks., 1983.
14. Census returns Stokenchurch, 1841 and 1851, Jonathan Poole (see List of Makers).
15. George Dean, letter dated 25.10.1955, Reading Museum of Rural Life.
16. Oral transcript, Mr & Mrs W. Stevens, Radnage, Bucks., 1983.
17. Ivan Sparkes, *The English Country Chair,* Spur 1973.
18. George Dean, letter dated 25.10.1955, Reading Museum of Rural Life.
19. Nancy Goyne Evans, 'English Windsor Furniture', *FHS Journal,* 1979.
20. Daniel Defoe, *Tour through the whole Island of Great Britain,* 1724-27.
21. Nancy Goyne Evans, 'English Windsor Furniture', *FHS Journal,* 1979.
22. Ambrose Heal, *London Furniture makers 1660-1840,* Batsford 1953.
23. Ibid.
24. J. Stabler, 'Two labelled Comb back Chairs', *Antique Collecting,* April 1977.
25. Ibid.
26. Nancy Goyne Evans, 'English Windsor Furniture', *FHS Journal* 1979.
27. R.W. Symonds, 'The Windsor Chair', *Apollo,* August 1935.
28. Ibid.
29. Ivan Sparkes, *The Windsor Chair,* Spur 1975.
30. George Bowes, London accounts 1733-34. Durham County Record Office, D/Strathmore/V 1390.
31. J. Stabler, 'A new look at the bow-back Windsor', *Connoisseur,* December 1974.
32. Ibid.
33. Pauline Agius, 'English Chair-makers listed in General and Trade Directories, 1790-1851', *FHS Journal* 1976.
34. L.J. Mayes, *The History of Chair making in High Wycombe,* RKP 1960.

35. K.R. Pearce, Prior family tree, Uxbridge Local History Society.
36. *Pigot's Directory,* Middlesex 1823.
37. K.R. Pearce, Prior family tree, Uxbridge Local History Society.
38. *Kelly's Trade Directory,* Middlesex 1845.
39. *Slater's Trade Directory,* Cricklewood 1851.
40. J. Fricker, 'Two Uxbridge Chairs', *Uxbridge Record,* no.38, 1982.
41. *Kelly's Trade Directory,* Middlesex 1842.
42. Ibid.
43. K.R. Pearce, Prior family tree, Uxbridge Local History Society.
44. *Kelly's Directory of Essex,* 1855-74.
45. Oral transcript, Philip Puddifer, 1983.
46. Census return High Wycombe 1841.
47. Census return High Wycombe 1861.
48. Census return Oxford 1841.
49. *Slater's Directory,* Oxfordshire, 1839.
50. Census return Oxford 1851.
51. John Badcock, *Origin, History and Description of Summertown,* 1832.
52. Census return Oxford 1851.
53. *Hunt & Co's Oxford Directory,* 1846.
54. *Shrimpton's Oxford Directory,* 1875.
55. Pauline Agius, *101 Chairs,* catalogue, Divinity School, Oxford, March 1968.
56. Oral transcript, Glenisters, High Wycombe, 1985.
57. Census return High Wycombe 1841.
58. *Kelly's Directory,* Oxford, 1899.
59. Census return Stokenchurch 1881.
60. Census return High Wycombe 1851.
61. Census return High Wycombe 1861.
62. Glenister & Gibbons, Price List, catalogue no.6, c.1865-79.
63. Ivan Sparkes, *The Windsor Chair,* Spur 1975.
64. Glenister & Gibbons, catalogue no.6, c.1865-79. High Wycombe Chair Museum.
65. Ibid.
66. Ibid.
67. Ibid.
68. *Kelly's Trade Directory,* Buckinghamshire, 1899.

Chapter 3
North East Region
Lincolnshire

1. See Index of Chair makers, Northamptonshire: March, John and Williams, R., John March, of Geddington. *F.H.S. Journal,* Vol.XII, 1976.
2. See Index of Chair makers, Lincolnshire, for trade directory source detail.
3. Mitchell 1801; Pigot 1828; Ward 1850; Whellan 1856; Kelly 1858 and 1894.

4. Census Report 1921, H.M.S.O.
5. T. Crispin, 'English Windsor Chairs', *F.H.S. Journal,* Vol.XIV, 1978.
6. B.D. Cotton, 'Regional influences among Windsor chairs', *Antique Dealer and Collectors' Guide,* February 1984.
7. See Index of Chair makers, Lincolnshire, for trade directory source detail.
8. Ordnance Survey map of Grantham 1866, Grantham Public Library.
9. *British Universal Directory,* Lincolnshire, 1790.
10. *White's Directory,* Lincolnshire, 1826.
11. Ibid.
12. Ibid.
13. *Pigot's Directory,* Lincolnshire, 1841.
14. *White's Directory,* Lincolnshire, 1842.
15. Census return Sleaford, 1861.
16. *Sleaford Gazette,* September 1865, quoted in *Mid-Victorian Sleaford,* ed. C. Ellis, Lincolnshire Library Service, 1981.
17. See Index of Chair makers, Lincolnshire.
18. Ibid.
19. White 1851; P.O. 1855; Kelly 1861; White 1872; Kelly 1885 and 1892.
20. Boston and Alford baptismal records. Census return Boston 1851.
21. Boston and Alford baptismal records. Census return Boston, 1851.
22. See Index of Chair makers, Lincolnshire, for details.
23. Census return Grantham 1841.
24. See Index of Chair makers, Lincolnshire, for details.
25. Census return Grantham, 1851.
26. Census return Grantham, 1841.
27. J.W. Shadford's workshop notebook, Lincoln Archives Office.
28. Ibid.
29. Census return Grantham, 1841.
30. Census return Caistor, 1861.
31. Ibid.
32. J.W. Shadford's workshop notebook, Lincoln Archives Office.
33. See Index of Chair makers, Lincolnshire, for biographical details of Ashtons.
34. Boston Marriage Register 1820.

Nottinghamshire

35. Wills of William Baker, 1753, and Thomas Hodson, 1759, of East Retford, Nottingham Record Office.
36. *Holden's Directory,* 1805.
37. *White's Directory,* 1932.
38. *Pigot's Directory,* Nottinghamshire 1822.
39. *Worksop Guardian,* 9.10.1936.
40. *Worksop Guardian,* 19.4.1929.

Nottinghamshire continued

41. Census returns Wellow and Ollerton 1841, 1851 and 1861.
42. *Worksop Guardian,* 5.8.1955.
43. Oral transcript, D.H. Godley, 1984, of Godley and Golding, Kilton Sawmills, Worksop.
44. M.J. Jackson, *Worksop of Yesterday,* Worksop Archaeological and Local History Society.
45. *Universal Directory,* Nottinghamshire.
46. *Worksop Guardian,* 9.10.1936.
47. Allsop v. Allsop, 1875. Public Record Office, Kew.
48. Census return Worksop, 1871.
49. Ibid., 1881.
50. Allsop v. Allsop, 1875. Public Record Office, Kew.
51. Ibid.
52. I. Allsop & Son's trade card, Worksop Library.
53. *Worksop Guardian,* 19.4.1929.
54. Ibid.
55. Oral transcript, D.H. Godley, 1984, of Godley and Golding, Kilton Sawmills, Worksop.
56. Ibid.
57. Census return Worksop, 1881.
58. M.J. Jackson, *Worksop of Yesterday,* Worksop Archaeological and Local History Society.
59. Allsop v. Allsop, 1875. Public Record Office, Kew.
60. Apprenticeship indenture from Wellow, Notts., 1830. Private Collection.
61. Allsop v. Allsop, 1875. Public Record Office, Kew.
62. Ibid.
63. *Retford and Gainsborough Times,* 18.3.1887.
64. Michael Jackson. *Worksop of Yesterday.* Worksop Archaeological and Local History Society.
65. *Pigot's Directory,* Nottinghamshire 1822.
66. Unrecorded after 1844.
67. Census return Worksop, 1851.
68. Ibid., 1881.
69. Census return Worksop, 1851.
70. Census return Worksop, 1881.
71. Will of John Gabbitass, Nottingham Record Office.
72. Census return Worksop, 1841.
73. Ibid., 1851.
74. Census return Worksop, 1841.
75. *Retford and Gainsborough Times,* 1898.
76. Census return Worksop, 1861.
77. Census return Worksop, 1881.
78. Ibid., 1851.
79. Ibid., 1881.
80. *Retford and Gainsborough Times,* 1898.
81. Census return Worksop, 1841.
82. Retford West Circuit Membership Book, 1803-1835.
83. B.J. Biggs, 'Chair-makers in Rockley', doctoral thesis research, May 1972.
84. *Pigot's Directory,* Nottinghamshire 1822.
85. Census return Gamston, 1861.
86. Census return Worksop, 1841.
87. *Pigot's Directory,* Nottinghamshire 1822.
88. Census return Worksop, 1841.
89. Ibid., 1851.
90. Ibid.
91. Ibid., 1861.
92. Ibid., 1881.
93. Ibid., 1861.
94. Ibid.
95. *Worksop Guardian,* 13.2.1948.
96. Ibid, 9.10.1936.

97. Census return Worksop, 1871.
98. *Kelly's Directory,* Brighouse, Yorks., 1881.
99. *Worksop Guardian,* 9.10.1936.
100. Voluntary examination of Robert Allsop of Worksop, 18.5.1842. Nottingham Record Office.
101. Ibid.
102. Census return Worksop, 1841.
103. *White's Directory,* Nottinghamshire 1832.
104. Allsop v. Allsop, 1875. Public Record Office, Kew.
105. Census return Worksop, 1841.
106. Ibid., 1851.
107. *Worksop Guardian,* 9.10.1936.
108. Allsop v. Allsop, 1875. Public Record Office, Kew.
109. Census return Worksop, 1861.
110. Census return Worksop, 1871.
111. Ibid.
112. Allsop v. Allsop, 1875. Public Record Office, Kew.
113. Ibid.
114. Census return Worksop, 1871.
115. Allsop v. Allsop, 1875. Public Record Office. Kew.
116. Ibid.
117. Ibid.
118. Ibid.
119. Ibid.
120. Ibid.
121. Ibid.
122. *Retford and Gainsborough Times,* 18.3.1887.
123. Ibid.
124. Ibid.
125. Ibid.
126. Ibid.
127. Wills of William Baker, 1753, and Thomas Hodson, 1759, of East Retford, Nottingham Record Office.
128. Census return Retford, 1851.
129. Ibid., 1861.
130. *Pigot's Directory,* Nottinghamshire 1822.
131. *Kelly's Directory,* Nottinghamshire 1891.
132. Census return Wellow, 1841.
133. *White's Directory,* Nottinghamshire 1853.
134. B.J. Biggs, 'Chair-makers in Rockley', doctoral thesis research, May 1972.
135. *Pigot's Directory,* Nottinghamshire 1822.
136. B.J. Biggs, 'Chair-makers in Rockley', doctoral thesis research, May 1972.
137. B.J. Biggs, *Rockley Methodist Chapel 1875-1975.* Centenary Souvenir, 1975.
138. Ibid.
139. B.J. Biggs., *Rockley Methodist Chapel 1875-1975,* Centenary Souvenir, 1975.
140. Retford West Circuit Membership Book, 1803-1835.
141. B.J. Biggs, *Rockley Methodist Chapel 1875-1975,* Centenary Souvenir, 1975.
142. Askham Parish baptismal register.
143. Census return Gamston, 1841.
144. B.J. Biggs., *Rockley Methodist Chapel 1875-1975,* Centenary Souvenir, 1975.
145. B.J. Biggs, 'Methodism in a Rural Society; North Nottinghamshire, 1740-1851', doctoral thesis University of Nottingham. May 1975.
146. B.J. Biggs, *Rockley Methodist Chapel 1875-1975,* Centenary Souvenir, 1975.
147. Census return Rockley, 1841.
148. Census return Worksop, 1851.
149. Ibid.
150. *White's Directory,* Nottinghamshire 1848.
151. *Kelly's Directory,* Nottinghamshire 1891.
152. Census return Rockley, 1851.
153. *White's Directory,* Nottinghamshire 1853.
154. Census return Worksop, 1871.
155. Census return Rockley, 1871.

Yorkshire

156. *Kelly's Directory,* Yorkshire 1881.
157. *Pigot's Directory,* Yorkshire 1816.
158. I. Allsop & Son's trade card, fl.1871-1887. Worksop Library.
159. Catalogue of William Brear & Sons, Addingham, via Leeds, c.1920.
160. I. Allsop & Son's trade card, fl.1871-1887. Worksop Library.
161. Catalogue of William Brear & Sons, Addingham, via Leeds, c.1920.
162. Ibid.
163. *Mitchell's Directory,* town and county of Newcastle, 1801.
164. *Directory of Newcastle,* 1824.
165. *Pigot's Directory,* Northumberland and Durham, 1834.
166. *Kelly's Directory,* Northumberland and Durham, 1873.
167. Ibid., 1858 and 1879.

Chapter 4
East Anglia

1. *Pigot's Directory,* Suffolk 1822/3 and Cambridge 1839.
   Robson's Directory, Suffolk 1839.
   Kelly's Directory, Cambridge 1847.
2. *Pigot's Directory,* Suffolk 1822/3.
   Robson's Directory, Suffolk 1839.
3. *Pigot's Directory,* Cambridge 1839.
   Kelly's Directory, Cambridge 1847.
4. *Pigot's Directory,* Essex 1822/3 and 1832.
5. Ibid., 1839.
6. Census return Colchester, 1841.
7. *Norwich Chair-makers' Book of Prices,* 1801. Central Library, Norwich (Norfolk Library Service).
8. Thomas Sheraton, *Cabinet Maker and Upholsterer's Drawing Books,* 1791-1802.
9. *Norwich Chair-makers' Book of Prices,* 1801, pp.2-3.
10. Ibid., p.2.
11. Collection of the Norfolk Rural Life Museum, Beech House, Gressenhall. Inventory no. N.C.M. 587.974.5.
12. *Norwich Chair-makers' Book of Prices,* 1801, p.3.
13. Ibid.
14. Ibid.
15. Ibid., pp.2-3.
16. George Edwards, *From Crow-scaring to Westminster.* Labour Publishing Co., 1922, reprinted National Union of Agricultural Workers, 1957, p.16.
17. *Norwich Chair-makers' Book of Prices,* 1801, p.2.
18. Ibid., pp.4-5.
19. Ibid., p.7.
20. George Hepplewhite, *Cabinet Maker and Upholsterer's Guide,* 1788.
21. Thomas Chippendale, *Gentleman and Cabinet-Maker's Director,* 1754.
22. Rose Tenent, *Essex Countryside,* Vol. 30, June 1982, pp.54-55.
23. *Norwich Chair-makers' Book of Prices,* 1801, p.v.
24. Ibid.
25. *Kelly's Directory,* Norfolk 1883-1904.
26. Census return North Walsham, 1861.
27. *Kelly's Directory,* Norfolk 1883-1904.
28. *Norwich Chair-makers' Book of Prices,* 1801.
29. Ibid., p.60.
30. Ibid.
31. Ibid., p.57.
32. Ibid. p.54.

FOOTNOTES

East Anglia continued

33. J.E.G. Mosby and P.E. Agar, *Wymondham Old and New,* Wymondham, 1949, pp.6-7.
34. Thomas Crispin, '10th December 1838', *Antique Collecting,* November 1980.
35. Marriage register, Mendlesham, 1756.
36. Burial register, Mendlesham, 1838.
37. *White's Directory,* Suffolk 1844 and 1855.
38. Marriage register, Mendlesham, 1756.
39. Baptismal register, Mendlesham, 1791.
40. Death certificate for Richard Day, 10-12-1838, aged 55.
41. *Pigot's Directory,* Suffolk 1830.
42. Burial register, Mendlesham, 1838.
43. Baptismal register, Earl Soham, 1818.
44. Burial register, Mendlesham, 1820.
45. Thomas Sheraton, *Cabinet Maker and Upholsterer's Drawing Book,* 1791-94.
46. Thomas Crispin, '10th December 1938', *Antique Collecting,* November 1980.
47. *Pigot's Directory,* Suffolk 1830.
48. Census return Rickinghall Superior, 1841.
49. *Kelly's Directory,* Suffolk 1847.
50. Census return Stonham Aspal, 1851.
51. Ibid, 1861.
52. Burial register, Stonham Aspal.
53. *White's Directory,* Suffolk 1844.
54. Census return Old Newton, 1851.
55. B. Everitt, *Cluster Analysis,* Heineman 1974.
56. Ibid.

Chapter 5
South West Region

1. Brown, R.D., 'Devonians and New England Settlement before 1650', *Transactions of the Devonshire Association,* Vol.95, 1953.
2. *Kelly's Directory* of Cornwall, 1856.
3. *Pigot's Directory* of Devonshire, 1844.
4. Santore, Charles, *The Windsor Style in America, 1730-1830,* Running Press, Philadelphia, 1981 (ISBN 0 89471 136 9).
5. Baptismal records for Yealmpton, 1795-1812.
6. Holloway, Peter, *Yealmpton Yesterday,* Private Publication, May 1981.
7. Banns of marriage, Yealmpton, 1754-1812.
8. Ibid.
9. Baptismal records, Yealmpton, 1813-1852.
10. Census for Yealmpton, 1841.
11. Census for Holberton, 1841.
12. Census for Newton Ferrers, 1841.
13. *Plymouth, Eyre,* and *Kelly's Directories.*
14. *Tryhall, Kelly, Eyre, Plymouth,* and *White's Directories.*
15. *Exeter Pocket Journal,* and *Pigot's Directories.*
16. Santore, Charles, *The Windsor Style in America, 1730-1830,* Running Press, Philadelphia, 1981.
17. Ibid.
18. Brown, R.D., 'Devonians and New England Settlement before 1650', *Transactions of the Devonshire Association,* Vol.95, 1963.
19. Kirk, J.T., *American furniture and the British tradition to 1830,* Alfred A. Knopf, New York, 1982 (ISBN 0 394 40038 0).
20. Santore, Charles, *The Windsor Style in America, 1730-1830,* Running Press, Philadelphia, 1981.

21. Baptismal records for Yealmpton, 1754-1852.
22. Brown, R.D., 'Devonians and New England Settlement before 1650', *Transactions of the Devonshire Association,* Vol.95, 1963.
23. Pain, Howard, *The heritage of Upper Canadian Furniture,* Van Nostrand Reinhold Ltd., 1978, p.112 (ISBN 0 442 29829 3).
24. Census for Yealmpton, 1851.
25. *Kelly's Directory,* 1882.
26. *Eyre's Directory* of Plymouth, 1882.
27. *Oral Tradition,* Mr. Francis Snawdon, 1983.
28. Census for Yealmpton, 1881.
29. *Oral Tradition,* Mr. Francis Snawdon, 1983.
30. Census for Holcombe Rogus, Burlescombe and Uffculme, 1841.
31. Dedamess, Eve, 'The Holcombe Rogus Craftsmen', unpublished essay.
32. Census for Holcombe Rogus, Burlescombe and Uffculme for 1871.
33. *Devon and Somerset News,* 8.4.1964.
34. Ibid.
35. *Western Enterprise,* 1908.
36. *Oral Tradition,* Mr. Jack Drake, Holcombe Rogus, 1983.
37. *Western Enterprise,* 1908.
38. Ibid.
39. *Devon and Somerset News,* 8.4.1964.
40. *Kelly's Directory* for Devonshire, 1887.
41. *Kelly's Directory* for Devonshire, 1919.

Chapter 6
West Midlands

1. F.C. Morgan, 'Philip Clisset, A Bosbury chair maker', *Fownehope Society Journal,* 1946.
2. *Lewis's Directory* of Worcestershire, 1820.
3. *Pigots Directory* of Worcestershire, 1829.
4. Offenham Parish Register of Baptisms, 1751.
5. Census for Evesham, 1841.
6. Ibid.
7. *Kelly's Post Office Directory,* Worcestershire, 1854.
8. Census for Evesham, 1861.
9. Census for Evesham, 1851.
10. Census for Birtsmorton, 1841.
11. Census for Castlemorton, 1851.
12. Birtsmorton Parish Register of Baptisms, 1817.
13. Census for Castlemorton, 1851.
14. Census for Eastnor, 1851.
15. Census for Bosbury, 1851.
16. F.C. Morgan, 'Philip Clissett, A Bosbury Chairmaker', *Fownehope Society Journal,* 1946.
17. Ibid.
18. 1921 Census Report, H.M.S.O.
19. Ledbury circuit Wesleyan Records.
20. Bosbury Parish Register of Baptisms, 1825.
21. Census for Bosbury, 1871.
22. Census for Bosbury, 1881.
23. F.C. Morgan, 'Philip Clissett, a Bosbury Chair maker', *Fownehope Society Journal,* 1946.
24. Census for Bosbury, 1851.
25. Census for Bosbury, 1861.
26. F.C. Morgan, 'Philip Clissett, A Bosbury Chair maker', *Fownehope Society Journal,* 1946.
27. Ibid.

28. *Architectural Review,* vol.13, 1903.
29. Exhibition Catalogue, Ernest Gimson, Leicester Museum, 1969.
30. F.C. Morgan, 'Philip Clissett, A Bosbury Chair maker', *Fownehope Society Journal,* 1946.
31. Ibid.
32. Census for Bransford, 1841.
33. Barrie Trinder and Jeff Cox, *Yeoman and Colliers in Telford,* Phillimore, 1980.
34. Ibid, p.339.
35. Census for Wellington, 1841.
36. Census for Wellington, 1861.
37. Photograph by Edwin Smith, by kind permission of Olive Cook (Mrs. Olive Smith).
38. By kind permission of Phillips, London.
39. Census for Clun, 1841.
40. Tom Beardsley, Clun Town Trust.
41. Ibid.
42. *Slaters Directory,* 1840.

Chapter 7
North West Region

1. H.M.S.O., Census Report, 1921.
2. Children's Employment Commission, H.M.S.O., 1865.
3. Reid, Richard, *Shell Book of Cottages,* Michael Joseph, 1977.
4. Kirk, John T., *American Furniture and the British Tradition to 1830,* Knopf, New York, 1982.
5. *Universal Directory,* 1790.
6. Petition of Mark Chippindale to the Preston Quarter Sessions, April 1813. Lancashire Records Office, Preston, Lancs.
7. Will of James Thomas Tomlinson of Lancaster, April 1848. Lancashire Records Office, Preston, Lancs.
8. Petition of Mark Chippindale to the Preston Quarter Sessions, April 1813. Lancashire Records Office, Preston, Lancs.
9. Ibid.
10. Ibid.
11. Ibid.
12. Hammond, J.L. and B., *The Skilled Labourer,* Longman, 1919.
13. Invoice from Ducket and Westhead, 1857. See Figure NW67.
14. Petition of Mark Chippindale to the Preston Quarter Sessions, April 1813. Lancashire Records Office, Preston, Lancs.
15. Ibid.
16. Ibid.
17. Will of James Thomas Tomlinson of Lancaster. April 1848. Lancashire Records Office, Preston, Lancs.
18. Holt, John, *General View of the County of Lancaster.* 1795. Reprinted David & Charles, 1969.
19. Ibid.
20. Ibid.
21. Edlin, H.L., *Woodland Crafts in Britain,* Batsford, 1949.
22. Ibid.
23. Petition of Mark Chippindale to the Preston Quarter Sessions, April 1813. Lancashire Records Office, Preston, Lancs.
24. Ibid.
25. Dickinson, Joseph, *Flora of Liverpool,* Liverpool University, 1850.
26. *Mannex Directory,* Preston, 1854, p.102.
27. *Gore's Directory of Liverpool,* 1813, Appendix.

North West Region continued

28. Wilmslow Churchwardens' Accounts, 1625.
29. Congleton Town Accounts, 1607.
30. Burton, Alfred, *Rush Bearing*, Brook & Chrystal, Manchester, 1891.
31. Ibid.
32. Ibid.
33. Ibid.
34. Hartly, M., & Ingleby, J., *Old Hand-Knitters of the Dales*, Dalesman Publishing Co., 1951.
35. See Index of Chair makers and Turners, Lancashire/Cheshire.
36. Ibid.
37. Baptismal Register, Mobberley, Cheshire, 1850, 1858.
38. Census return, 1851, Mobberley, Cheshire.
39. Baptismal Register, Mobberley, Cheshire, 1872.
40. Census return 1851, Sandbach. *Kelly's Cheshire Directory*, 1857. *White's Cheshire Directory*, 1860.
41. *White's Cheshire Directory*, 1860.
42. Census return 1851, Rochdale; *Slater's Lancashire Directory*, 1864.
43. *Raffald's Manchester Directory*, 1772.
44. *Universal Directory for Cheshire*, 1790.
45. *Pigot's Cheshire Directory*, 1834, and Census return, Altrincham, 1841.
46. *Pigot's Directory for Manchester*, 1804.
47. *White's Cheshire Directory*, 1860.
48. *Bagshaw's Cheshire Directory*, 1850.
49. *Slater's Yorkshire Directory*, 1861.
50. *Raffald's Manchester Directory*, 1772.
51. Census return, 1841, Sandbach.
52. *Pigot's Cheshire Directory*, 1824.
53. *Dean's Manchester Directory*, 1808.
54. *Pigot's Manchester Directory*, 1813.
55. *Pigot's Cheshire Directory*, 1824.
56. Census return, 1841. Sandbach.
57. *Dean's Manchester Directory*, 1808, and *Pigot's Manchester Directory*, 1813.
58. Will, Cheshire Record Office.
59. Baptismal Register, Manchester Cathedral, 1774, and *Pigot's Manchester Directory*, 1825.
60. *Pigot's Cheshire Directory*, 1834.
61. *Slater's Cheshire Directory*, 1850, and Census return, 1851, Middlewich, Cheshire.
62. Census return, 1851, Sandbach.
63. *Pigot's Cheshire Directory*, 1822.
64. *Pigot's Cheshire Directory*, 1828, 1834.
65. *History and Directory of Macclesfield*, 1825.
66. Census return, 1841, Sandbach.
67. Ibid.
68. *Pigot's Cheshire Directory*, 1824.
69. *Dean's Manchester Directory*, 1808.
70. *Pigot's Manchester Directory*, 1813.
71. Gillows of Lancaster. Estimate Sketch-book, 344/98 P1620. Westminster City Library.
72. Ibid.
73. *Dean's Manchester Directory*, 1808, and *Pigot's Directory*, 1813.
74. Cheshire Quaker Records, 1691.
75. *Universal Directory*, 1790, and Baptismal and Marriage Registers, Hardshaw East Quaker Meeting House, Manchester.
76. Prestbury Parish Registers.
77. Hardshaw East Quaker Records.
78. Will of John Bancroft, 1824. Lancashire Records Office, Preston, Lancs. Proved 1833.
79. See Leicester entries in Index of Chair makers and Turners, Lancashire/Cheshire.
80. Cheshire Quaker Records.
81. Hardshaw West Quaker Burial Records, Manchester.
82. Hardshaw East Quaker Records, Manchester.
83. Will of John Bancroft, 1824. Lancashire Records Office, Preston, Lancs. Proved 1833.
84. Hardshaw East Quaker Meeting House Records.
85. Ibid.
86. Will of John Bancroft, 1824. Lancashire Records Office, Preston, Lancs. Proved 1833.
87. *Pigot's Manchester Directory*, 1804.
88. *Dean's Manchester Directory*, 1808.
89. Hardshaw East Quaker Records.
90. *Pigot's Cheshire Directory*, 1819.
91. Will of John Bancroft, 1824. Lancashire Records Office, Preston, Lancs. Proved 1833.
92. Quaker Records, Prestbury, Cheshire.
93. *Kelly's Cheshire Directory*, 1858.
94. See Index of Chair makers and Turners from Lancashire/Cheshire.
95. Boram, J., *The Leicesters of Macclesfield*, Cheshire History, Spring 1984.
96. See Index of Chair makers and Turners, Lancashire/Cheshire.
97. *Pigot's Cheshire Directory*, 1838, and *Slater's Cheshire Directory*, 1887.
98. Census returns, 1841 and 1851, Macclesfield.
99. Census return, 1851, Macclesfield.
100. See Index of Chair makers and Turners, Lancashire/Cheshire.
101. Baptismal Register, Lower Peover, Great Budworth, 1844.
102. Ibid and Census return, 1841, Hyde.
103. Census return, 1861, Plumley; and *Morris' Cheshire Directory*, 1874.
104. See Index of Chair makers and Turners, Lancashire/Cheshire.
105. Register of Marriages, Billinge Parish.
106. Census return, 1861, Billinge.
107. Census returns, 1871 and 1881, Lamberhead Green and Pemberton.
108. See Index of Chair makers and Turners, Lancashire/Cheshire.
109. Register of Marriages, Billinge.
110. Ibid.
111. Census return, 1841, Billinge.
112. Ibid.
113. Census return, 1851, Billinge.
114. Ibid.
115. Ibid.
116. *Gore's Liverpool Directory*, 1810.
117. Census return, 1851, Billinge.
118. Ibid.
119. *Worrall's Lancashire Directory*, 1869.
120. Census return, 1871, Lamberhead Green.
121. See Index of Chair makers and Turners, Lancashire/Cheshire.
122. Census return, 1861, Billinge.
123. Ibid.
124. Parish Register, Billinge.
125. Marriage Register, Billinge.
126. *Pigot's Lancashire Directory*, 1816.
127. Will, 1837. Lancashire Records Office, Preston, Lancs.
128. Census return, 1841, Wigan.
129. Census return, 1861, Billinge.
130. Guest, R., *A Compendious History of the Cotton Manufacture*, 1823.
131. Sheraton, T., *Cabinet-makers' and Upholsterers' Drawing Books*, 1791-1794.
132. Oral transcript, 1985. Colin Stock, Rainford.
133. *Slater's Lancashire Directory*, 1887.
134. Ibid.
135. See Index of Chair makers and Turners, Lancashire/Cheshire.
136. Ibid.
137. Hartly, M., and Ingleby, J., *The Old Hand-Knitters of the Dales*, Dalesman Publishing Co., 1951.
138. *Gore's Liverpool Directory*, 1851, and *Slater's Manchester Directory*, 1887.
139. Brear, William, of Addingham, nr. Leeds. Catalogue, c.1920.
140. See Index of Chair makers and Turners, Lancashire/Cheshire.
141. See Index of Chair makers and Turners, Lancashire/Cheshire.
142. Ibid.
143. *Kelly's Lancashire Directories*, 1858 and 1873.
144. *Preston Directory*, 1877.
145. See Index of Chair makers and Turners, Lancashire/Cheshire.
146. Ibid.
147. Ibid.
148. Ibid.
149. Gilbert, C., *Common Furniture*, Temple Newsam, Leeds, 1982.

INDEX:
Regional Chair Makers and Turners 1700~1900

The index of chair makers, turners, and others engaged in the chair making trade was compiled from regional trade directories, census returns and other specialised forms of documentation, including military rolls, parish baptismal, marriage and burial records, wills, probate inventories, and some eighteenth and early nineteenth century references were taken from the *Dictionary of Furniture Makers, 1660-1840* (Furniture History Society).

Not all areas of England had established chair making traditions, since some major centres, such as High Wycombe in Buckinghamshire, were so prolific, that they reduced the development of traditions in the surrounding areas. For this reason, there are some counties for which the Index shows few or no recorded makers. However, further research may yet reveal traditions from these or other already identified areas, and in these terms, the Index is intended as a starting point for research, rather than a final statement.

The Index has a number of potential research uses beyond that of providing information about a maker's identification marks found on chairs. Other uses include providing demographic data about which makers were working where, and when. This information can provide a starting point for research which seeks to study local traditions which are as yet undiscovered. The record of makers' flourishing periods also indicates the rise and decline in regional chair making traditions, and through this, a method of attributing the manufacturing dates of chairs is provided.

LIST OF ABBREVIATIONS

B.	*Bagshaw's Directory*	Cassey.	*Cassey's Directory*
Bailey.	*Bailey's Directory*	Cent. Lib.	Central Library
Baines.	*Baines Directory*	Chase.	*Chase's Directory*
Barfoot & Wilkes	*Barfoot & Wilkes Directory*	Ch. D.	*Chester Directory*
Bar.	*Barrett's Directory*	Chesh. Dir.	*Cheshire Directory*
Barnes.	*Barnes Directory*	Ch. M.	chair maker
Billings.	*Billings Directory*	Ch. Man.	chair manufacturer
Blackwell.	*Blackwell's Sheffield Directory*	Cooks.	*Cook's Directory*
Boyles.	*Boyles Directory of Newcastle*	C.R.O.	Chester Record Office
Bragg.	*William Bragg's Directory*		
Br. Dr.	*British Directory*		
Broster.	*Broster's Chester Directory*	D.	*Dean's Directory*
Brown.	*Brown's Commercial Directory*	Dearden.	*Dearden's Directory*
Brownell.	*Brownell's Directory*	Derby Tr. Dir.	*Derby Trade Directory*
Bulmer.	*Bulmer's Directory*	Dir.	Directory
		Dir. Linc.	*Directory of Lincoln*
c.	Census	Drake.	*Drake's Directory*
CAB.	cabinetmaker	Dutton Allen.	*Dutton Allen's Directory*

E.P.J.	*Exeter Pocket Journal*
Eyre.	*Eyre's Directory of Plymouth*
F.H.S.	Furniture History Society (*Dictionary of English Furniture Makers 1660-1840*)
G.	*Glover's Directory*
Gl.	glazier
Gore.	*Gore's Directory of Liverpool*
Grundy.	*Grundy's Directory*
Hanley.	*Hanley's Newcastle and Potteries Directory*
Harrods.	*Harrods Directory*
Hillingdon Lib.	Hillingdon Library
Hist. Gaz.	*History, Gazetteer & Directory of Oxfordshire*
Holden.	*Holden's Directory*
Hunt.	*Hunt's Directory*
Hunt & Parsons.	*Hunt & Parsons Directory*
Ihler.	*Ihler's Directory of Newcastle & Gateshead.*
Ipswich Journal.	*Ipswich Journal*
J.	joiner
J.M.B.	J.M. Boram. Private researches.
J.O.J.	*Jackson's Oxford Journal*
Jones.	*Jones's Directory of the Potteries*
J.W.S. Diary.	John William Shadford's Diary, Caistor.
K.	*Kelly's Directory*
L.	*Lewis's Directory*
L. & H.	*Lascelles & Hagar's Directory*
Lanc. R.O.	Lancaster Record Office
Lancs. G.D.	*Lancashire General Directory* (Rogerson)
Lascelles.	*Lascelles Directory*
Leic. Dir.	*Directory of Leicestershire*
Leics. R.O.	Leicestershire Record Office
Lincoln Poll Book.	*Lincoln Poll Book*
Lincs. Dir.	*Directory of Lincoln*
Littlebury.	*Littlebury's Directory*
L.R. & S. Mercury.	*Lincoln, Rutland & Stamford Mercury*
L.R.O.	Lincoln Record Office
M.	*Morris's Directory*
Mackenzie.	*Mackenzie & Dent's Directory*
Man.	*Mannex Directory*
Man. Tr. Dir.	*Manchester Trade Directory*
Marshall.	*Marshall's Directory*
Mathieson.	*Mathieson's Directory*
Melville.	*Melville's Directory*
Meth. Records.	Methodist Records
Mitchell.	*Mitchell's Directory*
Mussan & Craven.	*Mussan & Craven's Directory*
Newland.	*Newland's Directory*
N.R.O.	Norwich Record Office

Ora.	*Orange Directory of Nottingham*
P.	*Pigot's Directory*
Parry.	*Parry's Chester Directory*
Pa. & Wh.	*Parson & White's Directory*
Parson.	*Parson & Bradshaw's Directory*
Pearce.	*Pearce's Directory*
Peck.	*Peck's Directory of Birmingham*
Ph. & Gd.	*Phillipson & Golder's Directory of Chester*
Pl.	plumber
Ply. Dir.	*Thorne's Plymouth Directory*
Poll.	*Poll Book* (local)
Posse Com.	*Posse Commission*
P.R.	Parish Register
Preston R.O.	Preston Record Office
P.R.O.	Public Record Office
R.	*Rogerson's Directory*
Raffalds.	*Raffald's Directory of Manchester*
Red. Bk.	*Red Book*, Grantham
Ret. & Gains.	*Retford and Gainsborough Times*
R.O.	Record Office
Robson.	*Robson's Directory*
S.	*Slater's Directory*
S. & W.	*Slater & White's Directory*
Scholes.	*Scholes Directory of Manchester & Salford*
Sleaford Gaz.	*Sleaford Gazette*
Slde. & Roeb.	*Slade & Roebuck's Directory*
Sl. H.P.O.	*Slade & Hagar's Directory*
Spalding Gent. Soc.	Spalding Gentlemen's Society
Stratford.	*Stratford's Directory of Worcester*
Sutton.	*Sutton's Directory*
T.	turner
Tr. Dir.	*Trade Directory*
Tryhall.	*Tryhall's Directory of Plymouth*
Underhill.	*Underhill's Directory*
Univ.	*Universal Directory*
W.	*White's Directory*
Wa. & Pr.	*Wardle & Pratt's Directory*
Walker.	*Walker's Directory*
Ward.	*Ward's Directory of Northumberland*
Wardle & Bentham.	*Wardle & Bentham's Directory*
Webster.	*Webster's Directory*
Wells & Manton.	*Wells & Manton's Directory*
West.	*West's Birmingham Directory*
Wh.	*Whellan's Directory*
Wheeler & Day.	*Wheeler & Day's Directory*
Whittle.	*Whittle's Directory of Preston*
Williams.	*Williams Directory of York* *Williams Commercial Directory of Cornwall*
Wksop. Gar.	*Worksop Guardian*
Wor.	*Worrall's Directory*
Wr.	*Wright's Directory*
Wrightson.	*Wrightson's Directory of Birmingham*
W.T.	wood turner

INDEX

Thames Valley continued

BROWN, Richard   T.
1868 Cassey 2 Gt. Knollys St., Reading
BROWN, Richard   Ch.M.
1824-31 P.R. 4 daughters baptised
1838 P.R. Son baptised
BROWN, William   Ch.M.
1851 Slater. Wing
1887 K. Lacel Green, Tring
1895 K. Lacel Green, Tring
BRUTON, James   Ch.M.
1851 Slater Amersham
BRYANT, James   Ch.M.
1851 C. Hammesley La., High Wycombe
(age 16)
BRYANT, William   Ch.M.
1841 C. Bird-in-Hand, West Wycombe
(age 25)
1851 C. Bird-in-Hand, West Wycombe
(age 35)
BRYANT & FRYER   Ch.Man.
1895 K. St. Mary's St., Wycombe
1899 K. St. Mary's St., Wycombe
BRYANT (Briant), John   Ch.M.
1841 C. Lanes Row, High Wycombe
(age 27)
1851 C. High Wycombe (age 37)
1861 C. High Wycombe (age 46)
1877 K. Hughenden Rd., High Wycombe
(& Co.)
1891 K. Hughenden Rd., High Wycombe
BRYANT, William   Ch.M.
1841 C. West Wycombe (age 25)
BUCK, Francis   Ch.M.
1861 C. High Wycombe (age 39)
BUCKINGHAM CHAIR CO.   Ch.M.
1877 K. St. Peters St., Gt. Marlow
1883 K. St. Peters St., Gt. Marlow
1887 K. St. Peters St., Gt. Marlow
1891 K. St. Peters St., Gt. Marlow
1895 K. St. Peters St., Gt. Marlow
1899 K. St. Peters St., Gt. Marlow
BUCKINGHAM, Michael   Ch.M.
1798 Posse Com., High Wycombe
BUDELL, Joseph   Ch.M.
1851 C. Hammersley La., High
Wycombe (age 34)
BUDD, Joseph   Ch.M.
1841 C. Newland, High Wycombe
(age 22)
BULLER, John   Ch.M.
1841 C. Downley, High Wycombe
(age 20)
BULLER, William   Ch.M.
1841 C. Downley, High Wycombe
(age 50)
BULLER, William   Ch.M.
1841 C. Downley, High Wycombe
(age 15)
BULLOCK, Ebenezer   Ch.M.
1841 C. Hamersley La., High Wycombe
(age 45)
BULLOCK, John   Ch.M.
1778-79 F.H.S. Turnham Green
BUNCE, Henry   Ch.M.
1861 C. High Wycombe (age 17)
BUNKER, Daniel   T.
1830 P. High St., Chesham
1863 Dutton Allen, Chesham
BUNKER, Ezra   T.
1868 Cassey Iffley Rd., Oxford
BURGESS, Robert   Ch.M.
1825 F.H.S. Stokenchurch
BUN(LER), John   Ch.M.
1841 C. West Wycombe (age 45)
BURNARD, Joseph   Ch.M.
1861 C. High Wycombe (age 17)
BURNET, Alfred   Ch.M.
1841 C. Hillary St., High Wycombe
(age 25)
BURNET, William   Ch.M.
1841 C. Hillary St., High Wycombe
(age 35)
BURNHAM, J.   Ch.M.
1899 K. Desboro Rd., Wycombe
BURNHARD, John   Ch.M. (seats)
1851 C. Newland, High Wycombe
(age 12)
BURRETT, James   Ch.M.
1830 P. 15 High St., Eton
BURTON, James   Ch.M.
1841 C. Rises, Chinnor (age 40)
1847 K. Chinnor
BURTON, James   Ch.T.
1883 K. Henton, Chinnor
1907 K. Chinnor
BUSBY, W.   Ch.M.
1847 K. Gerrards Cross
1861 C. Gerrards Cross (age 45)

BUTLER, Abraham   Ch.M.
1851 C. Stokenchurch (age 17)
BUTLER, Archippins   Ch.M.
1851 C. Stokenchurch (age 21)
BUTLER, Edward   Ch.M.
1851 C. Stokenchurch (age 39)
BUTLER, Edward   Ch.T.
1841 C. Church St., Stokenchurch
(age 25)
BUTLER, G.   Ch.T.
1895 K. The City, Radnage
1899 K. Radnage
BUTLER, Harry   Ch.M.
1881 C. Stokenchurch (age 20)
BUTLER, Henry   Ch.M.
1851 C. Stokenchurch (age 24)
BUTLER, James   Ch.M.
1861 C. High Wycombe (age 40)
BUTLER, John   Ch.M.
1851 C. West Wycombe (age 58)
BUTLER, Samuel   Ch.M.
1851 C. Stokenchurch (age 11)
BUTLER, Silvanus
1851 Stockenchurch (age 15)
BUTLER, Thomas   Ch.Bott.
1851 C. Stokenchurch (age 33)
BUTLER, William   Ch.M.
1841 C. Downley, West Wycombe
(age 50)
1851 C. West Wycombe (age 62)
BUTLER, William   Ch.M.
1841 C. Swilley Hse., Stokenchurch
(age 20)
1851 C. Swilley Hse., Stokenchurch
(age 29)
BYE, Thomas   Ch.M.
1861 C. Newland, High Wycombe
(age 33)
1877 K. Newland, High Wycombe
1883 K. Newland, High Wycombe
CAFFALL & KEEN   Ch.Man.
1891 K. West End Rd., Wycombe
also 5 Tabernacle St., London
1899 K. Queens Rd., Wycombe
CAFFALL, Joseph Hobbs   Ch.M.
1851 C. Temple End, High Wycombe
(age 34)
1853 Mussan & Craven, High Wycombe
CANNON, Charles   Ch.M.
1823 P. Pauls Row Yd., High Wycombe
1827 P.R. Daughter baptised
1830 P. London End, High Wycombe
1841 C. Jolly Miller, High Wycombe
(age 60)
1844 P. Jolly Miller, High Wycombe
CANNON, George   Ch.M.
1834 P.R. 2 daughters baptised
1841 C. Tylers Green, High Wycombe
(age 25)
CANNON, John   Ch.Man.
1798 Posse Com., High Wycombe
1814-24 P.R. 2 daughters baptised
1816-21 P.R. 2 sons baptised
1841 C. High Wycombe (age 60)
1851 C. Tylers Row, High Wycombe
(age 71)
CANNON, John   Ch. Seat Man.
1851 C. Newland, High Wycombe
(age 35)
CANNON, Joseph   Ch.M.
1815-26 P.R. 3 daughters baptised
1823 P.R. Son baptised
CANNOR, Charles   Ch.M.
1841 C. High Wycombe (age 60)
CAPILL, John   Ch.M.
1861 C. High Wycombe (age 32)
CAPON, William   Ch.M.
1780-98 F.H.S. Newport Pagnell
CAREY, John   Ch.M.
1851 C. Newland, High Wycombe
(age 23)
CARR, Ann   Ch.M.
1841 C. Newland, High Wycombe
(age 35)
CARR, Joseph   Ch.M.
1844 P. High Wycombe
1847 K. Newland, High Wycombe
1851 Slater High Wycombe
1851 C. (Sarah), High Wycombe
(master) (age 33)
1853 Mussan & Craven, High Wycombe
CARRS, Henry   Ch.M.
1841 C. Newland, High Wycombe
(age 22)
1851 C. Newland, High Wycombe
(age 31)
CARTER, Edmund   Ch.M.
1851 C. West Wycombe (age 32)
CARTER, H.   T.
1889 Cosburn, Thatcham

CARTER, William   Ch.M.
1841 C. Radnage (age 30)
CARTIS, John   Ch.M.
1861 C. High Wycombe (age 33)
CARTWRIGHT, B.   Ch.M.
1877 K. Mendy St., High Wycombe
1883 K. Mendy St., High Wycombe
1887 K. Mendy St., High Wycombe
1891 K. Mendy St., High Wycombe
1895 K. Mendy St., High Wycombe
1899 K. Mendy St., High Wycombe
CARTWRIGHT, B.W.   Ch.Man.
1883 K. Prestwood, Gt. Missenden
CARTWRIGHT, John   Ch.M.
1841 C. High Wycombe (age 15)
CARTWRIGHT, W.   Ch.Man.
1861 C. High Wycombe (age 24)
1869 K. Mendy St., High Wycombe
CASTLE, John   Ch.M. & J.
1851 C. Newland, High Wycombe
(age 22)
CATMAN, Alfred   Ch.M.
1899 K. Desboro Row, High Wycombe
CATTON, Amos   Ch.M.
1864 K. La. End, High Wycombe
1869 K. La. End, High Wycombe
1877 K. La. End, High Wycombe
1883 K. La. End, High Wycombe
1887 K. La. End, High Wycombe
1891 K. La. End, High Wycombe
1895 K. La. End, High Wycombe
CATTON, Elizabeth   Ch.Man.
1841 C. Marlow (age 40)
CHAHKMAN, Enoch   Ch.M.
1841 C. Voilers Ct., Wycombe (age 16)
CHALFORD, Henry   Ch.M.
1851 C. West Wycombe (age 15)
CHAPMAN, Daniel   Ch.M.
1861 C. High Wycombe (age 33)
CHAPMAN, Enoch   Ch.M.
1851 C. Newland, High Wycombe
(age 25)
1861 C. Newland, High Wycombe
(age 35)
CHAPMAN, John   Ch.M.
1851 C. Newland, High Wycombe
(age 17)
CHAPMAN, John   Ch.M.
1861 C. High Wycombe (age 31)
CHEESE, William   Ch.M.
1861 C. High Wycombe (age 19)
CHEESR(?), John Jnr.   Ch.M.
1899 K. Worlds End, Wycombe
CHESTERMAN, Henry   Ch.M.
1851 C. Oxford Rd., High Wycombe
(age 28)
CHILD, Edmond   Ch.M.
1899 K. 27 Baker St., Wycombe
CHILDS, Henry   Ch.M.
1861 C. High Wycombe (age 17)
CHILDS, William   Ch.Lab.
1851 C. Newland, High Wycombe
(age 42)
CHILTON, E.   Ch.T.
1869 K. Parslows Hill, Monks Risborough
1877 K. Parslows Hill, Monks Risborough
1883 K. Parslows Hill, Princes Risborough
1887 K. Parslows Hill, Princes Risborough
CHILTON, Thomas   Ch.M.
1851 C. Newland, High Wycombe
(age 33)
CHILTON, Thomas   Ch.M.
1841 C. Canal, High Wycombe
(age 34)
1861 C. High Wycombe (age 47)
CHURCH, Daniel   Ch.M.
1877 K. Duke St. High Wycombe
CLARIDGE, J.   T.
1862 K. Twickenham
CLARK, C.   Ch.M.
1869 K. Mendy St., High Wycombe
1877 K. Mendy St., High Wycombe
1883 K. Mendy St., High Wycombe
1887 K. Mendy St., High Wycombe
1891 K. Mendy St., High Wycombe
CLARK, Charles   Ch.M.
1833-37 P.R. 2 sons baptised
1834-39 P.R. 2 daughters baptised
1841 C. Treachers Row, High Wycombe
(age 35)
1851 Slater. Treachers Row, High
Wycombe
1864 K. Newland, High Wycombe
1869 K. Newland, High Wycombe
1877 K. Newland, High Wycombe
(Ch.Man.)
1883 K. Hendy St., High Wycombe
1887 K. Hendy St., High Wycombe
1891 K. Hendy St., High Wycombe

CLARK, Charles   Ch.M.
1851 C. Oxford Rd., High Wycombe
(age 41)
CLARK, Charles   Ch.M.
1851 C. Canalside, High Wycombe
(age 48)
CLARK, Daniel   Ch.M.
1861 C. High Wycombe (age 34)
CLARK, George   Ch.M.
1831 P.R. Daughter baptised. High
Wycombe
1841 C. Carthage Hall, Radnage
(age 40)
CLARK, Henry   Ch.M.
1861 C. High Wycombe (age 19)
CLARK, J.   Ch.M.
1863 Dutton Allen, Canalside, High
Wycombe
CLARK, John   Ch.M.
1861 C. High Wycombe (age 23)
CLARK, Joseph   Ch.M.
1835-38 P.R. 2 sons baptised
1837-40 P.R. 2 daughters baptised
1841 C. High St., High Wycombe
(age 26)
CLARK, Joseph   Ch.M.
1841 C. High Wycombe (age 20)
CLARK, Joseph   Ch.Man.
1861 C. High Wycombe (age 56)
CLARK, Thomas   Ch.M.
1861 C. High Wycombe (age 28)
CLARK, Thomas   Ch.M.
1814-38 P.R. 3 sons baptised
1823-28 P.R. 2 daughters baptised
1830 P. Queens Sq., High Wycombe
1844 P. High Wycombe
CLARK, Thomas   Ch.M.
1851 C. Canalside, High Wycombe
(age 17)
1861 C. High Wycombe (age 28)
CLARK, Thomas   Ch.M.
1841 C. Treachers Row, High
Wycombe (age 20)
CLARK, Samuel   Ch.M.
CLARK, William   Ch.M.
1815 P.R. Daughter baptised
1816-18 P.R. 2 sons baptised. High
Wycombe
CLARK, William   Ch.M.
1851 C. Oxford Rd.m High Wycombe
(age 42)
CLARKE, Charles   Ch.M.
1841 C. Carthage Hall, Radnage (age 12)
CLARKE, Charles   Ch.M.
1861 C. Newland, High Wycombe
(age 47)
1863 Dutton Allen, Newland, High
Wycombe
1864 Cassey, Newland, High Wycombe
CLARKE, George   Bath Ch.M.
1863 Dutton, 5, Bear La., Oxford
CLARKE, James   Ch.M.
1834-35 P.R. 2 sons baptised
1841 C. High Wycombe (age 34)
CLARKE, Joseph   Ch.M.
1851 C. Newland, High Wycombe
(age 36)
CLIMPSON, Edward   Ch.M.
1823 P. Wilding St., Amersham
1830 P. Wilden St., Amersham
1842 P. High St., Amersham (& Son)
1844 P. High St., Amersham
CLIMPSON, William   Ch.M.
1851 Slater Amersham
CLINKERBERRY, Daniel   Ch.M.
1851 C. Hammersley La., High
Wycombe (age 47)
CLINKERBERRY, Charles   Ch.M.
1861 C. High Wycombe (age 15)
COCK, Rueben   App. Ch.M.
1851 C. West Wycombe (age 14)
COKERILL, William   Ch.M.
1881 C. Stokenchurch (age 24)
COGGS, William   T.
1868 Cassey Thatcham
COLE, Thomas   T.
1868 Cassey 16 Coley Pl., Reading
COLEMAN, John   Ch.M.
1861 C. High Wycombe (age 23)
COLEMAN, Joseph   Ch.Worker
1851 C. Radnage (age 18)
COLEMAN, Joseph   Ch.M.
1861 C. High Wycombe (age 21)
COLES, George   Ch.M.
1861 C. High Wycombe (age 22)
COLES, Henry   Ch.M.
1861 C. High Wycombe (age 44)
COLES, James   Ch.M.
1823 P. Wendover
1830 P. Aylesbury St., Wendover

Thames Valley continued

DEAN, James   Ch.M.
1881 C. Stokenchurch (age 23)
1899 K. Stokenchurch
DEAN, James   Ch.M.
1881 Stokenchurch (age 61)
DEAN, Joseph   Ch.M.
1851 C. Stokenchurch (age 40)
DEAN, William   Ch. T. App.
1851 C. Temple End, High Wycombe
(age 15)
DEAN, William   Ch.M.
1881 C. Stokenchurch (age 18)
DEANE, George   Ch.M.
1841 C. Gt. Marlow (age 20)
DEANE, George   Ch.M.
1851 C. Hammersley La., High Wycombe
(age 23)
DEAN, Geo.   Ch.M.
1881 C. Stokenchurch (age 14)
DEANE, John   Ch.M.
1841 C. Horsleys Grd., Stokenchurch
(age 22)
DEANE, Richard   Ch.M.
1881 C. Stokenchurch (age 35)
DEAR, Charles & Son   Ch.M.
1839 F.H.S. Brentford
DELL, J.   Ch.T.
1899 K. Turville Henley
DENNETT, Thomas   Ch.M.
1824 P.R. Son baptised
1826 P.R. Son baptised, High Wycombe
DIDCOCK, John   Ch.M.
1851 C. Newland, High Wycombe
(age 22)
DIMMOCK, Henry Ch. M. Employee
1851 C. West Wycombe (age 15)
DIMMOCK, John   Ch.M.
1841 C. Newland, High Wycombe
(age 35)
1851 C. Newland, High Wycombe
(age 45)
DIMMOCK, P.   Ch.M.
1899 K. Totteridge Rd., Wycombe
DIPROSE, John   Ch.M.
1845 K. Cranford
DITEN, John   Ch.M.
1841 C. Carthage Hall, Radnage (age 45)
DITTON, John   W.T.
1851 C. Stokenchurch (age 59)
DITTON, Samuel   Ch.M.
1852 Hist. Gaz. Kingston Blount, Thame
DIX & CO.   Ch.M. Tool Maker
1895 K. 16-17 Church St., High
Wycombe
DIX, William   Ch.M.
1798 Posse Com., High Wycombe
DIXEY, George   Ch.M.
1833 P.R. Son baptised High Wycombe
DOBBIN, Reuben   Ch. Framer
1851 C. Stokenchurch (age 44)
DOBBINS, Reuben   Ch.M.
1841 C. Middle Row, Stokenchurch
(age 30)
DOBSON, Arthur   Ch.M.
1851 C. West Wycombe (age 20)
DOBSON, Edward   Ch.M.
1851 C. West Wycombe (age 22)
DOBSON, John   Ch.M.
1851 C. West Wycombe (age 24)
DOIL, George   Ch.M.
1861 C. High Wycombe (age 27)
DONNALD, Thomas   Ch.M.
1826 P.R. Daughter baptised
1828 P.R. Daughter baptised High
Wycombe
DORMER, E.   Ch.T.
1895 K. Common Radnage
1899 K. Common Radnage
DORMER, Thomas   Ch.M.
1814-26 P.R. 3 daughters baptised
1841 C. Bird-in-Hand, High Wycombe
(age 50)
1861 C. Bird-in-Hand, High Wycombe
(age 76)
DORMOT, George   Ch.M.
1861 C. High Wycombe (age 28)
DORSET(T), John   Ch.M.
1844 P. Bell End; Princes Risboro
1847 K. Princes Risboro
1851 Slater Princes Risboro
DOVER, William   Ch. Man.
1863 Dutton Allen, Bradenham
DOWLING, William   Ch.M.
1851 C. Newland, High Wycombe
(age 32)
DOWLING, William   Ch.M.
1861 C. High Wycombe (age 39)

DRASON, Edward   Ch.M.
1861 C. High Wycombe (age 21)
DRICEY, George   Ch.M.
1835 P.R. Son baptised High Wycombe
DUDLEY & BRISTOW   Ch.M.
1864 K. West Wycombe
1864 Cassey West Wycombe
DUDLEY, James   T.
1851 C. West Wycombe (age 14)
DUDLEY, John   T.
1851 C. West Wycombe (age 16)
DUDLEY, John Clough   T.
1851 C. West Wycombe (age 53)
1864 Cassey West Wycombe
DUDLEY, P.   Ch.M.
1869 K. Stokenchurch
DUDLEY, W.   Ch.Man.
1883 K. Queens Rd., High Wycombe
1891 K. Queens Rd., High Wycombe
1895 K. Queens Rd., High Wycombe
1899 K. Queens Rd., High Wycombe
DUKE, Samuel   Ch.M.
1861 C. High Wycombe (age 21)
DULLEY, Henry   Ch.M.
1830 P. Woburn
1844 P. Woburn
DUNKELEY, W.H.   T.
1862 K. Uxbridge
EALES, Robert   Ch.M.
1851 Slater. Wycombe
EARL, Richard   Ch.M. & T.
1861 C. High Wycombe (age 48)
EAST, Alfred   Ch.M.
1861 C. High Wycombe (age 17)
EAST, Daniel Russell   T.
1830 P. High St., Chesham
1863 Dutton Allen Chesham
EAST, John   Ch.M.
1851 C. Oxford Rd., High Wycombe
(age 37)
1861 C. Oxford Rd., High Wycombe
(age 47)
EAST, Richard   Ch.Man.
1851 C. High Wycombe (Ch.T.)
(age 37)
1887 K. 14 Mendy St., Wycombe
1891 K. 14 Mendy St., Wycombe
1895 K. 14 Mendy St., Wycombe
1899 K. 14 Mendy St., Wycombe
EAST, Samuel   Ch.M.
1841 C. Hillary St., High Wycombe
(age 20)
EAST, Thomas   Ch.T.
1841 C. Lower Chinnor (age 30)
EAST, William   Ch.M.
1813-22 P.R. 3 daughters baptised
1815-18 P.R. 2 sons baptised
1841 C. Lanes Row, High Wycombe
(age 63)
EAST, William   Ch.M.
1841 C. Lower Marsh, High Wycombe
(age 35)
EAST, Will & Job   T.
1830 P. White Hill, Chesham
EAST, William Jnr.
1830 P. Padmor, Mead End, Chesham
EASTACE, J.   Ch.M.
1847 K. Chinnor
EDEN, Edward   Ch.M.
1851 Slater Amersham
EDGERLEY, Henry   Ch.M. & J.
1851 C. Newland, High Wycombe
(age 20)
EDGERLEY, Samuel   Ch.M.
1851 C. Newland, High Wycombe
(age 17)
EDGERLEY, William   Ch.Man.
1863 Dutton Allen Newland, High
Wycombe
1877 K. Newland, High Wycombe
1883 K. Newland, High Wycombe
1887 K. Newland, High Wycombe
1891 K. Newland, High Wycombe
1895 K. Newland, High Wycombe
1899 K. Newland, High Wycombe
EDMONDS, George   Ch.M.
1841 C. Bird-in-Hand, High Wycombe
(age 37)
EDMONDS, George   Ch.M.
1851 C. West Wycombe (age 47)
EDMONDS, George   Ch.M.
1851 C. West Wycombe (age 17)
EDMONDS, John   Ch.T.
1861 C. High Wycombe (age 18)
EDMONDS, William   Ch.M.
1775 J.O.J. no.1173. High St., Oxford
EDMONDS, William
1775-79 F.H.S. Burford
EDMUNDS, Thomas   T.
1830 P. 13 Gun St., Reading

EDWARDS, George   Ch.Man.
1887 K. Totteridge Rd., Wycombe
1891 K. Totteridge Rd., Wycombe
EELE, John   Ch.M.
1851 C. Newland, High Wycombe
(age 23)
1861 C. High Wycombe (age 32)
1877 K. Easton St., High Wycombe
EELE, Robert   Ch.M.
1851 C. Newland, High Wycombe
(age 25)
1853 Mussan & Craven High Wycombe
EELES, Jacob   Ch.Lab.
1851 C. Stokenchurch (age 14)
EELES, Robert   Ch.Man.
1861 C. High Wycombe (age 34)
EGERLY, W. & S.   Ch.Man.
1869 K. Newland, High Wycombe
1877 K. (as Edgerley) High Wycombe
ELLIOT, John   Ch.M.
1861 C. High Wycombe (age 44)
ELLIOT, Thos.   Ch.M.
1851 C. West Wycombe (age 30)
ELLIOTT, James   Ch.M.
1899 K. 125 West End Rd., Oakmead,
Wycombe
ELLIS, George   Ch.M.
1841 C. Park La., West Wycombe
(age 15)
1887 K. Prestwood, Chesham
1899 K.
ELLIS, George Albert   Ch.M.
1899 K. 38-40 Desboro Rd., Wycombe
ELLIS, William   Ch.Man.
1887 K. Desboro Rd., Wycombe
1891 K. West End Rd., Wycombe
1895 K.
1899 K. (Ellis Bros.)
ELLWOOD, Joseph   Ch.M.
1798 Posse Com., High Wycombe
1841 C. Newland, High Wycombe
(age 75)
ELSDEN, Charles   Ch.M.
1853 Lascelles. Fish St., Babury
EMERY, Charles   T.
1823 P. Broad St., Reading
1830 P. Black Horse Yd., London St.,
Reading
EMERY, Robert   T.
1868 Cassey. 7 Caversham Rd., Reading
1883 K. 22 Caversham Rd., Reading
ENDELL, Walter F.   Ch.Man.
1887 K. Oxford Rd., Wycombe
ESSEX, Richard   Ch.Man.
1861 C. High Wycombe (age 15)
EUSTACE, Wm.   Ch.T.
1841 C. Chinnor Rd., Chinnor (age 15)
EVANS, James   Ch.T.
1851 C. Temple End, High Wycombe
EVANS, Richard   Ch.T.
1841 C. High Wycombe (age 25)
1851 C. High Wycombe (age 36)
FANE, George   Ch.M.
1877 K. West End Rd., High Wycombe
1883 K. West End Rd., High Wycombe
1887 K. West End Rd., High Wycombe
1891 K. West End Rd., High Wycombe
1895 K. West End Rd., High Wycombe
1899 K. West End Rd., High Wycombe
FARGUSON, John   Ch.M.
1851 C. Stokenchurch (age 49)
FARRANT, R.E.   T.
1866 Wheeler & Day 26 High St., Oxford
1868 Cassey Oxford
FAULKENER, Joseph   Ch.T.
1841 C. Church St., Stokenchurch
(age 60)
1851 C. Stokenchurch (age 77)
FEHRENBACK, Henry   Ch.M.
1841 C. High Wycombe (age 20)
FEHRENBACK, Joseph   Ch.M.
1841 C. High Wycombe (age 30)
FEHRENBACK, William   Ch.M.
1851 C. Easton St., High Wycombe
(age 18)
FENNER, E.   Ch.M.
1863 Dutton Allen Chalfont St. Giles
1864 K. Chalfont St. Giles
1869 K. Chalfont St. Giles
FENNER, George
1846 Hunt Thame
1847 K. Park St., Thame
1853 Lascelles Park St., Thame
1863 Dutton Park St., Thame
FENNER, Robert   Ch.M.
1861 C. High Wycombe (age 22)
FENNER, William   Ch.M.
1851 C. Crown La., High Wycombe
(age 18)
1863 Cassey Chalfont St. Giles

FERRALL, Job   Ch.M.
1851 C. Haverfalls Row, High
Wycombe (age 34)
FIEFIELD, John   Ch.M.
1851 C. Newland, High Wycombe
(age 35)
FIELD & PALMER   Ch.M.
1847 K. High St., Amersham
1851 Slater Amersham (Field only)
FLETCHER, Henry   Ch.M.
1861 C. High Wycombe (age 30)
FLETCHER, J.   Ch.M.
1899 K. Westbourne St., Wycombe
FLETCHER, Thomas   Ch.M.
1851 C. Easton St., High Wycombe
(age 44)
FLETCHER, William   Ch.M.
1851 C. Easton St., High Wycombe
(age 20)
FOLLEY, J.   Ch.M.
1847 K. Chinnor
FOLLEY, John   Ch.M.
1851 C. West Wycombe (age 22)
FOLLY, Frederick   Ch.M.
1851 C. West Wycombe (age 21)
FOLLY, George   Ch.M.
1851 C. West Wycombe (age 23)
FOLLY, George   Ch.M.
1851 C. Stokenchurch (age 15)
FOOTE, Richard   Ch.M.
1813 P.R. Son baptised
1841 C. Newland, High Wycombe
(age 50)
1851 C. Crendon La., High Wycombe
(age 65)
FORD, Mrs. Ann   Ch.M.
1863 Dutton Allen Railway Pl., Wycombe
1864 K. Newland, High Wycombe
1864 Cassey Newland, High Wycombe
FORD, B.   Ch. Back Maker
1899 K. West End Rd., Wycombe
FORD, Mrs E.   Ch.Man.
1895 K. 55 West End Rd., Wycombe
1899 K. 65 West End Rd., Wycombe
FORD, Henry   Ch.M.
1840 P.R. Daughters baptised
1841 C. Newland, High Wycombe
(age 20)
1851 Slater High Wycombe
1853 Mussan & Craven High Wycombe
1861 C. Newland, High Wycombe
(age 48)
FORD, Henry   Ch.Man.
1851 C. Haverfalls Row, High Wycombe
(age 51)
FORD, James   Ch.M.
1841 C. Bowden La., Wycombe (age 15)
FORD, Richard   Ch.M.
1841 C. Downley, West Wycombe
(age 50)
1851 C. Downley, West Wycombe
(age 63)
FORD, Richard   Ch.M.
1841 C. Downley, West Wycombe
(age 30)
1887 K. Downley, West Wycombe
1891 K. Downley, West Wycombe
FORD, Richard   Ch.M.
1851 C. Newland, High Wycombe
(age 21)
1861 C. Newland, High Wycombe
(age 32)
FORD, Richard   Ch. Back Maker
1891 K. West End Rd., Wycombe
1895 K. West End Rd., Wycombe
FORD, Samuel   Ch. Man. & Carp.
1822 P.R. Son baptised
1824-26 P.R. 2 sons baptised
1841 C. Bowdens La., High Wycombe
(age 50)
1851 C. Bowdens La., High Wycombe
(age 69)
FORD, Samuel   Ch.Man.
1861 C. West End Rd., High Wycombe
(age 18)
1877 K. West End Rd., High Wycombe
1883 K. West End Rd., High Wycombe
1887 K. West End Rd., High Wycombe
1891 K. Queens Rd., High Wycombe
1895 K. Queens Rd., High Wycombe
1899 K. Queens Rd., High Wycombe
FORD, William   Ch.Man.
1891 K. West End Rd., Wycombe
FORRESTOR, Ann   Ch.M.
1841 C. South St., Stokenchurch (age 55)
FORTNAM, Thomas   Ch.T.
1891 K. Cadmore End, Wycombe
1895 K. Cadmore End, Wycombe

INDEX

Thames Valley continued

JANES, G. Ch.M.
1869 K. Gt. Kingshill, Prestwood, Amersham
1877 K. Gt. Kingshill, Prestwood, Amersham
1883 K. Gt. Kingshill, Gt. Missenden
1887 K. Gt. Kingshill, Chesham
1895 K. Gt. Kingshill, Chesham
1899 K. Gt. Kingshill, Chesham
JANES, George Ch.T.
1841 C. Lower Chinnor (age 25)
JANES, Jacob Ch.T.
1851 C. Temple End, High Wycombe (age 29)
JANES, James Ch.T.
1883 K. Prestwood, Gt. Missenden
1887 K. Prestwood, Chesham
JANES, Martin Ch.T.
1851 C. Tylors Green, High Wycombe (age 35)
JARVIS, George Ch.Man.
1891 K. Hunridge, Chesham
1895 K. Church St., Chesham
1899 K., Chesham
JARVIS, James Ch.T.
1851 C. Stokenchurch (age 46)
JARVIS, James Ch.M.
1823 P. London St., Reading
1841 C. Gt. Marlow (age 40)
1847 K. La. End, Wycombe
1851 Slater, Wycombe
1863 Dutton Allen. West Wycombe
1864 K. La. End, High Wycombe
1869 K. High Wycombe
JARVIS, Joseph Ch.Man.
1864 Cassey. La. End, High Wycombe
1877 K. La. End, High Wycombe
1883 K. La. End, Hgh Wycombe
JARVIS, Leonard Ch.Man.
1887 K. La. End, Wycombe
1891 K. Wycombe
1895 K. Wycombe
1899 K. Wycombe
JARVIS, Michael Ch.T.
1851 C. Stokenchurch (age 35)
JARVIS, Thomas Ch.T.
1851 C. Stokenchurch (age 18)
JARVIS, William Ch.M.
1841 C. Gt. Marlow (age 30)
JENNING, William Ch.T.
1899 K. Prestwood, Gt. Missenden
JERVIS, James Ch.M.
1841 Beacons Bottom, Stokenchurch (age 35)
JOHNSON & BIRCH Ch.Man.
1877 K. West End Rd., High Wycombe
JOHNSON, Ann Ch.M. & Bott.
1851 C. Stokenchurch (age 31)
JOHNSON, Henry Ch.M. Benchman
1851 C. Newland, High Wycombe (age 26)
JOHNSON, James Ch.M.
1881 C. Stokenchurch (age 27)
JOHNSON, John Ch.M.
1881 C. Stokenchurch (age 35)
JOHNSON, Joseph Ch.M.
1851 C. Stokenchurch (age 25)
JOHNSON, Thomas Ch.M.
1841 C. Horsleys Gn., Stokenchurch (age 24)
1851 C. Horsleys Gn., Stokenchurch (age 34)
1881 C. Horsleys Gn., Stokenchurch (age 64)
JOHNSON, William Ch.Frames
1861 C. High Wycombe (age 28)
JOHNSON, W. Ch.Man.
1883 K. West End Rd., High Wycombe
1887 K. West End Rd., High Wycombe
1891 K. West End Rd., High Wycombe
1895 K. West End Rd., High Wycombe
1899 K. West End Rd., High Wycombe
JONES, Alfred Ch.M.
1861 C. High Wycombe (age 13)
JONES, C. & A. Ch.Man.
1877 K. Saffron Platt, High Wycombe
1883 K. Queen St., High Wycombe (Jones Bros.)
1895 K. Queen St., High Wycombe
1899 K. Queen St., High Wycombe
JONES, Charles Ch.M.
1861 C. High Wycombe (age 21)
JONES, J. Ch.M.
1851 C. Easton St., High Wycombe (age 50)
1863 Dutton Allen. Easton St., High Wycombe

JONES, John Ch.Man.
1839 P.R. Son baptised
1841 C. Newland, High Wycombe (age 30)
1851 Slater. Newland, High Wycombe
1853 Mussan & Craven. High Wycombe
JONES, John Ch.M.
1851 C. Mount Pleasant, High Wycombe (age 21)
JONES, John Ch.Man.
1861 C. High Wycombe (age 57)
JONES, Phillip Ch.M.
1841 C. Beacons Bottom, Stokenchurch (age 40)
JONES, Samuel Ch.M.
1861 C. High Wycombe (age 19)
JONES, Thomas Ch.M.
1861 C. High Wycombe (age 19)
JOYNSON, Frederick Ch.Man.
1891 K. Newland St., Wycombe
1895 K. Newland St., Wycombe (Joynson, Holland & Co.)
1899 K. Newland St., Wycombe
JOYNSON, William Ch.Man.
1891 K. 76 Easton St., Wycombe
JUDGE, Edwin Ch.T.
1881 C. Stokenchurch (age 20)
1899 K. Stokenchurch (age 20)
JUDGE, Hannah Ch.Bott.
1851 C. Stokenchurch (age 22)
JUDGE, James Ch.J.
1841 C. Church St., Stokenchurch (age 25)
JUDGE, James Ch.T.
1851 C. Stokenchurch (age 30)
JUDGE, John Ch.M. & J.
1841 C. Church St., Stokenchurch (age 40)
1851 C. Church St., Stokenchurch (age 55)
1864 K. Stokenchurch (Ch.T.)
JUDGE, John Ch.T.
1881 C. Stokenchurch (age 22)
JUDGE, Richard Ch.M.
1851 C. Stokenchurch (age 42)
1881 C. Stokenchurch (age 75)
JUDGE, Thomas Ch.M.
1851 C. Stokenchurch (age 22)
1868 Cassey. Stokenchurch
1881 C. Stokenchurch (age 53)
1883 K. Stokenchurch
1891 K. Stokenchurch
1895 K. Stokenchurch
1899 K. Stokenchurch
KEELEY, Josiah Ch.M.
1861 C. High Wycombe (age 12)
KEEN, Alfred Ch.M.
1851 C. West Wycombe (age 18)
KEEN, Edward Ch.M.
1851 C. West Wycombe (age 14)
KEEN, George Ch.M.
1851 C. West Wycombe (age 15)
KEEN, George Ch.M.
1851 C. West Wycombe (age 32)
KEEN, Henry Ch.Man.
1851 West Wycombe (age 26)
1891 K. Bird-in-Hand, West Wycombe
1895 K. Bird-in-Hand, West Wycombe
KEEN, J. Ch.T.
1864 K. Coleshill, Amersham
1869 K. Coleshill, Amersham
KEEN, John Ch.Man.
1851 C. High Wycombe (age 21
1883 K. West End Rd., High Wycombe
1887 K. West End Rd., High Wycombe
1891 K. West End Rd., High Wycombe
1895 K. West End Rd., High Wycombe
1899 K. West End Rd., High Wycombe
KEEN, Joseph Ch.M.
1851 C. West Wycombe (age 21)
KEEN, Joseph Ch.M.
1841 C. High St., High Wycombe (age 36)
1851 C. High St., High Wycombe (age 46)
KEEN, William Ch.Man.
1861 C. Wycombe (age 23)
1895 K. 61 Desboro Rd., Wycombe
1899 K. 61 Desboro Rd., Wycombe
KENNEDY, C. Ch.T.
1863 Dutton Allen, Bradenham, High Wycombe
1864 K. Bradenham, High Wycombe
1869 K. Bradenham, High Wycombe
KENNEDY, George Ch.M.
1861 C. High Wycombe (age 49)
KENNEDY, John Ch.M.
1720 F.H.S. Windsor
KENNEDY, William Ch.M.
1861 C. High Wycombe (age 32)

KENT, John Ch.M.
1742 F.H.S. Stony Stratford
KENT, Richard Ch.M.
1840 F.H.S. Newbury
KEYTE, Richard Ch.M.
1826 F.H.S. Uxbridge
KIBBLES, Charles Ch.M.
1851 C. Newland, High Wycombe (age 56)
KIBBLES, Charles Ch.M.
1851 C. Newland, High Wycombe (age 17)
KIBBLES, Henry Ch.M.
1851 C. Newland, High Wycombe (age 19)
KIBBLES, William Ch.M.
1861 C. High Wycombe (age 89)
KIBBLES, William Ch.M.
1851 C. Newland, High Wycombe (age 21)
KING — Ch.Frame Mkr.
1736 F.H.S. Bicester
KING, Edward Ch.M.
1841 C. Newland, High Wycombe (age 65)
KING, Thomas Ch.M.
1841 C. White House, Chinnor (age 35)
1847 K. Chinnor
1852 Hist. Gaz. Chinnor
KIRBY, Joseph Ch.M.
1861 C. High Wycombe (age 24)
KIRBY, Thomas Ch.M.
1861 C. High Wycombe (age 30)
KIRBY, William Ch.Framer
1861 C. High Wycombe (age 43)
LACEY, James W.T.
1861 C. Chesham (age 30)
1863 Dutton Allen. Chesham
LACEY, John Ch.M.
1825 P.R. Daughter baptised. Princes Risborough
LACEY, Samuel Ch.M.
1851 C. West Wycombe (age 20)
LAMBDEN, John Ch.M.
1798 Posse Com., West Wycombe
LAMBOURN, James Ch.M.
1851 C. Newland, High Wycombe (age 25)
1861 C. Newland, High Wycombe (age 35)
LAMBOURN, James Ch.M.
1851 C. Oxford Rd., High Wycombe (age 14)
LAMBOURN, John Ch.M.
1851 C. Oxford Rd., High Wycombe (age 16)
LAMBOURN, John T.
1853 Lascelles. Friday St., Henley
1854 K. Friday St., Henley
1863 Dutton. Friday St., Henley
LAMBOURNE, John Ch.M.
1823 P. Bell St., Henley
1839 P. Bell St., Henley
1839 Robson. Bell St., Henley
1842 P. Bell St., Henley
1844 P. Bell St., Henley
LAMBOURNE, Joseph Ch.M.
1861 C. High Wycombe (age 55)
LANCASTER, Joseph Ch.M.
1816 P.R. Son baptised
1822 P.R. Son baptised High Wycombe
LANE, Charles Ch.M.
1840 P.R. Son baptised
1841 C. Newland, High Wycombe (age 25)
1851 C. Newland, High Wycombe (age 36)
LANE, George Ch.M. & T.
1853 Lascelles. Northfield End, Henley
1864 K. Northfield End, Henley
1883 K. 14 New St., Henley (T)
LANE, Richard Ch.M.
1847 K. Northfield End, Henley
1852 Hist. Gaz. Northfield End, Henley
1854 K. Northfield End, Henley
LANER, Jonah Ch.M.
1881 C. Stokenchurch (age 33)
LANGLES, John Ch.M.
1841 C. West Wycombe (age 40)
LANGLEY, Charles Ch.M.
1851 C. West Wycombe (age 20)
LANGLEY, George Ch.M.
1861 C. High Wycombe (age 17)
LANGLEY, James Ch.M.
1851 C. West Wycombe (age 37)
LANGLEY, James Ch.M.
1851 C. West Wycombe (age 22)
LANGLEY, John Ch.M.
1814 P.R. Son baptised
1841 C. High St., High Wycombe (age 40)

1851 C. High St., High Wycombe (age 54)
LANGLEY, Thomas Ch.M.
1841 C. Downley, High Wycombe (age 35)
1851 C. Downley, High Wycombe (age 49)
LANTES, Edward Ch.M.
1851 C. Stokenchurch (age 19)
LANTES, Henry Ch.M.
1851 C. Stokenchurch (age 19)
LARNER, Henry Ch.M.
1841 C. Oakley, Chinnor (age 30)
LARNER, J. Ch.T.
1881 C. Stokenchurch (age 40)
1883 K. Stokenchurch
1899 K. Stokenchurch
LARNER, Jonah Ch.T.
1881 C. Stokenchurch (age 37)
1891 K. Stokenchurch
1895 K. Stokenchurch
LARNOR, William Ch.M.
1851 C. Stokenchurch (age 26)
LARRIE, Henry Ch.M.
1861 C. High Wycombe (age 24)
LASNER, Henry Ch.M.
1851 C. Stokenchurch (age 32)
LASNER, William Ch.M.
1851 C. Stokenchurch (age 40)
LAVERNO, Thomas W.T.
1863 Dutton Allen. Chesham
LAWLESS, James & Son T.
1823 P. Cross St., Reading
1830 P. 29, Cross St., Reading (James only)
LAWRENCE, John Ch.M.
1841 C. Mid Row, Stokenchurch (age 30)
LAWRENCE, Thomas Ch.Framer
1851 C. Newland, High Wycombe (age 24)
LAWRENCE, T. T.
1862 K. Rawlston
LAWRENCE, William Ch.M.
1851 C. Newland, High Wycombe (age 20)
1861 C. Newland, High Wycombe (age 30)
LEDGELEY, George Ch.M.
1851 C. Newland, High Wycombe (age 27)
LEE, George Ch.T.
1851 C. Stokenchurch (age 21)
LEE, Jacob Ch.T.
1883 K. Goring
1889 Cossburn Crays Rd., Goring
1895 K. Goring Heath, Reading
1899 K. Goring Heath, Reading
LEE, James Ch.M.
1861 C. High Wycombe (age 23)
LEE, John Ch.M.
1840 P.R. Married
1841 C. High Wycombe (age 20)
LESTER, George Ch.M.
1851 C. West Wycombe (age 19)
LEWIS, Caleb Ch.M.
1851 C. Newland, High Wycombe (age 17)
LINDSEY, Francis Ch.M.
1851 C. West Wycombe (age 35)
LINDSEY, John Ch.M.
1841 C. High St., West Wycombe (age 53)
1851 C. High St., West Wycombe (age 63)
LINE, Isaac Ch.M.
1851 C. High Wycombe (age 19)
1863 Dutton Allen. Marsh Green, High Wycombe
1864 Cassey. London Rd., High Wycombe
1877 K. Marsh Green, High Wycombe
1883 K. Marsh Green, High Wycombe (& Sons)
1891 K. Marsh Green, High Wycombe (Isaac & Sons)
1895 K. Marsh Green, High Wycombe
1899 K. Marsh Green, High Wycombe
LINE, T. Ch.Man.
1869 K. Frogmoor Gdns., High Wycombe
LINE, William Ch.M.
1899 K. Slater St., Wycombe
LINE, William Ch.M.
1823 P. Wilding St., Amersham
1830 P. Wilden St., Amersham
1839 P. Wilden St., Amersham
1842 P. Wilden St., Amersham
1844 P. Wilden St., Amersham
LINFORD, William Ch.M.
1798 Posse Com., West Wycombe

Thames Valley continued

TILBURY, Stephen   Ch.M.
1841 C. Collins Row, High Wycombe
   (age 20)
TILBURY, W.   Ch.Man.
1851 C. High Wycombe (age 21)
1877 K. Desboro St., High Wycombe
1883-99 K. 16 Slater St., High
   Wycombe
TILBY, John   Ch.M.
1840 P.R. Daughter baptised, High
   Wycombe
TIMBERLAKE, Edwin   Ch.M.
1851 C. Newland, High Wycombe
   (age 22)
TIMBERLAKE, Frederick   Ch.M.
1851 C. Newland, High Wycombe
   (age 16)
1861 C. Newland, High Wycombe
   (age 26)
TIMBERLAKE, Isaac   Ch.M.
1851 C. Newland, High Wycombe
   (age 20)
TIMBERLAKE, James   Ch.M.
1841 C. Tylers Grn., Wycombe
   (age 20)
1851 C. Tylers Grn., Wycombe
   (age 31)
1861 (Ch.Framer)
TIMBERLAKE, James   Ch.M.
   (Timberlie)
1841 C. Newland, High Wycombe
   (age 45)
1851 C. Newland, High Wycombe
   (age 56)
1861 C. Newland, High Wycombe
   (age 63)
TOMKINS, J.   Ch.T.
1869 K. Prestwood, Amersham
1877-99 K. Prestwood, Amersham
TOMLYN, Thomas   Ch.M.
1851 C. St. Marys St., High Wycombe
   (age 21)
1861 C. St. Marys St., High Wycombe
   (age 30)
TOMLYN, William   T.
1851 C. 33 St. Marys St., High
   Wycombe (age 23) (Ch.M.)
1883 K. 33 St. Marys St.
TOMS, John   Ch.M.
1861 C. High Wycombe (age 29)
TOOVEY, Dan   Ch.M.
1851 C. Oxford Rd., High Wycombe
   (age 35)
TOOVEY, James T.   Ch.M.
1863 Dutton Allen. Bury End,
   Amersham
1899 K. Bury End, Amersham
TOOVEY, Samp   Ch.M.
1823 P. High St., Amersham
1830 P. High St., Amersham
1842 Wilden St., Amersham
1844 P. Wilden St., Amersham
1847 K. Union St., Amersham
1851 Slater. Amersham
1864 K. Bury End, Amersham
TOOVEY, Samuel   Ch.M.
1864 Cassey. Bury End, Amersham
1864 K. Coleshill, Amersham
1869 K. Bury End, Amersham
1891 K. Bury End, Amersham
1895 K. Bury End, Amersham
TOOVEY, Theophilus   Ch.Man.
1883 K. Bury End, Amersham
1887 K. Bury End, Amersham
TOOVEY, William   Ch.M.
1823 P. Northbroke St., Newbury
1830 P. Parrs Yd., Newbury
1840-42 F.H.S. Newbury
TOWERTON, John   Ch.M.
1861 C. High Wycombe (age 14)
TOWERTON, W.   Ch.M.
1887 K. Stokenchurch
TOWERTON, Mrs William
1891 K. Stokenchurch
1895 Stokenchurch
1899 Stokenchurch
TRANTER, Henry   Ch.M.
1881 C. Stokenchurch (age 42)
TRANTER, James   Ch.M.
1851 C. Stokenchurch (age 30)
TRANTER, T.   Ch.M.
1847 K. Nettlebed, Henley
1863 K. Nettlebed, Henley (T)
1864 K. Nettlebed, Henley
1868 Cassey. Nettlebed, Henley
1869 K. Nettlebed, Henley

TRANTER, Thomas   Ch.M.
1868 Cassey. Nettlebed
TREACHER, Daniel   Ch.M.
1784 Bailey. High Wycombe
1790 Iniv. High Wycombe
1798 Posse Com., High Wycombe
TREACHER, Francis   Ch.M.
1840 P.R. Daughter baptised
1841 C. High Wycombe (age 27)
1847 K. Oxford Rd., Wycombe
1851 Slater. Wycombe
1853 Musson & Craven. Wycombe
1861 C. Wycombe (age 46)
1864 K. Wycombe
1869 K. Wycombe
TREACHER, Henry   Ch.M.
1841 C. High Wycombe (age 21)
1851 C. Canalside, High Wycombe
TREACHER, James   Ch.M.& Man.
1798 Posse Com., West Wycombe
1830 P. West Wycombe
1841 C. West Wycombe (age 60)
TREACHER, John   Ch.M.
1798 Posse Com., High Wycombe
1823 P. High St., High Wycombe
1830 P. High St., High Wycombe
TREACHER, Samuel   Ch.M.
1784 Bailey. High Wycombe
1790 Univ. High Wycombe
1798 Posse Com., High Wycombe
1823 P. Temple Place, High Wycombe
1830 P. Temple Place, High Wycombe
1840 P. Temple Place, High Wycombe
TREACHER, Samuel   Ch.M.
1832 P.R. Son baptised
1834 P.R. Son baptised
1841 C. Frogmore Hard, High Wycombe
   (age 33)
1834 Oxford Rd., High Wycombe
1844 Oxford Rd., High Wycombe
TREACHER, Thomas   Ch.M.
1830 P. High St., High Wycombe
1841 C. High St., High Wycombe
   (age 50)
TREACHER, Thomas & Co.   Ch.M.
1798 Posse Com., High Wycombe
1822-24 P.R. 2 daughters baptised
1820-34 P.R. 5 sons baptised
1823 P. High St., High Wycombe
1825 P. High St., High Wycombe
1830 P. High St., High Wycombe
1844 P. High St., High Wycombe
TREACHER, William
           Ch.M. & Ch.Leg T.
1768 Marriage registered
1784 Bailey. High Wycombe
1790 Univ. High Wycombe
TREACHER, William Henry   Ch.Man.
1815-24 P.R. Sons baptised
1818-27 P.R. Daughters baptised
1841 C. High Wycombe (age 50)
1847 K. Oxford Rd., Wycombe
TRENDALE, Edward   Ch.M.
1841 C. Sprigg Alley, Chinnor (age 37)
1847 K. Sprigg Alley, Chinnor (Trendall)
TRENDLE, James   Ch.M.
1841 C. Town End, Radnage (age 24)
1851 C. Town End, Radnage (age 37)
TRENDALL, G.   Ch.T.
1864 K. Radnage, Stokenchurch
1864 Cassey. Radnage Stokenchurch
1877 K. Radnage, Stokenchurch
TRENTHAM, James   Ch.M.
1851 C. Hammersley La., High Wycombe
   (age 27)
TRIACHS, Henry   Ch.M.
1841 C. Oxford St., High Wycombe
   (age 25)
TUCKER, Nathaniel   Ch.M.
1841 C. Newland , High Wycombe
   (age 30)
1851 C. Oxford Rd., High Wycombe
   (age 41)
1861 C. High Wycombe (age 52)
TUCKER, William   Ch.M.
1830 P. High St., Amersham
1834 P. High St., Amersham
TUCKING, William   Ch.M.
1861 C. High Wycombe (age 27)
TUCKWELL, David   T.
1883 K. 14 Ardenham St., Aylesbury
TUFFELL, J.   Ch.M.
1847 K. Newland, High Wycombe
TUNDALE   Ch.M.
1841 C. Rises, Chinnor (age 30)
TURNER, J.   Ch.T.
1863 Dutton Allen. Radnage
1864 K. Radnage
1864 Cassey. Radnage

TURNER, James   Ch.M.
1851 C. Radnage (age 49)
TURNER, James   Ch.M.& Caner
1838 P.R. Son baptised
1841 C. High Wycombe (age 25)
TURNER, Thomas   Ch.M.
1854 K. Nettlebed
TURRUND, Charles   Ch.M.
1861 C. High Wycombe (age 14)
URWING, John   Ch.M.
1851 C. Stokenchurch (age 25)
VARLEY, John S.   Ch.Man.
1861 C. Wycombe (age 16)
1891 K. Temple End, Wycombe
1895, 99 K. Temple End, Wycombe
VARNEY, James Jnr.   Ch.T.
1877 K. High St., Wendover
VARNEY, Thomas   Ch.M.
1834 P.R. Son and daughter baptised
1841 C. Randals Passage, High Wycombe
   (age 35)
VARNEY, William   Ch.Bow.
1851 C. Oxford Rd., High Wycombe
   (age 44)
VARVANNE, John   Ch.T.
1881 C. Stokenchurch (age 17)
VASLEY, Robert   Ch.M.
1861 C. High Wycombe (age 25)
VEARY, James   Ch.M.
1841 C. West Wycombe (age 25)
1851 C. Pauls Row, Wycombe
1861 C. High Wycombe (age 47)
VENABLES, George   Ch.M.
1841 C. Collins Row, High Wycombe
   (age 15)
1851 C. Newland, High Wycombe
   (age 27)
VENABLES, George   Ch.M.
1851 C. Oxford, High Wycombe
   (age 35)
1861 C. Oxford, High Wycombe
   (age 45)
VENABLES, Thomas   Ch.M.
1851 C. Canalside, High Wycombe
   (age 18)
VERNEY, William   Ch.M.
1861 C. High Wycombe (age 41)
VERNON, Richard   Ch.M.
1851 C. Stokenchurch (age 43)
VERNON, Richard   Ch.T.
1841 C. Middle Row, Stokenchurch
   (age 40)
VERNON, Richard   Ch.T.
1881 C. Stokenchurch (age 24)
VERSIN, Robert   Ch.M.
1851 C. Oxford Rd., High Wycombe
   (age 52)
VICKERS, George   Ch.M.
1861 C. High Wycombe (age 16)
VOLLUM (Vollum)   Ch.M.
1815-27 P.R. 4 daughters baptised
WADDLE, W.   Ch.M.
1839 Robson. Summertown, Oxford
WAFLER, Edward   Ch.M.
1861 C. High Wycombe (age 27)
WALBUM, William   Ch.M.
1851 C. Newland, High Wycombe
   (age 29)
WALKER, Frederick   Ch.M.
1861 C. High Wycombe (age 18)
WALKER, Henry   Ch.M.
1861 C. High Wycombe (age 24)
WALKER, John   Ch.Framer
1851 C. Pauls Row, High Wycombe
   (age 18)
1861 C. Pauls Row, High Wycombe
   (age 29)
WALKER, John   Ch.M.
1851 C. West Wycombe (age 16)
WALKER, John   Ch.M.
1861 C. High Wycombe (age 29)
WALKER, Michael   Ch.M.
1818 P.R. Son baptised
WALKER, Thomas   Ch.M.
1851 C. Pauls Row, High Wycombe
   (age 20)
WALL, John   Ch.T.
1883 K. Chinnor
1891 K. Chinnor
1895 K. Chinnor
1899 K. Chinnor
WALL, Joseph   Ch.M.
1861 C. Oxford Rd., High Wycombe
   (age 39)
1864 Cassey. Oxford Rd., High
   Wycombe
WALL, Joseph   Ch.T.
1841 C. Chinnor St., Chinnor (age 20)
1851 C. Chinnor St., Chinnor (age 30)

WALL, William   Ch.M.
1841 C. Horsleys Grn., Stokenchurch
   (age 27)
1851 C. Horsleys Grn., Stokenchurch
   (age 40)
WALLAN, Alfred   Ch.M.
1861 C. High Wycombe (age 13)
WALLAN, William   Ch.M.
1861 C. High Wycombe (age 48)
WALLER, Henry   Ch.M.
1841 C. Newland, High Wycombe
   (age 20)
WALLER, Stephen   Ch.M.
1841 C. Newland, High Wycombe
   (age 18)
WALLIN, Thomas   Ch.M.
1821 P.R. Son baptised
WALLING, Thomas   Ch.M.
1813 P.R. Daughter baptised
WALLUM, William   Ch.M.
1841 C. Newland, High Wycombe
   (age 20)
WALTERS, Edward   Ch.M.
1841 C. High Wycombe (age 25)
WALTER, Henry   Ch.Man.
1851 C. St. Mary St., High Wycombe
   (app., age 12)
1883 K. Oxford St., High Wycombe
WARD, Charles   Ch.Man.
1877-83 K. Speen, Tring
1891-99 K. Brook St., Wycombe
WARD, John   Ch.T.
1877 K. Gt. Hampden, Amersham
1883 K. Gt. Hampden, Amersham
1887 K. Gt. Hampden, Amersham
WARDELL, George W.   Ch.M.
1861 C. High Wycombe (age 23)
WARDELL, William E.   Ch.M.
1839 Slater. Summertown, Oxford
   (Waddle)
1841 C. Church St., Oxford (age 35)
1842 P. Summertown, Oxford
1844 P. Summertown, Oxford
1846 Hunt. Summertown (Ch.Man.)
1847 K. Summertown
1850 Slater. Summertown
1851 C. (age 47)
1853 Lascelles. Summertown
1854 K. Summertown
1861 C. High Wycombe (age 60)
WARDLE, James   Ch.M.
1841 C. Great Marlow (age 35)
WARLEY, George   Ch.M.
1861 C. High Wycombe (age 24)
WARNER, W.   Ch.M.
1847 K. Toddington
WARREN, H.H.   Ch.T.
1869 K. Radnage Common
1877 K. Radnage Common
1883 K. Radnage Common
WARREN, S.   Ch.T.
1883 K. The Common, Radnage
WARREN, William   Ch.M.
1861 C. High Wycombe (age 49)
WATERS, Edward   Ch.M.
1861 C. High Wycombe (age 48)
WATKINS, Edmund   Ch.Seat Man.
1851 C. Pauls Row, High Wycombe
   (age 16)
1861 C. High Wycombe (age 25)
1887 K. Mill St., Wycombe
WATSON, Burton   Ch.Man.
1891 K. Seer Grn., Beaconsfield
1895 K. Seer Grn., Beaconsfield
1899 K. Seer Grn., Beaconsfield
WATSON, Henry   Ch.M.
1861 C. High Wycombe (age 20)
WATSON, Matthew   Ch.M.Framer
1851 C. Newland, High Wycombe
   (age 30)
WATSON, William   Ch.M.
1851 C. West Wycombe (age 23)
WATTS, T.   Ch.M.
1847 K. Bierton, Aylesbury
1863 Dutton Allen. Aylesbury
1864 Cassey. Bierton, Aylesbury
1869 K. Bierton, Aylesbury
WAVENEY, James   Ch.Factor
1861 C. High Wycombe
WAY, F. & T.
1895 K. Beacons Bottom
1899 K. Beacons Bottom
WAY, Richard   Ch.M.
1863 Dutton Allen. Beacons Bottom
1864 K. Beacons Bottom
1868 Cassey. Beacons Bottom (Ch.T.)
1883 K. Beacons Bottom
1891 K. Beacons Bottom
WAY, William   Ch.M.
1841 C. Town End, Radnage (age 60)

Nottinghamshire continued

LAWSON, Matthew   **Ch.M.**
1818 Sutton. Listergate, Nott'm.
1840 Ora. Listergate, Nott'm.
1843 P. Listergate, Nott'm.
1844 G. Sawyers Arms Yd., Listergate
1848 L. & H. Sawyers Arms Yd.
1850 S. Listergate
1854 Wr. Listergate
1862 Wr. Walnut Tree Lane, Nott'm.
1871 C. 11 Chesterfield St. (age 67)
LAWSON, Thomas   **Ch.M.**
1815 Will. Listergate, Nott'm.
1825 G. Red St., Nott'm.
LAWSON, William   **Ch.M.& T.**
1719 F.H.S. Nott'm.
LEADHAM, George   **Ch.M.**
1876 K. 4 Carvers Fact., Ashforth St.,
    Nott'm.
LEAVESLEY, J.   **W.T.**
1864 K. Mortimer St., Nott'm.
LEEDHAM, George   **Ch.M.**
1871 C. 8 Gt. Freeman St., Nott'm.
    (age 45)
1881 K. 4 Carvers Fact., Ashforth St.,
    Nott'm.
LEEDHAM, William   **Ch.M.**
1871 C. 8 Gt. Freeman St., Nott'm.
    (age 20)
LESTER, John   **Ch.M.**
1832 W. Leeming St., Mansfield
LESTER, John   **T.**
1834 Dearden. Parliament St., Nott'm.
LEWERS   **T.**
1818 Sutton. Mary's Gate, Nott'm.
LODER, Thomas   **Ch.M.**
1841 C. Wellow (age 60)
LONGMAN, Sam   **T.**
1832 W. 19 New St., Nott'm.
1834 Dearden. 19 New St., Nott'm.
LORRIMAN, George   **Ch.M.**
1854 Wr. 27 Markergate, Nott'm.
LOVERSUCH   **T.**
1818 Sutton. Kington Ct., Nott'm.
1832 W. Mansfield Rd., Nott'm.
1834 Dearden. Trim Ct., Nott'm.
LYMAN (LYMN), George   **W.T.**
1851 C. Millgate, Newark (age 36)
1861 C. 52 Millgate, Newark (age 46)
1871 C. 47 Millgate, Newark (age 56)
LYMAN (LYMN), William   **W.T.**
1861 C. Millgate, Newark (age 22)
MARLOW, Joseph   **Ch.M.**
1881 C. Kilton Rd., Worksop (age 28)
MEADOWS, S.   **Ch.M.**
1818 Sutton. Mount St., Nott'm.
1825 G. Mount St., Nott'm.
1832 W. Mount St., Nott'm.
1840 O.R. Leanside, Nott'm.
MEADOWS & SON
    Ch.M. (Fancy & Windsor)
1819 P. Rout St., Nott'm.
1822 P. Nott'm.
MILES, Will   **Ch.M.**
1819 P. Balderton Gate, Newark
1832 Balderton Gate, Newark
1843 Balderton Gate, Newark
MILLS, J.   **W.T.**
1853 W. Kirkgate, Newark
MILLS, John   **W.T.**
1871 C. 11 Province Ct., Nott'm.
    (age 33)
MITCHELL, John   **Ch.M.**
1812 F.H.S. Nott'm.
1815 Will. Garness Hill, Nott'm.
1818 Sutton. Garness Hill, Nott'm.
1819 P. Butcher St., Nott'm.
1825 G. Garners Hill, Nott'm.
1828 F.H.S. Nott'm.
MOORE, William   **Ch.M.**
1871 C. 49 Marple St., Nott'm. (age 14)
MOSS   **T.**
1818 Sutton. North St., Nott'm.
MOSS, George   **Ch.M.**
1841 C. Bridge St., Worksop (age 30)
1843 Bridge St., Worksop
MOSS, James   **Ch.M.**
1841 C. Gateford Rd., Worksop (age 58)
MOSS & ALSOP   **Ch.M.**
1832 W. Potter St., Worksop
MUK(?), James   **Ch.M.**
1841 C. Newark (age 25)
MURRAY, Joseph   **W.T.**
1861 C. Abbey St., Worksop (age 34)
MYERS, P.   **T.**
1832 W. Pelham St., Nott'm.
NARTAGE, James   **Ch.M.**
1876 K. 10 Clumber St., Nott'm.

NEALE, George   **Ch.M.**
1861 C. Potter St., Worksop (age 51)
NEEDLE, James   **Ch.M.**
1871 C. 60 Curzon St., Nott'm.
    (Boarder) (age 56)
NEWELL, James   **Ch.M.**
1822 P. Nott'm.
NICHOLSON, George   **Ch.M.**
1832 W. Rockley
1841 C. Rockley
NICHOLSON, John   **Ch.M.**
1851 C. Lodging with John Stocks,
    Lowtown, Worksop (age 30)
NICHOLSON, Thomas   **W.T.**
1785 Will. South Collingham
NICHOLSON, William   **Ch.M.**
1841 C. Balderton Gate, Newark
    (age 50)
1851 C. (Ch.T. & lodging house keeper)
    (age 61)
NICKELS, John   **Ch.M.**
1876 K. 126 Stockwell Gate, Mansfield
NORMAN, Aaron   **W.T.**
1861 C. Worksop (age 33)
NORTON, Roderick   **W.T.**
1853 W. Lockside, Newark
NULL (NUTT), Thomas   **Ch.M.**
1861 C. Church Gate, East Retford
    (age 37)
1871 C. East Retford (age 45)
NUTT (see Muk), James   **Ch.M.**
1848 York St., Newark
1853 W. Balderton Gate, Newark
1861 C. Balderton Gate, Newark (age 50)
1864 K. (W.T.) Balderton Gate, Newark
1876 K. Balderton Gate, Newark
1871 C. Balderton Gate, Newark (age 60)
1874 Wr. Balderton Gate, Newark
NUTT, Thomas   **W.T.**
1874 Wr. 9 Balderton Gate, Newark
PACEY, James   **T.**
1861 C. Mill Lane, Newark (age 51)
PALMER, John   **Ch.M.**
1841 C. Wellow (age 24)
PARKER, John   **T.**
1832 W. 50 Barker Gate, Nott'm.
1834 Dearden. 50 Barker Gate, Nott'm.
PAYNE, James   **Ch.M.**
1841 C. Retford (age 35)
1843 St. John St., Retford
PERVIL, Thomas   **W.T.**
1871 C. 14 Poplar St., Nott'm. (age 14)
PHEASEY (PHESEY), Edward **W.T.**
1871 C. 30 Hawkridge St., Nott'm.
    (age 14)
1888 K. 70 Alfred St., Nott'm.
1891 K. 22 Robin Hood St., Nott'm.
PHILLIPS, John   **Ch.M.**
1881 C. Rock Cott., Cheapside,
    Worksop (age 20)
PLUMBRIDGE, James   **Ch.M.**
1841 C. Wellow (age 45)
POGSON, William   **Ch.M. (Windsor)**
1851 C. Norfolk St., Worksop (age 23)
1861 C. 17 Castle St., Worksop (age 33)
1871 C. 3 South Cotts., Worksop
    (age 43)
1881 C. Cheapside, Worksop (age 53)
PORTER, John   **Ch.M.**
1840 O.R. Sheridan St., Nott'm.
PRATT?   **Ch.M.& T.**
1719 F.H.S. Holme
PREETON, Henry   **W.T.**
1881 C. Worksop (age 47)
PRICE, William   **W.T.**
1864 W. Parkinson St., Nott'm.
PROCTOR, Henry   **W.T.**
1871 C. Kilton St., Worksop (age 37)
PRUDEN, John   **Pol.**
1871 C. 53 Cheapside, Worksop (son of
    Robert) (age 17)
PRUDEN, Robert   **Ch.M.**
1841 C. Wellow (age 20)
1851 C. Wellow (age 31)
1861 C. Cheapside, Worksop (C.T.)
    (age 41)
1871 C. Cheapside (Ch.M.) (age 51)
1881 C. Worksop (Ch.Pol.) (age 61)
PRUDEN (PRUDENCE), Sam **Ch.M.**
1841 C. Wellow (age 30)
1843 Wellow
1848 Wellow
1851 C. Wellow (age 42)
PRUDEN, Thomas   **Ch.M.**
1841 C. Wellow (age 15)
PYE, Thomas   **W.T.**
1874 Wr. Victoria St., Mansfield
1876 K. Victoria St., Mansfield
RADFORD, Thomas   **Ch.M.**
1871 C. 6 Warren Ct., Nott'm. (age 29)

RAINES, George   **Ch.M.**
1861 C. Lodger at Red Lion, Wellow
    (age 40)
RALPH, John   **Ch.M.**
1832 W. (& Victualler). Wellow
1843 Wellow
REY, Walter   **Ch.M.**
1871 C. 17 Cathcart St., Nott'm.
    (age 17)
RICHARDS, Arthur   **Ch.M.**
1871 C. 8 Ivy Row, Nott'm. (age 35)
RICHARDSON, Henry   **Ch.M.**
1861 C. 26 Union St., Worksop (age 24)
RICHARDSON & CROFTS   **Ch.M.**
1848 Wellow
RIDALE, Robert   **Ch.M.**
1841 C. North Collingham (age 79)
RILEY, Will   **W.T.**
1871 C. Lodger at Poplar Sq., Nott'm.
    (age 53)
RING, Michael   **Ch.M.**
1861 C. 39, Norfolk St., Worksop
    (age 25)
RIPPON, Will.   **W.T.**
1871 C. 17 Warren Ct., Nott'm.
    (age 21)
ROBINSON, George   **Ch.M.**
1871 C. 15 Rippon's Pl., Nott'm.
    (age 17)
ROCLIFF, Ellis   **Ch.M.**
1841 C. Wellow (age 28)
ROGERS, Sam   **T.**
1836 Indenture App. to John Hibbert,
    Newark
ROGERS, William   **W.T.**
1861 C. St. Martins La., Newark
    (age 45)
1871 C. St. Marks La., Newark (age 55)
ROPPIN, John   **W.T.**
1871 C. 21 Union St., Nott'm. (age 27)
ROWLAND, William   **T.**
1841 C. Worksop (age 25)
1881 C. East Gate, Worksop (age 66)
RUSHWORTH, William   **Ch.M.**
1835 F.H.S. Nott'm.
1843 New Lenton, Nott'm.
RUTHERFORD, John   **W.T.**
1871 C. 23 Lomas Yd., Nott'm. (age 22)
SANDAGE, Peter   **Ch.M.**
1832 W. Old Sun Yd., Retford
SANDERSON, Henry   **T.**
1841 C. Beardsall's Row, Retford
    (age 21)
SANDERSON, James   **Ch.M.& T.**
1830 F.H.S. (Saunderson) Turn La.,
    Retford
1832 W. Turn La., Retford
1841 C. East Retford (age 47)
1848 Retford (Ch.M.)
1851 C. Beardsells Row, Retford (as
    Master T.& Ch.M.) (age 57)
1861 C. Retford (W.T.) (age 67)
1864 K. (& Son) Beardsell's Row,
    Retford
SANDERSON, John   **T.**
1851 C. Retford (age 13)
1861 C. Beardsell's Row, Retford
    (age 23)
1871 C. Beardsell's Row, Retford
    (age 33)
1876 K. Beardsell's Row, Retford
1881 K. Beardsell's Row, Retford
1888 K. Beardsell's Row, Retford
1891 K. Beardsell's Row, Retford
SANDERSON, William   **Ch.M.**
1848 L. & H. Retford
1851 C. Retford (age 27)
SANSOM, Ben   **W.T.**
1871 C. 5 King St., Nott'm. (age 30)
1881 K. Woolpack La., Nott'm.
1888 K. 27 Woolpack La., Nott'm.
1891 K. 25, 29 Woolpack La., Nott'm.
SANSOM, Richard   **Ch.M.**
1828 F.H.S. Stockwellgate, Mansfield
1832 W. Stockwellgate, Mansfield
1843 Stockwellgate, Mansfield
SANSOM, Thomas   **Ch.M.**
1832 W. Rose Court, Mansfield
1843 Church St., Mansfield
SANSOM, William   **Ch.M.**
1832 W. Market, Warsop
SAXTON, Honers   **Ch.M.**
1848 L. & H. Greasley
SAXTON, W.   **Ch.M.**
1888 K. Beauvale Newthorpe, Nott'm.
1891 K. Beauvale Newthorpe, Nott'm.
SCATTERGOOD, Henry   **W.T.**
1871 C. Poplar St., Nott'm. (age 18)
SEALES, Luke   **Ch.M.**
1871 C. 117 Alfred St., Nott'm. (age 28)

SENIOR, Thomas   **Ch.M.**
1848 Talbot Yd., Nott'm.
1850 S. Talbot Yd., Nott'm.
1854 Wr. Long Row, Nott'm.
SHACKLETON ?   **Ch.M.& T.**
1715 F.H.S. Newark
SHARP, Sam   **Ch.M.**
1832 W. Park St., Worksop
SHARP, Sam   **W.T.**
1871 C. 13 Lake Yd., Nott'm. (age 20)
SHAW, John   **Ch.M.**
1851 C. Worksop (age 24)
1861 C. Carlton Rd., Worksop
SHAW, Will   **W.T.**
1871 C. 2 Mount Sq., Nott'm. (age 38)
SHAW, William   **Ch.M.**
1854 Notts. Crossland St., Leanside,
    Nott'm.
SHERATON, Ralph   **T.**
1832 W. Derby Rd., Nott'm.
1840 F.H.S. Nott'm.
SIMPSON, G. Snr.   **Ch.M.**
1841 C. Lowtown, Worksop (age 15)
1851 C. Lowtown Sth., Worksop (age 28)
SIMPSON, George Jnr.   **Ch.M.**
1861 C. Cheapside, Worksop (age 16)
1871 C. Worksop (age 26)
SIMPSON, Stephen   **W.T.**
1871 C. 6 Norton St., Nott'm. (age 21)
SIMPSON, Thomas   **Ch.M.**
1841 C. Lowtown, Worksop (age 20)
1861 C. Cheapside, Worksop (age 42)
1871 C. Gear Hill Rd., Worksop
    (age 52)
SIMPSON, Thomas   **W.T.**
1832 W. Westgate, Mansfield
SKELTON, William   **T.**
1832 W. Toll St., Nott'm.
SLACK, Will   **W.T.& Ch.M.**
1861 C. 93 Kilton Rd., Worksop
    (age 46)
SMART, Francis   **Ch.M.**
1838 F.H.S. Nott'm.
SMART, Thomas   **Ch.M.**
1814 F.H.S. Nott'm.
1815 Will. Red Lion Sq., Nott'm.
1818 Sutton. Butcher St., Nott'm.
1822 P. Nott'm.
1825 G. Red Lion Sq., Nott'm.
1832 W. Fishergate, Nott'm.
1834 Dearden (CAB & T.), Nott'm.
SMART, Sarah   **Ch.M.**
1840 O.R. Nott'm.
1843 Fishergate
1844 W. Fishergate
1848 L. & H. Fishergate
1850 S. 28 Fishergate, Nott'm.
SMITH, Charles   **Ch.M.**
1841 C. Wellow (age 30)
SMITH, George   **W.T.**
1871 C. Worksop (age 18)
1881 C. Kilton Rd., Worksop (age 28)
SMITH, Graham   **Ch.M.**
1851 C. Wellow (age 58)
SMITH, Jonathon   **Ch.M.**
1841 C. Wellow (age 48)
SMITH, Kiddale   **W.T.**
1881 C. Kilton Rd., Worksop (age 24)
SMITH, William   **Ch.M. (Windsor)**
1848 Retford
1861 C. Moorgate, Retford (age 35)
1864 K. Moorgate, Retford
1876 K. Moorgate, Retford
1881 K. Moorgate, Retford
1888 K. Moorgate, Retford
1891 K. Moorgate, Retford
SMITH, William   **Ch.M.**
1841 C. (App. to G. Nicholson) Rockley
    (age 15)
1853 W. Rockley
SOAR, John   **T.**
1832 W. Pearl Yd., Nott'm.
SPENCER, John   **W.T.**
1871 C. 18 Poplar Sq., Nott'm.
    (age 18)
SPRIGGS, Sam   **Ch.M.**
1841 C. Worksop (age 20)
SQUIRES, James   **Ch.M.**
1841 C. Guildhall St., Newark
    (age 25)
SQUIRES, Will. Snr.   **Ch.Mkr.**
1841 C. George St., Newark (age 60)
1848 George St., Newark
STAINTON (STENTON), John Snr.
    Ch.M.
1851 C. Eastgate, Worksop (age 44)
STAINTON (STENTON), John Jnr.
    Ch.M.
1851 C. Lodger, Worksop (age 21)

INDEX

Leicestershire & Rutland continued

BUCKLEY, William   T.
1888 K. 60 Church Gt., Leicester
1891 K. 18 Erskin St. and Lower Hill St., Leicester
BURWELL, John   T.
1835 P. Warf St., Leicester
BURWELL, Thomas   T.
1835 P. Warf St., Leicester
BUTLIN, Thomas   T.
1841 P. Back St., Melton Mowbray
CANT, James   Ch.M.& T.
1835 P. High St., Uppingham, Rutland
CANT, R.   Ch.M.
1843 Tr. Dir. Leicester
CANT, Robert J.   Ch.M.
1841 P. High St., Uppingham, Rutland
1843 Tr. Dir. High St., Uppingham
1846 W. High St., Uppingham (& T.)
1851 S. High St., Uppingham
1864 K. High St., Uppingham
CARRINGTON, John   T.
1841 P. Canning St., Leicester
CATTELL, S.   W.T.
1864 K. Baxtergate, Loughborough
1876 K. Baxtergate, Loughborough
1881 K. Baxtergate, Loughborough
1888 K. Baxtergate, Loughborough
1891 K. Baxtergate, Loughborough
CATTELL, Thomas   T.
1846 W. 120 Belgrave Gt., Leicester
1851 S. 120 Belgrave Gt., Leicester
1861 Drake. 156 Belgrave Gt., Leicester
CHETTLE, John   W.T.
1881 K. Bargate, Castle Donington
CLAXTON, Sam   CAB & Ch.M.
1822 P. Wisbeach, Rutland
CLEMENTS, John   Ch.M.
1808-15 F.H.S. Leicester
CLEMENTS, John Jnr.   Ch.M.
1826-40 F.H.S. Leicester
1846 W. Town Hall La., Leicester
CLEMENTS, Joseph   T.
1835 P. High Cross St., Leicester (Ch.M.)
1841 P. Cart La., Leicester
1861 Drake. 32 High Cross St., Leicester
1864 K. 32 High Cross St., Leicester
1876 K. 43 Sanvey St., Leicester
CLEMENTS, Williams   T.
1888 K. 32 High Cross St. & 19 Thornton, Leicester (see Clements & Son)
1891 K. 32 High Cross St.
CLEMENTS & SON   W.T.
1876 K. 32 High Cross St., Leicester
COOK, Thomas   Ch.M.
1835 P. Adam & Eve St., Market Harborough
1841 P. Adam & Eve St., Market Harborough (& T.)
1843 Leics. Dir. Adam & Eve St., Market Harborough
COWPER, John   T.
1835 P. Old Bond St., Leicester
1841 P. East Bond St., Leicester
1846 W. New Bond St., Leicester
COWPER, Nathaniel A.   T.
1861 Drake. Burley's La., Leicester
COX, John   W.T.
1881 K. 65 Royal East St., Leicester
CRAIG, Henry   W.T.
1891 K. 23 Wanlip St., Leicester
CURTIS, John & Son   CAB & Ch.M.
1822 P. Wisbeach, Rutland
CURTIS, Thomas   CAB & Ch.M.
1822 P. Wisbeach, Rutland
DARNELL, Joseph   T.
1835 P. Northampton St., Leicester
1841 P. Northampton St., Leicester
DEACON, William   T.
1851 S. Victoria, Oakham, Rutland
DEACON, W.   W.T.
1861 Drake. 48 Belgrave Gate, Leicester
1864 K. 8 Hill St., Leicester
DEWBERRY, Thomas   T.
1841 P. Mill St., Loughborough
1846 W. Mill St., Loughborough
1851 S. Ward's End, Loughborough
ELLIOTT, John   Ch.M.
1713 F.H.S. Leicester
ELLIOTT, William   T.
1861 Drake. 20 Applegate St., Leicester
ELLIS, William   CAB & Ch.M.
1841 P. Belgrave Gate, Leicester
1846 W. Belgrave Gate, Leicester
1851 S. 11 Belgrave Gate, Leicester
1861 Drake. 13 Belgrave Gate, Leicester

EXTON, John   Ch.M.
1835 P. Hallaton
1841 P. Hallaton
1843 Leics. Dir. Hallaton
1846 W. Hallaton
1851 S. Hallaton
1864 K. Hallaton
FARMER, E.   Ch.M.& T.
1822 P. Ashby de la Zouch
1835 P. Church St., Ashby de la Zouch
1841 P. Lower Church St., Ashby de la Zouch
1846 W. Bath St., Ashby de la Zouch
1851 S. Bath St., Ashby de la Zouch
1864 K. Bath St., Ashby de la Zouch
1876 K. Kilwardby St., Ashby de la Zouch
1881 K. Kilwardby St., Ashby de la Zouch
1888 K. Kilwardby St., Ashby de la Zouch
1891 K. Kilwardby St., Ashby de la Zouch
FARMER, J.   W.T.
1876 K. Market St., Ashby de la Zouch
1881 K. Market St., Ashby de la Zouch
1891 K. The Green, Ashby de la Zouch
FARMER, Richard   Ch.M.
1795 F.H.S. Loughborough
FEWKES, Joseph   T.
1784 F.H.S. Leicester
FINDLEY, William   CAB & Ch.M.
1835 P. Up. Charles St., Leicester
1841 P. Rutland St., Leicester
1846 W. Colton St., Leicester
1851 S. King St., Leicester
1861 Drake. 6 Free School La., Leicester
FOX, Joseph   T.
1835 P. Northgate St., Leicester
1841 P. Applegate St., Leicester
FOXTON, James   W.T.
1876 K. Leicester St., Uppingham
FROST, Thomas   W.T.
1876 K. Andrew St., Leicester
1881 K. Andrew St., Leicester
1888 K. Andrew St., Leicester
GASKELL, Thomas   Ch.M.
1835 P. Castle Donnington
1851 S. Castle Donnington
GEE, George   Ch.M.
1835 P. Mountsorrell
1841 P. Mountsorrell
1843 Leic. Tr. Dir. Mountsorrell
1851 S. Mountsorrell
GIEHR, Robert   W.T.
1891 K. 15 Kate St., Leicester
GILBERT, Thomas   Ch.M.
1790 Univ. Ashby de la Zouch
1791 Barfoot & Wilkes. Ashby de la Zouch
GILBERT, William   Ch.M.
1790 Univ. Ashby de la Zouch
1791 B. & F. Ashby de la Zouch
GIMSON, Benjamin   T.
1841 P. Welford Rd., Leicester
GOSLING, John   Ch.M.
1861 Drake. 1 Caroline St., Leicester
GRANT, J.   T.
1822 P. Belgrave Gt., Leicester
GREEN, Joseph   CAB & Ch.M.
1818 P. Leicester
1822 P. High Cross St., Leicester
1835 P. High Cross St, Leicester
1846 W. High Cross St., Leicester
1851 S. High Cross St., Leicester
1861 Drake. High Cross St., Leicester
GREEN, Joshua   Ch.M.
1822 F.H.S. Leicester
GREEN, W.   W.T.
1864 K. 35 Gravel La., Leicester
GROOCOCK, James   T.
1835 P. Welford St., Leicester
1841 P. Welford St., Leicester
HADDON, William   Ch.M.& T.
1790 F.H.S. Hinkley
1822 P. Castle St., Hinkley
1829 F.H.S. Hinkley
HALES, William   T.
1841 P. Bakehouse La., Lutterworth
1851 S. High St., Lutterworth
HALFPENNY, George   CAB & Ch.M.
1861 Drake. 25 Church Gate, Leicester
HALFPENNY, Joseph   Ch.M.
1822 P. Belgrave Gate, Leicester
1828 F.H.S. Leicester
HARLEY, James   T.
1835 P. Belgrave St., Leicester
HARRIS, Ralph   T.
1784 F.H.S. Mount Sorrell

HARRISON, Robert   CAB & Ch.M.
1822 P. Wisbeach, Rutland
HEADLEY, Edward   T.
1846 W. Church Gate, Leicester
1851 S. 99 Church Gate, Leicester
HENSON, Cornelius   Ch.M.
1841 P. Belgrave Gate, Leicester
1843 Leic. Tr. Dir. Belgrave Gate, Leicester
1846 W. Church Gate, Leicester
1848 Tr. Dir. Church Gate, Leicester
1851 W. Church Gate, Leicester
HIGGINS, Charles   Ch.M.& T.
1829 F.H.S. Ashby de la Zouch
1846 W. Kilwardby St., Ashby de la Zouch
1851 S. Ashby de la Zouch
HIND, W.   T.
1822 F.H.S. Market Harborough
HODGES, Thomas   T.
1846 W. Belvoir St., Leicester
1851 S. Church Gate, Leicester
HOLLAND, Sarah   T.
1861 Drake. Barston St., Leicester
HOLLAND & ROGERS   W.T.
1861 Drake. Painter St., Belgrave Rd., Leicester
1864 K. Painter St., Belgrave Rd., Leicester
HOLMES, Thomas   Ch.M.
1835 P. Northampton St., Leicester
HUDSON, J.F.   Ch.M.
1864 K. Bottesford
JACKSON, John   Ch.M.& T.
1835 P. High St., Uppingham, Rutland
1841 P. High St., Uppingham, Rutland
1843 Tr. Dir. High St., Uppingham
1846 W. High St., Uppingham
1864 K. High St., Uppingham
JEE, George   Ch.M.& T.
1822 P. Mount Sorrell
JEE, Samuel   Ch.M.& T.
1787 F.H.S. Mount Sorrell
JEFFS, Henry   Ch.M.
1846 W. East Bond St., Leicester
1851 S. East Bond St., Leicester (CAB)
JOHNSON, Joseph   T.
1861 Drake. Gas St., Leicester
KING, Daniel   T.
1790 Univ. Loughborough
KING, William   T.
1790 Univ. Loughborough
KIRK, William   W.T.
1891 K. Frog Isle, Leicester
KISBEE, George   T.
1846 W. Tinwell, Rutland
KNOTT, Thomas   T.
1822 P. Bond St., Leicester
LANGHAM, William   T.
1822 P. Melton Mowbray
1841 P. Nott'm St., Melton Mowbray
1851 S. Nott'm St., Melton Mowbray
LEWIN, William   T.
1841 P. Colton St., Leicester
LODGE, Thomas   T.
1861 Drake. 14 Church Gate, Leicester
LOVETT, George   Ch.M.
1876 K. 276 Birstall St., Leicester
1881 K. 65 Upper Brunswick St.
1888 K. 65 Upper Brunswick St.
1891 K. 65 Upper Brunswick St.
MADDER, J.   W.T.
1861 Drake. 2 West Bond St., Leicester
1864 K. 2 West Bond St., Leicester
1876 K. 772 Humberstone Gate, Leicester
1888 K. Upper Brunswick St., Leicester
1891 K. Upper Brown St., Leicester
MEADOWS, John   Ch.M.
1827-28 F.H.S. Leicester
MEIGH, W.   Ch.M.& W.T.
1851 S. Upper Bond St., Huckley
1864 K. Upper Bond St., Huckley
MOON, J.   W.T.
1876 K. Kenyon St., Leicester
MOORE, Charles   T.
1846 W. 169 Belgrave Gate, Leicester
MOORE, John   T.
1835 P. Colton St., Leicester
1841 P. Colton St., Leicester
1846 W. 28 Cotton St., Leicester
1861 Drake. 32 Colton St., Leicester
MOORE, J.   T.
1891 K. 4 Edward St., Leicester
MOORE, William   Ch.M.
1815 F.H.S. Leicester
1822 P. Yeoman St., Leicester
1846 W. Syston, Leicester
1848 Tr. Dir. Syston, Leicester

1876 K. Cramp St., Syston
1881 K. Cramp St., Syston
MORRIS, William   W.T.
1876 K. Castle Donington
MOY, John   CAB & Ch.M.
1822 P. Wisbeach, Rutland
MUSTON, John   CAB & T.
1851 S. The Borough, Hinkley
NEWBURY, Richard   T.
1822 P. Ashby de la Zouch
1835 P. Derby St., Ashby de la Zouch
NICHOLES, Charles   CAB & Ch.M.
1822 P. Wisbeach, Rutland
NORMAN, John   T.
1835 P. Husbands, Bosworth
PAINTER, William   T.
1835 P. Bakehouse La., Lutterworth
PEARSON & TOMPSON   W.T.
1864 K. 33 Bedford St., Leicester
PEGG, Amos   W.T.
1881 K. Mill St., Loughborough
PEGG, George   T.
1822 P. Mill St., Loughborough
1846 W. Churchgate, Loughborough
1851 S. Fennel St., Loughborough
PEGG, James   T.
1888 K. Clapgun St., Castle Donington
PEGG, Jap   W.T.
1888 K. 8 Mill St., Loughborough
1891 K. 8 Mill St., Loughborough
PEGG, John   Ch.M.
1835 P. Castle Donington
1841 P. Castle Donington
1843 L. Dir. Castle Donington
1846 W. Apesgate, Castle Donington
1851 S. Apesgate, Castle Donington
1876 K. Castle Donington
PEGG, John   W.T.
1846 W. Mill St., Loughborough (Ch.M.& T.)
1851 S. Mill St., Loughborough
1876 K. Mill St., Loughborough
PEGG, John   T.
1888 K. Packington Hill, Kegworth
1891 K. Packington Hill, Kegworth
PEGG, Joseph   T.
1822 P. Church Gate, Loughborough
1835 P. Church Gate, Loughborough
PEGG, Joseph   W.T.
1876 K. Kegworth
PEGG, William   T.
1822 P. Mill St., Loughborough
1835 P. Mill St., Loughborough
1841 P. Mill St., Loughborough
1854 Will. Leic. Rec. Off.
PEGG, William   Ch.M.
1841 P. Kegworth
1843 L. Dir. Kegworth
1851 S. Kegworth (& T.)
1876 K. Kegworth
PEGG, William   Ch.M.
1840 F.H.S. Castle Donington
PERRY, William   W.T.
1888 K. Nott'm St., Melton Mowbray
POTTER, William   Ch.M.
1841 P. Belgrave Gate, Leicester
1843 Leic. Dir. Belgrave Gate, Leicester
POWELL, C.   Ch.M.
1848 Tr. Dir. St. Nicholas St., Leicester
1851 S. St. Nicholas St., Leicester (CAB)
1861 Drake. 6 St. Nick's St., Leicester
POWELL, Joseph   Ch.M.
1828 F.H.S. Leicester
POWELL, William George   CAB & Ch.M.
1835 P. Belgrave Gate, Leicester
POWERS, Edmund   Ch.M.
1746-52 F.H.S. High St., Leicester
PRESTON, John   T.
1861 Drake. 62 Churchgate, Leicester
PRESTON, Thomas   T.
1835 P. Eaton St., Leicester
PUDDIFER, Joseph   Ch.M.
1861 Drake. 22 East Bond St., Leicester
RAWSON, William   T.
1835 P. Churchgate, Leicester
1841 P. Churchgate
READ, Susannah   T.
1835 P. St. Nicholas St., Leicester
REYNOLDS, William   Ch.M.& T.
1835 P. High St., Uppingham, Rutland
RIMMINGTON, John   T.
1851 S. Quorndon, Loughborough
ROBINSON, Jonathan   T.
1835 P. Angel Yd., High St., Leicester
1841 S. Freeschool La., Leicester
1846 W. Freeschool La., Leicester
1851 S. Freeschool La., Leicester

INDEX

Cornwall continued

NODDER, W. & J.   T.
1856 K. Church La., Truro
1873 K. 2 Church La., Truro (W. only)
1883 K. 2 Church La., Truro
PHILLIPS & NANCARROW
    T. & Carvers
1847 Williams. Penryn St., Redruth
POLKINGTON, John   T.
1830 P. Green Mkt., Penzance
ROWE, Mark   T.
1823 P. 18 Boscawen St., Truro
SALTER, John   T. & Carver
1847 Williams. Fore St., Redruth
SCANTLEBURY, John   T.
1873 K. Hessenford, St. Germans
1883 K. Hessenford, St. Germans
SMITH, Frederick   Ch.M.
1902 K. 49 Calnick St., Truro
SOLOMAN, Richard   T.
1873 K. Dean St., Liskard
TARR, N.   T.
1856 K. Pydar St., Truro
1873 K. Pydar St., Truro
1883 K. Jobs Crt., Pydar St., Truro
TREBILOCK, Richard   Ch.M.
1798 F.H.S. Truro
WHALE, H.   Ch.M.
1856 K. Trewint, Alternun, Launceston
1873 K. Trewint, Alternun, Launceston
1883 K. Trewint, Alternun, Launceston
1889 K. Trewint, Alternun, Launceston
WHALE, Thomas   Ch.M.
1862 Billings. Alternun, Launceston
WHETFORD, Philip   T.
1830 P. Moon's Row, Truro
WHITFORD, Philip   T.
1830 P. Moon's Row, Truro

Devon

AGLAND, Edwin   Ch.M.
1861 C. Uffculme
1871 C. Uffculme
ALGAR, John   Ch.M.
1827 F.H.S. Died. Plymouth
ALGAR, William & Son   Ch.M.
1814-23 F.H.S. Plymouth
1823 P. 11 Cornwall St., Plymouth
AMERY, John   W.T.
1830 P. Bampton St., Tiverton
ANTHONY, Robert   Ch.M.
1850 W. Morley Pl., Plymouth
1856 K. 5 Raleigh St., Plymouth
ANTHONY, William   Ch.M.
1850 W. Richmond St., Plymouth
AVIS, Thomas   Ch.M.
1850 W. Kingswear
BECK, David   T.
1823 P. St. Peters St., Tiverton
1830 P. St. Peters St., Tiverton
BEER, William   Ch.M.
1851 C. Sharland Row, Holcombe Rogus
BELL, E.   Ch.M.
1862 Billings. 34 Russel St., Plymouth
BEWS, John   T.
1830 P. Hatherleigh
BLACKWELL & SON   Ch.M.
1902 20 Cross St., Barnstaple
BODDINGTON, S.   Ch.M.
1856 K. Jessima La., Devonport
BRAY, John   T.
1823 P. Morice St., Plymouth
BROWN, William   Ch.M.
1850 W. 14 Hr. Batter St., Plymouth
BURD, James   T.
1823 P. Paul St., Exeter
1830 P. Paul St., Exeter
BURNAFORD, Thomas   Ch.M.
1751 F.H.S. Exeter
CARTER, G.   Ch.M.
1883 K. 12 Lower Middon St., Bideford
1889 K. Lower Meddow St., Bideford
    (Ch.caner)
1893 K. Lower Meddow St., Bideford
1897 K. Lower Meddow St., Bideford
CHAMBERS, Henry   Ch.M.
1832 R.O. Yealmpton
CHAMBERS, John   CARP.
1841 C. Newton Ferrers
CHAMBERS, Thomas   Ch.M.
1803 P.R. Married. Yealmpton (Carp.)
1841 C. Yealmpton
1844 P. Yealmpton
1851 C. Yealmpton
CHANNON, Otho   Ch.M.
1698-1756 F.H.S. Exeter

CHURLEY, Robert   W.T.
1830 P. Bampton St., Tiverton
CLARKE, Charles   Ch.M.
1851 C. 151 Golden Hill, Holcombe
  Rogus (age 17)
COTTERALL, Charles   Ch.M.
1871 C. Holcombe Rogus
COTTERALL, Richard   Ch.M.
1861 C. Twitchet Cott., Holcombe
  Rogus (age 14)
COTTERALL, Thomas   Ch.M.
1841 C. Holcombe Rogus
1851 C. 73 Twitchens, Holcombe Rogus
1861 C. Twitchens Cott., Holcombe
  Rogus
COOK, John   Ch.M.
1850 W. 7 Phoenix St., Devonport
COOK, Richard   Ch.M.
1850 W. Morley La., Plymouth
CRADDOCK, William   Ch.Repairer
1902 K. 135 King St., Plymouth
CRICK, William   Ch.M.
1841 C. Holcombe Rogus
1851 C. 61 Golden Hill, Holcombe Rogus
DAVEY, James   Ch.M.
1829 P.R. Bapt. children. Westleigh,
  Burlescombe
1831 P.R. Bapt. children. Westleigh,
  Burlescombe
EAST, John   Ch.M.
1784 F.H.S. Exeter
EGFORD, W.H.   Ch.M.
1873 Ply. Dir. 1 Vennel St., Plymouth
ELLIS, Thomas   Ch.M.
1830 P. 104 James St., Plymouth
1850 W. 4 James St., Plymouth
ENDICOTT, John   Ch.M.
1819-24 F.H.S. Exeter
EVANS, William   Ch.M.
1851 C. 55 Golden Hill, Holcombe Rogus
EVERY, James   Ch.M.
1838 F.H.S. Devonport
1844 P. 43 Marlborough St., Devonport
1850 W. 42 Marlborough St., Devonport
EYRES, John   Ch.M.
1791 F.H.S. Exeter
FANE, Edwin   Ch.M.
1881 C. Yealmpton
FLORIDA, C.S.   Ch.M.
1866 K. 158 King St., Plymouth
1871 Tyrhall. Plymouth
1882 Eyre. Plymouth
FOSTER, John   Ch.M.
1822 E.P.J. West Quarter, Exeter
1823-24 P. West Quarter, Exeter
1827 P. West Quarter, Exeter
1833, 34, 36 as above
1838 P. Spicers Cott., Forest Hill
1841 P. Fore St. Hill
1846 P. Fore St. Hill
1856 P. West Gate Quarter
1860 P. West Quarter
FOSTER, John   Ch.M.
1831-46 Marshall, Exe Island (then as
  CAB in Bartholomew St.)
FROST, Richard   Ch.M.& CAB
1823 P. Cullompton
1830 P. Cullompton
1841 C. Fore St., Cullompton (age 50)
GALE, George   Ch.M.
1830 P. Bampton Tiverton
1856 K. Bampton Tiverton
1866 Bampton Tiverton
GILLEY, G.   Ch.M.
1856 K. High St., Sidmouth
GORDEN, Richard   Ch.M.
1763-74 F.H.S. Exeter
GORMULLY, William   T.
1830 P. 63 Granby St., Devonport
GOSS, W.   Ch.M.
1856 K. 110 Bourport St., Barnstaple
1862 Billings. 110 Bourport St.,
  Barnstaple
1873 K. 108 Bourport St., Barnstaple
GOVER, Samuel & John   Ch.M.& T.
1823 P. Crediton
GRANT, James   Ch.M.
1841 C. Holcombe Rogus
1850 W. Holcombe Rogus
1851 C. Pound Hills, Holcombe Rogus
  (age 33)
GRANT, Thomas   Ch.M.
1851 C. 50 Golden Hill, Holcombe Rogus
GRANT, William   Ch.M.
1841 C. Holcombe Rogus (age 26)
GRANVILLE, Robert   T.
1830 P. 20 King St., Devonport
HALLET, William   W.T.
1830 P. Bridge Town, Totnes

HANSON, Samuel   Ch.M.
1851 C. Lower Head, Burlescombe
HARDING, William   Ch.M.
1851 C. Burlescombe
HARE, Catherine   Ch.M.
1838 F.H.S. Devonport
1844 P. 16 James St., Devonport
1850 W. 16 James St., Devonport
HARE, Richard   Ch.M.
1823-24 P. 17 James St., Devonport
1830 P. 16 & 17 James St., Devonport
HARE, William   Ch.M.
1836-38 F.H.S. Plymouth
HARPER (or HOOPER), Thomas
                    Ch.M.
1861 C. Uffculme
HARRIS, William   Ch.M.
1798 Univ. Ottery St. Mary
1830 P. Younder St., St. Mary
HATCHARD, John   Ch.M.
1841 C. Holcombe Rogus
HEARSON, George & Charles   Ch.M.
1823 P. High St., Barnstaple
1830 P. Pitton High St., Barnstaple
  (George only)
HENSON, Dan   Ch.M.
1851 C. Uffculme
1871 C. Uffculme (Carp.)
HENSON, Robert   Ch.M.
1841 C. Uffculme
1851 C. Uffculme
1861 C. Uffculme
1871 C. Uffculme (Carp.)
HENSON, Sam   Ch.M.
1841 C. Maidenhead Cott., Burlescombe
HOLLAND, John   Ch.M.
1841 C. Uffculme
HOLLAND, John   Ch.M.
1841 C. Burlescombe
HOLLEY, John   W.T.
1851 C. Burlescombe
HOOPER, Charles   Ch.M.
1851 C. Twitchens, Holcombe Rogus
  (age 31)
1861 C. Holcombe Rogus
1871 C. Uffculme
HOOPER, Thomas   Ch.M.
1851 C. Burlescombe
1871 C. Uffculme
HORNE, Uriah   Ch.M.
1841 C. Little Westhall Cott., Appledore
HOWARD, Nathaniel   Ch.M.
1758 F.H.S. Plymouth
HUSBAND, Phillip   Ch.M.
1837 F.H.S. Yealmpton
JACOMB, George   W.T.
1830 P. Buckfastleigh
JONES, Henry   Ch.M.
1861 C. Holcombe Rogus
JONES, John   Ch.M.
1871 C. 31 South St., Holcombe Rogus
JONES, Richard   Ch.M.
1871 C. 31 South St., Holcombe Rogus
JUDD, Henry   Ch.M.
1881 C. Yealmpton
KERSLAKE, John   W.T.
1871 C. Tinswells Cott., Holcombe
  Rogus (age 16)
1881 C. Tinswells Cott., Holcombe
  Rogus
KERSLAKE, John   Ch.M.
1841 C. Holcombe Rogus
1851 C. Holcombe Rogus
1893 K. Holcombe Rogus
KERSLAKE, Thomas   Ch.M.
1851 C. Holcombe Rogus
1861 C. Holcombe Rogus
1871 C. Tinswells Cott.
1881 C. Tinswells Cott., Holcombe
  Rogus
KERSLAKE, Thomas Jnr.   Ch.M.
1861 C. Holcombe Rogus (age 16)
1871 C. Tinswells Cott.
1881 C. Holcombe Rogus
KEYS, Thomas   T.
1823 P. Bartholomew St., Exeter
1830 P. Bartholomew St., Exeter
KIMBER, William   Ch.M.
1844 P. King St., Plymouth
LANE, John   T.
1822 F.H.S. Devonport
1830 P. 27 Tavistock St., Devonport
LANE, William   Ch.M.
1841 C. Uffculme
LANGDON, John   Ch.M.
1808-12 F.H.S. Barnstaple
LASKEY, John   Ch.M.
1791-1811 F.H.S. Exeter
LAVERS, George   Ch.M.
1873 Plymouth

LAVERS, William   Ch.M.
1873 K. 58 Richmond St., Plymouth
  (listed until 1902 at same address)
1882 Eyre. Also at 10 Russell St.
1893-97 58 Richmond St., Plymouth
LAVERS, William & Henry   Ch.M.
1877 Tryhall. 58 Richmond St.,
  Plymouth
1885-93 at both addresses
LEACH, John   Ch.M.App.
1861 C. Holcombe Rogus
LEE, John & Co.   Ch.M.
1850 W. Bourport St. & Edgecombe Rd.,
  Barnstaple
LEIGH, T.   Ch.M.
1877 Tryhall. 45 Cecil St., Plymouth
LETHERBY, William   Ch.M.
1830 P. Molton
MACKEY, Richard   T.
1830 P. 26 New St., Devonport
MARCOMBE, John   T.
1830 P. 15 Queen St., Devonport
MARSHALL, James   Ch.M.
1831-40 F.H.S. Exeter
1831-46 Exe Island (then as CAB
  Bartholomew St., Exeter)
MARTIN, George   Ch.M.
1818-22 F.H.S. Lower North St., Exeter
MEAD, R.   Ch.M.
1899 Eyre. 58 Richmond St., Plymouth
MEDLAND, George   Ch.M.
1873 Ply. Dir. 23 Raleigh St., Plymouth
1877 Tryhall. 23 Raleigh St., Plymouth
1882 Eyre. 23 Raleigh St., Plymouth
MELHUISH, Edwin   T.
1836 F.H.S. Exeter
MILLMAN, William   Ch.M.
1811 Yealmpton
1812 Plymouth
MOGRIDGE, J.   Ch.M.
1856 K. Paignton
NOSWORTHY, John   Ch.M.
1844 P. Paignton
1856 K. Paignton
1862 Billings. Winner St., Paignton
OTTON, John   T.
1818-23 F.H.S. Exeter
1823 P. Preston St., Exeter
PADFORD, Henry   Ch.M.
1851 C. Burlescombe
PALFREY, Richard   Ch.M.
1830-38 F.H.S. Exmouth
PAPPS, Richard George   Ch.M.
1883 K. Bampton St., Tiverton
PAWLBY, John   T.
1823 P. Portland St., Plymouth
PAYNE, William   Ch.M.
1861 C. Fore St., Holcombe Rogus
1871 C. 6 Fore St., Holcombe Rogus
PERRY, James   Ch.M.
1841 C. Holcombe Rogus (age 35)
PHILLIPS, John   Ch.M.
1830 P. 96 James St., Devonport
1844 P. 95 James St., Devonport
1850 W. James St., Devonport
PICKARD, John   T.
1830 P. Silver St., Bideford
PILMAN, R.   T.
1823 P. Preston St., Exeter
1830 P. Preston St., Exeter
POCOCK, L.   Ch.M.
1829 F.H.S. Ottery St. Mary
POLESTON, Edward   Ch.M.
1836-38 F.H.S. Plymouth
POOLE, James   Ch.M.
1881 C. Fore St., Holcombe Rogus
POSLING, Fred.   Ch.M.App.
1881 C. Yealmpton
POTTER, Edward   Ch.M.
1851 C. 42 Pond Cl., Holcombe Rogus
PRIEST, Charles   Ch.M.
1881 C. Yealmpton
PULLISTON, Edward   Ch.M.
1830 P. 17 Green St., Plymouth
RADFORD, Henry   Ch.M.
1841 C. Uffculme
1850 W. Uffculme
1856 K. Uffculme
1861 C. Uffculme
1862 Billings. Appledore, Uffculme
1866-93 as above
RADFORD, Henry   Ch.M.
1861 C. Burlescombe (age 37)
RADFORD, John   Ch.M.App.
1861 C. Uffculme
RADFORD, William   Ch.M.
1841 C. Culmstock
RICE, Samuel   Ch.M.
1841 C. Little Westhill Cott.,
  Appledore

Herefordshire continued

GRIFFITHS, Jane   Ch.M.& T.
1850 S. Bridge St., Kington
1859 S. Bridge St., Kington
GRIFFITHS, Richard   Ch.M.& T.
1835 P. Bridge St., Kington
1840 Robson. Bridge St., Kington
GRIFFITHS, Thomas   Ch.M.& T.
1830 P. Kington
HALL, Henry   T.
1851 Lascelles. West St., Leominster
HALL, Thomas   Ch.M.& T.
1835 P. Bridge St., Kington
1840 Robson. Bridge St., Kington
1850 S. Bridge St., Kington
1851 Lascelles. Bridge St., Kington
1856 K. Bridge St., Kington
1858 Cassey. Bridge St., Kington
1859 S. Bridge St., Kington
HATTON, John   T.
1876 Littlebury. Duke St., Kington
1879 K. Duke St., Kington
1885 K. Duke St., Kington
1891 K. Duke St., Kington
HENRY, Roger   Ch.M.& T.
1847 Hunt. 45 Eign St., Hereford
HODGES, Richard   Ch.M.& T.
1830 F.H.S. Ledbury
1835 P. Homend, Ledbury
1847 Hunt. Homend, Ledbury
1851 Lascelles. Homend, Ledbury
1856 K. Homend, Ledbury
HUGHES, Henry   Ch.M.& T.
1830 P. Little Berrington St., Hereford
1840 Robson. Eign St., Hereford
1850 Lascelles. Eign St., Hereford
1856 K. Bewell St., Hereford
1858 Cassey. Bewell St., Hereford
1859 S. Bewell St., Hereford
JONES, Richard   T.
1900 K. Walford, Ross. See Sims & Jones
JUCKES, Charles   Ch.M.
1847 Hunt. High St., Ledbury
LEWIS, William   W.T.
1876 Littlebury. 7 West St., Hereford
MORRIS, William   Ch.M.
1851 Lascelles. Duke St., Kington
1856 K. Duke St., Kington
1858 Cassey. Duke St., Kington
1859 S. Duke St., Kington
1863 K. Duke St., Kington
NASH, James   Ch.M.& T.
1830 P. West St., Leominster
1835 P. West St., Leominster
1840 Robson. West St., Leominster
NELMES, James   W.T.
1876 Littlebury. Widemarsh, Hereford
1879 K. Widemarsh, Hereford
1885 K. Widemarsh, Hereford
1891 K. Widemarsh, Hereford
OAKLEY, George & Olive
  Ch.M.& T.
1859 S. New St., Ledbury
OAKLEY, Thomas   Ch.M.
1847 Hunt. New St., Ledbury
OWEN, James   Ch.M.
1822 P. Hereford
1830 P. Builts Bldgs., Hereford
1835 F.H.S. Hereford
PALMER, Benjamin   Ch.M.
1851 Lascelles. Shereford St., Bromyard
PARKER, Phillip   Ch.M.
1826 F.H.S. Hereford
PAYNE, S.   T.
1856 K. West Town, Leominster
PERKINS, Richard   Ch.M.
1754 F.H.S. Hereford
POOLE, William   W.T.
1879 K. Commercial Rd. Sawmills, Hereford
RUSBATCH, John   Ch.M.& T.
1851 Lascelles. Bridge St., Kington
1856 K. Bridge St., Kington
1858 Cassey. Bridge St., Kington
1859 S. Bridge St., Kington
1863 K. Bridge St., Kington
1868 Littlebury. Bridge St., Kington
1870 K. Bridge St., Kington
1876 Littlebury. 60 Bridge St., Kington
SIMS, Charles   T.
1885 K. Wolford, Ross
1891 K. Wolford, Ross.
  See Sims C. & Jones R.
SIMS & JONES
1895 K. Wolford Ross
1896 K. Wolford Ross
STANLEY, William   T.
1876 Littlebury. 65 Eign St., Hereford

SYMONDS, James   Ch.M.
1777-78 F.H.S. Hereford
THOMAS, George   W.T.
1858 Cassey. Blue School La., Hereford
1859 S. ("By steam power.")
TIMS, Thomas   Ch.M.& T.
1835 P. Brookside, Hereford
WALTERS, George   Ch.M.
1870 K. Broad St., Bromyard
1879 K. Cruxwell St., Bromyard
WATKINS, Thomas   Ch.M.& T.
1835 P. Packers La., Hereford
WEBB, Alfred   T.
1885 K. Widemarsh, Hereford
1891 K. Widemarsh, Hereford
1895 K. Widemarsh, Hereford
1896 K. Widemarsh, Hereford
1900 K. 17 East St., Hereford
WILKES, Thomas   Ch.M.
1822 P. Hereford
1830 P. Broad St., Hereford
1835 P. Broad St., Hereford
1850 S. Eign St., Hereford
WILKINS, George   T.
1858 Cassey. Chapel Walk, Hereford
1859 S. St. Owen St., Hereford
WINNOT, William   Ch.M.& T.
1859 S. Woolhope

Shropshire

ABSLOW, James   Ch.M.
1850 S. Wellington
ADAMS, George   Ch.M.
1841 C. King St., Wellington (age 65)
ADAMS, W.   T.
1856 K. Upper Goalford, Ludlow
1858 Cassey. Upper Goalford, Ludlow
1863 K. 69 Lower Goalford
ALLKINS, L.   T.
1856 K. Mill Works, Newport
ANSLOW, James   Ch.M.
1835 F.H.S. Wellington
1841 C. New St., Wellington (age 37)
1843 P. New St., Wellington
ANSLOW, John   Ch.M.
1822 P. Wellington
1828 F.H.S. Wellington
ANSLOW, Thomas   Ch.M.
1822 P. Shrewsbury
ARROWSMITH, Thomas   Ch.M.
1822-35 F.H.S. Wellington
AUSTIN, Joseph   T.
1861 C. Wellington (age 27)
BENNETT, Richard   Ch.M.& T.
1840 S. Ludlow
BETTLEY, William   Ch.M.
1822 P. Wem, Nr. Whitchurch
BEVAN, William   Ch.M.
1741-61 F.H.S. Shrewsbury
BLANT, C.   Ch.M.
1851 C. St. John's Hill, Shrewsbury
BOUGHEY, T.   T.
1856 K. Church Aston, Newport
BOWEN, Edward   W.T.
1891 K. Court St., Madeley
BRIGHT, E.   Ch.M.
1856 K. Bishop's Castle, Shrewsbury
1863 K. Bishop's Shrewsbury
1870 K. Bishop's Shrewsbury
BROWN, J.   Ch.M.
1856 K. Madeley, Wellington
1863 K. Madeley, Wellington
1870 K. Madeley, Wellington
CHAPMAN, William   T.
1861 C. Wellington (age 27)
COLLEY, James   Ch.M.
1822 F.H.S. Bridgenorth
COLLEY, James   Ch.M.
1843 P. Cartway, Bridgenorth
COLLEY, Joseph   Ch.M.
1840 F.H.S. Broseley
1843 P. Broseley
DAVIS, Owen   Ch.M.
1797-1805 F.H.S. Bridgenorth
EDGE, John   Ch.M.& T.
1840 S. Greenend, Whitchurch
EDGE, W.   T.
1856 K. Greenend St., Whitchurch
1863 K. Greenend St., Whitchurch
EDWARDS, William   Ch.M.
1755 F.H.S. Wosbury
GAD, Thomas   Ch.M.& T.
1840 S. Shropshire St., Drayton
1843 P. Shropshire St., Drayton
1856 K. Shropshire St., Drayton
1863 K. Shropshire St., Drayton
1870 K. Shropshire St., Drayton
1891 K. Shropshire St., Drayton

GADD, Richard   Ch.M.
1822 P. Market Drayton
GREEN, Richard   Ch.M.
1840 S. Church St., Bishops Castle
1841 C. Church St., Bishops Castle (age 31)
1856 K. Church St., Bishops Castle
GROOM, John   Ch.M.& T.
1840 S. New St., Wellington
1841 C. New St., Wellington
1843 P. New St., Wellington
1850 S. New S., Wellington
1861 C. New St., Wellington
GROOM, Richard   Ch.M.
1841 C. New St., Wellington (age 22)
1863 K. Shropshire Works, Wellington (Richard & Thomas)
1870 K. Shropshire Works, Wellington (Richard & Thomas)
HALL, Robert   T.
1851 C. Upper Bar (age 33)
HARLEY, Cornelius   T.
1861 C. Wellington (age 35)
HARPER, John   T.
1840 S. Ludlow
HAYNES, William   T.
1851 C. Newport (age 28)
HEAFORD, Thomas   Ch.M.& T.
1840 S. New St., Wellington
1843 P. New St., Wellington
1850 S. New St., Wellington
HIGGINSON, Samuel   T.
1861 C. Wellington (age 41)
HILL, Alex   T.
1870 K. Abbey Foregate, Shrewsbury
HINE, E.   T.
1891 K. Gravel Hill, Ludlow
HOOD, John   Ch.M.
1834 F.H.S. Shrewsbury
HOODS or HOWS, Francis   Ch.M.
1841 C. Walker St., Wellington (age 25)
HOODS or HOWS, William   Ch.M.
1841 C. Walker St., Wellington (age 15)
HUGHES, George   Ch.M.
1828-40 F.H.S. Whitchurch
HULL, Robert   T.
1861 C. Wellington (age 43)
HUMPHRIES, Philip   T.
1851 C. Upper Bar (age 33)
HUXLEY & BUCKLEY   T.
1840 S. Newport
JONES, Charles   T.
1840 S. Oswestry
JONES, Edward   T.
1861 C. Wellington (age 27)
JONES, Thomas   T.
1840 S. Oswestry
1841 C. Oswestry
1843 P. Beatrice St., Oswestry
1863 K. Leg St. & Upper Brook St., Oswestry
JONES, William Henry   T.
1870 K. Perseverance Works, Wellington
LANGFORD, E.   T.
1863 K. North St., Bridgenorth
1870 K. 17 Northgate, Bridgenorth
LEECH, Henry   T.
1851 C. Edgmond
LIGGITT, Fred   T. App.
1861 C. Wellington (age 15)
LONGFORD, John   Ch.M.
1840 F.H.S. Bridgenorth
LONGFORD, John   Ch.M.
1841 C. Northgate, Oswestry
LONGFORD, Sarah   T.
1840 S. Bridgenorth
MACHIN, William   T.
1861 C. Wellington (age 39)
MANNING, John   T.
1870 K. Butchers Row, Shrewsbury
1891 K. 4a Castle St., Shrewsbury
MEDLICOT, Samuel   Ch.M.
1840 S. Church St., Bishop's Castle
1841 C. Church St., Bishop's Castle (age 30)
MEDLICOTT, Thomas   Ch.M.
1836 F.H.S. Bishop's Castle
MILES, Charles   Ch.M.
1840 F.H.S. Wellington
1843 P. New St., Wellington
MILLWARD, James   Ch.M.
1828 F.H.S. Market Drayton
MILLWARD, Stephen   Ch.M.
1797-98 F.H.S. Newport
MILLWOOD, James   Ch.M.& T.
1840 S. Crown St., Whitchurch
MOORE, Elizabeth   Ch.M.
1835-36 F.H.S. Wellington

MOORE, Richard   Ch.M.
1822 P. Wellington
1828 F.H.S. Wellington
MOORE, William   Ch.M.
1828-35 F.H.S. Wellington
1841 C. King St., Wellington (age 40)
MOORE, William   Ch.M.& T.
1840 S. New St., Wellington
1841 C. New St., Wellington (age 17)
MOORES, John   Ch.M.
1828 F.H.S. Whitchurch
NEITH, John   T.
1851 C. Upper Bur
NEWILD, John E.   T.
1861 C. Wellington (age 21)
NICHOLLS, Richard & Thomas
  Ch.M.& T.
1828 F.H.S. Shrewsbury (Richard only)
1840 S. Shrewsbury
1863 K. Castle St., Shrewsbury (Thomas only)
NORTH, Henry   T.
1861 C. Wellington (age 15)
NORTH, John   T.
1861 C. Wellington (age 44)
OWEN, Edward   Ch.M.
1841 C. ChurchSt., Clun (age 26)
PAGE, Charles   Ch.M.
1841 C. New St., Wellington (age 15)
1863 K. New St., Wellington
PAGE, Francis   Ch.M.& T.
1840 S. New St., Wellington
1843 P. New St., Wellington
1850 S. Wellington
1861 C. Wellington (age 77)
PAINE, Joseph   Ch.M.
1831 F.H.S. Newport
1861 C. Wellington (age 30)
PARKER, Isaac   T.
1861 C. Wellington (age 30)
PATERSON, Edward & Sons   T.
1870 K. Millbank Sawmills, Wellington
PATERSON, John & Son   T.
1891 K. Onibury, Craven Arms
PEMBER, John   T.
1840 S. Newport
POOLE, Richard   T.
1861 C. Wellington (age 43)
PRICE —   Ch.M.
1818 F.H.S. Whitchurch
PRICE, P.   Ch.M.
1841 C. Oswestry
RAY, Uriah   Ch.M.
1822 P. Market Drayton
1840 S. Cheshire St., Market Drayton
REEVES, John   Ch.M.
1851 C. Suffolk St., Newport (age 40)
RICHARDS, James   T.
1822 P. Shrewsbury
RICHARDS, Thomas   Ch.M.
1840 S. Church St., Bishop's Castle
1841 C. Church St., Bishop's Castle (age 50)
1843 P. Church St., Bishop's Castle
RICHARDS, W.   Ch.M.
1856 K. Bishop's Castle
1863 K. Bishop's Castle
1870 K. Bishop's Castle
ROBINSON, Edward   Ch.M.& T.
1840 S. Woodbine Tavern Yd., Ludlow
ROBINSON, Herbert   T.
1861 C. Wellington (age 24)
SANKEY, Francis   T.
1861 C. Wellington (age 20)
SANKEY, William   T.
1861 C. Wellington (age 58)
SCARATT, Homer   Ch.M.
1841 C. New St., Wellington (age 60)
SHEPERD, Isaac   CAB & T.
1861 C. Wellington
1863 K. New St., Wellington
SHEPPARD, Robert   Ch.M.& T.
1840 S. New St., Wellington
1841 C. New St., Wellington (age 40)
1843 P. New St., Wellington
1850 S. New St., Wellington
1856 K. New St., Wellington
1861 C. New St., Wellington (age 69)
SHEPPERD, Richard   Ch.M.
1835 F.H.S. Wellington
SMITH, William   T.
1861 C. Wellington (age 36)
SPENCER, Thomas   Ch.M.
1841 C. New St., Wellington (age 24)
STEVENS, G.   T.
1861 K. Mardol, Shrewsbury
1870 K. Mardol, Shrewsbury
STEVENS, William   T.
1840 S. Shrewsbury
SWINE(C)HATT, Job   Ch.M.
1822-28 F.H.S. Market Drayton

Derbyshire continued

LOWE, John   Ch.M.
1829 G. Sadler Gate, Derby
1842 Derby Tr. Dir. Bold La., Derby
1843 G. Start Garter Yd., Derby
1846 B. Crt 11, Bold La., Derby
LUNN, George   W.T.
1881 K. Wharncliffe, Eckington
1888 K. Wharncliffe, Eckington
MAPLEBECK, John   Ch.M.
1822 P. Wirksworth
1829 G. Wirksworth
MARPLES, Thomas   T.
1835 P. Woodhaft, Dronfield
MARSHALL, Charles   T.
1843 G. Rivett St., Derby
MOORE, Charles,   Ch.M.& T.
1857 W. Guild St., Burton on Trent
MORRIS, T.   Ch.M.
1846 B. Hartshorn, Burton on Trent
1864 K. Hartshorn, Burton on Trent
MORTON, George   T.
1871 W. 2 Bridge St., Derby
MORTON, George   T.
1845 W. Eckington
1876 Derby Tr. Dir. Eckington
1881 K. Wharncliffe, Eckington
1888 K. Wharncliffe, Eckington
MOSEDALE, William   T.
1835 P. Nun St., Derby
NOON, William   T.
1846 B. Anderstaff La., Burton on Trent
1857 W. Anderstaff La., Burton on Trent
OAKDEN, Henry   T.
1846 B. Butts, Belper
OAKDEN, Thomas   T.
1822 P. Belper
1829 G. Market Pl., Belper
1835 P. High St., Belper (Ch.M.& T.)
PEGG, John   Ch.M.& T.
1829 G. Melbourne
1835 P. Melbourne
1857 W. Market Pl., Melbourne
1864 K. 17 Traffic St., Derby
PERKINS, John   C.T.
1846 B. Meachan
POLLER, S.   W.T.
1864 K. Curzon St., Derby
POTT, Ed.   Ch.M.& T.
1823-29 F.H.S. Derby
POTTER, David   T.
1843 G. Talbot Yd., Derby
1846 B. Talbot Yd., Derby
POTTER, David   Ch.M.& T.
1818 P. Friar La., Derby
1823 P. Friar La., Derby
1829 G. Curzon St., Derby
1835 P. Curzon St., Derby
1842 Derby Tr. Dir. Curzon St., Derby
1843 G. Curzon St., Derby
1857 W. Curzon St., Derby
POTTER, Edward   Ch.M.
1823 F.H.S. Derby
1829 G. Friar Gate, Derby
POTTER, Samuel   W.T.
1888 K. Curzon St., Derby
1891 K. Curzon St., Derby
POTTS, Benjamin   Ch.M.& T.
1835 P. Nottingham Rd., Derby
1842 Derby Tr. Dir. Nottingham Rd., Derby
1843 G. Nottingham Rd., Derby
RENSHAW, Francis   T.
1857 W. Dronfield
RHODES, John   T.
1835 P. 25 London Rd., Derby
ROBINSON, James   T.
1829 G. St. Mary's Gate, Derby
1835 P. Wright St., Derby
1843 G. 6 Wright St., Derby
1846 B. St. Mary's Gate, Derby
ROBINSON, John   T.
1829 G. St. Mary's Gate, Derby
ROE, Edward   T.
1829 G. St. Mike's La., Derby
ROE, William   Ch.M.& T.
1842 Derby Tr. Dir. Nottingham Rd., Derby
1843 G. Nottingham Rd., Derby
1846 B. Nottingham Rd., Derby
1850 S. Derby
1857 W. Nottingham Rd., Derby
1864 K. Nottingham Rd., Derby
1871 Wright. 40, Nottingham Rd., Derby
1876 Derby Tr. Dir. Nottingham Rd., Derby
ROE & OAKLY   Ch.M.& T.
1846 B. Siddals La., Derby

ROE'S TIMBER CO.   W.T.
1881 K. Siddals Rd. Yd., Mortledge and Exeter St., Derby
1888 K. 87 Siddals Rd
1891 K. 87 Siddals Rd., Derby
ROOTH, George   W.T.
1881 K. Saltergate, Chesterfield
ROYLANCE, P.   Ch.M.
1818 P. Mealhouse Brow, Stockport
SAUNDERSON, H.   W.T.
1876 Derby Tr. Dir. Sheffield Rd., Chesterfield
1881 K. Sheffield Rd., Chesterfield
SAUNDERSON, W.   W.T.
1864 K. Newbold Rd., Chesterfield
SHARLOCK, Joseph   T.
1843 G. Peach's Row, Derby
SHARP, Samuel   Ch.M.
1829 G. South St., Chesterfield
1833 F.H.S. Chesterfield
1842 Derby Tr. Dir. Lord's Mill St., Chesterfield
1845 W. South St. (T.)
1846 B. South St. (CAB)
SHARP, Thomas   Ch.M.
1842 Derby Tr. Dir. South St., Chesterfield
SHARP, William   Ch.M.
1835 P. South St., Chesterfield
1845 W. Beetwell St., Chesterfield (T.)
1846 B. Beetwell St., Chesterfield
1848 Derby Tr. Dir. South St., Chesterfield
SIMPSON, Thomas   Ch.M.& T.
1857 W. Guild St., Burton on Trent
SIMPSON, William   Ch.M.& T.
1846 B. High St., Burton on Trent
1857 W. High St., Burton on Trent
SLACK, Job   Ch.M.
1846 B. Calver
1857 W. Calver
SLACK, John   Ch.M.
1822 P. Alfreton
1829 G. Alfreton (& T.)
1835 P. Alfreton
1842 Derby Tr. Dir. Alfreton
SLACK, Martin   Ch.M.
1845 W. Barlow, Chesterfield
1846 B. Moor Hall, Little Barlow
1848 Derby Tr. Dir. Barlow
SMITH, George Senior   Ch.M.& T.
1818-35 F.H.S. Derby.
1818 P. St. Peter's Gate, Derby
1822 P. St. Peter's St., Derby
1825 P. Derby
1829 G. St. Peter's St., Derby
1835 P. St. Peter's St., Derby
SMITH, George Junior   Ch.M.& T.
1829 G. Sadler Gate, Derby
1835 P. 31 London Rd., Derby
1842 Derby Tr. Dir.31 London Rd., Derby
1843 G. London Rd., Derby
1846 B. London St., Derby
SMITHARD, Simeon   Ch.M.
1843 G. Liversage St., Derby
SOAR, George   T.
1800-07 F.H.S. Derby
SOAR, John   T.
1843 G. Darley La., Derby
1846 B. Darley La., Derby
1848 Derby Tr. Dir. Darley La., Derby
STUBBS, Charles   T.
1818 P. St. Peter's Gate, Stockport
SUMMERS, Charles   Ch.M.& T.
1857 W. New St., Burton on Trent
TAYLOR, John   Ch.M.
1846 B. Sheeplea, Brampton
TAYLOR SONS & CO.   W.T.
1888 K. Walton, Chesterfield
1891 K. Walton Mills, Chesterfield
TRANTER, Thomas   T.
1871 Wr. 35 Nottingham Rd., Derby
TURNER, Jos.   Ch.M.
1752 F.H.S. Derby
VANSTONE, Francis   T.
1843 G. Wilmot St., Derby
WAIT, Francis   T.
1846 B. City Rd., Derby
WALKER, William   T.
1843 G. 22 Nun's St., Derby
WATKINS, Edward   W.T.
1888 K. Fritchley, and Bull Bridge, Derby
1891 K. Bull Bridge and Amber Gate
WEST, Thomas   Ch.M.& T.
1857 W. Bridge St., Burton on Trent
WESTON, J.   W.T.
1864 K. Jewry St., Derby

WIGHTMAN, Joseph   T.
1857 W. Fritchley, Crich Township
WILLIAMSON, Joseph   Ch.M.
1822 P. Gandy La., Ashbourne
1829 G. White Swan, Ashbourne
1835 P. Ashbourne Green
WILSON, George   T.
1845 W. Eckington
1857 W. Windmill Hill, Eckington
1864 K. Eckington, Chesterfield
1876 Derby Tr. Dir. Eckington, Chesterfield (& Sons)
1888 K. Eckington
1891 K. Churchfield, Eckington
WOOD, John   T.
1818 P. Portwood, Stockport
WOODHOUSE, Thomas   T.
1829 G. Ashbourne
WRAGG, John   Ch.M.
1767 F.H.S. Chesterfield
WRIGHT, J.   Ch.M.
1888 K. 8 Babbington La., Derby
1891 K. 8 Babbington La., Derby
YOUNG, Thomas   Ch.M.& T.
1857 W. Chapel St., Belper
1864 K. Butts, Belper
YOUNG, Thomas   Ch.M.
1846 B. 8 St. Helen's St., Derby

Lancashire & Cheshire

AARLAN (Aarlam), Joshua   Ch.M.& W.T.
1878 K. Witton St., Northwich
ABRAM, Henry   Ch.M.
1882 K. 52 Spear St., Manchester
1887 S. 52 Spear St., Manchester
ABRAM, William   Ch.M.
1868 M. 53 Portland Sq., Manchester
1871 S. 52 Spear St., Manchester
1873 K. 52 Spear St., Manchester
1879 S. 53 Spear St., Manchester
ACTON, Eliz.   T.
1888 S. Lower Park St., Congleton
ACTON, George   W.T.
1851 C. Back Park St., Congleton
1860 W. Lower Park St., Congleton
1874 M. Lower Park St., Congleton
ADDISON, John   Ch.M.
1800 F.H.S. Lancaster
1807 Free Burgess of Lancaster (from Skipton)
ADDISON, John   Ch.M.
1816 Colne
1818 La. Gen. Dir. Clayton St., Colne
ADLEY, William   Ch.M.
1848 S. Congleton
1856 S. West St., Congleton
ADSHEAD, Richard   Ch.M.
1874 M. Adswood, Cheadle
AGLAND, James R.   Ch.M.
1887 S. 15 Ribston St., Hulme
AIRAY, John   Ch.M.
1848 S. Lancaster
ALDRIDGE, Joseph   Ch.M.
1887 S. 3 Pomona St., Livepool
1891 K. 22 Smithdown, Liverpool
ALLANSON, William   Ch.M.
1882 K. 95 Moor La., Bolton
1887 S. 95 Moor La., Bolton
1891 K. 95 Moor La., Bolton
ALLANSON, William   Ch.M.
1873 K. Wilson Terr., Clitheroe
ALLCOCK, J.   Ch.M.
1850 B. Over La., Winsford
1856 S. Over La., Winsford
1857 K. Over La., Winsford
1860 W. Over La., Winsford (W.T.)
ALLEN, John   T.
1887 S. 65 Steel St., Liverpool
ALLEN, Thomas   Ch.M.
1810-35 F.H.S. Liverpool
ALLEN, John   W.T.
1850 B. Pepper St., Mobberley
1851 C. Pepper St., Mobberley (age 46)
ALLEN, Thomas   W.T.
1851 C. Pepper St., Mobberley (age 16, son of John)
ALLEN, Thomas   W.T.
1850 B. Limekiln La., Tranmere
ALLEN, T.   T.
1858 K. 3 George St., Liverpool
1864 K. 3 George St., Liverpool
1873 K. 3 George St., Liverpool
ALLEN & JOHNSON   T.
1882 K. 127a St. James St., Liverpool
ALMOND, G. & G.   T.
1858 K. Porter St., Preston

1860 B. Porter St., Preston
1864 K. Preston (G. only)
ALMOND, George   T.
1837 Whittle. Avenham St., Preston
1854 Man. 25 Avenham St., Preston
1855 Man. 25 Avenham St., Preston
1858 K. 6 Avenham St., Preston
1860 Br. 6 Avenham St., Preston
1864 K. 6 Avenham St., Preston
1866 Man. 28 Avenham St., Preston
1881 K. Preston
1882 Bar. 45 Crown St., Preston
1887 S. 45 Crown St., Preston
AMOS, W.   W.T.
1864 K. 62 Cable St., Liverpool
AMSON, Thomas   W.T.
1860 W. Moody St., Congleton
1865 K. Canal St., Congleton
ANDERSON, George   Ch.M.
1828-34 F.H.S. Northwich
ANION, W.   W.T.
1858 K. 62 Cable St. & 31 Glos. St., Liverpool
ARCHER, Ralph   Ch.M.
1796-1803 F.H.S. Liverpool
ARKWRIGHT, J.   W.T.
1864 K. London Rd., Manchester
ARMSTRONG, Edward   Ch.M.& T.
1887 S. New Union St., Ancoats, Manchester
ARMSTRONG, George Jnr.   Ch.M.& T.
1887 S. 1 Hood St., Ancoats, Manchester
ARMSTRONG, William   T.
1887 S. 43 St. James Rd., Liverpool
ARNFIELD, James H.   T.
1888 S. 7 Grosvenor St., Stalybridge
ARNOLD, Thomas   Ch.M.
1808 P.R. St. Helens
ASHBY, John   Ch.M.
1887 S. 11 Blossom St., Manchester
ASHCROFT, David   T.
1830 Man. Tr. Dir. Bk. Lloyd St., Manchester
ASHCROFT, S.   Ch.M.
1852 Man. Tr. Dir. 11 Cross St., Hanover
1871 S. 3 Hood St., Ancoats, Manchester
1887 S. 23 Cotton St., Ancoats, Manchester
ASKEW, J.   T.
1858 K. 124 North St., Preston
1864 K. Preston
ASPINALL, Robt.   Ch.M.
1813 F.H.S. Liverpool
ASPINALL, Wm.   Ch.M.
1806-1826 F.H.S. Liverpool
ASPINDLE, Richard   Ch.M.
1819 P. Friar Gate, Preston
ASPINWALL, James   Ch.M.
1871 S. 64 Tib St., Manchester
1873 K. 64, 66 Tib St., Manchester
1879 S. Tib St., Manchester
ASPINWALL, T.W.   Ch.M.
1858 K. 24 Thomas St., Manchester
1868 M. 24 Thomas St., Manchester
ASTON, Philip   Ch.M.
1841 C. Knutsford (age 40)
ATHERTON, John   W.T.
1827 Will. CRO Chester, Altringham
ATHERTON, William   Ch.M.
1814 F.H.S. Lime St., Liverpool
1824 Baines. 66 Lime St., Liverpool
1825 P. Liverpool
1827 Gores. 69 Lime St., Liverpool
ATKINSON, Francis   Ch.Bott.
1818 R. Mount St., Blackburn
ATKINSON, John   Ch.M.
1800-02 F.H.S. Manchester
ATKINSON, John   Ch.M.
1834 P. Chipping
ATKINSON, Robert   Ch.M.
1813-19 F.H.S. Manchester
ATKINSON, Robert   Ch.M.
1815-28 F.H.S. Manchester
AUKLAND, B.   W.T.
1873 K. Warrington
AVERY, Edward   Ch.M.
1835-37 F.H.S. Liverpool
AVERY, John R.   Ch.M.
1878 Bar. Old Barracks, King St., Blackburn
1882 K. Old Barracks, King St., Blackburn
1887 S. (& T.) Paradise St., Blackburn
1891 S. Paradise St., Blackburn
AXON, J.   W.T.
1858 K. Red Bank, Manchester

Lancashire & Cheshire continued

DALE, Thomas   T.& Ch.M.
1851 C. Love La., Nantwich (age 31)
1881 C. Daisy Bank, Macclesfield (age 61)
DALY, Patrick   Ch.M.
1882 K. 155 Smithdoen La., Liverpool
DAMPHELL, William   W.T.
1851 C. School Common, Wigan (age 39)
DANPHILL, William Jnr.   Ch.M.
1851 C. School Common, Wigan (age 17)
DANIELS, P.   Ch.M.
1864 K. 39 Gill St., Liverpool
DANIELS, William   T.
1833 Man. T.D. 15 Fleet St., Manchester
1836 Man. T.D. 24 Oxford St., Manchester
1852 Man. T.D. 74 George St., Manchester
DANSON, Richard   Ch.M.
1796 F.H.S. Liverpool
1819 P. 10 Haymarket, Liverpool
1822 P. 6 Old Haymarket
1824 Baines. 6 Old Haymarket
1825 P. 6 Old Haymarket
1827 Gores. 6 Old Haymarket
DARBYSHIRE, Thos.   Ch.M.
1814-39 F.H.S. Liverpool
DARCEY, C.   Ch.M.
1864 K. 15 Stanley St., Liverpool
DARCY, Thomas   Ch.M.
1844. Liv. T.D. 15 Stanley St., Liverpool
1858 K. 15 Stanley St., Liverpool
1873 K. 9 St. Stephen's La., Liverpool
DARLINGTON, Joseph   W.T.
1864 K. 12 Slater St., Liverpool
1873 K. 12 Slater St., Liverpool
1882 K. 14, 16 Slater St., Liverpool
1887 S. 14, 16 Slater St., Liverpool
1891 K. 12, 14, 16 Slater St., Liverpool
DAVENPORT, James   Ch.M.
1879 S. 1a Cooke St., Manchester
1887 S. 1a Cooke St., Manchester
DAVENPORT, John Henry   Ch.M.
1891 K. 25 Milton St., Hulme, Manchester
DAVENPORT, Thomas   Ch.M.
1841 C. Chester Rd., Macclesfield
1850 B. Broken Cross, Macclesfield
1856 S. 49 Chester Rd., Macclesfield
1857 K. Chester Rd., Macclesfield
1860 W. 49 Chester Rd., Macclesfield
1865 K. 49 Chester Rd., Macclesfield
DAVIES, Cyrus   T.
1861 S. 24a Deansgate, Manchester
DAVIES, Horatio   T.
1871 S. Little Peter St., Manchester
1873 K. Little Peter St., Manchester
1879 S. opp. Ordsall La. Station, Salford
1887 S. opp. Ordsall La. Station, Salford
DAVIES, Hugh   T.
1850 Man. T.D. 14 Cupid's Alley, Manchester
1852 Man. T.D. 14 Cupid's Alley, Manchester
1864 K. Gaythorn
1879 S. Knot Mill, Little Peter St.
DAVIES, John   T.
1834 Preston R.O. Will. Preston
DAVIES, John   Ch.M.
1835-37 F.H.S. Liverpool
DAVIES, Thomas   W.T.
1858 K. Islington Pl., Liverpool
1891 K. 13 Wakefield St., Liverpool
DAVIS, Robert   Ch.M.
1854 Man. North Rd., Preston
1858 K. 82 North Rd., Preston
1866 Man. Lord St., Preston
1882 Bar. 53 Lord St., Preston
DAVIS, William   W.T.
1873 K. 76 Port St., Manchester
DAWSON, Abraham   T.
1858 K. Springfield Wks., Bury
DAWSON, Edward   Ch.M.
1871 S. 24a Hanover St., Shudehill, Manchester
1873 K. 24a Hanover St., Shudehill, Manchester
1879 S. 24a Hanover St., Shudehill, Manchester
DAWSON, Sam   T.
1887 S. Pilsworth Rd., Heywood
DAWSON, William   T.
1887 S. Grimshaw Park, Blackburn
DEAN, Henry   Ch.M.
1824-25 F.H.S. Blackburn
DEAN, M.   W.T.
1864 K. 70 Port St., Manchester

DEAN, Thomas   Ch.M.
1804 P. Shudehill, Manchester
DEAN, Thomas   Ch.M.
1781 F.H.S. Manchester
1790 Univ. Longmill Gate, Manchester
1797 Scholes. 17 Swan St., Manchester
1804 P. 17 Swan St., Manchester
DEAN, William H.   T.
1888 S. 5 Albert St., Chestergate
DEAN & JUDGE   T.
1861 S. 70 Port St., Manchester
DEAN & STEELE   Ch.M.
1815 F.H.S. Manchester
DEGG, A. & CO.   T.
1871 S. 74 Port St., Manchester
DEKIN, George   Ch.M.
1825 F.H.S. Longdendale
DELANEY, Peter   T.
1887 S. 66 Jersey St., Ancoats, Manchester
DELANY, Michael   W.T.
1874 M. 126 Brook St., Birkenhead
1878 K. 2 St. Anne St., Birkenhead
1891 K. Abbey Crt., Abbey St.
1888 S. Abbey St., Birkenhead
DELAUNAY, Michael   T.
1850 Man. T.D. Major St., Manchester
1852 Man. T.D. 56 Major St., Manchester
1855 Man. T.D. 85 Silver St.
1858 K. 88 Major St.
1861 S. 88 Major St., Manchester
1864 K. Portland St., Manchester
DENNY, William   W.T.
1891 K. 23a Duke St., Liverpool
DENNY & SIMPSON   T.
1882 K. 54 Seel St., Liverpool
DERBYSHIRE, Thomas   Ch.M.
1816 Liverpool
1819 P. 1 Pall Mall, Liverpool
1822 P. 3 Pall Mall, Liverpool
1824 Baines. 3 Pall Mall, Liverpool
1825 P. 3 P-ll Mall, Liverpool
1841 G. _ Pall Mall, Liverpool
1848 S. 9 Pall Mall, Liverpool
1851 Gores. 3 Pall Mall, Liverpool
DISLEY, Richard   Ch.M.
1742 P.R. Rufford
DITCHFIELD, William   Ch.M.
1808 F.H.S. Manchester
DIXON, Aaron   Ch.M.
1841 C. Chapel End, Billinge (age 55)
1851 C. Billinge Slack (age 70)
DIXON, E.   Ch.M.
1851 C. Actons Crt., Wigan
DIXON, Edward   W.T.
1882 K. Lancaster
DIXON, Edward   W.T.
1891 K. Tateham
DIXON, James   Ch.M.
1810 Gores. 79 Byrom St., Liverpool
1811 Gores. 69 Byrom St., Liverpool
1813 Gores. 78 Byrom St., Liverpool
1814 Gores. 78 Byrom St., Liverpool
1816-21 Gores. 79 Byrom St., Liverpool
DIXON, James   Ch.M.
1841 C. Chapel End, Billinge (age 30)
1851 C. Billinge (age 45)
DIXON, Mary   Ch.M.
1822 P. Liverpool
DIXON, Thomas   Ch.M.
1818 Lan. G.D. 18 Friargate, Preston
1825 P. Preston
DIXON, William   Ch.M.
1841 C. Scholes St., Wigan
1851 C. Actons Crt., Wigan
1861 C. Lodging with John Jackson. Billinge (age 62)
DIXON, William   Ch.M.
1861 C. Living and working for John Jackson (age 51)
DOBSON, S.   W.T.
1864 K. Blackburn
1873 K. Blackburn
1882 K. Blackburn
DOBSON, W.   T.
1858 K. Whalley
DOBSON, W.H.   Ch.M.
1824 Baines. 7 Parr St., Liverpool
1825 P. Liverpool
DOLBY, George   Ch.M.
1850 Man. T.D. 83 George St., Manchester
DOODSON, Joseph   Ch.M.
1861 S. 12a Hanover St., Shudehill, Manchester
DRAPER, Thomas   T.
1854 Man. White Lion Brow, Bolton
1858 K. 5 Moor La., Bolton
1864 K. 5 Moor La., Bolton

1873 K. 5 Moor La., Bolton
1882 K. 5 Moor La., Bolton
1887 S. 15 White Lion Brow
1891 K. Bolton
DRAPER, William F.   Ch.M.
1871 S. 52 Miller St., Shudehill, Manchester
DREW, Sidney   Ch.M.
1887 S. 11 Virgil St., City Rd., Hulme, Manchester
1891 K. 9 Eastnor St., Cornbrook, Manchester
DRIVER, Edward   W.T.
1879 S. 62 Hardman St., Manchester
DUDLEY, Miss Anna   Ch.M.
1873 K. 53 Renshaw St., Liverpool
DUDLEY, Frederick   Ch.M.
1858 K. 85 Duke St., Liverpool
DUDLEY, R.   Ch.M.
1864 K. 53, 55 Renshaw St., Liverpool
DUDLEY, Thomas   Ch.M.
1896 K. Higher Bebington, Chester
DUDLEY, William   Ch.M.
1891 K. 27 Clare St., Liverpool
DUFFEY, James   Ch.M.
1861 S. 45 Goulden St., Manchester
1868 M. 15 Cable St., Manchester
1871 S. 13 Cable St., Manchester
DUFFYN, James   Ch.M.
1873 K. 57 Miller St., Manchester
DUKE, Henry   Ch.M.
1848 S. Liverpool
1851 Gores. 49 Hotham St., Liverpool
DUNBABIN, John   Ch.M.
1790-1822 F.H.S. Liverpool
DUNBAVIN, James   T.
1871 S. Brownsfield Mill, Gt. Ancoats St., Manchester
DUNCALF, John   W.T.
1840 Man. T.D. Batemans Buildings, Manchester
1845 Man. T.D. Clowers St., Salford
1852 Man. T.D. Sunnyside, Salford
DUNCALF, John   W.T.
1850 B. Kinsey St., Congleton
1851 C. Kinsey St., Congleton
DUNCALF, Joseph   T.
1818 Lancs. G.D. Soup St., Ashton under Lyne
DUNCALF, Thomas   Ch.M.
1819 Chester R.O. Will. Congleton
DUNCALF, W.   W.T.
1857 K. Canal St., Congleton
DUNCAN, John   T.
1836 Man. T.D. 17 Thomas St., Manchester
1850 Man. T.D. 17 Thomas St., Manchester
1852 Man. T.D. 17 Thomas St., Manchester
1855 Man. T.D. 72 Port St., Manchester
1868 M. 40 Little Ancoats St.
1871 S. Brownsfield Mill, Ancoats
1873 K. Gt. Ancoats St., Manchester
DUNCAN, Nathan   T.
1833 Man. T.D. Oak St., Macclesfield
1841 C. Beach La., Macclesfield
DUNCAN (Duncalf), Thomas   T.
1841 C. Beach La., Macclesfield (age 40)
1850 B. Beach La., Macclesfield
1851 K. Beach La., Macclesfield
1865 K. Beach La., Macclesfield
DUNCAN, Thomas   T.
1879 S. Brownsfield Mill, Gt. Ancoats St., Manchester
1887 S. Kenyon St., Rochdale Rd.
DUNN, John   Ch.M.
1824 P. 107 Chestergate, Macclesfield
1825 Hist. T.D. Macclesfield
1834 P. 107 Chestergate, Macclesfield
1841 P. 107 Chestergate, Macclesfield
1848 S. 107 Chestergate, Macclesfield
1857 K. 107 Chestergate, Macclesfield
DUNN, Thomas   Ch.M.
1860 W. 99 Chestergate, Macclesfield
DUTTON, Joseph   Ch.M.
1803 F.H.S. Nantwich
1819 P. Hospital St., Nantwich
1822 P. Nantwich
1828 P. Hospital St., Nantwich
1834 P. Hospital St., Nantwich
EASWOOD, George   T.
1888 S. 98 Chapel St., Edgeley
ECCLES, James   W.T.
1891 K. 11 Napier St., Blackburn
EDMONDSON, Peter   Ch.M.
1824 Baines. 14 Old Ropery, Liverpool
1825 P. Liverpool
1841 Gores. 4 Hart St., Liverpool

EDMUNDSON, J.   Ch.M.
1811 F.H.S. Lancaster
EDMONDSON & CO.   T.
1852 Man. T.D. 1 Charles St., Manchester
EDWARDS, John   W.T.
1873 K. Gt. Ancoats St., Manchester
EDWARDS, Len   W.T.
1882 K. Jersey St. Mill, Manchester
EDWARDS, Thomas   Ch.M.
1840 Man. T.D. 7 Beswick Row, Manchester
1848 S. Manchester
1850 Man. T.D. 7 Riggs St., Hanover St.
1852 Man. T.D. 7 Riggs St., Hanover St.
1861 S. 61 Charter St., Shudehill
ELCOCK, Joseph   Ch.M.
1743 F.H.S. Warrington
ELLISHAW, James   Ch.M.
1818 F.H.S. Liverpool
1824 Baines. 14 St. James St., Liverpool
1825 P. Liverpool
1827 Gores. 16 St. James St., Liverpool
1834 P. 17 St. James St., Liverpool
1841 Gores. 43 St. James St., Liverpool
1848 S. Liverpool
ELSTON, Robert   Ch.M.
1812 Free Burgess of Lancaster
EMPSON, T.   Ch.M.
1858 K. 19 Wolstenholme St., Liverpool
ENTWHISTLE, Isaac   T.
1854 Man. 8 Union St., Preston
1855 Man. 8 Union St., Preston
ETCHELLS, William   T.
1852 Man. T.D. 78 Fleet St., Manchester
EVANS, Charles   Ch.M.
1794 F.H.S. Manchester
1819 P. Apple Market, Manchester
1825 Baines. 67 Thomas St., Manchester
1830 Man. T.D. 67 Thomas St., Manchester
1833 Man. T.D. 67 Thomas St., Manchester
1834 P. 18 Thomas St., Manchester
1836 Man. T.D. 18 Thomas St., Manchester
1845 Man. T.D. 152 Long Millgate
1848 S. Warrington
1850 Man. T.D. 263 Rochdale Rd., Warrington
1852 Man. T.D. 263 Rochdale Rd., Warrington (T.)
EVANS, John   Ch.M.
1796 F.H.S. Liverpool
EVANS, John   T.
1852 Man. T.D. 18 Union St., Ancoats, Manchester
1861 S. New Islington, Manchester
EVERY, Edward   Ch.M.
1839 F.H.S. Liverpool
EYLES, Charles   Ch.M.
1891 K. 73 Virgil St., Liverpool
FAIRCLOUGH, Henry   T.
1769 Gore. Thomas St., Liverpool
FALLOWS, John   Ch.M.
1808 F.H.S. Manchester
1816 P. Manchester
1825 Baines. 7 Thomas St., Manchester
1825 P. Manchester
1834 P. 2 Cable St., Manchester
1836 Man. T.D. 2 Cable St., Manchester
1848 S. Manchester
1850 Man. T.D. 5 Oak St., Manchester
1852 Man. T.D. 5 Oak St., Manchester
1855 Man. T.D. 5 Oak St., Manchester
1858 K. 9 Oak St., Shudehill
FALLOWS, Joseph   Ch.M.
1835 F.H.S. Liverpool
1848 S. Liverpool
FARNELL, George   T.
1879 S. 8 Jordan St., Gaythorn, Manchester
1882 K. 8 Jordan St., Gaythorn, Manchester
1887 S. 8 Jordan St., Gaythorn, Manchester
FARRAND, John P.   CAB & Ch.M.
1887 S. Robert St., Cheetham, Manchester
FARRAND, Roger   T.
1830 Man. T.D. Bk. Lloyd St., Manchester
1833 Man. T.D. Bk. Lloyd St., Manchester
1836 Man. T.D. Bk. Lloyd St., Manchester
1840 Man. T.D. Bk. Lloyd St., Manchester
1845 Man. T.D. 16 Lloyd St., Manchester
1855 Man. T.D. Jacksons Row, Deansgate
1858 K. Dickinson St.
FARRELL, Patrick   Ch.M.
1841 C. Scholes, Wigan
1851 C. Union St., Wigan
FARRIES, Henry   W.T.
1891 K. Green Bank St., Preston

Lancashire & Cheshire continued

ROBERTS, Frank   T.
1887 S. 66 Jersey St., Ancoats, Manchester
ROBERTS, George   T.
1879 S. New Islington, Manchester
1882 K. New Islington, Manchester
1887 S. 187 Every St., Ancoats
ROBERTS, Mrs Jane   W.T.
1878 Bar. St. Peters St., Blackburn
ROBERTS, John   T.
1850 Man. T.D. 3 Watson St., Manchester
ROBERTS, Rod.   W.T.
1878 K. 33 Parkfield Ave., Birkenhead
ROBERTS, Thomas   CAB & Ch.Warehouse
1804 P. 20 Gt. Newton St., Manchester
1804-17 F.H.S. Manchester
ROBERTS, William   T.
1887 S. Melbourne St., Accrington
ROBINSON, Charles   T.
1804 P. 23 Cumberland St., Manchester
1830 Man. T.D. 34 Cumberland St., Manchester
1833 Man.T.D. 18 Cumberland St., Manchester
1836 Man. T.D. 23 Cumberland St., Manchester
1840 Man. T.D. 18 Cumberland St., Manchester
1845 Man. T.D. 18 Cumberland St., Manchester
ROBINSON, George   Ch.M.
1772-1807 Liverpool
ROBINSON, J.   W.T.
1873 K. 57 Cable St., Liverpool
ROBINSON, John   Ch.M.
1816 Preston
1818 Lanc. G.D. 42 Lord St., Preston
1819 P. 42 Lord St., Preston
1822 P. Preston
1825 P. Preston
1834 P. Lord St., Preston
1837 Whittle. 44 Lord St., Preston
1848 S. Preston
ROBINSON, John   Ch.M.
1790 Univ. 23 Mt. Pleasant, Liverpool
1794 Liverpool
1816 Liverpool
1825 P. Liverpool
1830 Lanc. R.O. Will. 'The Stained Chair Maker'
ROBINSON, John & Joseph   Ch.M.
1796-1818 Liverpool
ROBINSON, Joseph   Ch.M.
1790 Univ. 39 Gerard St., Liverpool
1794 Liverpool
1816 Liverpool
1819 P. 55 Whitechapel, Liverpool
1824 Baines. 55 Whitechapel, Liverpool
1825 P. Liverpool
1827 Gore. 55 Whitechapel, Liverpool
ROBINSON, Mary   T.
1861 S. 70 Oxford St., Manchester
1864 K. 70 Oxford St., Manchester
ROBINSON, Sam   Ch.M.
1868 M. Jersey St., Manchester
ROBINSON, Thomas   Ch.M.
1837 Whittle. 5 Pedders Crt., Preston
ROE, Peter   Ch.M.
1851 C. Mill St., Congleton (also Henry, brother, App.Ch.M.)
1850 Bag. Mill St., Congleton
1856 S. Mill St., Congleton
1857 K. Mill St., Congleton
1860 W. Mill St., Congleton
1864 M. Canal St., Congleton
1869 S. Canal St., Congleton
ROGERS, Andrew   Ch.M.
1806 Nantwich
ROGERS, Moses   T.
1819 P. 38 Sir Thomas' Blds., Liverpool
ROPER, John   Ch.M.
1818 Lanc. G.D. 18 Shambles, Preston
1819 P. 18 Shambles, Preston
1822 F.H.S. 18 Shambles, Preston
ROTHWELL, J.   W.T.
1858 K. Cable St., Manchester
1861 S. 44 Cable St., Manchester
ROTHWELL, J.   T.
1861 S. 57 Gt. Ancoats St., Manchester
1864 K. 57 Gt. Ancoats St., Manchester
ROTHWELL, James & Son   T.
1887 S. Mason St., Bury
ROTHWELL, John   W.T.
1782 Wigan P.R. Daughter baptised

ROW, Peter   W.T.
(see Peter Roe)
1850 Bag. Mill St., Congleton
1857 K. Mill St., Congleton (Ch.M.)
1860 W. Mill St., Congleton
ROWBOTTOM, William   W.T.
1882 K. Over Darwin
ROWE, Robert   Ch.M.
1815 Lanc. R.O. Will
ROWE, William   Ch.M.
1851 C. Warringtons La., Wigan (age 25)
ROWEN, William   Ch.Bott.
1851 C. Wellington St., Wigan (age 22)
ROWLAND, E.   Ch.M.
1851 C. School Common, Wigan (age 21)
1858 K. 17 Schofield La., Wigan
1861 S. 17 Schofield La., Wigan
ROWLAND, James Snr.   Ch.M. (Master)
1851 C. Wigan (age 40)
1854 Man. Water Leys, Wigan
ROWLAND, James   Ch.M.
1851 C. Greenhough Terr., Wigan (age 14)
1882 K. 15 Boswell La.
1891 K. Wigan
ROYLANCE, Charles   Ch.M.
1869 S. 46 Edward St., Stockport
1874 M. 46 Edward St., Stockport
ROYLANCE, Ellen   Ch.M.
1821 P. Mealhouse, Stockport
1825-27 F.H.S. Stockport
ROYLANCE, James   Ch.M.& T.
1850 S. 51 Carr Green, Stockport
ROYLANCE, John   Ch.M.
1834 P. 7 Barnford St., Stockport
1841 C. Upton Court, Stockport (age 35)
ROYLANCE, P.   Ch.M.
1816-20 F.H.S. Stockport
1818 P. Mealhouse Brew, Stockport
ROYLE, George & Thomas   T.
1861 S. Bourne's Blds., Tib St., Manchester
1871 S. Bourne's Blds., Tib St., Manchester
1882 K. 61 Oldham Rd., Manchester
1887 S. 54 Granby Rd., Manchester
1891 K. 54 Granby Rd., Manchester
ROYTON, James   Ch.M.
1841 C. Stockport (age 40)
RYDER, Edward   Ch.M.
1851 C. Hospital St., Nantwich (age 33)
SADLER, William   Ch.M.
1834-35 Liverpool
SAMPSON, Thomas   Ch.M.
1829-39 F.H.S. Liverpool
1848 S. Liverpool
SAMPSON, William   Ch.M.
1837 Liverpool
SANDERS, Annie   Ch.M.
1887 S. 2 Boundary Pl., Liverpool
SANDERS, Richard   T.
1819 P. 32 Thomas St., Liverpool
SANDHAM, James   W.T.
1891 K. Sherbourne Mill, Chorley
SANDWELL, Samuel   W.T.
1891 K. 75 Park Rd., Preston
SANDWELL, Stephen Jnr.   W.T.
1882 Bar. 26 Avenham St., Preston
1882 Preston
1887 S. 26 Avenham St., Preston
1891 K. 26 Avenham St., Preston
SANKEY, John   W.T.
1887 S. 84 Bostock Rd., Liverpool
1891 K. 84 Bostock Rd., Liverpool
SARRATT, Sam   CAB & Ch.M.
1816 F.H.S. Chester
1818 P. Northgate St., Chester
1840 Parry. Watergate Back Row, Chester
1850 Bag. Watergate Back Row, Chester
1870 Ph. & Gd. 38 Frodsham St., Chester
SAUNDERS, John   Ch.M.
1844 Freeman of Hull, from Liverpool
1844 Liv. T.D. 76 Limekiln St., Liverpool
SAUNDERS, William   Ch.M.
1868 M. 29 Gravel La., Salford
1871 S. 27 Gravel La., Salford
SAWYER, George   Ch.M.
1882 K. 87 Oldham Rd., Manchester
SAWYER, Walter   Ch.M.
1887 S. 39a Gun St., Ancoats, Manchester
SAYER, John   Ch.M.
1824 Freeman of Hull, from Liverpool
1824 Baines. Tarlton Crt., Liverpool
1825 P. Liverpool

SAYER, John Jnr.   Ch.M.
1888 S. Market St., New Mills
SAYERS, John   Ch.M.
1839 F.H.S. Liverpool
SCHOFIELD, Charles   T.
1836 Man. T.D. 45 Newton St., Manchester
SCHOFFIELD, John   T.
1833 Man. T.D. 4 Silver St., Ancoats, Manchester
1840 Man. T.D. 29 Newton St., Ancoats
1850 Man. T.D. 29 Newton St., Ancoats
1852 Man. T.D. 29 Newton St., Ancoats
SCHOLFIELD, G.   W.T.
1891 K. Canal Bridge, Stanley Rd., Bootle
SCHOLFIELD, John   T.
1827 Lanc. R.O. Will. Preston
SCORN, J.   W.T.
1865 K. Commercial Hall, Frodsham St., Chester
SCOTT, W.   Ch.M.
1887 S. 57 Water St., Bridge St., Manchester
SCOTT, William   W.T.
1873 K. Bootle
SEDDON, J.P.   W.T.
1891 K. Goit Pl., River St., Rochdale
SEEL, George   Ch.M.
1794 Liverpool
SEEL, Thomas   Ch.M.
1790 Univ. Cockgates, Manchester
1794 Manchester
1797 Scholes. 37 Cockgates, Manchester
SELL, Thomas   Ch.M.
1780 P.R. Lancs.
SHANNON, Martin   Ch.M.
1818 Lanc. G.D. 15 Bolton St., Preston
SHARP, Sam   Ch.M.
1887 S. 17 Strand St., Ancoats
SHARPE, Mrs Sarah   Ch.M.
1891 K. Strand St., Manchester
SHARPLES, James   W.T.
1878 Bar. Bk. Water St., Blackburn
SHARPLES, James   Ch.M. & T.
1864 K. 37 Larkhill, Blackburn
1870 Wor. 37 Larkhill & Fisher St., Blackburn
1878 Bar. 49 Ainsworth St., Blackburn
1878 Freeman of Hull, from Blackburn
1887 S. 41 Ainsworth St., Blackburn
SHARPLES, Thomas   Ch.M.
1824 Baines. 8 Queen St., Liverpool
1825 P. Liverpool
1836 Lanc. R.O. Will (CAB)
SHARWIN, James   T.
1850 Man. T.D. 61 Lees St., Manchester
SHARWIN & SON   T.
1850 Man. T.D. 77 Hanover St., Manchester
1852 Man. T.D. 79 Hanover St., Manchester
1855 Man. T.D. Ainsworth Crt., Long Millgate
SHAW, James   W.T.
1891 K. Corporation St., Stalybridge
SHAW, James   T.
1845 Man. T.D. 15 Clarence St., Manchester
SHEARS, Henry   Ch.M.
1861 S. 21 Ashley St., Manchester
SHERRATT, Joseph   Ch.M.
1851 C. Spring Gdns., Nantwich
SHERRIFF, William   Ch.T.
1850 P.R. Daughter baptised. Mobberley
SHORT, William   Ch.M.
1873 K. 22 Roscoe St., Liverpool
SILL, Thomas   Ch.M.
1811 Free Burgess of Lancaster
SIMPSON, Mrs Ann   Ch.M.
1873 K. 56 Moor La., Lancaster
SIMPSON, G.   Ch.M.
1851 Gores. 14 Brown St., Liverpool
SIMPSON, Henry   Ch.M.
1858 P. 12 Larkhill, Blackburn
SIMPSON, J.   W.T.
1873 K. Lancaster
SIMPSON, James   Ch.M.
1848 S. Lancaster
1848 Freeman of Hull
1858 K. St. Nicholas St., Lancaster
SIMPSON, James   W.T.
1873 K. Barrow
SIMPSON, Mrs Jane   W.T.
1891 K. Grizebeck, Carnforth
SIMPSON, John   T.
1887 S. 54 Seel St., Liverpool
SIMPSON, Moses   T.
1829 W. Mkt. Pl., Broughton in Furness, Ulverston

1858 K. Mkt. Pl., Broughton in Furness, Ulverston
1864 K. Mkt. Pl., Broughton in Furness, Ulverston
1882 K. Mkt. Pl., Broughton in Furness, Ulverston
1891 K. Upper Brook St., Ulverston
SIMPSON, Robert (R.H. & J.) Ch.M.
1848 S. Lancaster
1858 K. St. Nicholas St., Lancaster (CAB)
1864 K. 20 St. Nicholas St., Lancaster
1873 K. 18 St. Nicholas St., & 8 Friargate
1887 S. St. Nicholas St. & 6 Friar St.
SIMPSON, Sophie   Ch.M.
1848 S. Liverpool
SIMPSON, T.   Ch.M.
1882 K. 39 Summerseat, Liverpool
1891 K. 39 Summerseat, Liverpool
SIMPSON, Thomas   Ch.M.
1825 Baines. St. Nicholas St., Lancaster
1825 P. St. Nicholas St., Lancaster
1834 P. St. Nicholas St., Lancaster
1864 K. 28 St. Nicholas St., Lancaster
SIMPSON, Thomas Hartley   W.T.
1882 K. Broughton-in-Furness
1882 K. Also at Carnforth
1892 K. Broughton Mills, Broughton-in-Furness
SIMPSON, Thomas James   W.T.
1891 K. 54 Seel St., Liverpool
SIMPSON, Thomas Johnson   W.T.
1873 K. 54 Roscoe St., Liverpool
SIMPSON, William   Ch.M.
1763 Married Esther Gurnall. Goosnargh
SIMPSON & DUKE   Ch.M.
1841 Gores. 4 Mitchell P., Liverpool
SIMNOR, John   T.
1834 Lanc. R.O. Will. Manchester
SIM(M)S, Thomas   Ch.M.
1813-14 Liverpool
SINGLETON, Joseph   T.
1854 Man. 132 Blackburn St., Bolton
SKELLERN, Hugh   T.
1818 Lanc. R.O. Will. Rochdale
SKERWIN, William   T.
1861 S. 45 Edge St., Manchester
SKULL, Abraham   T.
1848 S. Liverpool
SLACK, Henry   T.
1850 Man. T.D. 15 China La., Manchester
1852 Man. T.D. 15 China La., Manchester
SLATER, C.   Ch.M.
1858 K. Little Mill, Chipping, Preston
1864 K. Little Mill, Chipping, Preston
1873 K. Little Mill, Chipping, Preston
1882 K. Little Mill, Chipping, Preston
1887 S. Hesketh La., Chipping, Preston
1891 K. Little MIll, Chipping, Preston
SLATER, Giles   Ch.M.
1817 Lanc. C.C. Died Church St., Blackburn
SLATER, John   Ch.M.
1816 Freeman of Hull, from Burnley
1819 P. Yorkshire St., Blackburn (& T.)
SLATER, Joseph   Ch.Bott.
1797 Manchester
SLATER, Luke   Ch.M.
1816 Blackburn
1816 Holden. 40 Church St., Blackburn
1818 R. 40 Church St., Blackburn
1819 P. Church St., Blackburn
1824 Baines. 44 Church St., Blackburn
1825 P. 44 Church St., Blackburn
1828 P. 44 Church St., Blackburn
1834 P. 44 Church St., Blackburn
1848 S. 44 Church St., Blackburn
1854 Man. 19 Church St., Blackburn
SLATER, Sam   Ch.M.
1798 F.H.S. Blackburn
1809 Lanc. R.O. Will. Preston
SLATER, Thomas   Ch.M.
1882 K. 14 Spring Gdns., Blackburn
1891 K. 2 Old Chapel, Blackburn
SLATER, William   Ch.M.
1851 C. Roode Hill, Congleton
SMITH, Charles   Ch.M.
1882 K. 70 Hanover St., Manchester
SMITH, Edward   W.T.
1857 K. Victoria St., Crewe
1874 M. Whitegates, Crewe
1878 K. Whitegates, Crewe
1888 S. Market St., Crewe
SMITH, Ellis   W.T.
1891 K. 135 Rochdale Rd., Bury

505

BIBLIOGRAPHY

Abbott, M.,   *Green Woodwork,* Guild of Master
                            Craftsmen, 1989.

Agius, P.,   'English Chairmakers listed in
                            General and Trade Directories
                            1790-1851', *F.H.S. Journal,* 1976,
                            pp.1-16.
                            101 Chairs, catalogue, Divinity
                            School, Oxford, 2-9 March, 1968.

Alexander, J.D. Jnr.,   *Making a Chair from a Tree: An
                            Introduction to Working Green Wood,*
                            The Taunton Press, Conn., USA,
                            1981.

Anon.   'Craftsman Dies (H.E. Goodchild)',
                            Obituary, *Bucks. Free Press,*
                            8.12.1950.
                            Correspondence by D. Young &
                            F.G. Roe, 5.1.1951.

Banks, N.J.,   'Lancashire Chairmakers', *Lancashire
                            Life,* Nov. 1980, pp.54-55.

Boram, J.M.B.,   'The Leicesters of Macclesfield',
                            Cheshire History, Spring edition,
                            1984.

Bury, Hon. A.,   'Mr. Goodchild's Immortal Chairs',
                            Everybody's, 2.10.1948, pp.14-15.

Carruthers, A. (Ed.)   *Ernest Gimson and the Cotswold Group
                            of Craftsmen,* Leicestershire Museums
                            Publication 14, 1978.

Chinnery, V.,   *Oak Furniture — The British Tradition,*
                            Antique Collectors' Club, 1979.

Cotton, B.D.,   'Country Chairs', *Antique Finder,*
                            October 1973.
                            'Vernacular Design: The Spindle
                            back chair and its North Country
                            Origins', *Working Wood,* 1980.
                            'The North Country Chair making
                            tradition: Design Context and the
                            Mark Chippindale deposition',
                            Furniture History Society Journal,
                            Vol. XVII, 1981.
                            'Country Chairs and their Makers',
                            Collectors' Guide, 1983.
                            Catalogue: *The Chair in the North
                            West. Regional styles in the 18th and
                            19th centuries,* 1987. (ISBN 9512214
                            0 X.)
                            Catalogue: *The Chair in the North East.
                            Regional styles in the 18th and 19th
                            centuries,* Lincolnshire County
                            Council, 1987. (ISBN 0861111 30 3.)

                            Catalogue: *Cottage & Farmhouse
                            Furniture in East Anglia,* 1987. (ISBN
                            9512214 1 8.)
                            'Unconventional Windsors from the
                            Cotswolds', *R.F.S. Journal II,* 1988.
                            'Shadford, Shirley and the Caistor
                            Workshop', *R.F.S. Journal II,* 1988.
                            Catalogue: *Windsor Chairs in the South
                            West,* 1989. (ISBN 0 9513531 1 X.)

Cotton, G.   'Common chairs from the Norwich
                            Chair Makers Price Book of 1801',
                            R.F.S. Journal II, 1988.

Crispin, T.,   '10th December 1838' (The
                            Mendlesham Chair), *Antique
                            Collecting,* Nov., Vol.15, No.6, 1980,
                            pp.10-11.

Edwards, R.,   *Victoria and Albert Museum —
                            A History of the English Chair,* H.M.
                            Stationery Office, 1931.

Forman, B.M.,   *American Seating Furniture 1630-1730,*
                            Winterthur Museum, USA, 1988.

Gilbert, C.,   Catalogue: *An Exhibition of Town &
                            Country Furniture,* Temple Newsam,
                            Leeds, 1972.
                            Catalogue: *An Exhibition of back stairs
                            furniture,* Temple Newsam, Leeds,
                            1977.
                            Catalogue: *An Exhibition of School
                            furniture,* Temple Newsam, Leeds,
                            1978.
                            Catalogue: *An Exhibition of Common
                            Furniture,* Temple Newsam, Leeds,
                            1982.
                            'Workhouse Furniture', *R.F.S.
                            Journal I,* 1987.

Gloag, J.,   *The Englishman's Chair,* Geo. Allen &
                            Unwin Ltd., London, 1964.

Goyne Evans, N.,   'A History and Background of
                            English Windsor Furniture', *F.H.S.
                            Journal,* 1979, pp.24-53.
                            'Design Sources for Windsor
                            Furniture', *Antiques,* 1988.

Harris, M., & Sons,   *The English Chair,* M. Harris &
                            Sons, London, 1937.

Haworth-Booth, M.,   'The dating of 18th century
                            Windsor chairs', *Collectors' Guide,*
                            1973, pp.63-69.

Heal, A.,   *London Furniture Makers 1660-1840,*
                            B.T. Batsford Ltd., London, 1953.

Hennell, T.,   *The Countrymen at Work. The Windsor Chair Maker*, Architectural Press, 1947, pp.73-75.

Hewison, L.,   'Search for a Norfolk Seat', article in *Eastern Daily Press*, 1.6.1983.

Jackson, M.J.,   'A Bygone Craft', (Worksop Chair Makers), *Life and Leisure*, Nov/Dec 1980, p.13.
'The Last of the Worksop Chair-makers', *Nottinghamshire Countryside*, Dec. 1973.

Jekyl, G., & Jones, S.   *Old English Household Life*, Batsford, 1939.

Jenkins, J.G.,   *Traditional Country Craftsmen*. 'The Chair Bodger', Routledge & Kegan Paul, London, 1965, pp.10-17.
Traditional Country Craftsmen. 'The Chair Maker', Routledge & Kegan Paul, London, 1965, pp.113-121.

Jervis, S.,   'Sussex Chairs in 1820', *F.H.S. Journal*, Vol.10, 1974.
'The First Century of the English Windsor chair, 1720-1820', *Antiques*, 1979.

Kelsale, G.,   'The English Country Chair', *Antique Collector*, Feb. 1977, pp.60-64.

Loudon, J.C.,   *Encyclopaedia of Cottage, Farm, and Villa Architecture*, Longman, 1833.

Massingham, H.J.,   *Men of Earth. The Chair Maker*, Chapman & Hall Ltd., London, 1943, pp.104-121.
Where Man Belongs. Goodchild of Naphill, Collins, London, 1946, pp.130-140.

Mayes, L.J.,   *The History of Chairmaking in High Wycombe*, Routledge & Kegan Paul, London, 1960.
'Some Customs in the Chair-making Trade', *Woodworker*, Sept. 1960, pp.175-176; Oct. 1960, pp.213-215.
'The Windsor Chair-maker', *Woodworker*, March 1957, pp.66-67.

Morgan, F.S.A,   *Philip Clissett. A Bosbury Chair-Maker*. Paper read 21.3.1946. Held by Hereford Public Library.

Mullet, Bert.,   *60 Years a Chair-maker*, Typescript notes, High Wycombe Public Library.

Noble, R.,   'The Chairs of Sutherland and Caithness: a Northern tradition of chair making', *R.F.S. Journal I*, 1987.

North, B.,   *Autobiography of Benjamin North*, 1882.

North, L.,   'Goodbye to the Chair Bodgers', *Reading Mercury*, 15.7.1962.

Norwich Chair Makers Book of Prices, 1801, Norwich Reference Library.

Roe, F.G.,   *Windsor Chairs*, Phoenix House Ltd., London, 1953.

Riley, N.,   'The Mysterious Mendlesham Chair', *Country Life*, 24.6.1976, p.1724.

Sandford, A.,   'Philip Clisset. The Bosbury Chairmaker', *Herefordshire Country Life*, Vol.1, No.9, Feb. 1979.

Santore, C.,   *The Windsor style in America*, Running Press, Philadelphia, USA, 1981.
The Windsor style in America, Vol.II, Running Press, Philadelphia, USA, 1987.

Sheraton, T.,   *Cabinet Makers and Upholsterers' Drawing Books*, 1794.

Skull, C.E.,   'Fifty Years in the Furniture Trade', *South Bucks. Free Press*, 8.10.1915.

Skull, E.,   Large Illustated Broadsheet: Edwin Skull Manufacturer of Every Description of Chairs. High Wycombe. No Connection with Any Other House. *Post*, Oct. 1865.

Sparkes, I.,   *The English Country Chair*, Spurbooks Ltd., Bourne End, Bucks., 1977.
The Windsor Chair, Spurbooks Ltd., Bourne End, Bucks., 1975.
The Wycombe Armchair, Information Sheet No.2, High Wycombe Museum.

Snow, C.F.F.,   'Chairs from the Chilterns' (H.E. Goodchild), *Country Life*, 6.2.1942, pp.250-251.

Stabler, J.,   'A New Look at the Bow-back Windsor', *Connoisseur*, Dec. 1974, pp.238-245.
'Two Labelled Comb-back Windsor Chairs', *Antique Collecting*, April, Vol.II, No.12, 1977, pp.12-14.
'An early Pair of Wheel-back Windsor Chairs', *Furniture History*, Vol.IX, 1973, pp.119-122.

Symonds, R.W.,   'English Cane Chairs', *Antique Collector*, May 1937.
'The Windsor Chair', *Apollo*, August 1935, pp.67-71; Nov. 1935, pp.261-267.

Trent, R.F.,   *Hearts and Crowns*, New Haven Colony Historic Society, Conn., USA, 1977.
'Connecticut Plain High-Style seating of the 18th century', *R.F.S. Journal I*, 1987.

Wight, M.,   'The Maker of Wooden Chairs', *Country Quest*, Vol.9, No.7, Dec. 1968.

Woods, K.S.,   *The Rural Industries Round Oxford, Chair-leg Turnery and Chair Making*, Clarendon Press, 1921, pp.102-115.

Pattern Books held at Temple Newsam House, Leeds.

Birch, W.,   (early 20th century). Various seating furniture catalogues.

Cox, J. & Son,   (early 20th century). Chair catalogues.

Gibbons, C.,   (early 20th century). Large illustrated sheets.

Glenister, T.,   (early 20th century). Various catalogues.

Hearn Bros.,   (early 20th century). Chair catalogue.

Mealing Bros.,   (early 20th century). Sheet. Wooden chairs and stools.

North, B., & Sons,   Furniture catalogue, 1915.

Skull, W., & Sons,   (early 20th century). Catalogue of chairs and stools.

Held in the Chair Museum, High Wycombe

B.N. Benjamin North   (c.1860), *Antique & Plain & Ornamental Chairs*, High Wycombe Chair Museum.

Glenister, T.,   *Chair Designs* (book of watercolour drawings), T. Glenister Ltd., High Wycombe.

Glenister & Gibbons,   (c.1865), *Patterns of Cane, Windsor, Fancy and other Chairs*, T. Glenister Ltd., High Wycombe.

Skull, W.,   (c.1849), *Chair Designs* (book of watercolour drawings), High Wycombe Public Library.